MW01221723

# Handbook for Aquaculture Water Quality

**Claude E. Boyd**
**School of Fisheries, Aquaculture and Aquatic Sciences**
**Auburn University, Alabama USA**


**Craig S. Tucker**
**USDA-ARS Warmwater Aquaculture Research Unit**
**Stoneville, Mississippi USA**

Copyright ©2014. All rights reserved.
No portion of this book may be reproduced, by any process or technique, without the express written consent.

ISBN: 978-0-692-22187-7

Cover photograph courtesy of Eugene L. Torrans

Printed by Craftmaster Printers, Inc., Auburn Alabama.

"Any opinions, findings, conclusions, or recommendations expressed in this publication are those of the authors and do not necessarily reflect the view of the United States Department of Agriculture. Mention of trade names is for descriptive purposes only and does not imply endorsement or approval by the United States Department of Agriculture to the exclusion of other products that may also be suitable."

# Table of Contents

# Common and Scientific Names of Aquaculture Species

| Common name | Scientific name |
|---|---|
| Atlantic cod | *Gadus morhua* |
| Basa | *Pangasius bocourti* |
| Bighead carp | *Aristichthys nobilis* |
| Black tiger prawn | *Penaeus monodon* |
| Blue catfish | *Ictalurus furcatus* |
| Blue tilapia | *Oreochromis aureus* |
| Buffalofish | *Ictiobus* spp. |
| Channel catfish | *Ictalurus punctatus* |
| Common carp | *Cyprinus carpio* |
| Fathead minnow | *Pimephales promelas* |
| Grass carp | *Ctenopharyngodon idella* |
| Hybrid striped bass | *Morone chrysops* x *M. saxatilis* |
| Kuruma shrimp | *Marsupeneaus japonicus* |
| Largemouth bass | *Micropterus salmoides* |
| Malaysian prawn | *Macrobrachium rosenbergii* |
| Milkfish | *Chanos chanos* |
| Nile tilapia | *Oreochromis niloticus* |
| Northern pike | *Esox lucius* |
| Pacific white shrimp | *Litopeneaus vannamei* |
| Paddlefish | *Polyodon spathula* |
| Rainbow trout | *Oncorhynchus mykiss* |
| Silver carp | *Hypophthalmicthys molitrix* |
| Striped bass | *Morone saxatilis* |
| Swai | *Pangasianodon hypophthalmus* |
| Threadfin shad | *Dorosoma petenense* |

# Preface

We began our careers in aquaculture water quality about 50 and 40 years ago, respectively. Although it was possible at that time to analyze water quality variables almost as accurately as today, little was known about how to interpret the results of water quality analyses with respect to the wellbeing of aquaculture animals. Even less was known about what to do if it was decided that the water quality data suggested an abnormality that could possibly harm the culture animals. Fish kills related to low dissolved oxygen concentration in particular were commonplace. Since those early days, aeration has become a powerful tool for enhancing water quality in aquaculture, and many research findings have been published in scientific journals describing relationships among aquaculture inputs, concentrations of water quality variables, effects of water quality variables on culture species, and approaches to improving water quality. Impaired water quality is still a major concern in aquaculture, but the effect usually is stress that affects aquatic animal health and growth rather than causing acute mortality

We embarked on this project with the intention of writing a small handbook outlining the best available practices that have been shown effective through research for maintaining or improving water quality in aquaculture production systems. We soon realized that application of these practices required knowledge of the principles behind them. Water quality is a multidisciplinary science that involves concepts of aquatic chemistry, ecology, microbiology, botany, soil science, and toxicology. Few aquaculture scientists and producers have found the time or motivation to obtain the requisite training to become proficient in this complex science. Although they know the names of the variables and how to acquire water quality data, they seldom understood the factors controlling water quality or the results that can be expected from a particular treatment for improving water quality. Moreover, they cannot evaluate the often outrageous claims of vendors promoting amendments for improving water quality.

We decided that a discussion of the scientific and technological principles needed for managing aquaculture water quality was essential and the manuscript for the small handbook grew. By the time it was complete, it was no longer a small handbook. Nevertheless, we attempted to separate the background information from the practices so that those who choose to ignore our plea about learning fundamentals can plunge ahead and apply the practices. It seems to be human nature to do things without first reading the instructions—the choice is yours.

We express our sincere appreciation to June Burns who typed, proofread, and organized the entire manuscript and to Rawee Viriyatum who made many of the drawings. Without their help this effort could not have been accomplished. The subject of water quality has become almost too broad for any one person to know completely, and what we know is the sum of the knowledge we obtained from our many friends, teachers, and colleagues. In that regard, we are especially grateful for discussions of subject matter over the years with David Brune, George Chamberlain, John Hargreaves, C. Kwei Lin, Aaron McNevin, Martine van der Ploeg, Julio F. Queiroz, Steven Summerfelt, David Teichert-Coddington, Les Torrans, Barnaby Watten, Bambang Widigdo, and C. Wesley Wood. We also would like to acknowledge the contributions of the many graduate students who have collaborated with us over the years. Their studies have been the basis for much that has been learned about water quality in aquaculture. We also thank the administration of Auburn University, Mississippi State University, and the Agricultural Research Service of the United States Department of Agriculture for their support while we wrote this book.

We greatly enjoyed writing this handbook, and we hope that it will be of benefit to the aquaculture industry.

Claude E. Boyd
Craig S. Tucker

# Chapter 1

# Introduction

Aquaculture is an important segment of world fisheries production, providing about half of fisheries products for human consumption. Global capture fisheries has reached or possibly exceeded its sustainable yield, while world population is expected to increase from about 7 billion in early 2012 to 9.1 billion by 2050—an increase of 30%. Assuming that people continue to consume fisheries products at the present rate, annual fisheries production must increase by 30% over the next 40 years. Because capture fisheries will not increase, future increases in seafood supply must come from aquaculture.

A large proportion of aquaculture, possibly more than 75% of fish production, is realized from ponds. There are about 8,500,000 ha of freshwater ponds and 2,500,000 ha of brackishwater ponds in the world.[1] Considerably more land and freshwater could be devoted to aquaculture, but most of the available land and water is located in areas where aquaculture is not commonly practiced.[2] Average annual production for all types of pond aquaculture is estimated at 2,492 kg/ha. This is a rather unimpressive average considering that better producers often report yields above 5,000 kg/ha and annual yields in modern, intensively aerated ponds may approach 20,000 kg/ha. Much of the future increase in aquaculture production is likely to result from intensification of production in existing ponds and increased culture of fish in cages in freshwater lakes, reservoirs, and the sea rather than from the expansion of pond area.

Aquaculture sites ideally should have an abundant supply of high quality water satisfactory for culture of fish, crustaceans, or other aquaculture species. However, in order to make aquaculture economically feasible, aquaculturists must seek ways to increase the yield of culture species above that possible from natural productivity. Production intensification depends on providing additional food and maintaining an environment that promotes healthy, fast-growing animals—a process called *water quality management*.

The term *water quality* encompasses all physical, chemical, and biological variables that influence the suitability of water for any intended use. There are literally hundreds of water quality variables. Fortunately, comparatively few are important in aquaculture. These variables are mainly dissolved inorganic substances important as osmoregulators, plant nutrients, toxic natural or anthropogenic substances, suspended particles that influence turbidity and light penetration, dissolved gases—particularly oxygen and carbon dioxide, particulate and dissolved organic matter, plankton, and of course, temperature and pH. These variables must remain within suitable ranges, or the culture species will not have adequate natural food, be stressed, or even die.

Aquaculture water quality management has three general goals: providing food for the cultured species, maintaining a good environment for animal growth, and lessening pollution by wastes produced during culture. The relative importance of these goals changes as aquaculture production increases.

The first level of increase in production is achieved through application of plant nutrients in fertilizers to increase primary productivity and natural food for the culture species. Depending upon the species cultured, yields may be increased from 50 to 200 kg/ha in unfertilized ponds to 500 to 2,000 kg/ha in fertilized ponds.[3] In many areas, however, pond soils are acidic and waters are low in total alkalinity and total hardness concentration. Liming materials should be applied to such ponds to allow effective use of fertilizers.[3]

Feeds are used to increase production to greater levels than possible with fertilization. However, a large fraction of nutrients in feeds enter pond waters in uneaten feed and in feces and metabolic wastes of the culture species. These nutrients stimulate phytoplankton productivity, leading to dense phytoplankton blooms and low dissolved oxygen concentration during nighttime.[3] For most species, low dissolved oxygen concentration will limit production in ponds with feeding alone to 2,000 to 3,000 kg/ha.

Mechanical aeration can be installed in ponds with feeding to increase the supply of dissolved oxygen and allow much greater production—up to 10,000 kg/ha is not uncommon.[4] Large feed inputs to aerated ponds lead to problems with high concentrations of carbon dioxide and ammonia in the water from aerobic respiration by fish and microorganisms. Elevated concentrations of other toxic metabolites such as nitrite and sulfide also may enter the water as a result of microbial activity in anaerobic zones within pond bottoms. The amount of aeration that can be applied to ponds is often limited, because aerators erode embankments and resuspend sediment creating turbidity in water.[3] Increasing the level of aquaculture production in ponds leads to progressive deterioration of water quality. Therefore, water quality management becomes increasingly important as the intensity of pond aquaculture increases.

Modifications of traditional culture ponds such as partitioned aquaculture systems (PAS), split ponds, in-pond raceways (IPR), plastic-lined, heterotrophic ponds (floc systems), and other outdoor, water-reuse systems allow greater production than possible in traditional aerated and fed pond systems. Although the emphasis of this book is on water quality management in traditional aquaculture ponds, we have included chapters on emerging pond technologies that may soon become commonplace.

Cage culture and raceway production are time-honored aquaculture methods, and fish survival and growth in both are extremely sensitive to water quality conditions. Cage culture sometimes is conducted in ponds, and earthen raceways occasionally have been combined with ponds. More recently, recirculating aquaculture systems have gained considerable attention. Although recirculating systems offer many advantages over more traditional forms of aquaculture, production costs are high and products often cannot compete in the same markets as those grown in other systems. We have included brief overviews of water quality issues in raceways, cages, and recirculating systems. There are also large amounts of saline groundwater, surface water, or both in many arid, inland areas.[5] Saline groundwater also may be found in humid regions.[6] It has recently been demonstrated that penaeid shrimp and other brackishwater and marine species can be successfully cultured in saline water at inland sites.[6] Some saline waters are suitable directly, but others must be remediated by mineral supplementation to correct ionic imbalances.[6] We therefore included a chapter on low-salinity, inland aquaculture because of its future potential.

We chose, however, not to consider the culture of mollusks, seaweed, and other organisms that are 'planted' in open waters of estuaries and seas. Although water quality is important in the culture of these species, aside from rejection of sites with impaired water quality, little can be done by aquaculturists to manage water quality in open reaches of coastal water.

As aquaculture production intensified over the last 25 years, mitigation of pollution by aquaculture effluents has become an important aspect of water quality management. Although fish and crustaceans often convert feeds into body tissue more efficiently than warm-blooded animals, large-scale aquaculture—like all animal agriculture—generates considerable waste. These wastes can cause eutrophication and sedimentation when discharged into other water bodies.

Some production systems are a greater pollution threat than others.[7] Ponds have long hydraulic retention times and natural in-pond physical, chemical, and biological processes assimilate wastes and lessen the proportion of feed wastes discharged into natural waters. Recirculating aquaculture systems are similar to ponds in that most wastes produced during culture are treated within the facility rather than discharged directly to other water bodies. Raceways and cages have very short hydraulic retention times and culture units have direct hydrological connections to effluent-receiving water bodies. The potential for pollution is greater from these systems than for most pond and recirculating aquaculture systems.

The successful aquaculturist must understand which water quality variables are important, learn the factors that control these variables, and strive to manage production systems so that important variables remain within tolerable ranges. Some water quality problems can be solved through application of specific substances or procedures. In many instances, however, expertise in water quality management is most important because it allows the manager to predict how specific site conditions, culture methodologies, and management interventions will influence water quality in production systems. In the case of aquaculture water quality management, knowing what to expect is equally as important as knowing what treatment or procedure to apply.

Although a few adverse water quality conditions—such as turbidity and excessive phytoplankton—can be detected visually, water of impaired quality for aquaculture often appears the same as water of good quality. An experienced aquaculturist may suspect that a water quality problem exists in a pond from the appearance of the water or by the reaction of the culture species, but there is no alternative to water analysis for verification, and in many cases, water analysis is the only way of detecting the problem. Moreover, water quality may deteriorate gradually, and regular, routine water analyses can alert managers to impending problems so that remedial measures can be taken to ward off abnormalities before they seriously impact survival or growth. There is increasing use of water analyses by aquaculturists, but analyses are not helpful unless the manager knows how to interpret the results and how to respond when one or more variables indicate deteriorating culture conditions.

This book is a summary of pond water quality management information that the authors have developed individually or collaborated on in the past. One of our recent efforts resulted in what we thought was an excellent book describing all aspects of pond water quality and its management.[3] Unfortunately, the book is so expensive that hardly anyone purchased it. Moreover, the level of detail in that book is far greater than necessary for those seeking practical solutions to water quality problems in ponds and other culture systems. Chemical, physical, and biological processes interact in aquaculture facilities like in all other ecological systems; thus, explanations of water quality dynamics are complex. Nevertheless, this time, we tried to present an easy to understand, practical account of aquaculture water quality management in an affordable book.

# References

1. Verdegem, M. C. J. and R. H. Bosma. 2009. Water withdrawal for brackish and inland aquaculture, and options to produce more fish in ponds with present water use. Water Policy 11 (supplement 1):52-68.
2. Boyd, C. E., L. Li, and R. Brummett. 2012. Relationship of freshwater aquaculture production to renewable freshwater resources. Journal of Applied Aquaculture 24:99-106.
3. Boyd, C. E. and C. S. Tucker. 1998. *Pond Aquaculture Water Quality Management*. Kluwer Academic Publishers, Boston, MA.
4. Boyd, C. E. 1978. Pond water aeration systems. Aquacultural Engineering 18:9-40.
5. Boyd, C. A., P. L. Chaney, C. E. Boyd, and D. B. Rouse. 2009. Distribution of ground water suitable for use in saline-water aquaculture in central and west-central Alabama. Journal of Applied Aquaculture 21:228-240.
6. Roy, L. A., D. A. Davis, I. P. Saoud, C. A. Boyd, H. J. Pine, and C. E. Boyd. 2010. Shrimp culture in inland low salinity water. Reviews in Aquaculture 2:191-208.
7. Boyd, C. E., C. Tucker, A. McNevin, K. Bostick, and J. Clay. 2007. Indicators of resource use efficiency and environmental performance in aquaculture. Reviews in Fisheries Science 15:327-360.

# Chapter 2

# Fundamentals of Water Science

## Introduction

Aquaculturists should have a basic understanding of water science, because water is the medium for culture of fish and other species. This chapter provides an overview of water science with emphasis on topics important in water quality management in aquaculture.

## Properties of Water

### Structure of Water Molecules

The water molecule, $H_2O$, consists of two hydrogen atoms covalently bonded to an oxygen atom (Fig. 2.1). The angle made by the H−O−H covalent bonds is 105°, which, in effect, places both hydrogen atoms on the same side of the oxygen atom. Although the water molecule has no net electrical charge, its electrons are not distributed uniformly— the heavier oxygen nucleus pulls the hydrogen electrons relatively closer to it and away from the hydrogen nuclei. This gives the hydrogen atoms a weak positive charge and the

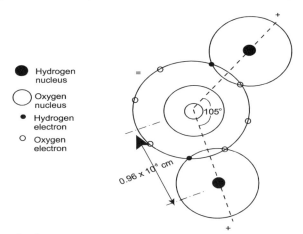

Hydrogen nucleus
Oxygen nucleus
Hydrogen electron
Oxygen electron

105°

$0.96 \times 10^8$ cm

**Fig. 2.1.** The water molecule.

oxygen atom a weak negative charge. Molecules with charge separation such as this are called *dipoles*, meaning 'two poles.' Opposite charges attract, and the negatively charged side of one water molecule attracts a positively charged side on another. The attraction between two water molecules is called a *hydrogen bond*. Hydrogen bonds cause liquid water molecules to form loose, polymer-like aggregates that continuously form and then break part in picosecond timeframes. To emphasize the fleeting, polymer-like structure of liquid water, the formula is sometimes denoted $(H_2O)_n$. Although weaker than ionic bonds, hydrogen bonds are stronger than van der Waals attractions that occur between molecules of all substances. Hydrogen bonding results in water having unique properties discussed below.

## *Thermal Characteristics*

Molecular energy declines with decreasing temperature, and as it does, molecular vibrations decrease and bond-lengths shrink. At standard atmospheric pressure (760 mm Hg), molecular movements decline sufficiently at 0°C for each water molecule to form hydrogen bonds with three other water molecules and produce the tetrahedral structure of ice (Fig. 2.2). The freezing point of water is much higher than that of other substances of similar molecular weight.

Warming increases vibration of molecules and causes bonds to stretch. Heat energy input to ice increases molecular activity and causes its tetrahedral structure to collapse forming liquid water. The phase change from ice to liquid water—without a change in temperature—requires 80 cal/g (the *latent heat of fusion*). The latent heat of fusion of water is much higher than that of other liquids of similar molecular weight.

Continued warming of water will raise its temperature. An energy input of 1 cal/g is required to raise its temperature by 1°C. The amount of energy necessary to increase temperature of 1 g of a substance by 1°C is called the *specific heat*; water has a high specific heat compared to most other substances. When temperature reaches 100°C at standard atmospheric pressure, water boils—it changes from a liquid to a gas. The vapor pressure of water at 100°C is equal to standard atmospheric pressure, and water

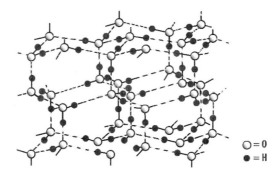

**Fig. 2.2.** Tetrahedral structure of ice.

molecules have enough energy to escape into the air as single $H_2O$ molecules. However, to completely break all hydrogen bonds and allow the phase change from liquid to gas requires an energy input of 540 cal/g without temperature change. This quantity of energy is the *latent heat of vaporization*. Water also has a greater latent heat than other liquids of similar weight.

The boiling point of water, because of hydrogen bonding, also is much higher than that of other compounds of similar molecular weight. Water exists on the earth's surface because of hydrogen bonding, without which it would be vapor at normal temperatures and would have diffused into space.

To summarize, to change ice at 0°C to water vapor at 100°C requires 80 cal/g to melt the ice, 100 cal/g (100°C × 1 cal/g/°C) to raise the temperature from 0° to 100°C, and another 540 cal/g to transform liquid water to water vapor.

## *Density*

Ice at 0°C, as a result of its open tetrahedral structure (Fig. 2.2), has a density of 0.9168 g/cm³ as compared to 0.99984 g/cm³ for liquid water at the same temperature. When the tetrahedral lattice of ice collapses, the volume of liquid water is less than that of the ice from which it came. There are remnants of the crystalline lattice in liquid water at 0°C, and the density of water will increase as these remnants continue to collapse. Water reaches a maximum density of 1.0000 g/cm³ at 3.94°C. Above this temperature, vibration of molecules and stretching of bonds have a greater influence on density than does the continuing breakup of the crystalline lattice. The density of water decreases with increasing temperature above 3.94°C (Table 2.1). The density of water also increases with increasing salinity (Table 2.2).

Density relationships resulting from hydrogen bonding cause ice to float and prevent water bodies from freezing solid from the bottom upward. They also are responsible for thermal stratification of water bodies, a topic discussed in Chapter 12.

**Table 2.1.** Density of freshwater (g/cm³) at different temperatures between 0 and 40°C.

| °C | g/cm³ | °C | g/cm³ | °C | g/cm³ |
|----|-------|----|-------|----|-------|
| 0 | 0.99984 | 14 | 0.99925 | 28 | 0.99624 |
| 1 | 0.99990 | 15 | 0.99910 | 29 | 0.99595 |
| 2 | 0.99994 | 16 | 0.99895 | 30 | 0.99565 |
| 3 | 0.99997 | 17 | 0.99878 | 31 | 0.99534 |
| 4 | 0.99998 | 18 | 0.99860 | 32 | 0.99503 |
| 5 | 0.99997 | 19 | 0.99841 | 33 | 0.99471 |
| 6 | 0.99994 | 20 | 0.99821 | 34 | 0.99437 |
| 7 | 0.99990 | 21 | 0.99800 | 35 | 0.99403 |
| 8 | 0.99985 | 22 | 0.99777 | 36 | 0.99309 |
| 9 | 0.99978 | 23 | 0.99754 | 37 | 0.99333 |
| 10 | 0.99970 | 24 | 0.99730 | 38 | 0.99297 |
| 11 | 0.99961 | 25 | 0.99705 | 39 | 0.99260 |
| 12 | 0.99950 | 26 | 0.99678 | 40 | 0.99222 |
| 13 | 0.99938 | 27 | 0.99652 | | |

**Table 2.2.** The density of water (g/cm$^3$) of different salinities at selected temperatures between 0 and 40°C.

| °C | Salinity (parts per thousand) | | | | |
|----|---------|--------|--------|--------|--------|
|    | 0 | 10 | 20 | 30 | 40 |
| 0  | 0.99984 | 1.0080 | 1.0160 | 1.0241 | 1.0321 |
| 5  | 0.99997 | 1.0079 | 1.0158 | 1.0237 | 1.0316 |
| 10 | 0.99970 | 1.0075 | 1.0153 | 1.0231 | 1.0309 |
| 15 | 0.99910 | 1.0068 | 1.0144 | 1.0221 | 1.0298 |
| 20 | 0.99821 | 1.0058 | 1.0134 | 1.0210 | 1.0286 |
| 25 | 0.99705 | 1.0046 | 1.0121 | 1.0196 | 1.0271 |
| 30 | 0.99565 | 1.0031 | 1.0105 | 1.0180 | 1.0255 |
| 35 | 0.99403 | 1.0014 | 1.0088 | 1.0162 | 1.0237 |
| 40 | 0.99222 | 0.9996 | 1.0069 | 1.0143 | 1.0217 |

## Surface Phenomena

Hydrogen bonding is responsible for water exhibiting both *cohesion* (attraction between like molecules) and *adhesion* (attraction between unlike molecules). A familiar event illustrates these properties. Water adheres to dry, unpainted wood because it forms hydrogen bonds with molecules of the wood. Water forms beads on painted wood because the cohesive force among water molecules are greater than adhesive attraction between water molecules and the painted surface.

Cohesive forces cannot act above a water surface, and molecules at the surface cohere to adjacent molecules and molecules below. The surface molecules act as a skin, causing the effect known as *surface tension*. The combined effects of adhesion, cohesion, and surface tension are responsible for *capillary action* that causes water to rise in thin glass tubes or in pores of soil and other porous media. In a thin tube, water adheres to the walls and spreads upward as much as possible. Water moving upward in the tube coheres to molecules of surface film which in turn cohere to molecules below. As adhesion drags the surface film upward, it pulls water up the tube against the force of gravity. Capillarity in some finely-grained soils can cause water to rise a few centimeters to several meters above the water table.

Capillarity also is influenced by the internal resistance of water to flow or its viscosity. Cohesion of water molecules is one of the factors determining viscosity. Both viscosity and surface tension decrease with increasing water temperature, favoring capillarity.

## Dielectric Constant

Water molecules are dipolar and therefore attracted to charges—the positive (hydrogen) side of the water molecule is attracted to negative charges and the negative (oxygen) side of the molecule to positive charges. This principle can be illustrated by determining the voltage that must be applied to obtain a charge of 1 volt on condenser plates immersed in pure water. The water molecules orient themselves around the positive and negative plates of the condenser to neutralize part of the applied charge. The *dielectric constant* represents the ratio of battery voltage:condenser plate voltage for condenser plates exposed to different media. The dielectric constant for water is 81 volts compared to 1.0000 volt in a vacuum and 1.0006 volts in air.

A crystal of table salt (NaCl) maintains its crystalline structure in air because of electrical attraction between anions and cations: $Na^+ + Cl^- = NaCl$. Salt dissolves readily in water because the attractive forces between anions and cations are 81 times less in water than in air. Water insulates ions from each other because water molecules are attracted to dissolved ions. Each anion attracts the positive sides of several water molecules, and each cation attracts the negative sides of other water molecules (Fig. 2.3). Ions can each attract several water molecules because ionic charges are much stronger than the charges on opposite sides of water molecules. Water is said to *hydrate* ions, and hydration neutralizes charges on ions just as the water molecules neutralize the charge on a condenser plate. Because of its high dielectric constant and dipolar properties, water is an excellent solvent for most inorganic and many organic substances.

Water's polarity also affects the behavior of many non-ionic molecules. An important interaction of this type occurs between water and carbon dioxide. Pure carbon dioxide consists of linear molecules (O=C=O) that are nonpolar. Like other nonpolar compounds, carbon dioxide should not be very soluble in water (a polar solvent). However, when carbon dioxide dissolves in water, the strong dipole in the water molecule induces a temporary dipole in the carbon dioxide molecule, which increases its polarity and water solubility. As a result of this 'dipole-induced dipole,' carbon dioxide is about 30 times more soluble in water than oxygen and about 50 times more soluble than nitrogen.

## Vapor Pressure

*Vapor pressure* is the pressure a substance exerts when in equilibrium with its vapor. Heating increases molecular energy of water and more molecules escape the surface to increase vapor pressure (Table 2.3). Warm air has the capacity to hold more water vapor than cooler air.

## Pressure

Just as the weight of the atmosphere exerts pressure on a point at the earth's surface, water exerts a pressure on points beneath its surface. Water pressure may be expressed as the weight of the water column above a small surface area ($g/cm^2$, for example) but more

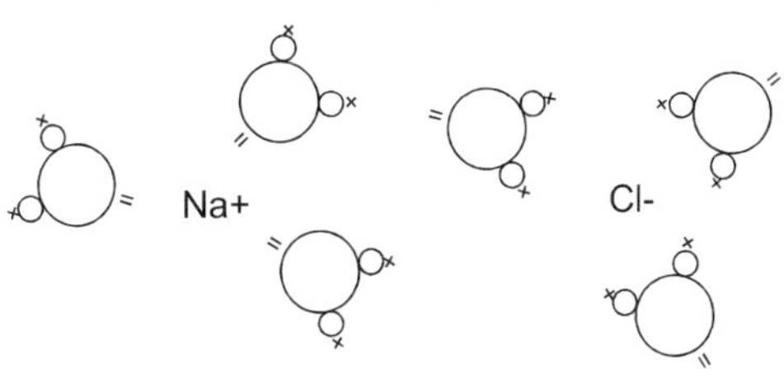

**Fig. 2.3.** Hydration of dissolved ions by water molecules.

**Table 2.3.** Vapor pressure of water in millimeters of mercury (mm Hg) at different temperatures (°C).

| °C | mm Hg | °C | mm Hg | °C | mm Hg |
|----|-------|----|-------|-----|-------|
| 0  | 4.579  | 35 | 42.175 | 70  | 233.7 |
| 5  | 6.543  | 40 | 55.324 | 75  | 289.1 |
| 10 | 9.209  | 45 | 71.88  | 80  | 355.1 |
| 15 | 12.788 | 50 | 92.51  | 85  | 433.6 |
| 20 | 17.535 | 55 | 118.04 | 90  | 525.8 |
| 25 | 23.756 | 60 | 149.38 | 95  | 633.9 |
| 30 | 31.824 | 65 | 187.54 | 100 | 760.0 |

commonly it is simply expressed as the depth of water. Of course, water also can have potential energy (pressure) as the result of elevation above a reference plane, kineticenergy as a result of velocity of flow, and pressure can be applied to water by a pump. Water pressure often is referred to as *head* of water, expressed as the depth or height of a water column.

## *Light Penetration*

Light refers to the visible wavelengths of the electromagnetic spectrum. These wavelengths, which fall between 400 to 700 nm, are also the wavelengths of solar radiation that drive photosynthesis, the most important reaction on earth. All points on the earth's surface have equal annual hours of day and night, but day length varies with the longest duration ranging from 12 hours at the equator to 6 months at the poles. Although annual hours of daylight are equal everywhere, the amount of solar energy received on a given surface area over a given time (*insolation*) is a function of latitude, season, slope of surface, and the tendency for cloud cover. In winter and at high latitudes, the sun's rays are more oblique than in summer and at low latitudes. The more perpendicular the rays are to the earth's surface, the greater the amount of insolation. Cloud cover also absorbs, scatters, and reflects sunlight — persistent clouds throughout the day can reduce insolation by more than half. The amount of solar radiation striking the earth's surface also varies with time of day. On a cloudless day, radiation increases from sunrise until solar noon and then decrease until the sun sets. In addition to these factors, water has additional effects on light by rapidly diminishing overall intensity and changing light's spectral qualities as it passes through water.

The amount of solar radiation entering water is greatest when the surface is smooth and the sun's rays are vertical. Light penetration decreases with greater surface turbulence and increasing departure from vertical by the sun's rays. Light is absorbed and transformed into heat as it passes through water—only about 50% of light striking the surface of pure water penetrates to a depth of 1 m. Light in the infrared and red wavelengths are most strongly absorbed by pure water. Impurities in water increase the rate of light quenching. Small amounts of dissolved organic matter strongly absorb blue and green wavelengths; plankton and other suspended solids absorb and scatter light in various wavelengths depending on the size and nature of the particles. Because light energy is rapidly diminished as it passes through water, photosynthesis by aquatic plants and algae is restricted to near-surface waters. Rapid quenching of light in ponds with plankton blooms also heats surface water faster than deeper water, favoring thermal stratification (Chapter12).

Underwater light meters can be used to measure light penetration at different depths. However, in aquaculture, the limit of visibility into water is often expressed as *Secchi disk visibility* (Secchi disk visibility is the depth in meters where a 20-cm black and white disk disappears when lowered into the water; Fig. 2.4). The extinction coefficient of light in water can be calculated from Secchi disk visibility:

$$K = \frac{1.7}{Z_{SD}} \tag{2.1}$$

where K = extinction coefficient (1/m); $Z_{SD}$ = Secchi disk visibility (m).

### *Conductivity*

Conductivity is the ability of a substance to convey an electrical current. In water, electrical current is conveyed by the dissolved ions. Thus, pure water is a poor conductor. Natural waters contain dissolved ions and are good conductors. Conductivity increases in direct proportion to dissolved ion concentrations.

# Water Temperature

Water has a high specific heat, and a large input of solar energy is required to increase the temperature of a large water body. A large amount of heat also must be lost to the

**Fig. 2.4.** A Secchi disk.

atmosphere for the temperature of a large water body to decrease. Because of the resistance to temperature change caused by the high specific heat of water, water temperature lags air temperatures in lakes. In the temperate zone, waters in lakes remain cool into late spring or early summer and warm until late fall or early winter. Aquaculture ponds have relatively small volumes, and as illustrated in Fig. 2.5, water temperature tends to follow air temperature fairly closely and seldom lags by more than 1 or 2 weeks.[1]

Water temperature usually is lower than air temperature as depicted in Fig. 2.5. Plankton blooms encourage higher water temperature[2], but even in ponds with dense plankton blooms, maximum daily temperature of surface water usually is several degrees less than that of the overlaying air.

## Hydrologic Cycle

The natural water cycle is illustrated in Fig. 2.6. Rain falling on the earth is either intercepted by vegetation and other above-ground surfaces or strikes the ground. Intercepted rainfall evaporates or drips to the ground. Rain reaching the ground may infiltrate into the soil, flow downslope as overland flow, or evaporate. Water infiltrating into soil becomes soil moisture, moves laterally to enter streams, or infiltrates until it intercepts the water table and becomes groundwater. Soil moisture either evaporates from the ground surface or is transpired into the air by plants. Overland flow and groundwater move in response to gravity and enter streams—becoming runoff. Runoff in streams evaporates or flows into the ocean. Groundwater and runoff may be withdrawn for use in human activities; this water usually evaporates or is discharged back into streams after being used. Water flowing into the oceans also eventually evaporates. Water that is evaporated into the air is caught up in the general atmospheric circulation. When air rises, it expands, cools, becomes saturated with water vapor, and clouds form. Water droplets in clouds coalesce and grow until they become raindrops or frozen precipitation and fall to the earth—the cycle continues.

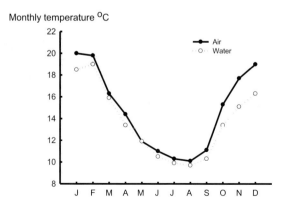

**Fig. 2.5.** Monthly air and pond water temperature in Western Australia.[1]

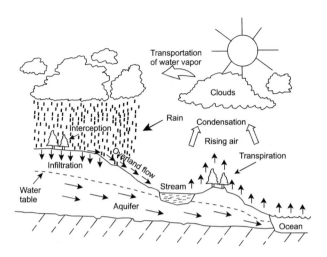

**Fig. 2.6.** The hydrologic cycle or water cycle.

## *Watersheds*

The *watershed* is the basic unit of surface water hydrology. It is the entire area that yields runoff to a particular point. Inside the watershed boundary, all runoff will flow downslope. The runoff from a watershed can be estimated by determining the amount of water flowing from it. The simplest form is the unit watershed (Fig. 2.7) from which runoff collects and flows to a first-order perennial or permanent stream. A *first-order stream* has no tributaries. In Fig. 2.7, a small pond has been constructed to capture and store runoff from the watershed. The overflow from this pond could be measured to estimate watershed runoff.

A *second-order* stream receives water from two or more first-order streams; a *third-order* stream receives water from two or more second-order streams, and so on. If the flow of a larger stream to which many unit watersheds contribute overland flow and base flow is measured, the entire area that contributes to flow at the point of measurement may also be called a watershed. Such watersheds also may be referred to as *stream basins* or *catchments*.

Watershed characteristics such as topography, soil type, underground geology, vegetative cover, and land use practices greatly influence the amount of runoff and its quality. Efforts to enhance water quality in streams focus on watershed management to reduce erosion and prevent pollution from all sources.

## *Evaporation*

Evaporation occurs from any moist surface exposed to the air, but it mostly occurs from free water surfaces and leaves of living plants. Water loss from plants is called

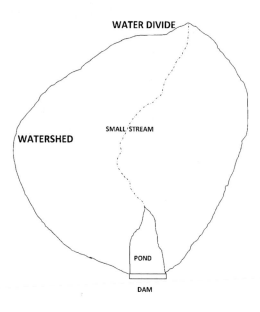

**Fig. 2.7.** A first order watershed containing a small pond.

*transpiration*, and the term *evapotranspiration* encompasses all water evaporated from a watershed. Water molecules evaporate into the air above a surface until the pressure of water molecules in air equals the saturation vapor pressure or 100% relative humidity. (Note that water can evaporate from a surface with a temperature less than 100°C because the energy content of water molecules in a particular mass of water do not all have the same energy content. Those with the greatest energy content will escape the water surface. The energy to evaporate 1 g of water molecules will equal the energy necessary to raise water temperature from that of the water surface to 100°C plus the energy necessary for the latent heat of vaporization). Evaporation from water bodies increases with higher water temperature, lower relative humidity, and greater wind speed. These factors, plus certain characteristics of plants such as large leaf area and roots extending into the capillary fringe above the water table, also favor greater evaporation from the land. Evaporation from land, however, often may be limited by a lack of moisture.

Evaporation or evapotranspiration usually is assessed by measuring water loss from a permanent water surface or from a well-watered container of soil containing plants called a *lysimeter*. Potential evapotranspiration often is estimated from mean monthly air temperatures and day lengths by the Thornwaithe method.[3] The most common device for measuring evaporation from a free, water surface is a *Class A evaporation pan* (Fig. 2.8). The daily loss of water from the pan is measured with a hook gauge and adjusted for rain falling into it to provide an estimate of potential evaporation. Studies have shown that Class A pan evaporation multiplied by 0.7 is a good estimate of pond evaporation,[4] but the factor 0.81 is a better estimate of evaporation from ponds.[5]

**Fig. 2.8.** Class A evaporation pan (left) and hook gauge (right).

Pan evaporation tends to be closely related to air temperature. For example, along a north-south transect of the United States from south Texas (26°N latitude) to the Canadian border (49°N latitude), evaporation decreases from nearly 200 cm/year to about 75 cm/year.[6] At a given location, pan evaporation and potential evapotranspiration both closely follow the annual march of air temperature (Fig. 2.9).

Evaporation is not measured as frequently as precipitation, but in the United States, there usually are several stations in each state where pan evaporation is measured. Pan evaporation rates for the continental United States that extends from about 25°N to 50°N latitude illustrate the range in potential evaporation from water surfaces. Average annual evaporation ranges from about 80 to 320 cm/year. The lowest values are in cold, inland

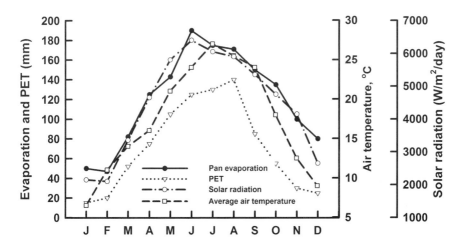

**Fig. 2.9.** Monthly solar radiation, air temperature, potential evapotranspiration (PET), and pan evaporation at Auburn, Alabama.

areas and the highest are in hot, arid places where windy conditions prevail (Table 2.4). A pond located in an area where pan evaporation is about 180 cm/year would lose an average of 145.8 cm/year (180 cm/year × 0.81) or 0.49 cm/day to evaporation. On a day with good conditions for evaporation, the loss might reach more than twice the average daily rate. Maximum evaporation from ponds seldom exceeds 1.25 cm/day (about 0.5 in/day).

Aquaculture systems provide excellent environments for evaporation because light absorption by plankton blooms elevates surface water temperatures and aerators splash water into the air to increase the surface area for evaporation. Evaporation is a cooling process, for a large amount of heat energy is required to raise the thermal energy of water molecules and supply the latent heat of vaporization. This energy is removed from the water body in escaping water molecules. Aerated ponds often have slightly cooler water than un-aerated ones.

## *Precipitation*

Water evaporated from the earth's surface is caught up in the general atmospheric circulation. When air rises because of mountains or other topographic barriers, cold fronts forcing warmer, lighter air upward, or differential heating of the land surface, precipitation often occurs. If the air temperature is above freezing, the precipitation will be rain.

The equatorial zone receives more solar radiation than other zones. Intensive heating increases the moisture holding capacity of air and also causes air to rise, and most equatorial locations tend to have much rainfall. In the zone around 30°N and 30°S latitude, air tends to fall—the great deserts of the world occur in this zone. Precipitation declines with increasing latitude because of lower air temperature. For example, in the United States, Alabama receives more precipitation than Ohio.

There are factors that cause many areas not to obey the general rainfall patterns described above. Mountainous terrain may result in high precipitation at almost any location where air must flow over it. Precipitation usually declines from coastal areas to inland areas on large land masses such as the United States. The further inland air travels, the greater the opportunity for it to lose moisture, and hence, a lower tendency for precipitation. A warm ocean offshore favors more precipitation on land than does a cold

**Table 2.4.** Class A pan evaporation rates for selected locations in the United States.

| Location | North latitude | Class A pan evaporation (cm/yr) |
|---|---|---|
| Northern Minnesota | 48° | 87 |
| Central New York | 45° | 98 |
| Coastal North Carolina | 35° | 142 |
| Central Alabama | 32° | 160 |
| South Florida | 25° | 195 |
| Central Kansas | 37° | 218 |
| Southwestern Arizona | 33° | 272 |
| Southwestern California | 33° | 312 |

ocean offshore. For this reason, the southern California coast with the cold Japanese current offshore has much less rainfall than North and South Carolina with the warm Gulf Stream offshore.

Rainfall is measured with a *rain gauge* (Fig. 2.10). The standard U.S. Weather Service-type rain gauge has an inner tube, an outer bucket, and a funnel top. The tube stands inside the bucket and receives water from the funnel top. The area of the funnel top is 10 times that of the inner tube. This concentrates rainfall in the tube to allow easy measurement of even small amounts of rainfall with a calibrated, dip stick. Once the tube is filled, it overflows into the bucket. The tube can be emptied and used to measure water captured in the bucket. There also are smaller rain gauges for unofficial data collection.

The depth and moisture content of snow can be used to convert its depth to a liquid water equivalent. Alternatively, the bucket of the rain gauge can be used to capture snow, the snow melted, and the water poured into the tube for measurement of water depth equivalent.

There are records of daily, monthly, and annual precipitation extending back for 50 to 100 years or more at many locations in the world. As already mentioned and as illustrated in Table 2.5, annual precipitation varies greatly with geography. Moreover, precipitation is not evenly distributed with time. Almost all locations have rainy days and dry days, but many locations have distinct wet seasons and dry seasons. For example, at Bangkok, Thailand, the rainy season is from May to October, and there is much less rainfall the rest of the year (Table 2.6).[7] Also, at most locations, some years have heavy rainfall, while other years have much less. Even one year with less than normal rainfall can lead to drought, and two or more years of low rain can cause extreme water shortages.

## *Soil Moisture and Groundwater*

Water that infiltrates the land surface becomes soil moisture or percolates deeper until it meets an impermeable, confining stratum and becomes groundwater (Fig. 2.11). The soil

**Fig. 2.10.** Standard U.S. Weather Service rain gauge (left); small rain gauge (right).

**Table 2.5.** Annual rainfall for selected cities.

| Location | cm/yr |
|---|---|
| Bangkok, Thailand | 149.2 |
| Bombay, India | 207.8 |
| Jakarta, Indonesia | 175.5 |
| Manila, Philippines | 179.1 |
| New Dehli, India | 71.5 |
| Brisbane, Australia | 109.2 |
| Perth, Australia | 88.9 |
| Edinburgh, Scotland | 67.6 |
| Madrid, Spain | 43.6 |
| Warsaw, Poland | 47.1 |
| Montgomery, Alabama | 126.6 |
| Dallas, Texas | 94.6 |
| Stockton, California | 36.0 |
| Mexico City, Mexico | 57.1 |
| Havana, Cuba | 122.4 |
| Bogota, Columbia | 94.2 |
| Manus, Brazil | 209.5 |
| Ankara, Turkey | 36.0 |

**Table 2.6.** Average monthly rainfall at Bangkok, Thailand.

| Month | cm | Month | cm |
|---|---|---|---|
| January | 0.89 | July | 17.78 |
| February | 2.90 | August | 19.08 |
| March | 3.38 | September | 30.58 |
| April | 8.89 | October | 25.48 |
| May | 16.58 | November | 5.69 |
| June | 17.09 | December | 0.69 |

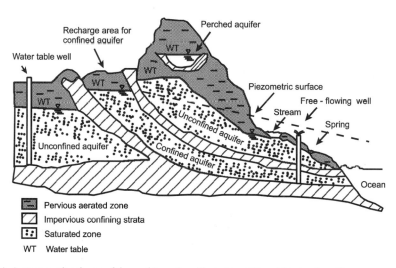

**Fig. 2.11.** A cross-sectional area of the earth's surface illustrating different kinds of aquifers.

has a finite capacity to hold water, and when it is saturated, water will move laterally through the soil and at places flows onto the land surface or enters streams. Water evaporates from moist soil, but much water loss from soil is through transpiration by plants.

Groundwater occurs in geological formations called *aquifers*. As in soil, water stands in the interstices or pore space between the solid particles comprising the formation. Groundwater moves downslope in response to gravity and it enters streams where their channels cut below the water table (top of an aquifer). This phenomenon, known as *base flow* sustains streams in dry weather.[8] Aquifers also may discharge into seas, lakes, and other water bodies. Aquifers hold a tremendous amount of water—much more than surface bodies of freshwater. Water removed from aquifers by wells is an important source of water for human activities.

## Surface Water

Water flows over the land surface in response to gravity when the rate of rainfall (or melting of snow) exceeds the rate that it can infiltrate into the soil. This water is called *overland flow*. Factors favoring large amounts of overland flow are heavy rainfall, water saturated soil, low temperature that reduces evapotranspiration, lack of vegetation or short grass as compared to tall grass or trees, soil of low infiltration capacity, frozen soil, cover of surfaces by pavement or other impermeable structures, and steep slopes.

Precipitation can be divided into three fractions: evapotranspiration, soil moisture and groundwater storage, and runoff. The amount of soil moisture and groundwater in storage normally is about the same from the beginning of one year to the next resulting in the following relationship:

$$\text{Precipitation} = \text{Evapotranspiration} + \text{Runoff} . \tag{2.2}$$

Average annual runoff estimated from stream flow data for 73 streams in Alabama[9] compared favorably to runoff estimated by subtracting annual potential evapotranspiration from precipitation (Table 2.7). Of course, Alabama normally has abundant rainfall, and because there usually is water in the soil to support evapotranspiration, potential evapotranspiration is similar to actual evapotranspiration. In semi-arid or arid climates, substituting potential evapotranspiration for evapotranspiration

**Table 2.7.** Runoff (in/yr) for regions of Alabama.

| Region | Measured stream discharge | Estimated P - PET |
|---|---|---|
| Appalachian Plateau | 23.49 | 20.72 |
| Blackland Prairie | 17.99 | 16.04 |
| Limestone Valleys | 22.05 | 19.08 |
| Lower Coastal Plain | 24.59 | 22.32 |
| Piedmont Plateau | 19.22 | 20.23 |
| Upper Coastal Plain | 20.80 | 18.93 |
| Average | 21.32 | 19.55 |

in Equation 2.2 will not provide a good estimate of runoff. However, an excellent estimation of annual evapotranspiration can be made in other climates by subtracting runoff from precipitation.

Runoff varies greatly among watersheds both within and between climatic regions. For example, in Alabama, runoff from 73 watersheds was 45.7 cm/year to 62.0 cm/year with an average of 52.7 cm/year.[9] In the central United States where rainfall is less, runoff is 12.7 to 38.1 cm/year, while in arid regions of the western United States runoff may be only 2.5 to 5 cm/year.[6] Runoff normally is 20 to 40% of annual precipitation, and base flow may account for 50% or more of runoff.

Runoff for a particular watershed varies with rainfall, and some months typically have greater flow than others. Moreover, drought years have much less annual runoff than normal.

The flow of water in streams is a function of average water velocity and cross-sectional area of flow:

$$Q = Av \qquad (2.3)$$

where Q = discharge (m$^3$/sec); A = cross-sectional area (m$^2$); v = water velocity (m/sec). Cross-sectional area and velocity at a particular point in a stream are directly proportional to stream depth. This relationship may be established for a range of depths and stream discharge can be estimated from depth.

Overland flow can be estimated from a *stream hydrograph* (Fig. 2.12). However, this method can only be used when streams have been gauged. The curve number method[6] allows estimation of overland flow from observation of soil features, vegetative cover, land use, hydrologic condition, antecedent rainfall, and amount of rainfall.

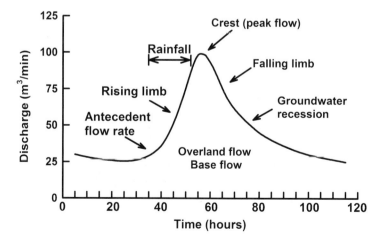

**Fig. 2.12.** A stream hydrograph.

## *Hydroclimate*

A plot of average, monthly rainfall and potential evapotranspiration for a location depicts a concept called *hydroclimate* that can be instructive about local hydrology. In the illustration of hydroclimate for a location in Alabama (Fig. 2.13), precipitation exceeds potential evapotranspiration during the period November through April, while the opposite occurs during other months. Normally, soil moisture and groundwater are recharged during winter and early spring. During May and June, soil moisture usually is adequate for plants, but water stress may occur during the period July through October. Although rainfall generally exceeds potential evapotranspiration in November and December, much of the available water is used in recharging soil moisture. Thus, groundwater recharges and overland flow may not be appreciable until winter. After April, stream flow declines because of lack of overland flow and a progressive decline in base flow.

Pond evaporation estimated from pan evaporation data can be plotted versus rainfall to illustrate periods when there is either a surplus or deficit of precipitation in comparison to water loss through evaporation. Such a plot is useful in predicting changes in water level only if data are available for gain or loss of water by seepage and gain of water by overland flow in watershed ponds and for seepage loss from embankment ponds.

## *Water Flow in Soil*

Soils and other geologic materials have interconnected voids (pore space) between their constituent particles. Water may flow through these pores in response to pressure and gravity. Minute channels through which water moves in porous materials are not straight but exhibit a random pattern. Hence, when a molecule of water passes through a porous

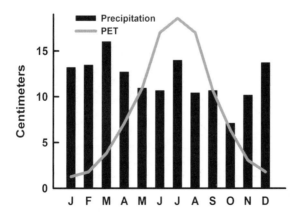

**Fig. 2.13.** Monthly precipitation and potential evapotranspiration at Auburn, Alabama.

cross-section of material does not permit flow; flow occurs only through voids. The *porosity* of soils or other porous media is defined as the ratio of the volume of voids to discharge of water through a cross-section of the material may be determined. Water material, the length of the path followed by the molecule is unknown, but the rate of molecules take various paths through the material, and their velocities differ. The entire the bulk volume.

Darcy's equation[6,10] states that seepage velocity (v) is proportional to a coefficient multiplied by the energy gradient—more often called the hydraulic gradient. That is,

$$v = Ki \tag{2.4}$$

where K = hydraulic conductivity (m/sec); i = hydraulic gradient (dimensionless). The hydraulic gradient is the head loss per unit length of travel through the porous medium.

The hydraulic conductivity of a porous material depends on the size and arrangement of particles in unconsolidated formations and on the sizes and arrangement of crevices, fractures, and solution caverns in consolidated formations. Any change in material characteristics influence the conductivity. For example, compaction of loose soil reduces K. Hydraulic conductivity usually is determined in the laboratory and expressed as the velocity of seepage through the permeable material under a hydraulic gradient of 1.00. The hydraulic conductivities of various materials are given in Table 2.8.

Sometimes, Darcy's equation is given in a slightly different form. Because Q = Av (Equation 2.3), we substitute Q/A for v in Equation 2.4 to give:

$$Q = KiA. \tag{2.5}$$

Use of Darcy's equation is illustrated in Example 2.1.

Seepage rates in ponds usually are measured rather than calculated, and they vary greatly. The most common way of measuring pond seepage is to measure the change in water depth over a period of several days when there are no inflows and evaporation and seepage are the only outflows. Under such conditions, seepage is equal to water level change minus pond evaporation. A literature review of pond seepage rates presented estimates of 2 to 100 cm/month with an average of 7 cm/month. Seepage rate categories based on the review are given in Table 2.9.

**Table 2.8.** Hydraulic conductivity of soil (K)

| Soil type | K (cm/sec) |
|---|---|
| Clean gravel | 2.5-4.0 |
| Fine gravel | 1.0-3.5 |
| Coarse, clean sand | 0.01-1.0 |
| Mixed sand | 0.005-0.01 |
| Fine sand | 0.001-0.05 |
| Silty sand | 0.0001-0.002 |
| Silt | 0.00001-0.0005 |
| Clay | $10^{-9}$-$10^{-6}$ |

> **Example 2.1**
> **Illustration of Seepage Velocity Estimation with the Darcy Equation**
>
> A 1-m deep pond has an excessively high seepage rate as the result of sandy soil in its bottom. A soil blanket of 20-cm depth is placed in the bottom of the pond. Assuming that the soil has a hydraulic conductivity of $10^{-6}$ cm/sec, estimate the lowest, daily seepage velocity that might be attained.
>
> $$v = Ki = (10-6 \text{ cm/sec})(86{,}400 \text{ sec/day})\left(\frac{1.0 \text{ m}}{0.2 \text{ m}}\right) = 0.432 \text{ cm/day}.$$

## Water Volume, Weight, and Flow Relationships

Quantities of water may be expressed several ways. In hydrology, the amount of water entering or leaving a watershed or other large area often is expressed in depth over a period of time; for example, 2 cm rainfall/24 hours or 56 cm potential evapotranspiration/year. Depth may be easily converted to volume by multiplying it by area, including the time period will provide an inflow or outflow rate for the variable (Example 2.2). In the English system of measure, depth is in inches or feet and area in acres. Equivalences among metric and English units are provided in Chapter 31.

Depending upon the size of aquaculture units, the volume of water usually is expressed in hectare-m (1 m of water spread over 1 ha), cubic meters, or liters; 1 ha-m = 10,000 $m^3$; 1 $m^3$ = 1,000 L. Volume in an aquaculture unit is easily calculated from surface area multiplied by average depth. For example, a 400 $m^2$ pond of 0.8 m average depth has a volume of 320 $m^3$. In the English system, volume may be given as acre-feet, cubic feet, or gallons: 1 acre-ft = 43,560 $ft^3$; 1 $ft^3$ = 7.48 gal.

Stream flow and discharge of pumps or pipes usually are given as volume per unit of time (such as liters per second or cubic meters per minute; 1 $m^3$/min = 1,000 L/min = 16.67 L/sec). The volume discharged over a period of time can be estimated by multiplying discharge rate by time of discharge (Example 2.3). In the English system, flow usually is expressed in cubic feet per second or gallons per minute: 1 $ft^3$/sec = 448.9 gpm.

**Table 2.9.** Seepage class categories for earthen ponds.

| Seepage class | Seepage rate (cm/month) |
|---|---|
| Normal | <20 |
| High | 20-40 |
| Excessive | >40 |

## Example 2.2
## Illustration of Watershed Discharge Calculation

A 500-ha watershed receives 120 cm/yr rainfall and ET in the region is 800 cm/yr. The annual discharge of the watershed will be estimated in both depth, volume, and flow rate units:

$RO = P - ET = (1,200 - 800)$ cm/yr $= 400$ cm/yr

The volume of runoff is:

0.40 m/yr × 500 ha × 10,000 m$^2$/ha $= 2,000,000$ m$^3$/yr.

The average discharge in cubic meters per minute is:

2,000,000 m$^3$/yr ÷ (365 day/yr × 1,440 min/day) $= 3.8$ m$^3$/min.

## Example 2.3
## Estimation of Pumping Time to Fill a Pond

A 1.5-ha pond of 1.2 m average depth will be filled from a pump that discharges 3 m$^3$/min. The combined loss by seepage and evaporation averages 2 cm/day. How long must the pump be operated to fill the pond?

Water loss is 0.02 m/day and equates to 0.21 m$^3$/min:

$$\frac{1.5 \text{ ha} \times 10,000 \text{ m}^2/\text{ha} \times 0.02 \text{ m/day}}{1,440 \text{ min/day}} = 0.21 \text{ m}^3/\text{min}.$$

Thus, the effective pump discharge is $(3.0 - 0.21)$ m$^3$/min $= 2.79$ m$^3$/min.

The time of pump operation is:

$$\frac{1.5 \text{ ha} \times 10,000 \text{ m}^2/\text{ha} \times 1.2 \text{ m}}{2.79 \text{ m}^3/\text{min} \times 60 \text{ min/hr}} = 107.5 \text{ hr}.$$

Concentrations of substances in water that will be discussed in the following chapters normally are given as weight per unit volume in milligrams per liter or ppm which are of the same value for freshwater because 1 L of water weighs 1 kg (1,000,000 mg), and 1 mg in 1,000,000 kg is 1 part in 1,000,000 parts. It also is important to note that 1 mg/L is the same as 1 g/m$^3$, because 1 m$^3$ has 1,000 L and 1,000 L of water containing 1 mg/L of a substance contains 1 g of that substance or 1 g/m$^3$. A hectare-meter of water is equivalent to 10,000 m$^3$; 1 mg/L in 1 ha-m is the same as 10,000 g/m$^3$ (10 kg/m$^3$). In the English system, 1 acre-ft contains 325,872 gal and weighs 2,711,000 lb. Thus, 1 ppm = 2.711 lb/acre-ft.

Determination of the dose to provide a particular concentration of a substance in an aquaculture unit is often necessary. Example 2.4 illustrates a dose calculation and shortcut methods are provided in Chapter 30.

---

**Example 2.4**
**Illustration of a Dose Calculation**

A 400-m$^2$ pond with an average depth of 85 cm must be treated with 0.1 mg/L copper using a commercial product that contains 20% copper.

$$\text{Dose} = \frac{400 \text{ m}^2 \times 0.85 \text{ m} \times 0.1 \text{ g Cu/m}^3}{0.2 \text{ g Cu/g product}} = 170 \text{ g product.}$$

---

# References

1. Morrissy, N. M. 1976. Aquaculture of marron, *Cherax tenuimanus* (Smith). Part 1. Site selection and the potential of marron for aquaculture. Fisheries Research Bulletin of Western Australia 17:1-27.
2. Idso, S. B. and J. M. Foster. 1974. Light and temperature relations in a small desert pond as influenced by phytoplanktonic density variations. Water Resources Research 10:129-132.
3. Thornthwaite, C. W. and J. R. Mather. 1957. Instructions and tables for computing potential evapotranspiration and the water balance. John Hopkins University, Publication in Climatology 10:185-311.
4. Hounam, C. E. 1973. Comparisons between pan and lake evaporation. Technical Note 126, World Meteorological Organization, Geneva, Switzerland.
5. Boyd, C. E. 1985. Pond evaporation. Transactions of the American Fisheries Society 114:299-303.
6. Yoo, K. H. and C. E. Boyd. 1994. *Hydrology and Water Supply for Aquaculture.* Chapma n and Hall, New York, NY.
7. Meteorological Department of Thailand. 1981. Climatological data of Thailand 30-year period (1951-1980). Ministry of Communications, Bangkok, Thailand.
8. Leopold, L. B. 1997. *Water, Rivers, and Creeks.* University Science Books, Sausalito, CA.
9. Boyd, C. E., S. Soongsawang, E. W. Shell, and S. Fowler. 2009. Small impoundment complexes as a possible method to increase water supply in Alabama. In: Proceedings of the 2009 Georgia Water Resources Conference, April 27-29. University of Georgia, Athens, GA.
10. Simon, A. L. 1976. *Practical Hydraulics.* John Wiley and Sons, New York, NY.

# Chapter 3

# Ecological Principles

## Introduction

Aquaculture is the deliberate alteration of an aquatic environment to increase animal or plant production or economic gain. Most 'unaltered' waters are relatively unproductive and providing more food is essential to increasing aquatic animal production. Food availability can be increased either by enhancing natural productivity within a water body or by providing supplemental food from external sources. Providing more food does not allow for unlimited increases in aquatic animal production because metabolic activities associated with increased animal biomass cause environmental conditions to deteriorate. After the animals' nutritional needs are met, dissolved oxygen availability is usually the first environmental factor to affect production because the gas is poorly soluble in water and only small amounts are available to meet respiratory demands—which may be large in intensive aquaculture systems. Aquatic animals also produce carbon dioxide, ammonia, and organic wastes as byproducts of metabolism. Waste accumulation affects production after oxygen needs are met. Overcoming limitations on aquaculture production requires resource inputs from outside the culture system. Those resources may be fertilizers, plant- or animal-derived feedstuffs produced in other ecosystems, or they may be direct inputs of industrial energy, mostly from fossil fuels. Industrial energy inputs may include, for example, electricity for aerators and water pumps to overcome limitations associated with oxygen supply and waste treatment.

## Food for Aquaculture Production

Organisms are categorized as *autotrophs, heterotrophs,* or *mixotrophs* based on how they obtain food and energy. Autotrophs obtain carbon for cell synthesis from inorganic carbon (carbon dioxide or bicarbonate) using energy from sunlight (photosynthesis) or from the oxidation of energy-rich, reduced inorganic compounds (chemosynthesis). Autotrophs are also called *primary producers*. Photosynthetic autotrophs are the most important (or only) primary producers in most environments. In this book, we will disregard chemosynthetic autotrophs in discussions of primary production, although they can be important in some specialized environments. Heterotrophs obtain energy and organic molecules for building cells by feeding on other organisms. Heterotrophs may feed either directly on primary producers (herbivores) or indirectly (detritivores and carnivores). Heterotrophs are sometimes called *consumers*, and include bacteria, fungi, protozoans, and animals. A few organisms (dinoflagellates and some other algae) are mixotrophs and synthesize new cells by either photosynthesis or heterotrophy.

Feeding habits are sometimes used to classify organisms into *trophic levels* that describe the succession of organisms that eat another organism and are, in turn, eaten themselves. Primary producers are said to be at the lowest trophic level. Various heterotrophs (herbivores, predators, carnivores) then occupy successively higher trophic levels. The trophic level concept is somewhat misleading because it implies that an organism feeds only on organisms occupying the next lowest trophic level (for example, predators eating herbivores). Most organisms have more complex feeding habits (omnivores may eat primary producers, herbivores, carnivores and other omnivores, for example). Feeding habits can also change as an organism grows.

Primary production is usually defined as the amount of carbon fixed in photosynthesis or the amount of chemical energy present in organic matter produced in photosynthesis. Gross primary production is the total amount of carbon or energy fixed in photosynthesis. Net primary production is gross production minus carbon or energy lost or used in respiration. The rate of primary production (that is, the amount of plant carbon or energy fixed per unit area in a given time) is called *primary productivity*.

Primary production may take place inside the aquatic ecosystem (*autochthonous* production) or it may occur outside the system (*allochthonous* production). The relative importance autochthonous and allochthonous primary production depends on the culture system and the organism under culture. Animal growth in fertilized ponds is based almost entirely on autochthonous food production. At the other extreme, animals grown at very high densities in water-recirculating or flow-through aquaculture systems depend entirely on high-quality manufactured feeds formulated from organic matter produced outside (often very far outside) the system.

## Factors Affecting Primary Production

Aquatic primary producers include algae and various vascular plants. Phytoplankton is the most common and generally the most preferred group of autotrophs in most aquaculture ponds. Other plants can be important in some ponds and are described in Chapter 19.

Phytoplankton are microscopic, photosynthetic organisms that are suspended or weakly swimming in water. A pond that is discolored and turbid because of phytoplankton is said to contain a *bloom*. Phytoplankton (and 'algae' in general) include true plants and *blue-green algae*, which are photosynthetic bacteria with plant-like chlorophyll. The currently accepted name for this group is *cyanobacteria* although most aquaculturists call them blue-green algae.

Phytoplankton productivity depends on the balance of growth rate and rate of cell loss. Colonization, water temperature, light, and nutrient availability are major factors affecting growth. Major losses include sinking (sedimentation), washout, and consumption by grazing zooplankton and fish.[1,2] All factors except water temperature can be managed to some degree although nutrient supply is clearly the easiest factor to control and is the subject of most attempts to manage phytoplankton productivity in aquaculture.

## Colonization

Phytoplankton cannot actively move from one water body to another, so colonization of new habitats is entirely passive, usually by transfer of propagules in the water supply or by airborne dispersal. When ponds are drained and refilled, pond bottom muds are an important source of inoculum because many species form reproductive bodies that are resistant to desiccation and can survive long periods in damp soil. Algal propagules also can be transported between water bodies by insects (which are a particularly important means of local transport), birds, and other animals. Algal colonization of new water bodies is rapid and it is usually not necessary to 'seed' new ponds to establish a community.

## Water Temperature

Phytoplankton are versatile organisms with respect to temperature requirements. Some algae can grow in snow and some can grow in hot springs at temperatures above 70°C. Optimum temperatures vary among species and, even within a particular species, the best temperature for growth depends on light intensity, nutrient availability, and other factors. For common species found in aquaculture ponds, growth rate approximately doubles as temperatures increase by 10°C over the range of 5 to 30°C. Seasonal changes in water temperature, which are often difficult to differentiate from seasonal changes in light availability, affect phytoplankton productivity, with higher growth rates in summer than winter. Water temperature can also be an important species-selection factor. For example, certain species of blue-green algae dominate phytoplankton communities when water temperatures are warm, yet these same species apparently do not compete effectively with other algae in cold water.

## Light

Although plant growth requires many resources, light availability ultimately limits food production in ponds. Relationships among aquatic plant metabolism and daily and seasonal changes in light availability (Chapter 2) also have important implications for pond management because photosynthesis affects concentrations of dissolved carbon dioxide and oxygen—two key water variables in aquaculture.

As discussed in Chapter 2, light—especially light in the infrared and red wavelengths—is rapidly absorbed as it passes through pure water. Selective absorption of light is important because wavelengths most strongly absorbed by water are also wavelengths most strongly absorbed by chlorophylls—the primary light-trapping pigments in plants. Dissolved and particulate impurities can lessen underwater light penetration even more by absorbing, reflecting, or scattering light. Because light energy is rapidly diminished as it passes through water, photosynthesis by aquatic plants and algae is a restricted to near-surface waters.

The minimum light requirement for phytoplankton growth is approximately 1% of full summer sunlight measured just under the water surface. The depth to which 1% of incident solar radiation penetrates is traditionally called the *light compensation point*, and corresponds to the depth where gross photosynthesis approximately equals respiration. The compensation point depth can be estimated as twice the Secchi disk visibility (Chapter 2; Fig. 2.4). The upper, illuminated layer of water above the compensation depth is called the *photic zone* and represents the volume of water with enough light to allow phytoplankton growth. Because oxygen is a product of photosynthesis and a reactant in respiration, the photic zone also represents the layer of water where more oxygen is produced in photosynthesis than is consumed in plant respiration during daylight. Below the compensation point, oxygen produced in photosynthesis is completely consumed in respiration and the only source of oxygen for organisms living in deep waters is mixing of oxygenated waters from the surface (see Chapter 12).

Light availability also influences the type of phytoplankton in the community. Some phytoplankton, notably certain species of blue-green algae, can grow well under low-light conditions because they have non-chlorophyll photosynthetic pigments that harvest light in wavelengths not used by other algae. Some phytoplankton can move up in the water column when light becomes limiting, either by actively swimming toward the surface or by changing cell density and floating upward. These organisms gain an advantage when phytoplankton standing crops become high and light becomes limiting.

## Nutrients

Although light ultimately limits aquatic primary productivity, availability of certain inorganic nutrients usually determines phytoplankton growth rate. Overall nutrient availability and the relative availability of critical nutrients also affect the type of algae present in the community.

Nutrients needed by all plants in relatively large amounts include C, N, P, S, K, Mg, and Ca. One other element—silicon—is a macronutrient for diatoms. Micronutrients are essential for growth but are required only in trace amounts. Micronutrients include Fe, Mn, Cu, Zn, B, Mo, and Co. Phytoplankton obtain carbon from dissolved carbon dioxide gas or bicarbonate ion ($HCO_3^-$). Other macronutrients (with one exception) are assimilated by phytoplankton as waterborne, dissolved ions. The exception is nitrogen, which is usually assimilated as ammonium ($NH_4^+$), nitrite ($NO_2^-$), or nitrate ($NO_3^-$) but can be obtained from dinitrogen gas ($N_2$) by some organisms in the process called *nitrogen fixation.*

Vascular aquatic plants can obtain nutrients from sources other than the water column. Aquatic plants with floating or aerial leaves use atmospheric carbon dioxide as the main carbon source and plants with roots can assimilate nutrients from sediment porewater. The relative availability of nutrients from the water column or sediment is a strong determinant of aquatic plant community type (Chapter 19).

Most nutrients are available in excess amounts and plant productivity is usually constrained by the availability of one or two nutrients that are in shortest supply relative to plant needs. If a water body has an abundant supply of all nutrients except one, incremental additions of that single nutrient will enhance growth whereas addition of other nutrients will have no stimulatory effect. This principle is known as *Liebig's Law of the Minimum*. As more of the limiting nutrient is added, plant growth continues to increase until there is adequate nutrient available for maximum growth. Adding more nutrient will not stimulate more growth, and may result in toxicity (Fig. 3.1) The concentration of the first limiting nutrient can be raised until a point is reached where a second nutrient becomes limiting. Further growth can be achieved by adding more of both nutrients (Fig. 3.1). The concept of limiting factors and ranges of tolerance also applies to other environmental factors, such as light intensity and water temperature.

Phosphorus is the growth-limiting nutrient in many fresh waters, although addition of nitrogen and phosphorus almost always causes a greater growth response than phosphorus alone. Nitrogen is the growth-limiting nutrient for phytoplankton growth in most of the ocean. These statements refer primarily to unpolluted water bodies where overall nutrient availability is low (such systems are often called *oligotrophic*). Generalizations regarding nutrient limiting factors must be interpreted carefully because individual ecosystems vary widely with respect to nutrient status and limiting factors. In waters with high nutrient loadings (*eutrophic* systems), phytoplankton growth may, for example, be limited by carbon or light availability. Carbon limitation occurs in systems with low total alkalinity (Chapters 6 and 9) because bicarbonate is not available as an alternative to dissolved carbon dioxide as a carbon source. Some intensively managed aquaculture ponds receive large amounts of nitrogen, phosphorus, and other nutrients as waste products derived from manufactured feed eaten by fish or shrimp (Chapter 11). If eutrophic ponds waters have high total alkalinity, all nutrients may be available in excess of phytoplankton needs and further growth is limited by light availability.

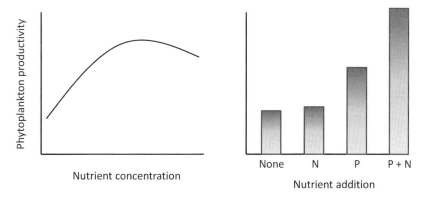

**Fig. 3.1.** (Left) Phytoplankton productivity in response to additions of a single limiting nutrient. (Right) Phytoplankton productivity in response to additions of nitrogen alone, phosphorus alone, and phosphorus plus nitrogen fertilization. Productivity in this hypothetical system was limited first by phosphorus availability. Adding nitrogen alone did not increase productivity until the requirement for the first growth-limiting nutrient—phosphorus—was met.

In addition to controlling phytoplankton growth rate, nutrient availability also influences the type of phytoplankton in the community because species have different nutrient requirements. The best-known example is the effect of silicon availability. Diatoms are unique among the algae because they require silicon, in the form of silicic acid, for construction of cell walls. Diatoms may become abundant when silicon is available but, as the nutrient becomes unavailable, other algae replace them. Another important example involves the ability of certain blue-green algae to use dinitrogen gas as a nitrogen source. Nitrogen-fixing species may become abundant when ionic sources of nitrogen ($NH_4^+$, $NO_2^-$, or $NO_3^-$) are scarce.

Nutrient sources for aquatic and marine ecosystems include 1) the atmosphere, for gaseous nutrient sources such as carbon dioxide and nitrogen gas; 2) runoff from land; 3) discharges from rivers and streams; 4) upwelling or mixing of nutrients in deep waters; 5) recycled nutrients from bacterial decomposition or excretion by grazing zooplankton or fish; and 6) intentional or unintentional additions from aquaculture management practices. Most undisturbed ponds and lakes have low nutrient loading and are relatively unproductive. Changes in catchment basin land use can increase nutrient inputs, leading to higher levels of primary productivity. Urban development (including lawns, gardens, and golf courses) and agriculture development (row-crops, improved pastures, and confined animal feed operations) involve the use of fertilizers in plant agriculture and landscaping or production of animal wastes—both of which can be sources of nutrients to downstream aquatic systems. Intentional fertilization of aquaculture ponds is a common practice to increase autochthonous primary production.

## *Sinking and Sedimentation*

Rapid attenuation of light as it passes through water restricts underwater photosynthesis to shallow depths, yet most phytoplankton are denser than water and will sink out of the photic zone unless resuspended by water currents or mixing. The abilities of different phytoplankton species to stay suspended in the photic zone plays a major role in determining which species are present in the community.

Phytoplankton have numerous adaptations to keep cells suspended. Small cells sink less rapidly than larger cells of the same density. Elongate cells or cells with appendages or spines sink slower than spherical cells because they have increased form resistance (drag). Some species can regulate buoyancy by accumulating low-density substances such as lipids or mucilage. Certain blue-green phytoplankton regulate buoyancy through light-mediated formation and collapse of gas-filled vesicles. The vesicles fill under low-light conditions and collapse when photosynthetic activity is high. The ability of some blue-green algae to regulate position in the water column helps them dominate poorly mixed, light-limited environments—such as eutrophic ponds with heavy algal blooms. Blue-green algae are generally undesirable in aquaculture ponds (Chapter 18) and the practice of water-column mixing (Chapter 12) attempts to change conditions so that buoyancy-regulating blue-green algae do not have a competitive advantage.

## *Hydraulic Retention and Washout*

Unattached, free-floating phytoplankton are susceptible to losses by washout when water bodies are rapidly flushed. Most aquaculture ponds have long hydraulic retention times (several months or more) and phytoplankton growth is not affected by cell losses to washout except during unusual precipitation events. When such events occur, community regrowth is usually rapid, although taxomonic composition of the community may change radically as a new community becomes established. At the extreme, outdoor raceway aquaculture systems have hydraulic retention times less than an hour (Chapter 26) and phytoplankton communities cannot become established at all.

The effects of flushing on nutrient concentrations are often more important than the direct affects on algal abundance. The impact of flushing on nutrient availability depends on flushing rate and inflow water quality, which in turn is influenced by catchment basin characteristics. For example, rapid flushing of a pond with stream flow from a forested catchment basin can leave a pond nutrient deficient and unproductive. Using chemical fertilizers to offset nutrients lost in outflow will be inefficient until the hydraulic residence time is increased, perhaps by diverting some of the flow around the pond. On the other hand, inflow from improved pastures, urban developments, and other sources of plant nutrients may result in increased algal growth rates that greatly offset physical losses of algal cells.

## *Grazing*

Harvest of phytoplankton by herbivorous zooplankton or fish is called *grazing*. Grazing is important in shaping phytoplankton community productivity, biomass, and species composition. Most planktivores graze by straining and concentrating suspended particles in specialized filtering structures. High grazing rates can decimate phytoplankton communities although modest grazing rates can actually increase phytoplankton productivity by rapidly recycling nutrients contained inside ingested phytoplankton cells and by preventing excessive phytoplankton biomass that can restrict light availability. Grazing may alter phytoplankton community structure through size-selective removal of certain species (filter feeding tends to remove larger particles most efficiently). The impact of grazing on phytoplankton communities is part of a concept called *top-down control* of ecosystem productivity and structure, and is described in the next section on food webs.

## Food Webs

Linkages among primary production and various consumers are described by *food webs*. The concept implies that as primary production either increases or decreases, so does production of organisms at higher trophic levels. This is the basis for adding chemical fertilizers to aquaculture ponds: inorganic fertilization increases phytoplankton primary production which in turn increases fish production.

## Top-Down and Bottom-Up Control of Productivity

Food webs depict the one-way flow of food through an ecosystem and are useful because they illustrate the concept that productivity and biomass of higher trophic levels depends on availability of organic matter produced in photosynthesis. This one-way flow of energy and materials is called 'bottom-up' control of ecosystem productivity and community structure. But, productivity and structure of aquatic plant and animal communities are also influenced by predation from higher trophic levels. This phenomenon is called 'top-down' control, and is based on the *trophic cascade hypothesis*.[3] For example, piscivorous fish eat planktivorous fish which, in turn, eat zooplankton and phytoplankton. Although potential ecosystem productivity is regulated by resource availability (bottom-up), actual biomass and productivity of all plants and animals in the system are affected by interactions between bottom-up and top-down effects.

Pond productivity can be manipulated using either bottom-up or top-down effects. Pond fertilization is an obvious example of increasing ecosystem productivity through bottom-up management. Adding top-level predators, such as largemouth bass, to a pond may decrease abundance of sunfish and other planktivores, allowing certain zooplankton species to increase. Increased grazing pressure by zooplankton may then reduce phytoplankton biomass. The relative importance of bottom-up and top-down control of ecosystem structure and productivity varies greatly among aquatic ecosystems.

## Animal Feeding Habits and Ecological Efficiency

When a unit of organic matter is consumed, some of the food energy and nutrients are used to make new tissue and some of the energy and nutrients are lost in respiration, excretion, or reproduction. Efficiency of organic matter conversion into new tissue is quite low, ranging from less than 2% to about 20% depending on quality of the food and the type of organism consuming the food. The practical implication of this well-known ecological principle is that efficiency of food use is much greater when the consumer is principally herbivorous rather than carnivorous.

Aquaculture production can be optimized by simultaneously culturing two or more animal species with different food habits. This strategy, called *polyculture*, makes more efficient use of the variety of natural foods available in ponds. For example, a possible combination of fish might be silver carp, grass carp, and common carp. Silver carp feed in the water column by filtering plankton; grass carp are adapted to feed on larger aquatic plants and added green fodders; and common carp are benthic omnivores that feed on detritus and benthic invertebrates. This combination makes efficient use of different foods available in fertilized ponds. The polyculture concept also can be used in ponds with feeding. For example, when channel catfish are co-cultured with blue tilapia, catfish feed on high-quality manufactured feeds and tilapia feed on phytoplankton, zooplankton, and insects produced within the pond. If tilapia are absent, the system becomes a catfish *monoculture* and most of the pond's natural productivity is unused.

## *Ponds with Chemical Fertilization*

Animal production in ponds with chemical fertilization (Chapter 10) relies primarily on autochthonous primary production. That is, nearly all the carbon eventually incorporated into the animal under culture is derived from carbon dioxide fixed in photosynthesis by plants (usually phytoplankton) growing in the pond. The link between plants and animals can be quite short. For example, Nile tilapia can graze directly on phytoplankton—a 'one-step' food web. Note that actual food webs are almost never that simple because no fish is strictly herbivorous. For example, Nile tilapia may also feed on detritus, zooplankton, and insects that grow in the pond (Fig. 3.2).

The link between primary production and animal production in ponds fertilized with chemical fertilizers can be more indirect and complicated than that for Nile tilapia. This complexity is exemplified by ponds managed for the popular sportfish, largemouth bass. Largemouth bass do not feed directly on plants; in fact, adult largemouth bass are considered to be carnivores. Sportfish ponds are fertilized to increase primary production, which then enhances production of zooplankton and insects, which, in turn, enhances production of forage fish, eventually culminating in increased growth of bass. The actual food web (Fig. 3.2) in sportfish ponds is more complex than described above because animals in the system feed on a variety of organisms.

Food webs become more complex when primary production is derived from plants other than phytoplankton. Most phytoplankton are of good food quality, with relatively high protein levels and low amounts of fiber and other indigestible matter. When communities are dominated by large vascular aquatic plants—some of which may be inedible or of poor food quality—food webs are often based on primary production by attached algae (periphyton) and detrital pathways dependent on death and decomposition of the larger plants. Decomposition converts plant material into high-quality food that is more accessible to various invertebrates (detritivores) that are then preyed upon by organisms at higher trophic levels.

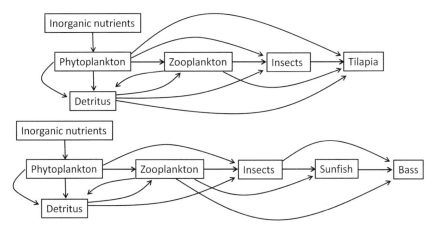

**Fig. 3.2.** Food webs in chemically fertilized ponds managed for tilapia production (top) or largemouth bass angling.

## *Ponds with Organic Fertilization*

Food webs can become very complex when ponds are fertilized with organic materials rather than simple chemical fertilizers. Organic fertilizers include a wide range of materials, including animal manure, green manure, fodders, composts, cereal grains, and seed meals. Some animal production in organically fertilized ponds is derived from direct consumption of the material added to the pond, although the material is often nutritionally inadequate, unpalatable, or too difficult to ingest to support high animal production through direct consumption. A more significant source of food in organically fertilized ponds is derived via *detrital food webs*, where low-quality organic materials are converted into higher quality food through the action of bacteria, fungi, and protozoans. Organic matter decomposition also releases inorganic nutrients (nitrogen, phosphorus, and others) in the process called *mineralization*. Mineralized nutrients then stimulate the growth of plants, which serve as the base of autotrophic food webs described above for ponds receiving chemical fertilizers. Organic material added to ponds therefore provides food for animals in three ways: 1) particulate organic matter may be consumed directly by animals; 2) the organic material provides a source of nutrients and organic matter for detrital food webs; and 3) the organic material provides mineral nutrients that stimulate plant growth as the base of autotrophic food webs.

## *Aquaculture Systems with Feeding*

Aquaculture yield in fertilized ponds is limited by primary productivity, which is ultimately limited by solar radiation. To increase aquaculture yield past that attainable in fertilized ponds, feed ingredients from outside the system must be obtained, formulated into a feed, and fed to cultured animals. Some systems are incapable of producing enough food to support even meager animal growth. As mentioned above, water flow through raceway systems is fast essentially no food is produced within the system. Animal production in highly intensive systems therefore depends entirely on manufactured feeds.

The quality of feeds added to ponds varies greatly depending on availability of resources, nutritional requirements of the cultured animal, and production economics. Inputs to some consist of low-quality organic matter that might otherwise be considered a waste product, such as animal manures, bedding (litter), and the by-products of processing agricultural plants. As mentioned above, only a portion of animal production may be derived from direct consumption of the organic material; much of the food is derived from autotrophic and heterotrophic food webs stimulated by addition of organic materials, and ponds are more properly classified as fertilized ponds rather than fed cultures. Some animals can efficiently use low-quality organic matter for growth, and direct consumption of those materials may account for a large portion of the food consumed. Grass carp is the best example of a commonly cultured animal that grows efficiently on inputs of forages and grasses. Most grass carp production relies on inputs of terrestrial or aquatic plants harvested from nearby land or water bodies and then processed to some degree (often by simply chopping into smaller pieces) and fed directly to fish in ponds or cages.

As culture intensity increases, from a nutritional standpoint, growth of cultured animals becomes limited first by the availability of dietary energy.[4] Therefore, providing supplemental inputs such as energy-rich cereal grains can complement natural foods and increase aquaculture production beyond that obtained by fertilization. As culture intensity increases further, protein quantity and quality become the next nutritional factors to limit production. Most fish and crustaceans grown in aquaculture cannot efficiently make direct use of low-quality organic matter, so feeds are manufactured to be a source of concentrated nutrients that are nutritious and highly digestible.

Autochthonous food production is meager in flow-though and recirculating aquaculture systems, and food webs are simple: animal eats feed. Feeds used in those systems must be nutritionally complete because they are the only nutrient source. Food webs in ponds with feeding are more complicated. Even when cultured animals are fed a nutritionally complete manufactured feed to satiety, animals in ponds have access to a variety of natural food organisms produced within the pond. Although consumption of natural food organisms is usually not expected to contribute significantly to total yield of animals fed manufactured feeds, natural foods can supply vitamins, essential fatty acids, or trace minerals important to animal growth, especially when manufactured feeds are not nutritionally complete. In the case of fed penaeid shrimp ponds, direct consumption of feed by shrimp is inefficient and a surprisingly large fraction of added feed functions as an organic fertilizer, stimulating the production of various natural food items that are subsequently consumed by shrimp.

## Life Support in Aquaculture Systems

The preceding sections emphasize that aquaculture production from ponds is initially limited by food availability. Providing food from outside the culture system obviously does not allow unlimited increases in aquaculture production because feeding causes unintended negative effects on water quality that eventually limit animal growth. A minority of the nutrients in feed is retained by aquatic animals and the remainder is excreted as waste (Chapter 11). Waste nutrients (nitrogen, phosphorus, and other minerals) and waste organic matter (feces and uneaten food) stimulate biological activity that exerts an oxygen demand inside the culture system. In addition, two waste products—carbon dioxide and ammonia—are potentially toxic to aquatic animals if allowed to accumulate. As aquaculture production is intensified by adding more animals to the system and providing more food to support good growth, production becomes limited by the capacity of the systems to provide oxygen and remove wastes.[5,6]

### Dissolved Oxygen

Of resources under control of the culturist, availability of dissolved oxygen is the next factor to limit production in ponds after meeting the animal's food requirements. Dissolved oxygen is needed in relatively large amounts to meet the respiratory demands of cultured animals and other organisms in the culture system. However, water saturated with oxygen contains relatively little oxygen to meet those needs (water contains 20 to 40 times less oxygen by volume than does air).

Two complimentary aspects of dissolved oxygen availability are important in aquaculture (Chapter 13). First, oxygen supply must be adequate to prevent concentrations from falling to levels that affect cultured animal growth and health. This criterion applies to all aquaculture systems. Beyond that, ponds and recirculating aquaculture systems rely on microbial processes to remove or transform metabolic waste products produced by animals during culture. These processes do not function efficiently unless adequate dissolved oxygen is available. For example, nitrification is an aerobic (oxygen-requiring) bacterial process occurring in ponds and recirculating systems that converts ammonia (a potentially toxic waste product) to nitrate (which is relatively non-toxic). If dissolved oxygen supplies are inadequate, nitrification rate decreases and ammonia accumulates. Maintaining oxygenated conditions near the sediment-water interface in ponds also helps minimize organic matter accumulation by enhancing bacterial decomposition rates.

## *Waste Treatment*

Fish and crustaceans produce wastes as a byproduct of growth, and the amount of waste produced is proportional to animal biomass and feeding rate. Fertilization or feeding practices used to increase aquaculture production therefore increase amounts of organic matter, solids, nitrogen, phosphorus, and other substances added to water.

Wastes produced during aquaculture must be removed to prevent degradation of the environment to the point where aquatic animal growth or health is negatively impacted. Some substances—such as carbon dioxide, ammonia, or nitrite—may accumulate and directly affect growth and health of cultured animals. Other substances have an indirect affect on growth or health. For example, organic materials added to the system (uneaten feed or feces) or produced during culture (phytoplankton) express an oxygen demand and compete with cultured animals for oxygen. Wastes produced during aquaculture also represent potential pollution if culture water is discharged from the facility. As such, waste-treatment processes in aquaculture, whether inherent in the production system or as an adjunct to culture, reduces the pollution potential of aquaculture effluents.

In pond aquaculture, waste nutrients and organic matter are continually removed by natural processes in the water and bottom sediment. Carbon dioxide is removed by plants in photosynthesis to produce organic matter. Organic matter added to ponds or produced in photosynthesis undergoes various transformations and is eventually decomposed by heterotrophic microbes to produce carbon dioxide. Ammonia is initially assimilated by plants and then removed from ponds through mineralization of organic nitrogen followed by coupled nitrification-denitrification (see Chapter 16). Phosphorus is assimilated by plants and removed from water when poorly soluble calcium, iron, or aluminum phosphate compounds precipitate in bottom sediments.

The capacity of pond ecosystems to remove wastes is limited and, because the initial step in waste removal often depends on assimilation of substances by plants, the capacity for waste treatment is limited by the rate of photosynthesis, which is ultimately limited by the finite energy from sunlight.[5,6] Further production intensification depends on removing excess organic matter and nutrients by means other than natural processes, such as exchanging degraded water with high-quality water (flow-through raceways or cages) or by treatment processes external to the culture unit (recirculating aquaculture systems).

## Culture Intensity and the Footprint of Aquaculture

The term *culture intensity* is used to classify agriculture systems based on annual crop yield per unit land or water area. Culture intensity varies over at least three orders of magnitude for commonly used aquaculture production systems. Water recirculating systems are capable of annually producing 1 to 2 million kg of fish per hectare of culture unit. The same fish production in flow-through raceways requires about 10 times more surface area and production in ponds may require 1,000 times the area of recirculating systems.

The concept of culture intensity also includes the broader context of resource inputs. Combining contexts of crop yield and resource use into the overall concept of culture intensity highlights the fact that differences in crop yields among aquaculture systems are not simply a function of systems with greater yields being more efficient or having inherently greater value than systems with lesser yields. Rather, a broader measure of culture intensity considers the extent to which the primary resources and ecological services needed to grow aquatic animals—food, life support, and waste treatment—are obtained from outside the culture facility.

The overall land or sea area occupied by the facility plus that needed to provide all resources to grow a crop is called the *ecological footprint*. In aquaculture, footprint includes areas for the facility, food production, and life support (which includes oxygen supply and waste treatment). Footprints may also include ecosystem requirements for other services, such as freshwater supply, forest or ocean areas for carbon dioxide sequestration, and, for some systems, nursery areas used to procure seedstock or brood animals.[7,8]

Low intensity culture systems have a low ratio of total support area to facility area whereas high-intensity systems require large areas external to the facility to support aquaculture production. For example, much of the ecosystem support for extensive pond aquaculture is inherent in the system. Traditional aquaculture ponds used in Chinese carp polyculture function not only to confine fish, but also to provide an internal area for food production, oxygen production, and waste treatment. That is, the overall ecological footprint is approximately equal to facility area. On the other hand, some aquaculture systems function only to confine the crop. Food for the confined animals is produced in external ecosystems and wastes are exported and treated outside the facility. In other words, the footprint of those systems is much larger than the facility area.

When considering the total ecosystem area needed to support a certain level of aquaculture production, apparent differences in culture intensity based on yield per unit area nearly disappear. Although ponds require hundreds or thousands of times the facility area as other systems, the other systems rely on hundreds or thousands of times the external ecosystem area to provide food and waste treatment compared with ponds.[5,7,8]

# References

1. Reynolds, C. S. 1984. *The Ecology of Freshwater Phytoplankton.* Cambridge University Press, Cambridge, UK.
2. Reynolds, C. S. 1997. *Vegetation Processes in the Pelagic: a Model for Ecosystem Theory.* Ecology Institute, Oldendorf/Luhe, Germany.
3. Carpenter, S. R., J. F. Kitchell, and J. R. Hodgson. 1985. Cascading trophic interactions and lake productivity. Bioscience 35:634-639.
4. De Silva, S. S. and T. A. Anderson. 1995. *Fish Nutrition in Aquaculture.* Chapman and Hall, New York, NY.
5. Tucker, C. S. and J. A. Hargreaves. 2012. Freshwater ponds, pages 191-244. In J. Tidwell (editor), *Aquaculture Production Methods.* Wiley-Blackwell, Ames, IA.
6. Hargreaves, J. A. and C. S. Tucker. 2003. Defining loading limits of static ponds for catfish aquaculture. Aquacultural Engineering 28:47-63.
7. Boyd, C. E., C. S. Tucker, A. McNevin, K. Bostick, and J. Clay. 2007. Indicators of resource use efficiency and environmental performance in fish and crustacean aquaculture. Reviews in Fisheries Science 15:327-360.
8. Tucker, C. S., J. A. Hargreaves, and C. E. Boyd. 2008. Aquaculture and the environment in the United States, pages 3-54. In C. S. Tucker and J. A. Hargreaves (editors), *Environmental Best Management Practices for Aquaculture.* Wiley-Blackwell, Ames, IA.

# Chapter 4

# Water Sources and Culture Systems

## Introduction

Water is a primary requirement for aquaculture and the features of the water supply should be considered in selecting species and production systems suitable for a particular location. Water temperature determines whether a site is suitable for coldwater, coolwater, warmwater, or tropical species. Of course, water temperature varies seasonally, and at some warmwater sites, it may be possible to also culture coldwater or coolwater species in winter and tropical species in summer. For example, tilapia can be cultured in summer and rainbow trout can be cultured in winter in central Alabama (32°N latitude). The range of species that can be cultured at a location also will be restricted by salinity (freshwater, brackishwater, or marine species) and seasonal differences in salinity may influence selection of culture species. More often than not, the kind of production system selected to culture a particular species at a given site results from the type of water source and its seasonal availability.

Water quality and water quantity also strongly influence selection of culture species and type of production systems. Moreover, water quality often changes in production systems as a result of aquacultural inputs to increase production.

## Ponds

Ponds are used widely for culture of fish and crustaceans. *Watershed ponds* are constructed by installing a dam to impound runoff. Many watershed ponds (Fig. 4.1) receive only overland flow following rains. Water levels in most watershed ponds vary with seasonal changes in rainfall or during drought. Ponds may be arranged in series to form a water-harvesting scheme where water that naturally flows and seeps from ponds at higher elevation maintains water levels in lower ponds during dry weather.[1] In areas with abundant groundwater, wells may be developed to supplement water supply for watershed ponds. Channel catfish farms in west-central Alabama and east-central Mississippi consist mainly of series of watershed ponds, and some farms have wells to supplement the supply of surface water.

Ponds usually have a water control structure to allow excess water to flow out and to drain ponds (Fig. 4.2). A grass-lined spillway should be provided to bypass large inflows and prevent overtopping of dams following unusually heavy rainfall events.

**Fig. 4.1.** Watershed pond showing the dam and a portion of the watershed (left); A complex of watershed ponds on the E. W. Shell Fisheries Station at Auburn University (right).

Some ponds are constructed by damming permanent streams. These ponds have stable water levels, but they also may have short retention times (high flushing rates). Short water retention time may reduce the effectiveness of liming and fertilization to enhance productivity. Deep-water intake structures that take in water from below the photic zone sometimes are installed in ponds to avoid discharge of nutrients and plankton after heavy rainfall (Fig. 4.3).

Ponds can be constructed by excavating a basin in which to store water (Fig. 4.4). *Excavated ponds* usually are small because of the large volume of earth that must be removed to form them. Water for filling these ponds may come from wells, streams or lakes, irrigation systems, or overland flow. Where the water table is shallow, excavated ponds may fill by ground water seepage. Excavated ponds cannot be drained, and their water levels may fall drastically in the dry season as the water table declines. Nevertheless, small excavated ponds are important for small-scale aquaculture in many Asian nations.

The most suitable type of pond for aquaculture is the *embankment pond* constructed by building an earthen embankment around an area in which to store water (Fig. 4.5). Ponds may be fitted with water control structures such as shown in Fig. 4.2, or water

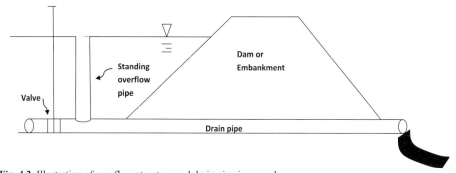

**Fig. 4.2.** Illustration of overflow structure and drain pipe in a pond.

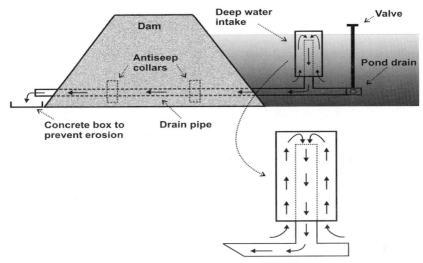

**Fig. 4.3.** Deep-water intake on overflow pipe.

gates with dam boards for controlling water level may be installed. Little overland flow enters embankment ponds because the only watershed is the sides and tops of embankments. There are few areas where rainwater and overflow will maintain water levels in embankment ponds. Water must be supplied from external sources such as wells, streams, lakes, irrigation systems, lakes, estuaries or the sea. For example, the channel catfish industry in western Mississippi and southeastern Arkansas uses embankment ponds filled by well water. Marine shrimp farming also is conducted in embankment ponds. Advantages of embankment ponds are that water levels can be controlled, ponds can be drained and refilled according to management schedules, and water exchange may be implemented to improve water quality.

**Fig. 4.4.** An excavated fish pond in Thailand.

**Fig. 4.5.** Embankment ponds used for channel catfish farming in the United States.

In areas where soils are highly permeable, clay blankets or impermeable plastic liners may be installed in ponds to reduce seepage loss (Fig. 4.6). In addition, plastic liners may be installed in heavily-aerated ponds to prevent erosion by aerator-generated water currents. Aquaculture using lined ponds is discussed in Chapter 25.

The intensity of aquaculture in ponds varies greatly. Yields of culture species based on natural productivity will be very low—seldom more than 50 to 200 kg/ha per year. Manures and fertilizers can be used to increase production—depending upon the species, production may reach 500 to 2,000 kg/ha. Much greater production can be achieved using feed, and the combination of feed and mechanical aeration provides the highest production. Fish and shrimp production in ponds with feeding alone normally ranges from 1,000 to 3,000 kg/ha, but with mechanical aeration, production often exceeds 5,000 kg/ha and may reach 15,000 to 20,000 kg/ha. Nevertheless, ponds have relatively low densities (0.3 to 1.3 kg/m$^3$) of culture animals.

**Fig. 4.6.** A plastic-lined pond.

In most kinds of pond culture, only a small fraction of the total volume of a pond is necessary to support the culture species. In extensive production, the remainder of the pond serves to produce food organisms for the culture species. In more intensive production with feed inputs, the remainder of the pond serves as an internal waste-treatment area. Where water exchange is used, a portion of the waste is flushed from the pond. In other words, the waste load is 'externalized' for treatment by natural waters.

Shapes, water surface areas, and depths of ponds vary greatly. Topography strongly influences the morphometry of watershed ponds, but as a general rule, watershed ponds take the shape of an irregular semi-circle, and average depth is about 0.4 times maximum depth. Water surface area may vary from a few hundred square meters to several hectares. Embankment ponds often are square or rectangular. There has been some use of round ponds (Fig. 4.7) because some feel that this shape enhances aeration-induced water circulation. Round ponds are more expensive to construct than rectangular or square ones, and a square pond is not greatly different from a round one. Bottoms of embankment ponds normally are constructed with gentle slopes and cross slopes to facilitate draining. Water depth quickly increases from edges to a depth of 0.75 m or more; maximum depths seldom exceed 2 to 3 m and average depths usually are 1.2 to 2.0 m. Excavated ponds normally are rectangular or square with depths of 1 to 3 m. Table 4.1 gives categories of water surface areas for the three major hydrologic types of ponds.

**Fig. 4.7.** Round ponds at a shrimp farm in Belize.

**Table 4.1.** Categories of ponds based on hectares of water surface area.

| Size | Hydrologic pond type | | |
| Category | Watershed | Embankment | Excavated |
|---|---|---|---|
| Small | <1 | <0.25 | <0.1 |
| Medium | 1-5 | 0.25-2.5 | 0.1-0.5 |
| Large | >5 | >2.5 | >0.5 |

## Partitioned Ponds

Intensive aquaculture ponds serve two simultaneous functions: 1) they confine the cultured animal and 2) they provide area for removal of wastes produced during culture. As mentioned above, only a small fraction of the total pond volume is necessary as 'living space' for the culture species and most of the pond area is essentially an aerobic waste-treatment lagoon. This is an elegant ecosystem but combining both functions in the same space can make ponds difficult to manage as animal production systems.

Outdoor, pond-based systems have been developed that physically separate the culture species from the waste-treatment area.[2] Water is then circulated between the two basins to remove wastes from the culture basin and return treated water. These systems are called *partitioned ponds* and are discussed in Chapter 24.

## Flow-Through Systems

Flow-through systems have continuous water inflow and outflow.[3] Suitable water quality for aquatic animal culture is maintained by the constant supply of oxygen in the incoming water and continuous removal of waste products in the outflow. Culture units in flow-through systems include raceways or tanks constructed from a variety of materials. Culture units can be arranged so that water passes through each unit once without reuse or in a series where water flows by gravity from one culture unit to another (Fig. 4.8). The most common water sources for commercial flow-through systems are artesian springs or water diverted from streams or rivers. Less commonly, water can be pumped from a water body, allowed to flow through the raceways or tanks, and then returned to the original body of water. Flow-through systems are most often used to produce trout and other salmonids. Some warmwater species are also produced in flow-through

**Fig. 4.8.** A trout raceway in the United States.

systems, but to a much smaller extent than salmonids. Raceways contain much higher densities of culture animals than do ponds. For example, Rainbow trout may be reared in raceways at densities of 80 to 160 kg/m$^3$—approximately 100 to 200 times greater than for fish in ponds.[2] Flow-through systems are described in Chapter 26.

## Cages and Net Pens

Fish often are produced in enclosures placed in natural water bodies, reservoirs, and ponds. The most common types of enclosures are cages and net pens. Cages range in size from about 1 m$^3$ to more than 1,000 m$^3$ (Fig. 4.9), and fish density may range from less than 20 to more than 200 kg/m.[3,4] Cages typically float in the water, and they are moored to the bottom. Water flows through cages to exchange waste-laden water and replenish dissolved oxygen used in respiration. Uneaten feed and feces fall through cages and settle to the bottom in the vicinity. Cages are periodically moved to new locations to allow benthic communities affected by sediment to recover—a process called fallowing.

Net pens are similar to cages, but they are made by placing netting around posts inserted in the bottom. Net pens may cover areas of a few to thousands of square meters, and extend into water up to 2 or 3 m in depth. Stocking density in net pens typically is much less than in cages. Cage culture is discussed in Chapter 27.

In-pond raceways are a variation of cage culture (they are also a variation of partitioned ponds and are described in Chapter 24). Fish are held at high density in floating or permanently installed raceways and water is flushed through raceways by paddlewheel aerators or air-lift pumps.

**Fig. 4.9.** Large cages in a lake (left); a small cage in a pond (right).

## Water Reuse Systems

Water reuse systems allow greater production per unit of water volume to improve the efficiency of water use. They also reduce the volume of effluents to lessen the pollution potential of aquaculture production facilities. Traditional ponds can be considered water reuse systems because wastes produced during culture are constantly removed by natural processes in the pond so that the water can be reused for indefinite periods (usually defined by the animal's culture cycle). The extent of water reuse in pond aquaculture can be increased by producing more than one crop of aquatic animals in the same water. Channel catfish farming in the United States is a good example of this practice. Ponds are not drained for harvest. Marketable-sized fish are removed with a grading seine, and additional fingerlings are stocked to replace them. Ponds typically are drained at intervals of 6 to 10 years.

Water passing through raceways and other culture systems can be pumped back to the grow-out units and reused. An example of this methodology is illustrated in Fig. 4.10. The water from culture units is passed through a sedimentation pond to remove the coarse solids and then held in a pond for natural water purification before reuse. In some systems, one or more additional species are cultured in the treatment pond.[5]

Water recirculation systems of much greater complexity are promoted by some innovators.[6] Recirculating aquaculture systems consist of a culture unit connected to a set of water-treatment units that allows some of the water leaving the culture unit to be reconditioned and reused in the same culture unit. Recirculating aquaculture systems minimally require water treatment processes to remove solids, remove or transform

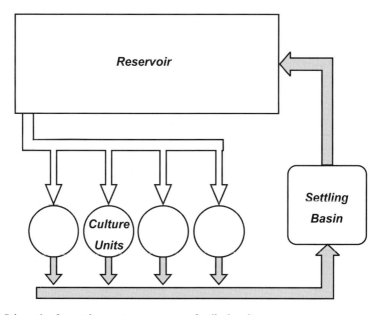

**Fig. 4.10.** Schematic of an outdoor, water reuse system for tilapia culture.

nitrogenous wastes, and add oxygen to the water. Other processes—such as temperature control, pH adjustment, gas removal, and disinfection—may also be required. Costs associated with construction and operation can increase production costs and commercial systems are therefore used to produce relatively higher value fish or in public facilities to produce fish for recreational stock enhancement or restoration of threatened and endangered species. Recirculating systems are described in Chapter 28.

## Mollusk and Seaweed Culture

Bivalve mollusks are produced by bottom culture methods in which spat are laid on sediment, rocks, or other solid surfaces for grow-out (Fig. 4.11). However, off-bottom culture is more efficient for it prevents benthic predators, eliminates sediment characteristics as a limiting factor, and allows three-dimensional use of the water column. Spat may be transferred to longlines attached to rafts, stakes, or racks for grow-out.

Floating or suspended culture of many species of seaweed is achieved by fixing seaweed propagules on ropes or nets and attaching them to rafts, nets, or longlines. A few species such as *Gracilaria* and *Caulerpa* normally are cultured in ponds.

**Fig. 4.11.** Oyster plots in the intertidal zone. Photo credit: David Cline.

## References

1. Boyd, C. E., S. Soongsawang, E. W. Shell, and S. Fowler. 2009. Small impoundment complexes as a possible method to increase water supply in Alabama. Proceedings 2009 Georgia Water Resources Conference, April 27-29, University of Georgia, Athens, GA.

2. Brune, D. E., C. S. Tucker, M. Massingill, and J. Chappell. 2012. Partitioned aquaculture systems, pages 308-342. In: J. Tidwell (editor), Aquaculture Production Methods. Wiley-Blackwell Publishing, Ames, IA.

3. Soderberg, R. W. 1994. *Flowing Water Fish Culture*. CRC Press, Inc., Boca Raton, FL.

4. Schmittou, H. R. 1993. High density fish culture in low volume cages. American Soybean Association, Singapore Office, Singapore.

5. Boyd, C. E., J. Queiroz, J. Lee, M. Rowan, G. N. Whitis, and A. Gross. 2000. Environmental assessment of channel catfish, *Ictalurus punctatus*, farming in Alabama. Journal of the World Aquaculture Society 31:511-544.

6. Timmons, M. B., J. M. Ebeling, F. W. Wheaton, S. T. Summerfelt, and B. J. Vinci. 2001. *Recirculating Aquaculture Systems*. Cayuga Aquaculture Ventures, Ithaca, NY.

Chapter 5

# Total Dissolved Solids, Salinity, and Major Ions

## Introduction

Water is an excellent solvent and is especially effective in dissolving substances that ionize. There usually is a much greater concentration of dissolved inorganic matter than of dissolved organic matter in natural waters. The inorganic fraction consists largely of a few major ions—calcium, magnesium, sodium, potassium, bicarbonate (and carbonate), sulfate, and chloride. These ions usually account for 90% or more of the weight of dissolved matter in natural waters.

Aquaculture species differ in their requirements for and tolerances of dissolved ion concentration. Thus, the suitability of water for aquaculture is influenced by the concentration of dissolved minerals or degree of mineralization. Aquatic organisms also have specific requirements for individual ion species and are affected by the proportions in which these ions occur. Moreover, the total concentration of dissolved ions influences the solubilities of gases and many other substances in water.

## Principles

### Total Dissolved Solids

The *total dissolved solids* (TDS) are the solids remaining in water after it passes a 2-µm filter.[1] A volume of filtered sample is measured into a tared dish and evaporated at 102°C. The weight of the residue in the dish expressed in milligrams per liter is the TDS concentration (Example 5.1). The residue in the dish can be ignited at 500°C, and the weight loss is the organic component of the TDS concentration (Example 5.1). The organic component is called the *total dissolved volatile solids* (TDVS), and it usually will be a small percentage of the TDS concentration.

There is tremendous variation in the concentrations of major ions in surface waters.[2] This results mainly from differences in geological and climatological factors. Major geological factors are the types and solubilities of minerals in surface soils and underlying formations. Main climatic factors are temperature, precipitation, and evaporation. In regions of high rainfall, and especially in the humid tropics and subtropics, most of the soluble mineral matter has gradually leached from the soil over time. In arid regions, evaporation in excess of rainfall concentrates dissolved substances, and certain minerals may precipitate as water becomes more concentrated in dissolved ions. Waters in areas with highly acidic, leached soils, sandy soils, or hard, insoluble rocks have low concentrations of most ions. Waters from fertile soils, and especially where soils contain limestone, have moderate TDS concentrations. In arid regions, waters tend to have the greatest concentration of TDS, and the proportions of major ions often are different from those found in waters of humid regions.

Total dissolved solids concentration is low in rain water. After falling on the earth's surface, it dissolves minerals and other substances and TDS concentration increases. Waters in different compartments of the hydrosphere tend to vary consistently with respect to dissolved matter. This can be illustrated by expressing typical TDS concentration for different hydrosphere compartments in orders of magnitudes: rainfall, 3 mg/L; runoff, 30 mg/L; groundwater, 300 mg/L, estuaries, 3,000 mg/L; oceans, 30,000 mg/L; closed-basin lakes, 300,000 mg/L. Although nice for visualization, categorizing TDS in this way does not reflect the great variation in TDS concentration within compartments of the hydrosphere.

---

**Example 5.1**
**Measurement of Total Dissolved Solids and Total Dissolved Volatile Solids**

Suppose that a 100 mL sample of water that passed a 2 μm filter is placed in an evaporating dish that weighs 40.20005 g. The water is evaporated and the dish and residue weigh 40.21108 g. The dish is then ignited at 500°C, and the dish and residue weigh 40.21056 g following ignition. The concentration of TDS and TDVS can be calculated as follows:

TDS:
| | |
|---|---|
| Weight dish and residue | 40.21108 g |
| Weight dish | 40.20005 g |
| Residue | 0.01103 g |

$$TDS\ (mg/L) = 0.01103\ g \times 10^3\ mg/g \times \frac{1{,}000\ mL/L}{100\ mL} = 110.3\ mg/L.$$

TDVS:
| | |
|---|---|
| Weight dish and residue | 40.21108 g |
| Weight dish and residue after ignition | 40.21056 g |
| Weight loss on ignition | 0.00052 g |

$$TDVS\ (mg\ /L) = 0.00052\ g \times 10^3\ mg/g \times \frac{1{,}000\ mL/L}{100\ mL} = 5.2\ mg/L.$$

Although rain water tends to have the lowest concentrations of TDS, these concentrations may vary from less than 1 mg/L in rural, inland areas with clean air to 30 mg/L or more in coastal areas where air contains salts from evaporation of wave spray and in heavily populated or industrial areas where air is polluted with dust, combustion products, and other impurities.

Concentration of TDS in streams in humid climates ranges from 10 to 100 mg/L in areas with sandy or highly leached soils. Values may reach 200 to 300 mg/L in areas with limestone or other relatively soluble minerals. In semi-arid regions, TDS concentration in streams often exceeds 300 mg/L, and the concentration above 1,000 mg/L may be found in streams in arid climates.[3] The TDS concentration increases from headwaters to lower reaches in streams because water dissolves minerals from the stream bed and the dissolved minerals are concentrated by evaporation as the water flows downstream. The TDS concentration usually decreases in relation to increasing discharge in a stream, because rainfall and overland flow causing the increase in discharge dilutes the water.[4] Moreover, during periods of dry weather, stream flow consists mainly of groundwater (base flow) that enters where stream beds intersect the water table, and groundwater usually is more concentrated in TDS than rainfall and overland flow.

Waters held in lakes or ponds also are affected by geologic and climatic factors in much the same way as streams. The hydraulic retention time of lakes and ponds has a particularly great effect on TDS concentrations. In general, the TDS concentration increases with greater hydraulic retention time. Lakes in arid regions sometimes have inflow but no outflow. In these closed basin lakes, TDS concentration may reach 200,000 mg/L or more. With respect to aquaculture ponds, TDS concentrations reflect interactions between source water and bottom soils.[5] In rain-fed ponds, the bottom soil is the main factor controlling TDS concentration (Table 5.1). Soils in the Limestone Valleys and Uplands and in the Blackland Prairie of Alabama often contain limestone. Soils of the Appalachian Plateau usually do not contain limestone, but they are not as highly leached as soils of the Coastal Plain and Piedmont Plateau. However, ponds may be filled from sources with high TDS concentration, such as mineralized groundwater or seawater. The TDS concentration in such ponds will be controlled by the TDS concentration in the source water. For example, channel catfish ponds in the Blackland Prairie region of Alabama have TDS concentrations of 200 to 300 mg/L when filled by rainfall and runoff; but concentrations of 2,000 to 5,000 mg/L when filled from saline aquifers.[6]

Groundwater often has a low redox potential and long contact with the geological formation in which it stands—factors favoring solubility of minerals.[7] Two major factors influence groundwater composition: 1) the composition and solubility of formations

**Table 5.1.** Total dissolved solids (TDS) concentration in water of ponds in different physiographic areas of Alabama.

| Physiographic region | TDS (mg/L) |
|---|---|
| Limestone Valley and Uplands | 112 |
| Blackland Prairie | 94 |
| Appalachian Plateau | 60.2 |
| Coastal Plain | 44.3 |
| Piedmont Plateau | 34.5 |

through which water infiltrated before reaching an aquifer; 2) the composition and solubility of minerals in the formation within which an aquifer occurs. Groundwater may vary tremendously in degree of mineralization. For example, water that has contacted only sand and gravel may contain as little as 10 to 20 mg/L TDS. Water that infiltrated through fertile soil and is contained in a limestone formation usually will have a TDS concentration of 250 to 500 mg/L. Water from a formation that contains salt will be saline—TDS concentrations often are above 1,000 mg/L and in some places may exceed 50,000 mg/L.[4]

The TDS concentration in an estuary typically increases from the upper tidal reach to the mouth of the estuary. Tidal action, however, causes TDS concentration at a particular location to change with the ebb and flow of the tide. Moreover, the TDS concentration may be greater at the bottom of an estuary than at the surface, because river water of lower TDS concentration and density will float above the more saline and denser ocean water. The TDS concentration in estuaries typically varies between the rainy and dry seasons (Fig. 5.1). Estuaries with large freshwater inputs may have very low salinity in the rainy season. Those with restricted openings to the sea may have hypersaline water in the dry season.

Seawater tends to have a relatively stable TDS concentration. The average for ocean water is 34,500 mg/L or 34.5 parts per thousand (ppt).

## Salinity

*Salinity* is the total concentration of dissolved ions in water. Therefore, concentrations of TDS and salinity usually are almost the same. In seawater, the direct determination of TDS concentration is impossible, because the salt remaining after evaporation of the sample is hydroscopic and cannot be weighed accurately. Moreover, determining the concentration of all ions to obtain the salinity of a sample is not practical, and indirect

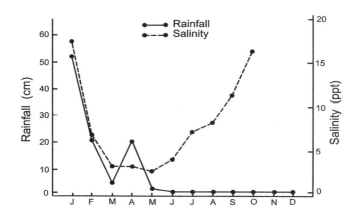

**Fig. 5.1.** Relationship between rainfall and salinity in coastal water near Guayaquil, Ecuador.

methods have been developed for estimating salinity.[8] The density of water increases with salinity, and salinity may be estimated from density as measured with a *hydrometer*. The concentration of ions affects the refractive index of water, and this relationship has been used to fabricate the popular *salinometer* (Fig. 5.2). In seawater and estuarine water, the relationship between chloride concentration and salinity is about 1.8, allowing salinity to be estimated from chloride concentration which can be easily measured by titration with mercuric nitrate. Salinity also can be estimated from specific conductivity; this variable will be discussed below.

## *Major Ions*

As mentioned earlier, the TDS concentration in natural waters results primarily from the presence of four cations (calcium, magnesium, sodium and potassium) and four anions (chloride, sulfate, bicarbonate, and carbonate). Bicarbonate and carbonate are ionic components of an equilibrium in which their proportions change with pH. Below pH 8.3, water contains only bicarbonate, but above this pH, carbonate occurs with bicarbonate. The proportion of carbonate relative to bicarbonate increases as pH rises. In addition to these ions, freshwaters may contain a relatively large amount of silicic acid largely in un-ionized form.[9] Concentrations of dissolved ions, like those of TDS and most other dissolved substances, are reported in milligrams per liter (mg/L) or its equivalent—parts per million (ppm).

The electrical charges of dissolved ions in water must balance. Most of the charge is from major ions, so the milliequivalents of major cations and major anions will nearly balance in most waters (Example 5.2). This relationship provides a simple procedure for checking the accuracy of analyses that include all of the major ions.

The proportions of the major ions varies considerably, but in humid regions, there usually is a greater abundance of calcium, magnesium, and bicarbonate (and carbonate) than of other ions. In drier climates, waters become more concentrated in ions, and calcium and magnesium carbonate often precipitate. This results in a greater proportion of sodium, potassium, sulfate, and chloride than in water of humid regions.

**Fig. 5.2.** A refractometer or salinometer for measuring salinity.

---

**Example 5.2**
**Anion-cation balance**

The measured concentrations of major anions and cations for the sample listed below will be divided by their milliequivalent weight to obtain milliequivalent concentrations:

Anions:
| | | |
|---|---|---|
| $HCO_3^-$ | 121 mg/L ÷ 61 mg/meq | = 1.98 meq/L |
| $SO_4^{2-}$ | 28 mg/L ÷ 48 mg/meq | = 0.58 meq/L |
| $Cl^-$ | 17 mg/L ÷ 35.45 mg/meq | = 0.48 meq/L |
| | Σ anions | = 3.04 meq/L |

Cations:
| | | |
|---|---|---|
| $Ca^{2+}$ | 39 mg/L ÷ 20.04 mg/meq | = 1.95 meq/L |
| $Mg^{2+}$ | 8.7 mg/L ÷ 12.15 mg/meq | = 0.72 meq/L |
| $Na^+$ | 8.2 mg/L ÷ 23 mg/meq | = 0.36 meq/L |
| $K^+$ | 1.4 mg/L ÷ 39.1 mg/meq | = 0.04 meq/L |
| | Σ cations | = 3.07 meq/L |

---

Groundwater can have various proportions of major ions (Fig. 5.3). Sodium chloride deposits in underground formations can lead to saline water as in Sample A. A process known as *natural softening* of groundwater occurs when water infiltrates through limestone and enters aquifers with high concentrations of sodium in the geological matrix. Calcium is exchanged for sodium resulting in a water with low calcium concentration but high in sodium and bicarbonate concentration as illustrated by Sample B. High concentrations of dissolved carbon dioxide in groundwater can lead to high proportions of calcium, magnesium, and bicarbonate in water from limestone aquifers as seen in Samples C, D, and E. Saline groundwater often is deficient in potassium and magnesium when compared to seawater of similar TDS concentration.

Concentrations of major ions in some typical aquaculture waters are provided in Table 5.2. This table also provides the world average river water composition and the normal concentrations of major ions in seawater. It is important to understand that concentrations of major ions in water added to ponds will change as equilibrium is established among the added water, the pond soil, and the air above the water. For example, calcium carbonate often precipitates from water of high dissolved carbon dioxide and bicarbonate concentration when it is exposed to air. This phenomenon is not harmful to fish or shrimp in ponds, but in hatcheries, the precipitating calcium carbonate may settle on eggs or larval stages of the culture species and destroy them.

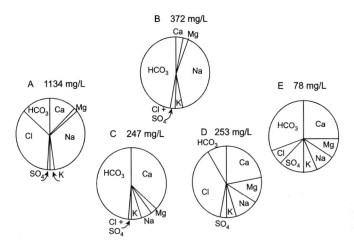

**Fig. 5.3.** Distribution of major ions in samples of groundwater of different total dissolved solid concentrations from wells in west-central Alabama.

## *Specific Conductance*

Electrical current is conducted through a substance via ions. Pure water has few ions and does not conduct electricity well. The conductivity of water increases as a function of increasing ionic concentration (Table 5.3). Thus, the *specific conductance* of water can be measured with a conductivity meter (Fig. 5.4) and used as an index of the degree of mineralization.[2] Up until the 1970s, units of specific conductance were micromhos/cm (μmhos/cm) after which they were changed to microsiemens per centimeter (μS/cm); 1 μmhos/cm = 1 μS/cm. Expression as μmhos/cm is still common.

**Table 5.2.** Concentrations of major ions and total dissolved solids (TDS) in three pond waters, river water, and seawater. All values are in milligrams per liter.

| Ion | Pond in humid area with highly-leached soil | Pond in humid area with calcareous soil | Pond in semi-arid area | River water (world average) | Normal seawater |
|---|---|---|---|---|---|
| $HCO_3^-$ | 14.1 | 107 | 244 | 58 | 142 |
| $SO_4^{2-}$ | 1.4 | 9.8 | 64 | 11.2 | 2,700 |
| $Cl^-$ | 2.6 | 12.8 | 7.6 | 7.8 | 19,000 |
| $Ca^{2+}$ | 2.71 | 34.8 | 53 | 15.0 | 400 |
| $Mg^{2+}$ | 1.40 | 4.0 | 15 | 4.1 | 1,350 |
| $Na^+$ | 2.6 | 4.3 | 34 | 6.3 | 10,500 |
| $K^+$ | 1.4 | 1.5 | 10 | 2.3 | 380 |
| TDS | 30 | 182 | 483 | 120 | 34,500 |

**Table 5.3.** Relationship between concentration of potassium chloride solutions and measured specific conductance at 25°C.[1]

| Concentration (N) | Specific conductance (μmho/cm) |
|---|---|
| 0 | 0 |
| 0.0001 | 14.94 |
| 0.0005 | 73.90 |
| 0.001 | 147.0 |
| 0.005 | 717.8 |
| 0.01 | 1,413 |
| 0.02 | 2,767 |
| 0.05 | 6,668 |
| 0.1 | 12,900 |
| 0.2 | 24,820 |
| 0.5 | 58,640 |
| 1.0 | 111,900 |

The TDS concentration is mainly the result of the concentration of major ions. Thus, there usually is a good correlation between specific conductance and TDS concentration (Fig. 5.5). However, there are differences in the capacity of different ions to conduct electricity. For example, one milliequivalent of potassium ions will conduct more current than one milliequivalent of sodium ions. Thus, the relationship between TDS concentration and specific conductance for inland waters often varies among regions as a result of differences in the proportions of major ions. The factor for converting specific conductance to TDS concentration usually is in the range of 0.55 to 0.9 for inland waters.[1] Normal seawater has a specific conductance of about 50,000 μmhos/cm, and estuarine and ocean waters have relatively constant proportions of major ions—the factor for converting specific conductance to TDS concentration is about 0.7.

**Fig. 5.4.** A laboratory bench conductivity meter (left) and a portable conductivity meter (right).

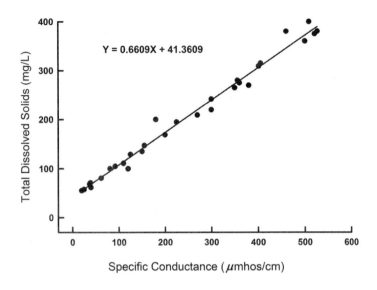

**Fig. 5.5.** Regressions between specific conductance and total dissolved solids in surface water in Alabama.

## *Freshwater, Brackishwater, and Seawater*

These three terms frequently are used in aquaculture, but they seldom are defined. Seawater is easy to define if it is considered to be water in the sea far enough from land not to be influenced by rivers. Seawater is said to have an average TDS (salinity) concentration of 34,500 mg/L. Brackishwater can be considered as less saline than seawater, and more saline than freshwater. There does not seem to be a general consensus on the definition of freshwater. However, we suggest using 1,000 mg/L TDS as the separation between freshwater and brackishwater. This TDS concentration usually would correspond to a specific conductance of about 1,500 μmhos/cm. Note that all inland waters are not freshwaters.

## *Osmotic Pressure*

The major influence of total dissolved solids or salinity on organisms results from their effect on osmotic pressure. The osmotic pressure of solutions increases as the concentration of dissolved particles increases. This variable may be visualized by considering two solutions of different particle concentrations separated by a semi-permeable membrane (Fig. 5.6). The membrane will allow water molecules to pass but not dissolved particles. On the side of the membrane facing the more concentrated solution, the membrane will be bombarded with more solute particles than on the other side, and this will result in more water molecules passing from the less concentrated side to the more concentrated side. The net movement of water from the concentrated side to the less concentrated side will continue until an equilibrium state exists between the two sides. The external pressure that would have to be applied to the more concentrated side to avoid net movement of molecules from the less concentrated side is the osmotic pressure.

The surfaces of an aquatic organism can be thought of as the impermeable membrane (Fig. 5.6). Freshwater species have body fluids more concentrated in solute particles than the water in which they live. Thus, they must retain solute and excrete water to maintain normal osmotic pressure of body fluids. Brackishwater and marine animals live in an environment that is more concentrated in solute than their body fluids. They must continually take in water and excrete ions to maintain normal osmotic pressure.

When freshwater animals find themselves in water of high TDS concentration or brackishwater or marine species move to water of low TDS concentration, they must exert energy to conduct physiological processes necessary to maintain normal osmotic pressure. This detracts from energy that would otherwise be used for other physiological purposes including growth. When the energy requirements for osmoregulation increase, animals become stressed, eat less, grow slower, and finally die.[10]

Freshwater fish usually do best at TDS concentrations below 1,000 mg/L, but many species can tolerate concentrations of 5,000 mg/L or higher. Brackishwater species usually are quite tolerant to fluctuating salinity and some species, such as marine shrimp, can be cultured in waters ranging from slightly greater salinity than freshwater to salinities above those of normal seawater. Truly marine species, however, do not survive and grow well at low salinity.

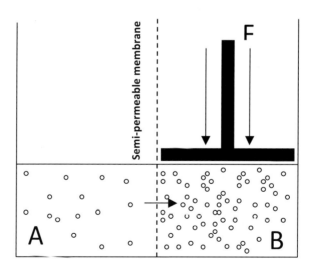

**Fig. 5.6.** Illustration of osmotic pressure. The force (F) that must be applied to the piston to prevent water from moving across the semi-permeable membrane from the less concentrated solution (A) to the more concentrated solution (B) is equal to the osmotic pressure.

# Management

The TDS (salinity) concentration is an important issue in selection of sites and species for aquaculture and in operating hatcheries and grow-out facilities. Individual concentrations of some major ions also can influence the growth and survival of aquatic animals.

## *Site and Species Selection*

The water at a particular site obviously should have a TDS concentration within the optimum range of the species to be cultured. Most freshwater species do well at TDS concentrations up to 1,000 to 2,000 mg/L, and some grow well at higher concentrations. Most marine species do best at salinities near those of normal seawater. However, most estuarine species can tolerate wide ranges in salinity. Many species of marine shrimp survive and grow well at salinities of 1 or 2 ppt up to 40 ppt. Nevertheless, most species of marine shrimp will not survive or grow well in freshwater.

In selecting a site, it is important to know the seasonal changes in TDS concentration and the extremes that may occur during unusually wet or dry periods. For example, many shrimp farms have suffered severe losses during unusually wet years when source water salinity was unacceptably low for several weeks.

In arid climates, waters of freshwater ponds may rise to unacceptably high TDS concentration during the dry season. This situation can be avoided where there is adequate water of lower salinity to flush ponds. However, use of freshwater from wells to dilute salinity in coastal aquaculture ponds has lead to groundwater depletion, land subsidence, and saltwater intrusion into freshwater aquifers in Taiwan and several other locations.

There are cases where the salinity of water is increased to allow culture of brackishwater species in normally freshwater areas. Application of salt to adjust salinity in hatcheries is a fairly common practice, because the volume of water to be treated usually is rather small. In the United States, production of striped bass in small ponds has been improved through the addition of crusher-run rock salt (NaCl). This product contains about 97 to 98% sodium chloride, and each 1 mg/L increase in TDS will require about 1 mg/L of this salt. In Thailand, shrimp production is often done in inland ponds where salinities of 2 to 5 ppt were achieved by mixing brine solution (150 to 250 ppt) from coastal seawater evaporation ponds with freshwater from irrigation systems.[11] Inland culture of shrimp and other brackishwater species has been done in the United States, Ecuador, China, Australia, Thailand, and possibly in other countries using brackish groundwater from wells.[12] Caution should be exercised in the use of brackishwater at inland sites to avoid salinization of nearby soils and streams.[13] Case studies of salinization by inland, brackishwater aquaculture have been made in the United States and in Thailand.[12,13] Best management practices presented in those studies may be implemented to lessen the likelihood of salinization.

## *Acclimation*

Small fish or shrimp larvae from hatcheries often are stocked into grow-out systems of different salinity. When this is done, the animals should be gradually acclimated to the new salinity. There is much variation in the acclimation time used by different managers, but in general, the acclimation time should not be less than 1 hour/ppt salinity, and even longer time should be used to acclimate hatchery animals produced in near full strength seawater for stocking in low-salinity culture systems. Shrimp larvae produced at 34 ppt salinity, for instance, should be acclimated to water of 2 ppt salinity over a period of 2 or 3 days for best results.

## *Seawater Equivalent Concentrations of Major Ions*

Saline water is available in many inland areas, and there is increasing effort to use these waters for culture of marine- and brackishwater species. However, such waters tend to be low in concentrations of potassium and magnesium resulting in death or poor growth of the culture species. Ideal concentrations of potassium, magnesium, and other major ions for culture of marine and brackishwater species are not known, but one would assume that they would do well at ionic proportions similar to those of normal seawater. Experience and research have revealed that adjustment of potassium and magnesium concentrations to the approximate concentrations that would be found in seawater diluted to the same salinity as the culture water usually allows marine shrimp to survive and grow normally.[14]

The following equation may be used to adjust the concentration of major ions in low-salinity water to their *seawater equivalent concentrations* (SEC):

$$\text{SEC (mg/L)} = \text{Salinity of water (ppt)} \times \frac{\text{Seawater concentration (mg/L)}}{34.5}. \qquad (5.1)$$

The normal concentrations of major ions in seawater are listed (Table 5.2). The calculation is illustrated in Example 5.3.

---

**Example 5.3**
**The Seawater Equivalent Concentration (SEC)**

Water in a pond for low-salinity culture of marine shrimp has a salinity of 4.2 ppt. The potassium and magnesium concentrations are 6.8 and 33.1 mg/L, respectively. The SEC is calculated using Equation 5.1:

$$\text{SEC}_K = 4.2 \times \frac{370}{34.5} = 45.0 \text{ mg/L}$$

$$\text{SEC}_{Mg} = 4.2 \times \frac{1,350}{34.5} = 164.3 \text{ mg/L}.$$

---

Two fertilizers, muriate of potash and sulfate of potash magnesia have been widely used for increasing potassium and magnesium concentrations in ponds for inland culture of marine shrimp. Muriate of potash is primarily potassium chloride (KCl) and contains about 50% potassium—a 1 mg/L increase in potassium will require 2 mg/L muriate of potash. Sulfate of potash magnesia is often sold under the trade name K-Mag®, and this product contains 17.8% potassium, 10.5% magnesium, and 21% sulfate-sulfur. Each 1 mg/L increase in potassium requires 5.62 mg/L of K-Mag®, and this amount of K-Mag® will increase magnesium by 0.59 mg/L. An alternate source of potassium is potassium sulfate, and magnesium can be supplied by magnesium sulfate (Epsom salt).

Although concentrations of other major ions normally are not adjusted in waters for inland, low-salinity aquaculture, a few sources of the other ions will be listed. They are as follows: sodium and chloride are usually derived from common salt (NaCl); calcium can be derived from calcium sulfate or calcium chloride; sulfate from sulfate of potash magnesia, magnesium sulfate, or calcium sulfate; and bicarbonate from liming materials or sodium bicarbonate.

## *Other Applications of Major Ions*

In hatcheries, low concentrations of calcium in water supplies have been associated with poor egg hatchability. In channel catfish hatcheries, it is recommended that calcium concentration be at least 4 mg/L (a calcium hardness of 10 mg/L as $CaCO_3$).[15] Water may be treated with liming materials or with calcium sulfate or calcium chloride to increase calcium concentration.

Major ion concentrations are increased in waters of culture systems for several other reasons than obtaining seawater equivalent concentrations. Calcium, magnesium, and bicarbonate concentrations are increased in acidic waters by adding liming materials. Calcium concentration must be increased in some waters to avoid excessively high pH, and calcium is used to remove suspended clay particles from water. Chloride applications often are used in channel catfish ponds to avoid nitrite toxicity in fish. These uses of major ion amendments will be discussed in other chapters.

## *Monitoring*

Although it is useful to have data on normal concentration of TDS and major ions in freshwater culture systems, concentrations change slowly in most waters and routine monitoring of TDS and major ions is not necessary. In arid regions where waters may become brackish when held for long periods in ponds or other grow-out units, in inland, low-salinity aquaculture, and in coastal, brackishwater aquaculture, TDS concentration may vary considerably and monitoring is necessary. The most practical way of monitoring is with a hand-held salinometer (Fig. 5.2) or a conductivity meter (Fig. 5.4). Measurements made at weekly or even monthly intervals usually are sufficient. It should be emphasized that salinometers do not provide reliable estimates of salinity below 5 ppt (5,000 mg/L).

It is necessary to monitor potassium and magnesium concentration in low-salinity waters for culture of brackishwater species.[14] For best results, samples should be taken at monthly intervals, at least initially, and sent to a laboratory for analysis. Water analysis kits also are available for measuring potassium. It also is possible to estimate magnesium concentration by measuring total hardness and calcium hardness with water analysis kits. The difference in total hardness and calcium hardness is the magnesium hardness (in mg/L $CaCO_3$). Magnesium hardness divided by 4.12 equals the magnesium concentration.

# References

1. Eaton, A. D., L. S. Clesceri, E. W. Rice, and A. E. Greenberg. 2005. *Standard Methods for the Examination of Water and Wastewater, 21st Edition*. American Public Health Association, Washington, DC.
2. Boyd, C. E. 2000. *Water Quality, An Introduction*. Kluwer Academic Publishers, Boston, MA.
3. Livingstone, D. A. 1963. Chemical composition of rivers and lakes. United States Geological Survey, Prof. Paper 440-G. United States Government Printing Office, Washington, DC.
4. Hem, J. D. 1970. Study and interpretation of the chemical characteristics of natural water. United States Geological Survey, Water-supply Paper 1473. United States Government Printing Office, Washington, DC.
5. Arce, R. G. and C. E. Boyd. 1980. Water chemistry of Alabama ponds. Bulletin 505, Alabama Agricultural Experiment Station, Auburn University, AL.
6. Silapajarn, K. C. E. Boyd, and O. Silapajarn. 2004. Physical and chemical characteristics of pond water and bottom soil in channel catfish ponds in west-central Alabama. Bulletin 655, Alabama Agricultural Experiment Station, Auburn University, AL.
7. Garrels, R. M. and C. L. Christ. 1965. *Solutions, Minerals, and Equilibria*. Harper and Row, New York, NY.
8. Brown, J., A. Colling, D. Park, J. Phillips, D. Rothery, and J. Wright. 1989. *Seawater: Its Composition, Properties, and Behavior*. Pergamon Press, New York, NY.
9. Hutchinson, G. E. 1957. *A Treatise on Limnology: Vol. I. Geography, Physics, and Chemistry*. John Wiley and Sons, New York, NY.
10. Boyd, C. E. and C. S. Tucker. 1998. *Pond Aquaculture Water Quality Management*. Kluwer Academic Publishers, Boston, MA.
11. Limsuwan, C., T. Somsiri, and S. Silarudee. 2002. The appropriate salinity level of brine water for raising black tiger shrimp under low-salinity condition. Department of Fisheries, Bangkok, Thailand, Aquatic Animal Health Research Institute Newsletter 11(1):1-4.
12. Boyd, C. E. and T. Thunjai. 2003. Concentrations of major ions in waters of inland shrimp farms in China, Ecuador, Thailand, and the United States. Journal of the World Aquaculture Society 34:524-532.
13. Boyd, C. A., C. E. Boyd, A. A. McNevin, and D. B. Rouse. 2006. Salt discharge from an inland farm for marine shrimp in Alabama. Journal of the World Aquaculture Society 37(4):345-355.
14. McNevin, A., C. E. Boyd, O. Silapajarn, and K. Silapajarn. 2004. Ionic supplementation of pond waters for inland culture of marine shrimp. Journal of the World Aquaculture Society 35:460-467.
15. Tucker, C.S. and J.A. Steeby. 1993. A practical calcium hardness criterion for channel catfish hatchery water supplies. Journal of the world Aquaculture Society 24:396-401.

# Chapter 6

# Total Alkalinity and Total Hardness

## Introduction

Total alkalinity and total hardness, together with salinity and total dissolved solids, are defining characteristics in assessing the quality of water. Although aquaculturists frequently measure concentrations of these two variables and manage ponds to maintain adequate alkalinity and hardness, few have a clear understanding of what they are measuring and managing. This possibly is because alkalinity and hardness are not actual dissolved substances in water—they are indices of concentrations of groups of variables that influence water quality and production of culture species. The purpose of this chapter is to explain the sources, measurement, and importance of total alkalinity and total hardness. Management of these two variables will be discussed primarily in other chapters.

## Definitions

### Alkalinity

*Total alkalinity* is the total quantity of titratable bases in water.[1] Bases react with hydrogen ions ($H^+$); thus, any substance that reacts with $H^+$ contributes alkalinity as illustrated below for anions commonly found in natural waters:

| | |
|---|---|
| hydroxide | $OH^- + H^+ = H_2O$, |
| carbonate | $CO_3^{2-} + H^+ = HCO_3^-$, |
| bicarbonate | $HCO_3^- + H^+ = H_2O + CO_2$, |
| ammonia | $NH_3 + H^+ = NH_4^+$, |
| phosphate | $HPO_4^- + H^+ = H_2PO_4^-$, |
| silicate | $H_3SiO_4^- + H^+ = H_4SiO_4$, |
| borate | $H_2BO_3^- + H^+ = H_3BO_3$. |

Bicarbonate and carbonate are present in natural waters at much greater concentrations than other anions listed above, and total alkalinity results primarily from these two ions.

Dissolved carbon dioxide ($CO_{2(aq)}$), bicarbonate, and carbonate exist in water in a pH-dependent equilibrium:

$$CO_{2(aq)} + H_2O = H^+ + HCO_3^- \qquad\qquad K = 10^{-6.35} \qquad\qquad (6.1)$$

$$HCO_3^- = H^+ + CO_3^{2-} \qquad\qquad K = 10^{-10.33}. \qquad\qquad (6.2)$$

There is no measurable bicarbonate in water with pH below 4.5; the proportion of carbon dioxide decreases and bicarbonate increases until bicarbonate comprises essentially 100% of the dissolved inorganic carbon at pH 8.3 (Fig. 6.1). Above pH 8.3, the proportion of bicarbonate declines and that of carbonate increases. Water with pH below about 4.5 does not contain total alkalinity. The total alkalinity in water of pH 4.5 to 8.3 consists almost entirely of bicarbonate. Above pH 8.3, both bicarbonate and carbonate contribute total alkalinity, with the contribution of carbonate increasing as pH rises. At pH 10.33, proportions of bicarbonate and carbonate are equal.

Alkalinity is commonly expressed in fisheries and aquaculture in units of equivalent calcium carbonate (mg/L as $CaCO_3$) or, in some fields of science, as milliequivalents (1 meq/L = 50 mg/L as $CaCO_3$). Expression as calcium carbonate is based on the idea that water of a certain alkalinity has the same acid-neutralizing capacity as a solution with a chemically equivalent amount of calcium carbonate dissolved in it, even if the water actually contains no calcium or carbonate. Alkalinity is expressed as equivalent calcium carbonate throughout this book.

The amount of acid that must be added to a water sample to depress pH to 4.5 is a practical measure of total alkalinity. Acid is consumed primarily in neutralizing bicarbonate and carbonate, but there will be small quantities of other bases in natural waters. Alkalinity measurement by acid titration is described in the last section of this chapter.


## Hardness

*Total hardness* is an index of the total concentration of divalent cations in water. These include calcium, magnesium, strontium, iron, and manganese. There is little strontium in most waters, and divalent iron and manganese are present in only trace amounts in water containing dissolved oxygen. Therefore, total hardness results primarily from calcium and magnesium. Divalent ions can be measured by titration with the chelating agent EDTA (ethylenediamine tetraacetic acid). The amount of EDTA required to bind (chelate) the divalent cations in water is equivalent to total hardness.

Excess hardness results in two undesirable reactions for domestic and industrial water.[2] Divalent cations react with soap, precipitating it and preventing it from forming lather. Accordingly, hardness is sometimes defined as the 'soap-wasting' property of water. A precipitate of calcium and magnesium carbonate will form in vessels where water high in total alkalinity and total hardness is boiled—this precipitate is known as boiler scale. The origin of the term 'hard water' possibly lies in these two features of water with a high concentration of calcium and magnesium.

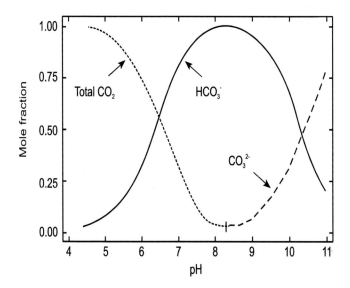

**Fig. 6.1.** Effects of pH on the relative proportions of total $CO_2$, $HCO_3^-$, and $CO_3^{2-}$. The mole fraction of a component is its decimal fraction of all the moles present.[1]

Various units of measure are used to describe water hardness. In the United States, hardness is most commonly expressed as equivalent calcium carbonate (mg/L as $CaCO_3$). Note that although alkalinity and hardness both are expressed as equivalent $CaCO_3$, they refer to distinctly different properties of water. Individual concentrations of calcium and magnesium may be expressed in mg/L of each of these constituents or in hardness units. When expressed as equivalent $CaCO_3$, the terms *calcium hardness* and *magnesium hardness* should always be used, rather than simply 'calcium' or 'magnesium.' Through this book, when we use the term 'hardness' it is assumed that units are calcium carbonate equivalents.

## Sources of Alkalinity and Hardness

Total alkalinity and total hardness usually originate from dissolution of limestone. There are three forms of limestone. *Calcite* or *calcitic limestone* is calcium carbonate ($CaCO_3$). *Dolomite* or *dolomitic limestone* consists of nearly equal parts of calcium and magnesium carbonate ($CaCO_3 \cdot MgCO_3$). *Ordinary limestone* is a mixture of calcium and magnesium carbonates in some proportion other than 1:1 as in dolomite.

Rain falling on the earth's surface is saturated with carbon dioxide, and water containing dissolved carbon dioxide reacts with limestone as illustrated below:

$$CaCO_3 + CO_{2(aq)} + H_2O \rightleftharpoons 2HCO_3^- + Ca^{2+} \tag{6.3}$$

**67**

$$CaCO_3 \cdot MgCO_3 + 2CO_{2(aq)} + 2H_2O \rightleftharpoons 4HCO_3^- + Ca^{2+} + Mg^{2+}. \tag{6.4}$$

Dissolution of limestone imparts chemically equivalent amounts of bicarbonate (total alkalinity) and calcium or calcium and magnesium (total hardness).

Water in equilibrium with atmospheric carbon dioxide and solid calcium carbonate will contain about 70 mg/L bicarbonate, 23 mg/L calcium, and have a pH of 8.3. It will contain very little dissolved carbon dioxide or carbonate. If more carbon dioxide is added to the system at equilibrium, more calcium carbonate will dissolve. Calcium carbonate will precipitate if carbon dioxide is removed from the system at equilibrium.

In many areas of the world, there is no limestone to provide alkalinity and hardness. In such places, calcium silicate minerals often are the main source of alkalinity and hardness:[3]

$$CaSiO_3 + 2CO_{2(aq)} + 3H_2O \rightarrow Ca^{2+} + 2HCO_3^- + H_4SiO_4. \tag{6.5}$$

As can be seen from Equation 6.5, dissolution of calcium silicate results in chemically equivalent amounts of calcium and bicarbonate.

Feldspars are common aluminosilicate minerals found in acidic soils. The following equation shows the dissolution the sodium feldspar, albite, resulting in sodium bicarbonate, silicic acid, and kaolinite:[1]

$$2NaAlSi_3O_8 + 2CO_{2(aq)} + 11H_2O \rightarrow 2Na^+ + 2HCO_3^- + 4H_4SiO_4 + H_2Al_2Si_2O_9. \tag{6.6}$$

Note that the weathering of albite yields total alkalinity but it does not provide total hardness.

## Alkalinity and Hardness in Natural Waters

Rainfall is naturally acidic because it is saturated with dissolved carbon dioxide, but it may contain traces of alkalinity and hardness. Rainwater dissolves minerals in rocks and soils, but in humid areas, and especially in warm climates, soils have been highly leached by rainfall. Unless limestone deposits are present, surface waters usually have relatively low concentrations of alkalinity and hardness. This is illustrated with data from five physiographic provinces of Alabama (Table 6.1). Ponds in sandy soils of the Coastal Plain and acidic soils of Piedmont Plateau had average total alkalinity and total hardness

**Table 6.1.** Concentrations of total alkalinity and total hardness in pond waters from different physiographic provinces of Alabama[4].

| Province | Total alkalinity (mg/L) | Total hardness (mg/L) |
|---|---|---|
| Piedmont Plateau | 11.6 | 12.3 |
| Coastal Plain | 13.2 | 12.9 |
| Appalachian Plateau | 18.9 | 22.0 |
| Limestone Valleys and Uplands | 42.2 | 49.2 |
| Prairies | 51.1 | 55.5 |

concentrations less than 15 mg/L, and those in the Appalachian Plateau, also an area where acidic soils are common, were only slightly higher. Higher concentrations of the two variables were found in ponds of the Blackland Prairie and Limestone Valleys and Uplands where soils often contain limestone.

Except during floods, streams often have higher concentrations of total alkalinity and total hardness than ponds in the same area. For example, streams in the Piedmont Plateau of Alabama had an average total alkalinity and hardness of 24.2 mg/L and 17.9 mg/L, respectively—almost twice as much as ponds. Streams in the Appalachian Plateau averaged 76.6 mg/L alkalinity and 81.6 mg/L hardness—more than three times higher than in ponds. This difference results from base flow of groundwater containing greater concentrations of alkalinity and hardness than surface water into streams.[4]

As a general rule, in humid areas, concentrations of total alkalinity and total hardness are positively correlated with increasing total dissolved solids concentration and specific conductance of surface waters. This results because alkalinity anions and hardness cations often comprised more than half of the dissolved matter in water, and soils and surface rocks that are more soluble are good sources of other major ions in water.

When liming materials are used in aquaculture ponds in regions with acidic soils and waters, concentrations of total alkalinity and total alkalinity in ponds will be above ambient levels in non-managed ponds and streams. In Thailand, tilapia ponds built in areas with acidic soils had average total alkalinity and hardness concentrations of 227 mg/L and 261 mg/L, respectively, because of large inputs of liming materials over several to many years.[5] Liming also resulted in total alkalinities of 79 to 117 mg/L and total hardnesses of 137 to 184 mg/L in ponds for hybrid, air-breathing catfish, carp, and freshwater prawn in Thailand.[6]

In semi-arid and arid regions, there is insufficient rainfall to cause extensive leaching and salts precipitate in the soil profile. Runoff will dissolve some of the salts, and evaporation will further concentrate dissolved substances in surface waters. Concentrations of total hardness and total alkalinity often are above 200 mg/L.

Solubility products of certain minerals are exceeded as ions concentrate in water through evaporation. Carbonates precipitate first resulting in concentrations of total hardness greater than those of total alkalinity. For example, a pond in west Texas with a total suspended solid concentration of about 2,000 mg/L had a total alkalinity of 126 mg/L and total hardness of 476 mg/L.

Water infiltrating the land surface becomes soil moisture or percolates deeper to become groundwater. Water passing through soil often becomes supersaturated with dissolved carbon dioxide from respiration of soil organisms. A high dissolved carbon dioxide concentration favors solubility of limestone, calcium silicate, and feldspars—the sources of alkalinity and hardness. Waters from aquifers in limestone formations often have higher total alkalinity and total hardness concentrations than can be maintained in waters at equilibrium with atmospheric carbon dioxide. Calcium and magnesium carbonates precipitate when such groundwaters are brought to contact with the atmosphere. For example, total alkalinity and total hardness in groundwater supplied to aquaculture ponds at a farm in west central Alabama were 273 mg/L and 318 mg/L, respectively. In ponds, concentrations declined to 120 mg/L total alkalinity and 168 mg/L total hardness within a few days even though bottom soils contained limestone.

Along coastal plains, water may infiltrate through limestone and then through clay of marine origin with a high concentration of exchangeable sodium.[7,8] Water is charged with bicarbonate and calcium (and possibly magnesium) while passing through limestone, and calcium and magnesium are exchanged for sodium within the underlying clay formation. Aquifers in such an area will yield waters of high total alkalinity and low total hardness concentration (Table 6.2). Such groundwater is said to be *naturally softened.*[7] Concentrations of alkalinity and hardness changed when the water was put in ponds. However, ponds had higher alkalinity than hardness (Table 6.2).

Water infiltrating through soils in semi-arid and arid regions may pass through layers where limestone, gypsum, and other minerals have deposited. Water from aquifers in such areas may have high alkalinity and hardness, and many times, concentrations of hardness may exceed those of alkalinity.

The nature of limestone influences the proportions of calcium to magnesium in inland waters.[4] For example, waters in ponds in the Blackland Prairie of Alabama where limestone has a high Ca:Mg ratio typically have around 25 to 35 mg/L calcium and 2 to 3 mg/L magnesium (Ca:Mg ratio averaged 13.1:1). In the Limestone Valleys and Uplands region of Alabama, calcium concentrations in ponds usually are 10 to 14 mg/L and magnesium concentrations often range from 3 to 6 mg/L (average Ca:Mg ratio = 2.5).

The average total alkalinity of river water ranges from 25.4 mg/L in South America to 77.9 mg/L in Europe; the world average is 47.5 mg/L. Corresponding values for total hardness are 20.9 mg/L in Australia to 100.9 mg/L in Europe with a world average of 54.4 mg/L. The average Ca:Mg for river water is 3.7:1 ranging from 1.4:1 in Australia to 5.6:1 in Europe.[9]

Normal seawater has a total alkalinity of 116 mg/L, while its total hardness is 6,570 mg/L.[1] The ratio of calcium to magnesium in normal ocean water is roughly 0.3:1. Compared to ocean waters, waters in estuaries usually have greater Ca:Mg ratios and lower concentrations of total alkalinity and total hardness.

**Table 6.2.** Composition of naturally softened groundwater from wells and waters in ponds supplied by the wells.[8]

| Sample | Total alkalinity (mg/L as CaCO$_3$) | Total hardness (mg/L as CaCO$_3$) | Calcium hardness (mg/L as CaCO$_3$) |
|---|---|---|---|
| Wiggins, SC | | | |
| Well | 313.2 | 37.4 | 11.3 |
| Pond | 93.2 | 26.9 | 17.1 |
| Ruffin, SC | | | |
| Well | 85.0 | 9.14 | 7.8 |
| Pond | 92.4 | 26.1 | 20.1 |
| Williams, SC | | | |
| Well | 60.1 | 14.1 | 12.5 |
| Pond | 59.2 | 17.1 | 11.9 |
| Meridian, MS | | | |
| Well | 136.0 | 21.8 | 17.1 |
| Pond | 93.0 | 15.1 | 11.5 |

# Alkalinity and Hardness in Aquaculture Systems

When water is added to aquaculture systems, the total hardness and total alkalinity can change as the result of several processes as follows:

1. Equilibrium of high alkalinity groundwater with atmospheric carbon dioxide level results in precipitation of calcium and magnesium carbonates and a loss of alkalinity and hardness as mentioned above.

2. Hardness and alkalinity concentrations can decline because calcium and magnesium carbonate precipitate in response to photosynthetic removal of carbon dioxide as will be discussed later in this chapter.

3. Large amounts of calcium may be removed from water bodies by dense standing crops of mollusks. Uptake of calcium and magnesium by other animals and by plants usually do not affect hardness appreciably.

4. Neutralization of total alkalinity occurs during nitrification—this is especially significant in intensive aquaculture in ponds and in water reuse systems where nitrification rates are high.

5. Calcium and magnesium concentrations may be altered by exchange of these two ions between pond water and bottom soil.

6. Alkalinity is neutralized by reaction of pond water with acidic, bottom soils.

7. Rainfall and runoff into culture systems may reduce alkalinity and hardness concentrations, while evaporation rates greater than inflow rates may concentrate alkalinity and hardness.

8. Alkalinity and hardness may be increased intentionally by applications of liming materials, gypsum, and other mineral amendments or inadvertently by applications of feed and other aquacultural inputs.

# Effects in Aquaculture Systems

The carbon dioxide-bicarbonate-carbonate system buffers water against pH change. The greater the alkalinity, the larger the buffering capacity of water. Nevertheless, as total alkalinity increases, the ambient pH of water increases. Water with total alkalinity of 10 mg/L might have an ambient pH of 6.5 or 7 in the early morning, but afternoon pH may reach 9.5 or 10 when phytoplankton photosynthesis is intense. Water with total alkalinity of 100 mg/L may have an ambient, morning pH of 7.5 to 8, but in the afternoon, phytoplankton photosynthesis usually will not cause pH to rise above 8.5 or 9. Buffering capacity of total alkalinity also depends upon water containing calcium. When pH increases to 8.3 as result of carbon dioxide depletion, plants begin to remove carbon dioxide from bicarbonate resulting in formation of carbonate. Carbonate hydrolyzes, and this causes a further increase in pH:

$$2HCO_3^- = CO_2 + CO_3^{2-} + H_2O \tag{6.7}$$

$$CO_3^{2-} + H_2O = HCO_3^- + OH^-. \tag{6.8}$$

The increase in carbonate (and pH) is moderated by precipitation of calcium carbonate:

$$Ca^{2+} + CO_3^{2-} \rightleftharpoons CaCO_3. \tag{6.9}$$

The calcium carbonate precipitate settles slowly, and it often re-dissolves at night when carbon dioxide concentration increases. In naturally softened water (Table 6.2), there are low concentrations of calcium and magnesium, and alkalinity anions usually are balanced by sodium and potassium. Sodium and potassium do not precipitate carbonate as calcium and magnesium do. Thus, photosynthesis causes very high pH in waters with high alkalinity and low hardness.

Alkalinity contributes to the supply of inorganic carbon for photosynthesis. At a given pH, the greater total alkalinity, the more carbon dioxide and bicarbonate available as a carbon source for photosynthesis (Table 6.3).

In water with a high calcium concentration, and especially if pH is high, phosphate will precipitate as insoluble calcium phosphate:

$$5Ca^{2+} + 3H_3PO_4 + H_2O \rightleftharpoons Ca_5(PO_4)_3OH + 7H^+. \tag{6.10}$$

Seawater has a high calcium concentration and a pH near 8. Thus, phosphorus fertilizers are not highly soluble in seawater. Ponds with acidic bottom soil have low total alkalinity and calcium concentrations. In such ponds, phosphate is removed from water by reaction with aluminum and iron in soil minerals. The optimum soil pH for solubility of phosphorus from pond bottom soils is 6.5 to 7 (Fig. 6.2).

**Table 6.3.** Factors for converting total alkalinity to milligrams of available carbon per liter. Multiply factors by total alkalinity.[10]

|  | Temperature (°C) | | | | | |
| --- | --- | --- | --- | --- | --- | --- |
|  | 5 | 10 | 15 | 20 | 25 | 30[a] |
| 5.0 | 8.19 | 7.16 | 6.55 | 6.00 | 5.61 | 5.20 |
| 5.5 | 2.75 | 2.43 | 2.24 | 2.06 | 1.94 | 1.84 |
| 6.0 | 1.03 | 0.93 | 0.87 | 0.82 | 0.78 | 0.73 |
| 6.5 | 0.49 | 0.46 | 0.44 | 0.42 | 0.41 | 0.40 |
| 7.0 | 0.32 | 0.31 | 0.30 | 0.30 | 0.29 | 0.29 |
| 7.5 | 0.26 | 0.26 | 0.26 | 0.26 | 0.26 | 0.26 |
| 8.0 | 0.25 | 0.25 | 0.25 | 0.24 | 0.24 | 0.24 |
| 8.5 | 0.24 | 0.24 | 0.24 | 0.24 | 0.24 | 0.24 |
| 9.0 | 0.23 | 0.23 | 0.23 | 0.23 | 0.23 | 0.23 |

[a]Estimated by extrapolation.

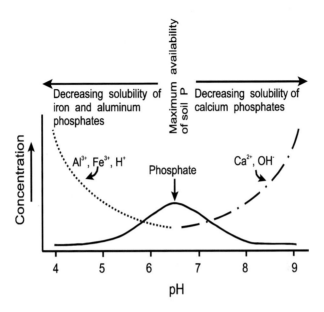

**Fig. 6.2.** Relationship between pH and available phosphorus in sediment.[1]

The cupric ion ($Cu^{2+}$) is highly toxic to algae, and copper sulfate or chelated copper compounds are used as algicides in aquaculture.[11] The solubility of $Cu^{2+}$ in water decreases with increasing pH, and as pH rises the copper carbonate ion pair ($CuCO_3^0$) forms further decreasing the amount of $Cu^{2+}$ available to kill algae. Thus, as total alkalinity increases, the dosage of copper sulfate for algal control must be increased.

Clay particles have a net negative charge and repel each other—a phenomenon that can lead to persistent turbidity and less light for photosynthesis. Calcium and magnesium ions neutralize changes on clay and other particles encouraging their coagulation and sedimentation.[11] Therefore, hard waters often are clearer than other waters. Natural, vegetative extracts (humic substances) impart a color to water similar to that of weak coffee or tea, and low alkalinity, acidic waters are more likely to be highly colored than wasters of moderate to high alkalinity. Humic substances possibly are mildly toxic to phytoplankton and they also restrict light penetration.

Total alkalinity and total hardness obviously effect several water quality variables related to phytoplankton productivity in both natural and managed water bodies. In unpolluted freshwaters, productivity tends to reach a maximum at about 150 mg/L total alkalinity (Fig. 6.3). This relationship, however, is more complex than it appears. High productivity requires nitrogen, phosphorus, and other nutrients in addition to adequate total alkalinity. The total alkalinity of surface waters tends to increase as the fertility of soils increase[4], and waters in contact with fertile soil will dissolve higher concentrations of nitrogen, phosphorus, and other nutrients. The fact that fertilized sportfish ponds with 25 to 50 mg/L total alkalinity can be highly productive (Fig. 6.3) is evidence that water bodies of relatively low alkalinity can be highly productive if nutrients are abundant. It

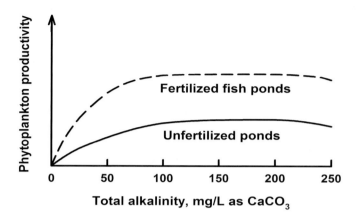

**Fig. 6.3.** Relationship between phytoplankton productivity and total alkalinity in unfertilized ponds and in fertilized fish ponds.

should be noted that unpolluted natural waters have much lower productivity than waters of aquaculture systems.

Phytoplankton productivity tends to decrease at total alkalinities above 150 to 200 mg/L. This also is probably an indirect relationship because total hardness tends to increase as total alkalinity increases. High calcium concentration associated with high hardness would lessen phosphorus solubility and reduce productivity.

In the southeastern United States, sportfish ponds typically are limed where total alkalinity concentration is less than 20 mg/L.[11] However, better results likely could be achieved if total alkalinity is increased to 50 mg/L. In ponds for crustacean and food fish culture, 75 to 100 mg/L is the minimum acceptable alkalinity.[11] Total hardness concentration is important because calcium is necessary to moderate pH, and calcium and magnesium also are required nutrients for plants and animals. Thus, in aquaculture waters, total hardness should not be less than total alkalinity, but there is no harm when total hardness greatly exceeds total alkalinity.

## Management

Liming materials are used to increase alkalinity and hardness. Calcium sulfate may be used where alkalinity is adequate, but hardness needs to be increased. Magnesium hardness can be increased with magnesium sulfate. In intensive culture systems, sodium bicarbonate sometimes is used to replace alkalinity lost as a result of acid produced during nitrification. In such systems, the application of a product that increases only alkalinity is acceptable because the neutralization of bicarbonate by nitrification does not affect total hardness.

It seldom is feasible to reduce total alkalinity and total hardness in ponds, flow-through systems, or waters for cage culture. In Israel, acidic fertilizers have been applied to ponds to reduce alkalinity, but there is no evidence of benefits from this procedure. Alum (aluminum sulfate) may be applied to ponds with high pH and high ammonia concentration to reduce pH (Chapter 8) and lower the proportion of potentially toxic un-ionized ammonia. One milligram per liter of alum will neutralize about 0.5 mg/L of alkalinity. Alum treatment at a rate of twice the phenolphthalein alkalinity will lower pH to 8.3.

Alkalinity reduction is feasible in hatcheries and intensive grow-out units. Total alkalinity concentration also can be lowered by adding a strong acid such as sulfuric or hydrochloric (Example 6.1). Ion exchange processes involving zeolite filters can remove hardness from water. The soda ash-lime process often is used in municipal water treatment plants to reduce hardness[2], but we know of no examples of the use of this process in aquaculture.

# Measurement

Total alkalinity, calcium hardness, and total hardness concentrations should be measured in production units for aquaculture species. If concentrations are not within desirable ranges, treatments should be applied. During production, the concentrations of alkalinity and hardness may fall below acceptable limits. Monitoring is necessary in many kinds of aquaculture, but the frequency of sampling will vary among systems (Table 6.4).

---

**Example 6.1**
**Calculation of the Volume of Sulfuric Acid Necessary to Lower Total Alkalinity**

A hatchery tank containing 50 $m^3$ of water has a total alkalinity of 200 mg/L. Merchant grade sulfuric acid (35 N) will be used to reduce the alkalinity to 100 mg/L.

The required reduction in total alkalinity of 100 mg/L is equivalent to

$$100 \text{ g } CaCO_3 / m^3 \times 50 \text{ m}^3 = 5{,}000 \text{ g } CaCO_3$$

$$5{,}000 \text{ g } CaCO_3 \div 50 \text{ g } CaCO_3/eq = 100 \text{ eq } CaCO_3.$$

Neutralization of 100 eq $CaCO_3$ will require 100 eq of $H_2SO_4$.

$$\frac{100 \text{ eq } H_2SO_4}{35 \text{ eq } H_2SO_4/L} = 2.86 \text{ L } H_2SO_4.$$

---

**Table 6.4.** Suggested monitoring frequency for alkalinity and hardness in aquaculture systems.

| Type of culture system | Suggested monitoring frequency |
|---|---|
| Sportfish ponds | Annually |
| Food animal ponds | |
| Earthen lined: | |
| Humid climate, acidic soil | Semi-annually |
| Humid climate, calcareous soil | Not necessary in extensive and semi-intensive culture; monthly in intensive culture |
| Area with potential acid-sulfate soil | Monthly |
| Semi-arid or arid region | Usually not necessary |
| Plastic lined | Monthly for semi-intensive culture, weekly for intensive culture |
| Flow-through systems | |
| Supplied by springs | Occasionally |
| Supplied by streams in humid climates | After heavy rainfall |
| Supplied by streams in semi-arid regions | Usually not necessary |
| Water reuse systems | Once or twice weekly |
| Water bodies for cage culture | Seasonally |

Standard methodology for measuring the forms of alkalinity and hardness is simple, but some laboratory apparatus and reagents are needed. Water analysis kits based on standard methods are sufficiently accurate for most aquacultural purposes.

Total alkalinity has traditionally been measured by titrating a 100-mL water sample to pH 4.5, the methyl orange endpoint, with 0.02 N sulfuric acid and expressing the results in terms of equivalent calcium carbonate (Example 6.2). Some authorities on water analysis recommend using a slightly higher pH (4.8 to 5.1) for the endpoint of the alkalinity titration. The calculations used in Example 6.2 may be arranged as an equation:

$$\text{Total alkalinity (mg/L as CaCO}_3) = \frac{(V)(N)50,000}{S} \tag{6.11}$$

where V = volume of sulfuric acid (mL); N = normality of sulfuric acid (meq/mL); S = sample volume (mL).

If the pH of a sample is above 8.3, the titration sometimes is done in two steps—titration to pH 8.3, the phenolphthalein endpoint, followed by titration to pH 4.5. The volume of titrant used in the first step is used to calculate the phenolphthalein alkalinity. The total alkalinity is calculated from the total volume of acid used in both steps of the titration. Phenolphthalein alkalinity alone has little meaning in aquaculture and is seldom measured as an independent property of water.

Total hardness concentration usually is determined by titration of a water sample with 0.01M EDTA to the eriochrome black-T endpoint (Example 6.3). A convenient formula for the calculation is:

$$\text{Total hardness (mg/L as CaCO}_3) = \frac{(V)(M)100,000}{S} \tag{6.12}$$

where V = volume of EDTA (mL); M = molarity of EDTA (mmole/mL); S = sample volume (mL).

**Example 6.2**
**Calculation of Total Alkalinity from Titration of Water Sample**

A 100-mL water sample requires 8.75 mL of 0.022 N sulfuric acid for titration to the methyl orange endpoint. The total alkalinity will be calculated.

$8.75 \text{ mL} \times 0.022 \text{ meq H}^+/\text{mL} = 0.192 \text{ meq H}^+$

$0.192 \text{ meq H}^+ \times 50 \text{ mg CaCO}_3/\text{meq} = 9.6 \text{ mg CaCO}_3$

$9.6 \text{ mg CaCO}_3 \times \dfrac{1{,}000 \text{ mL/L}}{100 \text{ mL sample}} = 96 \text{ mg/L as CaCO}_3.$

*Notice:* Normality (N) can be expressed as equivalents per liter or milliequivalents per milliliter, e.g. 0.022 N sulfuric acid is the same as 0.022 meq $H^+$/mL. Also, the equivalent weight of calcium carbonate, a compound consisting of the divalent entities $Ca^{2+}$ and $CO_3^{2-}$, is the formula weight divided by 2.

It is possible to precipitate magnesium from a water sample by raising pH above 12 and measuring only hardness resulting from calcium by titration with EDTA to the murexide endpoint. Magnesium hardness can be estimated as total hardness minus calcium hardness.

Hardness also may be calculated from calcium and magnesium concentrations. Conversion factors are 2.5 for calcium hardness ($CaCO_3/Ca = 100.08/40.08$) and 4.12 for magnesium hardness ($CaCO_3/Mg = 100.08/24.31$). A sample with 10 mg/l $Ca^{2+}$ and 1 mg/L $Mg^{2+}$ has calcium hardness of 25 mg/L, magnesium hardness of 4.12 mg/L, and total hardness of 29.12 mg/L.

**Example 6.3**
**Calculation of Total Hardness from Titration of a Water Sample**

A 100-mL water sample requires 12.15 mL of 0.0097 M EDTA for titration to the eriochrome black-T endpoint. The total hardness will be calculated.

$12.15 \text{ mL} \times 0.097 \text{ mmole/mL} = 0.118 \text{ mmole}$

$0.118 \text{ mmole} \times 100.08 \text{ mg CaCO}_3/\text{mmole} = 11.81 \text{ mg CaCO}_3$

$11.81 \times \dfrac{1{,}000 \text{ mL/L}}{100 \text{ mL sample}} = 118.1 \text{ mg/L as CaCO}_3.$

*Note:* Molarity (M) may be expressed as moles per liter or millimoles per milliliter. The molecular weight of a compound, in this case $CaCO_3$, is the same as its formula weight.

# References

1. Boyd, C. E. 2000. *Water Quality, An Introduction*. Kluwer Academic Publishers, Boston, MA.
2. Sawyer, C. N. and F. L. McCarty. 1967. *Chemistry for Sanitary Engineers*. McGraw-Hill Book Company, New York, NY.
3. Ittekkot, V. 2003. A new story from the Ol' Man River. Science 301 (July):56-58.
4. Arce, R. G. and C. E. Boyd. 1980. Water chemistry of Alabama ponds. Bulletin 505, Alabama Agricultural Experiment Station, Auburn University, AL.
5. Thunjai, T., C. E. Boyd, and M. Boonyaratpalin. 2004. Bottom soil quality in tilapia ponds of different age in Thailand. Aquaculture Research 35:698-705.
6. Wudtisin, I. and C. E. Boyd. 2006. Physical and chemical characteristics of sediments in catfish, freshwater prawn, and carp ponds in Thailand. Aquaculture Research 37:1,202-1,214.
7. Hem, J. D. 1970. Study and interpretation of the chemical characteristics of natural water. United States Geological Survey, Water-supply Paper 1473. United States Government Printing Office, Washington, DC.
8. Boyd, C. E., J. W. Preacher, and L. Justice. 1978. Hardness, alkalinity, pH, and pond fertilization. Proceedings of the Annual Conference of Southeastern Association of Game and Fish Commissioners 107:605-611.
9. Livingstone, D. A. 1963. Chemical composition of rivers and lakes. United States Geological Survey, Prof. Paper 440-G. United States Government Printing Office, Washington, DC.
10. Saunders, G. W., F. B. Trama, and R. W. Bachmann. 1962. *Evaluation of a Modified C-14 Technique for Shipboard Estimation of Photosynthesis in Large Lakes*. Institute of Science and Technology, University of Michigan, Ann Arbor, MI.
11. Boyd, C. E. and C. S. Tucker. 1998. *Pond Aquaculture Water Quality Management*. Kluwer Academic Publishers, Boston, MA.

# Chapter 7

# Carbon Dioxide

## Introduction

Carbon dioxide is involved in vital biological and chemical transformations of carbon in aquatic and marine ecosystems. Plants use carbon dioxide to produce organic matter that is the foundation of terrestrial and aquatic food chains. The gas is released during oxidation of organic matter in animal and plant respiration and bacterial decomposition. Dissolved inorganic carbon is lost from water during biological and chemical precipitation of calcium and magnesium carbonates, which is the first step in formation of limestones. Carbon dioxide reacts with water to form weak solutions of carbonic acid that dissolve limestones and other basic minerals. Substances released when these minerals dissolve are the major dissolved inorganic constituents of fresh waters. Bicarbonate and carbonate dissolved from carbonate minerals interact with dissolved carbon dioxide to regulate the pH of most waters near neutrality (Chapter 8).

The practical implications of carbon dioxide in aquaculture are limited primarily to its role as a potential stressor of aquatic animals and the influence of the dissolved gas on pH. These topics will be the focus of this chapter. Readers interested in carbonate geochemistry and ecological processes involving carbon dioxide should consult standard water chemistry and limnology textbooks.

## Solubility of Carbon Dioxide

Carbon dioxide is about 30 times more soluble in water than oxygen and about 50 times more soluble than nitrogen. Nevertheless, concentrations in pure water exposed to air are low because carbon dioxide is a minor constituent of the atmosphere (about 0.040% by volume in 2013, compared to 21% oxygen and 78% nitrogen).

The equilibrium expression for carbon dioxide dissolving in water is:

$$CO_{2(g)} = CO_{2(aq)} \qquad K_H = 10^{-1.47} \tag{7.1}$$

where $K_H$ is Henry's constant at 25°C in units of mol/L-atm.

In 2014, the atmosphere contained approximately 0.04% carbon dioxide, which is equal to a partial pressure of $10^{-3.40}$ atmospheres. From Equation 7.1, the concentration of dissolved carbon dioxide in equilibrium with air at 25°C is:

$$(CO_{2(aq)}) = (K_H)(CO_{2(g)}) = (10^{-1.47} \text{ mol/L-atm})(10^{-3.40} \text{ atm}) = 10^{-4.87} \text{ mol/L}. \qquad (7.2)$$

Multiplying the molar concentration ($10^{-4.87}$ mol/L) by the molecular weight of carbon dioxide (44 g/mol) gives the concentration in g/L, which can be converted to useful units of mg/L by multiplying by 1,000 mg/g:

$$(10^{-4.88} \text{ mol/L})(44 \text{ g/mol})(1,000 \text{ mg/g}) = 0.59 \text{ mg/L}. \qquad (7.3)$$

This value, 0.59 mg/L, is the concentration of carbon dioxide dissolved in pure water in equilibrium with dry air, both at 25°C. After correcting the atmospheric pressure for the vapor pressure of water, the effect of water temperature on gas solubility, and the salting-out effect of dissolved ions, concentrations of carbon dioxide in waters of various temperatures and salinities in contact with moist air at 760 mm Hg are shown in Table 7.1.

Henry's Law, which is embodied in Equation 7.1, states that the amount of gas dissolved in a liquid is proportional to the partial pressure of the gas in equilibrium with the liquid. As atmospheric carbon dioxide concentrations continue to rise as a result of human activities, dissolved carbon dioxide concentrations at equilibrium with the atmosphere will also increase. Information in Table 7.1 is therefore correct only for conditions in 2014, but can be corrected for new conditions by multiplying values in the table by the ratio of the ambient percentage atmospheric carbon dioxide divided by 0.04, the percentage atmospheric carbon dioxide in 2014. Equilibrium concentrations in Table 7.1 can also be corrected for the effects of altitude or barometric pressure as described for dissolved oxygen in Chapter 13.

## Reactions of Carbon Dioxide in Water

Dissolved carbon dioxide is involved in many important reactions in water. These reactions determine, to a large degree, the water's pH and ionic composition.

**Table 7.1** Solubility of carbon dioxide (mg/L) in water at different temperatures and salinities exposed to moist air containing 0.04% carbon dioxide at a total air pressure of 760 mm Hg.

| Temperature | Salinity ppt | | | | | | | | |
|---|---|---|---|---|---|---|---|---|---|
| (°C) | 0 | 5 | 10 | 15 | 20 | 25 | 30 | 35 | 40 |
| 0 | 1.34 | 1.31 | 1.28 | 1.24 | 1.21 | 1.18 | 1.15 | 1.12 | 1.09 |
| 5 | 1.10 | 1.08 | 1.06 | 1.03 | 1.01 | 0.98 | 0.96 | 0.93 | 0.89 |
| 10 | 0.93 | 0.91 | 0.87 | 0.85 | 0.83 | 0.81 | 0.79 | 0.77 | 0.75 |
| 15 | 0.78 | 0.77 | 0.75 | 0.73 | 0.70 | 0.68 | 0.66 | 0.65 | 0.64 |
| 20 | 0.67 | 0.65 | 0.63 | 0.62 | 0.61 | 0.60 | 0.58 | 0.57 | 0.56 |
| 25 | 0.57 | 0.56 | 0.54 | 0.53 | 0.52 | 0.51 | 0.50 | 0.49 | 0.48 |
| 30 | 0.50 | 0.49 | 0.48 | 0.47 | 0.46 | 0.45 | 0.44 | 0.43 | 0.42 |
| 35 | 0.44 | 0.43 | 0.42 | 0.41 | 0.40 | 0.39 | 0.39 | 0.38 | 0.37 |
| 40 | 0.39 | 0.38 | 0.37 | 0.36 | 0.36 | 0.35 | 0.35 | 0.34 | 0.33 |

Dissolved carbon dioxide reacts with water to form carbonic acid:

$$CO_{2\,(aq)} + H_2O = H_2CO_3 \qquad K = 10^{-2.8}. \qquad (7.4)$$

Carbonic acid then dissociates to produce hydrogen ions and bicarbonate:

$$H_2CO_3 = H^+ + HCO_3^- \qquad K_{a,1} = 10^{-3.5}. \qquad (7.5)$$

The acid-dissociation constant at 25°C ($K_a = 10^{-3.5}$) indicates that carbonic acid is a stronger acid than nitrous ($K_a = 10^{-4.5}$) and acetic ($K_a = 10^{-4.7}$) acids. However, solutions of carbon dioxide dissolved in water are generally considered to be weak acids (a fact that should be appreciated by anyone standing outside in the rain). This apparent discrepancy can be explained by rearranging the equilibrium expression in Equation 7.4:

$$\frac{(H_2CO_3)}{(CO_{2(aq)})} = 10^{-2.8}. \qquad (7.6)$$

Equation 7.6 shows that the ratio of carbonic acid to dissolved carbon dioxide is a small number. In fact, the concentration of carbonic acid is less than less than 0.2% of the concentration of dissolved carbon dioxide. Because dissolved carbon dioxide cannot be distinguished from carbonic acid by common analytical procedures, it is convenient to consider dissolved carbon dioxide plus carbonic acid as a hypothetical species, sometimes written as $H_2CO_3^*$. The 'apparent' acid-dissociation constant for $H_2CO_3^*$ (as contrasted to the 'true' acid-dissociation constant for carbonic acid) at 25°C is given by this expression,

$$H_2CO_3^* = H^+ + HCO_3^- \qquad K_{a,1} = 10^{-6.35}. \qquad (7.7)$$

Comparing the apparent acid-dissociation constant for the hypothetical combined species ($10^{-6.35}$) with the true acid-dissociation constant for carbonic acid ($10^{-3.5}$) shows that dissolved carbon dioxide acts as a weak acid because most of the hypothetical species $H_2CO_3^*$ consists of dissolved carbon dioxide gas rather than carbonic acid. The carbonic acid concentration is not measurable, but carbon dioxide concentration can be measured. Thus, Equation 7.7 usually is written as:

$$CO_2 + H_2O = H^+ + HCO_3^- \qquad K = 10^{-6.35}. \qquad (7.8)$$

Water containing carbonic acid is a more powerful solvent than pure water. For example, pure calcite ($CaCO_3$, a common constituent of limestone) is poorly soluble in pure water, dissolving to produce a calcium concentration of only about 5 mg/L. When pure water at 25°C is equilibrated with air containing $10^{-3.40}$ atmospheres of carbon dioxide, it will contain about 0.6 mg/L dissolved carbon dioxide (Equations 7.2 and 7.3). The small amount of carbonic acid produced under those conditions increases the solubility of calcite four-fold, to about 23 mg $Ca^{2+}$/L (which is an increase from about 12.5 to 50 mg/L as $CaCO_3$ when expressed as calcium hardness; see Chapter 6).

As explained in Chapter 6, dissolved carbon dioxide and carbonic acid react with and dissolve carbonate and silicate minerals in rocks and soil to produce bicarbonate, which is then in multiple, simultaneous, pH-dependent equilibria with dissolved carbon dioxide, carbonic acid and carbonate. With relatively rare exceptions, the pH of fresh water is determined by these simultaneous equilibria. Other bases influence the pH of seawater, but the carbonate system remains the major buffer system.

Carbonic acid formed when carbon dioxide reacts with water causes pH to decrease (Equations 7.4 and 7.5). When dissolved carbon dioxide is extracted from water by plants during photosynthesis or removed from water by degassing to the atmosphere, pH increases because loss of carbon dioxide forces this reaction to the right:

$$2HCO_3^- = CO_2 + CO_3^{2-} + H_2O. \qquad (7.9)$$

Carbonate ions then hydrolyze and generate hydroxyl ions, causing pH to rise:

$$CO_3^{2-} + H_2O = HCO_3^- + OH^-. \qquad (7.10)$$

The extent to which pH changes when carbon dioxide is added or removed from water depends on the amount of carbon dioxide added or removed and the water's acid-neutralizing capacity (which is called the water's 'alkalinity'; see Chapters 6 and 8).

## Carbon Dioxide in Aquatic Ecosystems

Carbon dioxide is gained or lost from water through four processes: 1) respiration, 3) photosynthesis, 3) chemical reactions with acids or bases, and 4) molecular diffusion between water and the gas in contact with the water. Dissolved carbon dioxide present in water at any particular time is the net result of these four processes.

Respiration by aquatic animals, plants, and bacteria adds carbon dioxide to water. The amount of gas respired depends primarily on the biomass of respiring organisms and water temperature. Photosynthesis by aquatic plants and algae removes carbon dioxide. Rates of photosynthesis depend on plant biomass, water temperature, light intensity, and other factors.

Addition of acids or bases alters dissolved carbon dioxide concentrations because carbon dioxide is part of the carbonate acid-base equilibrium system. Acid addition decreases pH and increases dissolved carbon dioxide concentrations whereas base addition increases pH and reduces concentrations (see Fig. 6.1 for a graphic illustration of the relationship of pH and the components of the carbonate system).

Diffusion between water and air may also either add or remove dissolved carbon dioxide. The direction of change depends on relative differences in partial pressures between the gas and liquid phases. For example, if the partial pressure of the dissolved gas in water is greater than the partial pressure in the atmosphere above the water (that is, the water is supersaturated with carbon dioxide), then carbon dioxide will diffuse from water to the atmosphere in the process called *degassing* or *stripping*. On the other hand, carbon dioxide will be absorbed from the atmosphere if the gas partial pressure is lower in water than in the overlying atmosphere.

## Natural Waters

In unpolluted surface waters, biological activity is relatively low and dissolved carbon dioxide concentrations are influenced primarily by gas exchange with the atmosphere. Concentrations are usually less than 2 mg/L, with relatively little daily or seasonal variation. When waters are polluted or otherwise enriched with nutrients and organic matter, biological activity increases and dissolved carbon dioxide dynamics are influenced by underwater respiration and photosynthesis. Concentrations vary daily and seasonally in response to changes in biological activity.

Bottom waters of deep, thermally stratified lakes and reservoirs may become enriched with dissolved carbon dioxide originating from decomposition processes in or near bottom muds (see Chapter 12). Carbon dioxide accumulates in the deeper waters because insufficient light is available for significant removal of carbon dioxide by plant photosynthesis and the lack of mixing with surface waters prevents loss of the gas to the atmosphere.

Dissolved carbon dioxide concentrations are often higher in groundwaters than in surface waters, ranging from 0 to over 100 mg/L with most values in the range of 5 to 50 mg/L.[1] Most carbon dioxide in groundwaters originates from biological activity in the aquifer recharge zone. Root respiration and decomposition of organic matter enriches soil air with carbon dioxide and, as water percolates through the soil, considerably more carbon dioxide goes into solution compared with water exposed to the atmosphere. Enrichment with carbon dioxide and, consequently, carbonic acid provides groundwaters with greater mineral-dissolving power than atmospheric precipitation or most surface waters. Groundwaters from aquifers composed of silicate minerals often have higher concentrations of dissolved carbon dioxide than waters from limestone aquifers because some carbon dioxide is removed in reactions with carbonates in limestone (see Chapter 6).

## Aquaculture Systems

Aquaculture ponds have high rates of biological activity and dissolved carbon dioxide concentrations are dominated by aquatic plant (usually phytoplankton) metabolism, much like dissolved oxygen dynamics. In fact, dissolved carbon dioxide concentrations almost always cycle in a daily pattern opposite that of dissolved oxygen (Fig. 7.1). Factors leading to increases in one variable usually cause decreases in the other. Conditions that favor rapid rates of photosynthesis (abundant plants or phytoplankton, bright sunlight, and warm water) cause rapid removal of carbon dioxide during daylight. Dissolved carbon dioxide often becomes essentially depleted from water on warm, sunny afternoons in ponds with moderate to dense plant or phytoplankton communities. At night, photosynthesis ceases and carbon dioxide from respiration accumulates. Dissolved

**83**

carbon dioxide concentrations in aquaculture ponds usually range from less than 1 mg/L in the afternoon to 5 to 10 mg/L, or more, at dawn, although the amplitude of daily fluctuations depends on the relative rates of photosynthesis and respiration, which depends on phytoplankton and fish standing crops and climatic conditions. Daily changes in dissolved carbon dioxide concentrations then affect the water's pH, with lowest values corresponding to periods of high dissolved carbon dioxide concentrations. The pH then rises during daylight as carbon dioxide is removed in underwater photosynthesis (Chapter 8). Maximum concentrations and variation with time increase as culture system intensity increases.

During extended periods of cloudy weather, daily net photosynthesis is low and carbon dioxide concentrations at dawn may increase from day to day until higher rates of photosynthesis resume with sunny weather. Highest concentrations of carbon dioxide in aquaculture ponds usually occur after phytoplankton die-offs. Sudden death of phytoplankton blooms may occur naturally or as the result of treatment with herbicides or other phytotoxic chemicals. Cessation of photosynthesis coupled with rapid decomposition of dead algal cells may result in dissolved carbon dioxide concentrations exceeding 20 mg/L for several days after the die-off.

Culture animals are the main source of dissolved carbon dioxide in flow-through and recirculating aquaculture systems. Decomposition of uneaten feed and fecal solids is also a source of carbon dioxide, but that contribution can be minimized through careful feeding and efficient solids removal practices. In recirculating aquaculture systems, ammonia is removed from water by autotrophic, nitrifying bacteria growing on the system's biofilter. Autotrophic bacteria consume carbon dioxide in this process, but considerable carbon dioxide is also produced by heterotrophic bacteria growing on biofilter surfaces. Carbon dioxide is also produced within recirculating aquaculture systems as an indirect result of the acid produced in the nitrification process. The total amount of carbon dioxide produced within the biofilter may account for up to 40% of the total carbon dioxide produced within a recirculating system.[2] Carbon dioxide in intensive aquaculture systems is discussed in Chapters 26 (recirculating aquaculture systems) and 28 (flow-through aquaculture systems).

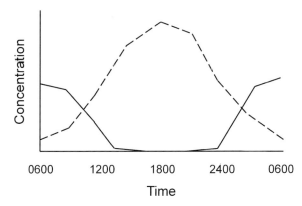

**Fig. 7.1.** Daily changes in dissolved oxygen (dashed line) and dissolved carbon dioxide concentrations (solid line) in ponds.

# Importance of Carbon Dioxide in Aquaculture

Exposure to high concentrations of carbon dioxide can be stressful or lethal to aquatic animals. Carbon dioxide also has indirect effects on aquatic animals because changes in dissolved carbon dioxide concentration affect the water's pH. Changes in pH related to dissolved carbon dioxide may directly impact animal well-being or may affect the pH-dependent toxicity of other substances.

Although direct and indirect physiological effects are the most important practical considerations of carbon dioxide in aquaculture, carbon in the form of carbon dioxide is a primary plant nutrient and lack of carbon may limit the productivity of some ponds. In fact, one of the goals of pond liming is to increase the supply of carbon for photosynthesis (Chapter 9).

## *Physiological Effects*

Aquatic animals excrete carbon dioxide produced in cellular respiration through their gills. Approximately 1 mol of carbon dioxide is excreted for every mol of oxygen consumed (on a mass basis, the ratio is 1.4 grams of carbon dioxide per gram of oxygen). When environmental carbon dioxide concentrations increase, the efficiency of carbon dioxide excretion across the gills decreases, leading to an increase in blood carbon dioxide levels (*hypercapnia*) and a decrease in blood or hemolymph pH (*acidosis*). These conditions decrease the affinity of respiratory pigments for oxygen, which reduces oxygen uptake by blood at the gills. In animals with hemoglobin as the respiratory pigment, the effect of blood acidosis or hypercapnia on the oxygen affinity of hemoglobin is known as the *Bohr effect*. Overall, exposure to high environmental dissolved carbon dioxide concentrations reduces respiratory efficiency and decreases the tolerance of animals to low dissolved oxygen concentrations.

Tolerance of fish and crustaceans to environmental dissolved carbon dioxide concentrations varies greatly. Many marine fish evolved in environments with stable, low dissolved carbon dioxide concentrations and are intolerant of dissolved carbon dioxide. Growth of Atlantic cod, for example, is significantly reduced upon long-term exposure to only 8 mg/L dissolved carbon dioxide, which also caused a high incidence of cataracts through some unknown mechanism.[3,4] Although poorly supported by experimental data, an upper limit of 20 mg/L dissolved carbon dioxide has been suggested for the health of salmonids,[5] although trout have been grown with no ill effects in water with constant dissolved carbon dioxide concentrations at least as high as 24 mg/L.[6] Warmwater fish evolved in environments where fluctuations in dissolved carbon are more common and, therefore, can tolerate higher concentrations. Concentrations of dissolved carbon dioxide greater than 60 to 80 mg/L have a narcotic effect on aquatic animals and even higher concentrations may cause death.

Prolonged exposure to elevated levels of dissolved carbon dioxide is implicated as causing calcareous deposits within fish kidneys, a condition known as *nephrocalcinosis*.[7] Although the condition rarely results in death, growth may be impaired. The mechanisms responsible for development of nephrocalcinosis are poorly understood, but appear to

**85**

depend upon diet composition and ionic composition of the water, as well as long-term exposure to relatively high concentrations of carbon dioxide (over 30 mg/L).

Studies of the physiological effects of dissolved carbon dioxide are almost always conducted by exposing fish to nearly constant concentrations for long periods. No studies have been made of the effects of short-term exposure of fish or crustaceans to varying carbon dioxide and oxygen concentrations, making it difficult to assess the importance of dissolved carbon dioxide exposure on fish and crustaceans raised in ponds where concentrations can vary over several orders of magnitude each day.

## *Carbon Dioxide and pH*

Addition of carbon dioxide causes pH to decrease and removal causes pH to increase. The extent to which pH changes depends on the amount of carbon dioxide added or removed and the water's buffering capacity (alkalinity). Changes in pH can impact aquatic animal health directly or, more commonly, indirectly through the effects of pH on other chemical reactions.

In waters of low alkalinity, carbon dioxide can depress pH to the point that the health of aquatic animals is affected. Problems with low pH related to excessive carbon dioxide accumulation do not occur in waters with modest amounts of alkalinity (Example 7.1)

Photosynthesis by underwater plants and algae removes dissolved carbon dioxide, causing pH to rise (Equations 7.9 and 7.10). This is a normal condition in ponds where dissolved carbon dioxide concentrations cycle daily in response to diurnal changes in solar radiation. Under some conditions, however, the increase in pH can be so dramatic or prolonged that aquatic animal health may be endangered. Problems with high pH in ponds are discussed in Chapter 8.

Because carbon dioxide and pH are interdependent, changes in dissolved carbon dioxide concentration affect all other pH-dependant equilibria in water. For example, changes in dissolved carbon dioxide concentrations affects ammonia toxicity and the toxicity of metals to aquatic animals. These interactions are discussed in the next chapter, but one aspect of the interaction between carbon dioxide and ammonia toxicity must be mentioned here.

Carbon dioxide and ammonia are excreted as waste products of aquatic animal metabolism, and both substances may become toxic if they accumulate.[8] The toxicity of ammonia is mainly attributable to the concentration of un-ionized ammonia ($NH_3$), which is in a pH- and temperature-dependent equilibrium with the ammonium ion ($NH_4^+$). Ammonium ion is considered much less toxic (see Chapter 15 for a discussion of ammonia toxicity). For a given concentration of total ammonia (ionized plus un-ionized), more of the total exists as toxic un-ionized ammonia as pH increases. Dissolved carbon dioxide depresses pH when it accumulates in aquaculture systems, changing the equilibrium between un-ionized ammonia and ammonium ion to reduce the fraction of un-ionized ammonia. Some aquaculturists make use of this relationship in fish transport tanks and serial-reuse flow-through systems by removing enough carbon dioxide to maintain safe levels, but allowing some dissolved carbon dioxide to remain so that the lower pH reduces the effects of the more toxic substance, un-ionized ammonia.

## Example 7.1
## Effect of Alkalinity on Acidification of Water by Carbon Dioxide

Even low levels of alkalinity will protect against dangerous decreases in pH due to carbon dioxide accumulation. Let's compare two waters at 25°C with both containing 20 mg/L dissolved carbon dioxide ($10^{-3.34}$ mol/L); one water has an alkalinity of 0 and the other an alkalinity of 10 mg/L as $CaCO_3$ (see Chapter 6 for an explanation of this manner of expressing alkalinity).

Equation 7.7 can be rewritten as

$$\frac{(H^+)(HCO_3^-)}{(H_2CO_3^*)} = K_{a,1} = 10^{-6.35}.$$

The pH of the first water can be calculated by assuming that $(H_2CO_3^*) \approx (CO_{2\,(aq)}) = 10^{-3.34}$ mol/L and that $(H^+) = (HCO_3^-)$ because equimolar amounts of hydrogen ion and bicarbonate are produced when carbonic acid dissociates:

$$\frac{x^2}{10^{-3.34}} = K_{a,1} = 10^{-6.35}$$

$$x^2 = 10^{-9.69}$$

$$x = (H^+) = 10^{-4.85}, \text{ or pH} = 4.85.$$

For the second water, we will assume that all the alkalinity is in the form of bicarbonate. Water with a total alkalinity of 10 mg/L as $CaCO_3$ has a bicarbonate concentration is $10^{-3.70}$ mol/L. Substitution into the same equation above gives

$$\frac{(x)(10^{-3.70})}{10^{-3.34}} = K_{a,1} = 10^{-6.35}$$

$$x = (H^+) = 10^{-5.99}, \text{ or pH} = 5.99.$$

Both waters contain 20 mg/L dissolved carbon dioxide—a concentration considered within the 'safe range' for most freshwater fish. However, in the water devoid of alkalinity, that amount of dissolved carbon dioxide depresses pH to 4.8—a level that may be stressful or lethal to fish (Chapter 8). A modest amount of alkalinity in the form of bicarbonate prevents the pH from falling below approximately 6, a level considered safe for most freshwater fish.

# Management

In the previous section 'Carbon Dioxide in Aquatic Ecosystems,' four processes were described that affect carbon dioxide concentrations. Three of those four processes remove carbon dioxide from water: photosynthesis, base addition, and diffusion to the atmosphere (degassing or gas stripping).

Most aquaculture ponds have high rates of biological activity and considerable carbon dioxide may be produced in respiration by fish, plankton, and the pond and sediment microbial community. Although much carbon dioxide may be produced, it does not accumulate in ponds because the gas is removed daily in photosynthesis and the carbon is incorporated into plant organic matter. Dissolved carbon dioxide concentrations occasionally increase over time when the balance of photosynthesis and respiration is upset, as might occur during long periods of cloudy weather or after phytoplankton bloom die-offs. Concentrations will increase and may remain high until plant growth resumes and the excess dissolved carbon dioxide is removed in photosynthesis.

Episodes of excessively high dissolved carbon dioxide concentrations are difficult to manage in aquaculture ponds. Photosynthesis—the process that normally keeps concentrations in check—is almost impossible to manage in aquaculture ponds. Removing dissolved carbon dioxide from ponds using degassing or addition of bases is also difficult in practice.

Dissolved carbon dioxide is difficult to strip from water because the gas is relatively soluble in water and its partial pressure in the normal atmosphere is low. When carbon dioxide-supersaturated water droplets pass through air or when bubbles pass through water, gas lost from the water accumulates in the gas phase and carbon dioxide partial pressure can quickly rise far above that in the atmosphere, especially if the volume of the gas phase is low compared to the volume of the liquid phase. When this happens, the carbon dioxide partial pressure gradient between water and air may disappear and no more gas can be stripped from the water. Most aerators used in pond aquaculture operate at intermediate gas-liquid ratios, and provide adequate quantities of oxygen to the culture animals by adding modest amounts of oxygen to large volumes of water. Because gas-liquid ratios are not high, aerators typically used in pond aquaculture are not very effective at removing carbon dioxide.[9]

To be effective at degassing dissolved carbon dioxide, aerators must be operated at high gas-liquid ratios. Open, cascade-type aerators (Fig 7.2) can provide high gas-liquid ratios, but the most common degassing devices are packed-column aerators with packing media having a large surface area. Water flows through the column by gravity and forced, counter-current air ventilation maintains low carbon dioxide partial pressures in the gas phase by quickly removing the carbon dioxide-enriched off-gas (Fig. 7.3).[10,11]

Dissolved carbon dioxide can be quickly removed from water by reaction with a base, such as sodium hydroxide (NaOH), sodium carbonate ($Na_2CO_3$) or calcium hydroxide, $Ca(OH)_2$—commonly called hydrated or slaked lime. The use of sodium hydroxide and sodium carbonate for carbon dioxide removal is discussed in Chapter 21. Hydrated lime is often more readily available to farmers, so its use is described here. Although base addition can be an effective treatment in aquaculture systems with small water volumes,

**Fig. 7.2.** A cascade-type aerator for removing super-saturated dissolved carbon dioxide from groundwater.

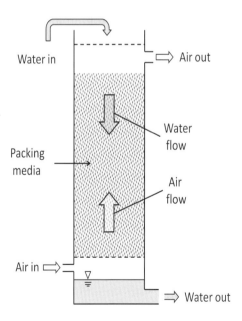

**Fig. 7.3.** A packed-column aerator used for adding dissolved oxygen and removing dissolved carbon dioxide from water.

there are two problems with this treatment in ponds, regardless of the type of base used: 1) large amounts of chemical may be required to remove substantial amounts of carbon dioxide from large aquaculture ponds and 2) the treatment is temporary.

The reaction of dissolved carbon dioxide with calcium hydroxide proceeds in two steps:

$$CO_2 + Ca(OH)_2 = CaCO_3 + H_2O \qquad (7.11)$$

$$CO_2 + CaCO_3 + H_2O = Ca^{2+} + 2HCO_3^-. \qquad (7.12)$$

The overall reaction is:

$$2CO_2 + Ca(OH)_2 = Ca^{2+} + 2HCO_3^-. \qquad (7.13)$$

The overall reaction indicates that 0.84 mg/L of calcium hydroxide will remove 1 mg/L of dissolved carbon dioxide. In practice, about twice that amount (1.6 mg/L) is needed to quickly remove 1 mg/L of carbon dioxide,[12] probably because the second step of the reaction (Equation 7.12) proceeds much slower than the first step. Consider a pond with a dissolved carbon dioxide concentration of 40 mg/L—a level sometimes reached after massive phytoplankton die-offs. To reduce that concentration to a presumed safe level of 20 mg/L in a 2-ha, 1.2-m-deep pond would require about 500 kg of hydrated lime. Using large quantities of caustic chemical such as hydrated lime is inconvenient, especially under emergency conditions. Further, using hydrated lime to remove carbon dioxide affords only temporary relief because it removes only the carbon dioxide present at the time of application. Treatment does not prevent subsequent problems because it does not address the reason carbon dioxide accumulated in the first place—high rates of community respiration.

Fortunately, problems with high dissolved carbon dioxide concentrations are rare in ponds and most fish species grown in ponds (carps, catfishes, tilapias) are relatively resistant to elevated levels. Because carbon dioxide affects oxygen use by fish and the two variables usually cycle opposite one another, most pond aquaculturists avoid problems by vigilant monitoring of dissolved oxygen concentrations and aerating ponds before the combined effects of low dissolved oxygen concentrations and elevated carbon dioxide concentrations kill fish. If conditions become critical, emergency treatment with hydrated lime can provide temporary relief.

Carbon dioxide accumulation is a common problem in intensive flow-through and recirculating aquaculture systems because of high rates of respiration in those systems. In low intensity systems, water exchange or vigorous aeration with air-contact aerators usually prevent dissolved carbon dioxide from accumulating to unsafe levels. As system carrying capacity is increased by using pure-oxygen systems to overcome oxygen limitations, carbon dioxide problems may occur due to the combination of high fish biomass, high levels of water reuse, and poor removal of carbon dioxide by oxygen-injection systems. Carbon dioxide management in recirculating aquaculture systems is discussed in Chapter 26 and in Chapter 28 for flow-through systems.

# Measurement

Dissolved carbon dioxide concentrations can change rapidly and concentrations may vary greatly with location within aquaculture systems. To be useful in management, analytical data should be collected routinely in a manner similar to that for dissolved oxygen. In ponds, the important measurements are those taken at dawn when concentrations of carbon dioxide are usually highest and concentrations of dissolved oxygen are lowest. In intensive production systems concentrations are usually highest in the hours after animals are fed. Measuring carbon dioxide concentrations daily is time-consuming because special care is needed to obtain water samples and analytical methods are laborious. Perhaps for those reasons, routine measurements are not made on most commercial facilities. Fortunately, dissolved carbon dioxide concentrations must be rather high to cause problems for most aquaculture species unless dissolved oxygen concentrations are low.

When carbon dioxide dissolves in water it forms an acid. Its concentration can therefore be determined by titration with a base. The overall reaction involves two reactions: first, the base (hydroxide in this example) reacts with carbonic acid to form bicarbonate:

$$H_2CO_3 + OH^- = HCO_3^- + H_2O. \tag{7.14}$$

Dissolved carbon dioxide then hydrates to replace the carbonic acid neutralized in Equation 7.13:

$$CO_{2\,(aq)} + H_2O = H_2CO_3. \tag{7.15}$$

The overall reaction is the sum of Equations 7.14 and 7.15:

$$CO_{2\,(aq)} + OH^- = HCO_3^-. \tag{7.16}$$

For practical reasons, sodium carbonate is the preferred titrant for dissolved carbon dioxide analysis. The overall reaction is

$$CO_3^{2-} + H_2O + CO_{2\,(aq)} = 2HCO_3^-. \tag{7.17}$$

The reactions in Equations 7.16 and 7.17 are complete at pH 8.3. The reaction endpoint is determined either potentiometically (i.e., using a pH meter) or by using phenolphthalein, a color indicator that is colorless at pH values below 8.3 and pink at higher pH values.[13] The color-indicator method is simple and suitable for practical use in freshwater aquaculture (Example 7.2). Most field test kits are based on this method.

The acid-base equilibrium system involving dissolved carbon dioxide, carbonic acid, hydrogen ions, and bicarbonate provides another method of determining dissolved carbon dioxide. This method requires determination of the water's pH, bicarbonate concentration (estimated as total alkalinity for most waters), temperature, and total dissolved solids concentration. The known values are then entered into a computer program or, more commonly, are used in a *nomograph* to calculate dissolved carbon dioxide concentrations. Nomographs are graphic diagrams used to estimate an unknown variable whose value depends on multiple interacting factors. The nomograph consists of scales for known values which are connected graphically with straight lines in a specified way, and the unknown variable (carbon dioxide in this case) is estimated from the point at which the final line crosses the scale for that variable. In practice, the nomograph method for estimating dissolved carbon dioxide concentrations is much easier to use than it is to describe. The nomograph method is more accurate than titration when the required variables are carefully measured and the nomograph is used correctly. The nomograph for estimating dissolved carbon dioxide concentrations is reproduced in any recent edition of *Standard Methods*.[13]

For practical use in most fresh waters, simplifying assumptions allow dissolved carbon dioxide to be estimated from pH and total alkalinity with one simple equation:

$$\text{Dissolved } CO_2 = (2)(\text{total alkalinity, mg } CaCO_3/L)(10^{(6\text{-pH})}) \tag{7.18}$$

For example, if the total alkalinity of a water is 125 mg/L as $CaCO_3$ and the pH is 7.2, the dissolved carbon dioxide concentration is 16 mg/L (the computed value is 15.77, but given the assumptions implicit in this method, rounding to the nearest whole number is justified). Strictly speaking, Equation 7.15 is valid only at 25°C and in fresh waters with low dissolved solids concentrations. Relatively little practical error is encountered, however, over temperatures from 15 to 35°C and dissolved solids concentrations from 0 to 500 mg/L. On the other hand, relatively large errors may result from mistakes in measuring pH and alkalinity when using either the nomograph or Equation 7.18.

---

**Example 7.2**
**Measuring Dissolved Carbon Dioxide by Titration with a Base.**

In the laboratory, dissolved carbon dioxide is conveniently titrated with a 0.0454 N sodium carbonate solution. Suppose a 100-mL water sample requires 2.52 mL of 0.0454 N sodium carbonate to titrate to the phenolphthalein endpoint. The dissolved carbon dioxide concentration is calculated as follows:

$$2.52 \text{ mL} \times 0.0454 \text{ meq } Na_2CO_3/mL = 0.114 \text{ meq } Na_2CO_3$$

$$0.114 \text{ meq} \times 22 \text{ mg } CO_2/meq = 2.52 \text{ mg } CO_2$$

$$2.52 \text{ mg } CO_2 \times \frac{1,000 \text{ mL/L}}{100 \text{ mL sample}} = 25.2 \text{ mg } CO_2/L.$$

The basis for using a 0.0454 N solution of sodium carbonate should now be apparent: when a 100 mL sample is used, the dissolved carbon dioxide concentration (in mg/L) can be rapidly calculated by multiplying the titration volume (in mL) times 10.

---

Salinity has a large effect on dissolved carbon dioxide concentrations measured by titration, nomograph, or Equation 7.18. For example, titration overestimates true dissolved carbon dioxide concentrations by a factor of 1.6 at full seawater salinity.[12] If relatively accurate measurements of dissolved carbon dioxide are needed in water with salinities greater than a few parts per thousand, methods have been developed based on establishing an equilibration between carbon dioxide partial pressures in the water and in a sealed gas phase inside an analyzer system. After gases equilibrate, carbon dioxide in the analyzer gas phase can be measured by a variety of techniques, although infra-red detection is common.[14] Portable meters based on gas equilibration and infra-red detection are now available. The meters are accurate and relatively simple to use, but are expensive and require long periods for equilibration, especially if the water velocity across the probe surface is slow. Measurement times between samples range from about 10 minutes at high water velocities to more than an hour for static samples.[15] Despite these shortcomings, meters based on liquid-gas partial pressure equilibration are the only practical alternative if accurate carbon dioxide measurements are needed in waters with salinities greater than a few parts per thousand.

Regardless of the method used to measure dissolved carbon dioxide, improper sampling can cause substantial errors. Gas can be quickly gained or lost from samples by diffusion or biological activity. The best advice is to sample with minimal agitation and contact with the atmosphere and to analyze the sample immediately after collection. Of greater concern, dissolved carbon dioxide concentrations often vary with location within a water body (especially with depth in ponds) and may change rapidly. Large spatial and temporal variation in dissolved carbon dioxide concentrations makes it difficult to design and interpret sampling programs. Meaningful sampling programs must be based on the purpose of sampling and knowledge of factors that affect concentrations.

# References

1. Matthes, G. 1982. *The Properties of Groundwater*. John Wiley and Sons, New York.
2. Summerfelt, S.T. and M.J. Sharrer. 2004. Design implications of carbon dioxide production within biofilters contained in recirculating salmonid culture systems. Aquacultural Engineering 32:171-182.
3. Moran, D. and J.G. Stöttrup. 2011. The effect of carbon dioxide on growth of juvenile Atlantic cod *Gadus morhua* L. Aquatic Toxicology 102:24-30.
4. Moran, D., L. Tubbs, and J.G. Stöttrup. 2012. Chronic $CO_2$ exposure markedly increases the incidence of cataracts in juvenile Atlantic cod *Gadus morhua* L. Aquaculture 364-365:212-216.
5. Colt, J. and K. Orwicz. 1991. Modeling production capacity of aquatic culture systems under freshwater conditions. Aquacultural Engineering 10:1–29.
6. Good, C. J. Davidson, C. Welsh, K. Snekvik, and S. Summerfelt. 2010. The effects of carbon dioxide on performance and histopathology of rainbow trout *Oncorhynchus mykiss* in water recirculation aquaculture systems. Aquacultural Engineering 42:51-56.
7. Landolt, M.L. 1975. Visceral granuloma and nephrocalcinosis in trout, pages 793-801. In: W.E. Ribelin and G. Migaki (editors), *The Pathology of Fishes*. University of Wisconsin Press, Madison, WI.

8. Tucker, C. S. and J. A. Hargreaves. 2004. Water quality management, pages 215-278. In C.S. Tucker and J.A. Hargreaves (editors), *Biology and Culture of Channel Catfish*. Elsevier, Amsterdam.

9. Eshchar, M., N. Mozes, and M. Fediuk. 2003. Carbon dioxide removal rate by aeration devices in intensive sea bream tanks. The Israeli Journal of Aquaculture–Bamidgeh 55:79–85.

10. Summerfelt, S.T., B. J. Vinci, and R.H. Piedrahita. 2000. Oxygenation and carbon dioxide removal in water reuse systems. Aquacultural Engineering 22:87-108.

11. Vinci, B.J., M.B. Timmons, S.T. Summerfelt, and B.J. Watten. 1998. *Carbon Dioxide Control in Intensive Aquaculture*. Northeast Regional Agricultural Engineering Service, Ithaca, NY.

12. Hansell, D.A. and C.E. Boyd. 1980. Uses of hydrated lime in fish ponds. Proceedings Annual Conference Southeastern Association Fish and Wildlife Agencies 34:49-58.

13. Eaton, A.D., L.S. Clesceri, E.W. Rice, and A.E. Greenberg, editors. 2005. *Standard Methods for the Examination of Water and Wastewater, 21st Edition*. American Public Health Association (APHA), American Water Works Association (AWWA), and the Water Environment Federation (WEF), Washington, DC.

14. Pfeiffer, T.J., S.T. Summerfelt, and B.J. Watten. 2011. Comparative performance of $CO_2$ measuring methods: marine aquaculture recirculating system application. Aquacultural Engineering 44:1-9.

15. Moran, D., B. Tirsgard, and J.F. Steffensen. 2010. The accuracy and limitations of a new meter used to measure aqueous carbon dioxide. Aquacultural Engineering 43:101-107.

# Chapter 8

# pH

## Introduction

The pH value is a mathematical transformation of the hydrogen ion concentration that conveniently expresses water's acidity or basicity. The pH of aquatic ecosystems varies within a particular range depending on the system's chemistry and biological activity. Freshwater and marine animals tolerate a range of environmental pH that may either be narrow or wide, depending on the ecosystem in which the animal evolved. Aquatic animals can become stressed or die when exposed to extremes of pH or when pH changes rapidly, even if the change occurs within a pH range that is normally tolerated. Fortunately, direct 'pH toxicity' is rare in aquaculture because farm sites and water supplies should be selected to provide an environment where pH is within the appropriate range. Nevertheless, all aquaculture systems are subject to conditions that may cause pH to rise or fall outside the tolerance range, causing injury or death of cultured animals. Indirect effects of pH and interactions of pH with other variables are usually more important in aquaculture than the direct toxic effects. Important interactions include the effects of pH on certain aqueous equilibria involving ammonia, hydrogen sulfide, chlorine, and metals. The fertility of aquatic ecosystems is also influenced by environmental pH because it affects the availability of key plant nutrients.

## The pH Concept

The term *pH* is defined as the negative logarithm of the hydrogen ion molar activity. The pH concept has its basis in the ionization of water:

$$H_2O = H^+ + OH^-. \tag{8.1}$$

The mass action expression for the ionization of water is:

$$\frac{(H^+)(OH^-)}{(H_2O)} = K. \tag{8.2}$$

Parentheses in Equation 8.2 denote molar activities, which in freshwater can be considered equal to molar concentrations. The degree of ionization of water is very small and does not change the concentration of water, and Equation 8.2 can be rewritten as:

$$(H^+)(OH^-) = K_w \tag{8.3}$$

Where $K_w$ is the special designation given to the equilibrium constant for the ionization of water.

In pure water, one hydrogen ion and one hydroxyl ion result from ionization of one water molecule; $(H^+)$ is calculated by substituting $(H^+)$ for $(OH^-)$ in Equation 8.3, and taking the square root of both sides of the following expression:

$$(H^+)(H^+) = K_w \tag{8.4}$$

$$(H^+) = \sqrt{K_w}. \tag{8.5}$$

Concentrations of hydrogen and hydroxyl ions at different temperatures are listed in Table 8.1. Although the $(H^+)$ of different waters varies greatly, the product of $(H^+)$ and $(OH^+)$ will always equal $K_w$, allowing $(OH^-)$ to be estimated from $(H^+)$:

$$(OH^-) = \frac{K_w}{(H^+)}. \tag{8.6}$$

In 1909, the Danish chemist S. P. L. Sørensen suggested taking the negative logarithm of the $(H^+)$ to avoid the cumbersome use of small molar concentrations when referring to $(H^+)$. The negative logarithm of $(H^+)$ was eventually called pH:

$$pH = -\log (H^+). \tag{8.7}$$

Each one-unit change in pH therefore represents a ten-fold change in hydrogen ion activity. Pure water at 25°C has $K_w = 1 \times 10^{-14}$ and, from Equation 8.5, $(H^+) = 1 \times 10^{-7}$. From Equation 8.7, the pH of pure water at 25°C is:

**Table 8.1.** Equilibrium constant for the ionization of water ($K_w$) and corresponding concentrations of hydrogen and pH in pure water of different temperatures. Note that $(H^+) = (OH^-)$ for pure water.

| Water temperature (°C) | $K_w$ | $(H^+)$ | pH |
|---|---|---|---|
| 0 | $10^{-14.94}$ | $10^{-7.47}$ | 7.47 |
| 5 | $10^{-14.73}$ | $10^{-7.36}$ | 7.36 |
| 10 | $10^{-14.53}$ | $10^{-7.26}$ | 7.26 |
| 15 | $10^{-14.35}$ | $10^{-7.18}$ | 7.18 |
| 20 | $10^{-14.17}$ | $10^{-7.08}$ | 7.08 |
| 25 | $10^{-14.00}$ | $10^{-7.00}$ | 7.00 |
| 30 | $10^{-13.83}$ | $10^{-6.92}$ | 6.92 |
| 35 | $10^{-13.68}$ | $10^{-6.84}$ | 6.84 |
| 40 | $10^{-13.53}$ | $10^{-6.76}$ | 6.76 |

$$pH = -\log (10^{-7.00}) = -(-7.00) = 7.00. \tag{8.8}$$

Pure water is neutral—neither acidic nor basic—because $(H^+) = (OH^-)$. Conditions become more acidic (that is, $(H^+)$ increases) as pH values decrease and more basic (that is, $(H^-)$ decreases) as pH increases. Note that the pH of pure water is 7.00 only at 25°C. At lower temperatures, the pH is above 7 at neutrality, and at higher temperatures, the pH is below 7 (Table 8.1). Although the pH scale is usually represented as ranging from 0 to 14, pH can extend past those values. It is possible to have negative pH values and pH values above 14. For example, at 25°C, a solution 2 M ($10^{0.3}$ M) in $H^+$ has pH = $-0.3$, while a solution 2 M in $OH^-$ has pH = 14.3.

## Processes Affecting pH

The pH of water is affected by innumerable reactions involving hydrogen ions but in most natural waters, the pH range is established by reactions involving carbon dioxide gas and the anions bicarbonate and carbonate. Photosynthesis and respiration influence pH because those processes affect dissolved carbon dioxide concentrations. Other biological reactions also affect the pH of waters; for example, bacteria-mediated oxidations such as nitrification and sulfur oxidation decrease pH whereas reductions such as denitrification and sulfate reduction increase pH. Strong acids or bases may also enter the water from pollution, either through direct waste discharge or indirectly, as in acidic precipitation. Water pH is also influenced by contact with acidic or basic soils. In fact, the most common water quality management practice in aquaculture involves adding limestone to ponds to neutralize acidic bottom soils.

### *Carbon Dioxide and the Carbonate System*

The pH of most waters is determined by simultaneous equilibria among dissolved carbon dioxide, carbonic acid, bicarbonate, carbonate, and, possibly, solid-phase carbonate-containing minerals. For fresh waters at equilibrium with atmospheric carbon dioxide, pH ranges from about 5.6 for waters with no alkalinity up to pH 8.4 for waters with a total alkalinity of 100 mg/L as $CaCO_3$. Seawater has an average total alkalinity of about 115 mg/L as $CaCO_3$ and a pH of about 8.1, which is lower than most fresh waters of the same alkalinity. This is the result of the effects of seawater's high ionic strength on equilibrium constants and because seawater is not a simple solution buffered only by the carbonate system (borate, for example, constitutes about 5% of the total alkalinity in seawater).

Alkalinity and the partial pressure of carbon dioxide in the atmosphere determine the 'initial' pH of most waters. The water's pH then changes as biological activity or gas transfer (diffusion) adds or removes dissolved carbon dioxide. Effects of carbon dioxide addition and removal on pH are discussed in Chapter 7. Briefly, carbon dioxide added to water forms carbonic acid, causing pH to decrease. Removal of carbon dioxide causes pH to increase. The extent to which pH changes depends on the amount of carbon dioxide added or removed and the water's buffering capacity (alkalinity). The effects of carbon dioxide addition and removal on pH can be calculated from knowledge of the various chemical species present.[1,2,3]

## Exchangeable Acidity

Poor growth of fish or crustaceans in ponds built on acidic soils may be the most common water quality problem in aquaculture. Some soils become acidic over time as calcium and magnesium are leached, leaving soils enriched with aluminum. Acidic soils are especially common in areas with abundant rainfall, which speeds up the leaching process. Trivalent aluminum cations adsorbed to the surface of clays and organic matter (*exchangeable aluminum*) are in equilibrium with aluminum cations in the water surrounding soil particles. Dissolved aluminum hydrolyzes in water to produce acid:

$$Al^{3+} + 3H_2O \rightleftharpoons Al(OH)_3 + 3H^+. \tag{8.9}$$

The resulting pH depends on the amount of aluminum adsorbed at cation exchange sites, which is a function of the total cation exchange capacity of the soil and the relative proportion of exchangeable aluminum to other cations.

Ponds built on soils made acidic by exchangeable aluminum and filled with very poorly buffered, low-alkalinity water may have water-column pH values that are marginal for aquatic life. More commonly, however, water-column pH is not so low that it threatens aquatic life, but rather ponds built on acidic soils are infertile because low sediment pH and abundant soil aluminum cause phosphorus to become fixed in the soil, making that essential plant nutrient unavailable to support primary production in the water column. The concept of exchangeable acidity and its relationship to soil and water pH are subjects of Chapter 9.

## Nitrification, Denitrification, and Ammonia Volatilization

Nitrification and denitrification are bacterial processes important in transformations of nitrogen in water and soils. The processes are important in aquaculture systems because two forms of inorganic nitrogen (un-ionized ammonia, $NH_3$, and nitrite, $NO_2^-$) are potentially toxic to aquatic animals (Chapter 16). The two processes are also important because they affect pH and the alkalinity system. In aquaculture systems where nitrogen loading rates are high, considerable nitrogen may be nitrified or denitrified, and the effects on pH can be significant.

*Nitrification* is the sequential, two-step oxidation of ammonia to nitrate ($NO_3^-$) by chemoautotrophic bacteria that oxidize inorganic nitrogen to obtain energy and use carbon dioxide as a carbon source for cellular biosynthesis. The oxidation of ammonia to nitrite is carried out by one group of bacteria (primarily in the genera *Nitrosomonas*, *Nitrosococcus*, and *Nitrosospira*) and the oxidation of nitrite to nitrate by a second group (primarily in the genera *Nitrobacter* and *Nitrospira*). The overall nitrification reaction is:

$$NH_4^+ + 2O_2 \rightarrow NO_3^- + 2H^+ + H_2O. \tag{8.10}$$

Each mole of ammonia nitrified produces two moles of hydrogen ions that reduce pH. The hydrogen ions produced in nitrification destroy alkalinity:

$$2HCO_3^- + 2H^+ \rightleftharpoons 2H_2O + 2CO_{2(aq)}. \tag{8.11}$$

Thus, each mole of ammonia nitrified produces two equivalents of acid that destroys two equivalents of alkalinity, or, in concentration units, 1 mg/L of ammonia-N fully nitrified to nitrate destroys 7.14 mg/L alkalinity expressed as $CaCO_3$.

*Denitrification* is the reduction of nitrate to dinitrogen gas ($N_2$) or other nitrogen gases. The process occurs when molecular oxygen concentrations are very low and common heterotrophic bacteria use nitrate instead of oxygen as a terminal electron acceptor in respiration. With respect to effects on pH, denitrification consists of two half-reactions: 1) the oxidation of organic matter, which produces hydrogen ions and carbon dioxide, and 2) the reduction of nitrate to nitrogen gas, which consumes hydrogen ions. The overall reaction, with $CH_2O$ representing generic organic matter, is:

$$4NO_3^- + 5CH_2O + 4H^+ \rightarrow 2N_2 + 5CO_{2(aq)} + 7H_2O. \tag{8.12}$$

Each mole of nitrate denitrified consumes one mole of hydrogen ions. The effect of denitrification on pH and alkalinity is more easily seen when Equation 8.12 is combined with the equation for ionization of water,

$$4H^+ + 4OH^- = 4H_2O \tag{8.13}$$

giving the overall reaction

$$4NO_3^- + 5CH_2O \rightarrow 2N_2 + 5CO_{2(aq)} + 3H_2O + 4OH^-. \tag{8.14}$$

Equation 8.6 shows that each mole of nitrate denitrified produces one equivalent of hydroxyl ions, or one equivalent of alkalinity. Or, stated another way, 1 mg/L of $NO_3$-N denitrified produces 3.57 mg/L alkalinity expressed as $CaCO_3$. When nitrification and denitrification are coupled, as they often are in aquatic and aquaculture systems, denitrification can potentially restore half the alkalinity destroyed by acid produced in nitrification.

Ammonia gas ($NH_3$) can be volatilized to the atmosphere when water pH is high:

$$NH_4^+ + OH^- \rightleftharpoons NH_{3(g)} + H_2O. \tag{8.15}$$

When combined with equation for ionization of water, the reaction is:

$$NH_4^+ \rightleftharpoons NH_{3(g)} + H^+ \tag{8.16}$$

showing that loss of ammonia gas by volatilization causes pH to decrease. Equation 8.8

occurs to a significant degree only when environmental pH is very high (>10) and the water is vigorously agitated. Under typical aquaculture conditions, the effect of ammonia volatilization on pH is insignificant compared with the effects of other processes.

## Sulfur Oxidation

Hydrogen sulfide ($H_2S$) is produced when sulfur-containing organic compounds decompose or when sulfate ($SO_4^{2-}$) is reduced under anaerobic conditions in a process analogous to denitrification of nitrate, described above. Hydrogen sulfide is thermodynamically unstable when oxygen is present and accumulates only under anaerobic conditions. Hydrogen sulfide reacts with metal ions to form metallic sulfides, usually iron pyrite (FeS) because iron is common in most environments. When soils containing iron pyrite are exposed to oxygen, chemoautotrophic bacteria called colorless sulfur bacteria in the genus *Thiobacillus* derive energy from the oxidation of reduced inorganic sulfur while using carbon dioxide (or, in some cases, simple organic compounds) as a carbon source in a process analogous to nitrification. An overall reaction for oxidation of iron pyrite is:

$$FeS_2 + 3.7O_2 + 3.5\ H_2O \rightarrow Fe(OH)_3 + 2\ SO_4^{2-} + 4H^+. \tag{8.17}$$

Soils containing abundant iron pyrite are common in coastal marshes and mangrove swamps and in the overburden of coal mines. When these soils or formations are exposed to air (as when ponds are built), considerable acid can be produced in the process described in Equation 8.17. Many sulfur-oxidizing bacteria are highly acid-tolerant and can grow at pH values as low as 1 or 2, so water leached from soils can have very low pH values. Acidic waters leached from coal mining operations are called *acid-mine waters*. Acidic soils in coastal areas are called *acid-sulfate soils* or *cat's clays*. Acid-sulfate soils are discussed in Chapters 9 and 17.

## Acid Rain

Rainwater, fog, snow, and other forms of precipitation are naturally acidic with a pH of about 5.5 because the water is saturated with atmospheric carbon dioxide. The terms *acid rain* or *acidic precipitation* refer, however, to a mixture of wet and dry precipitation made more acidic than solutions of dissolved carbon dioxide. The increased acidity is caused by acids produced when sulfur dioxide ($SO_2$) or nitrogen oxides ($NO_x$) react with water, oxygen, and other chemicals in the atmosphere to produce to produce weak solutions of sulfuric and nitric acid.[4] In arid areas or during dry periods, atmospheric acids may be incorporated onto dust and smoke particles that are deposited onto the ground, trees, and buildings forming acidic surface films that may be washed into lakes and streams in runoff.

The acidity of wet and dry precipitation depends on prevailing winds, population density, and upwind industrial development. Low pH values less than 2.0 have been recorded from areas with high levels of air pollution, but pH values of 4 to 5 are more common in precipitation considered acidic. In the United States, areas of lowest rainwater pH are located in the northeast where a dense human population and high concentration of power and industrial plants provide large inputs of gaseous sulfur and nitrogen oxide pollutants. Prevailing winds from west to east also bring pollution from the midwestern United States into the region.

## pH of Aquatic Ecosystems

Most groundwaters contain dissolved carbon dioxide, bicarbonate, and carbonate and have pH values between 5 and 9. In general, groundwaters in contact with silicate minerals have low concentrations of bicarbonate, a relatively high carbon dioxide content, and, consequently, a lower pH than waters from carbonate rock deposits. High pH values (>8.5) are usually associated with groundwaters that have high sodium carbonate content. Dissolved carbon dioxide cannot make water more acid than about pH 4.5, so pH values less than 4.5 are due to the presence of strong mineral acids. Strong acids may occur in water draining from some mines as a result of the oxidation of mineral sulfides to sulfuric acid, as described above. Low pH values also may occur in thermal waters which contain $H_2S$, $HCl$, or other volatile acids of volcanic origin.[5]

Most surface waters also are buffered by the bicarbonate-carbonate system and have pH values between 5 and 9. Very high pH values (>9) are common in lakes in arid regions, where the water has a high sodium carbonate content. High pH values can also result from high rates of carbon dioxide removal in photosynthesis. Low pH values (<4) are caused by the presence of mineral acids, especially sulfuric acid, and are typical of streams and lakes in volcanic regions or in waters receiving acid mine drainage or in contact acid-sulfate soils. Low pH values also are found in swamps and bogs that are rich in organic acids produced by decaying vegetation. Poorly buffered waters, such as those occurring in the mountainous regions of eastern North America, may have low pH values caused by acid precipitation.

Seawater is buffered by the bicarbonate-borate systems and has a relatively stable pH between 8.0 and 8.5. High rates of biological activity in nutrient-rich marine waters may result in higher or lower pH-values, but the pH is seldom lower than 7.5 or greater than 9.0.

The pH of most surface waters cycles diurnally depending on the relative rates of photosynthesis and respiration. During daylight, underwater aquatic plants and algae remove carbon dioxide in photosynthesis. Plants and animals continually release carbon dioxide into the water in respiration. During daylight, aquatic plants usually remove carbon dioxide from the water faster than it can be replaced by respiration, and pH increases. At night, carbon dioxide accumulates and pH declines. The diel cycle of pH resulting from carbon dioxide removal and evolution is illustrated in Fig. 8.1. The magnitude of daily pH fluctuation depends on the buffering capacity (total alkalinity) of the water and rates of photosynthesis and respiration. In some fertile, poorly buffered waters, pH can cycle between near pH 6 near dawn to over pH 11 in mid-afternoon. The pH of waters in aquaculture ponds is regulated by the same processes as in natural waters but biological activity usually has a greater effect on pH in aquaculture ponds than in most natural waters.

The pH of waters in flow-through systems is determined by the water's alkalinity and changes in carbon dioxide concentrations. Large amounts of carbon dioxide can be produced in intensive flow-through systems and unchecked accumulation may reduce pH to dangerous levels if the water has very low total alkalinity.[1] The pH of water in recirculating systems is also affected by alkalinity and changes in carbon dioxide concentrations, but additionally is affected by acid produced in biofilters during nitrification.[6] Some recirculating systems incorporate a denitrification process to remove nitrate produced in nitrification and help restore some of the alkalinity lost from acid produced in nitrification.[7]

## Effects of pH on Aquatic Animals

The optimum pH for growth and health of most freshwater aquatic animals is in the range of 6.5 to 9.0. The acid and alkaline death points are approximately pH 4 and pH 11. Marine fish evolved in the highly buffered seawater environment that is not subject to wide variation in pH and most marine animals typically cannot tolerate as wide a range of environmental pH as freshwater animals. Optimum pH for most marine animals is usually between pH 7.5 and 8.5. Fish and crustaceans living in brackish water are often exposed to a wide range of pH values as the relative amounts of freshwater and seawater

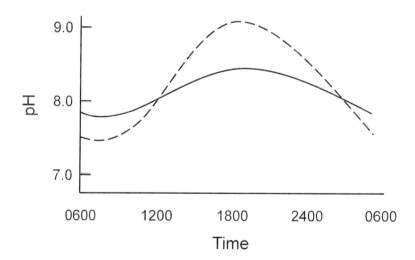

**Fig. 8.1.** Daily pH cycle in ponds with sparse (solid line) and abundant (dashed line) phytoplankton. These patterns are typical of sunny daytimes and water with a moderately high total alkalinity. Cloudy daytimes would dampen the amplitude and displace the curves slightly downward (i.e., lower average pH) because the amount of carbon dioxide removed from water during photosynthesis would be reduced. Amplitude of pH change would be greater in waters with lower total alkalinity.

change with variations in river discharge and tidal flow. Brackishwater inhabitants are therefore rather tolerant of extremes of pH. For instance, the acid and alkaline death points for most penaeid shrimp are roughly 4.5 and 10.5, and that the optimum pH range is 6 to 9.[8] If fish or crustaceans are transferred quickly from one water to another of drastically different pH, shock and death may occur even if the pH of the second water is within the normal pH tolerance range of the species.

Gills are the primary target of elevated hydrogen ion concentrations (low pH), which is not surprising considering their structural delicacy and their intimate contact with the external environment. The major effects of low pH are 1) changes in gill structure and function leading to decreased ability to maintain internal ion balance and 2) inhibition of gas exchange as a result of blood acidosis and changes in the structure of the gill epithelium.[9] Under mild acid stress, animals expend extra metabolic energy for maintenance of gill function at the expense of other processes such as growth and immune function. Under extreme acid stress, the animal is not capable of maintaining homeostasis and dies.

Gills of fish and crustaceans also are highly sensitive to high-pH solutions. High environmental pH impairs ion-exchange processes at the gills, leading to problems with osmoregulation and blood alkalosis. High environmental pH also hinders excretion of waste nitrogen because at high water pH, a large fraction of the ammonia immediately outside the gill will be in the form of un-ionized ammonia, thereby reducing the diffusive gradient for passive excretion of ammonia and causing blood ammonia levels to increase.[10]

Tolerance to extremes of pH can be influenced by other environmental factors. Fish and crustaceans generally tolerate a lower pH when the salinity of the external medium is near optimum for the species in question. Calcium is a particularly important modulator of pH toxicity because calcium affects the permeability and stability of biological membranes. The presence of high concentrations of waterborne calcium improves the survival of aquatic animals in acidified waters because it makes gill epithelial membranes less 'leaky,' thereby reducing passive loss of blood electrolytes.

Most waters used for aquaculture have pH values within the range considered desirable for fish production, and direct toxic effects from extremes of pH are seldom encountered. The two exceptions to this generality—acid produced from acid-sulfate soils and transient high pH in surface waters due to intense photosynthesis—have already been mentioned. More commonly, it is the indirect effects of pH and the interactions of pH with other environmental variables that are important in aquaculture. For example, the proportion of total ammonia ($NH_4^+ + NH_3$) existing in the toxic, un-ionized form ($NH_3$) increases as pH increases (Chapter 16). Environmental pH also affects the toxicity of hydrogen sulfide (Chapter 17), chlorine, and metals such as copper, cadmium, zinc, and aluminum (Chapter 20).

Environmental pH also has subtle, indirect effects on pond fertility. In many waters with low total alkalinity, pH is not low enough to harm fish, but it is low enough to reduce the amount of inorganic phosphorus and carbon dioxide available for plant growth. Liming is used to improve productivity in low alkalinity waters. On the other hand, high pH, especially in combination with high dissolved calcium concentrations, favors rapid precipitation of phosphate when fertilizers are applied to ponds.

# Managing pH in Ponds

## *Low pH in Ponds*

Ponds built on acid-sulfate soils may have water pH values less than 4.0, making them unsuitable for aquaculture. Methods exist for reclamation of ponds on acid-sulfate soils (Chapter 9) but the potential acidity of some acid-sulfate soils is so high that reclamation may be difficult and expensive. It is usually best to avoid areas sites with potential acid-sulfate soils for pond sites.

Ponds built on soils made acidic by exchangeable aluminum and filled with low-alkalinity water are often infertile and do not respond well to fertilization. Liming enhances the response to fertilization and generally improves environmental conditions for aquatic animals. Identification of ponds needing lime and the use of liming materials are discussed in Chapter 9.

Liming is most beneficial in ponds where fertilization will be used to improve productivity. The benefits of liming ponds where animals receive manufactured feeds are less obvious—unless ponds are so acidic that liming is needed to permit survival of fish and crustaceans (as in some ponds built on acid-sulfate soils). In mildly acidic waters typical of ponds built on soils with exchangeable acidity, there may be no benefit to liming ponds with feeding because the contribution of natural pond fertility to production is insignificant. Some believe that liming mildly acidic ponds improves conditions for animals receiving feed because increasing the total alkalinity poises the water's pH in a more desirable range. However, Murad and Boyd[11] found no difference in growth or yield of catfish raised in ponds with average total alkalinity of 2, 6, or 46 mg/L as $CaCO_3$, despite average pH values of less than 6 in ponds with the lowest total alkalinity. This study casts doubt on the need to manage pH in mildly acidic ponds where production is based on use of manufactured feeds.

In regions with sandy or rocky soils, acid rain can cause the pH of lakes in streams to be less than 5, affecting ecosystem productivity and, in extreme instances, fish survival. Surface waters with low total alkalinities (<10 mg/L as $CaCO_3$) are sensitive to the effects of acid rain. As a general rule, aquaculture ponds should be managed to maintain total alkalinity values above 20 mg/L, which should provide adequate buffering to counteract the effects of acid rain.

## *High pH in Ponds*

Daily photosynthesis is approximately equal to respiration in most ponds and pH cycles daily within a range tolerated by most animals. At times of rapid plant or algal growth, daily carbon dioxide removal in photosynthesis greatly exceeds carbon dioxide removal in respiration and pH may rise to abnormally high levels (>9) during the afternoon, perhaps even remaining high through the night. This condition may persist for many days, until photosynthesis decreases or respiration increases. Episodes of high pH are particularly common in ponds where filamentous algae or submerged macrophytes dominate the plant community. Ponds with underwater plants usually have clear water, allowing sunlight to penetrate into the water column and promote intense photosynthesis.

Managing high pH in aquaculture ponds is difficult and no specific management practice is always successful. In the narrowest sense, 'high pH' can easily be corrected simply by adding an acid—and this is sometimes done in emergency situations. However, 'high pH' is the result of an imbalance in processes that add and remove carbon dioxide. Reducing pH with an acid does not alter those processes, and therefore cannot address the underlying causes of high pH. The long-term solution to high pH problems in ponds is to alter pond biology so that net daily carbon dioxide uptake is near zero, by either reducing photosynthesis or increasing respiration. But changing community metabolism is difficult and greater success can be achieved by preventing or managing around pH problems rather than trying to correct problems after they occur.[12]

*Fill and prepare ponds early*

Problems with high pH are common in fry nursery ponds and in ponds used to grow freshwater prawns because fertilization practices are designed to promote fast-growing phytoplankton blooms. The early life stages of fish and crustaceans also are particularly susceptible to pH toxicity and, compared to older animals, juveniles are less able to avoid exposure to high pH by moving to areas of lower pH (such as deeper waters).

Problems with high afternoon pH commonly arise in the first few weeks after aquaculture ponds are filled because plant nutrients derived from feeds or fertilizers promote rapid photosynthesis and the biomass of respiring organisms is low. This leads to net daily removal of dissolved carbon dioxide and high pH. After the initial period of rapid plant growth, high afternoon pH values typically do not occur because rates of photosynthesis and respiration come into balance. If possible, ponds should be prepared as early as possible, preferably several weeks before stocking. This allows the initial flush of plant growth and corresponding high pH to occur before animals are introduced.

*Balance hardness and alkalinity*

Problems with high pH occur most often in waters with moderate to high total alkalinity (50 to 200 ppm as $CaCO_3$) and low calcium hardness (less than 25 ppm as $CaCO_3$). When plants remove carbon dioxide from water, carbonate concentration increases:

$$2HCO_3^- \rightleftharpoons CO_2 + CO_3^{2-} + H_2O. \tag{8.18}$$

Carbonate ions hydrolyze and generate hydroxyl ions, causing pH to rise:

$$CO_3^{2-} + H_2O \rightleftharpoons HCO_3^- + OH^-. \tag{8.19}$$

In waters where calcium is present, the increase in carbonate concentration eventually causes the solubility product of calcium carbonate to be exceeded and further increase in carbonate results in precipitation of solid, colloidal calcium carbonate. In waters where calcium concentrations are high, relatively little carbonate can be formed before the solubility product is exceeded, which limits the extent of pH increase (Equation 8.19). Sodium is usually the major cation in waters of high alkalinity and low hardness, and sodium carbonate is extremely soluble. Carbonate concentrations—and therefore pH—can rise to much higher levels than in high-calcium waters.[13] Also, sodium phosphates are more soluble than calcium phosphates, so more phosphorus is available to support plant growth in soft waters, leading to higher rates of photosynthesis which cause pH to increase rapidly.[14]

Deficiencies in hardness relative to alkalinity can be corrected by adding gypsum (calcium sulfate) as a source of calcium. The effectiveness of gypsum treatment in reducing pH is subject to debate and, at best, it is a preventative procedure rather than an emergency treatment. Hardness deficiencies should therefore be corrected before stocking, preferably as soon as the pond is filled in the spring. The amount of gypsum needed to roughly balance hardness and alkalinity is calculated by subtracting hardness from alkalinity and multiplying that value by two. For example, if hardness is 15 mg/L as $CaCO_3$ and alkalinity is 60 mg/L as $CaCO_3$, then 90 mg/L of gypsum will be needed to approximately balance the two values. Increased calcium levels following gypsum application may also benefit animals by helping them better physiologically respond to extremes of pH and other environmental stressors.

*Add alum*

Adding alum (aluminum sulfate) is an emergency treatment to quickly reduce high pH. Alum is a relatively safe, relatively inexpensive chemical that reacts in water to form an acid. In addition to the direct effect of alum on pH, it also flocculates and removes algae by sedimentation, thereby decreasing algal biomass and reducing photosynthesis. Alum may also help to reduce pH indirectly by removing phosphorus—an important nutrient for plant growth.

The effect of alum application is not permanent, and additional applications may be necessary until a reduction in plant or algal growth is realized. Precise reduction of pH through addition of alum is difficult because response is influenced by a number of conditions in the pond, especially the water's total alkalinity. Overtreatment with alum can cause a dramatic decrease in pH, possibly to levels more dangerous than the original high pH problem.

Boyd and Tucker[15] present an approach to reducing pond pH to values near pH 8.4 based on measuring the water's phenolphthalein alkalinity and then adding enough alum to neutralize that alkalinity. Phenolphthalein alkalinity (also called the carbonate alkalinity) is the amount of acid needed to reduce the pH of water to the phenolphthalein endpoint (pH 8.3; Example 8.1). Approximately 1 mg/L of alum will remove 1 mg/L of phenolphthalein alkalinity (expressed as equivalent $CaCO_3$). If alkalinity cannot be measured, a cautious empirical approach can be used where an initial dose of 10 mg/L alum is applied, followed by additional applications in 5 to 10 mg/L increments as needed. The effect of alum on pH is often temporary because it addresses the result rather than the cause of high pH. Alum should not be used in waters with total alkalinities less than 20 mg/L as $CaCO_3$ because even small alum additions may reduce pH to dangerous levels.

*Add a mineral acid*

An alternative to alum for reducing pH is merchant grade sulfuric acid (94% $H_2SO_4$). The dose of sulfuric acid necessary to lower pH to 8.3 is about 1 mg/L for each milligram per liter of phenolphthalein alkalinity. Merchant grade sulfuric acid has a density around 1.84, and on a volume basis, 0.54 μL/L would be needed for each milligram per liter of phenolphthalein alkalinity to reduce pH to 8.3. Concentrated sulfuric acid is more dangerous to store and handle than alum, but both chemicals should be used with extreme caution. Like alum, a strong acid will reduce pH but have no residual effect.

*Add organic matter*

Dissolved carbon dioxide concentrations can be increased through the decay of organic matter—such as cracked corn, soybean meal, or cottonseed meal—that is added to the ponds. Reduction in pH is not immediate, but organic input is a safe and relatively dependable practice. Application of about 15 kg/ha daily for about 1 week should prevent

---

**Example 8.1**
**Titration of Phenolphthalein Alkalinity with Results Expressed in Terms of Equivalent Calcium Carbonate**

A 100-mL water sample is titrated with 0.02 N sulfuric acid to the phenolphthalein endpoint. The titration requires 5.00 ml of acid. The phenolphthalein alkalinity (PA) is:

$$PA = \frac{[(N_{acid})(V_{acid})(50 \text{ mg } CaCO_3/\text{meq})(1{,}000 \text{ mL/L})]}{V_{sample}}$$

where $N_{acid}$ is the normality of the acid used to titrate the sample (meq/mL); $V_{acid}$ is the volume of acid used to titrate the sample to the phenolphthalein endpoint (mL); 50 mg $CaCO_3$/meq is the equivalent weight of calcium carbonate; $V_{sample}$ is the water sample volume (mL). For the example above,

$$PA = \frac{[(0.02 \text{ meq/mL})(5 \text{ mL})(50 \text{ mg } CaCO_3/\text{meq})(1{,}000 \text{ mL/L})]}{100 \text{ mL}} = 50 \text{ mg/L as } CaCO_3.$$

The phenolphthalein alkalinity is 50 mg/L as $CaCO_3$; approximately 50 mg/L of alum will reduce pH to about 8.3.

pH from rising to undesirable levels. This amount would be in addition to any concurrently assigned daily organic fertilization and the total daily application of organic matter should not exceed 50 kg/ha. The decay process that releases carbon dioxide into the water also uses dissolved oxygen, so make sure that dissolved oxygen concentrations are regularly measured and provisions are made to aerate the pond water to maintain satisfactory oxygen levels.

*Reduce plant growth rate*

Rapid plant growth causes high pH problems in ponds, so reducing plant growth rate will reduce pH. Using herbicides to kill algae or plants will eliminate high pH problems, but the benefits are often not worth the risks and costs. Decomposition of plants killed by herbicides causes oxygen depletion and accumulation of dissolved carbon dioxide and ammonia. Some herbicides are also relatively toxic to juvenile aquatic animals. For example, copper-containing products have a relatively low margin of safety between concentrations that kill plants and those lethal to juvenile fish or prawns. Reducing plant growth to manage high pH also conflicts with the goal of fertilization, which is to increase production of natural foods in the pond to support aquaculture production. Thus, using herbicides to reduce high pH is usually a poor substitute for proper pond management.

In general, herbicides should be used only to change one type of plant community to a more desirable type. For example, mats of filamentous algae are often responsible for excessively high pH in recently filled ponds. Filamentous algae are also undesirable because they interfere with pond management, particularly feeding and harvest. Certain herbicides can be cautiously used to eliminate the mat community in favor of a phytoplankton bloom.

High pH can also be reduced by reducing the amount of sunlight available for photosynthesis. Dyes sold commercially as weed-control agents tint the water blue to reduce light penetration and may effectively reduce pH for several weeks. Reducing light penetration into water may, however, favor the growth of mat-forming filamentous algae that float high in the water column where adequate light persists even in dye-treated water. Another approach to reduce the amount of light penetrating the water column is to keep the pond water turbid (a high level of suspended sediment) by using aerators or other devices to stir up mud from the pond bottom.

*Add sodium bicarbonate*

Sodium bicarbonate ($NaHCO_3$) is a good buffering agent and can be applied to exert some control on pH. However, rather large amounts of sodium bicarbonate must be added to waters of high pH to affect biologically meaningful pH reductions in large ponds. The amount necessary to reduce pH also increases with increasing water alkalinity (that is, if the water is highly buffered more sodium bicarbonate is required to reduce pH than in poorly buffered waters). For example, when added to pond waters with a pH of

10.0, 100 mg/L of sodium bicarbonate reduces pH to 9.6 in moderate alkalinity waters (50 mg/L as $CaCO_3$) and to 9.8 in high alkalinity waters (200 mg/L as $CaCO_3$).[16]

## Managing pH in Intensive Aquaculture Systems

Removal of dissolved carbon dioxide in photosynthesis is negligible or absent in flow-through and recirculating aquaculture systems and in fish transport tank. As such, problems with high pH do not occur in those systems. Intensive culture systems do, however, have high fish biomass loadings, resulting in high rates of carbon dioxide production. If total alkalinity is less than about 10 mg/L as $CaCO_3$, dissolved carbon dioxide accumulation can reduce pH below acceptable levels.[17]

Water-recirculating systems use nitrification biofilters to transform potentially toxic ammonia to less toxic nitrate. As described above, nitrification is an acid-forming process that reduces alkalinity and pH over time. Unchecked, acid produced in nitrification can destroy the system's alkalinity (Equation 8.3) and pH will fall to stressful or lethal levels. Alkalinity levels of 50 to 100 mg/L as $CaCO_3$ are maintained in recirculating systems to maintain pH in the desirable range of 7.5 to 8.2. Alkalinity is maintained by addition of bases such as calcium hydroxide (hydrated lime, $Ca(OH)_2$), sodium carbonate (soda ash, $Na_2CO_3$) or sodium bicarbonate (bicarbonate of soda, $NaHCO_3$) or by increasing the rate of new source-water addition (assuming the source water has relatively high alkalinity).[18] Management of pH in intensive systems is further discussed in Chapters 26 (flow-through systems) and 28 (recirculating systems).

## pH Measurement

Color indicators are often used in field test kits for quick, easy pH estimates. Often this is all that is needed to assess the suitability of a water for aquaculture. Indicators are organic compounds that change color as the solution pH changes. The color change may occur over a narrow or wide pH range depending on the specific indicator. Indicators for field use often consist of a combination of two or more individual indicators to extend the pH range over which the color change occurs. Some indicators are impregnated onto plastic or paper strips that are immersed into the sample. The strip's color is then compared to a color chart to determine approximate pH. Liquid indicator solution are also available that are added by dropper to the sample. The color of the resulting solution is then compared to permanent color standards supplied by the manufacturer. Visual determination of pH using color indicators is subjective and may be affected by ambient light conditions. Accuracy within 0.2 pH units is about the best that can be expected.

The most accurate common method of pH measurement uses a glass electrode and meter. The complex electrochemical theory of pH measurement with glass electrodes can be found elsewhere.[3,15,19,20] Water pH cannot be measured directly and the electrode-meter system must be carefully calibrated against one or, preferably, two solutions of precisely defined pH. Standards of various pH values are commercially available and should be selected to be within the range of expected sample pH or, if two standards are used, to closely bracket the expected sample pH range. Manufacturer's instructions for calibration and use of the pH meter must be carefully followed, including instructions for maintenance and storage of the electrode.

Temperature has two important effects on pH measurement. First, temperature affects the glass electrode response to the potential developed at the glass-sample surface. For all commercially available meters, this effect is compensated mechanically during calibration. A second temperature effect arises because the chemical reactions that buffer water at a certain pH are temperature dependant and pH measurements made at one temperature (room temperature, for example) will not be the same as those made on the same sample at a different temperature (the actual water temperature in the field, for example). If the measurement temperature and field temperature are relatively close, the difference between the measured pH and the actual pH is negligible for practical purposes. For example, consider a freshwater initially at 20°C that is sampled and then measured in the laboratory at 25°C. The measured pH will be about 0.05 pH units lower than the actual pH in the field—a difference that is usually well within the cumulative error associated with sampling and the accuracy of the pH meter itself. However, errors greater than 0.2 pH units occur when measurement temperature and field temperature differ by 20°C or more. An error of that magnitude is probably not meaningful when using pH data simply to assess the suitability of water for aquaculture, but it can be biologically significant when using pH data to assess the impacts of certain pH-dependant variables such as metal speciation and the ammonia/ammonium pair. Temperature correction methods are available if highly precise pH data are needed.[21,22]

Accuracy of pH measurement is also affected by salinity because electrode response is affected by the ionic strength of the solution in which it is immersed. Common buffers used for meter calibration have a much lower ionic strength than seawater, which introduces an error of about 0.1 pH unit[21]—an error that is not biologically meaningful for most aquaculture uses and is close to the practical limits of accuracy for most pH meters under normal conditions.[19] If extremely accurate pH data are needed, special buffers can be formulated for meter calibration and use in waters of various salinities.[23]

Errors caused by water temperature and salinity are usually less than those caused by improper sampling and sample handling. Water pH often varies greatly in time and space because the processes affecting dissolved carbon dioxide concentrations vary during the day and with pond depth and location. Meaningful sampling programs must be carefully designed to account for this variation. Gain or loss of dissolved carbon dioxide during sampling and in the interval between sampling and measurement can have significant effects on pH, especially for poorly buffered waters. Consider, for example, a water that has 100 mg/L total dissolved solids, an alkalinity of 20 mg/L as $CaCO_3$, a temperature of 20°C; and a dissolved carbon dioxide concentration of 20 mg/L. The pH of that water will be 6.6. If half the dissolved carbon dioxide is lost to the atmosphere during sampling and transport (as could easily happen as carbon dioxide is degassed from this supersaturated water), the resulting pH would be 7.3. The reverse is also common, with pH decreasing over time as plankton respiration adds carbon dioxide to samples held in the dark for long periods.

In general, pH should be measured immediately in the field for best results and reliable portable pH meters are available for that purpose. If immediate measurement is not possible, no longer than 1 hour should elapse between sampling and measurement. All sampling procedures should minimize contact with the atmosphere and samples should be stored in the dark at reduced temperature. At the time of measurement, samples should quickly be brought to the same temperature as calibration buffers and measurement should again be made with minimal agitation and air contact.

# References

1. Colt, J., B. Watten, and M. Rust. 2009. Modeling carbon dioxide, pH, and un-ionized ammonia relationships in serial reuse systems. Aquacultural Engineering 40:28-44.
2. Piedrahita, R. H. and A. Seland. 1995. Calculation of pH in fresh and sea water aquaculture systems. Aquacultural Engineering 14:331-346.
3. Snoeyink, V. L. and D. Jenkins. 1980. *Water Chemistry*. John Wiley and Sons, New York, NY.
4. Weathers, K. C. and G. E. Likens. 2006. Acid rain, pages 1549-1561. In: W. N. Rom (editor), *Environmental and Occupational Medicine, 4th Edition*. Lippincott-Raven Publishers, Philadelphia, PA.
5. Matthes, G. 1982. *The Properties of Groundwater*. John Wiley and Sons, New York, NY.
6. Summerfelt, S. T. 1996. Engineering design of a water reuse system, pages 277-309. In: R. C. Summerfelt (editor), *Walleye Culture Manual*. NCRAC Culture Series 101. North Central Regional Aquaculture Center Publications Office, Iowa State University, Ames.
7. Van Rijn, J., Y. Tal, and H. J. Schreier. 2005. Denitrification in recirculating systems: Theory and applications. Aquacultural Engineering 34:364-376.
8. Tsai, C. K. 1989. Water quality management, pages 56-63. In D. M. Akiyama (editor), *Proceedings of the Southeast Asia Shrimp Farm Management Workshop*. American Soybean Association, Singapore.
9. McDonald, D. G. 1983. The effects of $H^+$ upon the gills of freshwater fish. Canadian Journal of Zoology 61:691-703.
10. Wilkie, M.P. and C.M. Wood. 1994. The effects of extremely alkaline water (pH 9.5) on rainbow trout gill function and morphology. Journal of Fish Biology 45:87-98.
11. Murad, H. and C.E. Boyd. 1991. Production of sunfish (*Lepomis* spp.) and channel catfish (*Ictalurus punctatus*) in acidified ponds. Aquaculture 94:381–388.
12. Tucker, C. S. and L. R. D'Abramo. 2008. Managing high pH in freshwater ponds. Southern Regional Aquaculture Center Publication 4604, Southern Regional Aquaculture Center, Stoneville, MS.
13. Mandal, B. K. and C. E. Boyd. 1980. The reduction of pH in water of high total alkalinity and low total hardness. Progressive Fish-Culturist 42:183–185.
14. Wu, R. and C. E. Boyd. 1990. Evaluation of calcium sulfate for use in aquaculture ponds. Progressive Fish-Culturist 52:26–31.
15. Boyd, C. E. and C. S. Tucker. 1992. *Water Quality and Pond Soil Analysis for Aquaculture*. Alabama Agricultural Experiment Station, Auburn, AL.
16. Tucker, C. S. 2008. Misuses of sodium bicarbonate in pond aquaculture. Global Aquaculture Advocate 11(4):60-61.
17. Colt, J., Orwicz, K. 1991. Modeling production capacity of aquatic culture systems under freshwater conditions. Aquacultural Engineering 10:1-29.

18. Bisogni, J. J. and M. B. Timmons. 1994. Control of pH in closed cycle aquaculture systems, pages 235-246. In: M. B. Timmons and T.M. Losordo (editors), *Aquaculture Water Reuse Systems: Engineering Design and Management.* Elsevier, New York, NY.

19. Eaton, A. D., L. S. Clesceri, E. W. Rice, and A. E. Greenberg, editors. 2005. *Standard Methods for the Examination of Water and Wastewater, 21st Edition.* American Public Health Association, American Water Works Association, and the Water Environment Federation, Washington, DC.

20. Westcott, C. C. 1978. *pH Measurement.* Academic Press, San Diego, CA.

21. Grasshoff, K, K. Kremling, and M. Ehrhardt. 1999. *Methods of Seawater Analysis, 3rd edition.* Wiley-VCH, Weinheim, Germany.

22. Strickland, J. D. H. and T. R. Parsons. 1972. *A Practical Handbook of Seawater Analysis.* Fisheries Research Board of Canada, Ottawa, Canada.

23. Hansson, I. 1973. A new set of pH-scales and standard buffers for seawater. Deep Sea Research 20:479-491.

# Chapter 9

# Pond Liming

## Introduction

Aquaculture facilities may be supplied with water low in total alkalinity concentration. Such water has low buffering capacity and wide daily fluctuations in pH will occur when phytoplankton is abundant. Low total hardness concentration also is common in waters with low alkalinity. Low concentrations of these two variables are more common in waters from watersheds with highly leached, acidic soils in inland, humid regions than in coastal brackishwaters or in waters of semi-arid or arid inland areas. Moreover, acidity from oxidation of ammonia from fertilizers and feeds by nitrifying bacteria can result in low alkalinity.

Natural productivity is low and water quality unstable in water bodies with low alkalinity, and low pH and deficiencies of calcium and magnesium may have negative impacts on culture species. Most aquaculture species grow best at water pH between 6.5 and 9. Pond fertilizers have limited effectiveness in increasing natural productivity at alkalinity and hardness concentrations below 20 to 30 mg/L; foodfish species such as tilapia and carp grow best when alkalinity and hardness are above 50 to 60 mg/L; crustaceans need alkalinity and hardness above 75 to 100 mg/L for best performance. Agricultural limestone, lime, and other alkaline substances are applied to neutralize acidity and increase alkalinity, hardness, and pH.

## Liming Materials

Liming compounds contain bases such as carbonate, hydroxide, and oxide in combination with calcium and magnesium. Limestone, chalk, marl, seashells, and even ash can be used to make liming products, but limestone is the most common raw material. There are three forms of limestone:[1] calcitic limestone is mostly calcium carbonate ($CaCO_3$); dolomitic limestone consists of $CaCO_3$ and $MgCO_3$ in a 1:1 ratio; ordinary limestone has a $CaCO_3$:$MgCO_3$ ratio greater than 1:1 (Table 9.1).

Agricultural limestone is made by crushing limestone, and similar products are made by pulverizing chalk, marl, or seashells. The finer liming materials are crushed, the more quickly and completely they react in water to raise alkalinity (Fig. 9.1). Particles of agricultural limestone that passed a 0.106 mm sieve were as effective as particles passing smaller-meshed sieves and more effective than larger particles in raising pH and

**Table 9.1.** Description of different types of limestone based on calcium and magnesium concentrations.[1]

| Name | Ca (%) | Mg (%) |
|---|---|---|
| Pure calcitic limestone | 40 | 0 |
| Calcitic limestone | 38-40 | <1.2 |
| Pure dolomitic limestone | 21.7 | 13.2 |
| Dolomitic limestone | >20.3 | <12 |
| Ordinary limestone | Other compositions | |

 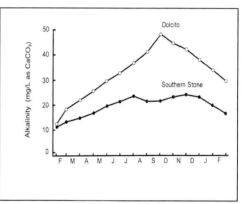

**Fig. 9.1.** Photograph of fine and coarse agricultural limestone samples with fineness values of 97% and 68%, respectively (left). When applied to ponds at the same rate, the fine agricultural limestone (Dolcito• brand) resulted in greater alkalinity concentration than the other (right).

increasing alkalinity.[2] Using the <0.106-mm particle-size class as the standard (100% efficiency), efficiency factors are calculated for larger particle-size classes in Table 9.2. The method for determining the *fineness value* (FV) of agricultural limestone based on particle-size distribution is illustrated in Example 9.1.

Burnt lime is made by heating limestone in a kiln at high temperature to drive off carbon dioxide. The residue is called burnt lime; it consists of calcium and magnesium oxides. Production of burnt lime from dolomitic limestone is illustrated below:

$$CaCO_3 \cdot MgCO_3 \xrightarrow{\Delta} CaO \cdot MgO + 2CO_2\uparrow. \tag{9.1}$$

Burnt lime is treated with water to produce hydrated or slaked lime as illustrated for calcium oxide:

$$CaO + H_2O \rightarrow Ca(OH)_2. \tag{9.2}$$

If limestone is burned properly, the resulting fine particles of lime will react quickly to neutralize acidity.

**Table 9.2.** Total alkalinity concentrations and efficiency factors for different particle-size classes of agricultural limestone applied to soil-water systems.[2]

| Particle-size class (mm) | USA standard testing sieve description of separates | | Class total alkalinity (mg/L) | Class efficiency factor (%) |
| | Passed | Retained on | | |
| --- | --- | --- | --- | --- |
| >0.85 | | 20 | 4.02 | 7.3 |
| 0.85 to 0.42 | 20 | 40 | 12.25 | 22.4 |
| 0.42 to 0.25 | 40 | 60 | 26.81 | 49.0 |
| 0.25 to 0.106 | 60 | 140 | 47.46 | 86.7 |
| <0.106 | 140 | | 54.74 | 100.0 |

**Example 9.1**
**Determining Fineness Value**

A sample of agricultural limestone is divided into separates of different particle-size classes by passing it through a nested stack of sieves. The separates are weighed, and the fineness value of the sample calculated using efficiency factors from Table 9.2.

| Class particle size range (mm) | Class separate | | Efficiency factor (%) | Weighted efficiency (%) |
| | g | Proportion | | |
| --- | --- | --- | --- | --- |
| >0.85 | 2.50 | 0.043 | 7.3 | 0.31 |
| 0.85-0.42 | 2.65 | 0.045 | 22.4 | 1.01 |
| 0.42-0.25 | 5.20 | 0.089 | 49.0 | 4.36 |
| 0.25-0.106 | 12.75 | 0.218 | 86.7 | 18.90 |
| <0.106 | 35.50 | 0.606 | 100.0 | 60.60 |
| | | | Fineness value (%) | 85.18 |

This sample would be only 85.18% as effective as a material with a fineness value of 100% (assuming equal neutralizing values).

Liming materials react with acidity as follows:

$$CaCO_3 + 2H^+ = Ca^{2+} + CO_2 + H_2O \quad (9.3)$$

$$CaO + 2H^+ = Ca^{2+} + H_2O \quad (9.4)$$

$$Ca(OH)_2 + 2H^+ = Ca^{2+} + 2H_2O. \quad (9.5)$$

The *neutralizing value* (NV) of a liming product represents its capacity to neutralize acidity in comparison to that of an equal quantity of calcium carbonate. Pure calcium carbonate is assigned a neutralizing value of 100% to facilitate comparison with other substances. One molecular weight of CaO, $Ca(OH)_2$, or $CaCO_3$ will neutralize two

**115**

molecular weights of hydrogen ion (Equations 9.3, 9.4, and 9.5). Molecular weights of these compounds are 56, 74, and 100 g, respectively. Neutralizing values of CaO and Ca(OH)$_2$ are 100/56 (174%) and 100/74 (135%), respectively, in comparison to CaCO$_3$.

Liming materials are not pure compounds, and it is necessary to measure their neutralizing values.[1] The amount of acid required to neutralize a given quantity of liming material is determined and expressed as percentage calcium carbonate equivalence (Example 9.2).

In summary, the two major types of liming materials are agricultural limestone and lime. Lime may be either unslaked or slaked (reacted with water). Liming materials will vary in chemical composition, neutralizing value, and particle-size distribution (Table 9.3) as a result of differences in the properties of raw material and in the manufacturing process.[1] Some other substances, such as sodium bicarbonate, silicate slag, and ash, have been used to a lesser extent as liming materials. Analyses of commercial liming products are provided in Table 9.3.

## *Reactions of Liming Materials in Water and Soils*

Neutralization of acidity by liming materials illustrated in Equations 9.3, 9.4, and 9.5 represents reactions in extremely acidic water. The more common reactions involve combination with dissolved carbon dioxide (CO$_{2(aq)}$), as illustrated below for calcium carbonate, calcium oxide, and calcium hydroxide:

$$CaCO_3 + CO_{2(aq)} + H_2O = Ca^{2+} + 2HCO_3^- \tag{9.6}$$

$$CaO + 2CO_{2(aq)} + H_2O = Ca^{2+} + 2HCO_3^- \tag{9.7}$$

$$Ca(OH)_2 + 2CO_{2(aq)} = Ca^{2+} + 2HCO_3^- . \tag{9.8}$$

### Example 9.2
### Measuring the Neutralizing Value of a Liming Product

A 500-mg sample of agricultural limestone is treated with 25.0 mL of 1.00 N HCl. The acid remaining after reaction with the sample required 15.20 mL of standard, 1.00 N NaOH for titration. The neutralizing value is calculated as follows:

(25.0 mL HCl)(1.00 meq/mL) – (15.20 mL NaOH)(1.00 meq/mL) = 9.80 meq acidity neutralized

The neutralizing value is expressed as the calcium carbonate equivalence of the acidity neutralized by the sample:

$$\frac{(9.80 \text{ meq acidity})(50 \text{ mg CaCO}_3/\text{meq}}{500 \text{ mg sample}} \times 100 = 98.0\%.$$

**Table 9.3.** Neutralizing value (NV), fineness value (FV), and percentages of calcium and magnesium in some liming materials used in Thailand.[1]

| Sample identification | NV (%) | FV (%) | Ca (%) | Mg (%) |
|---|---|---|---|---|
| Calcitic agricultural limestone | | | | |
| 1 | 98 | 96 | 36.9 | 1.9 |
| 6 | 101 | 95 | 37.6 | 1.3 |
| 9 | 81 | 55 | 33.4 | 1.1 |
| Dolomitic agricultural limestone | | | | |
| 11 | 107 | 95 | 21.4 | 12.0 |
| 16 | 108 | 96 | 21.8 | 13.0 |
| Marl | | | | |
| 27 | 94 | 77 | 35.7 | 0.0 |
| 28 | 71 | 63 | 29.1 | 2.7 |
| Pulverized seashells | | | | |
| 30 | 72 | 45 | 26.0 | 1.6 |
| 31 | 103 | 64 | 41.1 | 1.2 |
| Lime | | | | |
| 35 | 133 | 86 | 46.8 | 1.8 |
| 38 | 157 | 98 | 30.7 | 18.5 |
| 39 | 130 | 85 | 41.3 | 3.9 |

One molecular weight of each compound reacts to yield two bicarbonate ions and one calcium ion—sources of alkalinity and hardness, respectively. Thus, liming normally increases alkalinity and hardness by roughly equivalent amounts. The exception is for highly acidic water where the anionic fraction of liming material is consumed in neutralizing acidity, but the cations responsible for increasing hardness remains in solution (Equations 9.3, 9.4, and 9.5).

Liming materials also react with acidity in soil. *Exchangeable acidity* in soil is caused by aluminum ion ($Al^{3+}$) attracted to negatively-charged sites on soil colloids and in equilibrium with $Al^{3+}$ in the soil solution. Acidity results following hydrolysis of aluminum ion in the solution phase:

$$Al^{3+}\text{–Soil colloid} \rightleftarrows Al^{3+} + 3H_2O \rightleftarrows 3H^+ + Al(OH)_3\downarrow.$$

Solid phase     Solution phase     Solid phase
(Soil solution)

The capacity of soil colloids to attract cations is called the *cation exchange capacity* (CEC). The pH of soil declines as the ratio of exchangeable $Al^{3+}$:CEC, also known as the *base unsaturation* of soil colloids, increases.[3] This relationship is illustrated for Alabama pond bottom soils[4] in Fig. 9.2.

Liming products are applied to soil to decrease base unsaturation. Liming neutralizes acidity in the solution phase as illustrated with $CaCO_3$ in Fig. 9.3. Calcium ions released into the soil solution when $CaCO_3$ neutralizes acidity exchanges with aluminum ion on the soil resulting in a decrease in base unsaturation and an increase in soil pH (Fig. 9.3).

Base unsaturation of bottom soil and water-column alkalinity were related in Alabama ponds.[4] Water-column alkalinities were above 20 mg/L when base unsaturation was 0.2

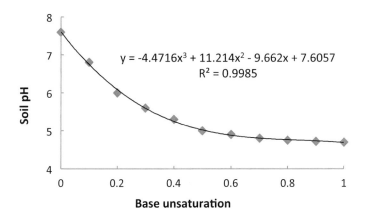

Fig. 9.2. Relationship between base unsaturation and pH of bottom soils in Alabama ponds. Modified from a data set from 145 ponds.[4]

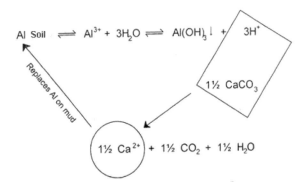

Fig. 9.3. A qualitative model of neutralization of acidic soil by calcium carbonate ($CaCO_3$).

or less. In ponds where base unsaturation was 0.0 to 0.1, alkalinity usually was above 50 mg/L. The concentration of alkalinity in distilled water at equilibrium between solid phase $CaCO_3$ and atmospheric carbon dioxide is 55 to 60 mg/L.[5] A higher alkalinity concentration may result from liming in ponds with an abundant supply of carbon dioxide from decay of organic matter. The extra carbon dioxide allows more liming material to dissolve than would be expected from equilibrium with atmospheric carbon dioxide.

Some soils, and especially those in coastal marshes, may contain iron sulfide (iron pyrite or $FeS_2$). When iron sulfide is exposed to air, it oxidizes to release sulfuric acid:

$$2FeS_2 + 3O_2 + 2H_2O = 2Fe^{2+} + 2H_2SO_4. \qquad (9.10)$$

Soils containing iron pyrite are known as *potential acid-sulfate soils*. They become active acid-sulfate soils when exposed to oxygen.[6]

The lime requirement of potential acid-sulfate soils is determined by the hydrogen peroxide oxidation method.[7] Lime requirement often is 50 to 100 tonnes/ha, but acidity is not expressed until iron pyrite oxidizes. Adding a single dose of liming material equal to the lime requirement is an ineffective way of neutralizing acidity in acid-sulfate soil. The lime particles will be lost from the soil or coated with iron and rendered insoluble before reacting completely.

Measures for preventing potential acid-sulfate soils from contacting air and drying can avoid the production of acidity and lessen the amount of liming material necessary. Procedures for mitigating acid-sulfate soils include: operating ponds without bottom dry-out between crops; establishing acid-tolerant grass on embankments; covering key areas with non-acidic soil; periodic liming. Nevertheless, sites with soil containing 1% or more total sulfur usually are not good places for aquaculture ponds.[8]

# Lime Requirement

The *lime requirement* of a pond is the amount of $CaCO_3$ (NV = FV = 100%) necessary to increase bottom soil pH and concentrations of alkalinity and hardness to desired levels. It is estimated by techniques modified from those used for agricultural soils. Soil pH in most soils is a function of the degree of base unsaturation (exchangeable $Al^{3+}$:CEC), but the amount of liming material necessary to provide a particular base unsaturation depends upon the CEC. Each type of clay mineral has a characteristic CEC, and soil organic matter has a high CEC. Thus, the amount of CEC in a soil is determined by the types of clay minerals present and the concentrations of clay minerals and organic matter in soil. Typical CEC values in aquaculture pond soil range from 1 or 2 meq/100 g to more than 40 meq/100 g. Reference to Fig. 9.2 reveals that two Alabama pond bottom soils of pH 4.9 each have a base unsaturation of about 0.5. The soil with the greater CEC, however, will have the larger lime requirement as illustrated in Example 9.3.

---

**Example 9.3**
**Cation Exchange Capacity and Lime Requirement**

Two soils of similar clay mineralology and base unsaturation (BUS) of 0.5 each have a pH of about 4.9 (Fig. 9.1). Soil A has CEC of 2 meq/100 g, while the CEC of soil B is 10 meq/100 g. The amount of calcium carbonate necessary to neutralize the exchangeable acidity (EA) and lower BUS to 0.0 will be calculated for the two soils.

Soil A:
EA to neutralize = 2 meq/100 g × 0.5 = 1 meq/100 g
Lime requirement = 1 meq/100 g × 50 mg $CaCO_3$/meq × 10 = 500 mg $CaCO_3$/kg

Soil B:
EA to neutralize = 10 meq/100 g × 0.5 = 5 meq/100 g
Lime requirement = 5 meq/100 g × 50 mg $CaCO_3$/meq × 10 = 2,500 mg $CaCO_3$/kg

---

One of the earliest methods for estimating lime requirement was based on soil pH and soil texture.[9] Lime requirement increases as soil pH declines, but at the same pH, finer textured soils have a greater lime requirement than coarser textured ones (Table 9.4). Shrimp ponds tend to have moderately fine to fine textured soils, and a lime requirement scale based solely on soil pH (Table 9.5) often is used.

A method for determining the lime requirement for raising bottom soil pH to 6 and increasing alkalinity and hardness above 20 mg/L was developed for sportfish ponds in Alabama and other states in the southern United States.[4] This method relies on determination of initial base unsaturation from soil-water pH and measurement of exchangeable acidity (exchangeable $Al^{3+}$) from the pH change caused by adding a small quantity of soil to a special buffer solution. The amount of exchangeable acidity (EA) that must be neutralized to decrease base unsaturation (BUS) to the desired level of 0.2 (pH 6) is estimated as follows:

$$\text{EA to neutralize} = \text{EA} \left( \frac{\text{Initial BUS} - \text{desired BUS}}{\text{Initial BUS}} \right). \tag{9.10}$$

The right-hand side of Equation 9.10 represents the fraction of the exchangeable acidity that should be neutralized. The lime requirement method above is not practical for wider use in aquaculture because data on the pH-base unsaturation relationship (Fig. 9.2) are not available for most locations. However, these data are not necessary if the lime requirement is based on complete neutralization of exchangeable acidity.[10] The alkalinity concentration usually will increase to at least 50 mg/L in ponds limed according to the results of this procedure.

Table 9.4. Lime requirements of pond soils based on pH and texture.[8]

| Mud pH | Lime requirement (kg/ha as $CaCO_3$) | | |
|---|---|---|---|
| | Heavy loams or clays | Sandy loam | Sand |
| <4.0 | 14,320 | 7,160 | 4,475 |
| 4.0-4.5 | 10,740 | 5,370 | 4,475 |
| 4.6-5.0 | 8,950 | 4,475 | 3,580 |
| 5.1-5.5 | 5,370 | 3,580 | 1,790 |
| 5.6-6.0 | 3,580 | 1,790 | 895 |
| 6.1-6.5 | 1,790 | 1,790 | 0 |
| >6.5 | 0 | 0 | 0 |

Table 9.5. Approximate lime requirements of bottom soils in shrimp ponds based on soil pH.

| Soil pH | Liming rate ($CaCO_3$ equivalent, kg/ha) |
|---|---|
| >7.5 | 0 |
| 7.0-7.5 | 500 |
| 6.5-6.9 | 1,000 |
| 6.0-6.4 | 1,500 |
| 5.5-5.9 | 2,000 |
| 5.0-5.4 | 2,500 |
| <5.0 | 3,000 |

The amount of liming material is based on the weight of the soil layer in which the liming material is expected to react. Liming materials react to a depth of about 15 cm over several months, and soil dry bulk density usually is around 1,200 kg/m$^3$ for this layer.[11] Example 9.4 shows how to calculate the amount of liming material (liming rate) necessary to completely neutralize exchangeable acidity.

Only 20 to 30% of nitrogen applied to aquaculture systems in feeds is recovered in biomass of culture animals. The remainder is transformed to ammonia through metabolic activities of microorganisms and the culture species. Ammonia is oxidized to nitrate by nitrifying bacteria (Chapter 16) in an acid-producing reaction. Hydrogen ions produced in this process neutralize alkalinity as illustrated below:

$$NH_4^+ + 2O_2 \rightarrow NO_3^- + 2H^+ + H_2O$$

$$CaCO_3 + 2H^+ \rightarrow Ca^{2+} + CO_2 + H_2O. \tag{9.11}$$

---

**Example 9.4**
**Estimation of Amount of Liming Material Necessary to Bring a Pond Soil to 100% Base Unsaturation**

A soil sample has an exchangeable acidity of 3.5 meq/100 g. Assuming that the liming material will react to a depth of 15 cm in the soil and the dry bulk density of the soil is 1,200 kg/m$^3$, the amount of agricultural limestone (NV = 98%; FV = 93%) will be estimated.

EA to neutralize = 3.5 meq/100 g × 50 mg CaCO$_3$/meq =

$$\frac{1{,}000 \text{ kg soil}}{100 \text{ g}} \times 10^{-6} \text{ kg/mg} = 0.00175 \text{ kg CaCO}_3/\text{kg soil}$$

Weight of soil = 1,200 kg/m$^3$ × 0.15 m depth × 10,000 m$^2$/ha = 1,800,000 kg/ha

Lime requirement = 1,800,000 kg soil/ha × 0.00175 kg CaCO$_3$/kg soil =

3,150 kg CaCO$_3$/ha

Liming rate = $\dfrac{3{,}185 \text{ kg CaCO}_3/\text{ha}}{(98/100)(93/100)}$ = 3,500 kg ha

of the agricultural limestone.

---

Oxidation of 1 mg/L of ammonia-nitrogen can neutralize 7.14 mg/L of alkalinity. Carbonate in bottom soil and alkalinity added to ponds during water exchange counteracts acidity from feeding, but alkalinity should be monitored regularly and liming materials added as necessary. The calculation of the lime requirement of feed is illustrated in Example 9.5. A general equation for estimating the lime requirement of feed follows:[12]

$$LR_{feed} = [N_f - (FCE \times N_a)]7.14 \qquad (9.12)$$

where $LR_{feed}$ = lime requirement of feed (kg $CaCO_3$/kg feed); FCE = feed conversion efficiency (kg of animal growth ÷ kg feed offered); $N_f$ and $N_a$ = decimal fractions of nitrogen in feed and culture species, respectively; 7.14 is ratio of $CaCO_3$:ammonia-nitrogen oxidized.

## *Application of Liming Products*

The first step in liming a pond is to determine the lime requirement of bottom soil and obtain a suitable liming material. Subsamples of the upper 15-cm layer of bottom soil should be obtained with a sediment corer or other device from 10 to 15 random locations in the pond. These subsamples should be combined and mixed thoroughly to make a composite sample for lime requirement analysis.[9,10]

---

### Example 9.5
### Lime Requirement of Feed

The lime requirement of feed will be estimated for a shrimp culture example in which the feed and shrimp contain 6% N (37.5% crude protein) and 2.75% N, respectively, and the feed conversion efficiency (FCE) is 0.556 kg shrimp/kg feed.

The difference in the nitrogen input and nitrogen in shrimp is the ammonia-N waste load:

1 kg feed × 0.06 = 0.06 kg N
0.556 kg shrimp/kg feed × 0.0275 = 0.0153 kg N/kg feed
Ammonia-N in waste = 0.06 – 0.0153 = 0.0447 kg/kg feed

Nitrification produces acidity equal to 7.14 kg $CaCO_3$/kg ammonia-N oxidized. Thus, the lime requirement for feed is:

0.0447 kg ammonia-N/kg feed × 7.14 kg $CaCO_3$/kg N = 0.319 kg $CaCO_3$/kg feed

---

The amount of liming material needed, the liming rate, can be determined from lime requirement and neutralizing value (NV) and fineness value (FV) of the material to be used:

$$\text{Liming rate, kg/ha} = \frac{\text{Lime requirement, kg } CaCO_3/\text{ha}}{(\% \text{ NV}/100)(\% \text{ FV}/100)} \tag{9.13}$$

For example, if the lime requirement is 2,000 kg/ha, and the liming material has a neutralizing value of 90% and a fineness value of 85%, 2,600 kg/ha of the material should be applied.

Liming materials and especially agricultural limestone react slowly, and several weeks or months may pass before maximum benefits are realized. Liming initially will remove phosphorus and suspended clay particles from water, which may encourage growth of underwater aquatic weeds. Liming should be done in late fall or early winter in temperate climates to allow the liming material time to react completely and increase alkalinity before the growing season begins. Fertilizer applications will be more effective following liming, and if made in early spring, fertilization will promote phytoplankton growth that will shade the bottom and prevent aquatic weed growth.

Water temperature in the tropics and subtropics is sufficient for phytoplankton growth year around. Liming should be done at the beginning of the production cycle, but fertilizers should not be applied until 2 or 3 days later to avoid phosphate precipitation.

Liming materials should be spread evenly over surfaces of ponds or other culture systems. Liming materials can be applied easily while ponds are empty between crops (Fig. 9.4), but applications should be made while soils are still moist. Liming materials also can be blended with the soil to a depth of 10 to 15 cm with a disk harrow (Fig. 9.4). Tilling is not essential, but it accelerates the reaction of liming material with the soil.

Fig. 9.4. Applying agricultural limestone to an empty pond (left) and tilling to mix lime into the upper, 15-cm soil layer (right).

Liming material should be spread uniformly over the water surface of ponds that cannot be drained. Liming material in bags may be poured directly over water surfaces from a boat, but bagging greatly increases the cost of materials. Bulk liming materials can be transported by truck and dumped near the pond. The bulk product should be loaded onto a platform mounted on a boat and spread over the pond surface—this can be done manually with a shovel or hydraulically (Fig. 9.5).

Liming to counteract acidity from nitrification is necessary mainly in intensive aquaculture and especially in plastic-lined ponds. Liming material can be applied near aerators and water currents will mix it throughout the water volume. In plastic-lined ponds with highly intensive production, one may want to consider using sodium bicarbonate as a liming material because it dissolves completely and quickly. Sodium bicarbonate has a NV of about 60%.

Liming should be done periodically, for alkalinity is consumed continually by reaction with acidity from bottom soil, organic matter decomposition, and nitrification, and it is lost in overflow and intentional discharge. Alkalinity measurement at the beginning of the growing season or crop cycle in extensive and semi-intensive ponds is usually sufficient for determining if liming should be repeated. In intensive ponds, alkalinity probably should be monitored monthly or more frequently and liming material applied as needed. Alkalinity also should be monitored monthly in ponds with acid-sulfate soils, for frequent liming usually is necessary.

**Fig. 9.5.** Loading agricultural limestone onto a platform on a boat (upper); spreading agricultural limestone manually (lower left) and hydraulically (lower right).

## *Pond Disinfection*

Lime—CaO or $Ca(OH)_2$—may be applied to pond bottoms between crops to increase soil pH to 10 or more (Fig. 9.6) and kill unwanted organisms and disease vectors that may survive in puddles or moist soil.[13] The usual procedure is to spread 1,000 to 2,000 kg/ha of lime uniformly over the soil surface. However, laboratory studies revealed that a treatment rate of 3,000 to 4,000 kg/ha was necessary to increase pH above 10 in many soils. This procedure is most effective when soil is moist and lime can dissolve and permeate the soil mass. The pH will quickly decline as lime reacts with carbon dioxide, and ponds can be refilled and stocked after 3 to 5 days. Lime applied for disinfecting pond bottoms also neutralizes soil acidity. Agricultural limestone does not raise pH above 8.3, and it is not useful for pond disinfection.

## *Improving Calcium Hardness*

High alkalinity water of low hardness concentration often has afternoon pH of 10 or above. Photosynthesis causes pH to rise until carbon dioxide depletion occurs at pH 8.3. Plants must then use carbon from bicarbonate causing carbonate concentration to increase. In absence of sufficient calcium to precipitate calcium carbonate, hydrolysis of soluble carbonate causes water pH to rise drastically. This can be avoided by increasing calcium concentration until hardness and alkalinity are approximately equal.[13]

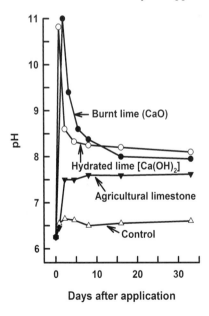

**Fig. 9.6.** Effects of liming materials on soil pH in bottoms of empty ponds. Liming materials were applied at 1,000 kg/ha.

Freshwater crustaceans need 50 to 75 mg/L hardness. Minimum, acceptable calcium concentration in water supplies for freshwater fish hatcheries vary with species from 10 to 200 mg/L calcium (25 to 500 mg/L as calcium hardness). Alkalinity often is adequate, and only calcium treatment is necessary.

The common source of calcium for increasing hardness is calcium sulfate. Application of 1.72 mg/L of calcium sulfate ($CaSO_4 \cdot 2H_2O$) will increase calcium hardness by 1.0 mg/L. It should be noted that calcium sulfate treatment is not a liming procedure for it does not neutralize soil or water acidity.

## Carbon Dioxide Removal

As explained in Chapter 7, lime may be applied when dissolved oxygen is low to remove carbon dioxide and allow fish or shrimp to use existing dissolved oxygen more efficiently.[13] Lime removes carbon dioxide from water by reactions illustrated in Equations 9.7 and 9.8. Quantities of calcium oxide and calcium hydroxide necessary to remove 1.0 mg/L of carbon dioxide are 0.64 mg/L and 0.84 mg/L, respectively. The treatment rate usually is increased by a factor of 1.5 or 2 to increase the speed of the reaction.[14] Agricultural limestone reacts too slowly to be of benefit in controlling high carbon dioxide concentration.

# References

1. Thunjai, T., C. E. Boyd, and M. Boonyaratpalin. 2004. Quality of liming materials used in aquaculture in Thailand. Aquaculture International 12:161-168.
2. Silapajarn, K., C. E. Boyd, and O. Silapajarn. 2004. An improved method for determining the fineness value of agricultural limestone for aquaculture. North American Journal of Aquaculture 66:113-118.
3. Adams, F. and C. E. Evans. 1962. A rapid method for measuring lime requirement of red-yellow podzolic soils. Soil Science Society of America Proceedings 26:355-357.
4. Boyd, C. E. 1974. Lime requirements of Alabama fish ponds. Bulletin 459, Alabama Agricultural Experiment Station, Auburn University, AL.
5. Boyd, C. E. 2000. Water Quality, An Introduction. Kluwer Academic Publishers, Boston, MA.
6. Fleming, J. F. and L. T. Alexander. 1961. Sulfur acidity in South Carolina tidal marsh soils. Soil Science Society of American Proceedings 25:94-95.
7. Boyd, C. E. 1995. Bottom Soils, Sediment, and Pond Aquaculture. Chapman and Hall, New York, NY.
8. Hajek, B. F. and C. E. Boyd. 1994. Rating soil and water information for aquaculture. Aquacultural Engineering 13:115-128.
9. Boyd, C. E. 1990. Water Quality in Ponds for Aquaculture. Alabama Agricultural Experiment Station, Auburn University, AL.
10. Pillai, V. K. and C. E. Boyd. 1985. A simple method for calculating liming rates for fish ponds. Aquaculture 46:157-162.
11. Munsiri, P., C. E. Boyd, and B. F. Hajek. 1995. Physical and chemical characteristics of bottom soil profiles in ponds at Auburn, Alabama, USA, and a proposed method for describing pond soil horizons. Journal of the World Aquaculture Society 26:346-377.

12. Boyd, C. E. 2007. Nitrification important process in aquaculture. Global Aquaculture Advocate 10(3):64-66.
13. Boyd, C. E. and K. Masuda. 1993. Characteristics of liming materials used in aquaculture ponds. World Aquaculture 25:76-79.

# Chapter 10

# Pond Fertilization

## Introduction

Phytoplankton productivity is the base of the food web for fish and other aquaculture species (Fig. 10.1). Concentrations of nitrogen and phosphorus in unmanaged ponds seldom are high enough to support adequate phytoplankton growth for efficient aquaculture. Potassium, calcium, magnesium, and sulfur and the minor nutrients, iron, manganese, zinc, copper, and boron, also may limit phytoplankton growth in some ponds. Chemical fertilizers for traditional agriculture are used as pond fertilizers to supply one or more limiting nutrients. Moreover, animal dung, grass, and agricultural wastes and by-products are applied to ponds as organic fertilizers. When organic fertilizers decompose, they release inorganic nutrients in the process called *mineralization*.

Fertilization results in 2- to 5-fold increases in aquaculture production, but greater increases can be achieved through application of feed. Fertilization is declining in aquaculture as feed-based aquaculture increases. Nevertheless, fertilization remains important in small-scale fish farming in Asia. It is also an aspect of most sportfish pond

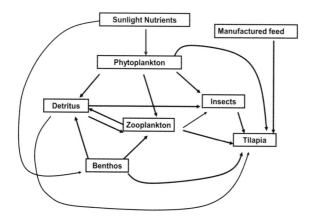

**Fig. 10.1.** Food web in a tilapia pond.

management in the United States and is a common practice in semi-intensive shrimp farming and in nursery ponds for culture of the early life stages of certain fish.

# Fertilizers

## *Chemical Fertilizers*

The main source of nitrogen for chemical fertilizer is industrial fixation of atmospheric nitrogen by the Haber-Bosch process. Natural gas is the hydrogen source to reduce nitrogen to ammonia:

$$N_2 + 3H_2 \rightarrow 2NH_3. \tag{10.1}$$

Ammonia is used to make ammonium and nitrate compounds and urea. Sodium nitrate also is extracted from caliche, a mineral found in the Atacama Desert of Chile and a few other deserts. Nutrilake® (SQM, Santiago, Chile) is a fertilizer made mainly from sodium nitrate and used in shrimp ponds in South and Central America.

The mineral apatite, often called rock phosphate, is the source of industrial and agricultural phosphorus. Phosphoric acid is made from apatite and sulfuric acid by the process illustrated here:

$$Ca_{10}(PO_4)_6F_2 + 10H_2SO_4 + 20H_2O \rightarrow 10CaSO_4 \cdot 2H_2O + 6H_3PO_4 + 2HF\uparrow. \tag{10.2}$$

Apatite is treated with sulfuric acid to produce superphosphate:

$$Ca_{10}(PO_4)_6F_2 + 7H_2SO_4 + 3H_2O \rightarrow 10Ca(H_2PO_4)_2 \cdot H_2O + 2HF\uparrow. \tag{10.3}$$

Triple superphosphate is made by treating apatite with phosphoric acid:

$$Ca_{10}(PO_4)_6F_2 + 14H_3PO_4 + 10H_2O \rightarrow 10Ca(H_2PO_4)_2 \cdot H_2O + 2HF\uparrow. \tag{10.4}$$

Potassium chloride is extracted from potassium-rich minerals such as sylvinite and carnalite; it also is made from natural brine solutions from closed basin lakes. Fertilizer grade potassium chloride is known as muriate of potash.

Ammonia, calcium phosphate, phosphoric acid, and muriate of potash are reacted with other substances to make a variety of fertilizer compounds (Table 10.1). Most fertilizers are solid, granular products, but phosphoric acid and ammonium polyphosphate are liquids. Liquid fertilizers are being used increasingly in both traditional agriculture and aquaculture.

Fertilizer compounds (Table 10.1) are blended to make mixed fertilizers with different ratios of the primary nutrients nitrogen, phosphorus, and potassium (Example 10.1). Concentrations of primary nutrients in fertilizers normally are reported in percentages of

Table 10.1. Approximate grades of common commercial fertilizer compounds.

| Chemical compound | Common name | Primary nutrients (%) | | |
|---|---|---|---|---|
| | | N | $P_2O_5$ | $K_2O$ |
| Urea [$(CO(NH_2)_2)$] | Carbamide | 45 | 0 | 0 |
| Calcium nitrate [$Ca(NO_3)_2$] | CAN | 15 | 0 | 0 |
| Sodium nitrate ($NaNO_3$) | Chile saltpeter | 16 | 0 | 0 |
| Ammonium nitrate ($NH4NO3$) | Nitrate of ammonia | 33-35 | 0 | 0 |
| Ammonium sulfate [$(NH_4)_2SO_4$] | --- | 20-21 | 0 | 0 |
| Phosphoric acid ($H_3PO_4$) | --- | 0 | 54 | 0 |
| Monocalcium phosphate [$Ca(H_2PO_4)_2 \cdot H_2O$ and $CaSO_4 \cdot 2H_2O$] | Superphosphate | 0 | 16 | 0 |
| Monocalcium phosphate [$Ca(H_2PO_4)_2 \cdot H_2O$] | Triple superphosphate | 0 | 44-54 | 0 |
| Monoammonium phosphate ($NH_4H_2PO_4$) | MAP | 11 | 48-52 | 0 |
| Diammonium phosphate [$(NH_4)_2HPO_4$] | DAP | 18 | 48 | 0 |
| Ammonium polyphosphate [$NH_4PO_3]n$ | APP | 11-13 | 37-38 | 0 |
| Potassium nitrate ($KNO_3$) | Salt peter | 13 | 0 | 46 |
| Potassium chloride ($KCl$) | Muriate of potash | 0 | 0 | 60 |
| Potassium sulfate ($K_2SO_4$) | Glaser's salt | 0 | 0 | 50 |

## Example 10.1
## Preparation of a 20-20-5 Fertilizer

A fertilizer containing 20% N, 20% $P_2O_5$, and 5% $K_2O$ can be made from diammonium phosphate (18% N and 48% $P_2O_5$), urea (45% N), muriate of potash (60% $K_2O$), and filler. The quantities of ingredients will be calculated for a 100 kg quantity:

| | |
|---|---|
| 20 kg $P_2O_5$ ÷ 0.48 kg $P_2O_5$/kg DAP = | 41.7 kg DAP |
| 41.67 kg DAP × 0.18 kg N/kg DAP = 7.5 kg N | |
| (20 kg N − 7.5 kg N) ÷ 0.45 kg N/kg urea = | 27. 8 kg urea |
| 5 kg $K_2O$ ÷ 0.60 kg $K_2O$/kg KCl = | 8.3 kg KCl |
| | |
| Fertilizers | 77.8 kg |
| Filler (agricultural limestone and anti-caking agent) | 22.2 kg |
| Total | 100.0 kg |

N, $P_2O_5$, and $K_2O$. A series of three numbers called the fertilizer analysis is prominently displayed on fertilizer bags or labels, e.g., 8-8-8, 35-0-10, or 20-20-5. These numbers are percentages of N, $P_2O_5$, and $K_2O$, respectively, in the fertilizer.

Secondary nutrients, calcium, magnesium, sulfur, and sodium, occur in some primary fertilizer compounds and fillers, and they are intentionally added in response to specific needs. Calcium and magnesium sulfates are soluble sources of secondary nutrients. Agricultural limestone is a less soluble source of calcium and magnesium, and it is often used as filler. Sodium silicate sometimes is included in fertilizers for shrimp ponds, for diatom abundance may be increased by silicate fertilization.[1]

Iron, manganese, zinc, copper, boron, and other trace elements are rarely included in aquaculture fertilizers because of their high cost. When included, trace metals usually are chelated with ethylenediamine tetraacetic acid (EDTA), triethanolamine (TEA), or some other chelating agent to enhance their solubility.

## Organic Fertilizers

Concentrations of nutrients in animal dung and agricultural wastes and byproducts (Table 10.2) are much less than in chemical fertilizers. Thus, application rates are high—about 700 kg/ha of fresh poultry manure are needed to provide as much phosphorus as contained in 20 kg/ha of triple superphosphate. Plant meals have much greater concentrations of nutrients, but they are more expensive than animal dung and agricultural wastes.

# Fate of Fertilizer Nutrients

The purpose of pond fertilization is to increase nutrient availability for phytoplankton. Although phytoplankton quickly assimilate nutrients, fertilizer nutrients are removed from water by other processes. Granular phosphate fertilizers are water soluble, but granules may settle to the pond bottom before completely dissolving.[2] Phosphate from fertilizer particles dissolving on the bottom is quickly absorbed by soil, and most of the adsorbed phosphorus is unavailable to phytoplankton. In acidic soils, phosphorus is sequestered by soil mainly through reaction with aluminum and iron. Calcium phosphates form in neutral and alkaline soils.

Fertilizers should be applied frequently, usually at 2- to 4-week intervals, to maintain adequate phosphorus concentrations. Phosphorus concentration in pond water can be increased most efficiently with liquid fertilizers or pre-dissolved granular fertilizers[3] (Fig. 10.2). This practice increases the availability of fertilizer phosphorus to phytoplankton.

**Table 10.2.** Fertilizer constituents in fresh animal dung, selected agricultural wastes, and two plant meals.

| Material | Moisture | N | $P_2O_5$ | $K_2O$ |
|---|---|---|---|---|
| | \multicolumn{4}{c}{Average composition (%)} | | | |
| Dairy cattle | 85 | 0.5 | 0.2 | 0.5 |
| Beef Cattle | 85 | 0.7 | 0.5 | 0.5 |
| Poultry | 72 | 1.2 | 1.3 | 0.6 |
| Swine | 82 | 0.5 | 0.3 | 0.4 |
| Sheep | 77 | 1.4 | 0.5 | 1.2 |
| Fresh cut grass | 70 | 0.78 | 0.14 | 0.64 |
| Peanut hulls, dry | 8 | 1.07 | 0.14 | 0.98 |
| Rice straw, dry | 7 | 0.56 | 0.21 | 1.08 |
| Potato peelings | 80 | 0.34 | 0.09 | --- |
| Sugar cane leaves | 74 | 0.21 | 0.16 | 0.91 |
| Soybean meal | 10 | 7.31 | 1.44 | 2.30 |
| Cottonseed meal | 7 | 6.93 | 2.45 | 1.74 |

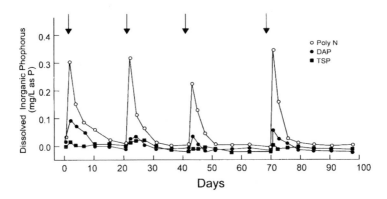

**Fig. 10.2.** Soluble inorganic phosphorus concentrations in ponds following applications of 9 kg $P_2O_5$/ha in liquid fertilizer (Poly N), and the granular fertilizers diammonium phosphate (DAP) and triple superphosphate (TSP). Arrows mark fertilization dates.[3]

Nevertheless, phosphorus added to water even in liquid fertilizers is sequestered in bottom soil rather quickly (Fig. 10.2). Sediment has a large capacity to bind phosphorus and pond bottoms usually are renovated with removal of sediment before their capacity to sequester phosphorus is filled.[4] Calcium phosphate will precipitate directly from water of high calcium concentration without involvement of sediment.[5]

Nitrogen fertilizers increase ammonia and nitrate concentrations in water. They are more soluble and less strongly adsorbed by sediment. Urea, a common fertilizer in aquaculture, quickly hydrolyzes to ammonia:

$$CO(NH_2)_2 + H_2O \rightarrow CO_2 + 2NH_3. \tag{10.5}$$

Un-ionized ammonia is in equilibrium with ammonium:

$$NH_3 + H^+ = NH_4^+. \tag{10.6}$$

Ammonium is the dominant form of ammoniacal nitrogen at normal pHs found in pond water.

Ammonia and nitrate not absorbed by plants undergoes transformations (Chapter 16). Ammonia diffuses from water into the air, a process favored by high afternoon pH.[6] Ammonia is oxidized by nitrifying bacteria. This process is a major source of acidity in fertilized ponds.[7] Nitrate applied in fertilizers or produced in nitrification is reduced to nitrogen gases by certain species of bacteria—gaseous nitrogen is lost to the atmosphere. Denitrification is an anaerobic process that normally occurs in sediment.

Potassium fertilizers are highly soluble.[2] Bottom soils remove potassium from water through cation exchange, and some 2:1 layered clays can fix potassium between the layers.[8] The greatest loss of potassium, however, is often by outflowing water.

Nitrogen, phosphorus, and potassium absorbed by phytoplankton move through the food web, and 10 to 30% of fertilizer nutrients are contained in aquatic animals harvested from ponds. Nutrients are bound in sediment organic matter and eventually recycled. They also exit ponds in overflow and intentional discharge.

Organic fertilizers decompose releasing nutrients which participate in processes mentioned above. Organic particles are food for zooplankton, and organic fertilization causes rapid increases in zooplankton abundance—this is desirable for early life stages of culture organisms that feed primarily on zooplankton. Filter-feeding fish consume organic particles and derive some nutritional value from them. However, decomposing organic fertilizers increase the oxygen demand, and this can cause low dissolved oxygen concentration.

# Fertilization Application Rates

## *Research Findings*

Few research stations have been willing to devote a large number of ponds to fertilization studies. Pioneering pond fertilization research was done at Malacca Malaysia; Auburn University, Alabama in the United States; and in Israel. The work at Auburn University has continued until the present. A number of pond fertilization studies also were conducted under auspices of the United States Agency for International Development (USAID) Aquaculture Collaborative Research Support Program (CRSP) in numerous projects at sites in Thailand, Philippines, Rwanda, Panama, and Honduras. There also has been considerable work on pond fertilization in India.

Studies in Malaysia were conducted in ponds with acidic soils that were limed to maintain alkalinity above 50 mg/L.[9] Fertilizers were broadcast over pond surfaces—a practice that reduces the effectiveness of phosphorus fertilization. The most efficient fertilization program was application of 44 kg $P_2O_5$/ha over a 6-month study period (about 7 kg $P_2O_5$/ha per month). Nitrogen and potassium fertilization was considered unnecessary. Ponds were thought to receive plenty of nitrogen from nitrogen fixation by blue-green algae and bacteria, and adequate potassium was available from the water supply and bottom soil.

Studies at Auburn University initially established that 10 to 12 broadcast applications of 45 kg/ha of granular 20-20-5 fertilizer (9 kg N, 9 kg $P_2O_5$, and 2.5 kg $K_2O$/ha per application) was optimum for sportfish ponds.[10] After 5 to 10 years of fertilization, plenty of nitrogen was available from nitrogen fixation and decomposition of organic matter in pond bottoms, and nitrogen fertilization was no longer essential.[11] It was later shown that phosphorus fertilization could be reduced to 4.5 kg $P_2O_5$/ha per application, or possibly less, by using liquid fertilizers or by pre-dissolving granular fertilizers.[3,12] In recent research,[13,14] maximum sunfish production was achieved in ponds with alkalinity of 30 to 50 mg/L from which sediment had recently been removed at applications of 3 kg $P_2O_5$/ha and 6 kg N/ha (Fig. 10.3)—this amounts to 30 to 36 kg $P_2O_5$ and 60 to 72 kg N/ha during the Alabama growing season. High nitrogen fertilization rates decreased fish production (Fig. 10.3) because ammonia toxicity reduced reproductive success of fish stocked in ponds. Potassium fertilization was unnecessary in pond waters at Auburn University, but waters contain 1.5 to 2 mg/L potassium, and this nutrient might be needed when ambient potassium concentrations are lower.

A standard fertilization dose of 60 kg/ha superphosphate and 60 kg/ha ammonium sulfate was recommended for ponds in Israel.[15] These rates equate to 11 kg $P_2O_5$ and 13 kg N/ha per application or 132 kg $P_2O_5$ and 156 kg N/ha over a 6-month period. More phosphorus was needed in hard waters in Israel than in softer waters at Malacca and Alabama. The response to phosphorus was much greater than to nitrogen, and fertilizer applications made at 2-week intervals were most effective.[16] Waters in Israel have high potassium concentration and inclusion of this nutrient in fertilizer was unnecessary.

Studies of the USAID Aquaculture CRSP project tended to use large fertilizer application rates. These high rates did not greatly increase fish production above that achieved in studies mentioned above.[17]

Pond fertilization studies in India demonstrated that pond bottom soil composition influences the response of pond waters to fertilizer applications.[18] A method for developing fertilizer nutrient application rates based on nutrient concentrations in pond bottom soils was recently suggested.[19]

## *Practical Fertilization Rates*

There is no widely-accepted method for determining the fertilizer application rate for ponds. Results presented above suggest that 6 kg N/ha and 3 kg $P_2O_5$/ha per application are sufficient nutrient inputs for ponds with total alkalinity above 30 to 40 mg/L and total hardness concentrations less than 150 mg/L. As a precaution, 2 kg $K_2O$/ha could be included for waters of low or unknown potassium concentration. The nutrients could be

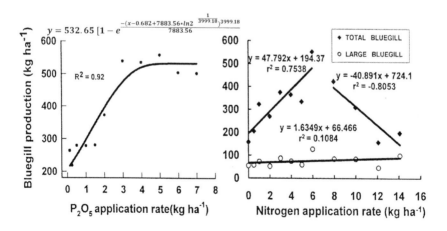

**Fig. 10.3.** Relationships between phosphorus application rate and sunfish production in ponds also treated with 8 kg N/ha per application[13] (left). Relationship between nitrogen application rate and sunfish production in ponds also treated with 3 kg $P_2O_5$/ha per application[14] (right).

supplied by mixed fertilizers (either liquid or solid) with analyses of 36-18-0 and 36-18-12, respectively, and applied at 16.7 kg/ha per application. Alternatively, nutrients could be achieved by applying appropriate amounts of two or three fertilizer compounds (Table 10.1) as illustrated in Example 10.2. Phosphorus application rates would likely need to be doubled or tripled in waters with hardness concentration above 150 or 200 mg/L. Because potassium unlikely would be limiting in such waters, one suitable treatment would be at 30 kg/ha per application of 20-20-0 fertilizer. Regardless of hardness concentration, in ponds with a history of fertilization, nitrogen fertilization can often be omitted.

The oxygen demand of organic fertilizers limits their application rate to a maximum of 60 to 80 kg dry weight/ha per day. The total input of fresh animal dung (10 to 30% dry weight) usually reaches several metric tons during a single grow-out period. Large treatment rate is an obvious disadvantage to most organic fertilizers. However, they are essential in small-scale aquaculture in Asia and a few other regions where animal dung and other agricultural wastes are cheap and locally available. Organic fertilization can result in greater fish production than possible with chemical fertilizers (Table 10.3).[20]

# Applying Fertilizers

Chemical fertilizers usually should be applied at 2- to 4-week intervals. Granular fertilizers should be pre-mixed in water to enhance their solubility. Liquid fertilizers have a density greater than that of water; they should be diluted before application to avoid

---

**Example 10.2**
**Calculating Amounts of Fertilizers**

A pond will be fertilized at the rate of 3 kg/ha of $P_2O_5$ and 6 kg/ha of N per application using urea (45% N) and triple superphosphate (46% $P_2O_5$). The necessary quantities of fertilizers per hectare are:

3 kg $P_2O_5$/ha ÷ 0.46 kg $P_2O_5$/kg TSP = 6.52 kg TSP

6 kg N/ha ÷ 0.45 kg N/kg urea = 13.3 kg urea

---

Table 10.3. Growth rates of fish in polyculture of Indian major carp in fertilized and fed ponds.[20]

| Treatment | Fish growth (kg/ha per day) |
|---|---|
| Control | 3.5 |
| Chemical fertilization | 10.4 |
| Pig dung | 18.0 |
| Feeding and chemical fertilization | 28.1 |
| Rural fish ponds treated with animal dung | 2.8 to 15.8 |

them from sinking before mixing with water. Fertilizer-water mixtures should be splashed over pond surfaces or discharged into the propeller wash of an outboard motor of a moving boat.[21]

Visibility into water as determined by a Secchi disk (Fig. 10.4) and water color are good indicators of phytoplankton abundance. The best range of Secchi disk visibility in fertilized ponds is about 25 to 40 cm. Low dissolved oxygen concentration is a risk at Secchi disk visibilities below 20 or 25 cm, and underwater weed problems are likely at Secchi disk visibilities above 40 or 50 cm. Secchi disk readings and water color observations allow one to follow the response of plankton to fertilization and to time fertilizer applications. Fertilization should be delayed if the Secchi disk visibility is too low. Excessive fertilization should be avoided, because heavy phytoplankton blooms can lead to DO depletion and fish kills.

Organic fertilizers also should be spread over the pond surface. However, they usually must be applied at more frequent intervals than chemical fertilizers.

## Pond Fertilization Problems

### Acidic, Low Alkalinity Waters

Liming is essential for a good response to fertilizers in ponds with low pH and total alkalinity. Pond liming is discussed in Chapter 9. It should be mentioned that calciumfrom liming materials precipitates phosphorus and, as such, fertilizer applications should not be made during the week after liming.

**Fig. 10.4.** A Secchi disk with line calibrated at 10-cm intervals.

## *Weed Problems*

Dense infestations of aquatic macrophytes should be controlled before fertilizers are applied. Otherwise, fertilizer nutrients may stimulate growth of aquatic macrophytes rather than phytoplankton. In temperate climates, initiation of fertilization in late winter or early spring can promote phytoplankton growth to create turbidity and prevent growth of underwater macrophytes. In sportfish ponds in the United States, grass carp often are used for aquatic weed control.

Organic fertilization precipitates clay turbidity from water and encourages underwater weeds. Organic particles also encourage the growth of filamentous algae such as *Spirogyra, Rhizoclonium, Pithophora*, and others (Chapter 19).

## *Turbidity*

High concentrations of suspended soil particles resulting from erosion in ponds or on their watersheds restrict light penetration and phytoplankton growth. Methods for controlling suspended clay turbidity in ponds are discussed in Chapter 15. Phytoplankton growth also may be limited in ponds with waters highly colored by humic substances. Humic stains usually occur in ponds with highly acidic water. Treatment with agricultural limestone (Chapter 9) often will reduce concentrations of humic substances and allow better response to fertilizers.

## *High Flushing Rate*

Ponds with hydraulic retention times less than 3 or 4 weeks usually will not respond well to fertilization because nutrients are flushed out too rapidly. This problem usually occurs where the watershed area:pond volume ratio is excessive. This ratio often can be lessened by diverting part of the runoff away from ponds with terraces or diversion ditches.

Deep water intake structures (Chapter 4, Fig. 4.3.) can be installed in ponds to prevent surface water overflow and loss of phytoplankton after heavy rains. Little can be done to avoid flushing plankton from ponds that have large inflow of stream or spring water.

## *Winter Kill*

Fertilization of sportfish ponds is not advisable in climates with extended periods of winter ice cover. Phytoplankton productivity increases in fertilized ponds resulting in greater input of organic matter to sediment. There is little dissolved oxygen production by photosynthesis under ice cover, and the larger oxygen demand for organic matter decomposition can lead to dissolved oxygen depletion and 'winter kill' of fish.

## *Excessive Phytoplankton Blooms*

In ponds with dense plankton blooms, low dissolved oxygen concentration may occur during the night, and especially during nights following cloudy days. Fertilized ponds may stratify thermally, and epilimnetic water will be depleted of dissolved oxygen. Heavy rainfall and strong winds associated with cold fronts can cause sudden destratification in summer. Blue-green algae sometimes die suddenly, and their decomposition can lead to dissolved oxygen depletion. This problem usually occurs when dense, surface scums of algae form during calm, clear weather.

Pond fertilization programs should focus on maintaining moderate levels of plankton abundance. Fertilizer applications should be reduced or delayed during periods when plankton blooms are excessively dense. Mechanical destratification devices (Chapter 12) can be installed in ponds to prevent thermal stratification, but these devices will not prevent low dissolved oxygen concentrations associated with excessive phytoplankton, cloudy weather, or massive phytoplankton die-offs. Mechanical aerators (Chapter 13) can be installed in sportfish ponds to prevent dissolved oxygen depletion, but they are expensive and require electrical services.

## *Nutrient Deficiencies*

Ponds usually are fertilized with nitrogen, phosphorus, and possibly potassium. A phytoplankton bloom may not occur because the application rate is too low or a limiting nutrient is missing from the fertilizer. Lacking a simple test for identifying limiting nutrients and optimum application rates, pond managers should increase fertilization rates or try adding other nutrients until the desired response is obtained.

## *Organic Fertilizers*

Low dissolved oxygen concentration and filamentous algae infestations associated with organic fertilization have been discussed, but there are other possible problems from these materials. Animal dung has relatively high concentrations of trace metals, and some may contain antibiotic residues. Aquaculture products from ponds treated with chicken dung have been reported to contain antibiotics. Off-flavor in fish has been observed in ponds receiving cattle dung. There also have been concerns over possible bacterial contamination resulting from fertilization with animal dung.

# References

1. Daniels, H. V. and C. E. Boyd. 1993. Nitrogen, phosphorus, and silica fertilization of brackishwater ponds. Journal of Aquaculture in the Tropics 8:103-110.
2. Boyd, C. E. 1981. Solubility of granular inorganic fertilizers for fish ponds. Transactions of the American Fisheries Society 110:451-454.

3. Boyd, C. E., Y. Musig, and L. Tucker. 1981. Effects of three phosphorus fertilizers on phosphorus concentrations and phytoplankton production. Aquaculture 22:175-180.
4. Masuda, K. and C. E. Boyd. 1994. Phosphorus fractions in soil and water of aquaculture ponds built on clayey, Ultisols at Auburn, Alabama. Journal of the World Aquaculture Society 25:379-395.
5. Hepher, B. 1958. On the dynamics of phosphorus added to fishponds in Israel. Limnology and Oceanography 3:84-100.
6. Gross, A., C. E. Boyd, and C. W. Wood. 1999. Ammonia volatilization from freshwater ponds. Journal of Environmental Quality 28:793-797.
7. Hunt, D. and C. E. Boyd. 1981. Alkalinity losses resulting from ammonium fertilizers used in fish ponds. Transactions of the American Fisheries Society 110:81-85.
8. Boyd, C. A., C. E. Boyd, and D. B. Rouse. 2007. Potassium adsorption by bottom soils in ponds for inland culture of marine shrimp in Alabama. Journal of the World Aquaculture Society 38:85-91.
9. Hickling, C. F. 1962. *Fish Cultures*. Faber and Faber, London.
10. Swingle, H. S. 1947. Experiments on pond fertilization. Bulletin 264, Alabama Agricultural Experiment Station, Auburn University, AL.
11. Swingle, H. S., B. C. Gooch, and H. R. Rabanal. 1963. Phosphate fertilization of ponds. Proceedings Annual Conference Southeastern Association Game and Fish Commission 17:213-218.
12. Metzger, R. J. and C. E. Boyd. 1980. Liquid ammonium polyphosphate as a fish pond fertilizer. Transactions of the American Fisheries Society 109:563-570.
13. Wudtisin, W. and C. E. Boyd. 2005. Determination of the phosphorus fertilization rate for bluegill ponds using regression analysis. Aquaculture Research 36:593-599.
14. Boyd, C. A., P. Pengseng, and C. E. Boyd. 2008. New nitrogen fertilization recommendations for bluegill ponds in the southeastern United States. North American Journal of Aquaculture 70:308-313.
15. Hepher, B. 1962.Ten years of research in fish pond fertilization in Israel. I.The Effect of fertilization on fish yields. Bamidgeh 14:29-38.
16. Hepher, B. 1963.Ten years of research in fish pond fertilization in Israel. II. Fertilization dose and frequency of fertilization. Bamidgeh 15:78-92.
17. Boyd, C. E. and C. S. Tucker. 1998. *Pond Aquaculture Water Quality Management*. Kluwer Academic Publishers, Boston, MA.
18. Banerjea, S. M. 1967. Water quality and soil condition of fish ponds in some states of India in relation to fish production. Indian Journal of Fisheries 14:113-144.
19. Banerjee, A., G. N. Chattaopahyay, and C. E. Boyd. 2009. Determination of critical limits of soil nutrients for use in optimizing fertilizer rates for fish ponds in red, lateritic soil zones. Aquacultural Engineering40:144-148.
20. Olah, J., V. R. P. Sinha, S. Ayyappan, C. S. Purushotaman, and S. Radheyshayam. 1986. Primary production and fish yields in fish ponds under different management practices. Aquaculture 58:111-122.
21. Boyd, C. E. and W. D. Hollerman. 1981. Methods of applying liquid fertilizers to fish ponds. Proceedings Annual Conference Southeastern Association of Fish and Wildlife Agencies 35:525-530.

# Chapter 11

# Feeds and Water Quality

## Introduction

Much of modern aquaculture relies on manufactured feeds to promote fast animal growth. Feeding allows greater animal production than in fertilized ponds where animals rely solely on in-pond food webs. Manufactured feeds are especially important when fish and crustacean species with commercial value do not efficiently use natural food webs (Chapter 3). Access to natural foods is meager or non-existent in cages, raceways, and water-recirculating systems. Animal production depends entirely on nutritionally complete manufactured feeds in those systems.

Feeds are expensive and considerable research has been conducted to optimize diets and feeding practices. This chapter will not address the nutritional aspects of feeding, which have been summarized many times. Rather, we will discuss the effects of feeding on water quality. Most feed eaten by aquatic animals is not converted to harvestable crop but rather is lost to the water as waste, with important impacts on water quality.

## Fate of Feed

*Feed conversion ratio* is a common measure of aquaculture production efficiency. The ratio, abbreviated FCR, is computed as the weight of feed offered to animals divided by net animal growth over some period of time. For example, if 4,500 kg of feed are fed and net animal growth is 3,000 kg, the FCR is 4,500/3,000 = 1.5 kg feed/kg animal production. Note that a lower FCR indicates better feed use efficiency than a higher ratio. Feed conversion ratios vary with species, feed quality, feeding practices, animal health, and environmental conditions. In commercial settings, FCR is also affected by how much feed is wasted during feeding and animal survival during culture. With careful feeding and good survival, FCRs of 1.2 to 2.0 are common and values less than 1.0 can be achieved under some conditions.

Although FCRs are useful for nutrition studies and comparative economics, they are misleading for water quality purposes. Aquatic animals are mostly water (fish average about 75% water) and feed is mostly dry matter (most feeds have 10% water, or less). When feed and production are both expressed on a dry-matter basis, actual feed conversions are not as good as implied when expressed on a wet-weight basis. For example, an FCR of 1.5 is a reasonably efficient feed conversion ratio in pond aquaculture, but 1.5 kg of feed contains about 1.35 kg dry matter and 1 kg of live fish contains 0.25 kg dry matter. The dry matter feed conversion ratio is 1.35/0.25 = 5.4. In other words, for every 1 kg of feed consumed, 0.73 kg of waste is produced. Even when FCR is 1.0 (which seems to imply that aquaculture can be a perpetual motion machine), considerable waste is produced. At an FCR of 1.0, the dry matter conversion is 3.6 and approximately 0.65 kg of waste is produced for every 1 kg of feed.

Wastes from feeding consist of organic matter, carbon dioxide, and compounds containing mineral nutrients such as nitrogen and phosphorus. Organic matter and nitrogen compounds that are not assimilated by the cultured animals express an oxygen demand that can reduce the production capacity of aquaculture systems. After the system's oxygen demand is met, accumulation of ammonia, carbon dioxide, or other waste products may limit animal growth and health. In fact, animal production in all aquaculture systems is ultimately limited by the system's capacity to remove or detoxify wastes resulting from feeding practices.

# Oxygen Demand of Feeding

Feeds added to aquaculture systems express an *oxygen demand* because organic matter in feed that is not converted to animal flesh is eventually oxidized to carbon dioxide, either in respiration by the cultured animal or during decomposition of feces and uneaten feed. Additional oxygen is used when ammonia—the major nitrogenous waste product for most aquatic animals—is oxidized to nitrate by nitrifying bacteria (Chapter 16).

Oxidation of feed organic matter to carbon dioxide requires the same amount of oxygen regardless of whether the oxygen is used in respiration by the cultured animal or in aerobic bacterial decomposition. Oxygen consumption during organic matter oxidation can be calculated from this general equation, where $CH_2O$ represents generic organic matter:

$$CH_2O + O_2 \rightarrow CO_2 + H_2O. \tag{11.1}$$

One mole of oxygen gas (32 g) is required to oxidize one mole of organic carbon (12 g), so on a mass basis, 2.67 units of oxygen are consumed per unit of carbon (32/12 = 2.67).

Oxygen is consumed in nitrification according to this process:

$$NH_4^+ + 2O_2 \rightarrow 2H^+ + NO_3^- + H_2O. \tag{11.2}$$

Two moles of oxygen gas (64 g) are consumed in the oxidation of one mole of ammonia-nitrogen (14 g), so 4.57 mass units of oxygen are consumed for each mass unit of nitrogen oxidized (64/14 = 4.57).

The oxygen demand of feed can be calculated by subtracting the amounts of carbon and nitrogen retained in animal from amounts in feed. The difference is the amount of carbon that can be oxidized to carbon dioxide by the animal or by bacteria and the amount of waste nitrogen that can be oxidized to nitrate by nitrifying bacteria. Those values are then be multiplied by the appropriate oxygen-demand factor from Equations 11.1 and 11.2 (Example 11.1).

Feed oxygen demand increases as FCR increases (that is, as FCR gets worse) because less organic matter and nitrogen are retained by the cultured animal and more enters the water. This is easily shown by expressing feed oxygen demand per weight of animal produced by multiplying oxygen demand per kg feed by FCR. Using the example above, the feed oxygen demand per kg of catfish produced at a feed conversion of 1.8 is

$$(1.21 \text{ kg } O_2/\text{kg feed})(1.8 \text{ kg feed/kg catfish}) = 1.92 \text{ kg } O_2/\text{kg catfish}. \qquad (11.3)$$

If the FCR increases (gets worse) to 2.4, feed oxygen demand increases to 3.02 kg $O_2$/kg catfish produced. To put this number into real-life perspective, the increase of 1.1 kg $O_2$/kg catfish amounts to an additional 26,400 kg of oxygen consumed in a 4-ha catfish pond during the production of 6,000 kg of catfish/ha. Efficient feeding has obvious economic benefits because feed is a large part of the cost of growing aquatic animals. Better feed conversion also improves water quality by decreasing the amount of oxygen consumed in various biological processes.

As mentioned above, feed oxygen demand has three components: animal respiration, bacterial decomposition of feces and uneaten feed, and the nitrogenous oxygen demand expressed by nitrifying bacteria. In general the average oxygen demand of aquaculture

---

**Example 11.1**
**Calculation of Feed Oxygen Demand**

Assume that channel catfish are grown on manufactured feed at a feed conversion ratio of 1.8 kg feed/kg fish. The feed contains 43% carbon and 5.2% nitrogen and catfish contains 8% carbon and 2.0% N. The oxygen demand of each kilogram of feed will be calculated.

The inverse of the FCR is called the *feed conversion efficiency* (FCE), with units of kg of fish produced per kg of feed. At an FCR of 1.8, the FCE is 1/1.8 = 0.556 kg fish/kg feed. One kilogram of feed contains 0.430 kg C and 0.052 kg N. Each kilogram of feed produces 0.556 kg of fish, which contains (0.556 kg fish)(0.08 kg C/kg fish) = 0.045 kg C, and (0.556 kg fish)(0.020 kg N/kg) = 0.011 kg N.

The amount of carbon not retained in fish is (0.430 kg in feed) − (0.045 kg retained in fish) = 0.385 kg C/kg feed; the oxygen demand of the unassimilated carbon per kilogram of feed is (0.385 kg C/kg feed)(2.67 kg $O_2$/kg C) = 1.03 kg $O_2$/kg feed.

The amount of unassimilated nitrogen is (0.052 kg in feed) − (0.011 kg retained in fish) = 0.041 kg N/kg feed; the oxygen demand of the unassimilated nitrogen is (0.041 kg N/kg feed)(4.57 kg $O_2$/kg N) = 0.18 kg $O_2$/kg feed.

The total oxygen demand of the unassimilated feed is 1.03 + 0.18 = 1.21 kg $O_2$/kg feed. This value is in the range of 1.2 to 1.3 kg $O_2$/kg feed suggested for general use in warmwater aquaculture.[1]

feed (1.2 to 1.3 kg $O_2$/kg feed) is proportioned as follows: animal respiration = 0.4 to 0.6 kg $O_2$/kg feed; bacterial decomposition = 0.4 to 0.6 kg $O_2$/kg feed; and nitrogenous oxygen demand = 0.15 to 0.25 kg $O_2$/kg feed. In other words, more than half the total feed oxygen demand is expressed by processes other than respiration by the cultured animal. This has important implications for aquaculture system design and management.

Flow-through and recirculating aquaculture systems are designed and operated to quickly remove uneaten feed and feces from the culture unit. Removing waste solids before they decompose in the culture unit reduces feed oxygen demand by half, or more. In effect, rapid solids removal allows greater animal production because more dissolved oxygen is available for animal respiration rather than being used for waste decomposition. Solid wastes removed from flow-through or recirculating systems can be collected, dried, and applied to land where they decompose using atmospheric oxygen. Solids are sometimes discharged to public waters or publically owned treatment works where the oxygen demand is met by aquatic processes external to the culture system. In pond aquaculture, most of the feed oxygen demand is expressed inside the culture system.

## Organic Matter and Nutrient Budgets

Waste budgets for feed organic matter and nutrients can be calculated by subtracting amounts in animal harvest from amounts in feed. The difference between inputs and outputs is the waste load. Waste loads as percentages of feed inputs vary depending on cultured species, feed quality, and other factors,[2] but using channel catfish as an example, about 80 to 90% of the carbon and 70 to 80% of the nitrogen and phosphorus in feeds is released to the culture unit as waste.[3]

Fates of excreted wastes and uneaten feed vary depending on culture system. Metabolic wastes and uneaten feed are rapidly removed from net-pen, flow-through, and recirculating aquaculture systems to maintain good water quality. In flow-through and net-pen systems, water flow transports organic solids and dissolved substances out of the culture unit. Recirculating aquaculture systems use discrete engineering processes, such as filters and degassers, to remove metabolic wastes. Because the systems are biologically simple, nutrient and organic matter budgets can be computed and used by engineers for precise system design. These concepts are discussed in appropriate chapters of this book but, as one example, most waste nitrogen is excreted as ammonia by most aquatic animals. Ammonia is potentially toxic if allowed to accumulate. In recirculating aquaculture systems, ammonia production rate is used to calculate the size of nitrification biofilters that transform ammonia into less toxic nitrogen compounds.

Eventual fates of organic matter and nutrients are much more complex in ponds than in other aquaculture systems (Figure 11.1). Ponds, by definition, have long hydraulic residence times and waste substances are retained for long periods where various biological, chemical, and physical processes transform or remove wastes from pond water.

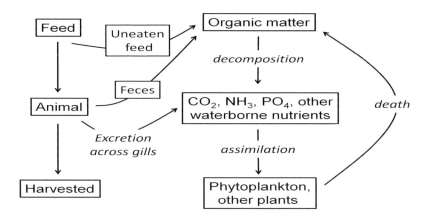

**Fig. 11.1.** Fate of feed offered to fish or crustaceans in aquaculture ponds. Oxygen-consuming processes include animal respiration; oxidation of organic matter derived from uneaten feed, animal feces, and dead plankton; and oxidation of ammonia to nitrate by nitrifying bacteria.

# Fates of Organic Matter and Nutrients in Ponds

Organic matter added to ponds initially consists of fecal material and uneaten feeds. These materials are quickly decomposed with consumption of dissolved oxygen, production of dissolved carbon dioxide, and liberation of dissolved nutrients in the process called *mineralization*. Unlike other aquaculture systems where feed oxygen demand is lessened by removing solids from the culture unit before they decompose, most or all of the feed oxygen demand is expressed inside the pond. Some of the demand is delayed because a portion of the organic matter from feeding may be stored temporarily in pond bottom muds before decomposing aerobically. Depending upon the pond hydraulic residence time, some fraction of the oxygen demand also may be transported to other water bodies when water is discharged.

Carbon dioxide, ammonia, various phosphorus compounds, and other nutrients released from decomposing organic matter contribute to the amounts of those substances excreted directly into water by the cultured aquatic animal. These nutrients have complex fates[2] but much of the carbon dioxide and inorganic nitrogen and phosphorus are initially assimilated by phytoplankton or other aquatic plants during the production of new organic matter. In most ponds with feeding, production of new organic matter in photosynthesis exceeds direct organic matter additions in feed wastes and uneaten feed. For example, in one study, about 1,500 kg of dry organic matter was produced as metabolic wastes during production of 1,000 kg of channel catfish, but 2,000 kg of new organic matter was produced in the form of phytoplankton.[3]

New organic matter produced in phytoplankton photosynthesis expresses an oxygen demand as the algae respire and when they die and decompose. Over the long term, the amount of oxygen used in phytoplankton respiration plus oxygen used in eventual

**145**

decomposition of dead algae is essentially equal to the amount of oxygen produced as a byproduct of photosynthesis during organic matter formation. The net oxygen demand of organic matter synthesized by phytoplankton (or other aquatic plants) is therefore near zero.

## Feeding and Water Quality in Ponds

Feed input is strongly correlated with deterioration of water quality in ponds. In general, as feed input increases, more metabolic waste enters the pond and phytoplankton abundance increases, concentrations of total ammonia and carbon dioxide increase, and persistent dissolved oxygen deficits develop.

Ponds with feed inputs less than approximately 30-40 kg/ha per day usually have few episodes of low dissolved oxygen concentrations (concentrations less than 3-4 mg/L) because feed oxygen demand is low and natural aeration of water is sufficient to keep dissolved oxygen concentrations near air-saturation levels.[4,5] As feed inputs increase, phytoplankton abundance increases because feed wastes contain nutrients that stimulate plant growth. As mentioned above, the net oxygen demand of organic matter produced in phytoplankton photosynthesis is zero but on a whole-community basis, oxygen produced in phytoplankton photosynthesis is obviously less than the combined oxygen demand of phytoplankton respiration, dead phytoplankton decomposition, and the components of feed oxygen demand (animal respiration, nitrogenous oxygen demand, and decomposition of feces and uneaten feed). When daily feed inputs consistently exceed about 30-40 kg/ha, total pond oxygen demand will eventually become so great that oxygen produced in daytime photosynthesis cannot prevent dissolved oxygen concentrations from falling at night to levels that may stress or kill the cultured animal. The daily shortfall between oxygen production and oxygen consumption will have to be offset by using mechanical aeration to keep animals alive and healthy.

As daily feed inputs increase above 30-40 kg/ha, the need for mechanical aeration to offset dissolved oxygen deficits increases, in theory, up to the point where continuous aeration is needed to offset total pond oxygen demand. In practice, however, when feeding rates become very high, accumulation of ammonia or carbon dioxide begins to affect animal performance even if mechanical aeration maintains dissolved oxygen levels above stressful levels.

The maximum feeding rate possible without accumulation of dangerous ammonia levels is difficult to determine because of the fate of waste nitrogen in ponds is complex and varies with water temperature, sunlight availability, and other factors that vary over time (Chapter 16). As an approximation, assume that most ammonia produced by aquatic animals is initially removed from water by phytoplankton as they assimilate the compound as a nitrogen source for growth. The nitrogen assimilation rate by phytoplankton can be estimated from the rate of carbon fixation in photosynthesis and the average ratio of carbon to nitrogen in algal tissue (6C:1N by mass). Photosynthetic rates range from less than 1 to more than 6 g $C/m^2$ per day.[6] Using 3 g $C/m^2$ per day as an average carbon fixation rate for phytoplankton in ponds with abundant nutrients, an estimated nitrogen assimilation rate can be calculated:

$(3 \text{ g C/m}^2 \text{ per day})(1 \text{ g N/6 g C}) = 0.5 \text{ g N/m}^2 \text{ per day.}$  (11.4)

Waste ammonia production rate for channel catfish (as an example) averages about 35 g N/kg of feed consumed,[7] so the maximum amount of feed that can be used without ammonia production exceeding phytoplankton assimilation capacity is

$$\frac{0.5 \text{ g N/m}^2 \text{ per day}}{35 \text{ g N/kg of feed}} \times 10,000 \text{ m}^2/\text{ha} \sim 140 \text{ kg of feed/ha per day} \qquad (11.5)$$

This amount, 140 kg of feed/ha per day, is based on a relatively high estimate of phytoplankton photosynthetic rate. In reality, average phytoplankton photosynthesis over long periods in static-water ponds is lower. Values of 90 to 110 kg feed/ha have been proposed for sustained maximum daily feeding rates without excessive ammonia accumulation in ponds.[6,7]

## Water Quality Management in Ponds with Feeding

To the extent possible, aquaculturists should strive to improve feed conversion and optimize nutrient retention by using high-quality feeds and feeding carefully to avoid wasting feed. However, water quality deterioration is inevitable in ponds with feeding, no matter how effectively animals are fed. Waste production is an unintentional and unavoidable consequence of feeding and, unlike other aquaculture systems where wastes can be quickly removed to prevent water quality deterioration, it is not economically feasible to remove wastes from ponds.

Managing water quality problems in ponds with feeding often consists of treating problems rather than addressing the cause of the problem. A good example is using mechanical aeration to offset dissolved oxygen deficits. In flow-through and recirculating culture systems, oxygen demand is lessened by quickly removing metabolic wastes and uneaten feeds from the culture unit. In ponds, however, the full feed oxygen demand is inevitably expressed and the only recourse is treating the problem's result (low concentrations of dissolved oxygen) because the problem's cause—waste loading from feeding—is uncontrollable.

Other than reducing waste loading by careful feeding, the key to successful pond aquaculture is operating within the limits of the inherent capacity of the pond ecosystem to provide dissolved oxygen and treat wastes. Initial challenges involve managing the increasingly severe dissolved oxygen deficits that develop as daily feed inputs increase above 30-40 kg/ha. As feeding rates increase, a point is reached where accumulation of metabolic byproducts (ammonia, nitrite, or carbon dioxide) begin to affect animal growth and health. Additional problems, such as production of toxins and odorous compounds by algae, also become more frequent in ponds with high feed inputs because blue-green algae tend to dominate phytoplankton communities of shallow, nutrient-rich ponds and lakes (Chapters 3 and 18). Toxic episodes and development of off-flavors in the crop can be serious economic risks in pond aquaculture and are very difficult to manage.

As rough guidelines for warmwater fish and shrimp, daily feeding rates should not exceed 30-40 kg/ha per day unless adequate aeration is available and should not exceed more than 100-150 kg/ha to prevent accumulation of ammonia. If more feed is needed to achieve greater animal production, systems designed for higher rates of waste assimilation must be used (Chapters 24-28).

# REFERENCES

1. Boyd, C. E. 2009. Oxygen demand of aquaculture feed. Global Aquaculture Advocate 12(6):44-45.
2. Boyd, C. E. and C. S. Tucker. 1998. *Pond Aquaculture Water Quality Management*. Kluwer Academic Publishers, Boston, MA.
3. Boyd, C. E., 1985. Chemical budgets for channel catfish ponds. Transactions of the American Fisheries Society 114:291-298.
4. Tucker, L., C. E. Boyd, and E. W. McCoy. 1979. Effects of feeding rate on water quality, production of channel catfish, and economic returns. Transactions of the American Fisheries Society 108:389-396.
5. Cole, B. A., Boyd, C. E., 1986. Feeding rate, water quality, and channel catfish production in ponds. Progressive Fish-Culturist 48: 25-29.
6. Brune, D. E., G. Schwartz, A. G. Eversole, J. A. Collier, and T. E. Schwedler. 2003. Intensification of pond aquaculture and high rate photosynthetic systems. Aquacultural Engineering 28:65-86.
7. Tucker, C. S. and J. A. Hargreaves. 2012. Freshwater ponds, pages 191-244. In J. Tidwell (editor), *Aquaculture Production Methods*. Wiley-Blackwell, Ames, IA.

# Chapter 12

# Thermal Stratification and Water Mixing

## Introduction

A goal of aquaculture water quality management is to provide a uniform culture environment that promotes rapid crop growth and efficient use of facility space. Some aquaculture systems come close to that ideal; for example, indoor recirculating aquaculture systems often provide relatively consistent water quality throughout the crop grow-out cycle and uniform environmental conditions throughout culture tanks. In contrast, pond environmental conditions vary greatly in time and space, with significant effects on crop growth. For example, daily and seasonal changes in sunlight and air temperature cause dissolved oxygen concentrations to vary over time, which is a key management consideration in pond aquaculture.

Sunlight and air temperature also cause pond water quality to vary with water depth. As light passes through water, much of its energy is reflected, scattered, or absorbed in the uppermost water layer, resulting in rapid attenuation of light with depth. Attenuation of light energy with depth can cause steep gradients in water quality between surface and bottom waters. Mechanical devices can disrupt those gradients and maintain completely mixed conditions, with possible benefits to aquaculture production.

## Thermal Stratification

The density of water is approximately 1 g/cm$^3$ but varies with temperature (Chapter 2). Maximum density occurs at approximately 4°C and density decreases as temperature increases. As sunlight is absorbed by water and transformed into heat, the upper layers become less dense than cooler bottom waters. In deep ponds or lakes, density differences can become so great that the warmer, upper layers do not mix with the cooler, denser waters near the bottom. The process by which layers of water develop resistance to mixing because of temperature-induced differences in water density is called *thermal stratification*.

Annual patterns of thermal stratification in deep, temperate lakes are described in all basic limnology text books. Briefly, cool or cold winter weather results in relatively uniform water temperatures and freely mixed conditions throughout the lake. If lakes remain ice-free in winter, mixing is facilitated by windy conditions as strong winter weather fronts move through the region. Although surface waters may heat on individual days, loss of heat to the atmosphere and to deeper waters prevents stable density differences. As weather warms and solar radiation increases with the approach of summer, surface waters absorb heat faster than is lost by conduction and mixing with deeper waters. Over time, surface waters become warmer than deeper waters and the density difference becomes so great that the two layers resist mixing by wind. The upper water layer—called the *epilimnion*—has relatively uniform water temperature and freely mixes within itself. The bottom layer—the *hypolimnion*—also has relatively uniform water temperature and freely mixes within itself. Between the two layers is a zone of rapid temperature change called the *metalimnion* or *thermocline* (Fig. 12.1). A stable state of thermal stratification persists until the onset of cooler weather in autumn when heat is lost from the epilimnion to the atmosphere and the density difference between upper and lower layers decreases. Eventually the entire lake mixes or *destratifies*. Loss of thermal stratification and subsequent mixing is sometimes described as a *turnover*.

Variations of the classic annual pattern of thermal stratification exist depending on climate and lake morphometry (principally water depth). Some water bodies never stratify while some—including most aquaculture ponds—stratify and destratify many times over the year.

Aquaculture ponds are shallower than lakes that develop persistent warm-weather thermal stratification. In ponds, heat is conducted rapidly between surface and bottom waters, simply because ponds are shallow and there is little distance between the surface and pond bottom. Also, because ponds have a high ratio of surface area to volume, relatively little wind is needed to mix the water. These characteristics do not favor long-term thermal stratification as seen in large, deep lakes. However, aquaculture ponds often have large amounts of suspended matter (usually in the form of phytoplankton) that

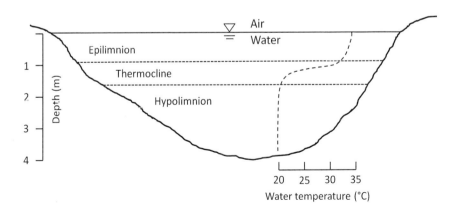

**Fig. 12.1.** Water temperature profile in a pond with strong thermal stratification. A warm layer of surface water (epilimnion) lies over a cooler, dense layer of deep water (hypomnion) with a transition zone (thermocline) where temperature rapidly decreases with depth.

absorb light and cause rapid heating of surface waters on calm, sunny days. This relatively weak state of thermal stratification may persist for hours to weeks, depending on water depth and weather conditions. During hot, sunny weather, shallow ponds (1- to 2-m deep) may stratify into layers that do not mix during the day, only to destratify at night when surface waters lose heat by conduction. Deeper ponds may remain stratified for longer periods if winds are calm, but strong winds or cold rains can cause complete mixing of surface and bottom waters.

## Chemical Stratification

Plant growth (usually in the form of phytoplankton) largely determines pond water quality. Plants produce oxygen and consume carbon dioxide and inorganic nitrogen—processes that are critical to maintaining a good environment for pond aquaculture. Energy driving these processes comes from sunlight. Because light energy is strongly attenuated in water, aquatic plant photosynthetic rate is highest near the surface and decreases with depth. The minimum light requirement for phytoplankton growth depends on many factors, but averages about 1% of full summer sunlight. The depth to which 1% of incident solar radiation penetrates is traditionally called the *light compensation point* and marks the approximate depth at which gross photosynthesis equals respiration. The layer of water above the compensation point is called the *photic zone*. In practical terms, the photic zone is the layer of water with net oxygen production. The compensation point depth can be estimated as twice the Secchi disk visibility (see Fig. 2.4).

If the light compensation point is deeper than the lake or pond depth, then the entire water body is in the photic zone (in other words, more than 1% of incident sunlight reaches all the way to the bottom). On the other hand, if the compensation point is shallower than the bottom, then part of the water column is in the photic zone and deeper waters are in a zone of net oxygen consumption. Turbid aquaculture ponds often have Secchi disk visibilities less than 0.25 m, meaning that oxygen is produced only near the surface and little or no oxygen is produced near the bottom. When the light compensation depth is shallower than the pond depth, oxygen produced in photosynthesis can reach the bottom only when oxygen-enriched surface waters are mixed with deeper waters. In the absence of vigorous mixing, dissolved oxygen concentrations vary greatly with depth and the pond is said to be *chemically stratified.*

## Potential Benefits of Mixing

Although thermal and chemical gradients develop independently, their relationship should be obvious. Thermal stratification prevents mixing of surface and bottom waters. If the photic zone lies in the epilimnion of a thermally stratified lake or pond, oxygen produced in photosynthesis near the surface cannot be distributed to bottom waters because density differences prevent mixing. The oxygen content of deeper waters becomes depleted by respiratory processes in deep waters and sediment. The potential benefits of mixing described below are related to disruption of these thermal and chemical gradients.

## Conserves Dissolved Oxygen

Photosynthesis in unmixed ponds with abundant phytoplankton is confined to near-surface waters because light energy is rapidly attenuated as it passes through turbid water. On sunny days, photosynthesis will be intense and dissolved oxygen concentrations often become supersaturated. Oxygen is lost from supersaturated surface waters when it diffuses to the atmosphere and is therefore not available for use by fish or other gill-breathing aquatic animals. Mixing constantly moves dissolved oxygen produced in surface waters into deeper water, thereby preventing oxygen loss to the atmosphere and increasing the total supply of oxygen available for the cultured species.

## Increases the Mass of Dissolved Oxygen

If the dissolved oxygen gradient is extremely steep with depth, a stratified pond will have a relatively small volume of oxygen-containing water near the surface. Conversely, the entire pond contains dissolved oxygen if the pond is thoroughly mixed. As such, the total mass of dissolved oxygen (the product of concentration and volume, integrated by depth) contained in a stratified pond may be much less than in a thoroughly mixed pond, even though the dissolved oxygen concentration near the surface might be much higher in the stratified pond (Fig. 12.2). When surface waters are undersaturated, mixing increases the rate of oxygen diffusion from air into water by constantly bringing deeper, oxygen-poor waters into contact with air. The overall effect of mixing is to increase the mass of oxygen in a lake or pond.

## Increases Habitat

When ponds are chemically stratified the entire water column may not be habitable by fish or crustaceans. In extreme cases where bottom waters are devoid of oxygen, animals can survive only by staying near the surface. Even if the oxygen gradient is not that extreme, animals seek out preferred areas and inhabit only a portion of the pond. The impacts of reduced habitat may be greater for bottom-dwelling animals, such as shrimp and freshwater prawns, that will be forced to the pond edges where crowding and predation may lead to crop loss.

Ponds tend to stratify most strongly during hot, calm weather. Under those conditions, surface water temperature may exceed local air temperature by several degrees because solar energy absorbed by water is transformed into heat faster than it can be dissipated to the air or conducted to deeper water waters. For example, in a channel catfish pond at Stoneville, Mississippi, water temperature at 5 cm depth was 39°C on a calm day when maximum air temperature was 34°C, and surface water temperatures exceeding 41°C

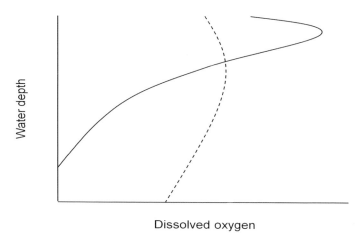

**Fig. 12.2.** Daytime dissolved oxygen concentrations in a pond with a well-mixed water column (dashed line) and a pond with strong chemical and thermal stratification (solid line).

have been recorded on several occasions. These values are in the range of the incipient upper lethal water temperatures for channel catfish. So, shallow chemical stratification during periods of hot weather will force animals to inhabit near-surface waters because of low dissolved oxygen concentrations in bottom waters but because chemical and thermal stratification co-exist under those conditions, the surface waters may be so warm that physiology or behavior are adversely affected.

In summary, mixing increases habitat for aquatic animals by distributing dissolved oxygen and heat throughout the water column. On hot, calm days, mixing will increase dissolved oxygen concentrations in bottom waters and decrease temperatures in surface waters relative to unmixed ponds.

## *Prevents Turnovers*

Shallow aquaculture ponds stratify daily during calm, hot periods, only to slowly destratify each night as surface waters cool. Deeper ponds may remain stratified for longer periods. In either case, ponds may suddenly destratify with serious consequences. Sudden strong winds or cold rains can rapidly mix the water column and mix the thin layer of oxygen-rich surface water with oxygen-deficient bottom water. These turnovers result in a completely mixed pond containing very little dissolved oxygen. Respiration of fish, plankton, and sediment may then quickly deplete remaining dissolved oxygen. Consequences of turnovers are usually more severe in deeper ponds because a proportionally larger volume of the pond may be oxygen-deficient than in shallow ponds. Continuous mixing of ponds, either by wind or mechanical devices, prevents turnovers by inhibiting the development of stratified conditions.

## *Reduces Organic Matter Accumulation*

Redistribution of dissolved oxygen from surface waters can affect processes occurring in or near pond sediments. Organic matter produced in photosynthesis eventually settles to the bottom where it decomposes, creating a demand for oxygen. Redistributing oxygen produced near the pond surface accelerates organic matter decomposition and reduces the rate of organic matter accumulation in pond sediments. In the absence of oxygen, organic matter decomposition results in the production of various organic compounds that may affect fish and shrimp growth. Mixing may prevent accumulation of anaerobic decomposition products.[1]

## *Reduces Algal Abundance*

Phosphorus availability often limits aquatic plant growth in freshwater ecosystems. Much of the water-column phosphorus supporting aquatic plant growth is internally recycled from sediments. Phosphorus is largely unavailable from aerobic sediments because oxidized ferric iron ($Fe^{3+}$) forms iron phosphates of very low solubility. Under anaerobic conditions, iron is reduced to soluble ferrous ($Fe^{2+}$) iron causing iron phosphates to be solubilized. In theory, mixing keeps dissolved oxygen concentrations relatively high near the pond bottom and the oxidized mud surface functions as a barrier to the diffusion of phosphorus from the mud into the overlying water. By creating conditions favorable for sequestering iron phosphates in pond muds, mixing may reduce the availability of phosphorus to phytoplankton. Although artificial mixing to reduce phosphorus availability is often suggested as a measure to counteract eutrophication in lakes, results are inconsistent.[2] Further, many aquaculture ponds have high external phosphorus loading from feeds, and reducing the supply of phosphorus recycled from sediments probably has little effect on phytoplankton growth.

## *Reduces Incidence of Blue-Green Algal Blooms*

Certain species of blue-green algae grow particularly well in poorly mixed waters with steep light gradients from top to bottom.[3] These species regulate cell buoyancy and control their position in the water column, allowing them to obtain adequate light to support growth when water is turbid. Blue-green algae also possess an array of primary and accessory photosynthetic pigments that allow them to use light in wavelengths that are not used by other algae. A thoroughly mixed water column negates these advantages by exposing all algae to the same underwater light climate, which theoretically favors other phytoplankton over slower-growing blue-green algae. Water-column mixing often suppresses blue-green algae blooms in deeper lakes and ponds, but results are inconsistent in shallow aquaculture ponds.[4]

# Mixing Devices

All aerators create flow and turbulence, and many are used for mixing as well as aeration. However, mechanical devices generally cannot be highly efficient at both oxygen transfer and mixing. If the primary goal is water circulation, devices designed for that specific purpose should be used. Mixing devices can be categorized as air-injection systems (bubblers or diffusers) or mechanical devices that induce either vertical or horizontal water currents.

## *Air-Injection Systems*

Air-injection systems use an on-shore compressor to deliver air to underwater diffusers. Unconfined air bubbles released from a single point entrain water as they rise to the surface, creating buoyant plumes of bubbles and water. Water may be detrained from the plume more or less continuously as plume rises, forming multiple cells of mixing. In shallow water, only one mixing cell forms as entrained water rises and spreads out across the surface. Water from the surface then moves downward to replace the rising water, forming a doughnut-shaped cell (a *torus*) of mixed water if air is released from a single point (Fig. 12.3). If air is released from a linear series of orifices (such as a perforated pipe), two cylindrical mixing cells develop on either side and parallel to the pipe. Size of the mixed zone increases as water depth and air flow increase and bubble size decreases.

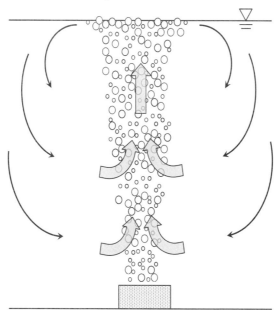

**Fig. 12.3.** Water mixing induced by a bubble plume.

Models incorporating those variables can be used to design systems to destratify entire lakes.[5] Air-injection systems are also used for aeration and have good oxygen transfer efficiencies when used in deep lakes. Aeration efficiency is relatively poor in waters less than 1 to 2 m deep (Chapter 13).

Bubble-plume destratifiers are the most common device used to mix large, deep lakes, but are not widely used in aquaculture ponds. Mixing efficiency is low in shallow water and diffusers must be spaced at close intervals over the entire pond bottom to completely mix the pond. The array of diffusers and air-supply lines may also interfere with crop harvest.

Air-lift pumps (Fig 12.4) are constructed of a length of pipe, called an eductor, that confines the bubble plume. Air from a low-pressure blower is released through a diffuser at the bottom of the eductor and rising bubbles lift water through the eductor, discharging it horizontally at the surface. Air-lift pumps are better mixers than unconfined bubble plumes in shallow ponds because they induce stronger horizontal currents. Most air-lift pumps are relatively small and useful only in small ponds or tanks. Oxygen transfer efficiency is poor in shallow waters and most air-lift pumps should be considered as mixing devices rather than aerators.

## *Vertical Water Mixers*

These devices mix water by producing currents that force surface water downward or pull deeper waters upward. A common example is a vertical impeller aerator (Fig 12.5). These aerators use a motor-driven impeller that draws water up and through the unit, producing a fountain-like spray. Although designed primarily for aeration, vertical impeller aerators are relatively effective mixing devices in small ponds.

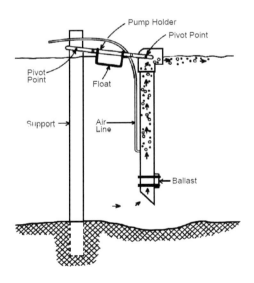

**Fig. 12.4.** Air-lift pump.

Better mixing efficiencies are obtained using devices that do not use energy to spray water high in the air. One such device is a commercially available, solar-powered circulator (Fig. 12.6) that uses a motor-driven impeller to draw water from a pre-determined water depth through a draft tube. The water then spreads radially across the

**Fig. 12.5.** Floating, vertical impeller aerator used to aerate and mix a small pond.

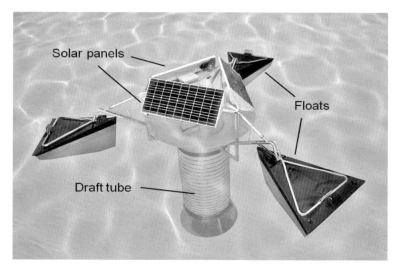

**Fig. 12.6.** Floating, solar-powered water circulator. Water is drawn upward through the draft tube by a motor-driven impeller (hidden by the solar panels), impinges on a deflector plate, and spreads radially across the water's surface (Photo courtesy of Medora Corporation, Dickinson, ND).

157

surface, away from the unit.[4] Other devices use a motor-driven impeller to draw surface water into a draft tube and discharges the water downward.[6] Devices that discharge water downward are not suited for shallow aquaculture ponds because energy imparted to water is lost when currents impact the pond bottom, reducing mixing efficiency. Down-welling currents could gouge holes beneath the device that will interfere with crop harvest.

### Horizontal Water Mixers

Mixers that generate horizontal currents are better suited for shallow ponds than those producing vertical currents. Paddlewheel aerators—the most common aerator in large-scale pond aquaculture—are often used to circulate pond water, although paddlewheel aerators are usually designed for good oxygen transfer efficiency rather than for high mixing efficiency. However, oxygen transfer and water flow are related variables for surface aerators because moving large volumes of water through the whitewater shear zone is necessary for high oxygen transfer rates. Paddlewheel aerators operated continuously, particularly if multiple aerators are placed in strategic locations, can keep a pond well mixed (Fig. 12.7).

Low-speed paddlewheels are more efficient mixing devices than paddlewheel aerators because energy is not used shear water into fine droplets and throw them through the air. Low-speed paddlewheels are efficient mixers for shallow basins because they move large water volumes at low velocity against a very low head. They are critical components of partitioned pond systems (Chapter 24) where they are used to pump water from a shallow pond through high-density fish culture raceways.

**Fig. 12.7.** Aerators used to aerate and circulate water in marine shrimp ponds. Photo credit: Marcos Kroupa, Aeration Industries International.

Various horizontal, axial-flow circulators have been used in aquaculture ponds (Fig. 12.8).[7,8] Water currents are generated by large-diameter impellers attached to a shaft inside a cylindrical housing. Other designs omit the housing and use impellers attached to the shaft of a submersible motor.

## Practical Considerations

The potential benefits of mixing are realized only if most of the pond water volume is mixed. Mixing a small area near the device does little good in a large pond. Complete mixing is easy in small ponds (<0.2 ha), where one or two, small (1-2 kW) vertical axial-flow or paddlewheel aerators can quickly mix the entire pond volume. Complete mixing of large ponds is difficult because currents emanating from a single point tend to become short-circuited in shallow ponds as outflows are redirected back towards the mixing device. The solution is to use multiple mixing devices in large ponds (Fig. 12.7). Another approach to increasing mixing efficiency is to abandon attempts to artificially mix traditional ponds and construct new systems with baffles to prevent short-circuited flows. This is the approach used in partitioned aquaculture system (Chapter 24).

Optimum timing and duration of mixing depends on the cultured species, pond size and depth, and the goal of mixing. Continuous mixing is standard practice in freshwater prawn and marine shrimp farming where the benefits of providing oxygen to a bottom-dwelling animal are obvious.[9,10] When properly implemented, water circulation will also improve sediment quality and control deposition of soft sediments that interfere with shrimp culture.[11,12]

In contrast to shrimp and prawn culture, most fish culture ponds are mixed intermittently, if at all. If the goal is to conserve dissolved oxygen produced in photosynthesis during the day and increase the total mass of dissolved oxygen in the

**Fig. 12.8.** Floating horizontal, axial-flow turbine water circulator.

pond, mixing is most effective when initiated before strong thermal gradients and supersaturated dissolved oxygen conditions develop,[13] and then continued for 6-8 hours through midday when conditions are best for photosynthesis. By preventing stratified conditions during the hottest part of the day, midday mixing reduces the probability of turnovers and catastrophic dissolved oxygen depletions in deeper ponds.

Mixing aquaculture ponds nearly always improves water quality and reduces reliance on nighttime aeration. Although mixing intensive shrimp ponds has proven economic benefits and is standard commercial practice, the benefits of mixing fish ponds are less clear. In one study, water was mixed in replicate 1-m-deep, 1.62-ha channel catfish ponds with 2.24-kW horizontal, axial-flow water circulators.[14] One circulator was positioned in a corner of each pond and discharge was directed along the long axis to establish a gyre within the pond. Circulators were operated approximately 6 hours each day from about 0900 to 1500 hours during the summers of 2 years. Aeration with paddlewheel aerators was used whenever dissolved oxygen concentrations were below 2 to 3 mg/L (usually at night). Relative to ponds without circulators, midday water temperatures and dissolved oxygen concentrations varied little with depth in mixed ponds. Most important, circulators reduced the need for nighttime aeration by a factor of 0.58. No other effects on water quality were noted. The reduced requirement for paddlewheel aeration in mixed ponds suggests that more dissolved oxygen was available to fish during nighttime hours than in un-mixed ponds and that fish were exposed to stressfully low dissolved oxygen levels at nighttime for less time in mixed ponds. Nevertheless, fish production and feed conversion ratio were not improved in ponds with circulators. Also, energy savings for reduced aeration in ponds with circulators were approximately offset by the energy cost of circulator operation.

Overall, it appears that water mixing to prevent strong gradients of temperature and dissolved oxygen is beneficial, but cost-effectiveness in ponds used to raise hardy warmwater fish (such as catfish, tilapia, and carps) is unclear. Future work should examine the effects of mixing on variables other than oxygen budgets. Improved processing of waste nitrogen and organic matter and improvements in fish flavor quality related to effects of mixing on phytoplankton community composition could dramatically improve the economic benefits of artificial pond mixing.

# References

1. Avnimelech, Y. and G. Ritvo. 2003. Shrimp and fish pond soils: processes and management. Aquaculture 220:549-567.
2. Gachter, R. and B. Wehrli. 1998. Ten years of artificial mixing and oxygenation: no effect on internal phosphorus loading of two eutrophic lakes. Environmental Science and Technology 32:3659-3665.
3. Paerl, H. W. and C. S. Tucker. 1995. Ecology of blue-green algae in aquaculture ponds. Journal of the World Aquaculture Society 26:109-131.
4. Hudnell, H. K., C. Jones, B. Labisi, V. Lucero, D. Hill, and J. Eilers. 2010. Freshwater harmful algal blooms (FHAB) suppression with solar powered circulation (SPC). Harmful Algae 9:208-217.

5. Schladow, S. G. 1993. Lake destratification by bubble-plume systems: design methodology. Journal of Hydraulic Engineering 119:350-368.
6. Quintero, J. E. and J. E. Garten. 1973. A low-energy lake destratifier. Transactions of the American Society of Agricultural Engineers 16:973-978.
7. Fast, A. W., D. K. Barclay, and G. Akiyama. 1983. Artificial circulation of Hawaiian prawn ponds. University of Hawaii Sea Grant Report IMIH-SEAGrant-CR-84-01, University of Hawaii, Honolulu, HI.
8. Howerton, R. D., C. E. Boyd, and B. J. Watten. 1993. Design and performance of a horizontal, axial-flow water circulator. Journal of Applied Aquaculture 3:163-183.
9. Garcia, A. and D. E. Brune. 1991. Transport limitation of oxygen in shrimp culture ponds. Aquacultural Engineering 10:269-279.
10. Rogers, G. L. and A. W. Fast. 1988. Potential benefits of low energy water circulation in Hawaiian prawn ponds. Aquacultural Engineering 7:155-165.
11. Avnimelech, Y. and G. Ritvo. 2001. Aeration, mixing, and sludge control in shrimp ponds. Global Aquaculture Advocate 4(3):51-53.
12. Boyd, C. E. 1992. Shrimp pond bottom soil and sediment management, pages 166-181. In J. Wyban (editor), *Proceedings of the Special Session on Shrimp Farming*. World Aquaculture Society, Baton Rouge, LA.
13. Szyper, J. P. 1996. Comparison of three mixing devices in earthen culture ponds of four different surface areas. Aquacultural Engineering 15:381-396.
14. Tucker, C. S. and J. A. Steeby. 1995. Daytime mechanical water circulation of channel catfish ponds. Aquacultural Engineering 14:15-28.

# Chapter 13

# Dissolved Oxygen and Mechanical Aeration

## Introduction

Dissolved oxygen is a critical variable in aquaculture systems because of its essential roles in respiration of culture animals and in oxidizing wastes. It also is important in water quality dynamics: when dissolved oxygen concentrations fall to low levels, reduced, potentially toxic microbial metabolites may enter the water column from sediment. Ponds in which fish production depends upon natural fertility usually have adequate dissolved oxygen from natural sources. Fertilized ponds experience low dissolved oxygen concentration in response to dense phytoplankton blooms, cloudy weather, sudden thermal destratification, and massive phytoplankton die-offs—problems caused by excessive fertilization. Feeding increases biomass of culture animals and the amount of waste. Mechanical aeration can provide additional dissolved oxygen to oxidize the feeding waste and prevent stressfully low dissolved oxygen levels.

This chapter presents basic principles of dissolved oxygen dynamics in aquaculture systems, discusses effects of dissolved oxytgen on culture animals, and provides information on mechanical aeration.

## Solubility of Oxygen

The atmosphere contains 20.946% oxygen. Standard atmospheric pressure is 760 mm Hg at sea level, and the partial pressure of oxygen is 159.2 mm (760 mm × 0.20946). Actual atmospheric pressure at a location may be measured with a barometer; it also can be estimated from elevation:

$$\log_{10} BP = 2.880814 - \frac{H}{19,748.2} \tag{13.1}$$

where BP = barometric pressure ( mm Hg); H = elevation above mean sea level (m).

Oxygen pressure in air forces oxygen molecules into water until the pressure of oxygen in water and air are equal. Water is said to be *saturated* with dissolved oxygen when this state is attained. Wind mixing accelerates oxygen-transfer to water bodies by mixing surface water with the water mass to prevent saturation of the surface layer from blocking oxygen-transfer. Turbulence caused by currents, water flowing over rocks and other irregular surfaces, and falling water favor oxygen exchange between air and water.

The amount of molecular oxygen in water usually is expressed in milligrams per liter instead of pressure units. The dissolved oxygen concentration at saturation in surface water in contact with moist air at 760 mm Hg (Table 13.1) decreases with both increasing

**Table 13.1.** The solubility of oxygen (mg/L) in water at different temperatures and salinities from moist air with pressure of 760 mm Hg.[1]

| Temp. (°C) | Salinity, parts per thousand (ppt) | | | | | | | | |
|---|---|---|---|---|---|---|---|---|---|
| | 0 | 5 | 10 | 15 | 20 | 25 | 30 | 35 | 40 |
| 0 | 14.60 | 14.11 | 13.64 | 13.18 | 12.74 | 12.31 | 11.90 | 11.50 | 11.11 |
| 1 | 14.20 | 13.73 | 13.27 | 12.83 | 12.40 | 11.98 | 11.59 | 11.20 | 10.83 |
| 2 | 13.81 | 13.36 | 12.91 | 12.49 | 12.07 | 11.67 | 11.29 | 10.91 | 10.55 |
| 3 | 13.44 | 13.00 | 12.58 | 12.16 | 11.76 | 11.38 | 11.00 | 10.64 | 10.29 |
| 4 | 13.09 | 12.67 | 12.25 | 11.85 | 11.47 | 11.09 | 10.73 | 10.38 | 10.04 |
| 5 | 12.76 | 12.34 | 11.94 | 11.56 | 11.18 | 10.82 | 10.47 | 10.13 | 9.80 |
| 6 | 12.44 | 12.04 | 11.65 | 11.27 | 10.91 | 10.56 | 10.22 | 9.89 | 9.57 |
| 7 | 12.13 | 11.74 | 11.37 | 11.00 | 10.65 | 10.31 | 9.98 | 9.66 | 9.35 |
| 8 | 11.83 | 11.46 | 11.09 | 10.74 | 10.40 | 10.07 | 9.75 | 9.44 | 9.14 |
| 9 | 11.55 | 11.19 | 10.83 | 10.49 | 10.16 | 9.84 | 9.53 | 9.23 | 8.94 |
| 10 | 11.28 | 10.93 | 10.58 | 10.25 | 9.93 | 9.62 | 9.32 | 9.03 | 8.75 |
| 11 | 11.02 | 10.67 | 10.34 | 10.02 | 9.71 | 9.41 | 9.12 | 8.84 | 8.56 |
| 12 | 10.77 | 10.43 | 10.11 | 9.80 | 9.50 | 9.21 | 8.92 | 8.65 | 8.38 |
| 13 | 10.53 | 10.20 | 9.89 | 9.59 | 9.30 | 9.01 | 8.74 | 8.47 | 8.21 |
| 14 | 10.29 | 9.98 | 9.68 | 9.38 | 9.10 | 8.82 | 8.56 | 8.30 | 8.04 |
| 15 | 10.07 | 9.77 | 9.47 | 9.19 | 8.91 | 8.64 | 8.38 | 8.13 | 7.88 |
| 16 | 9.86 | 9.56 | 9.28 | 9.00 | 8.73 | 8.47 | 8.21 | 7.97 | 7.73 |
| 17 | 9.65 | 9.36 | 9.09 | 8.82 | 8.55 | 8.30 | 8.05 | 7.81 | 7.58 |
| 18 | 9.45 | 9.17 | 8.90 | 8.64 | 8.39 | 8.14 | 7.90 | 7.66 | 7.44 |
| 19 | 9.26 | 8.99 | 8.73 | 8.47 | 8.22 | 7.98 | 7.75 | 7.52 | 7.30 |
| 20 | 9.08 | 8.81 | 8.56 | 8.31 | 8.07 | 7.83 | 7.60 | 7.38 | 7.17 |
| 21 | 8.90 | 8.64 | 8.39 | 8.15 | 7.91 | 7.69 | 7.46 | 7.25 | 7.04 |
| 22 | 8.73 | 8.48 | 8.23 | 8.00 | 7.77 | 7.55 | 7.33 | 7.12 | 6.91 |
| 23 | 8.56 | 8.32 | 8.08 | 7.85 | 7.63 | 7.41 | 7.20 | 6.99 | 6.79 |
| 24 | 8.40 | 8.16 | 7.93 | 7.71 | 7.49 | 7.28 | 7.07 | 6.87 | 6.68 |
| 25 | 8.24 | 8.01 | 7.79 | 7.57 | 7.36 | 7.15 | 6.95 | 6.75 | 6.57 |
| 26 | 8.09 | 7.87 | 7.65 | 7.44 | 7.23 | 7.03 | 6.83 | 6.64 | 6.46 |
| 27 | 7.95 | 7.73 | 7.52 | 7.31 | 7.11 | 6.91 | 6.72 | 6.53 | 6.35 |
| 28 | 7.81 | 7.59 | 7.39 | 7.18 | 6.98 | 6.79 | 6.61 | 6.42 | 6.25 |
| 29 | 7.67 | 7.46 | 7.26 | 7.06 | 6.87 | 6.68 | 6.50 | 6.32 | 6.15 |
| 30 | 7.54 | 7.34 | 7.14 | 6.94 | 6.76 | 6.57 | 6.39 | 6.22 | 6.05 |
| 31 | 7.41 | 7.21 | 7.02 | 6.83 | 6.65 | 6.47 | 6.29 | 6.12 | 5.96 |
| 32 | 7.29 | 7.09 | 6.90 | 6.72 | 6.54 | 6.36 | 6.19 | 6.03 | 5.87 |
| 33 | 7.17 | 6.98 | 6.79 | 6.61 | 6.44 | 6.27 | 6.10 | 5.94 | 5.78 |
| 34 | 7.05 | 6.86 | 6.68 | 6.51 | 6.34 | 6.17 | 6.01 | 5.85 | 5.69 |
| 35 | 6.94 | 6.75 | 6.58 | 6.41 | 6.24 | 6.07 | 5.92 | 5.76 | 5.61 |
| 36 | 6.82 | 6.65 | 6.47 | 6.31 | 6.14 | 5.98 | 5.83 | 5.68 | 5.53 |
| 37 | 6.72 | 6.54 | 6.37 | 6.21 | 6.05 | 5.89 | 5.74 | 5.59 | 5.45 |
| 38 | 6.61 | 6.44 | 6.28 | 6.12 | 5.96 | 5.81 | 5.66 | 5.51 | 5.37 |
| 39 | 6.51 | 6.34 | 6.18 | 6.03 | 5.87 | 5.72 | 5.58 | 5.44 | 5.30 |
| 40 | 6.41 | 6.25 | 6.09 | 5.94 | 5.79 | 5.64 | 5.50 | 5.36 | 5.22 |

water temperature and salinity.[2] Hydrostatic pressure is the weight of a water column pressing down on a point (Fig. 13.1). Hydrostatic pressure adds to atmospheric pressure resulting in a progressively higher dissolved oxygen concentration at saturation with increasing depth. Total pressure is calculated from barometric pressure, the specific weight of water (Table 13.2), and water depth:

$$TP = BP + [(\rho g)(Z)] \qquad (13.2)$$

where TP = total pressure (mm Hg); $\rho g$ = the specific weight of water (mm Hg/m) and is the product of water's density ($\rho$) and acceleration due to gravity (g); Z = water depth (m).

The dissolved oxygen concentration at saturation for a particular sampling station is estimated by adjusting tabular values of dissolved oxygen concentration (Table 13.1) for existing water temperature and total pressure:

$$DO_s = DO_t \left(\frac{TP}{760}\right) \qquad (13.3)$$

where $DO_t$ = tabular dissolved oxygen concentration from Table 13.1.

Aquatic organisms respond to the pressure of molecular oxygen, a variable directly proportional to percentage saturation of water with molecular oxygen:

$$PS = \left(\frac{DO_m}{DO_s}\right) = 100 \qquad (13.4)$$

where PS = percentage saturation with dissolved oxygen; $DO_m$ = measured dissolved oxygen concentration (mg/L); $DO_s$ = dissolved oxygen concentration at saturation (mg/L). The dissolved oxygen concentration may be equal to, less than, or greater than saturation. Water with a greater dissolved oxygen concentration than it should have at saturation is said to be supersaturated. It is not uncommon for surface waters of ponds to have dissolved oxygen saturation above 200% in the afternoon.[3]

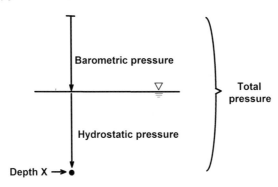

**Fig. 13.1** Illustration of total pressure below the water surface.

**Table 13.2.** Specific weight of water (mm Hg/m depth) as a function of temperature and salinity.[1]

| Temp. (°C) | Salinity, parts per thousand (ppt) | | | | | | | | |
|---|---|---|---|---|---|---|---|---|---|
| | 0 | 5 | 10 | 15 | 20 | 25 | 30 | 35 | 40 |
| 0 | 73.54 | 73.84 | 74.14 | 74.44 | 74.73 | 75.03 | 75.33 | 75.62 | 75.92 |
| 5 | 73.55 | 73.85 | 74.14 | 74.43 | 74.72 | 75.01 | 75.30 | 75.59 | 75.88 |
| 10 | 73.53 | 73.82 | 74.11 | 74.39 | 74.68 | 74.97 | 75.25 | 75.54 | 75.83 |
| 15 | 73.49 | 73.77 | 74.05 | 74.34 | 74.62 | 74.90 | 75.18 | 75.47 | 75.75 |
| 20 | 73.42 | 73.70 | 73.98 | 74.26 | 74.54 | 74.82 | 75.10 | 75.38 | 75.66 |
| 25 | 73.34 | 73.62 | 73.89 | 74.17 | 74.44 | 74.72 | 75.00 | 75.27 | 75.55 |
| 30 | 73.24 | 73.51 | 73.78 | 74.06 | 74.33 | 74.60 | 74.88 | 75.15 | 75.43 |
| 35 | 73.12 | 73.39 | 73.66 | 73.93 | 74.20 | 74.48 | 74.75 | 75.02 | 75.30 |
| 40 | 72.98 | 73.25 | 73.52 | 73.79 | 74.06 | 74.34 | 74.61 | 74.88 | 75.15 |

Calculations of barometric pressure, dissolved oxygen concentration in water at saturation, total pressure below the water surface, and percentage saturation are illustrated in Example 13.1.

# Dissolved Oxygen Concentration

## *Budgets*

Dissolved oxygen concentration at a particular place and time is the net result of several biological, physical, and chemical processes that add or remove oxygen from water. Oxygen is added in photosynthesis, inflow of water with more dissolved oxygen than the receiving water, movement of oxygen from air to water (*aeration*), and addition of pure oxygen (*oxygenation*). Oxygen is removed in movement of oxygen from water to air (*degassing*) and in respiration by animals, plants, and bacteria. Note that movement of oxygen between water and air can be either a gain or loss. When water is undersaturated with dissolved oxygen, it is aerated as oxygen enters from air. Aeration may be natural, such as water falling over a waterfall, or induced by mechanical devices. When water is supersaturated, oxygen is degassed from water to the air. Dissolved oxygen budgets can be used to model concentrations and, in some systems, to calculate allowable animal densities or design aeration systems.

The dissolved oxygen budget for flow-through aquaculture systems is simple. Significant oxygen sources are dissolved oxygen in the water inflow and oxygen added in aeration or oxygenation. Losses are animal respiration and oxygen lost in water outflow. Water temperature is relatively constant (at least in the short run) in most flow-through systems and these processes can be estimated with good accuracy. In fact, dissolved oxygen budgets are used to design flow-through systems (Chapter 26).

Oxygen budgets in recirculating aquaculture system are more complex than for flow-through systems because there are additional oxygen loss processes. Additional losses include oxygen used by nitrifying bacteria to convert ammonia to nitrate and oxygen used by bacteria during decomposition of fecal matter and uneaten feed. The system is still rather simple and constant water temperature allows accurate estimation of all processes.

Like flow-through systems, recirculating aquaculture systems can be designed to ensure adequate dissolved oxygen for culture (Chapter 28).

---

**Example 13.1**
**Dissolved Oxygen (DO) Calculations**

A freshwater pond located at an elevation of 730 m has water temperature of 22°C and a DO concentration of 6.50 mg/L throughout the water column. The approximate barometric pressure will be estimated, and the DO concentration at saturation will be calculated for surface and 1.5 m depth, and the percentage saturation computed for both depths.

Calculate BP with Equation 13.1:

$$\log_{10} BP = 2.880814 - \frac{730}{19{,}748.2} = 2.843849$$

BP = 698 mm Hg.

Calculate $DO_s$ for surface water using Equation 13.4:

$$DO_s = 8.73 \text{ mg/L} \times \frac{698 \text{ mm}}{760 \text{ mm}} = 8.02 \text{ mg/L}.$$

Calculate $DO_s$ at water at 1.5 m using data from Table 13.2 and Equation 13.4:

$$TP = 698 \text{ mm} + (73.39 \text{ mm/m})(1.5 \text{ m}) = 808.1 \text{ mm}$$

$$DO_s = 8.73 \text{ mg/L} \times \frac{808.1 \text{ mm}}{760 \text{ mm}} = 9.28 \text{ mg/L}.$$

Calculate $PS_{DO}$ with Equation 13.3:

Surface water:

$$PS_{DO} = \frac{6.50 \text{ mg/L}}{8.02 \text{ mg/L}} \times 100 = 81.0\%$$

Water at 1.5 m depth:

$$PS_{DO} = \frac{6.50 \text{ mg/L}}{9.28 \text{ mg/L}} \times 100 = 70.0\%.$$

---

Oxygen budgets for ponds are much more complex than for other aquaculture systems. Dissolved oxygen concentrations at any given time depend on relative rates of photosynthesis, mechanical aeration, cultured animal respiration, plankton respiration, respiration of organisms in sediment, and natural air-water gas transfer (which may be either gains or losses in the budget). Further complications arise because processes are affected by external factors, such as sunlight, water temperature, wind, and others (Table 13.3). These external factors vary daily and seasonally, and are difficult to predict and impossible to control. The complexity and unpredictability of processes affecting dissolved oxygen concentrations makes oxygen management much more difficult in ponds than in other aquaculture systems.

## Dissolved Oxygen in Ponds

The atmosphere is a vast reservoir of oxygen, but diffusion of oxygen into water is a relatively slow process—usually providing less oxygen than the amount used in respiration of the culture animals. Phytoplankton photosynthesis is a major source of dissolved oxygen during daytime in ponds and other water bodies; however, much

**Table 13.3.** Component processes in pond dissolved oxygen budgets and factors affecting the rate of each process.

| Component | Approximate magnitude (mg $O_2$/L per day) | Factors affecting process rate |
|---|---|---|
| *Oxygen sources* | | |
| Photosynthesis | 0-40 | Phytoplankton biomass |
| | | Sunlight |
| | | Water temperature |
| | | Non-algal turbidity (clay, etc.) |
| | | Phytoplankton species |
| Air-water gas exchange | 0-6 | Wind speed |
| | | Degree of dissolved oxygen undersaturation |
| Aeration | 0-20 | Aerator characteristics |
| *Oxygen losses* | | |
| Plankton respiration | 0-40 | Plankton biomass |
| | | Water temperature |
| | | Plankton species |
| Fish respiration | 0-5 | Fish biomass |
| | | Fish size |
| | | Water temperature |
| Sediment oxygen uptake | 0-4 | Benthos density |
| | | Organic matter content |
| | | Water temperature |
| | | Sediment chemistry |
| Air-water gas exchange | 0-6 | Wind speed |
| | | Degree of dissolved oxygen supersaturation |

oxygen released by photosynthesis is consumed in phytoplankton respiration. Other aerobic organisms in ponds also use dissolved oxygen in respiration. Photosynthesis normally exceeds respiration during most of the day, and dissolved oxygen concentration increases to a maximum by early afternoon (Fig. 13.2). Photosynthesis stops at night, and respiration causes dissolved oxygen concentration to fall—the lowest level is usually about dawn. Maximum daytime dissolved oxygen concentration increases and minimum nighttime dissolved oxygen concentration decreases with greater abundance of phytoplankton (Fig. 13.2).

Metabolic wastes resulting from feed inputs increase the availability of nitrogen, phosphorus, carbon dioxide, and other nutrients that stimulate phytoplankton growth. Increased phytoplankton abundance increases both the amounts of oxygen produced in photosynthesis and used in respiration—gains and losses of oxygen by the two processes eventually cancel each other. Bacterial oxidation of organic wastes and ammonia from feed impose an oxygen demand that increases as feeding rate increases (Chapter 11). Nighttime dissolved oxygen concentrations may become undesirably low in un-aerated ponds at feeding rates above 30 to 40 kg/ha per day.[4]

Low nighttime dissolved oxygen concentration is a common problem in ponds with dense phytoplankton blooms, especially when oxygen production by photosynthesis is limited by cloudy weather. Other phenomena causing low dissolved oxygen concentration are sudden massive phytoplankton die-offs, sudden thermal destratification, and algicide treatment. Phytoplankton die-offs usually occur in ponds with dense blooms of blue-green algae.[5] During calm, clear weather, algae float to the surface to form a

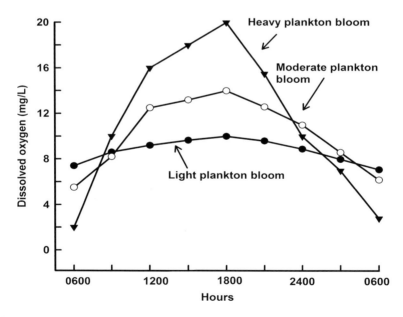

**Fig. 13.2.** Daily pattern of dissolved oxygen (DO) concentration in ponds with low moderate, and high phytoplankton abundance.

scum. Algae in surface scums sometimes are killed by excessive light. Decomposition of dead algae while photosynthesis is limited may deplete dissolved oxygen. Un-aerated ponds with maximum depths of about 3 m or more stratify thermally (Chapter 12). Heavy rains or strong winds may cause sudden destratification and mix anaerobic, hypolimnetic water of high oxygen demand with epilimnetic water resulting in low dissolved oxygen concentration. Decomposition of dead algae following algicide or herbicide application also can depress dissolved oxygen concentration.

## Dissolved Oxygen Requirements of Culture Animals

The amount of oxygen used by fish and other aquatic animals varies with species, size, water temperature, time since feeding, degree of activity, and other factors. Small individuals of a particular species consume more oxygen than larger ones (Table 13.4).[6] Oxygen consumption rate rises with increasing water temperature—it usually doubles with a 10°C increase within the range of dissolved oxygen tolerance of the culture animals. Active animals use more oxygen than resting ones. A study showed that tilapia respiration doubled when water velocity increased from 30 to 60 cm/second causing them to expend more energy to maintain their position.[7] Channel catfish consumed 680 mg $O_2$/kg fish/hour one hour after feeding but only 380 mg $O_2$/kg fish/hour following overnight fasting.[6] Lean fish consumed less oxygen than fat fish.[8]

Many studies have investigated fish respiration rates and made equations for estimating oxygen consumption by individual species. Fish and shrimp in aquaculture grow-out systems normally use 300 to 500 mg $O_2$/kg body weight/hour. A fish biomass of 5,000 kg might consume about 24 kg $O_2$/day, which is equivalent to 2.4 mg/L of dissolved oxygen per day in a 1-ha pond of 1-m average depth. Respiration by phytoplankton and bacteria in ponds may consume several times more oxygen than the culture animals.

**Table 13.4.** Respiration of channel catfish of different body weights under identical environmental conditions.[6]

| Fish size (g) | Respiration rate (mg $O_2$/kg fish/hr) |
|---|---|
| 5 | 1,225 |
| 10 | 1,050 |
| 50 | 750 |
| 100 | 625 |
| 500 | 480 |
| 1,000 | 340 |

Most aquatic animals are healthiest and grow fastest when dissolved oxygen levels are near air-saturation.[9] As dissolved oxygen concentrations fall below 60 to 70% of saturation (4.7-5.5 mg/L at 28°C and 6.0-7.0 mg/L at 15°C), animals compensate by changing behavior and physiology. These adaptations and responses allow healthy animals to survive for long periods even when dissolved oxygen levels are as low as 20 to 30% of saturation, but they eat less food, grow more slowly, and may be more susceptible to certain infectious diseases.[10,11] At 20 to 30% of saturation, dissolved oxygen concentrations are 1.5-2.3 mg/L at 28°C and 2.0-3.0 mg/L at 15°C. At some point (5 to 20% of saturation depending on species), compensatory responses are no longer sufficient and animals swim to the surface or crawl to the water's edge in an attempt to exploit oxygen in the surface film. Dissolved oxygen is near the lethal level when animals are seen at the surface.

The relationship between early morning dissolved oxygen concentration and feeding conversion ratio in pond experiments with channel catfish (Fig. 13.3) suggests that maintaining minimum, dissolved oxygen concentration between 3 and 4 mg/L should allow a feed conversion ratio of 2 or better.[4,12,13] In these experiments, feed was applied according to a feeding curve; no attempt was made to ascertain that fish consumed all the feed nor were uneaten feed pellets removed. The relationship between dissolved oxygen concentration and feed conversion ratio possibly was an artifact of overfeeding. Another study, however, suggested that a similar relationship existed in shrimp *Litopenaeus vannamei* ponds where feed was applied more conservatively (Table 13.3).[14]

Oxygen-transport proteins in blood (hemoglobin for fish; hemocyanin for crustaceans) leaving the gills are very nearly 100% saturated with oxygen when dissolved oxygen concentrations are near air-saturation. Higher dissolved oxygen levels therefore provide little benefit to fish or crustaceans. Extremely high dissolved oxygen concentrations (200 to 300% of saturation) can be harmful by causing gas bubble disease (Chapter 14).

In summary, aquatic animals use food more efficiently, grow faster, are less susceptible to disease, and survive better when dissolved oxygen concentration is adequate. Moreover, an abundant supply of dissolved oxygen promotes good water quality by favoring efficient oxidation of organic wastes and toxic microbial metabolites such as ammonia, ferrous iron, and hydrogen sulfide. In aquaculture systems with adequate dissolved oxygen concentration, most other water quality variables usually remain within a desirable concentration range.

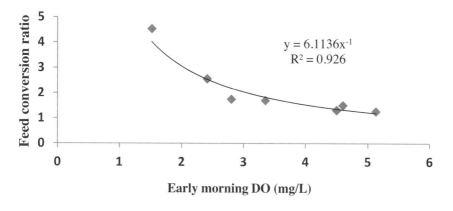

$$y = 6.1136x^{-1}$$
$$R^2 = 0.926$$

**Fig. 13.3.** Relationship between minimum daily dissolved oxygen (DO) concentration and FCR in channel catfish ponds.[4,12,13]

Managers should strive to maintain dissolved oxygen concentrations above 3 mg/L in warmwater culture systems and above 5 mg/L in coolwater and coldwater cultures. Dissolved oxygen management consists mainly of the following: select a reasonable stock density; install sufficient aeration to supply adequate dissolved oxygen concentration for the maximum expected feeding rate; select a good quality feed and apply it conservatively to avoid feeding more than fish will eat; monitor dissolved oxygen concentration, especially in early morning hours to assure that aeration is effective; maintain emergency aeration equipment for use if necessary. The effects of aeration on dissolved oxygen concentration in ponds are illustrated in Fig. 13.4.

## Dissolved Oxygen and Water Quality

Dissolved oxygen is so critical to culture species directly that we often forget its other important effects on water quality. Dissolved oxygen is essential for maintaining aerobic conditions at the bottom soil-water interface to prevent reduced substances (such as hydrogen sulfide, nitrite, ferrous iron, and reduced organic compounds) from entering the pond water. Aerobic sediment also is more effective than anaerobic sediment in removing phosphate from pond water. Although it is well known that oxygen is needed for aerobic, microbial degradation of organic matter, it is also required for nitrification of ammonia to nitrate. Ammonia will rapidly accumulate in ponds with chronically low dissolved oxygen concentration. Other microbial processes such as oxidation of sulfide, ferrous iron, and nitrite also require dissolved oxygen. The role of dissolved oxygen in each of the processes mentioned above is discussed in more detail in other chapters.

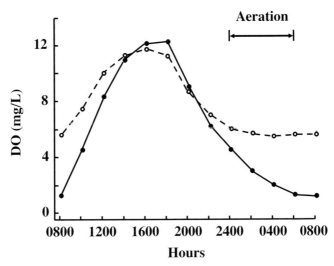

**Fig. 13.4.** Comparison of daily dissolved oxygen (DO) concentration pattern in aerated and un-aerated channel catfish ponds.[13]

Dissolved oxygen is the most critical 'single' variable in pond aquaculture water quality management. As stated in the introductory chapter, if pond managers assure that the dissolved oxygen concentration is satisfactory in aquaculture systems, other water quality problems are much less likely to develop. In extensive and semi-intensive aquaculture, dissolved oxygen management is affected primarily by adjusting stocking rates to levels at which the amount of wastes will not exceed the assimilative capacity of the system. In some cases, water exchange may be used to flush out waste and improve water quality. However, in intensive aquaculture, mechanical aeration is used to control dissolved oxygen concentration and enhance waste assimilation.

## Mechanical Aeration and Oxygenation

Mechanical aerators and oxygenators increase the rate of transfer of oxygen to water. Throughout this book, *aerators* will be defined as devices that either splash water or release fine air bubbles to enlarge the surface area between water and air for oxygen absorption. *Oxygenators* differ from aerators by using purified oxygen gas as the oxygen source rather than air.

Oxygen enters water through the gas-water interface, and the greater the pressure differential between oxygen molecules in the gaseous and aqueous phases, the faster oxygen enters water. The oxygen entry rate becomes slower as dissolved oxygen concentration nears saturation (Fig. 13.5). Aerators are not efficient after water reaches 70 or 80% saturation with oxygen. Aerators do not transfer oxygen to water at 100% saturation, and they strip oxygen from water supersaturated with oxygen.

Good aerators induce water currents that move oxygenated water away from the device, allowing it to be replaced by water of lower dissolved oxygen concentration. This prevents a reduction in aerator efficiency that would occur if dissolved oxygen concentration increased in water entering the aerator. It also mixes oxygenated water with the water mass, which enhances access to added oxygen by culture animals. Moreover, aerator-generated mixing delivers oxygenated water to pond bottoms and avoids anaerobic conditions at the sediment-water interface.

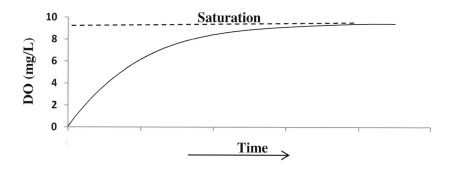

**Fig. 13.5.** Change in dissolved oxygen (DO) concentration with time of aeration.

Oxygenators increase dissolved oxygen concentration above the saturation concentration for water in contact with air. Air contains 20.946% oxygen; water in equilibrium with 100% oxygen has a dissolved oxygen concentration approximately five times higher than water in equilibrium with the atmosphere at the same pressure. Oxygenators usually function to add oxygen to a side stream of water to achieve a dissolved oxygen concentration of 20 to 100 mg/L, or sometimes more. The supersaturated water is blended back into the main stream of water of the culture system to produce a final dissolved oxygen concentration near saturation. Reliable technology for blending oxygen-enriched water with pond water is not available. Oxygenators are used primarily in fish-holding and transport tanks, hatchery tanks, raceways, and other flow-through culture systems.

## Air Contact Aerators

The simplest air-contact aerators are nozzles on ends of pipes to spray water, weirs over which water flows, and stacked screens through which water falls (see Fig. 7.2). Weirs are important in raceways where water flows by gravity from one production unit to the next (see Fig. 26.5). Water often is pumped to higher elevation for discharge onto screens. Well water for hatchery and ponds often is aerated with screens, and nozzles are used to aerate small discharges into hatchery tanks.

The most common mechanical, air-contact aerators are vertical impellers, paddlewheels, propeller-aspirator pumps, and air blowers with diffusers. A *vertical impeller aerator* has a submersible electric motor and impeller that jet water into the air (Fig. 13.6). These aerators usually are 0.5 to 2 hp in size, but much smaller units are available for hatchery tanks, and 5- and 10-hp units are sometimes used in ponds. Small, vertical impeller aerators, because of their light weight and ease with which they can be removed from one pond and installed in another, are widely used in small ponds at hatcheries and research stations. The main disadvantage of these devices is that they establish a zone of water circulation around the aerator and the same water tends to be continuously re-aerated, which reduces aeration efficiency.

**Fig. 13.6.** Vertical impeller aerator.

A *paddlewheel aerator* usually consists of a paddlewheel mounted on a floating frame. The paddlewheel can be driven by an electric motor mounted on the floating frame (Figs. 13.7 and 13.8 Right). It also may be driven by an internal combustion engine or electric motor mounted on the pond bank and attached to the paddlewheel by a drive shaft (Fig. 13.8 Left); this type often is called a 'long-arm' aerator. Paddlewheel aerators range in size from 1 to 15 hp. In Asian shrimp farming, 1- or 2-hp Taiwan-style and long-arm paddlewheel aerators are quite popular, while in channel catfish farming in the southern United States, 10-hp paddlewheel aerators (Fig. 13.8) are the standard aeration unit. Trailer-mounted, tractor-powered aerators (Fig. 13.9) also are used for emergency aeration of ponds.

The *propeller-aspiration-pump* aerator consists of a motor connected to a hollow, slotted, rotating tube with an air diffuser and propeller attached to its distal end. The tube is enclosed in a housing with an opening above the water line. The rapidly rotating propeller reduces pressure inside the housing and atmospheric pressure forces air into it. Air exits the diffuser in fine bubbles that are mixed into the water by the propeller (Fig. 13.10). These aerators are manufactured in sizes of 0.5 to 90 hp, but the most common sizes for aquaculture are 1 to 5 hp. These aerators direct water current towards the pond bottom, and they sometimes are installed in combination with paddlewheel aerators to enhance mixing.

**Fig. 13.7** Paddlewheel aerator of type used in channel catfish farming in the United States.

**Fig. 13.8.** Long-arm paddlewheel aerators: Left – long-arm aerator; Right – Taiwan paddlewheel aerator.

**Fig. 13.9.** Tractor-powered, paddlewheel aerator for emergency aeration.

**Fig. 13.10.** Propeller-aspirator-pump aerator.

A *diffused-air aerator* has a high volume, low pressure air blower connected by tubing to an air diffuser (Fig. 13.11). The rising air bubbles effect aeration, and they also mix the water column. One air blower can service many holding or grow-out units; thus, diffused-air aeration is used widely in fish hauling and holding tanks, hatcheries, and complexes of small ponds. The main disadvantage of these aerators in ponds is that bubbles rise to the surface too quickly for efficient oxygen transfer. Although this problem can be overcome by using many diffusers and releasing air slowly, such modification greatly increases aerator cost.[15] Moreover, diffusers and air lines become encrusted with fouling organisms, and the system cannot be easily removed to facilitate harvest. Although significant improvements have been made in diffuser design, diffused-air aeration systems are not as suitable as paddlewheel and propeller-aspirator-pump aerators for production ponds.

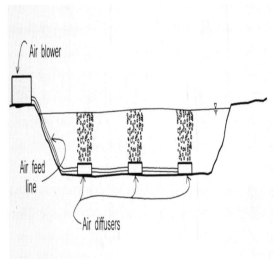 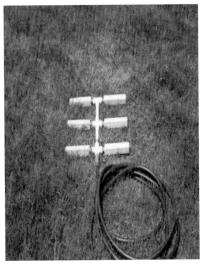

**Fig. 13.11.** Illustration of a diffused-air aeration system (left) and one type of diffuser with air-feeder line attached (right).

## *Oxygenators*

Pure oxygen can be purchased as bulk liquid or gas, or it can be produced on-site at the facility using *pressure-swing adsorption* (PSA) equipment.[16] Pressure swing adsorption uses adsorbent zeolites that attract and adsorb nitrogen more strongly than oxygen. As air passes through the zeolite bed under pressure, most of the nitrogen is adsorbed to zeolite and the gas coming out of the unit is enriched with oxygen. When the zeolite bed becomes nearly saturated with nitrogen, it is regenerated by reducing the pressure, thereby releasing the adsorbed nitrogen. The unit is then re-pressurized for another cycle of producing oxygen-enriched air. Choice of oxygen source is a compromise among economics, logistics (such as access to commercial sources of oxygen), and reliability. Pressure-swing adsorption equipment is initially expensive but may be a less expensive oxygen source in the long run. On the other hand, PSA equipment is, like any other equipment, subject to mechanical failure. Most recirculating aquaculture facilities use liquid oxygen because capital costs and risks are lower.

Many types of oxygenators have been developed for aquaculture, including various diffusers, aspirators, packed columns, U-tubes, oxygenation cones, and multistage low-head oxygenators.[16] Selection is based on effectiveness, cost, reliability, maintenance requirements, and the design and arrangement of other system components. Adding pure oxygen to water displaces other gases, principally nitrogen—the most abundant gas in water. Unless the displaced nitrogen is vented from the oxygenation unit, it may remain in solution, causing high total gas pressures that may cause gas bubble disease (Chapter 14).

A common oxygenator is the *packed-column absorber*.[16] It is a vertical column or tower filled with a high surface area medium—usually plastic spheres or cylinders with complex, open shapes. Water distributed over the top of the column flows downward through the packing. Oxygen gas released into the bottom of the column flows upward through the packing (see Fig. 13.12). The efficiency of oxygen absorption is 50 to 90%, and water discharged from packed columns usually contains 20 to 30 mg/L dissolved oxygen.

*U-tubes* consist of U-shaped conduit or a pair of annular pipes (a pipe within a pipe; Fig. 13.13) buried in the ground 10 to 50 meters. Oxygen is bubbled into water entering the U-tube and travels with the flow to the bottom of the device where gas absorption is maximized by additional pressure from the water column (hydrostatic pressure). At the bottom of the unit, water moves upward and exits the unit. Effluent dissolved oxygen concentration depends on conduit depth, water temperature, and system design. Typical oxygen absorption efficiencies are 30 to 80%, with efficiencies in the higher range achieved when oxygen-rich off-gas is recycled through the unit. Effluent dissolved oxygen concentrations are usually 20 to 40 mg/L. U-tubes have low energy requirements and resist clogging, but are costly and may be difficult to install. Systems may also produce waters with dangerous levels of total gas supersaturation because there is no opportunity for venting of nitrogen gas displaced by supersaturated oxygen when off-gases are recycled.

*Down-flow bubble contactors*, also called Speece cones, consist of an inverted cone-shaped vessel with water and oxygen injected at the top and oxygenated water removed at the bottom (Fig. 13.13). As water and oxygen bubbles move down the cone, the

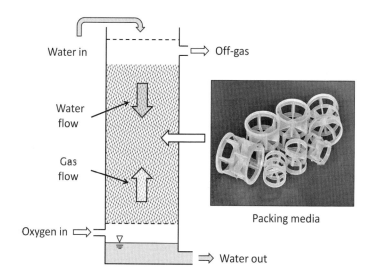

**Fig. 13.12.** A packed column absorber for oxygenation of water. The column is filled with high-surface-are-plastic media (insert) and pure oxygen gas is diffused into the column countercurrent to water flow. Off-gas may be recycled back through the column to increase oxygenation efficiency.

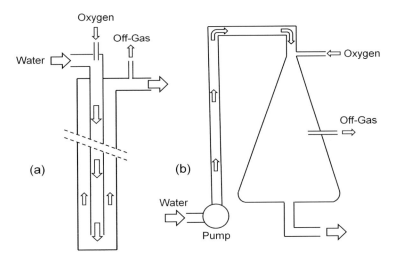

**Fig. 13.13.** (a) U-tube and (b) down-flow bubble contactor (Speece cone) for injecting pure oxygen into water.

downward water velocity decreases due to the increasing cross-sectional area of the cone until it equals the upward velocity of the bubbles. This allows a long contact time between water and oxygen, providing oxygen absorption efficiencies that may approach 100% with effluent dissolved oxygen concentrations of 20 to 40 mg/L. A vent can be installed in the lower half of the cone to remove some of the displaced nitrogen.

*Multistaged low-head oxygenators* (LHO) optimize oxygen absorption efficiency by reusing oxygen through a series of contact chambers.[16] Water is distributed across the top of the unit and cascades through multiple, vertical contact chambers (Fig. 13.14). Pure oxygen gas enters one end and oxygen with off-gases (mostly nitrogen and carbon dioxide) serially pass through each contact chamber before leaving the unit. Oxygen feed-gas is held within the contact chambers by pooled water above the distribution plate and pooled water at the bottom of the unit. Oxygen absorption efficiencies range from 60 to 90% depending on operational characteristics, with effluent dissolved oxygen concentrations 20 to 30 mg/L.

## Aerator Performance

Aerators are tested for oxygen-transfer capacity by deoxygenating water in a tank by adding sodium sulfite and cobalt chloride, and measuring the increase in dissolved oxygen concentration with time during aerator operation. The standard aeration efficiency (SAE) in kilograms of oxygen transferred per kilowatt·hour of aerator operation is estimated by a mathematical technique.[16,17] The SAEs measured for many aquaculture aerators are provided in Table 13.4.[18]

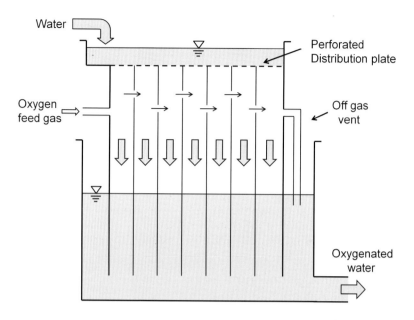

Fig. 13.14. Multistage low-head oxygenator for injecting pure oxygen into water.

**Table 13.4.** Summary of standard aeration efficiencies (SAEs) for electric aerators.[18]

| | SAE (kg O$_2$/kW·hr) | |
| --- | --- | --- |
| | Average | Range |
| Paddlewheel | 2.2 | 1.1-3.0 |
| Propeller-aspirator pump | 1.6 | 1.3-1.8 |
| Vertical pump | 1.4 | 0.7-1.8 |
| Pump sprayer | 1.3 | 0.9-1.9 |
| Diffused air | 0.9 | 0.7-1.2 |

The results of aerator performance tests such as summarized in Table 13.4 were obtained under optimum conditions for oxygen transfer—clean water and dissolved oxygen concentration initially near 0 mg/L. In a pond or other aquaculture production units, the water usually will not be clean and it will contain a modest oxygen concentration. The following equation can be used to adjust SAE values such as those shown in Table 13.4 to actual oxygen transfer efficiencies in ponds.

$$AE = SAE \left[ \frac{DO_{s,p} - DO_m}{DO_{s,20}} \right] (1.024^{t-20})(\alpha) \qquad (13.5)$$

where $DO_{s,p}$ = dissolved oxygen concentration at saturation in the pond (mg/L); $DO_m$ =

measured dissolved oxygen concentration in the pond (mg/L); $DOS_{,20}$ = dissolved oxygen concentration at 20°C (Table 13.1) for the salinity of pond water (mg/L); t = water temperature (°C); α = unitless ratio of oxygen-transfer rate of pond water:oxygen-transfer rate of clean water. An α-value of 0.92 is recommended for general use.[19] Example 13.2 shows how to convert SAE to AE for different water temperatures and dissolved oxygen concentrations.

## Aeration Rate

The SAE normally is given in kilograms of oxygen per kilowatt·hour, but aerator motor power generally is expressed in horsepower. Therefore, the aeration rate will be expressed here in horsepower per hectare.

The aeration rate for ponds usually is based on experience. A 1-hp Taiwan-style paddlewheel aerator is considered adequate for 400-500 kg of shrimp. A shrimp pond with a production goal of 6,000 kg/ha usually has 12 to 15 hp of aeration. Most or all

---

**Example 13.2**
**Aeration Efficiency (AE) Calculations**

An aerator with a standard aeration efficiency (SAE) of 2 kg $O_2$/kW•hr will be operated in a freshwater pond. The AE will be calculated for four combinations of water temperature and dissolved oxygen (DO) concentration using Equation 13.5.

At 22°C and 5 mg/L DO:

$$AE = 2.0 \text{ kg } O_2/\text{kW·hr} \left[ \frac{(8.73 - 5.0) \text{ mg/L}}{9.08 \text{ mg/L}} \right] (1.024^{22-20})(0.92) =$$
$$0.79 \text{ kg } O_2/\text{kW·hr}.$$

At 22°C and 3 mg/L DO:

$$2.0 \text{ kg } O_2/\text{kW·hr} \left[ \frac{(7.54 - 3.0) \text{ mg/L}}{9.08 \text{ mg/L}} \right] (1.024^{22-20})(0.92)$$

$$AE = 0.97 \text{ kg } O_2/\text{kW·hr}.$$

At 30°C and 5 mg/L DO; AE = 0.96 kg $O_2$/kW·hr.

At 30°C and 3 mg/L DO; AE = 1.16 kg O2/kW·hr.

Note: Increasing water temperature and decreasing DO concentration cause in an increase in AE.

aerators are operated day and night, but aerators often are turned off during feeding. Pond waters usually are above saturation with dissolved oxygen during daytime, and operating aerators is probably counterproductive for oxygenation. Shrimp live on pond bottoms, and water circulation to avoid low dissolved oxygen concentration near the sediment-water interface is important. Nevertheless, a portion of the aerators probably could be switched off during the day to save energy.

Channel catfish ponds in the United States usually are aerated at 4 to 8 hp/ha—about 1 hp/1,000 kg fish. There is no agreement on optimum aeration rate, but most farmers try to apply enough aeration to prevent dissolved oxygen concentration from falling below 2 mg/L. The 10-hp paddlewheel aerators usually are operated only at night unless dissolved oxygen concentration is low during daylight hours. Enough aeration should be provided to oxidize waste resulting from feed application. A method for estimating the biochemical oxygen demand (BOD) of feed has been developed[20] and is described in Chapter 11. The feed BOD varies with culture species, feed composition, and FCR, but it usually is about 1.25 kg $O_2$/kg feed. Because aerators will not transfer oxygen effectively during daylight hours, aeration rate should be based on nighttime aeration. But, dissolved oxygen concentration seldom is low enough for effective aeration more than 10 hour/night. An equation for aeration rate is:

$$AR = \frac{(1.25 \text{ kg } O_2/\text{kg feed})(FR)}{(AE)(0.746 \text{ hp/kW})(10 \text{ hr/day})} \tag{13.6}$$

where AR = aeration rate (hp/ha); FR = maximum daily feeding rate (kg/ha); AE = AE for the aerator used and the expected minimum dissolved oxygen concentration and salinity (kg $O_2$/kW·hr). Estimation of aeration rate is illustrated in Example 13.3.

---

**Example 13.3**
**Aeration Rate (AR) Calculation**

Marine shrimp will be cultured in a 1-ha aerated pond where a maximum daily feeding rate of 100 kg/ha is expected. Salinity is 20 ppt and water temperature will average 28°C. The dissolved oxygen concentration should not fall below 3 mg/L. The aeration rate is calculated for aerators with a standard aeration efficiency of 2.0 kg $O_2$/kW·hr.

Calculate AE (Equation 13.5):

$$AE = 2.0 \text{ kg } O_2/\text{kW·hr} \left[\frac{(7.38 - 3.0) \text{ mg/L}}{8.56 \text{ mg/L}}\right] (1.024^{22-20})(0.92) =$$

$$1.14 \text{ kg } O_2/\text{kW·hr}$$

Next, calculate AR (Equation 13.6):

$$AR = \frac{(1.25 \text{ kg } O_2/\text{kW·hr})(100 \text{ kg/ha/day})}{(1.14 \text{ kg } O_2/\text{kW·hr})(0.746 \text{ kW/hp})(10 \text{ hr/day})} \approx 15 \text{ hp/ha}$$

---

In flow-through systems and tanks, waste is regularly removed and there is little biological activity other than fish respiration. Aeration is applied to supply more oxygen to support a greater biomass. Aeration rate in such systems may be estimated as follows:

$$AR_f = \frac{(B)(R)(10^{-6})}{(AE)(0.746 \text{ hp/kW})} \tag{13.7}$$

where $AR_f$ = aeration rate to support fish respiration only (hp); B = fish biomass increase (kg); R = respiration rate (mg $O_2$/kg fish/hr); $10^{-6}$ = kg/mg. A calculation of aeration rate is provided in Example 13.4.

## Aeration Placement

Fish move into zones with high dissolved oxygen concentration, and aerators in fish ponds can be located in one part of the pond (Fig. 13.15a). This reduces the amount of electric cable and number of electrical services to reduce costs.

Shrimp spend most of their time on the pond bottom, and they are not as efficient as fish in finding zones of higher dissolved oxygen concentration. Thus, water circulation is more critical in shrimp ponds than in fish ponds. Aerators in shrimp ponds usually are arranged to cause a circular pattern of water currents throughout the pond (Fig. 13.15b,c). Much electrical cable and several electrical outlets are necessary for the aerators.

High aeration rates generate strong currents, and erosion of insides of embankments and pond bottoms occurs. Suspended soil particles, uneaten feed, dead plankton, and shrimp excrement settle in the central areas of ponds where water currents are weaker

---

**Example 13.4**
**Aeration Rate (AR) Calculation Based on Fish Respiration**

Fish biomass in a large, indoor tank will be 5,000 kg. Wastes will be constantly removed from the tank, and fish will be the main sink for dissolved oxygen. The aerator is expected to have an aeration efficiency of 1.4 kg $O_2$/kW·hr under conditions in the tank. Fish respiration is expected to be 400 mg $O_2$/kg body weight/hr. AR is estimated with Equation 13.7.

$$AR = \frac{(5,000 \text{ kg fish})(400 \text{ mg } O_2/\text{kg/hr})(10^{-6})}{(1.4 \text{ kg } O_2/\text{kW·hr})(0.746 \text{ kW/hp})} = 1.9 \text{ hp}$$

Note: About 2 hp of aeration will meet the respiratory oxygen requirements of 5,000 kg of fish. In a pond with feeding and a fish biomass of 5,000 kg/ha, AR would be 15 to 20 hp/ha. Fish respiration is a fairly small percentage of the oxygen demand in ponds.

(Fig. 13.16). This area becomes anaerobic because of microbial decomposition of sediment organic matter. Some shrimp producers partially or completely cover the inside slopes and bottom of ponds with plastic liners to minimize or prevent erosion.

Automation of aeration in aquaculture systems including ponds is becoming more common. In the past, the main technique was to use timers to turn aerators on and off in response to the normal pattern of daily changes in dissolved oxygen concentration. However, automated systems to turn aerators on and off in response to dissolved oxygen concentration measured by a polarographic dissolved oxygen probe are now available at a price that is affordable in several kinds of aquaculture systems. When the dissolved oxygen concentration falls or rises above set points, a signal from the dissolved oxygen

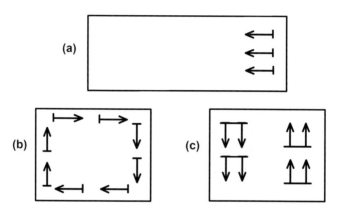

**Fig. 13.15.** Typical methods for positioning surface aerators in square and rectangular ponds.

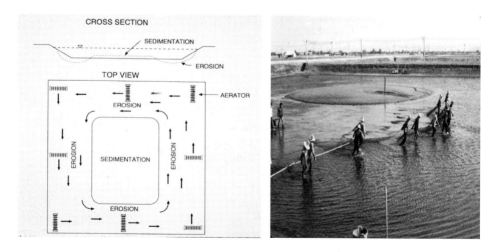

**Fig. 13.16.** Erosion of pond bottoms and embankment side slopes by aerator-induced water currents.

probe activates the aerators. This system can avoid unexpectedly low dissolved oxygen concentration and unnecessary aerator operation when dissolved oxygen concentration is high.[14] The automated controllers also provide a continuous record of dissolved oxygen concentration in ponds that allow producers to assess the effectiveness of aeration and add aerators if necessary. The aerator controllers also have an alarm that will notify managers when malfunctions occur.

## Dissolved Oxygen Measurements

Aquaculture facilities should have a means for measuring dissolved oxygen concentration. Portable test kits are available for those who do not make measurements frequently, but in intensive aquaculture where a biomass is high and dissolved oxygen concentration may fluctuate rapidly, a dissolved oxygen meter should be available. Dissolved oxygen meters are relatively easy to use and a single measurement can be made in 10 to 20 seconds.

Dissolved oxygen meters must be calibrated at intervals, and their reliability checked. This can be accomplished by comparing dissolved oxygen concentrations obtained with the dissolved oxygen meter to dissolved oxygen measurements by the Winkler technique for the same water. Samples with low, intermediate, and high dissolved oxygen concentrations can be prepared by aerating samples of dissolved oxygen-free distilled water for different periods of time. If it is not possible to compare results with those obtained by the Winkler technique, an alternative is to saturate a sample of distilled water with oxygen, 'air calibrate' the dissolved oxygen meter following the manufacturer's instructions, and compare the measured dissolved oxygen concentration to the theoretical dissolved oxygen concentration for the appropriate temperature and atmospheric pressure. It is difficult to bring the dissolved oxygen concentration in a water sample exactly to equilibrium with atmospheric oxygen. However, an approximate equilibrium can be attained by slowly stirring a sample of distilled water in a clean container for 15 or 20 minutes and then letting it stand undisturbed for a few hours.

The probe of traditional dissolved oxygen meters had oxygen sensing electrodes that were bathed in an electrolyte solution and separated from the pond water by a membrane. This membrane must be checked often for tears and bubbles that may appear under it. Either situation requires the membrane to be changed. Dissolved oxygen meters are now available with sensors that do not have membranes (fluorescent technology). This type of dissolved oxygen probe is gaining popularity in commercial aquaculture.

Dissolved oxygen recorders are used in aquaculture, but mainly as a component of automatic aerator controllers. Thus, the manager should develop an oxygen monitoring schedule that allows one or a few daily measures to suffice. The lowest dissolved oxygen concentration usually is in the morning, and the highest is normally in the afternoon. The procedure illustrated in Fig. 13.17 can be used to estimate when dissolved oxygen concentration may reach a particular concentration during the night. The important point is that aeration should be initiated before dissolved oxygen concentration reaches a critically low level.

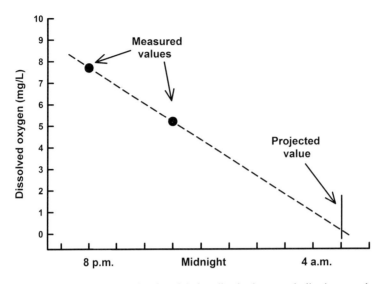

**Fig. 13.17.** Projection technique for estimating nighttime dissolved oxygen decline in aquaculture ponds.

# References

1. Colt, J. 1984. Computation of dissolved gas concentrations in water as functions of temperature, salinity, and pressure. Special Publication Number 14, American Fisheries Society, Bethesda, MD.
2. Benson, B. B. and D. Krause. 1984. The concentration and isotopic fractionation of oxygen dissolved in freshwater and seawater in equilibrium with the atmosphere. Limnology and Oceanography 29:620-632.
3. Boyd, C. E., B. J. Watten, V. Goubier, and R. Wu. 1994. Gas supersaturation in surface waters of aquaculture ponds. Aquacultural Engineering 13:31-39.
4. Tucker, L., C. E. Boyd, and E. W. McCoy. 1979. Effects of feeding rate on water quality, production of channel catfish, and economic returns. Transactions of the American Fisheries Society 108:389-396.
5. Boyd, C. E., E. E. Prather, and R. W. Parks. 1975. Sudden mortality of massive phytoplankton bloom. Weed Science 23:61-67.
6. Andrews, J. W. and Y. Matsuda. 1975. The influence of various culture conditions on the oxygen consumption of channel catfish. Transactions of the American Fisheries Society 104:322-327.
7. Farmer, G. J. and F. W. H. Beamish. 1969. Oxygen consumption of *Tilapia nilotica* in relation to swimming speed and salinity. Journal of the Fisheries Research Board of Canada 26:2,807-2,821.
8. Moss, D. D. and D. C. Scott. 1964. Respiratory metabolism of fat and lean channel catfish. Progressive Fish-Culturist 26:16-20.

9. Collins, G. 1984. Fish growth and lethality versus dissolved oxygen. Proceedings Specialty Conference on Environmental Engineering, June 25-27. ASCE, Los Angeles, CA.

10. Torrans, E. L. 2008. Production responses of channel catfish to minimum daily dissolved oxygen concentrations in earthen ponds. North American Journal of Aquaculture 50:371-381.

11. Andrews, J. W., T. Murai, and G. Gibbons. 1973. The influence of dissolved oxygen on the growth of channel catfish. Transactions of the American Fisheries Society 102:835-838.

12. Hollerman, W. D. and C. E. Boyd. 1980. Nightly aeration to increase production of channel catfish. Transactions of the American Fisheries Society 109:46-452.

13. Lai-fa, Z. and C. E. Boyd. 1988. Nightly aeration to increase the efficiency of channel catfish production. Progressive Fish-Culturist 50:237-242.

14. McGraw, W., D. Teichert-Coddington, D. B. Rouse, and C. E. Boyd. 2001. Higher minimum dissolved oxygen concentrations increase penaeid shrimp yields in earthen ponds. Aquaculture 199:311-321.

15. Boyd, C. E. and J. M. Moore. 1993. Factors affecting the performance of diffused-air aeration systems for aquaculture. Journal of Applied Aquaculture 2:1-12.

16. Boyd, C. E. and B. J. Watten. 1989. Aeration systems in aquaculture. Reviews of Aquatic Science 1:425-472.

17. American Society of Civil Engineers. 1992. *Measurement of Oxygen Transfer in Clean Water*. ANSI/ASCE 2-91, American Society of Civil Engineers, New York, NY.

18. Boyd, C. E. 1990. *Water Quality in Ponds for Aquaculture*. Alabama Agricultural Experiment Station, Auburn University, AL.

19. Shelton, J. L., Jr. and C. E. Boyd. 1983. Correction factors for calculating oxygen-transfer rates of pond aerators. Transactions of the American Fisheries Society 112:120-122.

20. Boyd, C. E. 2009. Estimating mechanical aeration requirement in shrimp ponds from the oxygen demand of feed, p. 81-85. In: C. L. Browdy and D. E. Jory (editors), *The Rising Tide, Proceedings of the Special Session on Shrimp Farming, World Aquaculture 2009*. World Aquaculture Society, Baton Rouge, LA.

# Chapter 14

# Gas Supersaturation

## Introduction

When water contains more dissolved gas than it should at equilibrium with air, the water is said to be *supersaturated* with the gas. Supersaturation is an unstable condition because the supersaturating gas will move from the water to the air, either by diffusing directly into the air across the water surface or by forming bubbles. Aquatic animals living in gas-supersaturated water may develop a stressful or lethal syndrome called *gas bubble disease* when bubbles come out of solution inside the animals' tissues.

## Terminology

Local barometric pressure (BP) is the sum of the partial pressures of nitrogen, oxygen, water vapor, argon, carbon dioxide, and all other atmospheric gases:

$$BP = (pN_2 + pO_2 + pH_2O + pAr + pCO_2 + ....)_g. \tag{14.1}$$

All atmospheric gases dissolve to some extent in water and *total dissolved gas pressure* (TGP) is the sum of the partial pressures of all gases dissolved in water:

$$TGP = (pN_2 + pO_2 + pH_2O + pAr + pCO_2 + ....)_{aq}. \tag{14.2}$$

When gas partial pressures in the atmosphere and water are equal, there is no net diffusion of gas molecules into or out of the liquid, and gases in the two phases are said to be at equilibrium. If the partial pressures of all gases in the atmosphere and water are equal, Equations 14.1 and 14.2 can be added together to give BP = TGP.

Gases are not always at equilibrium in water and air. If the partial pressure of a particular dissolved gas is greater than its partial pressure in air, the water is supersaturated with respect to that gas; if the partial pressure is less than in air, the water is undersaturated. Sometimes one or more dissolved gases are not at equilibrium with the atmosphere, and BP ≠ TGP. The difference between total dissolved gas pressure and local barometric pressure is called the *differential pressure* or "delta P" (ΔP):

$$\Delta P = TGP - BP. \tag{14.3}$$

Values for ΔP are most commonly expressed in aquaculture and fisheries in units of millimeters of mercury (mm Hg). Total gas supersaturation occurs when total dissolved gas pressure exceeds local barometric pressure (ΔP > 0 mm Hg).

Total dissolved gas pressure is sometimes reported as a percentage of local barometric pressure:

$$TGP\% = (TGP/BP)(100). \tag{14.4}$$

At saturation, TGP% = 100%, for supersaturated waters TGP% > 100%, and for undersaturated waters TGP% < 100%.

Values for ΔP and TGP% in Equations 14.3 and 14.4 are calculated with respect to conditions at the water's surface where gases are influenced only by barometric pressure. Gases dissolved in water are also influenced by hydrostatic pressure, which is the pressure exerted by the weight of overlying water. In effect, hydrostatic pressure helps keep gases in solution, so the tendency of a supersaturated water to form bubbles (described by the sign and magnitude of ΔP) must be corrected for hydrostatic pressure. The 'corrected' value of ΔP is called the *uncompensated ΔP* ($\Delta P_{uncomp}$):

$$\Delta P_{uncomp} = \Delta P - (\rho g)Z. \tag{14.5}$$

The quantity $\rho g$ is specific weight of water and is the product of water's density ($\rho$) and acceleration due to gravity (g). The quantity Z is the water depth of interest.

The uncompensated TGP% is

$$TGP\%_{uncomp} = \{(BP + \Delta P)/[BP + (\rho g)Z)]\}100. \tag{14.6}$$

In aquaculture and fisheries, hydrostatic head ($\rho g$) is usually expressed as mm Hg per meter and depth (Z) in meters. Hydrostatic head increases as water salinity increases and temperature decreases, but an average value of 74 mm Hg per meter is adequate for practical purposes.[1]

## Gas Bubble Disease

Supersaturation is an unstable condition and as gases come out of solution they form bubbles. If the blood of aquatic organisms becomes supersaturated with gases, bubbles (called emboli) may form in the circulatory system and other tissues.

Acute gas bubble disease occurs at high levels of supersaturation, usually at uncompensated ΔP values of 100 mmHg or greater.[2,3] Symptoms can develop within minutes of exposure depending on the level of supersaturation. Bubbles may form in eggs, causing them to float to the surface. In larvae and fry, high levels of gas supersaturation may cause hyperinflation of the swim bladder, exophthalmos ('pop-eye'), cranial swelling, swollen gills, blood in the abdominal cavity, gas bubbles in yolk sac, and distention and rupture of yolk sac membrane. In juvenile and adult fish, the most common symptoms of acute gas bubble disease are gas bubbles in the blood and other tissues (commonly in the gill filaments and on the head, in the mouth, and in fin rays), and protrusion of the eyes. Mortality rates may be very high, and death is caused by bubbles that restrict blood flow.

Chronic gas bubble disease develops when animals are exposed for long periods to moderate levels of supersaturation (uncompensated $\Delta P$ values of 25 to 75 mm Hg). Symptoms include bubbles in the gut and mouth, hyperinflation of the swim bladder, and low level mortality. Death may be caused by secondary, stress-related infections.

---

**Example 14.1**
**Calculation of Total Gas Pressure and $\Delta P$**

Total dissolved gas pressure is measured with instruments called *saturometers* that provide direct measurements of $\Delta P$ relative to local barometric pressure. Assume you measure $\Delta P$ of 70 mm Hg using a saturometer and the local barometric pressure is 755 mm Hg. What is the TGP% and the uncompensated $\Delta P$ experienced by a fish swimming at a depth of 0.9 m?

Rearranging Equation 14.3 gives:

TGP = BP + $\Delta P$ = 755 mm Hg + 70 mm Hg = 825 mm Hg.

The TGP% is calculated using Equation 14.4:

TGP% = [TGP/BP](100) = (825 mm Hg/755 mm Hg)(100) = 109%.

A value of $\Delta P$ = 70 mm Hg (109% of saturation in this example) can be a dangerous level of supersaturation for fish living near the surface. But, at a depth of 0.9 m the $\Delta P$ experienced by a fish is affected by hydrostatic pressure and is calculated using Equation 14.5 and an approximate value of 74 mm Hg/m for hydrostatic head.

$\Delta P_{uncomp}$ = $\Delta P$ – $(\rho g)Z$ = (70 mmHg) – (74 mm Hg/m)(0.9 m) = 3.4 mm Hg.

The degree of supersaturation expressed as uncompensated TGP% is calculated from Equation 14.6:

TGP%$_{uncomp}$ = {(755 mm Hg + 70 mm Hg)/[755 mm Hg + (74 mmHg/m)(0.9 m)]}(100) = 100.4%.

Values of $\Delta P_{uncomp}$ = 3.4 mm Hg and TGP%$_{uncomp}$ = 100.4% are negligible for biological purposes. This is an important point: fish living in deeper waters are not as susceptible to gas bubble disease as fish living in shallow water because hydrostatic pressure offsets some of the $\Delta P$ experienced by the animal. Put another way, gas concentration at saturation increases with increasing depth.

Development of gas bubble disease is strongly influenced by the depth of animals in the water column. Water depth has two important effects. First, as shown above, hydrostatic pressure increases with depth and tends to keep gases from coming out of solution. In supersaturated waters, bubbles may form near the surface, but at some depth, bubbles will not form because the sum of hydrostatic pressure and barometric pressure equals the gas pressure (that is, $\Delta P_{uncomp}$ at that depth is 0 mmHg). Animals confined to shallow depths (such as fish in shallow tanks or raceways in hatcheries) are particularly susceptible to gas bubble disease. Species or life stages that normally reside near the surface also are more susceptible to gas bubble disease.

In ponds, water depth also affects the risk of gas bubble disease because rates of photosynthesis and solar heating are greatest near the surface. Photosynthesis decreases with depth because light is absorbed as it passes through water. Thus, the $\Delta P$ resulting from high rates of oxygen production during photosynthesis also decreases with depth.

For a given $\Delta P$, gas bubble disease is less likely as the ratio of (nitrogen + argon):oxygen decreases. Stated another way, risk decreases as dissolved oxygen makes up a greater proportion of total dissolved gases. Dissolved oxygen is a biologically active gas and, as it diffuses across the gill membrane, some of the oxygen gas is consumed in cellular metabolism. Loss of arterial dissolved oxygen in respiration decreases the oxygen partial pressure in tissues and reduces the potential for emboli formation.

Tolerance to gas supersaturation varies among species based on physiological or behavioral differences. Generally, coldwater fish (especially salmonids) are more susceptible than warmwater fish, and species living near the bottom of the water column are less susceptible than those living nearer the surface. Tolerance also varies with life stages. These differences are species-specific, but eggs are relatively tolerant of gas supersaturation, larvae and fry are the most sensitive life stage, and adults are somewhat more tolerant than larvae.[2] Adult crustaceans are more tolerant of supersaturated conditions than fish because emboli in the open circulatory system of invertebrates have less effect on blood circulation than emboli in the vessels of the vertebrate circulatory system. Also, adult crustaceans cultured in ponds tend to reside near the bottom where susceptibility to gas bubble disease is reduced by hydrostatic pressure.

Water quality criteria for exposure to supersaturated conditions are difficult to formulate because risk depends on water depth, the relative contribution of dissolved oxygen partial pressure to total dissolved gas pressure, species, and other factors. In the 1960s, a TGP% criterion of 110% saturation ($\Delta P \sim 76$ mm Hg) was widely accepted as a maximum tolerance level,[4] but that value was based primarily on studies conducted in aquaria where fish are restricted to shallow depths. Fields observations consistently show greater tolerance to gas supersaturation than predicted from tank studies, primarily because fish may seek water depths where hydrostatic pressure reduces the risk of emboli formation. The 110% TGP criterion is still widely used, but some guidelines now incorporate water depth and dissolved oxygen partial pressure as contributing factors to the risk of gas bubble disease.[5]

# Causes of Gas Supersaturation

Gas supersaturation is caused by many natural and man-made phenomena, most of which are related to one of the following physical or biological processes.[2]

## *Air Entrainment*

Supersaturation is produced whenever air is mixed with water at pressures greater than local barometric pressure. One of the most common causes of gas supersaturation is entrainment of air in waters discharged below reservoir spillways (Fig. 14.1). As water flows over spillways, air bubbles mixed in the flow are carried into deep water at the base of the dam. The atmosphere in underwater air bubbles is under pressure from barometic pressure plus hydrostatic pressure, which forces more gas into solution than should be present at equilibrium with the local barometric pressure alone. The $\Delta P$ resulting from air entrainment depends on the depth of bubble submergence, the amount of air entrained, and the degree of mixing.

Water also can become supersaturated when submerged aerators (diffusers or bubblers) release bubbles beneath the water surface. The increase in $\Delta P$ depends on depth of diffuser submergence, amount of air released per water volume, and gas transfer efficiency. Fine-bubble diffusers produce higher levels of gas supersaturation than coarse-bubble diffusers. Bubbles formed in seawater are smaller than bubbles formed in

**Fig. 14.1.** Water flowing over a dam spillway is a common cause of gas supersaturation. The air-water mixture cascading down the spillway face is carried to great depths in the plunge basin at the dam's base where hydrostatic pressure drives gases into solution. Photo credit: United States Bureau of Reclamation.

**193**

freshwater, so problems are more likely in saltwater culture systems. Proper and efficient use of pure oxygen submerged aeration does not significantly increase ΔP, and may actually reduce high ΔP values by displacing other gases (such as nitrogen) with oxygen. Also, as explained above, the risk of gas bubble disease is less when dissolved oxygen partial pressure contributes a greater proportion of total dissolved gas pressure.

Supersaturation can also develop if there is a leak (such as a poorly glued joint in plastic pipe) on the suction side of a pump in a water supply line. Air can be drawn in through the leak and mixed with the water. As the water passes through the pump and is pressurized, some of the air is passed into solution resulting in supersaturation.

## Photosynthesis

Rapid oxygen production during photosynthesis by aquatic plants can increase total dissolved gas pressure. During periods of intensive photosynthetic activity, dissolved oxygen concentrations may exceed saturation values by a factor of three (20-30 mg/L) in surface waters. This corresponds roughly to ΔP values of about 300 mm Hg, assuming no change in other gases. Net oxygen production and ΔP values decrease with depth because of decreased light penetration.

## Heating

Gas solubility decreases with increasing temperature. If water near saturation is heated without allowing excess gases to escape completely, the water will be supersaturated at the final temperature. This may occur when calm surface waters rapidly warm due to solar heating, when water is heated in a boiler that is not exposed to the atmosphere, or when deep ground waters are heated by the internal heat of the earth. The ΔP resulting from heating waters initially saturated with atmospheric gases at 0, 10, 20, and 30°C are given in Table 14.1.

## Mixing Waters of Different Temperatures

Gas solubility is not linearly related to water temperature, so mixing waters of different temperatures can result in supersaturation even if both waters were initially at saturation.

**Table 14.1.** Values of ΔP (mm Hg) resulting from heating water initially at four different temperatures.

| Initial water temperature (°C) | Temperature change (°C) | | | | |
|---|---|---|---|---|---|
| | +2 | +4 | +6 | +8 | +10 |
| 0 | 40 | 81 | 123 | 165 | 207 |
| 10 | 33 | 67 | 100 | 133 | 167 |
| 20 | 28 | 55 | 84 | 111 | 139 |
| 30 | 23 | 46 | 68 | 91 | 113 |

However, relatively large differences in temperature (>15°C) are required to produce significant supersaturation and this is not often encountered in aquaculture.

## Ice Formation

As water cools, the solubility of gases increases and $\Delta P$ decreases unless gas diffuses into the water from the atmosphere. But, if ice forms, some gases are expelled from the ice and concentrated into the remaining water. If the ratio of ice volume to the total (ice + water) volume is quite high (>0.1), significant supersaturation may occur.

## Changes in Barometric Pressure

At a given total dissolved gas pressure, $\Delta P$ increases as barometric pressure decreases. Natural changes in barometric pressure with passing weather fronts occur slowly enough to allow gases to come to equilibrium with the new pressure. However, when air pressure changes quickly, as may occur when aquatic animals are transported in aircraft, the sudden reduction in air pressure may cause large increases in $\Delta P$.

# Gas Supersaturation in Natural Waters

Ground water $\Delta P$ values range from $-100$ to more than 300 mm Hg. Values depend on the amount of gas added or removed in the aquifer recharge zone and the changes in temperature as waters move into the aquifer. Some ground waters are highly supersaturated with carbon dioxide, but this contributes little to the overall total gas pressure because carbon dioxide is a minor constituent of water and it is very soluble. Geothermal heating of deep ground waters can, however, cause relatively high $\Delta P$ values.

Gases in turbulent streams and rivers are nearly at equilibrium with the atmosphere and $\Delta P$ values are usually less than 40 mmHg. Natural air entrainment in rapids or waterfalls may cause transient increases in $\Delta P$. In slow-moving rivers, air entrainment is normally less important, and heating of surface waters by sunlight and oxygen produced in photosynthesis may cause supersaturation. Dams or electrical generating facilities can affect the $\Delta P$ of surface waters. Air entrained in water flow over spillways is a common cause of supersaturation. Electrical generating facilities use cooling water and discharge warm effluent. The rapid temperature increase can cause significant increases in $\Delta P$. The $\Delta P$ of lake and reservoir surface waters is often strongly influenced by photosynthesis.

# Gas Supersaturation in Aquaculture

The $\Delta P$ of shallow aquaculture ponds is initially a function of the gas pressures in the source water but gases in water rapidly come to equilibrium with the atmosphere during and after the pond is filled. After that, gas pressures are affected primarily by photosynthesis and solar heating. In one study of warmwater fish ponds surface waters at dawn were usually undersaturated with oxygen, saturated with nitrogen plus argon, and supersaturated with carbon dioxide.[6] Average $\Delta P$ values were below saturation ($-40$ mm Hg; range $= -127$ to $+ 62$ mm Hg). In midafternoon, $\Delta P$ values increased to a mean of 111 mm Hg (range $= -46$ to 334 mm Hg). High afternoon $\Delta P$ values resulted primarily from dissolved oxygen supersaturation caused by phytoplankton photosynthesis. Supersaturation with nitrogen $+$ argon caused by solar heating of the surface waters also contributed to afternoon supersaturation, but to a much lesser extent.

A common cause of gas supersaturation in flow-through aquaculture systems is pre-existing gas supersaturation in the water supply because many facilities use ground water or water from tailwaters below dam spillways. Even if the source water is not supersaturated, air can be entrained at several points in the water-supply system, including vortexing at the water-intake structure caused by poor design or inadequate submergence of the intake. Supersaturation may also develop if the source water is heated before use. The most common causes of gas supersaturation in recirculating aquaculture systems are leaks in pipe connections on the suction side of pumps and heating of water. In all types of intensive aquaculture, gas supersaturation can result from aeration when bubbles are released by diffusers in deep water.

# Management

Fish losses caused by gas bubble disease are rare in aquaculture ponds despite frequent supersaturated conditions in surface waters (nearly every day during warm, sunny weather). Apparently, if gas supersaturation in surface water reaches harmful levels, animals move into deeper waters where saturation is less. Life stages with limited mobility or surface-dwelling habits may, however, be at risk.

The risk of gas bubble disease is greatest in intensive culture systems because 1) commonly used water supplies for flow-through culture may be supersaturated, 2) water distribution systems in flow-through and recirculating systems present multiple opportunities for supersaturation to develop, and 3) culture tanks are often shallow, particularly in flow-through systems. Using deeper culture tanks simply to avoid high $\Delta P_{uncomp}$ is seldom a reasonable design option, so potential problems in the water supply should be addressed by using good well-drilling practices and properly plumbing the water supply system to minimize opportunities for air entrainment.

Supersaturation in the water supply or caused by heating or other processes within the system can be corrected by removing supersaturated dissolved gases by exposing water to air in the process called *degassing*. The rate of degassing increases dramatically as the air-water surface area increases. This is usually accomplished by breaking the water into fine droplets or thin films and increasing the ratio of air volume to water volume. For example, gas supersaturated water flowing into hatchery tanks can be partially degassed by breaking the flow into a fine spray with a common garden-hose spray nozzle and spraying water into the hatching or rearing tank. This simple solution may be adequate bring the $\Delta P$ for moderately supersaturated water into a safe range.

Packed columns (see Fig. 7.3) are one of the simplest and most effective ways to manage gas supersaturation. Packed columns consist of a plastic or metal tube filled with a packing material that has a high void volume. Various packing media are specifically made for use in packed columns. A perforated support plate holds the packing media in at the bottom of the column and another perforated plate, called the distribution plate, is placed on top to evenly distribute the incoming water over the packing material. Water then trickles down through the column as a film or fine droplets, greatly increasing the air-water surface area. Packed columns often serve the dual roles of removing supersaturated gases and adding oxygen. If water is supersaturated with carbon dioxide, packed columns remove the potentially toxic gas and, for waters with very low alkalinity, degassing also prevents the water's pH from falling to dangerous levels by removing carbon dioxide and decreasing the concentration of carbonic acid.

Packed column design is based on water flow, the degree of supersaturation in the incoming water, and the desired reduction in $\Delta P$. Water flow determines the column diameter and gas removal effectiveness determines the column height. Obviously, high water flows and highly supersaturated waters require columns of greater diameter and height. Gas removal efficiency is enhanced if air is forced up through in the opposite direction (countercurrent) to water flow. Gas removal can further be increased if the system is operated in a vacuum, although this is seldom needed or cost-effective in most aquaculture applications. Detailed instructions for packed column design are found elsewhere.[7,8,9,10]

# Measurement

Gas supersaturation can sometimes be detected visually as milkiness or cloudiness caused by extremely small bubbles coming out of solution. Small bubbles often form on underwater surfaces (such as sides of tanks) that can be visualized by running your hand across the surface to release swarms of small bubbles. The only way to be sure that a problem exists is to measure $\Delta P$ directly using a saturometer.

Saturometers consist of a length of gas-permeable tubing connected to a pressure measuring device. Dissolved gases diffuse between water and the interior of the tubing and equilibrium is reached when the gas pressure inside the tubing equals the water's dissolved gas pressure. The pressure change is read from the pressure gauge. Equilibrium is reached slowly and operation instructions must be carefully followed to obtain accurate readings. Measurement must be made in place because diffusion of gases during sample transport and analysis can cause serious errors.

# References

1. Colt, J. 2012. *Dissolved Gas Concentrations in Water: Computation as Functions of Temperature, Salinity, and Pressure, 2nd Edition.* Elsevier, Waltham, MA.
2. Colt, J. 1986. Gas supersaturation—impact on the design and operation of aquatic systems. Aquacultural Engineering 5:49-85.

3. Shrimpton, J. M., D. J. Randall, and L. E. Fidler. 1990. Factors affecting swim bladder volume in rainbow trout (*Oncorhynchus mykiss*) help in gas supersaturated water.

4. United States Environmental Protection Agency. 1973. *Quality Criteria for Water*. United States Environmental Protection Agency, Washington, D.C.

5. Canadian Council of Ministers of the Environment. 1999. *Canadian Water Quality Guidelines for the Protection of Aquatic Life: Dissolved Gas Supersaturation*. Canadian Council of Ministers of the Environment, Winnepeg, Manitoba, Canada.

6. Boyd, C. E., B. J. Watten, V. Goubier, and R. Wu. 1994. Gas supersaturation in surface waters of aquaculture ponds. Aquacultural Engineering 13:31-39.

7. Huguenin, J. E. and J. Colt. 1989. *Design and Operating Guide for Seawater Systems*. Elsevier, Amsterdam, The Netherlands

8. Hackney, G. E. and J. E. Colt. 1982. The performance and design of packed column aeration systems for aquaculture. Aquacultural Engineering 1:275-295.

9. Colt, J. and G. Bouck. 1984. Design of packed columns for degassing. Aquacultural Engineering 3:251-273.

10. Hargreaves, J. A. and C. S. Tucker. 1999. Design and construction of degassing units for catfish hatcheries. Southern Regional Aquaculture Center Publication 191. Southern Regional Aquaculture Center, Stoneville, MS.

# Chapter 15

# Suspended Solids, Turbidity, and · Color

## Introduction

*Turbidity* is the word used to define the reduction in light penetration into water caused by dissolved, colloidal, or coarse suspended particles. The degree of turbidity is expressed most simply as the depth of visibility into a water body. The surface of a water body has color resulting from light reflected by dissolved substances (*true color*) or by suspended particles (*apparent color*). Turbidity in ponds is caused primarily by suspended soil particles, organic detritus, dissolved humic substances of vegetal origin, and living plankton. For example, ponds may be turbid with soil particles suspended by erosion that impart yellow, red, brown, or other colors. Ponds surrounded by woodlands often contain a high concentration of humic substances that restrict visibility and give the water a tea or coffee color. Dense phytoplankton blooms can make waters extremely turbid, and the apparent color usually will be some shade of green.

Aquaculture ponds should be moderately turbid with plankton. In fertilized ponds, phytoplankton is the base of the food web. Plankton turbidity limits underwater plant growth by restricting light penetration. This is a desirable occurrence in ponds where rooted, underwater plants often are considered weeds. In ponds with feeding, abundant plankton usually occurs as a result of nutrients from feed that is the nutritional base for the culture animals. Nevertheless, plankton turbidity is important for aquatic weed control in ponds receiving feed. Excessive phytoplankton growth and turbidity, however, cause low nighttime dissolved oxygen concentration and shallow thermal stratification in both fertilized and fed ponds.

Turbidity from humic substances or suspended soil particles also limits light penetration and can prevent infestations of underwater aquatic weeds, but it also restricts phytoplankton growth. Although undesirable in fertilized ponds, low phytoplankton abundance as a result of suspended soil particles or humic substances often is acceptable in fed ponds provided mechanical aeration is applied.

Extremely high turbidity resulting from suspended soil particles often leads to excessive sedimentation. Soil particles settle to the pond bottom and smother fish eggs and benthic organisms.[1] Sediment fills in deeper areas of ponds, creates a soft bottom into which feed pellets may sink, increases oxygen demand at the sediment-water interface, and interferes with harvesting.

The purpose of this chapter is to discuss turbidity management in source water for aquaculture facilities and in production ponds.

# Sources of Turbidity

## *External*

Erosion on watersheds is a common source of turbidity in ponds and other aquaculture facilities. There are two basic scenarios: the watershed with erosion and the aquaculture facility are part of the same property, or the erosion occurs on property not under ownership or control of the aquaculture facility. In the first case, managers of aquaculture facilities should control erosion on the watershed to reduce turbidity in the water supply. In the second case, managers of the aquaculture facilities should install a method for reducing turbidity of source water before using it.

The most effective means of controlling erosion on watersheds is establishment of vegetative cover on bare soil. Gullies may have developed in some watersheds, and regrading of steep slopes may be necessary for effective revegetation. Where water flows in defined channels, measures should be installed to prevent stream bed erosion. In instances where it is not practical to control erosion over the entire watershed, water from areas with uncontrolled erosion may sometimes be diverted from aquaculture facilities by installation of terraces or ditches.

## *Internal*

Internal sources of turbidity in ponds may be biological or physical in origin. Plankton blooms, especially phytoplankton blooms, are major sources of turbidity, and activity of fish and other organisms can suspend soil particles in ponds (*bioturbation*). Physical sources are wind and aerator-inducted water currents, rainfall on above-water parts of the earthen infrastructure, and erosion of inlet and outlet canals by flowing water.

Plankton turbidity can be controlled to some extent through limits on fertilization and feeding rates. Bioturbation by culture species also can be controlled by limits on stocking density.

Control of physical sources of turbidity requires attention to preventing erosion. Embankments should be sloped in accordance with soil properties and compacted at optimum moisture content as determined by the standard Proctor test. Grass should be established on the above-water parts of embankments. Canals should be constructed with appropriate hydraulic cross-sections and bottom slopes for the design discharge rate to avoid bottom scouring, erosion of sides, or sedimentation. Sections anticipated to be subject to strong currents should be lined with rip-rap, gabion, geofabric, or a combination of those materials.[2,3]

The above-water portions of canals also should be vegetated to stabilize the bank and reduce erosion. More specific information on design and construction features to avoid erosion is provided in Chapter 23.

Aerator-induced water currents are a major cause of erosion in ponds. Aerators should be positioned in water of at least 0.75-m depth and mounted at least 3 m beyond the toes of embankments. Aerators should not cause strong water currents to impinge on embankments. In highly intensive ponds, insides of embankments and parts or all of bottoms can be lined with impermeable, plastic liners to prevent aerator-induced erosion.[3]

## Sedimentation

Where turbidity cannot be controlled on watersheds, the common means of removing turbidity is sedimentation. Water should be held in a basin under quiescent conditions to allow a large proportion of the suspended soil particles to settle. Particles settle in relation to particle size and density. The time required to remove different-sized particles from still water can be estimated with the *Stokes' Law equation*.[3] This equation is:

$$V_s = \frac{g\, d_p^2 (\rho_p - \rho_w)}{18\, \mu} \tag{15.1}$$

where $V_s$ = velocity of particle (m/sec); g = gravitation acceleration (9.8 m/sec$^2$); $\rho_p$ = particle density (1,050 and 2,500 kg/m$^3$ for organic and mineral particles, respectively); $\rho_w$ = density of water (997 kg/m$^3$ at 25°C); $d_p$ = particle diameter (m); $\mu$ = viscosity of water (0.89 × 10$^{-3}$ N·sec/m at 25°C).

Diameters of different classes of mineral soil particles are provided in Table 15.1, but similar data are not available for organic soil particles. In waters of channel catfish ponds at the E. W. Shell Fisheries Center at Auburn University, in Alabama, the weight of suspended solids is about equally divided among organic and inorganic particles.[4] However, surface water entering aquaculture ponds usually would have a greater percentage of mineral particles because the source of suspended solids in most surface waters is soil erosion.

The *critical settling velocity* ($V_{cs}$) is the settling velocity necessary for a particle to settle before flowing out of a sedimentation basin. The value of $V_{cs}$ may be estimated by dividing the sediment basin depth by hydraulic retention time. Alternatively, the settling time necessary for a particle to be removed may be estimated as follows:

**Table 15.1.** Classification of soil particles according to the International and United States Department of Agriculture (USDA) Systems.

| Name of particle | Diameter limits (mm) | |
|---|---|---|
| | International System | USDA System |
| Gravel | Above 2.00 | Above 2.00 |
| Very coarse sand | | 2.00-1.00 |
| Coarse sand | 2.00-0.20 | 1.00-0.50 |
| Medium sand | | 0.50-0.25 |
| Fine sand | 0.20-0.02 | 0.25-0.10 |
| Very fine sand | | 0.10-0.05 |
| Silt | 0.02-0.002 | 0.05-0.002 |
| Clay | Below 0.002 | Below 0.002 |

$$\text{Settling time (hr)} = \frac{D}{(V_s)(3,600 \text{ sec/hr})} \qquad (15.2)$$

where $V_s$ = settling velocity (m/sec); D = settling distance (m).

Times required to remove particles increases rapidly as particle size decreases (Table 15.2). Mineral particles settle much faster than organic particles. Mineral particles 10 μm and larger and organic particles 20 μm and larger will settle 1 m in 24 hours. Smaller particles and especially small, organic ones require a very long time to settle.[5]

Settling basins should be large enough to provide time for coarse particles and some clay particles to settle (Fig. 15.1). The finest clay particles, organic detritus, and plankton settle so slowly that it is not practical to provide sufficient hydraulic retention time to remove them. Illustration of a quick method for estimating the necessary volume of a settling basin for treating a shrimp farm water supply is provided in Example 15.1. Settling basins should be large enough to provide the hydraulic retention time necessary to remove particles larger than a specified size. They also should have additional volume for sediment storage. Nevertheless, basins will eventually fill, and sediment must be removed to assure adequate hydraulic retention time for continued effectiveness.[3]

It is important that water is introduced at the surface on one side of a settling basin and discharged from the surface on the opposite side (Fig. 15.1). Baffles are sometimes installed in sediment basins to avoid short-circuiting of flow.

## Removing Residual Turbidity

Elimination of erosion and other sources of turbidity leads to clearing of pond water in most instances. Humic substances are dissolved and cannot be cleared from water by sedimentation. Humic-stained waters typically are acidic, and liming will decrease acidity and this often will enhance microbial degradation of humic substances and reduce turbidity. A long hydraulic retention time does not necessarily result in removal of most suspended solids; colloidal clay particles may remain suspended indefinitely. These particles are negatively charged and repulsion by like charges prevents them from flocculating and settling. Liming will increase calcium concentration, and this may

Table 15.2. Time (hour) necessary for mineral and organic particles of different sizes to settle 1 m at 25°C.

| Particle diameter (mm) | Time to settle 1 m (hour) | |
|---|---|---|
| | Mineral particles | Organic particles |
| 0.041 | 0.18 | 5.1 |
| 30.00 | 0.34 | 9.5 |
| 0.020 | 0.75 | 21 |
| 0.010 | 3.02 | 86 |
| 0.008 | 48 | 1,337 |
| 0.005 | 121 | 3,423 |

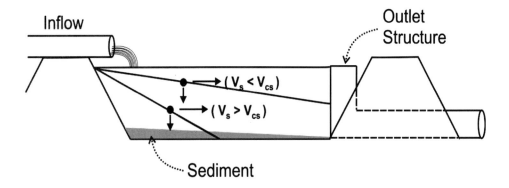

**Fig. 15.1.** Illustration of the relationship between critical settling velocity ($V_{cs}$) and terminal settling velocity ($V_s$) in a sedimentation pond. All particles have the same horizontal velocity, but particles with $V_s < V_{cs}$ will not settle before exiting the pond.

## Example 15.1
## Design of Influent Sedimentation Basin

A settling basin with a 4-hr hydraulic retention time is needed to remove coarse, mineral solids greater than 0.01 mm in diameter (Table 15.2) from the water supply of a small, shrimp farm. The inflowing water has an average TSS concentration of 200 mg/L, and sedimentation will reduce the concentration to 25 mg/L. The inflow to the basin will be 50 m³/min. The basin will be 1.0 m deep and should be designed to operate for 5 yr before clean-out is necessary.

The inflow is 5 m³/m, and the minimum volume necessary to provide a 4-hour HRT is:

$$50 \text{ m}^3/\text{min} \times 4 \text{ hr} \times 60 \text{ min/hr} = 12,000 \text{ m}^3$$

The volume of sediment that will accumulate in 5 yr is:

$$\frac{(200-25)\text{g}\frac{\text{TSS}}{\text{m}^3} \times \frac{50\text{m}^3}{\text{min}} \times 5 \text{ yr} \times 525,600 \frac{\text{m}^3}{\text{yr}} \times 10^{-3}\text{kg/g}}{2,500 \text{ kg/m}^3} = 9,198\text{m}^3.$$

Thus, to have a 4-hr HRT after 5 yr, the basin must have a volume equal to 12,000 m³ plus an additional 9,198 m³ for sediment storage. The minimum volume will be 21,198 m³. For a 1-m deep basin the water surface area will be 2.12 ha.

neutralize the charge on colloids allowing them to flocculate and settle. Sometimes, use of fertilizer will cause phytoplankton blooms at the surface of turbid waters, and changes in pH resulting from phytoplankton photosynthesis leads to flocculation of residual turbidity.

In cases where turbidity persists following elimination of major internal and external sources of suspended clay particles and application of both liming materials and fertilizers, coagulants such as calcium sulfate (gypsum), aluminum sulfate (alum), and ferric chloride may be applied to neutralize charges on colloids and cause them to floc together and precipitate.[1,3]

Calcium sulfate (gypsum) treatment is recommended most often for removing turbidity. The treatment rate usually is 100 to 300 mg/L requiring 1,000 to 3,000 kg/ha per meter of water depth applied by spreading the material over the entire water surface. In spite of the high treatment rate, calcium sulfate has the advantages of not being harmful to the pond ecosystem or to workers, and it has a long residual effect. However, coagulants containing aluminum or iron act faster and more predictably than gypsum.

The usual treatment rate is 20 to 40 mg/L for aluminum sulfate [$Al_2(SO_4)_3 \cdot 14H_2O$] and 5 to10 mg/L for ferric chloride ($FeCl_3$). Either coagulant should be pre-mixed in water, applied over the entire pond surface, and mixed into the water column with aid of an aerator or other mixing device. The mixing device should be stopped after 15 or 20 minutes to facilitate precipitation. The treatment should be made on a calm day without rainfall to favor precipitation and avoid resuspension of the precipitate. Flocculation will begin within 1 hour after alum or ferric chloride application, and precipitation of turbidity will be complete within 24 to 48 hours. There is no residual effect of alum or ferric chloride because the metal ion ($Al^{3+}$ or $Fe^{3+}$) quickly hydrolyzes and precipitates.[3]

The treatment rate can be determined by a dose-response test for water samples in beakers treated with a selected coagulant. To illustrate, a sample of turbid water from a pond is used to fill 11, clear, 1-L containers. A 10,000 mg/L alum solution is prepared (1 g alum/100 mL distilled water). Alum treatments of 0, 5, 10, 15, 20, 25, 30, 35, 40, 45, 50 mg/L are made by adding 0, 0.5, 1.0, 1.5, 2.0, 2.5, 3.0, 3.5, 4.0, 4.5, and 5.0 mL of the alum solution, respectively. The solutions are stirred thoroughly, and after 1 hour, the lowest alum concentration that caused clearing of turbidity from the water is ascertained.

Aluminum and iron coagulants are acidic because of hydrogen ions released during hydrolysis of the metal ions:

$$Al_2(SO_4)_3 \cdot 14H_2O + 6H_2O \rightarrow 2Al(OH)_3 + 6H^+ + 3SO_4^{2-} + 14H_2O \qquad (15.3)$$

$$FeCl_3 + 3H_2O \rightarrow Fe(OH)_3 + 3H^+ + 3Cl^-. \qquad (15.4)$$

The neutralizing effect is 0.5 mg/L and 0.92 mg/L of calcium carbonate for 1 mg/L of either aluminum sulfate or ferric chloride, respectively. In ponds, alkalinity usually drops by the expected amount within a few hours, but it usually recovers as water equilibrates with bottom soils over a period of days or weeks.

Aluminum sulfate and ferric chloride should be used with caution in low alkalinity water. They will depress pH. These compounds are less affective in clearing turbidity at pH below 6, and low pH also harms culture animals. The alum treatment rate should not exceed the total alkalinity concentration and the ferric chloride treatment rate should not be more than 50% of the total alkalinity concentration. In low alkalinity water, liming before application is a prerequisite before use of alum or ferric chloride. It is important that workers wear eye protection, rubber gloves, and avoid contact with alum or ferric chloride solutions which are strongly acidic. The solutions also are corrosive to metal surfaces that they may contact.

Iron and aluminum coagulants precipitate phosphorus from water as illustrated for aluminum in Fig. 15.2. Therefore, it may be necessary to fertilize ponds after application of coagulating agents to avoid a decline in natural productivity.

Organic matter also may be applied to ponds to precipitate turbidity. The process is not completely understood, but the particles of organic matter apparently stick to soil particles and microorganisms grow on the particles.[6] Microorganisms have gelatinous surfaces that stick together favoring flocculation of particles. Bacteria growth also possibly neutralizes charges on colloidal particles. Treatment rates for organic matter are quite high—1,000 kg/ha or more of hay or animal manure usually is necessary to clear a pond of turbidity.[7] Sedimentation of suspended particles following organic matter treatment usually is a gradual process requiring several days or even weeks before benefits are observable, and retreatment may be necessary to obtain a good result. Another major disadvantage is organic matter treatment for turbidity removal is the oxygen demand of the organic matter.

## Effluent Treatment

Elevated concentrations of suspended soil and organic matter particles from internal erosion of earthwork are typical in pond effluents. Particularly high concentrations of suspended solids occur during discharge of the final 20 to 25% of pond volume during

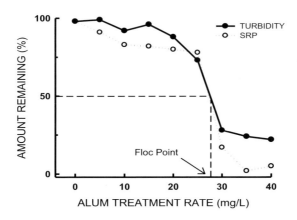

**Fig. 15.2.** Changes in concentrations of soluble reactive phosphorus (SRP) and turbidity in aliquots of a pond water sample treated with different concentrations of alum. Calculation of the floc point is illustrated.

draining for harvest (Fig. 15.3). This results because animals are crowded and swimming rapidly to avoid seining operations, and the high velocity of shallow, outflowing water also resuspends sediment.

Coarse particles can be removed from effluent by sedimentation. A hydraulic retention time of 1 hour usually is sufficient to remove suspended sand particles and the required settling basin area is relatively small (Example 15.2). Up to 2 days are required to remove the larger silt particles, and removal of fine silt and of clay particles requires a much longer hydraulic retention time. Settling pond areas for such long retention times would not be feasible in aquaculture.

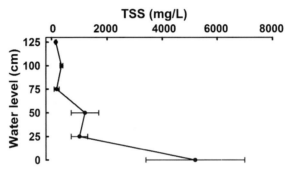

**Fig. 15.3.** Increase in total suspended solids (TSS) concentration during drawdown of water level in channel catfish pond in preparation for harvest.

## Example 15.2
## Design of Effluent Sedimentation Basin

The area of a 1-m deep settling basin with a 1-hr HRT necessary to remove soil particles of 0.02 mm diameter and greater from the last 25% of draining effluent from a 10-ha × 1.2-m deep aquaculture pond will be calculated. It will be assumed that the pond effluent will be completely discharged in 12 hr.

Effluent volume $= 10$ ha $\square$ $10{,}000$ m$^2$/ha $\times 1.2$ m $\times 0.25$ $= 30{,}000$ m$^3$/12 hr

The draining time is 12 times greater than the desired HRT, thus

$$\frac{30{,}000 \text{ m}^3/\text{draining event} \times 1.0 \text{ m}^2/\text{m}^3}{12} = 2{,}500 \text{ m}^2.$$

To prevent sediment accumulation from reducing HRT, the basin should be 1.5 or 2 times greater than the minimum value calculated above. On farms with several production ponds, the settling basin can be used for treating effluent from multiple ponds provided only one pond is drained at the time.

Production ponds sometimes can be operated to serve as settling basins. If it is possible to close the drain at 25% pond volume and harvest the culture species by seining, the water can be held to effect sedimentation. The remaining water must be drained slowly to avoid resuspension of sediment. Alternatively, it may be possible to transfer the draining effluent from a pond into an empty pond and hold it for sedimentation.

# Measurement

The most common technique for assessing turbidity in aquaculture ponds is the Secchi disk (Fig. 2.4), but this device will not distinguish among forms of turbidity. The disk is lowered into water until it just disappears, the depth is recorded, and the disk is then raised until it just reappears and that depth is recorded. *Secchi disk transparency* is the mean of the two depths. Water color often is observed and used to ascertain if turbidity is from suspended soil particles, high concentration of humic substances, or suspended soil particles.

Turbidity can be estimated instrumentally with a *turbidimeter*. There are several types of turbidimeters, but the most common device is a *nephelometer*. It compares the refraction of light at a 90° angle to the incident for a water sample with that of a sample of clear water. The procedure is calibrated against turbidity standards. The unit of turbidity normally is a *nephelometer turbidity unit* (NTU). Tap water usually has a turbidity of 1 or 2 NTU, and pond waters typically have values of 25 to 75 NTU. Waters of ponds receiving runoff from highly-erodible watersheds may have turbidities of 500 to 1,000 NTU following heavy rains.

An alternative to turbidity measurement is determination of the weight of suspended solids in water. This is done by filtering a water sample through a tared, 2-μm glass fiber filter. The dry weight of the residue on the filter is the total suspended solids (TSS). The TSS concentration normally is expressed in milligrams per liter. The filter and residue from the TSS determination may be incinerated in a furnace at 450°C to 500°C, and the weight loss, expressed in milligrams per liter, is the amount of particulate organic matter—sometimes called the *suspended organic solids*. Subtracting the concentration of particulate organic matter from total suspended solids gives the *particulate inorganic matter*. The measurement and calculation of total suspended solids and the suspended organic and inorganic solids are illustrated in Example 15.3.

Total suspended solids concentration in aquaculture ponds typically ranges from 10 to 100 mg/L, and there often are approximately equal proportions of inorganic and organic particles.[1,4] In ponds that are highly turbid with suspended clay particles, TSS concentration may be much higher, and inorganic solids will comprise most of the TSS.

Suspended solids, and especially the suspended inorganic solids, settle from water. The fraction of the solids that settles rapidly is called the *settleable solids*. This fraction is measured volumetrically in an *Imhoff cone* and reported as milliliters of settleable solids per liter of water.

**Example 15.3**
**Measurement and Calculation of Total Suspended Solids (TSS), Particulate Organic Matter (POM), and Particulate Inorganic Matter (PIM)**

A 100-mL water sample is passed through a tared, glass fiber filter weighing 5.0020 g. The filter and residue are dried at 102°C, cooled in a dessicator, and re-weighed (5.0120 g). The dry filter and residue are ignited in a muffle furnace at 450°C for 2 hr. After cooling in a dessicator, the filter and remaining residue weigh 5.0061 g.

$$TSS = \frac{(\text{weight of filter \& residue} - \text{tare weight})\ 10^3\ mg/g}{\text{Sample volume} \div 1,000\ mL/L}$$

$$TSS = \frac{(5.0120\ g - 5.0020\ g)\ 10^3\ mg/g}{100\ mL \div 1,000\ mL/L} = 100\ mg/L$$

POM =
$$\frac{(\text{Weight of filter \& residue before ignition} - \text{weight after ignition})\ 10^3\ mg/g}{\text{Sample volume} \div 1,000\ mL/L}$$

$$POM = \frac{(5.0120\ g - 5.0061\ g)\ 10^3\ mg/g}{100\ mL \div 1,000\ mL/L} = 59\ mg/L$$

$$PIM = TSS - POM = (100 - 59)\ mg/L = 41\ mg/L.$$

## Management Issues

Management of phytoplankton blooms and associated turbidity is discussed in other chapters. Excessive turbidity from suspended soil particles can be avoided by erosion control on watersheds and in ponds as discussed above. Nevertheless, erosion cannot be completely avoided except possibly by covering bottoms of ponds and canals with plastic liners.

Sediment that accumulates in settling basins or ponds must eventually be removed and disposed. Settling basins can be dredged while they are in operation, but their effectiveness will decline during dredging. The dredge discharge should be confined in a sedimentation area and allowed to dry rather than released into a natural water body. It is better to drain settling basins, let the sediment dry, and excavate the dewatered material.[2]

Sediment in ponds can be removed by washing pond bottoms with water discharge from hoses with high-pressure nozzles. The sediment-laden water should be treated in a settling basin. It usually is better to allow pond bottoms to dry and excavate the dry sediment.[1]

The sediment from settling basins, dredge discharge confinement areas, or ponds is mostly silt and sand and not ideal earthfill to repair pond embankments and other earthen infrastructure or for new construction on farms. Sometimes, there are construction projects near farms in which pond sediment can be used. If no uses for it can be found, sediment removed from sedimentation basins or from production ponds should be spread over vacant land and grass cover established to avoid erosion. Sediment from brackishwater ponds has a large salt burden. Disposal of such sediment in freshwater areas can lead to surface water and groundwater salinization when salts are leached by rainfall.

# References

1. Boyd, C. E. and C. S. Tucker. 1998. *Pond Aquaculture Water Quality Management.* Kluwer Academic Publishers, Boston, MA.
2. Yoo, K. H. and C. E. Boyd. 1994. *Hydrology and Water Supply for Aquaculture.* Chapman and Hall, New York, NY.
3. Boyd, C. E. 1995. *Bottom Soils, Sediment, and Pond Aquaculture.* Chapman and Hall, New York, NY.
4. Masuda, Y. and C. E. Boyd. 1994. Chemistry of sediment pore water in aquaculture ponds built on clayey, Ultisols at Auburn, Alabama. Journal of the World Aquaculture Society 25:396-404.
5. Ozbay, G. and C. E. Boyd. 2003. Particle size fractions in pond effluents. World Aquaculture 34(4):56-59.
6. Avnimelech, Y., B. W. Troeger, and L. W. Reed. 1982. Mutual flocculation of algae and clay: evidence and implications. Science 276:63-65.
7. Irwin, W. H. 1945. Methods of precipitating colloidal soil particles from impounded waters of central Oklahoma. Bulletin 42, Oklahoma Agricultural Mechanical College, Stillwater, OK.

# Chapter 16

# Nitrogen

## Introduction

Forms, concentrations, and transformations of nitrogen have important implications for aquaculture. Nitrogen is a major plant nutrient and ponds are often fertilized with nitrogen-containing materials to increase plant growth, which serves as the base of the food web leading to increased aquaculture production (Chapter 10). In cultures provided with manufactured feed, nitrogen is a constituent of feed protein, and large amounts of nitrogenous waste can be produced as a byproduct of feeding. Waste nitrogen may contribute to excessive phytoplankton growth in ponds (Chapter 11) and ammonia—the principle nitrogenous waste product of most aquatic animals—can be toxic to aquatic animals if it accumulates in the culture system. Ammonia can be converted to nitrite, which is also potentially toxic. Nitrogen gas is usually the major contributor to gas supersaturation, which may cause gas-bubble disease in aquatic animals (Chapter 14). Nitrogen is also of concern because waters discharged from aquaculture facilities may be enriched to the point where the effluent may degrade the quality of receiving waters (Chapter 29).

## Nitrogen Transformations

Relationships among various forms of nitrogen in aquatic and terrestrial environments constitute the *nitrogen cycle*. Many transformations in the cycle are biochemical oxidation-reduction reactions and are strongly interdependent because the rate of one process usually depends on the rate of substrate formation in a preceding process. All these transformations occur in ponds (Fig. 16.1). Nitrogen pathways are simpler in recirculating aquaculture systems where a specific nitrogen-transformation process is incorporated into the system to detoxify and remove ammonia produced as a byproduct of feeding. In net-pen and flow-through systems, the major processes are even simpler: ammonia is added to the water as metabolic waste and removed by mass transport in water leaving the culture unit.

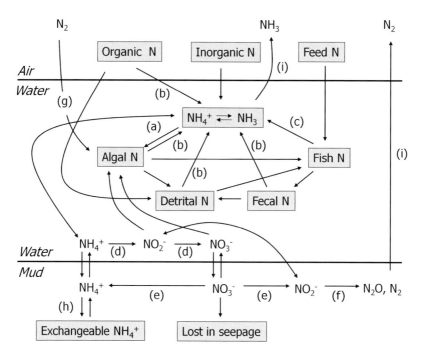

**Fig. 16.1.** The nitrogen cycle in aquaculture ponds. Major inputs may include nitrogen in organic fertilizers, inorganic fertilizers, or feed. Processes illustrated are (a) assimilation, (b) mineralization, c) excretion, (d) nitrification, (e) nitrate reduction, (f) denitrification, (g) biological nitrogen fixation, (h) cation exchange, and (i) volatilization.

## Un-ionized Ammonia-Ammonium Equilibrium

Ammonia exists in water in two forms—un-ionized ammonia (dissolved ammonia gas, $NH_{3(aq)}$) and ammonium ion ($NH_4^+$). For purposes of describing nutrient availability and nitrogen dynamics in ponds, we are usually interested in the total concentration of the two forms, which is referred to as 'total ammonia' or simply 'ammonia.' Sometimes it is important to differentiate between the two forms. For example, ammonia toxicity is related principally to the concentration of un-ionized ammonia. Un-ionized ammonia and ammonium ion exist in equilibrium:

$$NH_4^+ = NH_{3(aq)} + H^+; K = 10^{-9.3} \text{ at } 25°C. \tag{16.1}$$

The amount of $NH_{3(aq)}$ present as a proportion of total ammonia ($NH_{3(aq)} + NH_4^+$) increases as pH and temperature increase and salinity decreases.

## Nitrogen Fixation

*Nitrogen fixation* is the conversion of dinitrogen gas, $N_2$, into a biologically usable form of combined nitrogen. Nitrogen can be fixed (1) as a nitrogen oxide by atmospheric electrical discharges; (2) as organic nitrogen by symbiotic bacteria in the roots of legumes and certain nonlegumous plants or by certain free-living bacteria and blue-green algae; and (3) as synthetic nitrogen fertilizers produced by industrial fixation. The amount of nitrogen added to ponds as a result of fixation during atmospheric electrical discharges is inconsequential in aquaculture ponds but the other processes can be important.

Nitrogen fixation by symbiotic microorganisms associated with legumes is important because modern aquaculture depends strongly on feeds formulated with a high soybean meal content. Soybeans are legumes that derive much of their nitrogen for growth from atmospheric nitrogen fixed by bacteria in the genus *Rhizobium* living in nodules in the plant's root system. Nitrogen gas is also fixed by certain non-symbiotic bacteria and blue-green algae. Although nitrogen fixation by blue-green algae is important in many aquatic ecosystems, the process is suppressed when other sources of nitrogen are available. As such, nitrogen fixation by blue-green algae is relatively minor in aquaculture ponds. Industrial fixation of nitrogen is important to cultures using synthetic fertilizers to enhance primary production.

## Fertilization and Feeding

Most of the nitrogen in aquaculture systems is intentionally added as either fertilizer or feeds. In fertilized ponds, nitrogen is added as synthetic fertilizers or nitrogen-rich organic materials to enhance primary productivity. In culture systems with feeding, almost all the nitrogen originates from feed protein. The amount of nitrogen in feed that is recovered in aquatic animal production ranges from less than 25% to about 50% depending on animal species and size, feed quality, feeding practices, water temperature, and other factors. In other words, 50 to 75% of the nitrogen in feed is lost to the water as fish waste. Most of the waste nitrogen enters the ponds as ammonia, the primary nitrogenous waste product excreted by aquatic animals. Nitrogen also enters the water in fecal material and uneaten feeds, but ammonia is quickly liberated when those organic materials decompose. Assuming 40% retention of feed nitrogen and 35% protein in the feed, total waste nitrogen input to the pond water will be about 34 g N per kg of feed that is eaten.

## Assimilation of Combined Inorganic Nitrogen by Plants

Uptake by phytoplankton is the initial sink for most combined inorganic nitrogen in aquaculture ponds. Plants actively assimilate nitrogen as ammonium and nitrate. Net rates of nitrogen assimilation are roughly proportional to rates of net primary production, so factors affecting photosynthesis affect nitrogen assimilation in a qualitatively similar fashion. For instance, assimilation of combined inorganic nitrogen is reduced at night, during cloudy periods, when water temperatures are low, or when the availability of some other nutrient limits plant growth. Rates of uptake also vary diurnally with highest uptake during daylight. Long-term rates of nitrogen assimilation by phytoplankton can be approximated by assuming that phytoplankton assimilate nitrogen in the same proportion to carbon as the C:N elemental ratio of "average" phytoplankton tissue (this is the so-called *Redfield ratio* of C:N:P in algal tissue, which is 42:7:1 by weight). Net carbon fixation rates range from less than 0.5 to over 5 mg $C/m^2$ per day in aquaculture ponds, which would correspond to nitrogen assimilation rates of less than 80 to over 800 mg $N/m^2$ per day.

## *Mineralization and Ammonification*

Large amounts of nitrogen-containing organic matter may be produced in aquaculture. In ponds, organic matter is mostly living and dead phytoplankton cells, with lesser amount of fecal solids, uneaten feed, and other organic materials. In other systems, most of the particulate material is feces or detritus derived from fecal matter. Particulate organic matter is first broken down to soluble organic matter by decomposer microorganisms. Proteins liberated when the particulate material is solubilized are broken down to amino acids, which are then deaminated with the release of ammonia. The overall process is called *mineralization* and the last step, the release of ammonia, is called *ammonification*.

The rate of ammonia production from mineralization depends on temperature, pH, oxygen availability, and the quantity and quality of organic matter. Rates generally increase with increasing temperature up to about 40°C and decomposition rates are fastest at near-neutral to slightly basic pH. Mineralization of fresh, high-quality organic matter occurs at approximately equal rates under aerobic or anaerobic conditions. Ammonia production obviously increases as the amount of organic material undergoing decomposition increases, and more ammonia is released from high-quality, nitrogen-rich material than from nitrogen-poor material. In fact, if the organic matter is deficient in nitrogen relative to the nutritional needs of decomposer organisms (a carbon:nitrogen mass ratio of about 30:1 or greater), inorganic nitrogen will be removed (*immobilized*) from the environment by microorganisms that use the nitrogen to further the decomposition process.

In ponds, ammonia produced when organic matter is mineralized is available for further use in biological processes, such as reassimilation by phytoplankton. The continuous internal recycling of nitrogen through the processes of assimilation by phytoplankton, cell death, mineralization of organic nitrogen, and reassimilation by phytoplankton is an important aspect of the nitrogen dynamics in aquaculture ponds. In recirculating and flow-through systems, mineralization can be an important contributor to excessive ammonia production if fecal solids are not removed from the system in a timely fashion.

## *Ammonium Adsorption by Muds*

Ammonium ion is weakly attracted to and retained by negatively charged cation exchange sites of clays and organic colloids in pond bottom soils. This process is important because it reduces the opportunity for nitrogen to be lost in leaching waters and because adsorption by muds is a temporary sink for nitrogen. Ammonium adsorbed at mud exchange sites is not permanently lost from the overlying water because ammonium is weakly attracted to soil particles and adsorbed ammonium is readily released when sediment particles are temporarily resuspended into the water column. As such, the pool of exchangeable ammonium can be a small, but significant, source of nitrogen for biological processes in the sediment and water.

## *Ammonia Volatilization*

Un-ionized ammonia is a dissolved gas and can be lost from water by *volatilization* to the atmosphere. Rates of volatilization are greatest when partial pressures of dissolved ammonia gas are high (high concentrations of total ammonia and high pH), and when conditions favor gas transfer (such as turbulence and wave formation during periods of windy weather). It is likely that ammonia volatilization is significant only during afternoon periods of high pH and windy conditions.

## *Nitrification*

*Nitrification* is the sequential oxidation of ammonia to nitrite to nitrate by two groups of aerobic, chemoautotophic bacteria. Nitrifying bacteria derive metabolic energy from the oxidation of inorganic nitrogen compounds and obtain carbon for cell synthesis from carbon dioxide. The first step in nitrification is the oxidation of ammonia to nitrite. This reaction is carried out primarily by species of *Nitrosomonas*, *Nitrosococcus*, and *Nitrosospira* bacteria:

$$NH_{3(aq)} + 1.5O_2 \rightarrow H^+ + NO_2^- + H_2O. \tag{16.2}$$

The substrate for this reaction, $NH_{3(aq)}$, is in equilibrium with $NH_4^+$:

$$NH_4^+ = NH_{3(aq)} + H^+. \tag{16.3}$$

As $NH_{3(aq)}$ is assimilated by nitrifying bacteria, $NH_4^+$ in the water dissociates instantaneously to form more $NH_{3(aq)}$ and restore equilibrium. The overall reaction is the sum of Equations 16.2 and 16.3:

$$NH_4^+ + 1.5O_2 \rightarrow 2H^+ + NO_2^- + H_2O. \tag{16.4}$$

Nitrite is then oxidized to nitrate primarily by species of *Nitrospira* and *Nitrobacter*:

$$NO_2^- + 0.5\ O_2 \rightarrow NO_3^-. \tag{16.5}$$

The two-step nature of the reaction is important because rates can become unequal with the accumulation of the intermediate product, nitrite. Nitrite is toxic to many aquatic animals.

Nitrifying bacteria grow slowly because the energy yield in the oxidations is relatively low. Nitrification rates in ponds may also be slow because rapid uptake of ammonia by phytoplankton and other plants reduces substrate concentrations. Nitrifying bacteria are aerobic and rates of nitrification drop dramatically when dissolved oxygen levels fall below 1 to 2 mg/L. Nitrification occurs over a wide temperature range (from less than 5°C to over 40°C), but the optimum is 25-35°C. Nitrifying bacteria grow over a wide range of pH values (5.5-10) but the optimum range of pH 7.0-8.5 is rather narrow.

Nitrifying bacteria colonize surfaces and most nitrification in ponds occurs at the sediment-water interface. Rates of 'open-water' nitrification tend to be low unless clay particles or other attachment surfaces are suspended in the water. Recirculating aquaculture systems use nitrification biofilters to detoxify ammonia. Biofilters consist of a tank or chamber filled with media having a high specific surface area (i.e., a high ratio of surface area to volume), providing nitrifying bacteria with a large area to colonize. Ammonia in water pumped through the filter is oxidized to nitrate by bacteria growing on the media.

Equation 16.4 shows that the first step in nitrification produces acid that can react with bases (primarily bicarbonate, $HCO_3^-$) in the alkalinity system that buffers most waters in the pH range of 6.5 to 9. In high-intensity aquaculture systems that rely upon nitrification biofilters to remove large amounts of ammonia produced during culture, the amount of acid produced in nitrification can be so great that it neutralizes all the alkalinity and the water's pH may then fall quickly to levels that endanger aquatic animals. Rates of nitrification and, correspondingly, rates of acid production are much lower in pond aquaculture, so it is unlikely that nitrification will cause pH to decline to dangerous levels. However, over a period of several years, the acid produced in nitrification may cause the total alkalinity of the pond water to decline to the point where the pond becomes less fertile and does not respond well to fertilization.[1] This problem is easily corrected by liming (Chapter 9).

## *Denitrification and Nitrate Reduction*

In the absence of molecular oxygen, many common heterotrophic bacteria can use nitrate or other oxidized forms of nitrogen instead of oxygen as terminal electron acceptors in respiration. This process is termed nitrate reduction or nitrate respiration when nitrate is reduced to nitrite, hyponitrite, hydroxylamine, or ammonia. The process is called denitrification when gaseous forms of nitrogen are the products of reduction and lost from the system.

Denitrification depends on nitrate availability, so the rate is usually linked to the production of nitrate from nitrification. Denitrification rate also depends on the concentration of organic matter because the denitrifying bacteria are heterotrophs and need organic carbon for growth.

In ponds, most nitrate reduction occurs in bottom muds and not in the water column. A few recirculating systems incorporate denitrification bioreactors to remove nitrate produced in nitrification biofilters and to partially offset some of the alkalinity lost to acid produced in nitrification.[2] As shown in more detail in Chapter 8, the overall denitrification process is an acid-consuming process (shown here using $CH_2O$ as a generic organic matter):

$$4NO_3^- + 5CH_2O + 4H^+ \rightarrow 2N_2 + 5CO_2 + 7H_2O. \tag{16.6}$$

Denitrification can offset half the alkalinity destroyed as a result of acid produced in nitrification if all nitrate produced in nitrification is subsequently denitrified.

## Ammonia Toxicity, Management, and Measurement

Ammonia in aquaculture systems is derived from fertilizers, as the principal nitrogenous waste product excreted by fish and crustaceans, or from mineralization of organic matter. Ammonia is potentially toxic to fish and crustaceans, and the risk of intoxication increase as culture intensity increases because greater quantities of nitrogenous compounds are in flux among the various nitrogen-transformation processes.

Total ammonia concentrations are the net result of rates of ammonia input and rates of ammonia losses and transformations. The key to ammonia management in aquaculture is to assure, to the extent possible, that ammonia inputs do not exceed losses for more than brief periods.

### Ammonia Toxicity

The principal nitrogenous waste product of most fish and crustaceans is ammonia, carried in the blood primarily as ammonium ions and excreted as un-ionized ammonia, which diffuses across the gill epithelium in response to concentration gradients between un-ionized ammonia in blood and the external environment.[3] The gradient for un-ionized ammonia efflux is enhanced by the acidification of water at the external gill surface by respired carbon dioxide, which 'traps' excreted un-ionized ammonia as the ammonium ion, maintaining a favorable concentration gradient between internal and external un-ionized ammonia. As long as external un-ionized ammonia concentrations remain low, this passive process provides an energy-efficient mechanism for removing waste nitrogen from the blood. If external un-ionized ammonia concentrations increase, the diffusion gradient between blood and water decreases and ammonia begins to accumulate in the blood and tissues with serious physiological consequences.

The primary effects of acute ammonia intoxication are on the central nervous system.[4] Symptoms progress from hyperactivity and convulsions to lethargy, loss of equilibrium, and finally, coma. Long-term exposure to non-lethal concentrations of ammonia causes osmoregulatory disturbances, blood acidosis, and reduced respiratory efficiency, which reduces growth and increases susceptibility to infectious diseases.

At relatively high environmental pH values (above about pH 7.5), ammonia toxicity is related primarily to the concentration of un-ionized ammonia, which determines the diffusive gradient for ammonia efflux across the gills. Ammonia toxicity is often described in terms of the un-ionized ammonia concentration. However, ammonium ion contributes to toxicity at lower pH values and the combined effects of un-ionized ammonia and ammonium ion are best described by the 'joint toxicity model' used by the United States Environmental Protection Agency (USEPA) to define 'safe' ammonia levels for short- and long-term exposures.[5,6]

The USEPA[5] criteria for short-term (1-hr) exposures (called *criterion maximum concentrations*, or CMC) are expressed as maximum allowable total ammonia-nitrogen (TAN) concentrations as a function of pH. Salmonids are more sensitive to ammonia than non-salmonids, so two models are needed. Water temperature has relatively little impact on acute ammonia toxicity and is not included in either model. Table 16.1 presents acute criteria for ammonia exposure at different pH values as calculated the USEPA models.[5]

The USEPA[5] criteria for chronic exposures (*criterion chronic concentrations*, or CCC) are expressed as maximum allowable average total ammonia-nitrogen concentrations over a 30-day period. Although water temperature has little effect on acute ammonia intoxication, ammonia is more toxic in cold water than in warmer water for long-term exposures, so a temperature factor is included in the model as well as a pH factor. Two criteria are needed because tolerance to ammonia varies with life stage. In fish, early life stages are the most sensitive; eggs, juveniles, and adults are more tolerant. Some representative CCC values calculated with the USEPA models[6] are presented for fish early life stages (Table 16.2) and for fish populations where early life stages are absent (Table 16.3).

Marine fish may be slightly less tolerant of ammonia than freshwater fish[4] but criteria in Equations 16.7 through 16.10 should provide adequate protection. Ammonia toxicity to crustaceans of importance in aquaculture is generally within the same range as that for fish. Tolerance of crustaceans to ammonia increases as the animals mature and grow. Larvae are most sensitive, followed by postlarvae, juveniles, and adults.

Other environmental variables affect ammonia toxicity and these interactions are often more important than the differences among species and life stages. Obviously, pH and, to a much lesser extent, temperature affect ammonia toxicity. Concurrent exposure to low dissolved oxygen concentrations increases ammonia toxicity. High calcium concentrations and salinities near optimum for a particular species reduce toxicity.

Aquatic animals also have physiological strategies for tolerating elevated environmental ammonia levels and may acclimate upon continuous or repeated exposure.

Interpreting ammonia-toxicity criteria is difficult when animals are grown in ponds because pH and temperature changes quickly throughout the day (Chapter 8), which has large effects on ammonia toxicity. However, information on daily and seasonal changes

**Table 16.1.** Criterion maximum concentration (CMC, mg N/L) for non-salmonid and salmonid fish.[5] The CMC is the maximum allowable total ammonia-nitrogen concentration for 1-hour exposure at different pH values.

| | CMC (mg N/L) | | | CMC (mg N/L) | |
|---|---|---|---|---|---|
| pH | Non-salmonids | Salmonids | pH | Non-salmonids | Salmonids |
| 6.6 | 46.8 | 31.3 | 7.8 | 8.1 | 12.1 |
| 6.8 | 28.1 | 42.0 | 8.0 | 5.6 | 8.4 |
| 7.0 | 24.1 | 36.1 | 8.2 | 3.8 | 5.7 |
| 7.2 | 19.7 | 29.5 | 8.4 | 2.6 | 3.9 |
| 7.4 | 15.4 | 23.0 | 8.6 | 1.8 | 2.7 |
| 7.6 | 11.4 | 17.0 | 8.8 | 1.2 | 1.8 |

**Table 16.2.** Criterion chronic concentration (CCC, mg N/L) for early life stages of fish.[6] The CCC is the maximum allowable total ammonia-nitrogen concentration for a 30-day exposure at different pH and temperature values. At water temperatures of 15°C and above, CCC values when fish early life stages are absent are the same for when fish early life stages are present.

| | CCC (mg N/L) for fish when early life stages are present | | | | | |
|---|---|---|---|---|---|---|
| | Temperature (°C) | | | | | |
| pH | 0 | 14 | 18 | 22 | 26 | 30 |
| 6.5 | 6.7 | 6.7 | 5.3 | 4.1 | 3.2 | 2.5 |
| 7.0 | 5.9 | 5.9 | 4.7 | 3.7 | 2.8 | 2.2 |
| 7.5 | 4.4 | 4.4 | 3.5 | 2.7 | 2.1 | 1.6 |
| 8.0 | 2.4 | 2.4 | 1.9 | 1.5 | 1.2 | 0.9 |
| 8.5 | 1.1 | 1.1 | 0.9 | 0.7 | 0.5 | 0.4 |
| 9.0 | 0.5 | 0.5 | 0.4 | 0.3 | 0.2 | 0.2 |

**Table 16.3.** Criterion chronic concentration (CCC, mg N/L) for fish production when early life stages are absent.[6] The CCC is the maximum allowable total ammonia-nitrogen concentration for a 30-day exposure at different pH and temperature values. At water temperatures $\geq$ 15°C, CCC values when fish early life stages are absent are the same as those for fish early life stages (Table 16.2).

| | CCC (mg N/L) for fish when early life stages are absent | | | | | |
|---|---|---|---|---|---|---|
| | Temperature (°C) | | | | | |
| pH | 0-7 | 8 | 10 | 12 | 14 | 16 |
| 6.5 | 10.7 | 10.1 | 8.8 | 7.7 | 6.8 | 5.9 |
| 7.0 | 9.6 | 9.0 | 7.9 | 7.0 | 6.1 | 5.4 |
| 7.5 | 7.1 | 6.6 | 5.8 | 5.1 | 4.5 | 4.0 |
| 8.0 | 4.0 | 3.7 | 3.5 | 2.9 | 2.5 | 2.2 |
| 8.5 | 1.8 | 1.7 | 1.5 | 1.3 | 1.1 | 1.0 |
| 9.0 | 0.8 | 0.7 | 0.7 | 0.6 | 0.5 | 0.4 |

of total ammonia, pH, and temperature can be used to model the risks of ammonia intoxication in ponds. For example, considerable information is available on channel catfish pond water quality in the southeastern United States. When that information is combined with the USEPA model criteria, problems with ammonia toxicity are predicted to be most likely in winter (when conditions are unfavorable for ammonia uptake by phytoplankton), after sudden die-offs of phytoplankton blooms (when decomposition of algal cells releases ammonia into the water), and occasionally during late afternoons in summer (when pH is high).[7]

## Ammonia Management

Methods of preventing ammonia toxicity vary among culture systems, but the common goal is to maintain overall nitrogen loading rate within the limits of the system's capacity to remove or transform ammonia to a less toxic substance. In flow-through systems and net pens, the system's capacity to remove ammonia is defined by water flow relative to the amount of waste nitrogen produced in feeding (Chapter 26). In water-recirculating aquaculture systems, ammonia is treated by transforming it to nitrate in biological nitrification filters. The proper type and size of biological filter is determined by defining the facility's production goal, which defines the required feeding rate, which in turn defines the waste ammonia production rate (Chapter 28).

Ammonia is much more difficult to manage in ponds than in other aquaculture systems because nitrogen transformation rates vary daily and seasonally depending on water temperature, sunlight, wind speed, and other environmental variables that are impossible to control. Also, removing ammonia from pond water is difficult because of the large water volume in most ponds. Various treatments, some based on accelerating natural processes, have been proposed but most either do not work or are too expensive.[8] Ammonia can be removed by exchanging water and this is commonly practiced in some pond cultures. Water exchange may be continuous or occasional—often based on whenever the pond manager feels that fish health is threatened. The need for water exchange and the effectiveness of the practice as an ammonia-removal strategy is debatable in most pond aquaculture, particularly if ponds are large and water exchange rates are low (less than about 20% per day). Moreover, if frequent water exchange is required to maintain ammonia concentration at a non-threatening level, it is a clear indicator that the waste assimilation capacity of the pond has been exceeded. At that point, the system is no longer a pond, but rather a flow-through system.

Because ammonia is difficult to remove from pond water, the key to ammonia management in ponds is to minimize the probability of accumulation to toxic levels by operating within the assimilative capacity of the pond ecosystem. If ammonia concentration is routinely high in fertilized ponds, nitrogen is being supplied in excess of requirements for algal growth, which is wasteful of fertilizer and money. In ponds receiving feed, the risk of ammonia toxicity is reduced by using moderate stocking and feeding rates and using high-quality feeds and good feeding practices to maximize nitrogen retention by the cultured animals (see Chapter 11). Other than these general rules and using experience to determine the pond's assimilative capacity, it is difficult to precisely define nitrogen loading limits for ponds. As a rough estimate, the nitrogen assimilative capacity of a pond is roughly equivalent to the average rate of nitrogen uptake by phytoplankton. Nitrogen uptake rates vary from day to day, but a reasonable average daily uptake rate for warm, shallow, unmixed ponds is in the range of 300 to 500 $mg/m^2$. This corresponds to the amount of nitrogen excreted by fish when daily feeding rates for high-quality feed are in the range of 80 to 140 kg/ha. Algal nitrogen assimilative capacity must be increased (as it is in the Partitioned Aquaculture System, see Chapter 24) if greater feeding rates are sustained over long periods.

## *Ammonia Measurement*

All common analytical methods measure total ammonia. Three methods (Nesslerization, the phenate method, and the salicylate method) are based on reactions of ammonia with reagents that produce colored compounds. The color intensity varies with ammonia concentration and is measured with a spectrophotometer. Total ammonia can also be measured with gas-sensing or specific-ion electrodes. If information is needed on un-ionized ammonia concentrations, concurrent measurements must be made of pH, water temperature, and total dissolved solids (or salinity) which are then used to calculate un-ionized ammonia concentrations using equations based on the ammonium-ammonia equilibrium expressions.[9] For a particular water, factors for calculating un-ionized ammonia concentrations can be tabulated for convenience (Table 16.4). Strictly speaking, information in Table 16.4 applies only to fresh waters with total dissolved solids concentrations less than 250 mg/L but values in that table can be used for practical purposes with little error in all freshwaters. For precise work, online 'ammonia calculators' are available that compute un-ionized ammonia concentrations for any freshwater and saltwater condition (http://fisheries.org/hatchery).

# Nitrite Toxicity, Management, and Measurement

Nitrite ($NO_2^-$) is a naturally occurring, potentially toxic intermediate product in nitrification and denitrification. Nitrite is seldom detected in significant amounts in unpolluted ground or surface waters but is routinely found in aquaculture ponds and recirculating systems because large amounts of nitrogen are added as fertilizers or feeds. When nitrogen loading rates are high, relatively small changes in the individual reaction rates of multi-step processes can result in the accumulation of the intermediate product, nitrite.

**Table 16.4.** Decimal fractions of total ammonia-nitrogen existing as un-ionized ammonia-nitrogen at various pH values and water temperatures. Values were calculated using the "ammonia calculator" at http://fisheries.org/hatchery for a typical, dilute fresh water with a total dissolved solids concentration of 250 mg/L.

| pH | Temperature (°C) | | | | | | |
|---|---|---|---|---|---|---|---|
| | 5 | 10 | 15 | 20 | 25 | 30 | 35 |
| 7.0 | 0.001 | 0.002 | 0.003 | 0.004 | 0.005 | 0.007 | 0.010 |
| 7.5 | 0.004 | 0.005 | 0.008 | 0.011 | 0.016 | 0.023 | 0.032 |
| 8.0 | 0.011 | 0.017 | 0.024 | 0.035 | 0.050 | 0.069 | 0.093 |
| 8.5 | 0.035 | 0.051 | 0.073 | 0.103 | 0.141 | 0.189 | 0.246 |
| 9.0 | 0.103 | 0.146 | 0.200 | 0.267 | 0.342 | 0.424 | 0.507 |
| 9.5 | 0.266 | 0.350 | 0.442 | 0.535 | 0.622 | 0.699 | 0.765 |
| 10.0 | 0.534 | 0.630 | 0.715 | 0.784 | 0.839 | 0.880 | 0.911 |

## Nitrite Toxicity

Nitrite causes *methemoglobinemia* in some fish, which is a condition where nitrite enters the bloodstream across the gills and oxidizes iron in hemoglobin to the ferric state. Oxidized hemoglobin, called *methemoglobin*, cannot reversibly bind with oxygen, causing considerable respiratory distress because of the loss in blood oxygen-carrying capacity. Methemoglobin has a characteristic brown color that becomes grossly noticeable when the methemoglobin level in the blood exceeds about 20% of the total hemoglobin. This is the basis for a common name of the syndrome, 'brown-blood disease.'

Tolerance to nitrite exposure varies greatly among fish species. Freshwater fish in the families Cichlidae, Cyprinidae, Ictaluridae, and Salmonidae are particularly sensitive because nitrite is actively concentrated into the blood from the water by the same gill anion-uptake mechanism responsible for uptake of chloride from water. Note that this group of nitrite-sensitive fish includes tilapias, common carp, fathead minnows, channel catfish, and rainbow trout—some of the most important aquaculture species in the world. Species of Centrarchidae, Moronidae, and perhaps others concentrate chloride from the environment but nitrite is somehow excluded from the bloodstream and these fish are relatively tolerant to waterborne nitrite.[10]

Because chloride and nitrite are concentrated by the same mechanism in nitrite-sensitive species, the amount of nitrite entering the blood (and thus the amount of methemoglobin formed) depends on the ratio of nitrite to chloride in the environment. Either raising the chloride concentration or lowering the nitrite concentration will decrease nitrite uptake by competitive exclusion of branchial ion uptake. As such, practical exposure guidelines for nitrite-sensitive freshwater fish should be based on the ratio of environmental chloride to environmental nitrite, rather than on nitrite concentrations alone. For channel catfish, nitrite exposure can be tolerated for extended periods if the ratio of chloride (in mg $Cl^-/L$) to nitrite-nitrogen (in mg $NO_2^-$-N/L) exceeds 20:1.[11] This guideline seems to have broad application for many nitrite-sensitive fish. Centrarchids, moronids, and other fish that exclude nitrite from their blood are very tolerant of waterborne nitrite, and can withstand prolonged exposure to concentrations well over 25 mg $NO_2^-$-N/L even when environmental chloride levels are very low. Concentrations of nitrite that high will be rarely, if ever, encountered in pond aquaculture. Marine fish are likewise very tolerant of nitrite because of the high background level of chloride in seawater. Culturists should be aware however, that many euryhaline fish are sensitive to nitrite when raised in low-salinity water.

Nitrite is also toxic to crustaceans although the mechanism of toxicosis is poorly understood. Hemocyanin, rather than hemoglobin, is the blood oxygen-transport protein in crustaceans, and reactions of nitrite with hemocyanin have not been determined. Nitrite is concentrated into the blood of freshwater crayfish (*Procambarus* spp.) and is toxic at concentrations similar to those toxic to many freshwater fish.[12] Chloride ions also antagonize nitrite uptake, which indicates that nitrite probably enters crayfish by the same branchial anion uptake mechanism responsible for its uptake in freshwater fish. Nitrite is surprisingly toxic to marine shrimp, despite the observation that nitrite is only weakly concentrated into the hemolymph[13] and the expectation that the high chloride concentration in seawater should provide protection against nitrite toxicity. For example, 'safe' nitrite concentrations for *Penaeus monodon* are about 0.1 mg $NO_2^-$-N/L for larvae and 1.5 mg $NO_2^-$-N/L for postlarvae. Juvenile *P. monodon* are relatively more tolerant than larvae and postlarvae, with an estimated 'safe' concentrations of about 4 mg $NO_2^-$-N/L in water of 20 ppt salinity.[14,15]

## Nitrite Management

Most nitrite in aquaculture systems is derived from the nitrification process when the rate of ammonia oxidation (Equation 16.4) exceeds the rate of nitrite oxidation (Equation 16.5). Unequal oxidation rates typically occur when conditions are otherwise favorable for nitrification and ammonia concentrations suddenly increase. Sudden availability of ammonia stimulates the growth and activity of ammonia-oxidizing bacteria, and nitrite is produced. Growth of nitrite-oxidizing bacteria lags behind until sufficient substrate (nitrite) accumulates, after which nitrite is oxidized to nitrate. The lag time in development of active populations of the two groups of bacteria results in a characteristic pattern of elevated total ammonia levels followed by increases in nitrite and nitrate levels (Fig. 16.2).

In ponds, nitrite accumulation may occur following phytoplankton die-offs or after aquatic weeds are killed with herbicides. Decomposition of dead plant material releases large amounts of ammonia into the water, which stimulates the activity of ammonia-oxidizing bacteria, and nitrite is produced. In aquaculture ponds in temperate regions, nitrite may also accumulate with the onset of shorter days and cool weather. Poor conditions for phytoplankton growth causes increased ammonia concentrations and greater substrate availability for nitrification.[16]

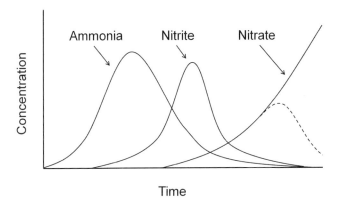

**Fig. 16.2.** Concentrations of total ammonia, nitrite, and nitrate when there is a lag time between the development of populations of ammonia-oxidizing and nitrite-oxidizing bacteria. The pattern with nitrate concentrations continuing to increase over time (solid line) is typical of recirculating systems with low water exchange rates. In systems where nitrate is assimilated by phytoplankton or removed in water exchange or denitrification, nitrate concentrations decline after an initial increase (dashed line).

Removing nitrite from large ponds is not practical but adding common salt to pond water to increase chloride concentration can prevent nitrite toxicosis. The required amount of chloride depends on the highest expected nitrite concentration and the fish species cultured. Elevated nitrite levels are a common problem in pond culture of Channel Catfish in the southeastern United States and salt is routinely added so that the chloride concentration is at least 20 times the highest expected nitrite-nitrogen concentration. Experience has shown that salt added to maintain a chloride concentration of about 100 mg/L protects fish from all but the most extreme episodes of nitrite accumulation. Salt treatment is relatively inexpensive and is long-lasting because chloride is lost from ponds only during overflow associated with excessive rains or intentional water exchange or pond draining.

In recirculating aquaculture systems, nitrite accumulates when the system is first put into operation. As ammonia is generated as a byproduct of feeding, the biofilter is first colonized by ammonia-oxidizing bacteria, causing temporary accumulation of nitrite until nitrite-oxidizing bacteria colonize the filter (Fig. 16.2). Nitrite toxicity to animals in the system can be avoided by developing active nitrifying populations within the biofilter before animals are stocked. The filter can be 'pre-seeded' with commercial cultures of nitrifying bacteria and solutions of ammonium and nitrite salts can be fed to the filter to accelerate development of nitrifying populations. Frequent measurements of ammonia, nitrite, and nitrate will show when the nitrification process is fully activated.

Nitrite toxicosis should never be a problem in flow-through or net-pen aquaculture. Nitrification is a slow process and ammonia produced during culture is removed from the culture unit by water flow before significant nitrite can be produced.

## Nitrite Measurement

Nitrite is measured colorimetrically using variations of the *diazotization* method. Two reagents added to water react with nitrite under acid conditions to form a highly colored dye whose color intensity is proportional to the amount of nitrite present. The method is sensitive and highly specific for nitrite.

# Nitrate

Nitrate concentrations are usually low in aquaculture ponds, especially when water temperatures are warm and plants are actively growing. Plant growth removes ammonia from the water thereby limiting the substrate levels for nitrification. Any nitrate produced in nitrification or added to the pond in nitrate-containing fertilizers is rapidly removed from the water by plants. In regions with temperate climates, low nitrate concentrations ($<5$ mg $NO_3^-$-N/L) may accumulate in the cooler months of the year when assimilation of ammonia and nitrate by plants is reduced.

Nitrate may accumulate to high levels in recirculating aquaculture systems as the end product of nitrification (Fig 16.2). Unless nitrate is removed in some way, all of the nitrogen as feed protein—minus that removed in the crop—will eventually end up as nitrate. Most recirculating systems operate with small but continuous water exchange and some nitrate will be lost as effluent. However, in systems operated with high water reuse ratios (i.e., very low rates of water exchange) to maintain water temperatures or conserve water, nitrate will accumulate to levels exceeding several hundred mg $NO_3^-$-N/L. Nitrate is considered to be the least toxic of the common forms of nitrogen found in aquaculture systems, with lethal concentrations exceeding 1,000 mg $NO_3^-$-N/L for most freshwater fish and crustaceans. There is, however, evidence that continuous exposure to high concentrations are detrimental to some aquatic animals[17] and some recirculating systems incorporate a denitrification process to remove nitrate by converting it to nitrogen gas. In addition to reducing potential toxic effects, removing nitrate from recirculating system water reduces nitrogen discharged and replenishes some of the alkalinity destroyed by acid produced in nitrification.[2]

# References

1. Hunt, D. and C. E. Boyd. 1981. Alkalinity losses from ammonia fertilizers used in fish ponds. Transactions of the American Fisheries Society 110:81-85.
2. van Rijn, J., Y. Tal, and H. J. Schreier. 2005. Denitrification in recirculating systems: Theory and applications. Aquacultural Engineering 34:364-376.
3. Wilkie, M. P. 1997. Mechanisms of ammonia excretion across fish gills. Comparative Biochemistry and Physiology 118:39-50.
4. Randall, D. J. and T. K. N. Tsui. 2002. Ammonia toxicity in fish. Marine Pollution Bulletin 45:17-23.
5. USEPA (United States Environmental Protection Agency). 1999. *1999 Update of Ambient Water Quality Criteria for Ammonia*. EPA-822-R-99-014. United States Environmental Protection Agency, Washington, D.C.
6. USEPA (United States Environmental Protection Agency). 2009. *2009 Update Aquatic Life Ambient Water Quality Criteria for Ammonia - Freshwater*. EPA-822-D-09-001. United States Environmental Protection Agency, Washington, DC.
7. Hargreaves, J. A. and C. S. Tucker. 2005. Conditions associated with sub-lethal ammonia toxicity in warmwater aquaculture ponds. World Aquaculture 36(3):20-24.
8. Hargreaves, J. A. and C. S. Tucker. 2004. Management of ammonia in fish ponds. Southern Regional Aquaculture Center Publication 4603. Southern Regional Aquaculture Center, Stoneville, MS.
9. Emerson, K., R. C. Russo, R. E. Lund, and R. V. Thurston. 1975. Aqueous ammonia equilibrium calculations: Effects of pH and temperature. Journal of the Fisheries Research Board of Canada 32:2379-2388.
10. Tomasso, J. R. 1994. The toxicity of nitrogenous wastes to aquaculture animals. Reviews in Fisheries Science 2:291-314.
11. Tucker, C. S, R. Francis-Floyd, and M. H. Beleau. 1989. Nitrite-induced anemia in channel catfish, *Ictalurus punctatus* Rafinesque. Bulletin of Environmental Contamination and Toxicology 43:295-301.
12. Gutzmer, M. P. and J. R. Tomasso. 1985. Nitrite toxicity to the crayfish *Procambarus clarkii*. Bulletin of Environmental Contamination and Toxicology 34:369-376.
13. Chen, J. -C. and S. -F. Chin. 1992. Effects of nitrite on growth and molting of *Penaeus monodon* juveniles. Comparative Biochemistry and Physiology 101C:453-458.

14. Chen, J. -C. and S. -C. Lei. 1990. Toxicity of ammonia and nitrite to *Penaeus monodon* juveniles. Journal of the World Aquaculture Society 21:300-306.

15. Chen, J. -C. and T. -S. Chin. 1988. Acute toxicity of nitrite to tiger prawn, *Penaeus monodon*, larvae. Aquaculture 69:253-262.

16. Hargreaves, J. A. and C. S. Tucker. 1996. Evidence for control of water quality in channel catfish *Ictalurus punctatus* ponds by phytoplankton biomass and sediment oxygenation. Journal of the World Aquaculture Society 27:21-29.

17. Camargo, J. A., A. Alonso, and A. Salamanca. 2005. Nitrate toxicity to aquatic animals: a review with new data for freshwater invertebrates. Chemosphere 58:1255-1267.

# Chapter 17

# Hydrogen Sulfide

## Introduction

Sulfur is an essential element for plants, animals, and bacteria. The element is present in natural waters and in waters of aquaculture systems mainly as the sulfate ion ($SO_4^{2-}$). The primary source of sulfate in inland, surface waters is dissolution of sulfate-containing minerals in watershed soils. In humid regions, sulfate concentrations usually are less than 50 mg/L, but in more arid regions, concentrations may exceed 100 mg/L. Seawater has a high concentration of sulfate averaging 2,700 mg/L.

Two amino acids—methionine and cysteine—contain sulfur; thus, feeds applied to aquaculture systems contain sulfur. Sulfur also is a component of several other materials commonly applied to ponds to include organic matter, the fertilizers superphosphate and ammonium sulfate, gypsum for increasing total hardness or precipitating suspended clay particles, and the algicide copper sulfate. However, sulfur is seldom a limiting nutrient for aquatic productivity and it usually is not applied to aquaculture systems for the specific purpose of increasing sulfur concentrations in soil or sediment.

The main sulfur-related issue in aquaculture is the occasional presence of toxic concentrations of sulfide—specifically hydrogen sulfide ($H_2S$)—in sediment or in the water column. The purpose of this chapter is to discuss the processes that result in elevated hydrogen sulfide concentrations, the toxicity of this substance to culture organisms, and the management practices for avoiding hydrogen sulfide toxicity.

## The Sulfur Cycle

A description of the global sulfur cycle (Fig. 17.1) is presented because several of the pathways in this cycle occur in aquaculture systems. Natural sources of sulfur to the atmosphere include volcanic activity that releases hydrogen sulfide and sulfur dioxide ($SO_2$), sulfate originating from evaporation of sea spray, dust from arid land that contains gypsum and sulfur anhydrides, hydrogen sulfide from decomposing organic matter, and sulfur dioxide from wild fires, burning of refuse, and combustion of fossil fuels. In the atmosphere, reduced forms of sulfur are oxidized to sulfate in sulfuric acid and the sulfuric acid reaches land and water surfaces in precipitation. Rainfall contaminated with sulfuric acid has a lower pH than possible from carbon dioxide (see Chapter 8). Such rainfall is the cause of the much publicized acid rain phenomenon.

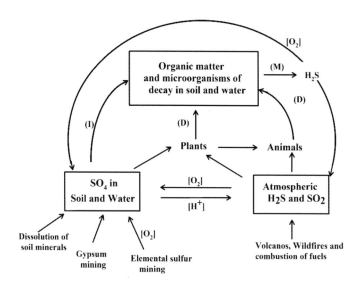

$[O_2]$ = oxidation ; $[H^+]$ = reduction ; (D) = death ; (I) = immobilization ; (M) = mineralization

**Fig. 1.** The sulfur cycle.

Acid rain in some regions has pH values of 2 to 4, but this is seldom a problem in pond aquaculture because liming materials typically are applied to maintain a suitable pH and alkalinity (see Chapter 9). Acid rain has sometimes caused unacceptably low pH in trout raceways supplied from mountain streams.

The main source of sulfur for plants is sulfate from dissolution of sulfur-containing minerals in soil, from the oxidation of sulfide from decaying organic matter, and from atmospheric deposition. Some plants can fix sulfur dioxide from the air by using it to make sulfur-containing amino acids in a process somewhat analogous to nitrogen fixation. Aquatic plants use sulfate from the water that originates from the same sources mentioned for terrestrial plants. Animals obtain their sulfur mainly from proteins in their diets.

Sulfur for industrial, agricultural, and other uses is obtained by mining deposits of elemental sulfur and gypsum or as a by-product of crude oil refining. Sulfur is a key resource for producing sulfuric acid needed for phosphate fertilizer manufacturing.

The decomposition of organic matter in aquatic ecosystems is a source of hydrogen sulfide in water, but most hydrogen sulfide in aquatic ecosystems—including aquaculture systems—comes from the reduction of sulfate by anaerobic, chemoautotrophic bacteria that use oxygen in sulfate as an alternative to molecular oxygen as an electron acceptor in respiration. When hydrogen sulfide from anaerobic zones in water bodies enters oxygenated water, it is oxidized to sulfate.

Anaerobic sediment often contains high concentrations of ferrous iron, manganous manganese, and other metal ions. Sulfide in anaerobic sediment reacts with metals to form highly insoluble metallic sulfides such as iron sulfide ($FeS_2$). These sulfides precipitate into the sediment, and this process is the origin of potential acid-sulfate soils mentioned in Chapter 9.

## *Sulfur Reductions*

Sulfur reductions occur in anaerobic environments in which sulfur-reducing bacteria such as species of the genus *Desulfovibrio* use oxygen from sulfate or partially oxidized sulfur compounds as electron and hydrogen acceptors in respiration. Some examples using skeleton-type reactions are:

$$SO_4^{2-} + 8H^+ \rightarrow S^{2-} + 4H_2O \tag{17.1}$$

$$SO_3^{2-} + 3H^+ \rightarrow S^{2-} + 3H_2O \tag{17.2}$$

$$S_2O_3^{2-} + 8H^+ \rightarrow 2SH^- + 3H_2O \tag{17.3}$$

The source of electrons, hydrogen ions, and energy for reactions 17.1 to 17.3 is organic matter. A representative complete reaction is:

$$CH_3CHOHCOONa + MgSO_4 \rightarrow H_2S + 2CH_3COONa + CO_2 + MgCO_3 + H_2O \tag{17.4}$$

## *Sulfur Oxidations*

Sulfur oxidations occur spontaneously in the presence of molecular oxygen, but oxidation of sulfur compounds is accelerated by various species of obligate or facultative chemoautotrophic, sulfur-oxidizing bacteria—such as species of *Thiobacillus*—capable of using energy released by sulfur oxidation to convert carbon dioxide to organic carbon. This process is analogous to nitrification in that organic carbon is synthesized by a non-photosynthetic process.

An example of a spontaneous sulfur oxidation is the transformation of hydrogen sulfide to sulfur dioxide in the atmosphere:

$$2H_2S + 3O_2 \rightarrow 2H_2O + 2SO_2 \tag{17.5}$$

Of course, $SO_2$ can be further oxidized to sulfuric acid.

Some reactions that may involve sulfur-oxidizing bacteria are:

$$S + 1\tfrac{1}{2}O_2 + H_2O \rightarrow H_2SO_4 \tag{17.6}$$

$$Na_2S_2O_3 + 2O_2 + H_2O \rightarrow 2NaHSO_4 \tag{17.7}$$

$$FeS_2 + H_2O + 3.5O_2 \rightarrow FeSO_4 + H_2SO_4 \qquad (17.8)$$

There are many other possible sulfur oxidations, and the products of most of these reactions are highly acidic. The most unique of the sulfur oxidations are those carried out by the green and purple sulfur bacteria that use light and sulfide to reduce carbon dioxide to organic carbon.

# Hydrogen Sulfide

## *Dissociation*

Hydrogen sulfide is a diprotic acid that ionizes as follows:

$$H_2S = HS^- + H^+ \qquad K = 10^{-7.01} \qquad (17.9)$$

$$HS^- = S^{2-} + H^+ \qquad K = 10^{-13.89}. \qquad (17.10)$$

The effect of pH on the distribution of the three forms of sulfide at 25°C is shown in Fig. 17.2. The dominant sulfide form varies with pH; $H_2S$ dominates up to pH 7.00, $HS^-$ is the major ion from pH 7.02 to pH 13.88, and beyond pH 13.89, $S^{2-}$ is the main form. The mass action form of Equation 17.9 will be used to estimate the percentage un-ionized sulfide ($H_2S$) at pH 6 (Example 17.1).

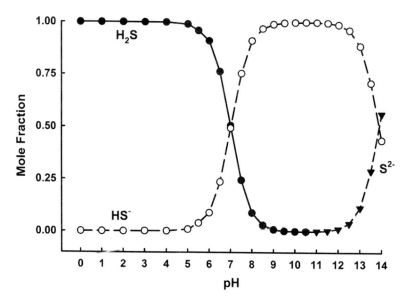

Fig. 17.2. Effects of pH on the relative proportions of $H_2S$, $HS^-$, and $S^{2-}$.

## Example 17.1
## Percentage Un-ionized Hydrogen Sulfide

The percentage un-ionized hydrogen sulfide ($H_2S$) will be estimated for pH 6.

$$\frac{(HS^-)(H^+)}{(H_2S)} = 10^{-7.01}$$

$$\frac{(HS^-)}{(H_2S)} = \frac{10^{-7.01}}{(H^+)} = \frac{10^{-7.01}}{10^{-6}} = 10^{-1.01} = 0.098$$

Thus, at pH 6, there will be 0.098 mole HS⁻ for each mole of $H_2S$. The percentage $H_2S$ will be:

$$\frac{1}{1 + 0.098} \times 100 = 91.1\%.$$

The proportions of un-ionized sulfide at different pH values and temperatures in freshwater are provided (Table 17.1). For use in seawater, the proportions of un-ionized sulfide from Table 17.1 should be multiplied by 0.90.[1] Suppose that the water temperature is 26°C, the pH is 7.5, and the sulfide concentration is 0.25 mg/L. From Table 17.1, the decimal fraction of hydrogen sulfide is 0.238, and the hydrogen sulfide concentration would be 0.25 mg/L × 0.238 = 0.06 mg/L (60 µg/L).

## Toxicity

Hydrogen sulfide inhibits oxidative phosphorylation in aquatic animals by blocking the reoxidation of reduced cytochrome $a_3$ by molecular oxygen.[1] The overall effect is inhibition of energy metabolism by cells—similar to the effect of hypoxia. Fish exposed to acutely lethal concentrations of sulfide increase ventilation rates, but ventilation soon stops, and fish die. Because of the effect of sulfide on oxidative processes, toxicity increases with decreasing dissolved oxygen concentration.[2]

It usually is assumed that $H_2S$ is the primary toxic form of sulfide to aquatic species, because the un-ionized molecule readily crosses cell membranes in contrast to ionized sulfide that is largely excluded by membranes.[1] Moreover, the HS⁻ ion was not toxic to the shrimp *Crangon crangon* while $H_2S$ was highly toxic.[3] There is no $S^{2-}$ ion at pH below 12 (Fig. 17.2); thus, $S^{2-}$ would not be present at the pH range found in aquaculture systems even if it was toxic. Because lower pH favors a higher proportion of un-ionized sulfide, hydrogen sulfide toxicity is more likely to occur in acidic environments than in neutral or alkaline ones.

**Table 17.1.** Decimal fractions (proportions) of total sulfide-sulfur existing as un-ionized hydrogen sulfide in freshwater at different pH values and temperatures.[1] Note: Multiply values by 0.9 for seawater.

| pH | Temperature | | | | | | | | |
|-----|------|------|------|------|------|------|------|------|------|
| | 16 | 18 | 20 | 22 | 24 | 26 | 28 | 30 | 32 |
| 5.0 | 0.993 | 0.992 | 0.992 | 0.991 | 0.991 | 0.990 | 0.989 | 0.989 | 0.989 |
| 5.5 | 0.977 | 0.976 | 0.974 | 0.973 | 0.971 | 0.969 | 0.967 | 0.965 | 0.963 |
| 6.0 | 0.932 | 0.928 | 0.923 | 0.920 | 0.914 | 0.908 | 0.903 | 0.897 | 0.891 |
| 6.5 | 0.812 | 0.802 | 0.792 | 0.781 | 0.770 | 0.758 | 0.746 | 0.734 | 0.721 |
| 7.0 | 0.577 | 0.562 | 0.546 | 0.530 | 0.514 | 0.497 | 0.482 | 0.466 | 0.450 |
| 7.5 | 0.301 | 0.289 | 0.275 | 0.263 | 0.250 | 0.238 | 0.227 | 0.216 | 0.206 |
| 8.0 | 0.120 | 0.114 | 0.107 | 0.101 | 0.096 | 0.090 | 0.085 | 0.080 | 0.076 |
| 8.5 | 0.041 | 0.039 | 0.037 | 0.034 | 0.032 | 0.030 | 0.029 | 0.027 | 0.025 |
| 9.0 | 0.013 | 0.013 | 0.012 | 0.011 | 0.010 | 0.010 | 0.009 | 0.009 | 0.008 |

Hydrogen sulfide is highly toxic to freshwater fish. For example, egg survival and fry development in northern pike were limited by 6 µg/L H$_2$S.[2] The 72-hr LC50s of H$_2$S to bluegill at 20-22°C were as follows: eggs, 20 µg/L; 35-day-old fry, 14 µg/L; juveniles, 51 µg/L; adults, 48 µg/L.[4] The 3-hr LC50 of H$_2$S at 25-30°C and pH 6.8-7.0 was 850 µg/L for channel catfish fry, 1,060 µg/L for fingerlings, 1,380 µg/L for advanced fingerlings, and 1,490 µg/L for adults.[5] Of course, the 96-hr LC50 would be much less than the 3-hr LC50. A literature review[6] reported 48-hr to 96-hr LC50 values for hydrogen sulfide to 11 species of freshwater fish of 4.2 to 34.8 µg/L. The United States Environmental Protection Agency[7] suggests a maximum hydrogen sulfide concentration of 2 µg/L for fish and other aquatic life.

Marine species apparently are more tolerant to hydrogen sulfide than are freshwater species. The 96-hr LC50 of milkfish in seawater at 26-30°C and pH 8-8.5 was 128 µg/L.[8]

The 96-hr LC50s of hydrogen sulfide to the marine shrimp *Metapenaeus dobsoni* and *Penaeus indicus* ranged from 63 to 342 µg/L and from 77 to 378 µg/L, respectively, at different pH values. The toxicity decreased (LC50 increased) from lower pH (6.0-6.3) to higher pH (8.1-8.3).[9] The 96-hr LC50 of hydrogen sulfide to the black tiger prawn was reported to be 51 mg/L.[10]

Chronic exposure to sublethal concentrations of hydrogen sulfide weakens the immune system making aquatic animals more susceptible to disease. For example, exposure of kuruma shrimp to 88 µg/L of H$_2$S for 144 hours did not result in mortality.[11] However, hydrogen sulfide reduced the shrimp's immune response, because 80% of animals injected with *Vibrio alginalyticus* died of vibriosis within 144 hours at the same hydrogen sulfide concentration. Similar results were obtained for the Pacific white shrimp.[12]

## Dynamics in Ponds

Because hydrogen sulfide is produced in anaerobic environments, it typically is found in the hypolimnion of eutrophic water bodies and in sediment. Aquaculture ponds usually are constructed shallow enough that they do not stratify thermally, or their waters are mixed by aeration preventing thermal stratification. Thus, anaerobic decomposition of organic matter in sediment is the main source of hydrogen sulfide in aquaculture ponds. Hydrogen sulfide must diffuse from sediment into the water column or be mixed into the water column by disturbances of the sediment by biological activity, erosion by aerators, or seine hauls. Hydrogen sulfide is quickly oxidized in waters with normal concentrations of dissolved oxygen, and unless the rate of delivery of hydrogen sulfide into the water column exceeds the rate of its oxidation, there will be no residual hydrogen sulfide. Of course, pH plays a major role in hydrogen sulfide toxicity, and the diffusion of hydrogen sulfide into acidic water would be more likely to cause toxicity to aquatic organisms than it would in waters of greater pH. A study in acidic lakes in northeast Texas[5] demonstrated that high concentrations of hydrogen sulfide were responsible for poor growth of channel catfish.

Large amounts of organic matter settle to the bottoms of aquaculture ponds producing an environment conducive for hydrogen sulfide production. The potential for sulfide production is especially great in ponds with high sulfate concentration such as those in semi-arid and arid regions and those filled with brackishwater or seawater. Of course, the presence of iron and manganese or other metals that are transformed to a reduced state under anaerobic conditions provides a damper on hydrogen sulfide concentration in sediment pore water through the precipitation of metallic sulfides.[6]

Hydrogen sulfide concentrations in sediment may be quite high. In laboratory soil-water systems (microcosms) maximum sulfide concentrations at 0.5 cm below the soil-water interface were 57 to 113 mg/L.[13] However, Pacific white shrimp in the microcosms were unaffected by the presence of large amounts of hydrogen sulfide in sediment provided the sediment surface remained oxidized and the overlaying water had 70% of dissolved oxygen saturation or more.[13] Other authors pointed out that at low dissolved oxygen concentration near the sediment-water interface, hydrogen sulfide toxicity to zoobenthos was more likely than at higher dissolved oxygen concentration.[6] Because zoobenthos productivity often is as important as natural food for culture species—even in ponds with feeding—hydrogen sulfide can indirectly affect aquacultural production.

# Avoiding Hydrogen Sulfide Toxicity

## *Monitoring*

It is not necessary to monitor hydrogen sulfide in the great majority of aquaculture ponds. However, if a toxic agent is suspected as the cause of poor growth or unexplained mortality, it may be desirable to make hydrogen sulfide analyses. Analytical procedures determine the total sulfide concentration, and the hydrogen sulfide concentration must be calculated for the pH and temperature of the water with the aid of Table 17.1. The most common laboratory procedure for measuring total sulfide is the methylene blue method[14], but water analysis kits for sulfide analysis are available—we cannot vouch for their accuracy.

It is difficult to measure total sulfide for several reasons: the methodology is rather complex (except for kits), concentrations are usually quite low, and contamination of samples with oxygen may result in oxidation of sulfide during the period between sampling and analysis. Often, it is unnecessary to make analyses to reveal the presence of $H_2S$, because the substance has an extremely strong odor similar to that of a rotten egg.

Sediment analyses for hydrogen sulfide usually are not necessary for aquaculture production operations. There is a common belief that black sediment contains hydrogen sulfide. This is not always correct; the black color is from ferrous iron. The redox potential must decline considerably below that necessary for the appearance of ferrous iron for the occurrence of hydrogen sulfide. Nevertheless, sediment must be black or at least dark in color to contain hydrogen sulfide.

## Management

The main practices that can be used to lessen the risk of hydrogen sulfide toxicity are as follow:

- Avoid siting ponds in areas of organic soils.

- If ponds will not be aerated, build them shallow enough to avoid thermal stratification.

- Lime acidic ponds to maintain soil and water pH above 7.

- Avoid overfeeding and the resulting accumulation of uneaten feed in ponds or other culture systems.

- Use enough aeration to prevent dissolved oxygen concentration for falling below 3 or 4 mg/L and to assure water movement over the bottom of culture units.

- Dry pond bottoms thoroughly between crops to encourage decomposition of organic matter and oxidation of sulfide.

Several other practices have been used to avoid $H_2S$ toxicity, but the effectiveness of these methodologies has not been thoroughly evaluated:

- Apply potassium permanganate to the water column to remove hydrogen sulfide according to the following reaction:

$$4KMnO_4 + 3H_2S \rightarrow K_2SO_4 + S + 3MnO_2 + 3H_2O. \qquad (17.11)$$

  The minimum potassium permanganate requirement for removing 1 mg/L $H_2S$ would be 6.19 mg/L.[1]

- Treat pond bottoms with a source of iron to encourage the precipitation of hydrogen sulfide as iron sulfide. For example, ferrous oxide (FeO) has been applied to pond bottoms in Japan at 1 kg/m$^2$ for this purpose.[1] Research in laboratory soil-water systems has shown that application of 4,000 ppm of ferrihydrite (Fe$_5$O$_3$·9H$_2$O) would suppress hydrogen sulfide release from anaerobic sediment.[15]

- Apply sodium nitrate to maintain nitrate concentration in water to serve as an oxygen source for denitrifying bacteria at the soil-water interface. This should poise the redox potential at the soil-water interface above the redox potential at which hydrogen sulfide can exist.

- Treat ponds with probiotics containing sulfur-oxidizing bacteria (it is, however, doubtful if this procedure, called *bioaugmentation*, will be effective; see Chapter 21)

# References

1. Boyd, C. E. and C. S. Tucker. 1998. *Pond Aquaculture Water Quality Management*. Kluwer Academic Publishers, Boston, MA.
2. Adelman, I. R. and L. L. Smith, Jr. 1970. Effect of hydrogen sulfide on northern pike eggs and sac fry. Transactions of the American Fisheries Society 99:501-509.
3. Vismann, B. 1996. Sulfide species and total sulfide toxicity in the shrimp *Crangon crangon*. Journal of Experimental Marine Biology and Ecology 204:141-154.
4. Smith, L. L., Jr., D. M. Oseid, G. L. Kimball, and S. M. El-Kandelgy. 1976. Toxicity of hydrogen sulfide to various life history stages of bluegill (*Lepomis macrochirus*). Transactions of the American Fisheries Society 105:442-449.
5. Bonn, E. W. and B. J. Follis. 1967. Effects of hydrogen sulfide on channel catfish, *Ictalurus punctatus*. Transactions of the American Fisheries Society 96:31-36.
6. Gray, J. S., R. S. Wu, and Y. Y. Or. 2002. Effects of hypoxia and organic enrichment on the coastal marine environment. Marine Ecology Progress Series 238:249-279.
7. United States Environmental Protection Agency (USEPA). 1977. *Quality Criteria for Water*. Office of Water and Hazardous Materials, USEPA, Washington, DC..
8. Bagarinao, T. and I. Lantin-Olaguer. 1999. The sulfide tolerance of milkfish and tilapia in relation to fish kills in farms and natural waters in the Philippines. Hydrobiologia 382:137-150.
9. Gopakumar, G. and V. J. Kuttyamma. 1996. Effect of hydrogen sulphide on two species of penaeid prawns *Penaeus indicus* (H. Milne Edwards) and *Metapenaeus dobsoni* (Miers). Environmental Contamination and Toxicology 57:824-828.
10. Chien, Y. 1992. Water quality requirements and management for marine shrimp culture, pp. 144-156. In: *Proceedings of the Special Session on Shrimp Farming*. World Aquaculture Society, Baton Rouge, LA.
11. Cheng, S., S. Hsu, and J. Chen. 2007. Effect of sulfide on the immune response and susceptibility to *Vibrio alginolyticus* in the kuruma shrimp *Marsupenaeus japonicas*. Fish and Shellfish Immunology 22:16-26.
12. Hsu, S. and J. Chen. 2007. The immune response of white shrimp *Penaeus vannamei* and its susceptibility to *Vibrio alginolyticus* under sulfide stress. Aquaculture 27:61-69.

13. Ritvo, G., J. B. Dixon, W. H. Neill, T. M. Samocha, and A. L. Lawrence. 2000. The effect of controlled soil sulfur concentration on growth and survival of *Litopenaeus vannamei*. Journal of the World Aquaculture Society 31:381-389

14. Eaton, A. D., L. S. Clesceri, E. W. Rice, and A. E. Greenberg. 2005. *Standard Methods for the Examination of Water and Wastewater, 21st Edition*. American Public Health Association, Washington, DC.

15. Ritvo, G., V. Shitumbanuma, and J. B. Dixon. 2004. Soil solution sulfide control by two iron-oxide minerals in a submerged microcosm. Aquaculture 239:217-235.

# Chapter 18

# Toxic Algae and Off-flavors

## Introduction

Some aquatic microorganisms produce substances that are toxic to aquatic animals or make the aquaculture crop unsafe or unpleasant to eat. These problems often are caused by problematic algal communities called *harmful algal blooms* (HABs). The term is used loosely, however, because some organisms considered to be harmful 'algae' are algae only in the broadest sense—and some are not algae at all. Toxin- or odor-producing aquatic microorganism are among the most economically important water quality problems in aquaculture. They are also among the most difficult problems to manage.

## Toxic Algae

Some toxins produced by algae affect the aquaculture crop directly by reducing growth or killing the cultured animal. Other algal toxins may not be harmful to the crop itself, but rather they accumulate in the tissues of animals that feed upon the algae and are transmitted through the food chain. Toxins passed along the food chain may be a health threat to humans who consume the product. Most toxin-producing algae are marine and are important in shellfish farming or cage culture of fish in bays and estuaries. Only a few species are important in freshwater pond aquaculture.

Most problems occur when populations of potentially toxic species increase dramatically in events called *blooms*. Dense algal blooms may cause localized dissolved oxygen depletions that kill fish, shellfish, and other aquatic microorganisms independent of toxin production. In many instances, fish kills caused by dissolved oxygen depletions are mistakenly attributed to algal toxins because of the coincidental occurrence of suspected toxin-producing algae.

### Toxin-Producing Algae

#### Blue-green algae

Blue-green algae are not true plants but are bacteria with plant-like chlorophyll. Most species inhabit freshwater, although there are many brackishwater and marine species.

Toxic species produce hepatotoxins (liver poisons), neurotoxins (nervous system poisons), or both.[1]

The most common hepatotoxins are called *microcystins* and are produced by species of *Microcystis*, *Anabaena*, and *Planktothrix* (formerly *Oscillatoria*) that are common in freshwater aquaculture ponds (Fig. 18.1). Microcystins cause severe, sometimes fatal, damage to the liver of birds, cattle, swine, horses, and dogs that drink water containing toxin-producing blooms. Microcystins also cause liver damage in fish, although death in microcystin-challenged fish may result from a combination of liver failure and toxin-induced gill damage. Fish injected with a lethal dose of microcystin become lethargic and ventilation becomes rapid and irregular. Death occurs within a day or two following a period of coma.[2]

Blue-green algal neurotoxins include *anatoxins* and *saxitoxins*. Anatoxins are produced primarily by species of *Anabaena* and disrupt the function of the neurotransmitter acetylcholine, resulting in overstimulation of muscle cells. Symptoms include convulsions, tetany, and disoriented swimming; death is caused by respiratory paralysis. Saxitoxins are produced by *Aphanizomenon* (Fig. 18.1) and other genera. These are the same toxins produced by marine dinoflagellates that cause paralytic shellfish poisoning. Saxitoxins, like anatoxins, disrupt neuromuscular communication, although saxitoxins do so by preventing the release of acetylcholine, thereby paralyzing muscle cells. Symptoms of intoxication are similar to those caused by anatoxins.[2]

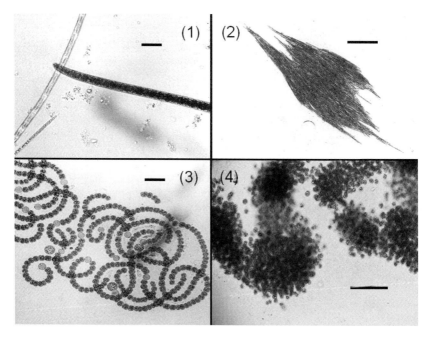

**Fig. 18.1.** Four common blue-green algae from aquaculture ponds: 1) *Planktothrix perornata* (bar = 10 µm); 2) *Aphanizomenon* sp. (bar = 50 µm); 3) *Anabaena* sp. (bar = 10 µm); and 4) *Microcystis* sp. (bar = 10 µm).

There are surprisingly few reports of fish kills that can be unequivocally attributed to toxin-producing blue-green algae, which is puzzling because toxin-producing blue-green algal strains are very common in warm, freshwater aquaculture ponds. Further, blue-green algal toxins are quite toxic to fish when injected directly. There is no good explanation for this paradox, although several factors may contribute to the apparent tolerance of fish to blooms of toxin-producing blue-green algae.[3]

*Euglenoids*

Some strains of *Euglena sanguinea* (and possibly *E. granulata*) produce a potent neurotoxin, *euglenophycin*, that has killed channel catfish and hybrid striped bass in freshwater ponds.[4] Fish exposed to toxin-producing *E. sanguinea* go through a rapid succession of symptoms including loss of appetite, disoriented swimming near the surface or at pond edges, followed by death. Although fish kills have been reported only from the United States, *E. sanguinea* is a common species found worldwide in a variety of temperate and tropical fresh waters (Fig. 18.2).

*Haptophytes (golden-brown algae)*

The Haptophyceae is a distinctive group of mostly marine, unicellular algae. Haptophytes have two flagella used for locomotion and a third appendage, called a haptonema, that enables cells to attach to surfaces and aids in food capture. Haptophytes have two golden-brown chloroplasts, giving the group its common name *golden-brown algae*. Haptophytes are mixotrophic, meaning they obtain food in photosynthesis and by ingesting dissolved

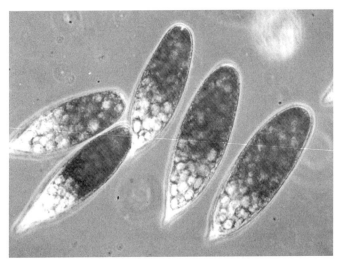

**Fig. 18.2.** *Euglena sanguina.* Cells are approximately 60-μm long. The darker, anterior portions of the cells (towards the upper right of each cell) are tinged with hematochrome, giving the cells a red coloration.

or particulate organic matter. Species in two genera, *Prymnesium* (Fig. 18.3) and *Chrysochromulina* produce toxins that have caused spectacular fish kills. Toxic species of *Chrysochromulina* inhabit estuaries and near-shore marine waters; *Prymnesium* is found most often in mineralized inland waters.

*Prymnesium parvum* (the most common *Prymnesium* species) produces potent toxins that kill gill-breathing animals, including fish, crustaceans, and shellfish; they have no effect on mammals, birds, or aquatic insects. The species has world-wide distribution and grows in waters with salinities of 2 to 50 ppt, with optimum salinities for growth and toxin production in the range of 3 to 25 ppt. Optimum growth temperature is in the range of 20° to 25°C, although fish kills related to *P. parvum* have occurred at water temperatures from less than 10°C to almost 30°C. *Prymnesium* produces several toxic substances collectively called *prymnesins*.[5] Toxins act by disrupting gill membrane permeability followed by toxin uptake across the gills. After the toxins cross the gill membrane, cytotoxic and hemolytic activities are expressed, including lysis of red blood cells and neurotoxic effects. Gills of affected fish are fragile and may bleed easily when touched. Hemorrhagic areas may be evident around the mouth, eyes, and base of fins. Intoxicated fish are lethargic and may swim to the bank where they lie in shallow water and possibly die. In the early stages of intoxication, fish may recover within an hour or two if transferred to clean water.

The genus *Chrysochromulina* comprises dozens of widely distributed species that are important in fresh water and marine food chains. At least two marine species produce ichthyotoxins that may be similar to those produced by *Prymnesium parvum*.[6] Under certain conditions populations can suddenly increase—usually in nearshore waters—and cause massive losses of net-pen cultured fish.[7]

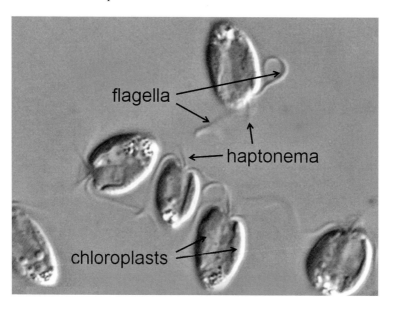

**Fig. 18.3.** *Prymnesium* sp. Cells are approximately 10-μm long.

*Raphidophytes*

Raphidophytes are small, bean-shaped cells with two flagella arising from near the middle of the cell—one flagella points forward and the other trails behind. Raphidophytes are usually inconspicuous in freshwater and marine environments, but some marine species including species of *Chatonella*, *Heterosigma*, and *Fibrocapsa* may suddenly bloom in nearshore waters and cause fish kills, including fish cultured in net pens.[7] Toxic raphidophytes produce neurotoxic and hemolytic toxins.

*Dinoflagellates*

Dinoflagellates are common, small, mostly marine, biflagellate organisms that are important in aquatic food chains. Species may be photosynthetic, heterotrophic, or mixotrophic (combining photosynthesis and feeding on particulate organic matter—often including live prey). Some are parasitic. A few species produce potent toxins that cause problems in fisheries throughout the world. Dinoflagellate blooms are often called *red tides* and usually consist of one species that suddenly increases rapidly in abundance. Red tides may be toxic or not depending on the species.

Some dinoflagellate species produce toxins that accumulate in shellfish and other filter-feeding invertebrates, often with no obvious ill effects on the filter-feeder. Toxins are passed through the food chain to consumers, including humans who may suffer potentially lethal neurological, gastrointestinal, and respiratory disorders.

When blooms of toxic dinoflagellates occur in areas with shellfish aquaculture facilities, the products may become toxic to humans and unmarketable, imposing serious economic hardships on shellfish growers and associated industries. Although it is often assumed that toxic dinoflagellates have little effect on shellfish (other than rendering them toxic to vertebrate consumers), blooms of certain species can cause slow growth or death of larval, juvenile, and adult oysters, mussels, and other bivalves.[8]

In addition to human food-safety problems caused by dinoflagellate toxins, fish may also be killed or stressed when exposed to toxic dinoflagellates. Some toxins can poison fish when they eat shellfish or crustaceans that have accumulated the toxins while feeding on the toxin-producing dinoflagellates. Toxins may also kill fish feeding directly on the toxic dinoflagellates. The heterotrophic dinoflagellates *Pfiesteria piscicida* and *P. shumwayae* produce ichthyotoxins and feed on tissues of live and dead fish. Blooms of *Pfiesteria* occur in estuaries worldwide and have been implicated in several fish kills, especially along the Atlantic coast of the United States.[9]

*Diatoms*

Diatoms are common algae with a two-part shell impregnated with silicon. They are important in marine and freshwater food chains. Marine species in the genus *Pseudonitzchia* produce domoic acid—a powerful toxin that causes amnesic shellfish poisoning in humans who eat shellfish growing in waters containing toxic strains of

*Pseudonitzchia*. Symptoms include abdominal cramps, disorientation, short-term memory loss, and, in some instances, death. Species of another marine diatom, *Chaetoceros*, have spines that can break off, penetrate, and damage the delicate epithelial tissues of fish gills (Fig. 18.4). Blooms of *Chaetoceros* have caused extensive losses of cage-cultured salmon.[10]

## Toxic Algae Management in Ponds

Harmful algal problems and their management differ among aquaculture systems. In ponds with long hydraulic residence times, harmful communities develop inside the culture system and the culturist has some control over bloom development and management of toxic episodes. In contrast, harmful algal communities may develop outside of flow-through systems and net pens where the culturist has no control. For example, a toxic dinoflagellate population may develop in an estuary and then be swept through a net pen facility by tidal currents. Toxic algae are not a problem in recirculating aquaculture systems because facilities can be made biosecure and microbial communities inside the system can be controlled.

Fish kills in ponds have been caused by species of blue-green algae, *Prymnesium*, and *Euglena*. These organisms, especially *Prymnesium*, may also cause toxic events in flow-through and net-pen aquaculture systems, although other taxonomic groups are usually more important in those systems.

### Managing toxic blue-green algae

Developing complex or expensive management practices to prevent blooms of toxic blue-green algae is probably not justified because toxin-producing species are very common in

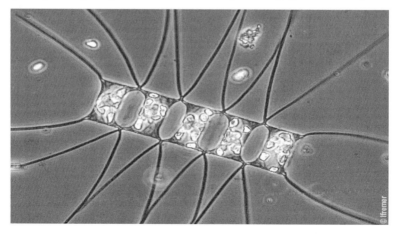

**Fig. 18.4.** *Chaetoceros* sp. Each cell possesses four silicified setae (spines) that overlap and link cells together into small colonies. Cells are approximately 10-μm wide. Photo credit: IFREMER.

in aquaculture ponds, yet there are few conclusive reports of toxin-related fish kills. The prevalence of potentially toxic blue-green algae can be reduced by decreasing nutrient loading rates, vigorous mixing, or culturing filter-feeding fish that selectively graze on large colonial phytoplankton (most toxin-producing blue-green algae form relatively large colonies or filaments). However, completely eliminating toxin-producing species is not possible. If problems with toxic blue-green algae are suspected, application of algicides will probably make conditions worse because large amounts of toxin will be released into the water when the algae die and lyse.

Anatoxins and microcystins are easily oxidized to non-toxic substances by relatively low doses of potassium permanganate.[11] If applied early in the toxic event, before fish receive a lethal dose of toxin, application of potassium permanganate may prevent or reduce fish losses to blue-green algal toxins. Potassium permanganate is a strong oxidant and is toxic to fish at concentrations not much higher than those needed to oxidize the toxins. It is also an expensive chemical. As such, the culturist must be certain that algal toxins are causing—or about to cause—a problem and that the risk and expense of treatment are justified.

The decision to treat can be difficult because strange fish behavior and fish kills can be caused by many conditions unrelated to algal toxins. When toxicosis is suspected, there is usually little time to gather conclusive evidence (such as toxin analysis) that algal toxins are the cause. Minimally, the decision to treat should be based on three lines of evidence: 1) clinical signs of intoxication that are consistent with those known for blue-green algal toxins; 2) one or more potential toxin-producing species are present in a water sample examined by a competent microbiologist; and 3) all other possible causes of the problem are ruled out.

Potassium permanganate treatment rates vary from pond to pond because the chemical is rapidly consumed in reactions with organic matter in water. Potassium permanganate must be applied to achieve a residual concentration 2 to 3 mg/L above the amount lost in those initial reactions. Ponds with low levels of organic matter in the water (sparse phytoplankton blooms) may require a total treatment of only 2 to 4 mg/L potassium permanganate whereas more than 6 mg/L may be required in a pond with abundant phytoplankton. Treatment rates are best estimated by performing a simple '15-minute potassium permanganate demand test' to determine the amount of chemical consumed in initial oxidation reactions and then adding 2 to 3 mg/L to that amount. The demand test is conducted by adding a standard potassium permanganate solution to a series of water samples in 1.0 mg/L increments, waiting 15 minutes, and then visually determining the lowest concentration of potassium permanganate that still has a faint pink color.[12] The estimated amount of chemical needed for treatment should not be applied to the pond in one dose, but rather applied in 1 or 2 mg/L increments to avoid overtreatment.

*Managing toxic euglenoids*

Control methods for *Euglena* toxic events are unknown. It appears that euglenophycins can be detoxified by potassium permanganate and limited field experience suggests that timely application of the chemical reduces fish mortality rates.[4] Follow the same procedure described above for treating blue-green algal toxicoses with potassium permanganate.

*Managing toxic prymnesiophytes*

*Prymnesium parvum* is responsible for killing more pond-raised fish than any other alga and considerable research has been conducted on control methods. Control depends on early detection, which may involve a continuous program of monitoring in waters highly susceptible to *Prymnesium* blooms. Detection methods includes microscopic examination of water samples for the organism, bioassays to detect toxins, visual indications that a bloom is present, and clinical signs of intoxication in fish.[13]

If *Prymnesium* is detected early (before populations become dense), copper-based algicides or applications of ammonium sulfate can be used to eradicate the algae. These methods should not be used when dense blooms are present because large amounts of intracellular toxins may be released into the water when cells lyse. The use of ammonia sulfate to kill *Prymnesium* is a unique and highly selective control measure. Sufficient ammonium sulfate is applied to increase un-ionized ammonia level to about 0.15 to 0.25 mg $NH_3$-N/L.[14] Apparently, un-ionized ammonia freely diffuses across *Prymnesium* cell membranes where it is protonated at the lower pH existing inside the *Prymnesium* cell. Eventually the internal concentration of ammonium ion reaches a point where the increased turgor pressure within the cell causes the cell to rupture. Although this is an effective and widely used method of controlling losses to *Prymnesium blooms*, it should be used cautiously since un-ionized ammonia is also toxic to fish and other aquatic animals. Prymnesins can be detoxified with potassium permanganate using the methods described above for detoxifying blue-green algal toxins with the chemical.[13]

Because of the potential toxicity of ammonia and copper-based algicides to fish, other control methods have been investigated. When freshwater or euryhaline fish or crustaceans are cultured, growth of *Prymensium* can be discouraged by reducing the salinity of pond waters to less than 2 ppt. *Prymensium* blooms also can be controlled by manipulating algal community structure to encourage other phytoplankton species. Apparently, *Prymensium* species gain a competitive advantage over other phytoplankton when nutrient levels are low, so frequent additions of inorganic or organic fertilizer can change community structure and discourage *Prymnesium* blooms.[15]

Many *Prymnesium* toxic events in ponds are caused by introduction of cells from surface water supplies. The most efficient risk-reduction strategy may be to monitor the water supply and treat incoming water to eliminate *Prymnesium* before it reaches the pond. These methods are discussed in the next section.

## Toxic Algae Management in Flow-though and Cage Systems

Flow-through systems and cages have open water exchange with the external environment and the aquaculture crop within the facility may be exposed to harmful algal blooms that develop outside the system. Animals in raceways, flow-through ponds, or cages are particularly susceptible to toxic blooms because they are held captive and cannot escape when winds or currents move blooms into areas near the facility.

Preventing or managing toxic events in open aquaculture systems is difficult because blooms may cover a large area (thousands of hectares, or larger) and develop far away from the facility, usually in waters that cannot be legally or logistically managed by the culturist. Also, the few management options available work only when the problem is detected early, yet toxic blooms are unpredictable and may develop rapidly. The best solution is to choose sites with a low probability of nuisance blooms. Site evaluation should include a thorough hydrographic survey including rates of water exchange (sites should be fully mixed and in contact with fully mixed sea areas), assessment of the nutrient status of the local waters and the accumulation of soft sediments (soft sediments indicate areas of poor circulation that may allow harmful blooms to remain in the vicinity of the facility for long periods), a survey of the phytoplankton community and previous problems related to harmful blooms, and a survey for the presence of cysts in local sediments (dormant cysts indicate that a bloom is possible).[16]

It is probably impossible to find sites for large-scale aquaculture that are completely risk-free because toxic algae occur in most brackish and marine environments and in many inland waters. Management therefore depends on early detection and developing a plan to minimize impacts if a harmful bloom develops in the water supply.

Several management options are available for land-based, flow-through systems using surface water supplies. These culture systems include tanks, raceways, or ponds with constant inflow from a discrete, controllable water supply (usually water pumped through pipes or open channels). The water supply should be monitored for potential toxin-producing algae and the culturist should watch for changes in the appearance of the water supply or changes in behavior of animals in the water supply or in the culture facility. Many countries and states maintain internet websites or telephone hot-lines with current information on harmful bloom status. When a problem is imminent, water inflow can be temporarily stopped until the bloom in the water supply dissipates. Aeration or oxygenation should be available to support animals in the absence of water flow. Feeding should be stopped and, if possible, animal standing crops should be reduced either by harvest or transport to a temporary refuge site not affected by the bloom. If toxin-producing algae or their toxins are introduced into the system, treatment with potassium permanganate (as described above) will kill the organism and oxidize most toxins. Use of algicides such as copper sulfate should be avoided because intracellular toxins will be released into the water when algal cells lyse.

In areas with recurrent harmful blooms, it may be cost-effective to treat the source water before it enters the facility. Ozone ($O_3$) and ultraviolet irradiation will kill harmful algae and most other organisms in the water. Ozone also oxidizes microcystins and anatoxins,[11] prymesins,[13] and brevetoxins produced by some dinoflagellates.[17] Saxitoxins—toxins produced by certain dinoflagellates and blue-green algae—resist ozone oxidation.[18] Ultraviolet irradiation kills algal cells but does not detoxify algal toxins, which limits its usefulness.

Control of bloom toxicity for cage facilities is much more difficult than for land-based systems with a controllable water supply. Cages are literally immersed in the environment, and it is nearly impossible to prevent entry of toxic blooms when they drift into the area by tidal or wind-driven currents. Proper siting to minimize risk is essential. It may be possible to surround pens or cages with an impervious barrier or tow the pen to a safe location. Such measures are feasible only for small pens. If adequate warning is given, it may be possible to reduce standing crops to minimize losses. The only mitigation strategy that has had some success is using clay slurries to co-flocculate toxic algae around cage culture facilities.[19] As the slurry settles through the water, it binds with algal cells forming aggregates that settle out of the water. Removal efficiency depends on the type of clay, water turbulence and velocity, salinity, and other factors. Small algae, such as *Prymnesium*, are difficult to flocculate unless clays are combined with aluminum salts or synthetic polymer flocculants.[20] Flocculation is a controversial practice because it may simply redistribute the algal cells and their toxins from the water column to sediments where toxicity is expressed to bottom-dwelling organisms. Also, the logistics of obtaining and applying clays limits the general usefulness of flocculation to small-scale applications in relatively confined areas.

# Off-Flavors

*Off-flavors* are objectionable tastes or odors in water or foods. Off-flavors in aquaculture products are often caused by spoilage or lipid oxidation after harvest and processing. Here we discuss off-flavors acquired before harvest. Some off-flavors are caused by substances in natural foods or feed ingredients. Most are caused by odorous compounds absorbed from the water.[21]

The most common off-flavors are caused by natural substances that are non-toxic to aquatic animals or human consumers. In that respect, off-flavor is different from other water quality problems in aquaculture because the concern is aesthetic rather than fish husbandry or human safety. Off-flavors are important because off-flavored fish or crustaceans should not be harvested, which reduces profits for the grower. If off-flavored seafood is inadvertently marketed, the negative consumer reaction may adversely affect long-term market demand for that product.

## *Types of Off-Flavor*

### *Off-flavors of microbial origin*

The most common aquaculture off-flavors are caused by the compounds *geosmin* or *2-methylisoborneol* (MIB) (Fig. 18.5). Geosmin has an earthy odor redolent of a damp basement or cellar, while 2-methylisoborneol has a unique, musty-medicinal odor, somewhat like camphor. They are among the most highly odorous compounds found in nature and are common in aquatic and terrestrial environments—for example, they give soil its characteristic odor. Both compounds are highly lipophilic and concentrated into fatty tissues. The combination of very low human sensory threshold and high bioconcentration means that geosmin and MIB cause flavor problems in fish or crustaceans even when present in water at trace levels. Geosmin and MIB are synthesized by a variety of fungi, actinobacteria, and blue-green algae. In ponds, they are nearly always produced by blue-green algae.[21]

Relatively few species of blue-green algae synthesize geosmin or MIB in aquaculture ponds. Geosmin is usually produced by species of *Anabaena* and *Aphanizomenon* and MIB by species of *Planktothrix* (Fig. 18.1). Flavor problems in cultured animals coincide with the development and disappearance of odor-producing populations. When odorous populations are present, waterborne geosmin or MIB are absorbed across the gills and stored in animal tissues. When odor-producing algae disappear from the phytoplankton community (or when fish are transferred to clean water), geosmin and MIB in fish or crustacean tissues are purged or metabolized. Rates of depuration depend primarily on water temperature and tissue fat content. Lean fish in warm water may completely depurate intense off-flavors within days, whereas fatty fish in cold water may remain off-flavor for months.

Off-flavors caused by geosmin and MIB are common in cultured and wild fish throughout the world. Most waters producing fish tainted with geosmin or MIB are static, nutrient-enriched fresh waters where blue-green algal communities are a natural consequence of prevailing environmental conditions. The species that produce geosmin and 2-methylisoborneol do not thrive in saline waters and earthy-musty off-flavors have been reported only for aquatic animals grown in fresh water or dilute brackish water.

In contrast to ponds in which geosmin and MIB are produced mainly by blue-green algae, earthy-musty off-flavors in freshwater recirculating systems are caused by species *Streptomyces* and *Nocardia*, which are aerobic actinobacteria with a filamentous, branching growth habit. They thrive in aerobic, organic-rich environments and frequently grow as biofilms on the surfaces of tanks, filters, or other components of recirculating aquaculture systems.[22,23]

In addition to geosmin and MIB, dozens of odorous compounds have been isolated from cultures of actinomycetes, blue-green algae, and eukaryotic algae. Some compounds have odors similar to those described from off-flavored fish, but few have been confirmed as the cause. Odorous compounds also are released into water during bacterial

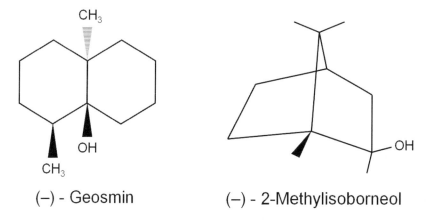

(−) - Geosmin          (−) - 2-Methylisoborneol

**Fig. 18.5.** Structures of geosmin and 2-methylisoborneol.

decomposition of organic matter, including offensive sulfur-containing mercaptans and sulfides, and noxious amino acid decomposition products. Fish from recirculating systems or ponds sometimes have faint off-flavors described as 'swampy' or 'sewage-like' that may be related to odorous compounds produced during organic matter decomposition.

*Off-flavors caused by pollution*

Some organic pollutants discharged into natural waters are highly odorous and can impair the flavor of aquatic animals. Off-flavor problems related to industrial pollutants are rare in cultured fish because it is easy to site aquaculture facilities to avoid exposure. However, petroleum products potentially may enter culture facilities in runoff contaminated with motor oils or fuels from accidental spills of fuels or lubricants from boats, pumps, or other equipment. Fish and other aquatic animals exposed to petroleum products develop characteristic off-flavors variously described as oily, diesel fuel, petroleum, kerosene, and so on.

Petroleum hydrocarbons are absorbed quickly from the water and stored in the fatty tissues for long periods after exposure. Fish exposed to petroleum products therefore develop off-flavors rapidly and lose the flavors slowly, persisting for weeks or months after exposure. Purging of the flavor is especially slow in cold water. As little as 2 L of diesel fuel spilled in a 1-ha pond can cause noticeable off-flavors in fish.

*Diet-related off-flavors*

Off-flavors can be caused by dietary components that are absorbed across the gastrointestinal tract and deposited in the flesh.[21] Diet-related off-flavors are rare in aquaculture because high-quality commercial feeds are formulated so that they do not cause flavor problems. However, animals in ponds (and perhaps other culture systems) occasionally eat foods other than manufactured feed, and some of those food items may cause flavor problems. For example, 'decay' or 'rotten' off-flavors are occasionally noted in pond-raised catfish during winter when many catfish farmers do not routinely feed their fish. These flavors probably develop when fish eat decaying organic matter as they forage for natural foods.

## Off-Flavor Management in Ponds

All aquatic animals can acquire off-flavors and risk does not depend on species, but rather on the culture environment. Animals grown in freshwater ponds are at high risk, because environmental conditions often favor development of blue-green algal communities. Off-flavors are also relatively common in freshwater recirculating aquaculture systems because they provide good conditions for actinobacteria. The risk of off-flavor in flow-through and cage aquaculture depends on the nature of the water supply. Animals in flow-through systems supplied with unpolluted ground water should not develop off-flavors, but animals in any facility connected to surface waters may become tainted with odors produced by microorganisms in the water supply. Accidental contamination of the culture water or water supply also can cause off-flavors in any culture system. The extent of contamination may be small (a few milliliters of hydraulic fluid from a leaky pump) or large (millions of liters of crude oil spilling from a grounded tanker).

Off-flavors are difficult to manage in pond aquaculture because "off-flavor" describes a variety of problems, each with a unique (and often unknown) origin. Problems cannot, therefore, be solved with a single management strategy. Control of off-flavor is also difficult because many aquaculture ponds are ideal habitats for blue-green algae—the most common cause of off-flavors in pond-raised fish and crustaceans.

Four approaches have been used to manage blue-green algal off-flavors in pond aquaculture: 1) avoid harvesting the crop during off-flavor episode, 2) biomanipulation of algal communities using plankton-feeding fish, 3) using algicides to kill odorous algae, and 4) moving fish to a clean environment where off-flavor are purged.[21] Off-flavors caused by inadvertent contamination with petroleum products are persistent and difficult to treat once they occur, and are most easily managed by prevention. Regardless of cause, off-flavors cannot be prevented with certainty. As such, overall risk management should always include routine pre-harvest monitoring of flavor quality to so that off-flavored products do not enter the marketplace.

*Avoid harvesting off-flavored animals*

The biomass and taxonomic composition of pond phytoplankton communities constantly changes. When an odor-producing species starts growing, fish become off-flavored. But when community composition changes and the odor-producing species disappears, MIB or geosmin are metabolized or purged from the flesh and flavor improves. Therefore, one way to manage the problem is to monitor flavor quality to find 'windows of opportunity' in which off-flavors are absent and the crop can be harvested. The disadvantage to this approach is that it is impossible to predict how long an odor-producing species will remain in the pond—they may disappear in a few days or they may persist for months.

*Biomanipulation*

Blue-green algae have a competitive advantage over other phytoplankton in warm, fresh waters with high nutrient loading rates. Drastically reducing nutrient loading rates can encourage the growth of other phytoplankton types but this is difficult in aquaculture ponds where high nutrient levels are a natural consequence of fertilization or feeding practices. Phytoplankton communities are also influenced by interactions with organism higher in the food chain. Using these interactions to control plankton abundance and water quality is called *biomanipulation*.

Biomanipulation in aquaculture uses plankton-feeding fish to alter phytoplankton community structure. Most plankton-feeding fish graze or feed most efficiently on larger food items, such as colonial phytoplankton and large-bodied zooplankton. Smaller phytoplankton species then thrive because of reduced competition from larger algae and less grazing pressure from large zooplankton. In theory, plankton-feeding fish should reduce the incidence of odor-producing blue-green algae, which are relatively large filamentous organisms.

Reports of off-flavor are rare in pond cultures of planktivorous Chinese carps and tilapias, indicating that planktivorous fishes do reduce the incidence of odor-producing blue-green phytoplankton. Also, adding blue tilapia or threadfin shad to channel catfish ponds reduces the abundance of odorous blue-green algae and reduces the incidence of geosmin and MIB off-flavors in catfish. But, tilapia and threadfin shad are cold intolerant and with when water temperatures fall below 10-15°C in winter, catfish develop "rotten-fish" off-flavors caused by feeding on dead fish. Using tilapia or threadfin shad for phytoplankton biomanipulation in channel catfish ponds therefore presents a dilemma: planktivore polyculture reduces catfish off-flavor incidence in warm months but causes off-flavors in the colder months.[24]

*Algicides*

Algicides can be used to kill odorous blue-green algae, which will allow geosmin or MIB to purge from fish. Under the right conditions this can be reasonably successful. The key to success is to confirm that blue-green algae are the cause of the problem. Obviously, algicides have no effect on off-flavors caused by compounds that are not produced by algae.

Copper sulfate and certain chelated or complexed copper products are the most commonly used algicides in aquaculture (see Chapter 19). Copper sulfate is not a selective algicide, so its use will probably kill all, or most, of the other algae in the pond. Dissolved oxygen depletion may follow and sufficient mechanical aeration must be available to cope with the problem. Copper sulfate is also potentially toxic to fish and crustaceans. These are ample reasons to be certain that blue-green algae are causing the flavor problem before deciding to use copper-based algicides. To be effective, the odor-producing species must be completely eliminated, which often calls for multiple treatments. The need for additional treatments can be confirmed by microscopic examination of a water sample taken a few days after the first treatment. If any odorous blue-green algae persist, additional treatment is needed.

Diuron is an organic herbicide that has been approved by the United States Environmental Protection Agency (EPA) for use as an off-flavor treatment in certain states. Diuron is algicidal at low concentrations (0.01 mg/L active ingredient) and can be an effective treatment for blue-green algal off-flavors. Multiple treatments may be necessary to completely eliminate the odor-producing species and the EPA-approved treatment protocol for diuron calls for no more than nine weekly treatments with 0.01 mg/L active ingredient in a calendar year.

*Depuration*

Moving off-flavor animals to clean water is the most dependable way of improving flavor quality. All off-flavors eventually disappear when the animal is no longer exposed to the odorous chemical, but the time for complete depuration varies greatly. Geosmin and MIB are eliminated fairly rapidly from fish and crustaceans. Other compounds, such as petroleum hydrocarbons, are more slowly eliminated, and weeks to months may be required for off-flavors to dissipate. Purging rates of all chemicals decrease at lower water temperatures and fatty animals purge more slowly than lean animals. Moving fish to clean environments is laborious and time-consuming, and always carries some risk that some animals may die from handling stress. Shrimp in particular may not withstand the rigors of harvest and transfer without significant loss.

## Managing Off-Flavors in Recirculating Systems

Off flavors caused by geosmin and MIB are found widely in coldwater and warmwater fish grown in recirculating systems. Biocides cannot be used to control off-flavors, because the nitrification biofilter is a common site of colonization by actinobacteria, and biocides could kill nitrifying bacteria as well as the odor-producing bacteria. Ozone has been proposed to oxidize geosmin and MIB in drinking water supplies, but ozone dosages considered safe to fish in recirculating systems do not reduce geosmin or MIB levels in culture water.[25] Higher levels of ozone may remove the odorous compounds, but the ozone residual in the contact chamber would have to be removed by ultraviolet irradiation before the water reaches fish culture tanks. At present, off-flavors that develop in recirculating aquaculture systems are most effectively managed by moving harvest-ready animals to a separate depuration facility supplied with odor-free water.

## Managing Off-Flavors Caused by Pollution

Off-flavors caused by pollution are not common in aquaculture products because it is easy—and prudent—to site aquaculture facilities where they can be supplied with unpolluted water. Nevertheless, off-flavors caused by polluted water are not completely avoidable in aquaculture, and some culture facilities, such as open water cages and shellfish beds, are particularly vulnerable to unanticipated pollution. Most problems are caused by relatively small spills of petroleum products. Prevention is the best management, because petroleum off-flavors are extremely difficult to purge from animals. Fuel and oil storage facilities should be located away from ponds and fitted with secondary containment to retain spills. Care should be exercised when refueling vehicles and other equipment, or when handling petroleum products near culture facilities. Farm workers should be aware that even small spills of diesel fuel and other petroleum products can cause noticeable off-flavors in fish.

# References

1. Hudnell, K. H. 2008. *Cyanobacterial Harmful Algal Blooms: State of the Science and Research Needs. Advances in Experimental Medicine and Biology, Volume 619.* Springer Science + Business Media LLC, New York, NY.
2. Malbrouck, C. and P. Kestemont. 2006. Effects of microcystins on fish. Environmental Toxicology and Chemistry 25:72-86.
3. Boyd, C. E. and C. S. Tucker. 1998. *Pond Aquaculture Water Quality Management.* Kluwer Academic Publishers, Boston, MA.
4. Zimba, P. V., P. D. Moeller, K. Beauchesne, H. E. Lane, and R. E. Triemer. 2010. Identification of euglenophycin—a toxin found in certain euglenoids. Toxicon 55:100-104.
5. Manning, S. R. and J. W. La Claire. 2010. Prymnesins: toxic metabolites of the golden alga *Prymnesium parvum* Carter (Haptophyta). Marine Drugs 8:678-704.
6. Houdan, A., A. Bonnard, J. Fresnel, S. Fouchard, C. Billard, and I. Probert. 2004. Toxicity of coastal coccolithophores (Prymnesiophyceae, Haptophyta). Journal of Plankton Research 26:875-883.
7. Smayda, T. 2006. *Harmful Algal Bloom Communities in Scottish Coastal Waters: Relationship to Fish Farming and Regional Comparisons—A Review.* Paper 2006/3 prepared for The Scottish Executive Environmental and Rural Affairs Department. Available at http://www.scotland.gov.uk/Publications/2006/02/03095327/0
8. Gainey, L. F., Jr. and S. E. Shumway. 1988. A compendium of the responses of bivalve molluscs to toxic dinoflagellates. Journal of Shellfish Research 7:623-628.
9. Burkholder, J. M. and H. G. Marshall. 2012. Toxigenic *Pfiesteria* species—updates on biology, ecology, toxins, and impacts. Harmful Algae 14:196-230.
10. Bruno, D. W., G. Dear, and D. D. Seaton. 1989. Mortality associated with phytoplankton blooms among farmed Atlantic salmon, *Salmo salar* L., in Scotland. Aquaculture 78:217-222.
11. Rodriguez, E., G. D. Onstad, T. P. J. Kull, J. Metcalf, J. L. Acero, and U. Von Gunton. 2007. Oxidative elimination of cyanotoxins: Comparison of ozone, chlorine, chlorine dioxide and permanganate. Water Research 41:3381-3393.
12. Boyd, C.E. 1979. *Water Quality in Warmwater Fish Ponds.* Alabama Agricultural Experiment Station, Auburn University, AL
13. Barkoh, A., D. G. Smith, and G. M. Southard. 2010. *Prymnesium parvum* control treatments for fish hatcheries. Journal of the American Water Resources Association 46:161-169.
14. Barkoh, A., D. G. Smith, and J. W. Schlechte. 2003. An effective minimum concentration of un-ionized ammonia nitrogen for controlling *Prymnesium parvum*. North American Journal of Aquaculture 65:220-225.
15. Kurten, G. L., A. Barkoh, L. T. Fries, and D. C. Begley. 2007. Combined nitrogen and phosphorus fertilization for controlling the toxigenic alga *Prymnesium parvum*. North American Journal of Aquaculture 69:214-222.
16. Shumway, S. E. 1990. A review of the effects of algal blooms on shellfish and aquaculture. Journal of the World Aquaculture Society 21:65-104.
17. Schneider, K. R. R. H. Pierce, and G. E. Rorick. 2003. The degradation of *Karenia brevis* toxins utilizing ozonated seawater. Harmful Algae 2:101-107.
18. Orr, P. T., G. J. Jones, and G. R. Hamilton. 2004. Removal of saxitoxins from drinking water by granular carbon, ozone, and hydrogen peroxide—implications for compliance with the Australian drinking water guidelines. Water Research 38:4455-4461.
19. Sengco, M. R. and D. M. Anderson. 2004. Controlling harmful blooms through clay flocculation. Journal of Eukaryotic Microbiology 51:169-172.

20. Sengco, M. R., J. A. Hagstrom, E. Graneli, and D. M. Anderson. 2005. Removal of *Prymnesium parvum* (Haptophyceae) and its toxins using clay minerals. Harmful Algae 4:261-

21. Tucker, C. S. 2000. Off-flavor problems in aquaculture. Reviews in Fisheries Science 8:45-88.

22. Guttman, L., and J. van Rijn. 2008. Identification of conditions underlying production of geosmin and 2-methylisoborneol in a recirculating system. Aquaculture 279:85-91

23. Schrader, K. K. and S. T. Summerfelt. 2010. Distribution of off-flavor compounds and isolation of geosmin-producing bacteria in a series of water recirculating systems for rainbow trout culture. North American Journal of Aquaculture 72:1-9.

24. Mischke, C. C., C. S. Tucker, and M. Li. 2011. Channel catfish polyculture with fathead minnows or threadfin shad: effects on pond plankton communities and catfish fillet flavor, color, and fatty acid composition. Journal of the World Aquaculture Association 43:208-217.

25. Schrader, K. K., J.W. Davidson, A. M. Rimando, and S. T. Summerfelt. 2010. Evaluation of ozonation on levels of the off-flavor compounds geosmin and 2-methylisoborneol in water and rainbow trout *Oncorhynchus mykiss* from recirculating aquaculture systems Aquacultural Engineering 43:46-50.

# Chapter 19

# Aquatic Plant Management

## Introduction

The role of aquatic plants in pond aquaculture has been mentioned many times throughout this book. Plants are the base of the food web in cultures relying on natural foods produced in the pond. In those cultures to increase aquaculture yield, plant growth is often encouraged through fertilization. Plant communities also function with other components of the ecosystem to maintain adequate water quality for aquaculture production. For example, oxygen produced in plant photosynthesis is a major source of dissolved oxygen in most ponds.

Although plants are desirable in most aquaculture ponds, some types of plants interfere with pond management, endanger the well-being of the animal under culture, or impair the quality of the aquaculture product. In those instances, plants become weeds, and aquaculturists often try to prevent them from developing or to eradicate them if they become established.

## Aquatic Plant Communities

Aquatic plants can be categorized based on growth form and location in the water column: 1) phytoplankton, 2) periphyton; 3) macrophytic filamentous algae, 4) submersed plants, 5) emergent plants, 6) free-floating plants, and 7) rooted floating plants. Some type of community will always be present because aquaculture ponds are ideal habitats for aquatic plants. The type of community that becomes established depends on the outcome of resource competition among different plants.

### Phytoplankton

Phytoplankton is the community of microscopic plants and plant-like bacteria suspended or weakly swimming in water. When the quantities of organisms become abundant enough to noticeably discolor the water, the communities are sometimes called *blooms*. Phytoplankton are efficient at using dissolved nutrients and communities grow rapidly under conditions of adequate nutrient availability, warm water temperatures, and good light penetration into the water.

Phytoplankton is usually the most desirable plant community in aquaculture ponds. Phytoplankton help prevent growth of less desirable plants by competing for nutrients and shading the water so that plants near the bottom do not have enough light to grow. Because of their microscopic size, phytoplankton does not interfere with harvest, feeding, or other pond management activities. Most phytoplankton are of high food quality and phytoplankton is generally a good base for food webs when cultures depend on natural foods produced in the pond. Phytoplankton can, however, become a weed problem when community standing crops become too high or when undesirable species are present.

Overabundance of phytoplankton causes imbalances in dissolved oxygen budgets resulting in large daily dissolved oxygen deficits (see Chapter 13). Some blue-green algae, notably certain species of *Microcystis* and *Anabaena*, form obnoxious scums on the surface of the water. Surface scums of blue-green algae are poor oxygenators because much of the oxygen produced in photosynthesis is lost to the atmosphere rather than dissolved in the water. Blue-green algal scums can suddenly experience what are called 'die-offs;' the entire community dies over a short period of time with catastrophic deterioration in water quality. In some aquaculture systems, the most economically important weed problems are the production of toxins or odorous compounds by phytoplankton (Chapter 18).

## Periphyton or Attached Algae

Periphyton is the community of microscopic algae growing on underwater surfaces (Fig. 19.1). The definition is often expanded to include communities of bacteria, fungi, protozoa, and other invertebrates associated with the attached algae. Communities are

**Fig. 19.1.** Communities of periphyton. Epiphytic algae (left) are attached to submersed aquatic plants and epilithic algae (right) are attached to rocks. Communities often appear as 'furriness' covering the substrate (arrows).

described by their substrate: epilithic algae grow on rocks, epiphytic algae on macrophytes (larger algae or vascular plants), and epipelic algae on sediment surfaces. Periphyton is an important contributor to productivity in some lakes and ponds, and is a primary food source for some juvenile fish and invertebrates. Periphyton is not objectionable in ponds, although the larger plants serving as substrate for epiphytic algae may cause problems.

## Submersed Vascular Plants and Filamentous Macroalgae

These two plant groups comprise distinctly different plants but are discussed together because the ecological conditions favoring their presence and the problems they cause in aquaculture ponds are similar. Submersed vascular plants grow underwater, although flowering parts may extend above the water surface (Fig. 19.2). Plants are usually rooted in the mud although masses of plants may tear loose and float free in the water.

Filamentous macroalgae differ from phytoplankton (many of which also form filaments) based upon size. Individual filaments of macroalgae are easily seen with the naked eye. Charophytes (*Chara*, *Nitella*, and others) are attached to the bottom and grow up through the water column (Fig. 19.3). Most other filamentous algae grow as unattached clouds or mats of finely divided, interwoven, cottony or slimy plant material. Mat-forming filamentous macroalgae, such as *Pithophora*, *Hydrodictyon*, and *Spirogyra*, usually begin growing on the pond bottom or among shoreline plants. Mats rise to the surface when gas bubbles become entrapped in the plant mass (Fig. 19.4).

**Fig. 19.2.** Submersed vascular plants: *Ceratophyllum* or coontail (left) and *Cabomba* or fanwort (right).

**Fig. 19.3.** Filaments of the algae *Chara* resemble vascular plants because of its size (often 0.5-1 m long) and whorls of branches. The plant often feels gritty due to calcium carbonate (lime) encrusted on the surface.

Communities of rooted submersed plants are favored over other plants in shallow ponds with low dissolved nutrient concentrations because these plants can use nutrients in bottom muds for growth. Also, ponds with low levels of water-borne nutrients are usually clear because they support sparse phytoplankton communities. Under these conditions, light penetrates to the bottom of shallow areas where submersed plants or filamentous macroalgae start growing. Established communities of submersed plants or filamentous macroalgae outcompete phytoplankton for nutrients and light, and some plants also produce substances that inhibit the growth of phytoplankton. The ability of submersed

**Fig. 19.4.** Floating mats of filamentous algae growing in a pond (left). A closer view (right) shows numerous bubbles trapped among the filaments.

plants and filamentous macroalgae to exploit environments with low concentrations of waterborne nutrients explains the common occurrence of those communities in new ponds or ponds that have been recently refilled after being drained.

Communities of submersed plants also tend to be more common in hard waters than in soft, acid water. In hard water, high concentrations of calcium and magnesium favor coagulation and precipitation of clays and organic colloids, and waters are often clear unless turbid with plankton. Dissolved calcium and relatively high environmental pH usually associated with hard waters also favor precipitation of phosphorus from the water and concentrations of water-borne orthophosphate tend to be low, which hinders development of phytoplankton communities.

Submersed plants and filamentous macroalgae are present in many ponds and cause no problems if growth is limited to small areas around pond margins. They can, however, interfere with pond management when communities occupy large areas. Harvest seines ride up over dense plant stands, allowing cultured animals to escape. Also, the weight of plant material caught in the seine may damage equipment or make harvest impossible. Even if weed biomass is low enough to allow harvest, animals that are captured may be so entangled in the mass of plants caught in the seine that it is difficult for workers to manually separate animals from weeds. If animals are to be harvested and transported live, captured animals will be stressed as workers tediously separate animals from plants, resulting in excessive mortality at some later time.

Extensive communities of submersed plants and filamentous macroalgae also interfere with fish feeding activities. Feed pellets distributed among the plant mass may not be found by animals under culture, resulting in wasted feed. In culture systems where forage fish are present, smaller fish can hide among the weeds and foraging by larger fish will be less effective, causing an imbalance of fish populations. In sportfishing ponds, mats of filamentous macroalgae or stands of submersed plants are highly undesirable because they interfere with angling.

Large areas of floating algal mats are also undesirable because water quality may deteriorate beneath the plants. Oxygen produced in photosynthesis by plants in the surface mat is lost to the atmosphere rather than dissolved in the water. Floating algal mats shade the water and reduce oxygen production by underwater plants. Decreased availability of dissolved oxygen may reduce aquaculture production or, in the extreme, endanger the animal under culture.

## Emergent Plants

Emergent plants are rooted in the bottom and extend above the water. Plants are rigid and not dependent on water for support. Many species can grow under strictly terrestrial conditions as well as in water. A wide range of plant types are included in this group, including grasses, rushes, sedges, cattails (Fig. 19.5), shrubs, and trees.

Emergent plants colonize shallow shoreline areas. They have roots and use nutrients in the sediments, so their initial establishment is favored by low nutrient levels in the water. Emergent plants may also develop in ponds with a limited supply of water relative to pond size. For example, in ponds with a watershed that is too small to provide adequate runoff, pond water levels may fluctuate greatly between large rains, providing an opportunity for shoreline area to be colonized by emergent plants. For the most part, emergent plants grow only along shallow shorelines and do not interfere with angling or fish culture activities unless growth becomes dense and widespread.

## Free-Floating Plants

Free-floating plants are not attached to the pond bank or pond bottom and float on, or just under, the water surface. Most have roots that hang into the water for nutrient uptake. Larger free-floating plants, such as water hyacinth (*Eichhornia crassipes*), water lettuce (*Pistia stratiotes*), and giant salvinia (*Salvinia molesta*) are notorious weed problems in large water bodies but seldom cause problems in aquaculture ponds because it is easy to prevent their introduction and, if a few plants become established, they are easily removed or killed before they begin to spread.

Smaller free-floating plants include waterferns (*Azolla* spp.), duckweeds (species of *Lemna*, *Landoltia*, and *Spirodela*), and watermeal (*Wolffia* spp.). These plants are found throughout the world and are continually introduced into ponds because they are small and easily carried from one body of water to another by birds, animals, and on equipment such as seines or nets. Smaller floating plants seldom form extensive communities in larger ponds and lakes because plants are continually washed ashore in exposed waters where they die from desiccation. They are most commonly found in sheltered areas among shoreline vegetation or in small ponds—especially those surrounded by trees and protected from winds (Fig. 19.6). Under the right conditions, duckweeds and watermeal can grow rapidly and cover a large area in a short time.

**Fig. 19.5.** Cattails growing along a pond shoreline.

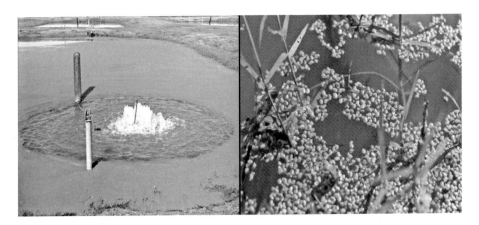

**Fig. 19.6.** (Left) A small fish pond nearly covered with duckweeds. Water currents from an aerator have opened up a small area of clear water in the foreground. (Right) Duckweed fronds floating among emergent vegetation. Individual fronds are 2-4 mm across.

Duckweeds and watermeal may clog small-mesh seines and nets, and interfere with harvest of smaller aquaculture species such as baitfish, ornamental fish, or fry and fingerlings. Extensive coverage by duckweeds is also undesirable because dissolved oxygen concentrations may be reduced. Oxygen produced by floating plants is lost to the atmosphere rather than dissolved in water and plants shade the water and reduce oxygen production by underwater plants.

### Rooted Floating Plants

Rooted floating plants include waterlilies (species of *Nuphar*, *Nelumbo*, and *Nymphaea*; Fig. 19.7), watershield (*Brasenia* spp.), and the floating-leaved pondweeds (such as variable-leaf pondweed *Potamogeton diversifolius*). Although limited stands of waterlilies, watershield, or pondweeds are not uncommon along the margins of aquaculture ponds, they seldom cause problems in well-managed aquaculture ponds because normal management activities—such as periodic pond draining and frequent harvesting—make conditions unfavorable for their establishment.

## Managing Aquatic Weeds

The usual goal of weed management in aquaculture ponds is to encourage phytoplankton and prevent or eliminate other vegetation. Although phytoplankton is usually the most desirable plant community, the community may become too abundant or consist of undesirable species. This section describes practices used to control larger aquatic plants; phytoplankton management is discussed later.

**Fig. 19.7.** A species of water lily, *Nymphaea*.

## *General Pond Management Practices*

Chemical weed control is risky in aquaculture ponds because water quality deterioration after weeds are killed may endanger the cultured animal. When possible, ponds should be managed to reduce opportunities for weed growth rather than relying on herbicides to treat problems after they develop.

Pond fertilization (Chapter 10) encourages phytoplankton growth and is the best method of preventing growth of troublesome weeds. In fact, many ponds and lakes are fertilized just for that reason. Phytoplankton blooms compete with other plants for light and nutrients, and usually prevent growth of submersed and emergent plants in all but the shallowest water. Fertilization to promote phytoplankton blooms can be used only to prevent weed infestations. If filamentous macroalgae or submersed plant communities are already established, fertilization will make conditions worse by stimulating further weed growth.

Submersed and emergent weeds start growing in shallow areas where light penetrates to the bottom. Deepening the edges of ponds discourages establishment of emergent or submersed weeds. Ponds should have an adequate supply of water and be filled as quickly as possible. By increasing water depth quickly, plants that start growing on the pond bottom have less opportunity to become established.

Nontoxic dyes can also be used to inhibit the growth of submersed plants. These dyes, which are available commercially for weed control, absorb light in wavelengths most effective at promoting plant photosynthesis. When used properly they shade the water and reduce growth of plants at depths greater than about 0.75 m. This technique is most effective when the dye is applied before weeds begin growing. Application may not control established stands of submersed plants or surface mats of filamentous macroalgae. Dyes are most useful in relatively deep ponds and the dye concentration should be maintained throughout the growing season, so it may be impractical (and expensive) to use in ponds with significant discharge.

Removing weeds mechanically or by hand may reduce the possibility of having to use other measures to control plants. Routine mowing of pond banks will help prevent the establishment of rank growths of shoreline plants and will also reduce habitat for snakes. Removing plants by handpulling or raking is often mentioned as a weed control practice but, in reality, manual weed control is possible only in small ponds and is seldom an option in commercial aquaculture. Even in small ponds, plants should be removed immediately as small areas become infested because it is time-consuming and laborious to manually remove established stands of weeds. Also, care should be taken to remove as much of the rootstock or rhizome as possible to minimize regrowth.

## Biological Control with Herbivorous Fish

Biological control of aquatic weeds includes the use of insects, fungi and other plant pathogens, birds, mammals, or fish to kill or eat plants. Fish are commonly used as weed control agents but most other approaches to biological control are impractical or untested in aquaculture ponds.

Grass carp are freshwater fish native to eastern Asia. They have been widely introduced throughout the world for weed control. Grass carp feed almost exclusively on larger plants and do not compete to a significant degree with plankton-feeding fish or fish fed manufactured feeds. They do not reproduce in ponds and tolerate a wide range of water temperatures and environmental conditions. Grass carp consume large quantities of plant material when water temperature are between 20 to 30°C and grow rapidly—as much as 2-5 kg per year. They stop feeding when water temperatures fall below about 10°C. Grass carp will eat filamentous macroalgae but, when given a choice, they prefer succulent submersed plants. They also readily eat duckweeds and watermeal. Fibrous plants such as grasses, cattails, sedges, and rushes are eaten only when other plants are unavailable. Stocking rates for weed control vary from 10 to more than 100 fish/ha depending on severity of weed problems. Grass carp may require a year or more to control dense weed infestations, so it is best to use the fish as a preventative measure or stock the pond with the fish before the weed problem becomes widespread. Grass carp are banned or tightly regulated in some countries. Even when it is legal to use the fish, discretion should be used and every effort made to prevent their escape into natural waters where the fish is not native.

Juveniles and adults of all five of the most widely cultured tilapias (*Oreochromis aureus*, *O. mossambicus*, *O. niloticus*, *Tilapia rendalli*, and *T. zilli*) consume macrophytic filamentous algae and submersed plants as parts of their overall, omnivorous diets. The latter two species, which are relatively small fish, appear to feed more or less exclusively on larger aquatic plants and are particularly effective at weed control. However, the tendency for tilapia species to overpopulate ponds is a major drawback to their use for weed control, especially in fry or fingerling nursery ponds where they compete for feed, natural foods, dissolved oxygen, and habitat with the aquaculture crop. Tilapias do not tolerate cold water temperatures and must be restocked each year if weeds persist in temperate ponds. On the other hand, some fish culturists consider the inability of the fish to overwinter as an advantage because the fish will not be a permanent inhabitant of the pond after weeds have been controlled.

Common carp control weeds by feeding directly on the plants and by stirring bottom muds, which increases turbidity and decreases light availability. Clay turbidity resulting from the feeding activities of carp is undesirable in most culture situations because it limits growth of desirable plants such as phytoplankton. Common carp also reproduce in ponds and may become excessively abundant. These disadvantages outweigh any advantages (such as hardiness or worldwide availability), and common carp are rarely used strictly for weed control.

## *Chemical Weed Control*

Using chemical herbicides is usually the quickest way to eradicate established weed communities. Many chemicals have been used to control aquatic weeds, but relatively few are legal to use in aquaculture ponds. Lists of legal herbicides differ among countries and legal status changes over time, so we will not discuss individual herbicides in this chapter. Detailed information is presented elsewhere.[1,2,3] Excellent online resources for aquatic plant management are also available, including websites managed by Texas A&M University's Aquaplant (http://aquaplant.tamu.edu) and the University of Florida's Center for Aquatic and Invasive Plants (http://aquat1.ifas.ufl.edu).

Effective weed control depends on correctly identifying the weed problem, selecting the most cost-effective herbicide, properly applying the chemical, and managing the effects of herbicide use on water quality. Correct weed identification is critical because herbicides effective on one species may be ineffective even on similar species. Weed identification can be difficult, and experts at local universities or private consulting firms can help identify the weed problem. Plant identification keys are available in the publications and websites listed above.

The printed information accompanying the herbicide container is called the 'label' and constitutes a legal document in most countries. Failure to use herbicides according to label instructions can lead to severe penalties. From a practical standpoint, misuse of herbicides can result in poor weed control; risks to people, the aquaculture crop, or wildlife; or herbicide residue problems in the aquaculture product. The label provides information on the active ingredient, directions for correct use on target plant species, warnings and use restrictions, and safety and antidote information.

Herbicide treatment rates are based on pond area or pond volume. Miscalculation causes either over-treatment or under-treatment. Carefully measure pond dimensions and keep up-to-date records of pond size and depth. Pond surface area tends to increase and pond depth tends to decrease over time because of erosion of embankments and sedimentation of pond bottoms. The only way to be certain of average pond depth is to measure water depth before treatment at several dozen random locations.

With the notable exceptions of copper-based herbicides and the methylamine formulations of the herbicide endothall, most aquatic herbicides are of low toxicity to most aquatic animals. However, using any herbicide in ponds can be dangerous because treatment of a plant-infested pond causes dramatic changes water quality that may endanger cultured animals. Decay of herbicide-killed plants may cause dissolved oxygen depletion and increased levels of dissolved carbon dioxide and total ammonia. The extent to which water quality is affected depends on the amount of plant material killed, the amount of plant material unaffected by the herbicide, the rate that death of plants occurs, water temperature, and other factors. Risks are greatest when treating dense stands of weeds during hot weather because the dead plant material is rapidly decomposed and the solubility of oxygen in water is low. If treatment is absolutely necessary under those conditions, only a portion of the pond should be treated at one time. After waiting a few days, another portion can be treated, and so on. Supplemental aeration should be available to prevent fish kills caused by low dissolved oxygen concentration any time herbicides are used.

# Phytoplankton Bloom Management

Ponds are usually managed to promote phytoplankton and discourage other plant growth. Phytoplankton can, however, become a weed problem when community biomass becomes excessive or when species are present that produce odors or toxins (see Chapter 18). Persistent overabundance of phytoplankton in fertilized ponds indicates that too much fertilizer is being applied, and the solution is to reduce fertilization. In pond cultures with feeding, abundant phytoplankton blooms and noxious blue-green algae are a natural consequence of culture practices because large amounts of nutrients are excreted into the water as metabolic waste (Chapter 11). Reducing nutrient input or removing nutrients from water to control blooms are difficult or expensive, and aquaculturists have resorted to chemical or biological treatments to control phytoplankton communities and improve water quality.

## Algicides

*Algicides* are herbicides used to kill algae. They are used to manage phytoplankton blooms for two distinctly different purposes. First, they are used to eliminate undesirable phytoplankton species from the community. This use of algicides, which is discussed in Chapter 18, can be relatively successful when managing algae-related off-flavors, but can be dangerous when treating toxin-producing algae. Toxins stored inside algal cells are released when cells are killed and lyse, causing a sudden—and potentially dangerous—increase in waterborne toxin concentrations.

The second use of algicides is to reduce overall phytoplankton biomass. This practice is based on the relationship between excessive phytoplankton biomass and poor water quality, and the apparently logical conclusion that environmental conditions can be improved simply by reducing algal biomass. Water quality may, in fact, be improved when phytoplankton cells are continuously removed from the water by physical means, such as washout using water exchange or grazing by filter-feeding fish. But using algicides to simply kill a portion of the phytoplankton community often causes worse environmental conditions than those prevailing before their use, and the frequent result of herbicide use is decreased aquaculture yield.[3,4,5]

## Copper Algicides

Herbicides with cupric ion as the active ingredient are commonly used in aquaculture, so a few comments are justified. Copper, as the cupric ion ($Cu^{2+}$), is an essential trace nutrient for plant growth. Exposure to higher levels inhibits growth or kills plants by binding with protein sulfhydryl groups causing inhibition of critical enzyme systems. Copper algicides are formulated as 1) copper sulfate pentahydrate ($CuSO_4 \cdot 5H_2O$), sometimes called bluestone or abbreviated CSP; 2) acidic solutions of copper; or 3) organically chelated copper.

Copper sulfate algicides are formulated as powders or crystals. Treatment rates range from about 0.06 mg/L as copper (0.25 mg/L as $CuSO_4 \cdot 5H_2O$) to over 0.5 mg/L as copper (2 mg/L as $CuSO_4 \cdot 5H_2O$) depending on the type of algae to be controlled and water chemistry. Copper tends to be more toxic to blue-green phytoplankton than to other groups. The filamentous macroalgae *Pithophora*—a common aquaculture pond weed problem—is notoriously resistant to copper algicides.

Copper toxicity to plants and aquatic animals is affected by water quality variables that reduce the amount of $Cu^{2+}$ in water or reduce uptake of $Cu^{2+}$ by the organism. In general, copper toxicity decreases as pH, alkalinity, calcium hardness, and dissolved and particulate organic matter concentrations increase. Briefly, as pH and alkalinity increase, $Cu^{2+}$ concentrations decrease because copper is precipitated or complexed as oxides, hydroxides, and carbonates at higher pH and alkalinity. Calcium ions compete with cupric ions for uptake across cell membranes, which reduces the amount of copper taken up by plants and animals. Organic matter forms complexes with $Cu^{2+}$, reducing the amount in solution. These interactions are much more complicated than described here and are discussed elsewhere.[3,6] To compensate for these interactions, suggested treatment rates increase with increasing water hardness or alkalinity. One suggested rate is based on total alkalinity:

Copper sulfate pentahydrate (mg/L) = total alkalinity (mg/L as $CaCO_3$) ÷ 100      (19.1)

This equation is based on practical experience rather than chemical principles; it ignores the effect of organic matter and assumes that alkalinity, pH, and calcium hardness vary together—which they do in many, but not all, waters. Precipitation as copper oxides and assimilation of cupric ion by algae rapidly reduce waterborne copper levels after treatment. Essentially all the copper applied to ponds ends up in pond bottom muds.[7]

Copper sulfate is applied by dissolving the chemical in water and distributing or spraying the concentrated solution over the pond (Fig. 19.8). The chemical may also be applied by placing copper sulfate crystals into cloth or burlap bags and towing the bags behind a boat while the chemical dissolves. Care must be taken to assure that undissolved crystals are not lost as the chemical is applied. Simply broadcasting copper sulfate crystals over the water is not efficient, because much of the chemical is lost to the bottom muds before it dissolves.

Some copper-based algicides are formulated as solutions of copper sulfate (or other copper salts) dissolved in acid. Because copper is already in solution as $Cu^{2+}$, using this formulation reduces the amount of copper lost as undissolved crystals during application. The acidic solution is applied directly to ponds or diluted with water. Formulation as an acidic solution does not enhance algicidal activity because the acid carrier is neutralized as soon as the product is applied to the pond, leaving $Cu^{2+}$—the same species initially present when solid copper sulfate dissolves in water. Toxicity of acidic copper solutions is affected by the same water quality variables that affect copper sulfate.

Chelated copper herbicides use organic compounds (such as ethanolamines) to bind $Cu^{2+}$ so that copper does not rapidly precipitate out of solution in waters of high pH. Label instructions for the use of chelated copper algicides call for applications rates of 0.2 to 0.5 mg/L as copper depending on the type of algae to be controlled. This is approximately the same treatment concentration range used for copper sulfate pentahydrate, but chelated products are claimed to be more effective than copper sulfate in water of high pH. The chemical is most commonly applied by diluting the liquid product with water and using a hand or power sprayer to spray course droplets over the pond surface.

**Fig. 19.8.** Spraying a concentrated solution of copper sulfate dissolved in water into a pond to eliminate blue-green algae causing off-flavor in fish.

## *Biological Control of Phytoplankton: Biomanipulation*

Phytoplankton community productivity and organization are influenced by resource availability and predation from higher trophic levels. The role of resource availability has been called 'bottom-up' control. The impact of predation is called 'top-down' control and is based on the trophic-cascade concept, which posits that predation from higher trophic levels affects the structure and biomass of communities at lower trophic levels.[8]

Phytoplankton community structure can therefore be manipulated either from the bottom up or the top down. Pond fertilization is an example of controlling ecosystem productivity from the bottom up. Fertilization increases phytoplankton productivity by increasing resource (nutrient) availability. Often, however, the goal is to reduce phytoplankton abundance or to eliminate undesirable species. It is difficult to use bottom-up control in aquaculture ponds with feeding because nutrient additions are more or less continuous and reducing nutrient loading rates is difficult, expensive, or may cause un-intended consequences. In systems with continuous, high nutrient loading, top-down control is an attractive possibility. Top-down control of plankton communities is sometimes called *biomanipulation.*

Biomanipulation in aquaculture ponds uses planktivorous fish such as silver carp or threadfin shad to reduce phytoplankton abundance and eliminate noxious species. Contrary to expectations, planktivorous fish usually do not reduce phytoplankton abundance but they often change plankton community structure. Planktivorous fish graze or feed primarily on larger phytoplankton and large-bodied zooplankton, which removes the primary consumers (larger zooplankton) and the primary resource competitors (large phytoplankton) of small phytoplankton. Since small algae generally grow faster and are more efficient at using sunlight and dissolved nutrients than larger algae, total phytoplankton biomass may increase.

Changes in phytoplankton community structure caused by planktivorous fish may be beneficial in aquaculture. Small phytoplankton have higher rates of net primary productivity than larger algae, which enhances dissolved oxygen production and assimilation of dissolved inorganic nitrogen. Also, size-selective filter feeding by some planktivorous fishes may reduce the abundance of large colonial or filamentous blue-green algae that produce odorous metabolites or toxins.[9,10] Even if planktivorous fish have minimal impact on noxious phytoplankton blooms, adding plankton-feeding fish to cultures of fish receiving manufactured feed increases overall fish production by converting a portion of otherwise unwanted phytoplankton production into edible fish flesh.

# References

1. Avery, J. L. 2012. Controlling plant pests before fertilization, pages 73-91. In C.C. Mischke (editor), *Aquaculture Pond Fertilization: Impacts of Nutrient Input in Aquaculture.* Wiley-Blackwell, Ames, IA.

2. Madsen, J. D., R. J. Richardson, and R. M. Wersal. 2012. Managing aquatic vegetation, pages 275-305. In J. W. Neal and D. W. Willis (editors), *Small Impoundment Management in North America*. American Fisheries Society, Bethesda, MD.

3. Boyd, C. E. and C. S. Tucker. 1998. *Pond Aquaculture Water Quality Management*. Kluwer Academic Publishers, Boston, MA.

4. Tucker, C. S. and C. E. Boyd. 1977. Consequences of periodic applications of copper sulfate and simazine for phytoplankton control in catfish ponds. Transactions of the American Fisheries Society 106:316-320.

5. Tucker, C. S., T. R. Hanson, and S. K. Kingsbury. 2001. Management of off-flavors in pond-cultured channel catfish with weekly applications of copper sulfate. North American Journal of Aquaculture 63:118-130.

6. Snoeyink, V. L. and D. Jenkins. 1980. *Water Chemistry*. John Wiley and Sons, New York.

7. Han F. X., J. A. Hargreaves, W. L. Kingery, D. B. Huggett, and D. K. Schlenk. 2001. Accumulation, distribution, and toxicity of copper in sediments of catfish ponds receiving periodic copper sulfate applications. Journal of Environmental Quality 30: 912–919.

8. Carpenter, S. R., J. F. Kitchell, and J. R. Hodgson. 1985. Cascading trophic interactions and lake productivity. BioScience 35:634-639.

9. Torrans, L. and F. Lowell. 1987. Effects of blue tilapia/channel catfish polyculture on production, food conversion, water quality, and channel catfish off-flavor. Proceedings of the Arkansas Academy of Science 41:82-86.

10. Mischke, C. C., C. S. Tucker, and M. Li. 2011. Channel catfish polyculture with fathead minnows or threadfin shad: effects on pond plankton communities and catfish fillet flavor, color, and fatty acid composition. Journal of the World Aquaculture Society 43:208-217.

# Chapter 20

# Trace Elements

## Introduction

*Trace elements* are elements that occur in water in very small concentrations, and if they are biologically essential, they are needed by plants and animals in relatively small amounts.[1] The proper term for biologically essential trace elements is *micronutrients*. Plants require nine micronutrients: boron, cobalt, copper, iron, manganese, molybdenum, selenium, vanadium, and zinc. Animals do not need boron, but in addition to the other micronutrients required by plants, some animals also need one or more of the following: iodine, fluorine, arsenic, chromium, nickel, and tin.

Although essential in small quantities to plants and animals, biologically essential trace elements can be toxic at higher concentrations.[1] Biologically unessential elements found in water such as aluminum, beryllium, cadmium, chromium, lead, mercury, and silver also can be toxic to plants and animals.

The ultimate sources of trace elements are minerals in the earth's crust. Aluminum, iron, and manganese make up 8.3, 6.2, and 0.1%, respectively, of the weight of the earth's crust. The other trace elements are present in the earth's crust in much smaller quantities but can be abundant in certain deposits.

Many trace elements are metals that are sparingly soluble in water of aquaculture systems. Deficiencies of biologically essential trace elements may occur, but because of low solubility, natural sources of trace elements seldom lead to toxicity. Copper often is applied to ponds as an algicide, and procedures for avoiding toxicity must be carefully followed (Chapters 18 and 19). Iron can be present at high concentration in groundwater, and when used in hatcheries, ferric hydroxide precipitation can lead to physical clogging of the gills of culture species. Trace elements also may enter culture systems in pollution.

## Chemistry

The concentration of a trace element in water usually is controlled by the solubility of a mineral compound of the elements (Table 20.1). An equilibrium will be established between the dissolved ionic form of the trace element and its controlling mineral.[2] For example, the solubility-controlling mineral for iron might be ferric hydroxide:

$$Fe(OH)_3 + 3H^+ = Fe^{3+} + 3H_2O. \tag{20.1}$$

**Table 20.1.** Solubility expressions of equilibrium constants (K) for minerals that control solubilities of selected microelements in water.[2]

| Name | Reaction | log $K^a$ |
|---|---|---|
| Fe (III) oxide | $Fe(OH)_3 + 3H^+ = Fe^{3+} + 3H_2O$ | 3.54 |
| Goethite | $FeOOH + 3H^+ = Fe^{3+} + 2H_2O$ | 3.55 |
| Hematite | $Fe_2O_3 + 6H^+ = 2Fe^{3+} + 3H_2O$ | -1.45 |
| Siderite | $FeCO_3 + H^+ = Fe^{2+} + HCO_3^-$ | -0.3 |
| Iron (II) hydroxide | $Fe(OH)_2 = Fe^{2+} + 2OH^-$ | -14 |
| Manganese (IV) oxide | $MnO_2 + 4H^+ = Mn^{4+} + 2H_2O$ | --- |
| Manganite | $MnOOH + 2H^+ = Mn^{3+} + 2H_2O$ | 0.3 |
| Manganese (II) hydroxide | $Mn(OH)_2 = Mn^{2+} + 2OH^-$ | -12.8 |
| Manganese carbonate | $MnCO_3 = Mn^{2+} + CO_3^{2-}$ | -9.3 |
| Malachite (copper hydroxyl carbonate) | $Cu_2(OH)_2CO_3 + 4H^+ = 2Cu^{2+} + 3H_2O + CO_2$ | 14.16 |
| Tenorite (copper oxide) | $CuO + 2H^+ = Cu^{2+} + H_2O$ | 7.65 |
| Zinc oxide | $ZnO + 2H^+ = Zn^{2+} + H_2O$ | 11.18 |
| Zinc carbonate | $ZnCO_3 + 2H^+ = Zn^{2+} + H_2O + CO_2$ | 7.95 |
| Cobalt carbonate | $CoCO_3 = Co^{2+} + CO_3^{2-}$ | -12.8 |

[a]To convert K to exponential form (power of 10), simply use the entry as the exponent, e.g., log K = -10.4 and K = $10^{-10.4}$.

The solubility of $Fe^{3+}$ from ferric hydroxide is 0.19 mg/L at pH 3, but at higher pH values common in aquaculture ponds, concentrations of $Fe^{3+}$ are less than 1 µg/L. Most metal ions have their greatest solubility at low pH, and some, like iron and manganese, are more soluble at low redox potential. Thus, when dissolved oxygen is depleted in sediment pore water, in the hypolimnion of stratified water bodies, and in groundwater, ferric ion and manganic manganese are reduced to soluble ferrous iron ($Fe^{2+}$) and manganous manganese ($Mn^{2+}$). When exposed to oxygen again, $Fe^{2+}$ and $Mn^{2+}$ will be oxidized back to highly insoluble forms.

In spite of the low concentration of free, trace element ions in water, total concentrations of trace elements found in water often are many times greater than estimated equilibrium concentrations.[3] This phenomenon is the result of reactions among the free ions and other substances in water to form soluble complexes.

Many elements—especially metals—hydrolyze to form metal hydroxides as illustrated below for ferric iron:

$$Fe^{3+} + OH^- = FeOH^{2+}$$
$$Fe^{3+} + 2OH^- = Fe(OH)_2^+$$
$$Fe^{3+} + 3OH^- = Fe(OH)_3^0$$
$$Fe^{3+} + 4OH^- = Fe(OH)_4^-.$$

These hydroxides are soluble, and they increase the concentration of iron found in water.

Trace elements also form *ion pairs* in which ions of opposite charge attract each other forming soluble associations in water that do not precipitate. Ion pairs may be charged or uncharged as illustrated with ferric and cupric ion:

$$Fe^{3+} + SO_4^{2-} = FeSO_4^-$$
$$Fe^{3+} + Cl^- = FeCl^{2+}$$
$$Cu^{2+} + SO_4^{2-} = CuSO_4^0$$
$$Cu^{2+} + CO_3^{2-} = CuCO_3^0.$$

Ion pairs also increase the total concentration of an element found in water.[3]

Certain organic molecules contain one or more pairs of electrons that can be shared with metal ions in solution.[3] These molecules are known as *ligands* or *chelating agents*, and the complexes formed between organic molecules and metals are called chelated metals. Humic and fulvic acids are common, natural chelating agents in waters, but because these acids are large, complex molecules, the structure of the chelation process is illustrated with iron and salicylic acid (Fig. 20.1). The presence of chelated metals in water can contribute greatly to the total concentrations of dissolved metal ions.

Free, trace element ions in water are in equilibrium with a controlling mineral as well as with exchangeable ions on soil colloids. Clay minerals and organic matter in bottom soil have a net negative charge (cation exchange capacity) and can attract and hold cations including trace metals such as $Fe^{2+}$, $Cu^{2+}$, and $Zn^{2+}$. If a large amount of $Cu^{2+}$ is added to the water, it may displace other ions from cation exchange sites on bottom soil. Hydrolysis products, ion pairs, and chelates also are in equilibrium with free ions in the water as illustrated for zinc (Fig. 20.2). There is an equilibrium between free $Zn^{2+}$, complexed forms, zinc attracted to cation exchange sites in bottom, and the controlling mineral as illustrated below:

$$\text{Mineral form} \leftrightarrow \text{free ion} \leftrightarrow \text{complexed and exchangeable forms.} \qquad (20.2)$$

Plants can remove free ions from the water, and they will be replaced by dissociation of ions from complexed forms (hydrolysis products, ion pairs, and chelates), release of ions from exchange sites in the bottom soil, and by dissolution of the controlling mineral. The complexed forms, however, usually represent a much larger supply of plant available trace elements than does the controlling mineral or the exchangeable ions in the bottom soil.

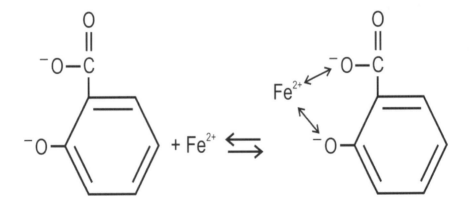

**Fig. 20.1.** Salicylic acid as an example of a chelating agent.

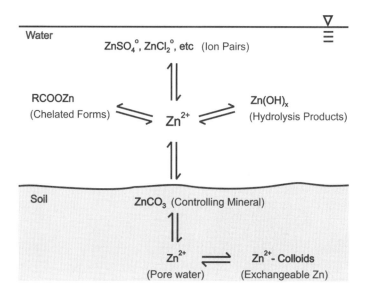

**Fig. 20.2.** Illustration of reactions of zinc in pond water and sediment.

Soluble compounds of most metals exist and can be applied to water to give high concentrations of free ions. For example, copper sulfate pentahydrate ($CuSO_4 \cdot 5H_2O$) is quite soluble in water, but its concentration ultimately will be determined by the most stable mineral form that can form under the prevailing water quality conditions. In the case of $Cu^{2+}$ in water of pH 7 and above, the controlling mineral is CuO (tenorite):

$$CuO + 2H^+ = Cu^{2+} + H_2O \qquad K = 10^{7.65}. \qquad (20.3)$$

At pH 7, the solubility of $Cu^{2+}$ from CuO is 28 µg/L; at pH 8, 0.28 µg/L; at pH 9, 0.0028 µg/L. Of course, the total dissolved copper concentration will be higher because of copper hydroxides, ion pairs, and chelates.

Copper sulfate often is applied to channel catfish ponds in the United States for controlling algae responsible for off-flavor.[4, 5] Treatment rates usually are in the range of 0.1 to 0.5 mg/L copper, but the concentration of dissolved copper quickly declines following treatment (Fig. 20.3). Many channel catfish ponds have been treated with copper sulfate several times per year for many years, but ambient concentrations in pond waters have not increased.[6]

Trace elements in fertilizers may be chelated with ethylenediamine tetraacetic acid (EDTA), citric acid, or lignin sulfonate to enhance their availability.[4] Copper for algal control also may be chelated—usually with triethanolamine (TEA). Chelation prevents the copper from precipitating from the water before it can kill algae. The free cupric ion is toxic, and in acidic water, copper algicides cannot be used because of potential toxicity to fish and other culture species. However, chelated copper compounds can be used in acidic waters for algal control without causing fish mortality.[4]

274

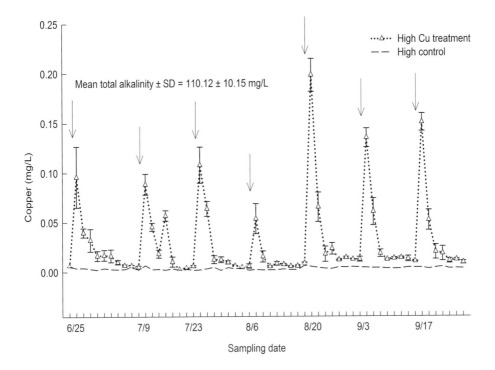

**Fig. 20.3.** Copper concentrations in control ponds and in ponds treated with copper sulfate[5].

Biologically essential trace elements are removed from water by algae or other aquatic organisms. When these organisms die, they settle to the pond bottom and the trace element contained in their remains is part of the organic matter in the sediment until recycled through microbial decomposition.

There is little evidence that micronutrients should be routinely included in pond fertilizers for freshwater ponds. It is more likely that trace elements—particularly iron and manganese—could limit phytoplankton productivity in fertilized ponds containing seawater. Nevertheless, there has been little work to establish the possible benefits of including micronutrients in fertilizers for brackishwater or seawater ponds.

## Concentrations and Toxicity

Typical concentration ranges for trace elements in freshwater are wide, and freshwater tends to have greater concentrations of most trace elements than average seawater (Table 20.2). This is mainly because seawater has a higher pH than most freshwaters, and high pH inhibits the solubility of many trace elements. Moreover, water of the open ocean is not as likely to be polluted with metals as is freshwater.

**Table 20.2.** Typical concentrations and maximum safe concentrations of trace metals in water.[4,7]

| Element | Concentration range found in literature for freshwater (μg/L) | Average seawater (μg/L) | Maximum safe concentration (μg/L) | |
|---|---|---|---|---|
| | | | Soft | Hard water and seawater |
| Aluminum | <1 | 10 | 1 | 1,000 |
| Beryllium | 0.01-1 | 0.0006 | 11 | 1,100 |
| Cadmium | 1-5 | 0.11 | 25 | 70 |
| Chromium | 1-50 | 0.05 | 100 | 100 |
| Cobalt | 1-10 | 0.5 | 50 | 50 |
| Copper | 5-50 | 3 | 25 | 70 |
| Iron | 0.01-500 | 10 | 1,000 | 1,100 |
| Lead | 1-20 | 0.03 | 200 | 4,000 |
| Manganese | 0.01-250 | 2 | 1,000 | 1,000 |
| Mercury | <0.02 | 0.03 | 0.1 | 0.1 |
| Nickel | 5-25 | 2 | 50 | 400 |
| Selenium | 0.1-5 | 4 | 20 | 20 |
| Silver | 0.01-0.3 | 0.3 | 0.05 | --- |
| Tin | 1-20 | 3 | --- | --- |
| Zinc | 10-100 | 10 | 50 | 100 |

Safe concentrations of trace metals also are provided in Table 20.2. Acceptable concentrations of several elements are higher in hard freshwater and seawater than in soft freshwater. This results because hard waters and seawater have a higher pH and greater degree of mineralization than soft water. Concentrations of the free metal ions—the toxic form—will be low because of elevated pH. Nearly all of the trace metal concentration will be the result of hydroxides, ion pairs, and chelates that are not toxic.

Trace element concentrations vary widely in bottom soil (Table 20.3), but there is no evidence that natural, ambient concentrations of trace metals have caused toxicity to culture species in ponds with slightly acidic to alkaline bottom soils and water. The possible effects of the higher concentrations of trace metals on benthic communities in aquaculture ponds have not been considered. In ponds constructed in acid sulfate soils, high concentrations of aluminum and other metals have been associated with low survival and production of fish and shrimp.

Guidelines for safe concentrations of selected trace elements in sediment have been reported by pollution control agencies in several countries (Table 20.4). The maximum safe concentrations tend to be higher than the maximum concentrations reported in Table 20.3 for aquaculture ponds.

High trace element concentrations always are considered a potential negative factor in hatchery water supplies. It is difficult to assess the likely effects of trace elements from water analyses, and concentration of trace metals could suddenly increase if there was a source from pollution. Therefore, hatchery operators—especially those producing shrimp postlarvae in coastal water—apply ethylenediamine tetraacetic acid (EDTA) to the incoming water at 5 to 10 mg/L to chelate trace metals and lessen their potential toxicity.

**Table 20.3.** Relative abundance categories of trace elements (ppm) in a series of soil samples from aquaculture ponds.[8]

| Variable | Decile | | | | |
|---|---|---|---|---|---|
| | 1st (very low) | 2nd and 3rd (low) | 4th-7th (medium) | 8th and 9th (high) | 10th (very high) |
| Freshwater ponds (n = 358) | | | | | |
| Iron | <10 | 10-50 | 50-130 | 130-210 | >210 |
| Manganese | <5 | 5-20 | 20-40 | 40-75 | >75 |
| Zinc | <0.2 | 0.2-1.5 | 1.5-2.5 | 2.5-5 | >5 |
| Copper | <0.3 | 0.3-1.25 | 1.25-2.5 | 2.5-6 | >6 |
| Silicon | <20 | 20-40 | 40-60 | 60-100 | >100 |
| Boron | <0.3 | 0.3-0.5 | 0.5-0.75 | 0.75-1.25 | >1.25 |
| Cobalt | <0.10 | 0.1-0.2 | 0.2-0.35 | 0.35-0.8 | >0.8 |
| Molybdenum | <0.1 | 0.11-0.15 | 0.15-0.2 | 0.21-0.35 | >0.35 |
| Aluminum | <3.5 | 3.5-75 | 75-120 | 120-200 | >200 |
| Barium | <0.5 | 0.5-1 | 1-1.5 | 1.5-4 | >4 |
| Chromium | <0.5 | 0.5-0.75 | 0.75-1 | 1-1.75 | >1.75 |
| Lead | <1 | 1-1.25 | 1.25-1.5 | 1.5-2.5 | >2.5 |
| | | | | | |
| Brackishwater ponds (n = 346) | | | | | |
| Iron | <60 | 60-200 | 200-750 | 750-1,200 | >1,200 |
| Manganese | <10 | 10-50 | 50-150 | 150-350 | >350 |
| Zinc | <2 | 2-5 | 5-8 | 8-14 | >14 |
| Copper | <1 | 1-2 | 2-8 | 8-11 | >11 |
| Silicon | <30 | 30-100 | 100-500 | 500-750 | >750 |
| Boron | <4 | 4-8 | 8-18 | 18-24 | 24 |
| Cobalt | <0.5 | 0.5-1 | 1-2.5 | 2.5-3.5 | >3.5 |
| Molybdenum | <0.3 | 0.3-0.5 | 0.5-0.9 | 0.9-1.2 | >1.2 |
| Aluminum | <100 | 100-200 | 200-500 | 500-600 | >600 |
| Barium | <0.5 | 0.5-1 | 1-1.5 | 1.5-3.5 | >3.5 |
| Chromium | <1 | 1-2 | 2-4 | 4-7 | >7 |
| Lead | <2 | 2-4 | 4-7 | 7-9 | >9 |

**Table 20.4.** Guidelines for maximum safe concentrations of selected elements in sediment.[9]

| Element | Concentration (mg/kg) | | |
|---|---|---|---|
| | MAFF[a] action level | EPA[b] threshold level | ANZECC[c] trigger value |
| Copper | 2 | 31 | 1.5 |
| Chromium | 100 | 25 | 65 |
| Iron | --- | --- | --- |
| Lead | 40 | 132 | 50 |
| Zinc | 200 | 760 | 200 |

[a]Ministry of Agriculture, fisheries, and Food, United Kingdom.
[b]United States Environmental Protection Agency.
[c]Australian and New Zealand Environmental and Conservation Council.

# Iron

Iron deserves special attention because it needs to be removed from some waters, and it affects the appearance of bottom soil often raising concerns about soil quality. In pond bottoms, the surface of sediment is oxidized because of contact with oxygenated water. Bacterial activity in sediment consumes dissolved oxygen from pore water faster than it can move downward through the pore space. Below a depth of a few millimeters, pond sediment usually is devoid of oxygen and has a low redox potential. This results in pore water often being high in ferrous iron concentration.

Ferric iron is changed to ferrous iron in the absence of oxygen in sediment. Ferrous compounds impart a dark color to sediment, and surface, aerobic sediment is lighter in color than underlying, anaerobic sediment (Fig. 20.4).

Ferrous iron in sediment often has a beneficial effect. Hydrogen sulfide is produced by microbial activity in reduced sediment, and this potentially toxic gas can diffuse into pond water. If ferrous iron is abundant in sediment pore water, it precipitates hydrogen sulfide as insoluble ferric sulfide (iron pyrite). Hydrogen sulfide toxicity is not likely to occur in shrimp ponds where bottoms were constructed of soil with high iron content. Treatment of pond sediment with iron slag, ferrous sulfate or ferrous oxide has been used as a hydrogen sulfide control technique.

Ferrous iron in pond soil is oxidized to the ferric form during the dry-out period between crops. The coloration of the soil can be used to follow the progress of soil oxidation. Oxidation of large amounts of ferrous iron to ferric iron often results in reddish deposits of ferric hydroxide on pond bottoms. This phenomenon is particularly common where water seeps out of the embankments of empty ponds. After refilling, the water in such ponds may contain a reddish suspension of ferric hydroxide for a few days. The suspended particles of iron hydroxide should be allowed to settle before stocking ponds with fish or shrimp.

**Fig. 20.4.** The dark area in the center of the figure resulted from removing the thin surface layer of aerobic soil to expose anaerobic soil underneath.

In ponds with acidic sediment, iron and manganese deposits can form on the exoskeletons and gills of shrimp. This can cause physical damage to the gills and unsightly blotches on shrimp at harvest. The most effective way of reducing iron concentrations in sediment pore water is application of agricultural limestone or lime to raise the pH.

Phosphate reacts with ferric iron to form relatively insoluble iron phosphate. However, when the redox potential declines, ferric iron is reduced to ferrous iron, releasing phosphate. Pore water of anaerobic sediment and oxygen-depleted pond water can have high concentrations of dissolved phosphate. Oxygenation of anaerobic water results in re-precipitation of ferrous iron as ferric hydroxide, and phosphate is adsorbed by the precipitating ferric hydroxide and removed from the water column.

Dissolved phosphate concentrations often increase in the bottom waters of ponds or lakes that thermally stratify in summer. In autumn, these water bodies destratify and the bottom water is mixed with oxygenated water in upper layers resulting in re-precipitation of phosphate. Nevertheless, the increase in phosphorus concentration in surface water for a brief period following the overturn often triggers a temporary phytoplankton bloom.

Groundwaters usually are depleted of dissolved oxygen, and waters from wells can have high concentrations of ferrous iron. When such water is exposed to air, ferrous iron is oxidized and precipitates. This process can cause brownish or reddish stains on objects in contact with the water. In some situations, slimy mats of iron-oxidizing bacteria may develop where wells discharge onto the land surface.

Iron is not directly toxic to organisms, and the precipitation of iron from well water entering ponds usually has no negative impacts. In hatcheries, however, precipitation of ferric hydroxide from well water can coat eggs or cause mechanical obstruction of the gills of fish. Well water that contains much ferrous iron can be treated by gravity aeration (Fig. 20.5) or mechanical aeration. The resulting ferric hydroxide floc can be removed by

**Fig. 20.5.** Illustration of aeration of well water by passing it through a stack of expanded metal trays.

sedimentation, but a settling time of one or two days may be necessary. Alternatively, the iron floc can be quickly removed by sand filtration.

Measurement of iron concentrations in pond soils and waters usually is not necessary. Acidic soils should be limed irrespective of iron content, and raising the pH by liming will reduce the solubility of iron. High concentrations of iron in well water can be detected by placing some of the water in a clear container and aerating it by stirring. Precipitation occurs quickly, and the amount of the precipitate will be proportional to the ferrous iron concentration. The dark color caused by ferrous iron also allows one to detect anaerobic zones in sediment.

# References

1. Pais, I. and J. B. Jones, Jr. 1997. *The Handbook of Trace Elements*. Saint Lucie Press, Boca Raton, FL.
2. Boyd, C. E. 1995. *Bottom Soils, Sediment, and Pond Aquaculture*. Chapman and Hall, New York, NY.
3. Boyd, C. E. 2000. *Water Quality, An Introduction*. Kluwer Academic Publishers, Boston, MA.
4. Boyd, C. E. and C. S. Tucker. 1998. *Pond Aquaculture Water Quality Management*. Kluwer Academic Publishers, Boston, MA.
5. McNevin, A. and C. E. Boyd. 2004. Copper concentrations in channel catfish *Ictalurus punctatus* ponds treated with copper sulfate. Journal of the World Aquaculture Society 35:16-24.
6. Silapajarn, O. and C. E. Boyd. 2006. Copper adsorption capacity of pond bottom soils. Journal of Applied Aquaculture 18(2):85-92.
7. Goldberg, E. D. 1963. Chemistry – the oceans as a chemical system, pages 3-25. In: M. N. Hill (editor), *Composition of Sea Water, Comparative and Descriptive Oceanography, Volume II, The Sea*. Interscience Publishing, New York, NY.
8. Boyd, C. E., M. Tanner, M. Madkour, and K. Masuda. 1994. Chemical characteristics of bottom soils from freshwater and brackishwater aquaculture ponds. Journal of the World Aquaculture Society 25:517-534.
9. Abdul-Wahab, S. A. and B. P. Jupp. 2009. Levels of heavy metals in subtidal sediments in the vicinity of thermal power/desalination plants: a case study. Desalination 244:261-282.

# Chapter 21

# Miscellaneous Treatments

## Introduction

Various chemical treatments for improving water quality have been discussed in other chapters—including liming, fertilization, flocculation of suspended soil particles, algicides for phytoplankton control, salt for counteracting nitrite toxicity, and many others. This chapter focuses on several less commonly used treatments for enhancing water quality. We also will consider some substances used for disease control and for wild fish eradication, because their effectiveness can be influenced by water quality or they may negatively impact water quality.

## Biological Amendments

The most common biological amendments used for the purpose of improving water quality in ponds and other production units are microbial products—cultures of living organisms or enzyme preparations. These microbial agents or derivatives are claimed by vendors to enhance rates of organic matter decomposition, nitrification, denitrification, and other microbial processes resulting in lower concentrations of ammonia, nitrite, and sulfide, higher dissolved oxygen concentration, and less blue-green algae. Vendors often market these products aggressively, claiming that they will alleviate most any water quality problem of interest to a potential customer.

### Living Microorganisms

*Bioaugmentation* is the application of living microorganisms produced in cultures to supplement the naturally occurring microbial community. This technique differs from *biostimulation* in which liming, mechanical aeration, nitrogen fertilization, or other treatments are used to improve environmental conditions and stimulate natural microbial processes. In aquaculture, it is common for microorganisms used for bioaugmentation to be called *probiotics*. This usage should be discouraged, because a probiotic is properly defined as a microorganism that provides a health benefit to its host.

Bioaugmentation is not unique to aquaculture—it has been used in terrestrial agriculture, waste treatment, and soil remediation.[1] Many different microbial organisms have been included in products for bioaugmentation. Several bacterial genera to include *Bacillus, Nitrobacter, Nitrosomonas, Pseudomonas, Aerobacter, Cellulomonas*, and *Rhodopseudomonas* have been applied to aquaculture systems for bioaugmentation. Of these, *Bacillus* species are the most common organisms used in bioaugmentation, perhaps because they are spore-forming organisms and therefore easier to produce, package, and store.

A survey of shrimp farmers in Asia[2] revealed widespread application of bioaugmentation; for example, 86% of farmers interviewed in Thailand applied living microorganisms to their ponds. Unfortunately, research on bioaugmentation has shown variable success for all applications, and results for aquaculture are particularly unimpressive.[1] A few studies have shown an increase in ammonia concentration and phytoplankton production in ponds following bioaugmentation, but these are not necessarily desirable changes. There are no reported instances where water quality or sediment condition in research ponds improved as a result of bioaugmentation, and no convincing evidence of increased shrimp or fish production.[1] It also seems noteworthy that the abundance of bacteria in pond water did not increase following inoculation with cultured bacteria.[3,4]

A bioaugmentation trial was conducted on a shrimp farm in Ecuador. Ponds were stocked with postlarval shrimp at roughly the same density and managed by identical practices. In 2009, 52 shrimp crops were produced on a single farm in ponds that received periodic applications of living bacteria or enzyme preparations, and eight crops were produced in control ponds (without bioaugmentation). In 2010, 65 shrimp crops were produced in ponds without bioaugmentation. Ponds receiving living microbial cultures and control ponds did not differ in shrimp production (Table 21.1). Moreover, shrimp production was as high in 2010 when no bioaugmentation was applied as it had been in 2009 in bioaugmented ponds. The on-farm study corroborates observations from research ponds that bioaugmentation does not increase aquacultural production.

In spite of the popularity of bioaugmentation of aquaculture systems in many countries, we agree with Mischke's[5] summation of the effectiveness of bioaugmentation: "Currently, the most efficient way to keep the pond environment suitable for microbial processes is through normal pond management. Maintaining adequate dissolved oxygen levels through aeration and careful feeding practices are more viable strategies for water quality maintenance than adding expensive commercial formulation."

The ineffectiveness of bioaugmentation is not surprising. Bacteria are ubiquitous in the environment; if you add substrate, bacteria capable of decomposing it will thrive. When the substrate has been used up, the bacterial community that was decomposing it

**Table 21.1.** Results of bioaugmentation on shrimp production at a commercial, semi-intensive farm in Ecuador.

| Year | Treatment | Number of crops | Shrimp production (kg/ha) |
|------|-----------|-----------------|---------------------------|
| 2009 | Microbial cultures | 33 | 866 ± 202 |
|      | Enzymes (no living bacteria) | 19 | 990 ± 276 |
|      | Control | 8 | 1,090 ± 206 |
| 2910 | No microbial cultures or enzymes | 65 | 1,066 ± 208 |

declines, but vegetative cells or spores will remain. If a common organic substrate such as those found in aquaculture ponds does not decompose readily, it is because of one or more environmental limitations on the organisms of decay (low temperature, low pH, low dissolved oxygen concentration, nutrient limitations, etc.) not because of a lack of bacteria.

## Microbial Extracts

### Enzymes

A *catalyst* is a substance that accelerates a specific chemical reaction. The catalyst is not altered in the reaction, and it can serve its function over and over again. Enzymes are organic catalysts that accelerate rates of biochemical reactions. Most enzymes catalyze reactions at the cellular level, but there are extracellular enzymes. Organic matter consists of complex molecules too large to be absorbed by microbial cells. Bacteria and other microbes excrete extracellular enzymes that can degrade complex organic molecules into fragments small enough to be absorbed. This process is similar to the action of enzymes in saliva that begins the digestion process before humans and many other animals swallow their food.

Commercial enzyme preparations usually are made from yeast extracts. Several companies sell enzyme preparations for use in aquaculture, but there is no documented evidence from research of the effectiveness of these products. The on-farm study of bioaugmentation at the Ecuadorian shrimp farm described above also failed to show benefits of enzyme augmentation on shrimp production (Table 21.1).

### Antimycin A

This compound is a natural antibiotic produced by the bacterium *Streptomyces griseus*. It inhibits aerobic respiration and is extremely toxic to fish—especially scaled fish. At one time a commercial formulation of antimycin A was available in the United States for aquaculture use as a selective piscicide. The chemical was especially useful in channel catfish farming because it could be applied at concentrations that selectively killed unwanted scaled fish without affecting catfish. The product is not currently available. The effective dose for fish eradication ranges from 3 to 20 µg/L depending upon species. Antimycin A is much less toxic to other pond organisms than it is to fish.

The toxicity of antimycin A declines with decreasing temperature and increasing pH. Following use of antimycin A, residues can be detoxified by potassium permanganate treatment—an application of 2 mg/L above the potassium permanganate demand (described later) is the usual dose.

## Plant Extracts

### Grapefruit seed extract

There has been considerable use of citrus extracts for treating shrimp ponds in Ecuador for the purpose of enhancing soil and water quality. One popular product, Kilol®, is an extract of grapefruit seed. It is either applied directly or mixed with lime before being applied to ponds. There is no published literature to verify the effectiveness of Kilol®. However, studies have shown that this product has antimicrobial properties, it has been approved by the United States Food and Drug Administration for use on human foods, and it does not cause environmental harm.

### Yucca extracts

Extracts of the yucca plant (*Yucca schidigera*) contain a gluco-fraction and a saponin fraction that can bind ammonia. A commercial yucca preparation known as De-odorase® (Alltech) is marketed for inclusion in animal feed to reduce the impact of ammonia on livestock and waste treatment systems. This product has sometimes been applied to aquaculture ponds—especially shrimp ponds—for ammonia removal. One of us (CEB) found that under laboratory conditions, 1 mg/L of a yucca extract reduced total ammonia-nitrogen concentrations by 0.1-0.2 mg/L in samples of pond water and total ammonia-nitrogen concentrations were slightly lower in ponds treated with yucca extract at 0.3 mg/L at 15-day intervals than in control ponds. Nevertheless, further research is needed to verify the benefits of this treatment.

### Rotenone

Rotenone is a complex organic compound extracted from the roots of *Derris elliptica*, *Lonchocarpus* spp., and a few other leguminous plants; it has been widely used as an insecticide. This substance is used in fisheries and aquaculture as a piscicide. Rotenone interferes with fish respiration and is extremely toxic—concentrations of 0.05 to 0.2 mg/L of actual rotenone are sufficient to eradicate fish from most water bodies. The commercial preparations for fish eradication usually contain only 2.5 to 5.0% rotenone.

Water quality affects the effective dose of rotenone. The dose must be increased in waters with a high pH or high alkalinity. Studies showed that the acute toxicity of rotenone increased threefold between pH 5 and pH 10. Also, fourfold more rotenone was required for fish eradication in soft, acidic waters than in waters of high alkalinity. Increasing water temperature increases the toxicity of rotenone, but it also increases the rate at which rotenone degrades to non-toxic form. The usual time for detoxification is 1 to 2 weeks in summer and 2 to 4 weeks or more in winter. Like antimycin A mentioned above, potassium permanganate also can be used to detoxify rotenone. A treatment rate of 2 mg/L above the potassium permanganate demand (described on page 293) will detoxify the usual concentrations of potassium permanganate used for fish eradication.

Rotenone does not have adverse effects on chemical water quality; it is extremely toxic to invertebrate fish food organisms, but invertebrate communities will recover rapidly after rotenone degrades.

# Chemical Amendments

Some of the chemical treatments discussed here are quite effective for improving specific water quality problems. However, the effectiveness of several others—despite their rather widespread use—has not been established through research.

## Oxidants and Disinfectants

These compounds oxidize reduced substances in water, kill microorganisms by reacting with their surface membranes, poise the redox potential in water or sediment, and some release molecular oxygen into the water.

### Peroxides

Three peroxide compounds, hydrogen peroxide ($H_2O_2$), calcium peroxide ($CaO_2$), and sodium carbonate peroxyhydrate ($2Na_2CO_3 \cdot 3H_2O_2$), have been used in aquaculture. Hydrogen peroxide is an extremely strong oxidant that has many applications ranging from being a bleach and cleaning agent to serving as a rocket propellant. In aquaculture, hydrogen peroxide can be employed to disinfect fish eggs, disinfect tanks and other containers, and it has occasionally been applied as an herbicide. However, the most common use is as an emergency source of dissolved oxygen. In water, hydrogen peroxide decomposes spontaneously to release molecular oxygen as follows:

$$2H_2O_2 \rightarrow 2H_2O + O_2. \tag{21.1}$$

Stoichiometry expressed in Equation 21.1 reveals that 2.1 mg/L hydrogen peroxide will release 1 mg/L molecular oxygen.

The cost of hydrogen peroxide prohibits its use as an alternative to routine mechanical aeration. Assuming a cost of about \$1.50/kg of pure $H_2O_2$ in bulk, enough hydrogen peroxide to add 1 mg/L molecular oxygen to a 1-ha pond of 1 m average depth would cost \$US 31.88. However, this cost would be reasonable in an emergency situation where a large quantity of fish or shrimp is at risk of suffocation. The other issue with hydrogen peroxide is its highly reactive nature and the resulting hazard of handling solutions with more than 30% active ingredient. Nevertheless, hydrogen peroxide has been used as an emergency source of dissolved oxygen in fish holding and hauling tanks and in raceways.

Calcium peroxide is a solid material that is less hazardous to handle than concentrated solutions of hydrogen peroxide. This compound is not appreciably soluble in water, but it reacts quickly in aqueous solution to release molecular oxygen as follows:

$$2CaO_2 + 2H_2O \rightarrow 2Ca(OH)_2 + O_2. \tag{21.2}$$

The oxygen yield ratio of calcium peroxide is 32/144, or 4.5 mg/L of $CaO_2$ will yield 1 mg/L molecular oxygen.

Calcium peroxide has an advantage over hydrogen peroxide by not releasing all of its oxygen at once. It can be used as a continuing source of molecular oxygen in holding and hauling vessels. In Japan, it has been applied to sediment in eel ponds at 25 to 100 g/m$^2$ at monthly intervals to oxidize sulfide produced in anaerobic sediment.[6]

Calcium peroxide is alkaline in water, because each 1.0 mg/L of $CaO_2$ applied will result in 1.03 mg/L of $Ca(OH)_2$ (Equation 21.2). This will raise the pH temporarily, but calcium hydroxide will react with dissolved carbon dioxide to form bicarbonate:

$$2Ca(OH)_2 + 4CO_{2(aq)} \rightarrow 2Ca^{2+} + 4HCO_3^-. \tag{21.3}$$

The pH will decline as a result of the reaction depicted in Equation 21.3. Bicarbonate from the reaction is a source of alkalinity; 1 mg/L $CaO_2$ will generate 1.39 mg/L total alkalinity.

Sodium carbonate peroxyhydrate—often called SCP—is a solid compound consisting of 2 parts sodium carbonate and 3 parts hydrogen peroxide. It is mainly used as a cleaning product. In water, the compound decomposes into sodium carbonate and hydrogen peroxide:

$$2Na_2CO_3 \cdot 3H_2O_2 \rightarrow 2Na_2CO_3 + 3H_2O_2 \tag{21.4}$$

Sodium carbonate reacts with dissolved carbon dioxide to form bicarbonate:

$$2Na_2CO_3 + 2CO_{2(aq)} + 2H_2O \rightarrow 4Na^+ + 4HCO_3^-. \tag{21.5}$$

Hydrogen peroxide from SCP will react as shown in Equation 21.1 to release molecular oxygen; 1 mg/L of SCP will release 0.15 mg/L molecular oxygen and increase alkalinity by 0.64 mg/L.

Sodium carbonate peroxyhydrate is legal to use as an algicide in the United States. Commercial formulations are 85% SCP (equivalent to 28% $H_2O_2$). Products are applied at 4 to 12 mg/L (as SCP) for phytoplankton control and 20 to 40 mg/L for control of filamentous macroalgae. The chemical is an attractive alternative to copper-based and organic algicides because it decomposes to innocuous residues. However, high treatment rates and cost have precluded routine use of SCP as an algicide in aquaculture ponds.

*Sodium nitrate*

Nitrate salts are strong oxidants and they are sometimes applied to ponds to oxidize bottom sediment. Sodium nitrate ($NaNO_3$) has been used more commonly for this purpose than has calcium or potassium nitrates, because it has a higher oxygen content than other nitrate salts. Sodium nitrate is highly soluble, and when added to ponds, it almost completely dissolves in the water column. Nitrate in water moving over the pond bottom will be used by denitrifying bacteria in sediment. In the presence of nitrate, redox potential will not fall low enough for more reduced substances, e.g., ferrous iron and sulfide, to enter the water column. Also, poising the redox potential by maintaining dissolved nitrate at the sediment surface prevents release of phosphate from anaerobic zones of the sediment into pond water.

Although sodium nitrate is a bottom soil oxidant, there is little evidence that its use in ponds leads to enough improvement in water quality to justify the cost of its routine use.[7] However, in ponds where anaerobic sediment is thought to be negatively affecting fish or shrimp, application of sodium nitrate to maintain a nitrate-nitrogen concentration above 1 mg/L may possibly be beneficial.

## Potassium permanganate

This compound ($KMnO_4$) has been used in aquaculture based on claims that it oxidizes reduced substances to lessen oxygen demand and that it releases molecular oxygen into the water. Although the claims are true under certain conditions, when applied to aquaculture ponds, potassium permanganate may actually harm water quality by killing phytoplankton and causing a decline in dissolved oxygen concentration.[8] Moreover, potassium permanganate is toxic to fish, and applications above 5 mg/L may sometimes cause fish kills. We do not recommend its use for improving water quality in ponds.

Potassium permanganate has often been used to detoxify rotenone and antimycin A used in fish eradication. The chemical has also been used to oxidize and destroy certain toxins produced by algae (Chapter 18).

## Chlorine

Chlorination is the most common way of disinfecting drinking water and wastewater. Chlorine also is widely used as a bleach. The common sources of chlorine are chlorine gas ($Cl_2$), sodium hypochlorite or household bleach (NaOCl), and calcium hypochlorite or high test hypochlorite (HTH) [$Ca(OCl)_2$].[9] Chlorine gas has rarely been used in aquaculture because of its hazardous nature—it is a deadly toxin and it must be handled, stored, and used according to strict procedures seldom possible on farms. Calcium hypochlorite, the chlorination agent often used in swimming pools, is the usual chlorination agent in aquaculture.

When chlorination chemicals are dissolved in water, four chlorine species ($Cl_2$, HOCl, OCl$^-$ and Cl$^-$) can result:

$$Cl_2 + H_2O = HOCl + H^+ + Cl^- \tag{21.6}$$

$$HOCl = OCl^- + H^+. \tag{21.7}$$

Chloride (Cl⁻) has no appreciable disinfecting power. The three other chlorine species—known as free chlorine residuals—vary in proportion with pH rather than the particular chlorine compound applied (Fig. 21.1). The pH also affects the total concentration of free chlorine residuals necessary for disinfection, because $Cl_2$ and HOCl have about 100-times greater disinfecting power than OCl⁻. In aquaculture applications, pH usually will be above 5, and only HOCl and OCl⁻ will exist in measurable concentration (Fig. 21.1). The minimum concentration of free chlorine residual for effective disinfection at pH 7 is about 1 mg/L, and the amounts of calcium hypochlorite (65% active ingredient) required to provide the equivalent of this dose at different pH values are provided in Table 21.2.

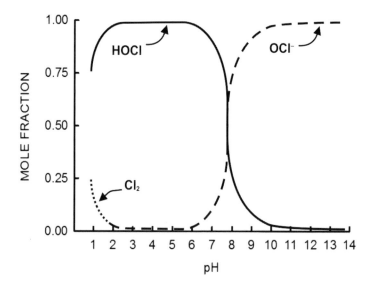

**Fig. 21.1.** Effect of pH on the concentration of free chloride residuals in water.

**Table 21.2.** Molar ratios of hypochlorous acid:hypochlorite ion at different pH values, and concentrations of free chlorine residual necessary to have disinfecting power equal to that of 1 mg/L free chlorine residual at pH 7.

| pH | HOCL:OCl⁻ | Free chlorine residual equivalent to 1 mg/L at pH 7 (mg/L) | Calcium hypochlorite (mg/L) |
|---|---|---|---|
| 5.0 | 316 | 0.76 | 1.17 |
| 5.5 | 100 | 0.77 | 1.18 |
| 6.0 | 32 | 0.78 | 1.20 |
| 6.5 | 10 | 0.84 | 1.29 |
| 7.0 | 3.2 | 1.00 | 1.54 |
| 7.5 | 1 | 1.52 | 2.34 |
| 8.0 | 0.3 | 3.06 | 4.71 |
| 8.5 | 0.1 | 7.68 | 11.82 |
| 9.0 | 0.03 | 19.0 | 29.22 |

Chlorination rates in Table 21.2 are for pure water. In pond water, chlorine residuals will be expended when they oxidize dissolved and particulate organic matter. Chlorine residuals also react with ammonia to form chloramines that have less disinfecting power than free chlorine residuals. Chloramine formation is illustrated by the following equations:

$$NH_3 + HOCl = NH_2Cl + H_2O \qquad (21.8)$$

$$NH_2Cl + HOCl = NHCl_2 + H_2O \qquad (21.9)$$

$$NHCl_2 + HOCl = NCl_3 + H_2O. \qquad (21.10)$$

Chloramines—$NH_2Cl$, $NHCl_2$, and $NCl_3$—are given the prefixes mono, di, and tri, respectively. In addition, chlorine residuals are transformed to nontoxic chloride by exposure to sunlight:

$$2HOCl = 2H^+ + 2Cl^- + O_2. \qquad (21.11)$$

Because of extraneous reactions, the calcium hypochlorite dose necessary for effective chlorination often is greater than suggested in Table 21.2.

Chlorine compounds are extremely toxic, so they should not be used in waters containing culture animals. The most common use of chlorine is to disinfect indoor holding and culture units in hatcheries. However, chlorination also has been used as a means of disinfecting water in hatchery ponds and in intensive culture ponds before introducing culture animals. The chlorination dose may be established by treating water samples with a series of calcium hypochlorite concentrations, and determining the dose that provides the desired concentration of free chlorine residual. Of course, this dose still should be adjusted for the effect of pH on disinfecting power (Table 21.2). The procedure usually is not practical for use at aquaculture facilities, and a treatment rate of 20 to 30 mg/L often is used. Because of the high doses necessary, chlorination of large volumes of water is quite expensive.

*Dichlorovos*

Dichlorovos is an organophosphorus insecticide;[10] it has the chemical name 2,2-dichlorovinyl dimethyl phosphate and is often referred to as DDVP. This compound provides a cheaper alternative to chlorination for eliminating microcrustacean vectors of aquatic animal diseases from water in aquaculture ponds. It is effective at a much lower concentration than chlorination; treatment rates of 1 to 3 mg/L are effective in destroying disease vectors. Of course, DDVP will not reduce the abundance of bacteria in water.

Because DDVP is an insecticide, its use in aquaculture alarms many people—especially environmentalists. However, within 3 or 4 days after application, DDVP concentration will decline to an undetectable level in water. In reality, DDVP is safer than chlorine compounds for use in pond waters.

DDVP is marketed in Asia as Pondvos or Crusticide for use in shrimp ponds. It is used either in reservoirs before water is transferred to ponds, or ponds are treated with DDVP after refilling but before they are stocked with postlarvae. In shrimp ponds, several months will have passed between treatment with DDVP and harvest, and there is no reason to be concerned about DDVP contamination of shrimp harvested from ponds previously treated with this compound.

## *Ammonia Removal*

### *Zeolites*

Zeolites are aluminosilicate clay minerals of high cation exchange capacity. They are used as cation ion exchange media for softening water, because sodium held to negatively-charged sites on zeolite molecules is exchanged for calcium and magnesium ions dissolved in hard water.[11] Other cations, including ammonium, can be exchanged for sodium, and zeolites have been used in commercial aquaria and fish hauling and holding tanks to remove ammonia. In these applications, a relatively small volume of water is continually passed through a zeolite column and back to the fish holding unit. When zeolite in the column becomes saturated with ammonium and other cations, backwashing with a strong sodium chloride solution will restore its capacity to absorb ammonium (and other cations).

The success of zeolite in the above applications led to the use of zeolite in ponds to remove ammonia. However, zeolite is ineffective for this purpose. Other cations compete with ammonium for adsorption by zeolite, and in highly mineralized freshwater, brackishwater, and seawater, other ions, and particularly sodium, far outnumber ammonium. The removal rate of ammonium nitrogen per gram of zeolite had the following relationship to salinity: freshwater, 9 g $NH_4$-N/kg zeolite; 4 ppt salinity, 0.12 g/kg; 8 ppt, 0.10 g/kg; 16 ppt, 0.08 g/kg; 32 ppt, 0.04 g /kg.[12] The amount of zeolite to remove 1 mg/L $NH_4$-N from a pond 1 ha in area × 1 m average depth would be 1,111 kg. Much more zeolite would be needed for a pond with brackishwater or seawater.

Zeolite often is applied to shrimp ponds in southeast Asia at rates up to about 200 kg/ha per month. Obviously, no benefit could be expected from such low treatment rates, and the cost of treatment doses high enough to significantly lower ammonium concentration would be excessive.

### *Formalin*

Shrimp ponds in southeast Asia are sometimes treated with formalin (40% formaldehyde solution) to remove ammonia. Formaldehyde reacts with ammonia to form hexamethylenetetramine and formamide, and formalin treatments of 5 to 10 mg/L reduced ammonia nitrogen concentrations by 50% or more in laboratory systems and ponds.[12] However, formaldehyde is a noxious chemical to apply, it is toxic to aquatic animals, it can kill phytoplankton and cause dissolved oxygen depletion, and it possibly could cause a residue problem in aquaculture products. More research is needed to ascertain if formalin treatment should be recommended for use in commercial aquaculture ponds.

## Carbon Dioxide Removal

Elevated concentrations of dissolved carbon dioxide usually are not harmful to aquaculture species when there is plenty of dissolved oxygen. But, concentrations of carbon dioxide typically are elevated when dissolved oxygen concentrations are low. Carbon dioxide interferes with uptake of oxygen by hemoglobin in fish blood (hemocyanin in shrimp blood); thus, a high dissolved carbon dioxide concentration makes a low dissolved oxygen concentration more harmful to the culture species.

Mechanical aeration strips carbon dioxide from water supersaturated with this gas, and high carbon dioxide concentration is usually not a problem in well-aerated ponds. However, it can be a serious problem in un-aerated ponds, and chemical removal of carbon dioxide can be used as an emergency measure. Oxygen stress in the culture species should be alleviated quickly, and although both agricultural limestone and lime will remove dissolved carbon dioxide from water (see Chapters 7 and 9), these products are not highly soluble. Thus, they do not react as quickly with carbon dioxide as does sodium hydroxide (NaOH) and sodium carbonate ($Na_2CO_3$) that are more water soluble. Reactions of sodium hydroxide and sodium carbonate with dissolved carbon dioxide are depicted below:

$$NaOH + CO_{2(aq)} = Na^+ + HCO_3^- \qquad (21.12)$$

$$Na_2CO_3 + CO_{2(aq)} + H_2O = 2Na^+ + 2HCO_3^-. \qquad (21.13)$$

Amounts of sodium hydroxide and sodium carbonate necessary to remove 1 mg/L of carbon dioxide are 0.91 mg/L and 2.41 mg/L, respectively; but, the rates are more easily remembered as 1 mg/L and 2.5 mg/L, respectively.

Sodium hydroxide is more alkaline and more dangerous to handle than sodium carbonate. Contact with sodium hydroxide solutions can cause serious damage to the skin and especially to the eyes of workers, and overdosing could cause pH in pond water to rise to a toxic level. Sodium carbonate also must be used with caution, but it does not have as strong an alkaline reaction as sodium hydroxide.

Effective removal of carbon dioxide requires the removal compound be mixed with water and splashed over the surface of the pond or other culture unit. Aeration can be used to facilitate mixing, but chemical removal of carbon dioxide is necessary mainly in systems without aeration.

It is not uncommon to hear of sodium bicarbonate ($NaHCO_3$) being added to water to remove carbon dioxide. However, sodium bicarbonate is totally ineffective for this purpose, because it does not react with carbon dioxide.[13]

## Sulfide Removal

Hydrogen sulfide is produced by microbial activity in anaerobic sediment, and it diffuses into the water where it is quickly oxidized. The rate of its release from sediment may sometimes exceed its rate of oxidation in water, and residual hydrogen sulfide concentrations of a few micrograms per liter may be toxic to culture animals. Hydrogen sulfide toxicity probably is more common in coastal aquaculture than in inland aquaculture, because brackishwater and seawater have a high sulfate concentration—the source of sulfide.

The best way of avoiding high sulfide concentration is to maintain plenty of dissolved oxygen in pond water and manage pond bottoms to avoid excessive concentrations of organic matter (see Chapter 23). Peroxides and potassium permanganate have been used to oxidize sulfide in water or sediment on an emergency basis, but a better approach is application of an iron source such as powered ferrous oxide (FeO) to the sediment to react with sulfide and precipitate it in nontoxic ferrous sulfide (FeS).[6] Application rates of 50 to 100 kg/ha have been used for this purpose.

Well waters used in hatcheries sometimes may be elevated in sulfide concentration. Vigorous aeration of these waters before use is the best way of eliminating sulfide.

## Control of pH

One of the most common water quality problems in aquaculture is low pH caused by building ponds on acidic soils. This problem, which is thoroughly discussed in Chapters 8 and 9, is controlled by liming. Robust rates of photosynthesis can remove dissolved carbon dioxide from pond water and cause extended periods of excessively high pH. This is a difficult problem to solve and various pond management practices and treatments have been used to reduce high pH. These treatments include the use of aluminum sulfate (alum), strong mineral acids, calcium sulfate (gypsum), algicides, dyes, and sodium bicarbonate—all of which are explained in Chapter 8.

One common recommendation to reduce high pH is to apply an acid-forming fertilizer such as ammonium sulfate. However, the resulting increase in un-ionized ammonia concentration in high pH water could be toxic to the culture species. Moreover, ammonia nitrogen must be nitrified to express the potential acidity of nitrogen fertilizers, and pH will not decline quickly following application of nitrogen fertilizers.

## Alkalinity Control in Water Recirculating Systems

Acidity caused by nitrification reduces alkalinity in culture units with water recirculation (Chapter 28). Because of its high solubility, sodium bicarbonate is widely used to replenish alkalinity in water recirculating systems.[13] One molecular weight of sodium bicarbonate (84 g) yields one mole of bicarbonate ion (61 g)—equal to one equivalent of calcium carbonate (50 g). Calcium carbonate is the unit of alkalinity, and it requires 1.68 mg/L of sodium bicarbonate to replenish 1.0 mg/L of total alkalinity.

The lime requirement resulting from nitrification of ammonia from feeding is about 0.32 kg CaCO₃/kg feed applied. Thus, in a water recirculating system, the sodium bicarbonate demand should be around 0.54 kg NaHCO₃/kg feed. It is more accurate, however, to measure total alkalinity and make sodium bicarbonate applications accordingly.

## *Therapeutants*

A number of antibiotics and other drugs are used in aquaculture for therapeutic purposes and applied in feeds (medicated feeds). A few compounds, however, are applied directly to the water of the culture system. The most common materials applied directly to water of culture systems are potassium permanganate and formalin.

### *Potassium permanganate*

Potassium permanganate is a common treatment for external bacterial diseases of fish.[8] The effective concentration in clean water is about 2 mg/L, but when added to a pond, considerable potassium permanganate is converted to manganese dioxide in oxidizing reduced substances—particularly dissolved and particulate organic matter. The potassium permanganate demand of the water should be estimated and a treatment dose of 2 mg/L more than the demand applied. The potassium permanganate demand can be estimated by treating samples of water in clear vessels with a series of concentrations of this chemical, e.g., 0, 1, 2, 3, 4, 5, 6, 7, and 8 mg/L. The lowest concentration in which the pink color of permanganate ion remains after 15 or 20 minutes is the permanganate demand. The potassium permanganate demand of aquaculture pond waters often is 3 to 5 mg/L.

### *Formalin*

Formalin is a liquid containing about 40% formaldehyde. This chemical is widely used in fish culture for control of fungi on fish eggs and external parasites on fish. It is relatively nontoxic to fish and is used at 1,000-2,000 µL/L (1,103-2,206 mg/L) for 15 minutes in constant flow baths, 167-250 µL/L (184-276 mg/L) in tanks or raceways for 1 hour, and 15-25 µL/L (16.5-27.6 mg/L) for indefinite periods in ponds.[14]

Formalin is applied to ponds as an external parasite treatment. The usual treatment rate of 15 mg/L (13.6 µL/L) may kill plankton and present a risk of dissolved oxygen depletion.[15] Depletion of dissolved oxygen following formalin treatment was more severe in fertilized and fed ponds which had heavy plankton blooms than in ponds that did not receive nutrient additions and had little plankton. Treatment of a channel catfish pond with a dense plankton bloom at Auburn University with 15 mg/L of formalin caused massive mortality of the phytoplankton bloom and several tonnes of fish died from oxygen depletion. Pond managers should monitor dissolved oxygen concentrations after formalin treatments and provide emergency aeration if necessary.

*Antimicrobial agents*

A number of antimicrobial compounds, e.g., glutaraldehyde (pentane-1,5 dial), benzalkonium chloride (benzyl-dimethyl-tridecylazanium chloride), and povidone-iodine (a stable complex of complex of polyvinylpyrrolidone and elemental iodine) are used to treat eggs of aquatic organisms and waters of culture systems for the purpose of reducing the loads of bacteria and other microorganisms. There is little published data to support the use of these compounds in small hatchery systems and no evidence that they are effective in ponds.

# References

1. Tucker, C. S., S. K. Kingsbury, and C. C. Mischke. 2009. Bacterial bioaugmentation of channel catfish ponds. North American Journal of Aquaculture 71:315-319.
2. Gräslund, S., K. Holmström, and A. Wahlström. 2003. A field survey of chemicals and biological products used in shrimp farming. Marine Pollution Bulletin 46:81-90.
3. Boyd, C. E., W. D. Hollerman, J. A. Plumb, and M. Saeed. 1984. Effect of treatment with a commercial bacterial suspension on water quality in channel catfish ponds. Progressive Fish-Culturist 46:36-40.
4. Queiroz, J. F. and C. E. Boyd. 1998. Effects of a bacterial inoculums in channel catfish ponds. Journal of the World Aquaculture Society 29:67-73.
5. Mischke, C. C. 2003. Evaluation of two bio-stimulants for improving water quality in channel catfish, *Ictalurus punctatus*, production ponds. Journal of Applied Aquaculture 14:163-169.
6. Chamberlain, G. 1988. Rethinking shrimp pond management. Coastal Aquaculture, Volume 2, Texas Agricultural Extension Service.
7. Chainark, S. and C. E. Boyd. 2010. Water and sediment quality, phytoplankton communities, and channel catfish production in sodium nitrate-treated ponds. Journal of Applied Aquaculture 22:171-185.
8. Tucker, C. S. and C. E. Boyd. 1977. Relationships between potassium permanganate treatment and water quality. Transactions of the American Fisheries Society 106:481-488.
9. White, G. C. 1992. *Handbook of Chlorination and Alternative Disinfectants, 3rd Edition*. Van Nostrand Reinhold, New York, NY.
10. Worthington, C. R. (editor). 1991. *The Pesticide Manual*. British Crop Protection Council, Berkshire, UK.
11. Silapajarn, O., K. Silapajarn, and C. E. Boyd. 2006. Evaluation of zeolite products used for aquaculture in Thailand. Journal of the World Aquaculture Society 37:136-138.
12. Chiayvareesajja, S. and C. E. Boyd. 1993. Effects of zeolite, formalin, bacterial augmentation, and aeration on total ammonia nitrogen concentrations. Aquaculture 116:33-45.
13. Tucker, C. S. 2008. Misuses of sodium bicarbonate in pond aquaculture. Global Aquaculture Advocate 11(4):60-61.
14. Boyd, C. E. and C. S. Tucker. 1998. *Pond Aquaculture Water Quality Management*. Kluwer Academic Publishers, Boston, MA.
15. Boyd, C. E. and C. S. Tucker. 1998. *Pond Aquaculture Water Quality Management*. Kluwer Academic Publishers, Boston, MA.

# Chapter 22

# Water Quality in Low-Salinity Aquaculture

## Introduction

Saline soils occur in arid regions of more than 100 countries, and surface waters and ground waters in such areas often have more than 1 ppt salinity.[1] Saline groundwater also may occur in regions of greater rainfall as a result of salt deposits, connate groundwater of marine origin, and saltwater intrusion in coastal areas.[2] In the United States, saline groundwater can be found at some depth beneath two-thirds of the country.[3] There is interest in producing brackishwater and marine aquaculture species in this previously un-utilized water resource. The effort focuses mostly on marine shrimp, particularly Pacific white shrimp, but some researchers and entrepreneurs also have produced other marine organisms in low-salinity, inland waters.[4]

In the United States, marine shrimp apparently were first successfully cultured in 1990 in Texas in ponds supplied with saline groundwater that was diluted with freshwater to maintain a salinity of 25 ppt.[5] Since then, inland culture of marine shrimp using saline well water with salinities of 1 to 15 ppt has become rather common in the United States with farms in Florida, Alabama, Texas, Arizona, and other states. Some of the farms have been in production for more than 10 years.

A number of farmers in Ecuador initiated projects to culture marine shrimp in saline well water at sites more than 100 km inland near Palestina and Santa Rosa in Guayas Province. Although good survival and growth of shrimp was possible, these facilities apparently are no longer in operation. There have been various reports of shrimp culture in saline, well water in Brazil and other South American nations[6], but no documentation of the current status of inland culture of shrimp in these countries was found.

In arid, agricultural areas, irrigation may cause the water table to rise to within 1 m or less of the land surface and this shallow groundwater often is saline. A pond excavated below the shallow water table will fill with groundwater to the level of the piezometric surface. In the early 1990s, a few farmers in northeastern Thailand successfully cultured black tiger prawn in excavated ponds where groundwater contained 5 to 10 ppt salinity, but the practice was not adopted.

There are extensive areas in the delta and flood plain of the Yellow River in Shandong Province, China, where cultivation of traditional agricultural crops formerly was not possible because of shallow, saline groundwater. Near Dong Ying, China, about 3,000 ha of land were reclaimed for productive use by digging ponds and placing the excavated earth around the ponds and above the original land surface (Fig. 22.1). The completed effort consists of 40% pond water surface, 40% elevated land area, and 20% roads and canals.[4] Salt leached from the excavated soil between the ponds, and after 2 or 3 years this soil was used for cultivating crops. The ponds fill to a depth of about 1.5 m with saline groundwater of 2 to 3 ppt salinity. Freshwater from the irrigation system may be added to ponds to dilute salinity when necessary. Tilapia were originally cultured in the ponds, but because of its higher value, Pacific white shrimp is now the main species.

There are projects in the Murry-Darling River Basin of Southern Australia and in the wheat belt of Western Australia in which saline groundwater is pumped from a network of bore holes to lower the water table and reclaim the land for agriculture. The saline water is placed in large, shallow ponds for evaporation and salt recovery. Considerable research has been conducted on the suitability of this water for commercial aquaculture. A review of these studies[7] suggests that the waters have considerable potential for culture of several marine finfish species, but the temperature climate in most of the salinity-affected areas of Australia is not conducive to marine shrimp culture.

In Thailand, a different approach has been used for obtaining low-salinity water for inland shrimp culture. Brine solution from coastal, seawater evaporation ponds is mixed with freshwater. The brine solution is obtained from evaporation ponds before its salinity exceeds 250 ppt and sodium chloride starts to precipitate from solution.[8] Salt from seawater evaporation ponds also may be added to ponds in Thailand to increase salinity. Pond waters there typically have 2 to 5 ppt salinity, and excellent survival and growth of shrimp usually is achieved. Nevertheless, a recent study[9] suggests that soil uptake of potassium and magnesium in ponds treated with brine solution may lead to ionic imbalance.

There has been an effort in Jiangsu, Shanghai, and Zhejiang Provinces of China, to culture marine shrimp in inland water with less than 1 ppt salinity.[10] Growth and production of shrimp has been highly variable and often low. Thus, some producers in these provinces add crushed rock salt to ponds to increase salinity.

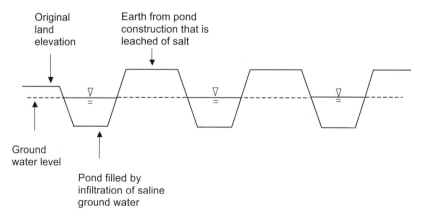

**Fig. 22.1.** Procedure for reclaiming saline areas of the Yellow River floodplain in Shandong Province, China.

# Saline Groundwater

In many countries, useful information on the depth and specific conductivity or chloride concentration of groundwater is available from well driller's logs that are kept in governmental archives. These data can be examined to identify areas where saline groundwater may be found. For example, examination of 2,527 well records of the Geological Survey of Alabama and the United States Geological Survey for 11 counties in central and west-central Alabama[2] revealed 238 wells with chloride concentrations of 136 to 94,000 mg/L. Saline groundwater in Washington, Choctaw, and Clarke Counties was not considered ideal for inland shrimp culture because of great depth and extremely high chloride concentration. In Dallas, Hale, Greene, Marengo, Wilcox, and Sumter Counties, water from wells supplied by the Eutaw, Gordo, McShan, and undifferentiated Eutaw-McShan formations had an average and standard deviation of 1,238 ± 615 mg/L chloride. Based on the frequency of saline-water wells, number of wells with water of chloride concentrations above 700 mg/L (about 2 ppt salinity), and relatively shallow well depths, it was concluded that Hale, Greene, Marengo, and Sumter Counties have the greatest potential for saline-water aquaculture in Alabama. Contour maps for chloride concentrations and depths of wells in these four counties were prepared to better delineate this potential water source for aquaculture. There were, however, areas in Lowndes, Tuscaloosa, and Wilcox Counties in Alabama with saline groundwater suitable for inland aquaculture.[2]

# Ionic Composition of Water

Interest in inland, low-salinity shrimp culture appears to have been stimulated mainly by the success of this practice in Thailand where pond waters were made saline by additions of brine solution. Shrimp producers from Thailand encouraged Ecuadorian producers to use saline groundwater for shrimp culture. The initial attempts to produce shrimp in low-salinity groundwater in Ecuador resulted in low survival of postlarvae. Analysis of the water revealed low potassium concentration, and supplementation with potassium resulted in improved survival.[10] Similar observations were made in the United States[11,12] and Australia.[7]

## *Seawater Equivalent Concentration*

A survey of the ionic composition of waters for inland, low-salinity culture of marine shrimp was conducted. Proportions of major ions were similar to those in normal seawater in Thailand where brine solutions from seawater evaporation ponds were used to raise salinity. Saline surface water and groundwater that occur naturally often have different ionic proportionalities than would be expected in seawater diluted to the same salinity because of differential precipitation of salts as water evaporates and removal of ions by reactions with soil and other geological material. Thus, ponds filled with saline groundwater in China, Ecuador, and the United States are quite different in ionic proportions when compared to seawater. In particular, saline water tended to be low in potassium, magnesium, and sulfate relative to concentrations expected in seawater diluted to the same salinity.[10]

Marine shrimp are native of coastal waters in which the proportionalities of major anions and cations resemble those of normal seawater. Shrimp can survive and grow well at salinities as low as 1 or 2 ppt, but the requirements for individual ions are not known. Practical experience has provided enough information about this issue to allow adequate culture conditions to be maintained while more exact information is sought through research. The concentrations of major ions that would be present in normal seawater diluted to the same salinity as a particular source of inland saline water for aquaculture may be estimated using the following equation:

$$SEC_x = (S_p)(R_x) \hspace{6cm} (22.1)$$

where $SEC_x$ = seawater equivalent concentration of ion x; $S_p$ = salinity of pond water; $R_x$ = ratio of concentration of ion X in seawater to salinity of normal seawater. Values for $R_x$ are provided in Table 22.1.

Data on well water composition, composition of water after equilibrium in ponds, and seawater equivalent concentrations for the pond water are provided for a shrimp farm in Alabama (Table 22.2). The loss of calcium and alkalinity from the well water after equilibration in the pond resulted from calcium carbonate precipitation. Salinity declined because of dilution by rainfall and soil uptake of ions. The pond water was especially low in potassium, magnesium, and sulfate concentration relative to the seawater equivalent concentration.

There is evidence from short-term exposures of postlarvae to different ionic concentrations in culture tanks that both potassium and magnesium additions to saline well water will enhance survival and growth of shrimp.[13] Nevertheless, treatment of pond waters on one shrimp farm in west Alabama with potassium was as effective in increasing shrimp production as was treatment of ponds with both potassium and magnesium. During 2001, no potassium was applied and shrimp survival was only 27% and production averaged approximately 750 kg/ha.[14] Potassium was applied to maintain the concentration between 35 and 50 mg/L in 2002, and survival increased to 67% and production to 3,500 kg/ha. In 2003, 2004, and 2005, both potassium and magnesium were applied, but production was no better than that achieved in 2002 (Fig. 22.2).

**Table 22.1.** Factors for estimating acceptable concentrations of individual ions for inland shrimp culture from salinity.[10]

| Ion | Factor[a] |
|---|---|
| Calcium | 11.6 |
| Magnesium | 39.1 |
| Potassium | 10.7 |
| Sodium | 304.5 |
| Bicarbonate[b] | --- |
| Chloride | 551.0 |
| Sulfate | 78.3 |

[a]Example: Sodium in mg/L = salinity in ppt × 304.5.
[b]Not be below 75 mg/L total alkalinity (92 mg/L bicarbonate).

**Table 22.2.** Concentrations of salinity, total alkalinity, and major ions in well water used to supply ponds at an inland shrimp farm in Alabama and concentrations of those variables in pond water at this farm in late April before potassium and magnesium salts were applied.[11]

| Variable | Well water[a] (n = 4) | Pond water (n = 5) | Seawater diluted to 2.56 ppt salinity |
|---|---|---|---|
| Salinity (ppt) | 3.70 ± 0.34 | 2.56 ± 0.51 | 2.56 |
| Total alkalinity (mg/L as CaCO₃) | 272.6 ± 30.3 | 119.9 ± 55.7 | 10.5 |
| Chloride (mg/L) | 1,982 ± 177 | 1,460 ± 117 | 1,410 |
| Sulfate (mg/L) | 0.46 ± 0.56 | 33.8 ± 18.7 | 200 |
| Calcium (mg/L) | 118.2 ± 5.6 | 59.8 ± 5.1 | 29.7 |
| Magnesium (mg/L) | 5.46 ± 0.92 | 4.61 ± 1.18 | 100 |
| Potassium (mg/L) | 11.6 ± 1.8 | 6.25 ± 2.44 | 27.4 |
| Sodium (mg/L) | 1,402 ± 110 | 971 ± 208 | 77.9 |

[a]Average of four samples collected between January and April 2002.

 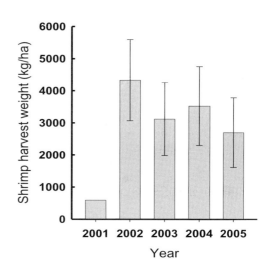

**Fig. 22.2.** Averages and standard deviations for shrimp production at an inland shrimp farm in Alabama – potassium supplementation was not used in 2001.

Total alkalinity concentration in pond waters should be 75 mg/L or more to provide adequate buffering capacity regardless of salinity—this equates to 90 mg/L bicarbonate in water with pH less than 8.3. Low concentrations of other ions could possibly have lesser negative impacts on shrimp growth and survival, and further research on this topic is needed. However, practical experience suggests that additions of potassium alone provide excellent remediation of ionic imbalance in ponds in Alabama filled with groundwater from wells or other sources.

In Thailand, however, water in ponds for inland shrimp culture tend to be lower in magnesium than potassium relative to SEC; magnesium supplementation lead to an increase in shrimp production in trials conducted on one farm.[9]

## Potassium and Magnesium Supplementation

The most common material for increasing potassium concentration in pond water is fertilizer-grade potassium chloride (KCl) often called muriate of potash. This material is about 50% potassium, so a treatment rate of 2 g/m$^3$ provides a potassium increase of about 1 g/m$^3$ (1 mg/L). Another fertilizer, sulfate of potash magnesia (K$_2$SO$_4$·2MgSO$_4$)— sold under the trade name K-Mag®—has been used as a source of both potassium and magnesium for treating inland shrimp ponds.[14] This product contains 10.5% magnesium, 17.8% potassium, and 63.6% sulfate. A treatment rate of 5.6 g/m$^3$ is necessary to cause a 1 mg/L increase in potassium—resulting increases in magnesium and sulfate are 0.59 mg/L and 3.5 mg/L, respectively.

The costs of muriate of potash and K-Mag® are similar per tonne, but because of differences in potassium content, use of K-Mag® for increasing potassium concentration is much more expensive than application of muriate of potash. To illustrate, ponds on a shrimp farm in Alabama are about 1.2 m average depth and contain 8 mg/L potassium and 20 mg/L magnesium (Table 22.2). To increase the potassium concentration to the seawater equivalent concentration of 41.7 mg/L would require 67.4 mg/L (809 kg/ha of muriate of potash), but it would require 2,480 kg/ha of K-Mag®. Attaining the seawater equivalent concentration of magnesium would require 9,000 kg/ha of K-Mag®—much more than necessary for adjusting potassium concentration to the seawater equivalent concentration. In Alabama, shrimp producers often use both muriate of potash and K-Mag® to increase potassium concentration slightly above the seawater equivalent concentration and to provide a modest increase in magnesium concentration—usually about 25% of the seawater equivalent.

## Potassium and Magnesium Uptake by Soils

Potassium and magnesium applied to pond waters are lost through overflow, seepage, draining at harvest, soil uptake, and shrimp harvest. During the grow-out period in Alabama, there was little outflow of water until ponds were harvested, and the observed, gradual decline in potassium and magnesium concentration was initially believed to result from adsorption of these ions on cation exchange sites in bottom soil. Potassium and magnesium budgets for ponds treated with muriate of potash and K-Mag® were prepared by assessing inputs and outputs of the two cations.[14,15] The increase in exchangeable potassium and magnesium in bottom soil was not sufficient to account for the removal of the two ions from the water (Table 22.3)—especially for potassium.

Laboratory soil-water systems were established in plastic tanks. Soil from a shrimp farm that was similar to pond bottom soil but never exposed to saline water was used. Saline water was obtained from the well that supplied ponds on the farm. The systems were treated with either potassium chloride to give 50 mg/L potassium[16] or magnesium sulfate to provide 80 mg/L magnesium.[17] Concentrations of ions were measured at intervals and retreatment with potassium or magnesium was made when concentrations fell below 30 mg/L and 50 mg/L, respectively. The rate of loss of ions from the water declined over time, but the uptake rate of potassium was still substantial after three treatments during a 10-month period.

**Table 22.3.** Average potassium and magnesium budgets measured for three ponds in Alabama used for inland culture of marine shrimp in low-salinity water.[14,15] The studies were done on the same farm, but in different years.

| Variable | Potassium Mean ± SD[a] (kg/ha) | Magnesium Mean ± SD (kg/ha) |
|---|---|---|
| Inputs | | |
| Muriate of potash | 596.8 ± 45.0 | |
| K-Mag | 220.6 ± 16.6 | 142.9 ± 16.8 |
| Well water | 130.2 ± 2.7 | 275.1 ± 69.7 |
| Feed | 55.0 ± 10.3 | 17.0 ± 9.7 |
| Rainfall and runoff | 18.6 ± 0.23 | 6.5 ± 0.2 |
| Sum | 1,021.2 ± 65.2 | 441.5 ± 78.2 |
| | | |
| Outputs | | |
| Harvest effluent | 347.9 ± 49.1 | 212.8 ± 67.4 |
| Seepage | 101.2 ± 16.2 | 74.6 ± 88.9 |
| Shrimp | 5.4 ± 1.5 | 5.3 ± 3.1 |
| Overflow | 2.0 ± 3.4 | |
| Sum | 456.5 ± 53.2 | 292.6 ± 24.2 |

[a]SD = standard deviation.

Analysis of potassium and magnesium loss from water in the tanks revealed that soils took up 4,982 mg potassium and 1,568 mg magnesium (Table 22.4). Exchangeable potassium increase in the soil accounted for 25.8% of the potassium loss from the water. The remainder of the potassium obviously was absorbed by the soil through a process other than ion exchange. Soils in the area where inland shrimp farming is conducted in Alabama have a high concentration of 2:1 layered, smectite clay. Such soil can fix potassium between the adjacent tetrahedral layers of the clay, and potassium fixed by this mechanism is essentially unavailable to the surrounding solution.[18]

Magnesium present in soil as exchangeable magnesium at the end of the study accounted for 91.8% of magnesium lost from the water in the tanks. Thus, the soils did not fix large amounts of magnesium within the interlayers of the clay. The laboratory soil-water study suggested that magnesium uptake by bottom soils should decline quicker than potassium uptake and possibly become insignificant after 1 or 2 years. Potassium uptake by bottom soils can be expected to be an important factor for a much longer time.

**Table 22.4.** Average potassium and magnesium loss from water and adsorption by soil in laboratory soil-water systems.[16,17]

| Variable | Potassium Mean ± SD | Magnesium Mean ± SD |
|---|---|---|
| Loss from water | | |
| (mg/L) | 89.0 ± 10.0 | 28.0 ± 2.8 |
| (mg/tank) | 4,982 ± 559 | 1,568 ± 155 |
| Soil weight (kg/tank) | 9.6 ± 1.32 | 5.5 ± 0.4 |
| Exchangeable ion absorption by soil | | |
| (mg/kg) | 136 ± 83 | 263.0 ± 67.4 |
| (mg/tank) | 1,284 ± 792 | 1,440 ± 274 |
| Ion absorption by soil through non-exchangeable processes | | |
| (mg/kg) | 385 | 23 |
| (mg/tank) | 3,698 | 128 |

Inland shrimp culture can be accomplished using water from various sources. Inland shrimp farmers are facing several different culture scenarios depending on a number of factors, including geographical location, length of production season, climate, availability of saline water, and other factors. Because environmental factors vary greatly by geographical location, there is no magic recipe that can be applied to all inland shrimp culture scenarios. When culturing shrimp in inland saline waters, farmers must tailor their production strategies to their specific culture conditions, and thus to their specific waters. As a result, a number of different production strategies have been utilized worldwide to culture shrimp in low-salinity waters.

The culture of shrimp in ponds is perhaps the most widespread production strategy for raising shrimp in low-salinity waters. In Thailand, for instance, shrimp are cultured in ponds prepared by mixing freshwater and brine solution from coastal seawater evaporation ponds to provide a salinity of about 5 ppt initially, but the salinity typically falls to about 2 ppt by harvest time.[9] In much of the United States and South America, inland, low-salinity ponds are filled from saline groundwater.[2,10] In this case, water of 2 to 15 ppt salinity is pumped from wells and used to fill production ponds. Some producers in Thailand and China mix granular salt (either from evaporation ponds or mines) with freshwater to prepare low-salinity water.[10]

Water utilized to culture shrimp in inland low-salinity waters can vary considerably both in salinity and ionic composition.[11,12] These differences were not only observed among pond waters located on different farms, but also among ponds from the same farm which draw water from the same low-salinity artesian well. Pond salinity and ionic composition is dependent on a number of factors, including initial salinity, initial concentrations of dissolved ions, different adsorption rates in pond bottom sediments, runoff, evaporation, rain and other contributing factors. These and other factors have resulted in a large variation in ionic profiles among farms. As a result, the farmer is forced to analyze the water of individual ponds before stocking in order to assess the viability of each pond for growing shrimp. This has resulted in large variations in survival, growth, and production among ponds.

## *Measuring Potassium and Magnesium Concentration*

Farmers should measure potassium and magnesium concentrations before each crop, and apply fertilizers as indicated by the results. Potassium concentration also should be monitored at 4- to 6-week intervals and retreatment with muriate of potash made as necessary. Magnesium concentration can be measured with water analysis kits for total hardness and calcium hardness. The magnesium ion concentration may be estimated as follows:

$$Mg = \frac{TH - CaH}{2.5} \qquad (22.2)$$

where Mg = magnesium concentration (mg/L); TH = total hardness (mg/L as $CaCO_3$); CaH = calcium hardness (mg/L as $CaCO_3$); 2.5 = ratio of weights of $CaCO_3$:Ca.

Potassium concentration in water normally is measured using a flame emission spectrophotometer. Farmers must send samples to a laboratory for analysis, and it may not be possible to obtain results in a timely manner. HANNA Instruments, Inc. (Ann Arbor, Michigan, USA) manufactures a relatively inexpensive potassium meter (Model HI 93750 Ion Specific Meter, Potassium) that measures potassium concentration by a colorimeteric method. Comparison of potassium concentration made with the meter and by flame emission spectrophotometry on samples of low-salinity water revealed that the meter provided sufficiently accurate results for use by inland shrimp farmers in assessing potassium concentrations in ponds.[19]

# Environmental Regulations and Control

Utilization of saline water sources has allowed shrimp aquaculture to expand into inland areas; however, there are concerns with discharging water containing high concentrations of total dissolved solids (TDS) into freshwater ecosystems. Though problems associated with salinization are typically associated with arid regions where irrigation of traditional, agronomic crops have lead to salinization of groundwater and caused water tables to rise, recent studies[20,21] have revealed that inland aquaculture in low-salinity water can result in stream salinization in humid climates. To illustrate, total salt input in saline well water, mineral amendments, feed, and rainfall and runoff to ponds of an inland shrimp farm in Alabama was 1,980.8 tonne over a 5-year period.[21] A residual of 270.4 tonne of salt remained in pond water and 38.3 tonne in bottom soil. Only 8 tonne of salt were removed in harvested shrimp. A total of 1,588 tonne of salt or 80.2% of the input was lost to the environment with roughly equal amounts exiting the ponds in seepage and overflow and in harvest effluent. The highest salinity was observed in the nearby stream when ponds were harvested. At this time, the stream water exceeded the Alabama Department of Environmental Management limit of 230 mg/L of chloride.

In Chachoengsao Province of Thailand low-salinity culture of shrimp occupies more than 8,400 ha of land and utilizes saline water transported inland from the coast.[20] The salt balance of these operations was evaluated both as they are currently managed, and through modeling a zero-discharge scenario. Under the then current management system, which utilized water exchanges to maintain water quality and further discharges at harvest, electrical conductivity of the irrigation canal water peaked well above levels that would negatively impact rice (2,000 μmhos/cm) and orchard crops (1,000 to 1,800 μmhos/cm) several times throughout the study. Employing a zero-discharge management system, was still expected to result in a nearly 50% loss of salts to the environment, mainly through lateral seepage. Currently, the Government of Thailand has placed a moratorium on inland marine shrimp farms in areas designated as freshwater ecosystems by provincial governments, because of the potential elevation of salts.

In the United States, effluent salinity, specific conductance, and TDS criteria and standards specific to aquaculture do not exist. However, United States Environmental Protection Agency (USEPA) suggests that in-stream chloride concentrations should not exceed 230 mg/L, and this chloride limit was adopted in Alabama. Recent investigations into salt discharges by marine shrimp farms in the Blackland Prairie region of Alabama revealed elevated electrical conductivity and chloride concentrations, above 230 mg/L, in both the groundwater and nearby streams. Electrical conductivity and chlorides remained elevated in streams near these production facilities throughout the year despite the absence of direct discharges into the streams, and appears to be the result of lateral seepage. Elevated chloride concentrations persisted as far as 4 km downstream at some locations, but were highly dependent upon freshwater inputs from base flow and runoff from storm events. A potential solution to this problem is to locate inland, mariculture facilities away from freshwater streams, and to properly construct ponds as to limit seepage of saline water.

Best management practices (BMPs) recommended for minimizing the potential of salinization by inland, low-salinity aquaculture[21] follow:

- Ponds should not be constructed in areas where soils have high infiltration rates.
- Construction techniques should include features to minimize lateral and downward seepage.
- Ponds should be operated to present, or minimize as much as possible, overflow after heavy rains.
- When a pond is drained for harvest, water should be stored in a reservoir or other ponds and reused in the next crop to prevent discharge of effluents into natural waters.

However, data collected at four aquaculture farms in Alabama that used saline groundwater suggested that BMPs recommended above were not adequate to protect streams during drought conditions when stream flow was low.[22] Lateral seepage from ponds entered streams resulting in in-stream chloride concentrations above 230 mg/L during a 2-year period that had the lowest rainfall expected for a 50-year return period. The only way of avoiding this avenue of stream salinization would be to site ponds further from streams—but, there were insufficient data to suggest a minimum distance that ponds should be separated from streams.

# References

1. Keren, R. 2000. Salinity, pages G1-G26. In: M. E. Summer (editor), *Handbook of Soil Science*. CRC Press, Boca Raton, FL.
2. Boyd, C. A., P. L. Chaney, C. E. Boyd, and D. B. Rouse. 2009. Distribution of ground water suitable for use in saline-water aquaculture in central and west-central Alabama. Journal of Applied Aquaculture 21:228-240.
3. Foth, J. H. 1970. Saline groundwater resources of the conterminous United States. Water Resources Research 6:1,454-1,457.
4. Roy, L. A., D. A. Davis, I. P. Saoud, C. A. Boyd, H. J. Pine, and C. E. Boyd. 2010. Shrimp culture in inland low salinity waters. Reviews in Aquaculture 2:191-208.
5. Smith, L. L. and A. L. Lawrence. 1990. Feasibility of penaeid shrimp culture in inland saline groundwater-fed ponds. Texas Journal of Science 42:3-12.

6. Nunes, A. J. P. and C. V. Lopez. 2001. Low-salinity, inland shrimp culture in Brazil and Ecuador – economics, disease issues move farms away from coasts. Global Aquaculture Advocate 4(3):62-64.

7. Partridge, G. J., A. J. Lymbery, and R. J. George. 2008. Finfish mariculture in inland Australia: a review of potential water sources, species, and production systems. Journal of the World Aquaculture Society 39:291-310.

8. Limsuwan, C., T. Somsiri, and S. Silarudee. 2002. The appropriate salinity level of brine water for raising black tiger prawn under low-salinity conditions. Department of Fisheries, Bangkok, Thailand, Aquatic Animal Health Research Institute Newsletter 11(1):2-4.

9. Wudtisin, I. and C. E. Boyd. 2011. Possible potassium and magnesium limitations for shrimp survival and production in low-salinity, pond waters in Thailand. Journal of the World Aquaculture Society 42: 766-777.

10. Boyd, C. E. and T. Thunjai. 2003. Concentrations of major ions in waters of inland shrimp farms in China, Ecuador, Thailand, and the United States. Journal of the World Aquaculture Society 34:524-532.

11. McNevin, A. A., C. E. Boyd, O. Silapajarn, and K. Silapajarn. 2004. Ionic supplementation of pond waters for inland culture of marine shrimp. Journal of the World Aquaculture Society 35:460-467.

12. Saoud, I. P., D. A. Davis, and D. B. Rouse. 2003. Suitability studies of inland well waters for *Litopenaeus vannamei* culture. Aquaculture 217:373-383.

13. Roy, L. A., D. A. Davis, I. P. Saoud, and R. P. Henry. 2007. Effects of varying levels of aqueous potassium and magnesium on survival, growth, and respiration of the Pacific white shrimp, *Litopenaeus vannamei*, reared in low salinity water. Aquaculture 262:461-469.

14. Boyd, C. A., C. E. Boyd, and D. B. Rouse. 2007. Potassium budget for inland, saline water shrimp ponds in Alabama. Aquacultural Engineering 36:45-50.

15. Pine, H. J. and C. E. Boyd. 2011. Magnesium budget for inland low salinity water shrimp ponds in Alabama. Journal of the World Aquaculture Society 42: 705-713.

16. Boyd, C. A., C. E. Boyd, and D. B. Rouse. 2007. Potassium adsorption by bottom soils in ponds for inland culture of marine shrimp in Alabama. Journal of the World Aquaculture Society 38:85-91.

17. Pine, H. J. and C. E. Boyd. 2010. Adsorption of magnesium by bottom soils in inland brackish water shrimp ponds in Alabama. Journal of the World Aquaculture Society 41:603-609.

18. Sparks, D. L. 2000. Bioavailability of soil potassium, pages D38-D53. In: M. E. Summer (editor), *Handbook of Soil Science*. CRC Press, Boca Raton, FL.

19. Chainark, S. and C. E. Boyd. 2009. Evaluation of a meter for testing potassium concentration in low-salinity aquaculture ponds. Journal of the World Aquaculture Society 41:102-106.

20. Braaten, R. O. and M. Flaherty. 2001. Salt balances of inland shrimp ponds in Thailand: implications for land and water salinization. Environmental Conservation 28:357-367.

21. Boyd, C. A., C. E. Boyd, A. A. McNevin, and D. B. Rouse. 2006. Salt discharge from an inland farm for marine shrimp in Alabama. Journal of the World Aquaculture Society 37:345-355.

22. Pine, H. J. and C. E. Boyd. 2011. Stream salinization resulting from inland brackish water aquaculture in Alabama. North American Journal of Aquaculture: 73:107-113.

# Chapter 23

# Pond Bottom Soil Management

## Introduction

Ponds should be built on sites where soils are suitable for building stable embankments and for forming bottoms that will not seep excessively. Water supplies for ponds usually contain suspended soil particles and soil particles are suspended by erosion of earthwork. These particles continually settle, forming sediment that quickly transforms to a 'pond soil' with a distinct profile.[1] Exchange of chemical substances between water and bottom soil influence pond water quality; bottom soil also is habitat for benthic biota and especially for microbial communities that decompose organic matter and recycle nutrients.

This chapter discusses soil limitations for aquaculture sites, explains how sediment develops and changes over time, and considers how water quality is influenced by bottom soil. It also provides practical information on pond bottom management.

## Site Selection

Visual inspection of the land surface and soils at a proposed aquaculture site reveals information about topographic features and gross soil properties. Cores should be taken to the expected depth of excavation at several places and examined to determine changes in the soil profile with depth, and to ascertain the presence or absence of large stones.[2] Samples also should be analyzed for texture (proportions of sand, silt, and clay), compactability, pH, and organic matter concentration. Particularly in coastal areas, soils should be examined for presence of potential acid-sulfate conditions. Results from the site inspection and soil evaluation should be used to ascertain whether or not one or more soil properties, if not corrected, would make the site unsuitable for pond aquaculture. In some cases it may be technically impossible or too expensive to correct one or more limitations in soil properties; such sites should be rejected.

Numerous factors related to terrain, geological formations, and soils can result in site limitations for pond construction.[2] A common problem is unsuitable topography for constructing ponds. Topography for watershed ponds must allow installation of a dam to capture runoff, while a relatively flat area and an external source of water is required for embankment ponds. Wetland sites should not be disrupted for pond construction for ecological reasons; it also is difficult to construct earthwork in wetland areas. Flood plains may be subject to flooding, and too many ponds in a flood plain may block flood water flow to increase flood levels.

There are several features of underlying geological formations that should be avoided.[2] Ponds built in sandy soils may seep excessively. High seepage rates also occur in ponds built in areas where bedrock is near the land surface or where there are rock outcrops. Limestone and other soluble rock formations are not suitable for pond bottoms, because solution caverns may develop and convey water from ponds. Large stones in soils can lead to seepage through pond bottoms, dams, and embankments. A soil of very high clay content seldom will seep excessively; however, clay is difficult to compact and does not bear loads well, causing dams or embankments to be unstable. In addition, a pond bottom with high clay content does not dry well during the fallow period between crops. Land with a shallow water table may not provide a good foundation for dams or embankments; moreover, water may seep into empty ponds preventing bottoms from drying between crops. Organic soil will decompose when exposed to the air resulting in deterioration of earthwork. Oxidation of iron pyrite in soils produces sulfuric acid and can cause soil pH to fall to 3 or less.

## Design and Construction

Aquaculture facilities should be designed to make best use of site features such as topography, shape and orientation of available space, access to water supply, mixing zone for effluent discharge, and soil characteristics.[3] The designer should assure that pond bottoms are above sea level, the water table, or other water surfaces to facilitate complete draining. Pond size should be in accordance with the production objective of the project. Ponds of several hectares in size may be used for semi-intensive culture, but ponds larger than 1 or 2 ha usually cannot be managed effectively for intensive culture. Ponds should be aligned so prevailing winds will not cause severe wave erosion of embankments. Embankments should be sloped and compacted with respect to soil particle size distribution to reduce erosion, seepage, and slip; embankments should be high enough to prevent flood waters or waves from overtopping them; enough freeboard also should be provided to prevent pond water from overflowing embankments during heavy rains. If soils are porous, pond bottoms and embankment slopes should be lined with suitable soil and compacted to reduce seepage. Inflow and outflow structures should be installed in each pond for water level control.

Canal design should minimize erosion by rainfall and prevent scouring of channel sides and bottoms by flowing waters—severe erosion will occur in undersized canals because of high water velocities when ponds are drained for harvest. The best hydraulic section for a trapezoidal channel[3] is:

$$b = 2y\left(\frac{\tan\varnothing}{Z}\right) \qquad (23.1)$$

where b = channel bottom width (m); y = depth of flow in channel (m); Z = side slope. The tangent of $\theta$ = 1/Z, and $\theta$ = $\tan^{-1}$ (1/Z). Maximum velocity to present scouring of earthen channels and minimum velocity to avoid sedimentation in channels can be calculated as follows:

$$V_{max} = 0.295G\ (y^{0.2}) \tag{23.2}$$

$$V_{min} = 0.192\ (y^{0.64}). \tag{23.3}$$

where $V_{max}$ = maximum permissible velocity (m/sec); $V_{min}$ = minimum permissible velocity (m/sec); G = erosion coefficients (Table 23.1).

Canals may be designed to avoid scouring of sides and bottoms, but serious erosion can result where one canal discharges into another or where canals discharge into natural water. Stone riprap can be installed to reduce erosion by lessening the force with which water strikes earthwork.

Soil characteristics should be considered in building earthwork, and design and construction techniques altered as necessary with respect to differences in soil properties across the area.[3] Precise cut and fill calculations prevent piles of excess soil and creation of borrow pits for earth fill. Good compaction of pond levees and canals is necessary, and the degree of compaction depends on the moisture content of the earth used. Earth fill should be compacted at the optimum moisture content as determined by the standard Proctor test.[4] Typical optimum moisture contents for compaction of different soil materials follow: sand, 6 to 10%; sandy silt, 8 to 12%; silt, 11 to 15%; clay, 13 to 21%. Attention to design and compaction of earthwork and reinforcement of potential problem areas with stone or other material will not prevent erosion caused by rainfall—grass cover on earthwork is the best protection against erosion by rain.

Slopes of embankment and canal sides also should be adequate to prevent erosion.[3] Recommended side slopes for embankments made of clay, clayey sand, silty sand, or clayey gravel are 3:1 (horizontal:vertical) on the wet side and 2:1 on the dry side; slopes of 3:1 should be provided on both sides of an embankment made of silty clay (Table 23.2).

There is a major misconception among aquaculturists that heavy clay soils are best for aquaculture ponds—some authors state that 25% or more of clay is needed. Actually, a well-graded soil (a soil with a wide range of particle sizes) with only 5 to 10% clay is often preferable over heavy clay soil for building stable, watertight embankments.

**Table 23.1.** Allowable side slope factors and erosion coefficients (G) for various channel materials.[3]

| Soil type | Z | Side slope (degrees) | G |
|---|---|---|---|
| Sandy loam | 3.0 | 18.4 | 2.0 |
| Silty clay | 3.0 | 18.4 | 2.5 |
| Silty sand | 2.0 | 26.5 | 2.5 |
| Soft shale | 2.0 | 26.5 | 3.2 |
| Stiff clay | 1.5 | 33.7 | 3.5 |
| Soft sandstone | 1.5 | 33.7 | 3.5 |
| Riprap lining | 1.0 | 45.0 | --- |
| Concrete lining | 0.5-1.0 | 63-45 | --- |
| Peat | 0.25 | 76.0 | --- |
| Rock | 0 | 90.0 | --- |

**Table 23.2.** Recommended side slopes for embankments.[3]

| Material | Slope (Z) | |
| --- | --- | --- |
| | Wet side | Dry side |
| Clay, clayey sand, clayey gravel, sandy clay, silty sand, and silty gravel | 3 | 2 |
| Silty clay and clayey silt | 3 | 3 |
| Well-graded soil | 1 or 2 | 1 or 2 |

In some places, embankment soils may be acidic and low in nutrients making them unfavorable for growth of grass. Top soil can be stockpiled during construction and placed back on above-water parts of canals and embankments and planted with grass species tolerant to the prevailing environmental conditions. Grass should be established on embankments if possible to avoid continual erosion by rainfall, but it is extremely difficult to establish grass cover on exposed earthwork made of saline soil.

Catfish and sportfish ponds in the United States normally are constructed by standard engineering procedures, and construction often is inspected by engineers of the USDA Natural Resources Conservation Service. Many of the sportfish ponds are now over 50 years old and some catfish ponds are over 25 years old. Most of these older ponds still have sound earthwork structures because proper design and construction were employed, and grass was established on levees. Conversely, it is common to see in many countries poorly designed and constructed aquaculture ponds with embankments and canals severely eroded and in need of major renovation after only 2 or 3 years.

# Pond Soils

## Development

Surface soil in the area to become the pond bottom usually is scraped off during construction and used as earth fill for embankments.[5] The newly finished pond bottom normally is subsoil low in concentrations of organic matter and nutrients. In areas with highly leached soils, pond bottoms may be high in clay content and of low pH.[1]

After filling with water, various processes begin to transform the bottom of a new pond into a pond soil. Erosion on watersheds suspends particles of mineral soil and organic matter that enter ponds in runoff. Wave action, rainfall, and water currents from mechanical aeration erode embankments and shallow edges of ponds to suspend soil particles. In addition, nutrients added to ponds in fertilizers, manures, and feeds cause phytoplankton blooms that increase the concentration of suspended organic particles. Suspended particles settle in ponds with sand particles settling first, followed by silt-sized particles, and finally clay particles and fine-divided organic matter. Water currents and activity of fish and other organisms continually resuspend particles from the bottom, and these particles settle again. Continuous input, deposition, resuspension, and redeposition of particles in a pond result in sorting of particles with fine clay and organic matter particles settling in deeper water and coarser particles settling in shallow water.[6,7]

Deeper areas gradually fill in, and ponds decrease in volume over time. Sediment thickness in embankment-style aquaculture ponds usually increases at an average of 1 to 2 cm/year over a period of 25 to 50 years.[1,8] The rate initially is very high, but it declines as ponds age. For example, in channel catfish ponds, sediment rate was 12.5 cm/year the first year, 3 cm/year for years 2-5, and only 1.3 cm/year after 20 years.[9] Natural channels and small streams often convey turbid runoff into the upper ends of watershed ponds; upon entering ponds, turbulence declines leading to sedimentation and filling in of the shallow area.

Organic matter settles to the bottom and simple carbohydrates, protein, and other cellular constituents are quickly degraded by the microbial community; complex carbohydrates and other cell wall components accumulate because they are resistant to decay. There is a continuous input of organic matter to the bottom, and microorganisms are continually decomposing both fresh, easily-degradable (labile) organic matter and older, resistant (refractory) organic matter. Because of the continuous resuspension and redeposition of particles and stirring of the pond soil surface by fish and other organisms, organic matter is rather uniformly mixed in the upper layer of soil, but organic matter concentration typically is greatest near the sediment surface.[1] There also is a flocculent layer of newly settled, fresh organic matter above the soil surface. The ratio of labile organic matter:refractory organic matter also is greatest in the flocculent layer and near the sediment surface.[9]

Organic matter concentration in pond soils will soon reach an equilibrium dependent upon aquacultural and natural inputs of organic matter and pond management practices and natural conditions affecting microbial decomposition.[10,11] New ponds usually have little organic matter in bottom soil, and the labile organic matter settling to the bottom each year will partially decompose. A considerable proportion of refractory organic matter will accumulate[11], and after a few crops, organic matter in the soil will reach a high enough concentration that the annual rate of organic matter loss through decomposition will equal the annual input of organic matter resulting in an equilibrium concentration of soil organic matter. The equilibrium concentration develops so quickly that it may not be possible to show a relation between pond age and soil organic matter concentration.

Dissolved oxygen cannot rapidly penetrate bottom soil, because it must diffuse through the tiny, water-filled pore spaces among soil particles. At a depth of only a few millimeters below the soil surface, the demand for dissolved oxygen by microorganisms exceeds the rate of diffusion of dissolved oxygen, and anaerobic conditions develop. The oxidized (aerobic) layer of surface sediment will have a lighter color than the deeper, reduced (anaerobic) sediment—anaerobic sediment usually is gray or black from the presence of ferrous iron.

Processes described above result in sediment forming distinct layers with respect to bulk density (weight of soil per unit volume, usually given in grams dry soil/cubic centimeter), organic matter concentration, and color. A core taken through the sediment and extending into the original bottom soil is called a *profile* and it contains distinct layers or *horizons* (Fig. 23.1). The F and S horizons are most important in aquaculture, because they exchange substances with overlaying water to influence water quality.

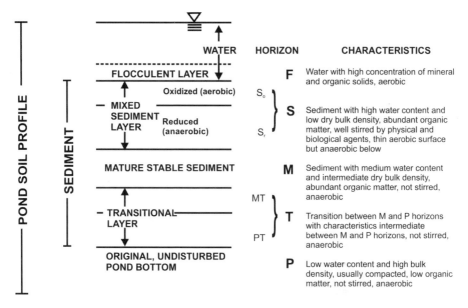

**Fig. 23.1.** Horizons in sediment profile.

## *The Oxidized Layer*

Metabolic products of aerobic decomposition are carbon dioxide, water, ammonia, and other nutrients, but in anaerobic sediment, some microorganisms decompose organic matter by fermentation and produce alcohols, ketones, aldehydes, and other organic compounds as metabolites. Other anaerobic microorganisms use oxygen from nitrate, nitrite, iron and manganese oxides, sulfate, and carbon dioxide to decompose by-products of fermentation and other organic matter, but they release nitrogen gas, ammonia, ferrous iron, manganous manganese, hydrogen sulfide, and methane as metabolites.[12] Some metabolites, and especially hydrogen sulfide and nitrite, can enter the pond water and be toxic to fish or shrimp. An oxidized layer at the soil surface lessens diffusion of toxic metabolites into pond water; they are oxidized to non-toxic form by chemical and biological activity while passing through the aerobic surface layer—nitrite to nitrate, ferrous iron to ferric iron, and hydrogen sulfide to sulfate. Methane and nitrogen gas seldom cause toxicity of aquatic organisms; they pass through the layer and diffuse from pond water to the atmosphere.

The oxidized layer is lost when soils accumulate large amounts of organic matter, and dissolved oxygen is used up within the flocculent layer (F horizon) before it can penetrate the soil surface. Even in ponds without high concentrations of soil organic matter, high rates of organic matter deposition from large, daily feed inputs and heavy plankton blooms can cause oxygen depletion in the F-horizon. Ponds should be managed to minimize accumulation of fresh organic matter in the F horizon, at the soil surface, and in the upper few millimeters of soil.

Toxic metabolites entering well-oxygenated pond water quickly oxidize. However, if the rate of release of toxic metabolites into water exceeds the rate that metabolites are oxidized, equilibrium levels of metabolites in water may become high enough to detrimentally affect culture animals.

## Soil Organic Matter Concentration

Organic soils contain recognizable plant remains resistant to microbial decomposition and have 25 to 40% organic matter. Such soils are not good for pond aquaculture and should be avoided in favor of soils with less organic matter known as mineral soils.

Methods of soil organic matter analysis do not distinguish among coarse plant remains, refractory organic matter, and labile organic residues—they measure the total concentration of organic matter. A soil with 10% organic matter may be perfectly acceptable for pond aquaculture if most of the organic matter is refractory, but unacceptable if the organic matter is mostly labile.

A classification of soil organic carbon concentration for pond aquaculture follows: >15%, organic soil; 3.1 to 15%, mineral soil, high organic matter content; 1.0 to 3.0%, mineral soil, moderate organic matter content, and best range for aquaculture; <1%, mineral soil, low organic matter content. Soil organic matter is about 50 to 58% carbon, so a rough approximation of organic matter concentration may be obtained by multiplying soil organic carbon concentration by 2.

## Nutrient Exchange Between Soil and Water

Nitrogen and phosphorus are key nutrients for phytoplankton productivity in ponds; the plant available forms are ammonium, nitrate, and orthophosphate. Ammonium may be absorbed by phytoplankton, converted to organic nitrogen, and transformed into nitrogen of fish protein via the food web. Ammonium also may be oxidized to nitrate by nitrifying bacteria, and nitrate may be used by phytoplankton or denitrified by anaerobic micro-organisms in sediment. Nitrogen gas from denitrification diffuses from sediment to pond water to the atmosphere. Ammonium is in equilibrium with ammonia, and ammonia also can diffuse from pond waters to the atmosphere. A small amount of ammonium may be adsorbed on cation exchange sites in pond bottom soils. Organic nitrogen in plankton and in aquatic animal feces may settle to the bottom to become soil organic nitrogen. Nitrogen in soil organic matter may be mineralized to ammonia and recycled to the pond water.

Phytoplankton can rapidly remove phosphate from water, and phosphorus in phytoplankton may enter the food web culminating in fish or shrimp. Pond soil strongly adsorbs phosphorus, and the capacity of pond soil to adsorb phosphorus increases as a function of increasing clay content.[13] More than half of phosphorus applied to ponds in feeds or fertilizers typically accumulates in bottom soils; this phosphorus is tightly bound and only a small amount is water soluble.[14] Although soil removes phosphorus from waters of fed ponds, phosphorus is applied daily in feeds, and soil uptake will not prevent excessive phytoplankton blooms.

## *Soil pH*

The best pH for pond soils is neutral or slightly basic.[12] Maximum availability of soil phosphorus usually occurs around pH 7, and many soil microorganisms, and especially soil bacteria, function best at pH 7.5 to 8. Soils in humid areas tend to be highly leached and acidic (Chapter 8). In semi-arid and arid regions, evaporation exceeds precipitation and salts accumulate in soils causing a neutral or basic reaction. In coastal aquaculture, ponds often are filled with seawater or brackishwater with moderate total alkalinity, but bottoms of coastal ponds may still be acidic and respond positively to liming—especially those in areas where soils contain iron pyrite. When such soil is exposed to air, pyrite oxidizes releasing sulfuric acid; these soils are known as acid-sulfate soils. They may have pH values of 5 to 7 when wet, but when dried, pH may fall to 2 or 3.[12] Acid-sulfate soils should not be used for aquaculture ponds if other alternatives are available.

## *Soil Texture*

*Texture* refers to the particle-size distribution in soil: a soil texture class can be assigned based on percentages of sand, silt, and clay using a soil triangle (Fig. 23. 2). The large number of textural classes that can be assigned with a soil triangle is useful in describing agricultural soils. It is not necessary to use so many soil texture classes for aquaculture pond soils. Classifying them as sandy, silty, sandy clay, silty clay, and clay is probably more than adequate.

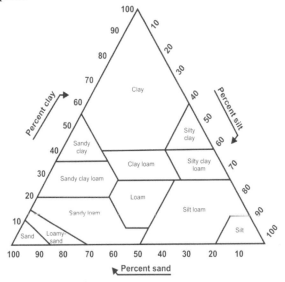

23.2. Soil triangle. To use, mark percentage clay and percentage sand on the appropriate axes. From these points, project a line inward from the clay axis and parallel to the sand axis and another line from the sand axis parallel to the silt axis. The interaction of the two projected lines will denote soil texture.

# Pond Soil Treatments

## Liming

Liming neutralizes acidity of bottom soils and increases total alkalinity and total hardness concentrations in water to enhance conditions for natural productivity and fish growth. Freshwater ponds with less than 40 or 50 mg/L total alkalinity, brackishwater ponds with total alkalinity below 75 mg/L, and any pond with soil pH below 7 usually will benefit from liming (see Chapter 9).

## Drying

Drying pond bottoms between crops (Fig. 23.3) reduces moisture content of soil, and air enters pore spaces among soil particles to improve aerobic decomposition of organic matter. After 2 to 3 weeks of dry out, most labile organic matter from the previous crop will decompose, and reduced inorganic compounds will be oxidized.[15]

The time required to dry a pond bottom depends upon soil texture, air temperature, wind conditions, rainfall, and infiltration of water from adjacent ponds or shallow water tables. Light-textured soils dry faster than heavy-textured soils; warm, dry weather and windy conditions hasten drying, while rainy weather or infiltration of water into ponds retards drying. Decomposition rate will increase up to the optimum moisture content and then decline upon further drying—it usually is not useful to dry pond bottoms for more than 3 or 4 weeks.

**Fig. 23.3.** Left: Water-logged soil in bottom of recently-drained pond. Right: Pond bottom following a 2-week dry-out period.

Soils with a high clay content or with deep layers of silty or clayey sediment crack into columnar blocks upon drying. Surfaces of these blocks may appear dry and oxidized, but inside they are still wet, black, and reduced (Fig. 23.4). Additional drying will be of little benefit, because dry surfaces are a barrier to evaporation.

## *Tilling*

Tilling bottom soils can enhance drying and increase aeration to accelerate organic matter decomposition and oxidation of reduced compounds. Agricultural limestone or other amendments can be mixed into soil by tilling. Large accumulations of organic matter or other substances in the surface layer of soil also can be mixed with deeper soils to reduce concentrations of the substances in the surface layer.

Ruts caused by operating tractor-drawn disk harrows in wet, soft sediment tend to fill with sediment and become anaerobic. Ruts also interfere with draining and increase the difficulty of drying pond bottoms. Where tractors are used for tilling, dual tires or extra-wide tires are recommended to prevent causing ruts.

Depth of tillage usually should be about 10 to 15 cm, so a disk harrow (Fig. 23.5) or rototiller can be used, but rototillers require much more energy than disc harrows. Mould board plows can be used to turn soil over—a practice useful if surface soil has unacceptably high concentrations of organic matter. A mould board plow should not be used for routine tilling for it requires more energy than a disk harrow.

Tilling can be counterproductive in ponds where mechanical aeration is used. Tilling loosens soil particles and favors greater erosion by aerator-induced water currents. This problem can be lessened by compacting pond bottoms with a heavy roller before refilling.

**Fig. 23.4.** Left: Columnar blocks of soil in bottom of dry pond. Right: Reduced (dark color) soil in center of soil block.

**Fig. 23.5.** Tilling bottom of pond with a disc harrow.

## *Sediment Removal*

Soft sediment is undesirable because it fills deeper areas causing ponds to lose volume, and it traps feed pellets and fertilizer granules. Anaerobic zones often occur in soft sediment, lessening its value as habitat for benthic organisms. Fish harvest also is hampered by soft sediment because it impedes seining operations.

Soft sediment should be removed before it reaches a troublesome thickness, but most ponds can be operated for 10 to 30 years before sediment removal is necessary. In a recent study at Auburn University, pond bottom soil characteristics following sediment removal from 30-year-old ponds were similar to those that existed when the ponds were new.[16] Sediment can be excavated with a variety of equipment ranging from shovels to bulldozers. Excavated sediment should not be put back on the areas of the earthwork from which it eroded, because it is mostly silt and sand. Sediment should be disposed of outside of ponds in a responsible way to prevent unsightly, ecologically-degrading, spoil piles that erode easily (Fig. 23.6).

**Fig. 23.6.** Improper and environmentally-degrading disposal of sediment from bottom of shrimp ponds.

317

In Asia, some farmers use high pressure streams from hoses to wash loose sediment from pond bottoms (Fig. 23.7). The wash water should be held in a sediment basin to remove suspended solids before release into natural waters.

## *Fertilization*

In ponds constructed on soils with high concentrations of fibrous organic matter, decomposition is slow because of low pH and the high C:N ratio of the organic matter. Urea spread over pond bottoms at 200 to 400 kg/ha at the beginning of the fallow period will accelerate decomposition in organic soil by providing nitrogen, thereby reducing the C:N ratio. Urea hydrolyzes to ammonia which diffuses into the air; thus, bottoms should be tilled after urea application to incorporate lime and urea into soil and lessen the opportunity for ammonia volatilization. Tilling also provides better aeration of the soil mass to encourage bacterial activity.

Areas in some ponds that will not dry sufficiently for optimum decomposition of organic matter and oxidation of reduced inorganic compounds. Sodium, potassium, or sodium nitrate can be applied to wet soil to encourage organic matter decomposition by denitrifying bacteria and to oxidize ferrous iron, manganous manganese, and hydrogen sulfide. The usual application rate is 20 to 40 g/m$^2$ over wet areas. Nitrate fertilizers are more expensive than urea and are not recommended where soils can be adequately dried.

Productivity of benthic organisms may be low in ponds with concentrations of organic carbon below 0.5 to 1.0%. Chicken litter or other animal manures applied at 1,000 to 2,000 kg/ha to pond bottoms during the fallow period can enhance growth of benthic organisms. An even better benthic response usually can be obtained by applying 250 to 500 kg/ha of higher quality organic matter, such as rice bran, soybean meal, crushed corn, or low-protein content animal feed. After organic fertilization of pond bottoms, ponds should be filled with 10 to 20 cm of water and a plankton bloom allowed to develop.

**Fig. 23.7.** Washing loose sediment from bottoms of shrimp ponds using high-pressure nozzles.

Water level should be increased and 1 or 2 weeks allowed for development of the benthic community before stocking ponds.

## *Bottom Raking*

Stirring the sediment surface of pond bottoms during the culture period is thought to improve contact with oxygenated water and help maintain the oxidized layer. Several methods have been used to introduce oxygenated water into surface sediment, but the two most popular techniques are manual raking in small ponds and dragging a heavy chain across the bottom of larger ponds. This practice usually is applied at weekly intervals.

Organic matter originating from dead algae, manure particles, or uneaten feed often accumulates in the windward corners of ponds and settles to the bottom to degrade the sediment surface. Some pond managers remove this material manually by raking.

## *Disinfection*

Bottom soils can harbor aquatic animal pathogens or their vectors between crops and thereby transmit diseases to the succeeding crop; it is common practice to attempt to disinfect pond bottoms following disease outbreaks. Dry out of pond bottoms eliminates most disease organisms, but the combination of drying and application of a chemical disinfectant is thought to be more effective. Treatment with calcium hypochlorite—often called high test hypochlorite or HTH (Chapter 21)—kills organisms by chlorine contact, while liming with calcium oxide or calcium hydroxide raises soil pH high enough to kill organisms. Calcium hypochlorite is the more expensive alternative, and liming is most commonly used. About 1,000 kg/ha is the minimum amount of lime to raise pH high enough for disinfection, and 2,000 to 3,000 kg/ha is a more reliable rate. Lime should not be applied after ponds are completely dry because it will not dissolve and increase pH. Uniform coverage of bottom soil is necessary; adding a few centimeters of water to the pond after lime treatment allows high pH water to penetrate the soil mass.

Liming for disinfection kills beneficial bacteria as well as pathogenic ones, but pH quickly declines following lime application and bacterial communities usually re-establish in 3 to 5 days. Ponds should be left fallow for 2 or 3 weeks following disinfection to promote organic matter degradation.

Some shrimp farmers refill ponds and disinfect the water with biocides before stocking postlarvae. Two common treatments are calcium hypochlorite at 20 to 30 mg/L or with the organophosphorus insecticide, Dichlorvos, at 2 to 3 mg/L. Although bottom soil is not treated directly, contact with biocide in the water will also disinfect the soil.

## *Bioaugmentation and Miscellaneous Treatments*

A number of products are promoted to enhance chemical and biological processes that improve soil quality. These products include cultures of living bacteria, enzyme preparations, composted or fermented residues, plant extracts, and other concoctions. There is no evidence from research that any of these products will improve soil quality. Nevertheless, most of them are not harmful to the culture species, surrounding environment, workers, or quality of aquaculture products. Some of these treatments are discussed in Chapter 21.

# References

1. Munsiri, P., C. E. Boyd, and B. F. Hajek. 1995. Physical and chemical characteristics of bottom soil profiles in ponds at Auburn, Alabama, USA, and a proposed method for describing pond soil horizons. Journal of the World Aquaculture Society 26:346-377.
2. Hajek, B. F. and C. E. Boyd. 1994. Rating soil and water information for aquaculture. Aquacultural Engineering 13:115-128.
3. Yoo, K. H. and C. E. Boyd. 1994. *Hydrology and Water Supply for Aquaculture*. Chapman and Hall, New York, NY.
4. McCarty, D. F. 1998. *Essentials of Soil Mechanics and Foundations: Basic Geotechnics*. Prentice Hall, Upper Saddle River, NJ.
5. Boyd, C. E. 1985. Hydrology and pond construction, pages 107-134. In: C. S. Tucker (editor), *Channel Catfish Culture*. Elsevier Scientific Publishing Company, Amsterdam, Netherlands.
6. Boyd, C. E. 1970. Influence of organic matter on some hydrosoil characteristics. Hydrobiologia 36:17-21.
7. Boyd, C. E. 1976. Chemical and textural properties of muds from different depths in ponds. Hydrobiologia 48:141-144.
8. Steeby, J. A., J. A. Hargreaves, C. S. Tucker, and S. Kingsbury. 2004. Accumulation, organic carbon, and dry matter concentration of sediment in commercial channel catfish ponds. Aquacultural Engineering 30:115-126.
9. Sonnenholzner, S. and C. E. Boyd. 2000. Vertical gradients of organic matter concentration and respiration rate in pond bottom soils. Journal of the World Aquaculture Society 31:376-380.
10. Avnimelech, Y. 1984. Reactions in fish pond sediments as inferred from sediment cores data. Publication Number 341, Technion Israel Institute of Technology, Soils and Fertilizer Research Center, Haifa, Israel.
11. Avnimelech, Y. J. R. McHenry, and J. D. Ross. 1984. Decomposition of organic matter in lake sediments. Environmental Science and Technology 18:5-11.
12. Boyd, C. E. 1995. *Bottom Soils, Sediment, and Pond Aquaculture*. Chapman and Hall, New York, NY.
13. Boyd, C. E. and P. Munsiri. 1996. Phosphorus adsorption capacity and availability of added phosphorus in soils from aquaculture areas in Thailand. Journal of the World Aquaculture Society 27:160-167.
14. Masuda, K. and C. E. Boyd. 1994. Phosphorus fractions in soil and water of aquaculture ponds built on clayey, Ultisols at Auburn, Alabama. Journal of the World Aquaculture Society 25:379-395.
15. Boyd, C. E. and S. Pipoppinyo. 1994. Composition of sediment from intensive shrimp ponds in Thailand. World Aquaculture 25:53-55.
16. Yuvanatemiya, V. and C. E. Boyd. 2006. Physical and chemical changes in aquaculture pond bottom soil resulting from sediment removal. Aquacultural Engineering 35:199-205.

# Chapter 24

# Partitioned Ponds

## Introduction

Ponds are elegant aquaculture systems because all resources needed to grow a crop are provided in one self-contained unit. First, ponds hold water and confine animals under culture, functioning like the walls of a tank or aquarium. Ponds also support animal growth by providing food, dissolved oxygen, and waste treatment. Although this appears to make ponds an ideal culture system, combining all ecosystem functions in the same space can make ponds difficult to manage.

Most aquatic animals can grow and thrive in a relatively small water volume if wastes are removed and adequate food and dissolved oxygen are provided. In ponds, food production, dissolved oxygen generation, and waste treatment are byproducts of algal photosynthesis, which is powered by sunlight. Sunlight energy is diffuse and a much larger area is needed to capture enough energy to produce dissolved oxygen and treat wastes than is needed just to hold the animals (Example 24.1). When animals are dispersed at low densities and roam freely throughout large ponds, they can be difficult to feed, protect from predators, treat when sick, and harvest. Most important, it is difficult to efficiently manage dissolved oxygen in large ponds. Several outdoor systems—which we collectively call *partitioned ponds*—have been developed that exploit the best features of ponds but make the system more controllable and efficient by confining animals in a small area that is separated from other ecological functions.

## Linked Polyculture Ponds

Early partitioned ponds were designed to facilitate polyculture of channel catfish and other species. Waste nutrients from feeding stimulate production of phytoplankton that is largely unused by catfish fed manufactured feeds. Adding plankton- or detritus-feeding fish to the pond improves ecological efficiency by making better use of feed nutrients that would otherwise be wasted in catfish monocultures. Fish production based on natural foods may also increase farm income by generating an additional crop at little extra expense. However, culturing more than one species in the same pond presents problems because the secondary fish crop may compete with catfish for food, oxygen, and other resources. From the farmer's perspective, the greatest disadvantage of co-culture is the additional time and labor required to harvest and sort fish for marketing.

**Example 24.1**
**Relative Pond Areas for Fish Living Space and Ammonia Removal**

Channel catfish can be grown in flow-through raceways at biomass densities greater than 100 kg/m$^3$. For a 1-m-deep pond, that means that 1,000 kg of catfish can be held in an area smaller than 10 m$^2$. If fish are fed 2% of body weight per day and ammonia excretion is 35 g N/kg of feed consumed, total ammonia-nitrogen (TAN) production is:

TAN production = (35g N/kg feed)(20 kg feed/day) = 700 g N/day.

Most ammonia is initially removed from water by phytoplankton as they assimilate ammonia as a nitrogen source for growth. The nitrogen-removal rate by phytoplankton can be calculated from a typical rate of carbon removal in photosynthesis (3 g C/m$^2$ per day) and the average ratio of carbon to nitrogen in algal tissue (the 'Redfield Ratio' which, by mass, is 6C:1N):

N removal rate (g N/m$^2$ per day) = (3 g C/m$^2$ per day)(1 g N/6 g C) = 0.5 g N/m$^2$ per day.

Therefore, the pond area required to remove ammonia excreted by 1,000 kg of channel catfish is

$$\frac{(700 \text{ g N/day})}{(0.5 \text{ g N / day})} = 1,400 \text{ m}^2.$$

The pond area needed to hold 1,000 kg of channel catfish (10 m$^2$) is at least 140 times smaller than the pond area needed to remove waste ammonia produced by that fish biomass (1,400 m$^2$).

The *polyculture production system* (PPS) was proposed in 1984 as a simple way to physically separate channel catfish from the polyculture species.[1] The PPS is built by dividing an existing catfish pond into halves with an earthen cross-levee. Catfish are grown in one half and one or more secondary species are grown in the other half. Secondary species might include bighead carp, silver carp, buffalofish, paddlefish, or freshwater prawns. Screened culverts or open channels connect the ponds and water is circulated between the two halves using paddlewheel aerators as pumps. In theory (the system was never tested), the PPS provides additional income from secondary species without harvest problems encountered when fish are mixed in the same pond. The ecological impacts of filter-feeding fish may also improve water quality in both sets of ponds, thereby providing better conditions for catfish culture.

In the late 1970s and early 1980s, two large catfish farms in Arkansas used *recirculating raceway systems* to produce catfish and a variety of plankton-feeding or detritus-feeding fishes.[2] These systems consisted of concrete raceways with water flowing by gravity from an elevated earthen pond (Fig. 24.1). Aeration in the raceways was provided by water falling over weirs between raceways and by liquid oxygen supplied by diffusers in each raceway. Raceways discharged into a series of earthen ponds connected with water flowing by gravity through culverts. Water from the lowest pond in the series was then pumped back up into the header pond for recirculation through the raceways. Channel catfish were grown on manufactured feed in the raceways. Ponds contained blue tilapia, paddlefish, silver carp, or bighead carp that fed on catfish wastes and natural foods. The system shown in Fig. 24.1 consisted of 108 raceways (36 parallel series of 3 raceways in a series) linked to seven ponds totaling 55 ha. Water flowed through the system at 115 $m^3$/minute.

The primary goal of the Arkansas recirculating raceway systems was to confine catfish in a system where they are easy to feed, grade by size, and harvest (Fig. 24.2). Overall catfish production (based on total water area of raceways and ponds) was similar to production achieved in well-managed traditional catfish ponds. Additional income was gained by selling the plankton-feeding fish.

## Partitioned Aquaculture System

The *partitioned aquaculture system* (PAS) developed at Clemson University was designed to optimize pond water quality and increase aquaculture production rather than

**Fig. 24.1.** An outdoor, recirculating raceway system in southeastern Arkansas in 1987. Raceways were supplied with water fed by gravity from an elevated 'header' pond on the right. Raceways discharged to the left into a series of seven earthen ponds linked by screened culverts. Water was pumped from the lowest pond back into the header pond for reuse.

**Fig. 24.2.** Harvesting channel catfish from an outdoor, recirculating raceway system in southeastern Arkansas.

simply to facilitate polyculture. The primary crop—either fish or penaeid shrimp—is confined at high densities in flow-through raceways where animals are easy to feed, protect, and harvest. The rest of the system is designed and managed to optimize phytoplankton photosynthesis. In essence, the PAS is an outdoor, recycled aquaculture system consisting of a high-density raceway system for holding the crop coupled to a much larger, high-rate algal oxidation ditch that was originally developed for domestic wastewater treatment. Components are linked with large volumes of water constantly recycled between the raceways and algal growth basin.[3,4,5]

Increased phytoplankton photosynthesis is the key to higher aquaculture production in the PAS. As explained in Chapter 3, pond aquaculture production is limited by the ecosystem's capacity to provide essential life-support functions. As pond aquaculture intensifies, these limiting factors progressively shift from food supply to oxygen production to waste removal. In commercial aquaculture of catfish, shrimp, and many other species, the first two limitations are overcome by providing manufactured feed and using mechanical aeration to supplement natural oxygen supplies. The ultimate limitation on pond aquaculture production is, therefore, removal or transformation of ammonia and carbon dioxide—two potentially toxic products of animal metabolism. In outdoor systems, ammonia and carbon dioxide are initially removed from water by phytoplankton, which use them as sources of nitrogen and carbon to support growth. Because carbon dioxide and ammonia assimilation rates are proportional to phytoplankton growth rate, the waste-treatment capacity of ponds (and therefore the upper limits on fish or shrimp production potential) can be increased by improving conditions for phytoplankton photosynthesis.

Phytoplankton growth rate depends on water temperature, sunlight intensity and duration, transmission of underwater light, nutrient availability, and cell loss.[6] Water temperature and sunlight depend on geographic location, climate, and season—factors that cannot be controlled by the culturist except through site selection. Nutrient availability seldom limits algal productivity in intensive pond aquaculture because large amounts of waste nutrients are produced as a byproduct of feeding. Underwater light conditions and cell loss can, however, be manipulated in the PAS to increase phytoplankton photosynthesis.

The PAS algal basin is shallow (~0.5 m) so that phytoplankton cannot sink below the well-lighted photic zone. Turbulent mixing throughout the algal basin constantly brings phytoplankton cells near the water's surface where light intensity is highest. Low-level turbulence also enhances nutrient assimilation by algal cells and disperses nutrients evenly throughout the basin. Loss of algal cells from the water column may either decrease or increase algal productivity depending on the loss rate relative to growth rate. Controlled, modest loss rates can increase algal productivity by decreasing average cell age, rapidly recycling nutrients, and by preventing excessive algal growth that may reduce underwater light availability in the process called 'self-shading.' Phytoplankton communities in the PAS are continually "cropped' using filter-feeding animals or by using physical processes such as coagulation and precipitation of algal biomass. The combination of a shallow basin, turbulent mixing, and continuous cropping of algal biomass results in a 3- to 4-fold increase in phytoplankton photosynthetic rates compared to traditional ponds, allowing a proportional increase in the upper limits of potential aquaculture production.

Continuous water flow throughout the PAS is critical. High-quality water must flow through the culture raceways to maintain good conditions for animal growth. Water flow in the algal basin also assures well-mixed conditions for phytoplankton photosynthesis. Water movement must be continuous throughout the PAS, so moving large water volumes with low energy input, minimal capital investment, and low maintenance costs is essential. Slow-turning (1-3 rpm) paddlewheels (Fig. 24.3) that move large water volumes against low head are the only pump type with those attributes.

**Fig. 24.3.** Slow-turning paddlewheels used to pump water through the partitioned aquaculture system (PAS) at Clemson University. Paddlewheels are 4.9-m long, 1.8-m diameter, and turn at 1 to 3 rpm with paddles immersed to a depth of 0.45 m. Photo credit: David Brune.

The 0.8-ha PAS illustrated in Fig. 24.4 was designed and operated to produce channel catfish as the primary crop. The fish-holding area consists of three parallel, concrete-block channels. The outer two channels comprise four raceway cells in a series, with water from the middle channel entering each cell through an adjustable gate. Gates are adjusted to provide water flow in proportion to fish oxygen demand within each cell. In addition to distributing water into the catfish raceways, the middle channel also holds tilapia, Water flow through the raceways is induced by a single 4.9-m-long, 1.8-m-diameter paddlewheel turning at 1 to 3 rpm with paddles immersed to a depth of 0.45 m. The algal basin is 0.45-m deep and water circulates around a center baffle at about 0.1 m/second. Water flow is induced by a gang of four paddlewheels (Fig. 24.3) with total length of 19.5 m. Individual paddlewheels had the same dimensions as the single paddlewheel used to pump water through the raceways. The gang of four paddlewheels in the algal basin pumps 90 m$^3$/minute, with a power requirement less than 1 kW. Catfish production averages between 15,000 and 20,000 kg/ha, which is 2- to 4- times that achieved in most conventional catfish ponds. Tilapia production provides an additional 5,000 kg/ha of fish biomass. Note that filter-feeding animals, such as tilapia, are not added to the PAS with the primary intention of producing a second crop, but rather they are used as a phytoplankton-management tool. Production of the secondary crop can, however, provide additional farm income.

The PAS concept has been adapted for production of marine shrimp, harvest of algal biomass for energy production, and wastewater treatment.[5] The PAS concept, especially the use of slow-turning paddlewheels as pumps, is also the starting point for the two systems described below.

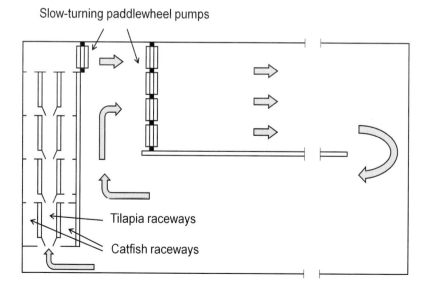

Fig. 24.4. Water flows in a partitioned aquaculture system (PAS).

# In-Pond Raceways

*In-pond raceways* (IPRs) confine fish at high densities in flow-through tanks installed in an existing earthen pond (Fig. 24.5). Water is pumped though the raceways from the main part of the pond, which provides the same functions as the algal basin in the PAS. In-pond raceways take advantage of certain features of the PAS, such as facilitating feeding, harvesting, and protecting the fish crop but are less expensive to build. The major difference between IPRs and the PAS is that the algal basin of the PAS is designed specifically to optimize phytoplankton photosynthesis whereas water depth and water flow characteristics in the pond used for IPRs vary depending on original pond morphology, location of the raceways within the pond, and modifications made to the pond during construction. As such, phytoplankton photosynthetic rate in most IPR systems will not be as high as in the PAS, which will reduce the system's waste-treatment capacity and fish-production potential relative to the PAS.

A variety of IPR designs have been used commercially. Raceways may be fixed, permanent concrete tanks[7] or floating plastic or plastic-lined tanks that are moored to a pier for access.[8] Water is circulated between raceways and pond using slow-turning paddlewheels, airlift pumps, or both. Aeration or oxygenation in the raceways is provided by mechanical surface agitators, air diffusers, pure-oxygen diffusers, or a combination of devices.

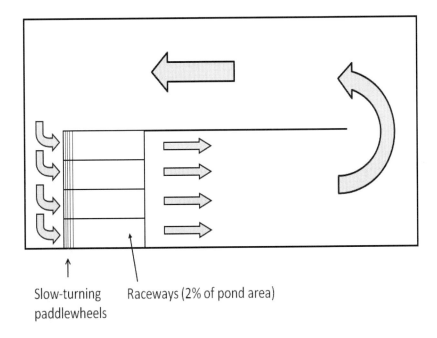

Slow-turning paddlewheels

Raceways (2% of pond area)

**Fig. 24.5.** Water flows in an in-pond raceway (IPR) system.[7]

An IPR system used for commercial catfish aquaculture in Alabama will be described as one example of the concept.[7] Six parallel raceways were built using concrete blocks on a reinforced concrete foundation in a 2.4-ha, 1.7-m-deep earthen pond (Fig. 24.6). Each raceway was 13.7-m long, 4.9-m wide, and 1.2-m deep. A slow-turning (1.2 rpm) paddlewheel at the head of the raceway pulled water from the pond at 9.3 $m^3$/minute, resulting in one water-volume exchange every 4.9 minutes. Average water velocity through the raceway was 0.026 m/second. A 1.12-kW regenerative blower delivered 2.5 $m^3$/minute of air through a diffuser grid at the head of the raceway. Fish were confined in raceways with two, plastic-coated steel screens extending across the upper and lower ends of each raceway cell. Feed from a bulk feed bin was delivered with an auger system to automatic feeders operated either manually or on a timer. Channel catfish or channel × blue catfish hybrids were grown in the raceways; tilapia and paddlefish were stocked into the pond. Over 1 year of study,[7] catfish production was 13,000 kg/ha and an additional 2,500 kg/ha of tilapia and paddlefish were produced. Feed conversion rate (weight of feed fed divided by fish growth) for catfish was approximately 1.5, which is excellent under commercial conditions.

## Split-Ponds

*Split-ponds* are modifications of the polyculture production system described earlier. Split-ponds are constructed by dividing an existing pond with an earthen levee but, unlike the PPS, split-ponds are divided unevenly and most split ponds are not used for polyculture, but rather used to grow channel catfish or channel × blue catfish hybrids in monoculture. They are, however, easily adapted to polyculture with tilapia or other fish.

**Fig. 24.6.** Raceways and slow-turning paddlewheel pumps in an in-pond raceway (IPR) system.[7] Photo credit: Travis Brown.

The original goal of the split-pond was to take advantage of the fish-confinement benefits of the PAS, such as facilitation of feeding, inventory, harvest, health management, and protection from predators. During development of the system in Mississippi, it became evident that fish production could be significantly greater in the split-pond than in traditional ponds. The split-pond thus represents an intermediate level of intensification between traditional earthen ponds and IPRs and the PAS.[5,9]

The split-pond has a relatively smaller algal basin (about 80-85% of the total area) and a larger fish-holding basin than IPRs or the PAS (Fig. 24.7). The levee dividing the two basins is breached with two conduits—either open channels or culverts—through which water circulates between the two sections. Barriers or screens in each conduit prevent fish escape. In the original split-pond design,[9] water was pumped with a large, slow-turning paddlewheel (Fig. 24.8) but systems have been built using high-speed screw pumps, high-speed axial-flow pumps, or high-speed paddlewheels to recirculate water. Aerators in the fish-confinement area provide supplemental dissolved oxygen at night.

The two critical design parameters for split-ponds are water flow rate between the two basins and the amount of aeration required in the fish-holding area. During daylight and early evening, oxygenated water from the algal basin is pumped through the fish-holding basin and return flow to the algal basin removes fish metabolic wastes. At night, when dissolved oxygen concentrations decrease in the algal basin, circulation between the two basins stops and oxygen is provided by mechanical aerators in the fish-holding area. No attempt is made to manage dissolved oxygen in the algal basin; during the summer growing season, dissolved oxygen concentrations fall below 1 mg/L nearly every night. In practice, pump and aerator operation are controlled by oxygen sensors located in both sections of the split-pond.

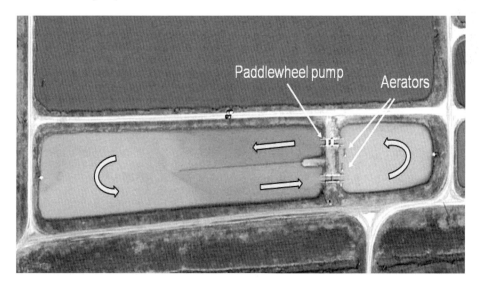

**Fig. 24.7.** Satellite photograph of a 2-ha split-pond in Mississippi. An earthen levee separates the fish-holding area on the right from the waste-treatment lagoon on the left. The levee is breached in two places with an open channel so that water can be recirculated between the basins.

**Fig. 24.8.** A slow-turning paddlewheel used to pump water between basins in a 2-ha split-pond. The paddlewheel is 3.7-m long and 1.8-m in diameter and turns at 2-3 rpm with paddles immersed to a depth of 1.2 m.

Pumping rate estimates are based on the assumption that fish oxygen requirements are met during daylight and early evening by oxygen in water flowing into the fish-holding area from the algal basin. A simple mass balance is used to calculate flow rate (volume/time) by dividing estimated fish respiratory rate (oxygen mass/time) by the minimum desired dissolved oxygen concentration (oxygen mass/volume). Required water flow varies with time as fish grow and water temperature changes.

Split-pond aeration requirements are determined by assuming that fish respiration is the only significant oxygen-consuming process in the fish holding area. This is a fair assumption because other sources and sinks of oxygen, such as free water surface diffusion and plankton and benthic metabolism are insignificant at the high fish biomass loading in the fish-holding area. Fish respiratory demand is then matched with aerator oxygen transfer. Standard oxygen transfer rates are available for several commonly used catfish pond aerators which can then be corrected to field conditions to determine aeration requirements (see Chapter 13).

As an example, a 2-ha pond in Mississippi was split into a 0.32-ha fish holding area and a 1.50-ha algal basin (the remaining area consisted of the new cross levee). The pond was designed for a maximum catfish biomass of approximately 36,000 kg. Aeration requirements were calculated based on a minimum dissolved oxygen concentration of 4.0 mg/L in the fish-holding area. For the brand of paddlewheel aerator that was used, 12 kW of aerator power input was required to match fish respiration during the summer growing season. That brand of aerator is available only as 7.5-kW units, so two aerators were installed in the fish-holding area of the split-pond (Fig. 24.9). The resulting 15 kW of aerator power was adequate to maintain dissolved oxygen above 4.0 mg/L throughout the summer. The required water flow rate between the fish-holding area and the algal basin was approximately 50 m³/minute, which was induced with a six-bladed, 3.70-m-long, 1.8-m-diameter paddlewheel operated at 2-3 rpm (Fig. 24.6). The paddlewheel was powered by a 1.1-kW electric gearmotor. Net annual catfish production ranged from 15,000 to more than 17,000 kg/ha based on total water area for the system, which is 2- to 4-times that achieved in traditional ponds and marginally less than in IPRs and the PAS. At stocking rates of 25,000 fish/ha (based on total water area), fish grew from an average initial weight of 50-70 g/fish to 0.80-0.90 kg/fish in a 7-month growing season. Feed conversion ratio was approximately 1.8, which is good for commercial conditions.

Although the split-pond cannot achieve the fish production obtained in the PAS, it offers several advantages over traditional ponds. Aerating the small fish-confinement area is more effective at maintaining adequate levels of dissolved oxygen than in traditional ponds. Fish in the confinement area also are easier to feed and harvest. These attributes, combined with greater fish production than in traditional ponds, make the split-pond an attractive alternative for certain types of aquaculture.

**Fig. 24.9.** Two, 7.5-kW paddlewheel aerators installed in a 2-ha split-pond.

# References

1. Torrans, L. 1984. Pond design for polyculture. Arkansas Aquafarming 2(2):3-4.
2. Tucker, C. S. and E. H. Robinson. 1990. *Channel Catfish Farming Handbook.* Van Nostrand Reinhold, New York, NY.
3. Brune, D. E., G. Schwartz, A. G. Eversole, J. A. Collier, and T. E. Schwedler. 2003. Intensification of pond aquaculture and high rate photosynthetic systems. Aquacultural Engineering 28:65-86.

4. Brune, D. E., G. Schwartz, A. G. Eversole, J. A. Collier, and T. E. Schwedler. 2004. Partitioned aquaculture systems, pages 561-584. In: C. S. Tucker and J. A. Hargreaves (editors), *Biology and Culture of Channel Catfish*. Elsevier, Amsterdam, The Netherlands.
5. Brune, D. E., C. S. Tucker, M. Massingill, and J. Chappell. 2012 Partitioned aquaculture systems, pages 308-342. In: J. Tidwell (editor), *Aquaculture Production Methods*. Wiley-Blackwell Publishing, Ames, IA.
6. Reynolds, C.S. 1984. *The Ecology of Freshwater Phytoplankton*. Cambridge University Press, Cambridge, UK.
7. Brown, T. W., J. A. Chappell, and C. E. Boyd. 2011. A commercial-scale, in-pond raceway system for *Ictalurid* catfish production. Aquacultural Engineering 44:72-79.
8. Masser, M. P. 2012. In-pond raceways, pages 387-393. In: J. Tidwell (editor), *Aquaculture Production Methods*. Wiley-Blackwell Publishing, Ames, IA.
9. Tucker, C.S., and S. Kingsbury. 2010. High-density split-pond systems offer high output, low maintenance. Global Aquaculture Advocate 13(2):64-54.

# Chapter 25

# Lined Ponds

## Introduction

Some sites are unsuitable for ponds because of issues related to soils. For example, sandy soils have high infiltration capacities, soils containing iron pyrite can be extremely acidic, and stable earthwork cannot be constructed from organic soils.[1] Bottom soils are important supplementary sources of inorganic nutrients for primary productivity and habitat for benthic food organisms in ponds with extensive and semi-intensive production. In intensive production, accumulation of organic matter and resulting anaerobic conditions in pond bottoms may negatively impact fish and shrimp survival and growth (see Chapter 23). Thus, as the level of production in ponds increases, the benefits of bottom soils decline and their liabilities increase.

Application of mechanical aeration improves dissolved oxygen concentration in the water and circulates oxygenated water over the bottom allowing fish and shrimp production to be increased. The amount that production may be increased depends—up to a point—upon the quantity of aeration applied. But, water currents generated by aerators erode embankments, cause turbidity in water, and lead to sediment accumulation in areas of ponds where water velocity declines (see Chapters 13 and 23). Erosion limits the amount of aeration that can be applied, and restricts the level of production that can be achieved in earthen ponds.

Seepage has no doubt been a concern since people learned how to impound water in earthen ponds. All earthen ponds lose water to seepage,[2] but the rate varies greatly from site to site (Fig. 25.1) depending upon soil characteristics of construction technique. Categories for pond seepage rates are given in Table 25.1. Common procedures for reducing seepage—installation of clay blankets or use of flocculating agents to seal pore spaces in soil—are not useful for reducing erosion from aerators. In fact, aeration would lessen the effectiveness of common seepage control measures.

Development of impermeable plastics offered an opportunity for lining aquaculture ponds. The liming material can be made of polyvinyl chloride (PVC), polyethylene (PE), ethylene propylene diene monomer rubber (EPDM), or similar plastics. These materials are flexible and come in rolls of sheeting that can be cut and joined easily during application. The pond area must be cleaned and smoothed. The liner is spread over the pond bottom; the edges usually are buried in a ditch dug in the tops of the embankments.

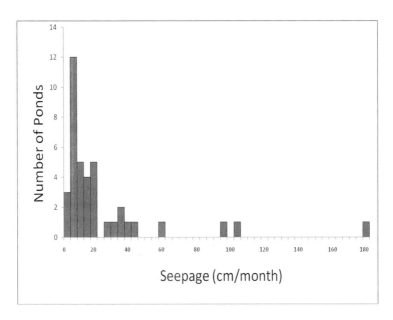

**Fig. 25.1.** Monthly seepage rates in aquaculture ponds.

**Table 25.1.** Seepage rate categories for aquaculture ponds.

| Category | Seepage rate (cm/month) |
|---|---|
| Low | <4 |
| High | 21-40 |
| Very high | 41-60 |
| Extreme | >60 |

A good example of the use of pond liners is provided by the Claude Peteet Mariculture Center, Gulf Shores, Alabama. This facility is located several kilometers from the ocean, but brackishwater (10 to 20 ppt) obtained via a pipeline supplies the small, research ponds. A grass farm located nearby uses groundwater to irrigate its fields. Because of the sandy nature of soils and underlying geological strata in the area, the pond seeped heavily, and the grass farm owner complained that seepage from the ponds was responsible for increasing salinity in groundwater used for irrigation. Ponds were lined with impermeable, plastic liners in 1988. The liners were effective in stopping seepage, and they are still in good condition and resisting seepage after more than 20 years. Impermeable plastic liners also may be installed in pond bottoms to lessen erosion and avoid contact of water with problem soils.

Pond liners are expensive—$10,000 to $100,000 per hectare depending upon type of liner and size of pond. In addition, they can lead to phosphorus accumulation in water and dense phytoplankton blooms. Phosphorus accumulates in the water because bottom soil uptake of phosphorus—the main sink for phosphorus in ponds—is blocked by the liner. Phytoplankton blooms tend to increase to a high density and are prone to sudden 'crashes.' Phosphorus is released from the dead plankton, and the process repeats itself.[3]

In the example from the Claude Peteet Mariculture Center given above, and at several other aquaculture research stations, pond liners were covered with a layer of soil— usually about 5- to 20-cm thick—to remove phosphorus from the water and lessen the frequency of oscillations in plankton abundance. Although the practice of covering pond bottoms with plastic liners and installing soil over the liners sometimes can be afforded by research stations and hatcheries, this approach is much too expensive for use in commercial aquaculture ponds operated at normal production levels. The main purpose of this chapter is to briefly discuss new procedures for intensive production in lined ponds. The possibility for using less expensive, permeable pond liners to avoid erosion also will be considered.

## Lined Ponds with Sediment Removal

Dissolved oxygen depletion resulting from dense, unstable phytoplankton blooms in lined ponds without soil can be overcome by mechanical aeration, and the expense of liners can be justified by using enough aeration to allow much greater production than possible in earthen-lined ponds. Dead phytoplankton accumulates in the bottom of lined ponds where it decomposes with release (mineralization) of ammonia and phosphate. The decomposition process consumes oxygen that could otherwise have been used by the culture species, and the nutrients from organic decomposition stimulate phytoplankton photosynthesis that produces more organic matter.

Ponds can be constructed with center drains, and aerators positioned to create circular water movement and cause dead phytoplankton and other organic wastes to accumulate in the area around the drain. The drain can be opened and organic sediment will be removed in outflowing water. This procedure is illustrated in Fig. 25.2 for a small, production unit, but in ponds larger than 200 to 400 m$^2$, waste accumulates over too large an area for effective removal by water currents resulting from water flowing towards the open drain. In larger ponds a sludge pump can be used to remove organic sediment. Alternatively, in some larger ponds with a center drain, it is possible to attach one end of a flexible tube to the drain creating a siphon so that the other end of the hose acts as a suction device. Workers can use the suction end of the hose to remove sediment from anywhere in the pond bottom.

Sediment removal from lined ponds spares dissolved oxygen and allows higher production. The benefits of this procedure are illustrated with observations made at a large shrimp farm in Indonesia. The 0.5-ha ponds are lined, stocked at 150 postlarvae/m$^2$ or more, 12 to 14 hp of aeration are applied, and sediment is removed from the ponds at about 2-week intervals. Each pond typically produces 7,000 to 9,000 kg shrimp per crop (14,000 to 18,000 kg/ha) per crop.

Although sediment removal can allow high levels of production in lined ponds, it does so because much of the waste load is exported. In a pond without sediment removal,

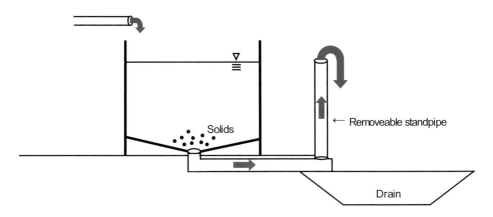

**Fig. 25.2.** Illustration of intensive fish culture unit with center drain. When the standpipe is removed, the solids will be flushed from the tank.

much of the dissolved oxygen provided by aerators is used by aerobic, saprophytic micro-organisms to oxidize uneaten feed, feces, and dead plankton. With sediment removal, a portion of the organic matter is taken from ponds before microbial oxidation occurs, allowing a greater proportion of dissolved oxygen supplied by aeration to be used by the culture species. In addition, the organic matter is removed before significant amounts of nitrogen and phosphorus are recycled, and there are less nutrients to stimulate organic matter production by phytoplankton photosynthesis.

Sediment removed from ponds cannot be separated easily from effluent, and it typically is discharged into natural waters. Organic matter decomposition that was avoided in ponds will occur in nature with consumption of oxygen and mineralization of nutrients. Obviously, sediment removal is not an 'environment-friendly' practice.

## Heterotrophic Systems

In lined ponds without sediment removal, production also can be increased by applying more aeration. In ponds operated at high density, the water becomes so turbid after a few weeks that light limitation greatly reduces phytoplankton abundance, and the phytoplankton bloom is replaced by a bacterial community.[4] The water changes from the greenish hue of phytoplankton blooms to a brownish-black hue imparted by the microbial flocs, also called *bioflocs* (Fig. 25.3). 

Commercial use of lined, heterotrophic ponds has focused mostly on culture of marine shrimp, but other species can be produced in these systems.[5,6] The culture animals eat manufactured feed applied to the system, but they also feed on the bacterial floc. Normally, an organic material of lower quality than aquaculture feed, e.g., crushed corn or other grain, is used to replace a portion of the daily feed input. In some cases, blackstrap molasses also may be applied as a carbon source for the bacteria. Organic matter and ammonia from pond water are used by bacteria, and protein in bacterial

**Fig. 25.3.** Microbial floc in water from a biofloc shrimp production system.

biomass can be used by shrimp or other species that feed on detritus and living particulate matter. The effective crude protein percentage of organic matter inputs to heterotrophic systems can be lowered by using a combination of standard feed, grain, and molasses as compared to applying standard aquaculture feed alone.

Although nitrogen input to heterotrophic systems is high, ammonia mineralized by shrimp metabolism and degradation of organic matter is largely bound in bacterial protein or oxidized to nitrate. Total nitrogen concentration is high in waters of floc systems, but concentrations of ammonia seldom are greatly elevated.[4,5,6] However, because of the high level of microbial and shrimp respiration and the low level of phytoplankton photosynthesis in floc systems, a large amount of aeration (often more than 40 hp/ha) must be used continuously. Dissolved oxygen depletion may occur within a few hours if aerators are not operating. Therefore, an emergency generator should always be available if aerators supplied with electricity from the grid are used.

Water exchange with the outside environment is not normally necessary in floc systems. In addition, when ponds are drained for harvest, the water can be transferred to a settling basin and returned to the pond after a few days for reuse.

## Other Applications

Liners also can be used to cover the insides of earthen raceways. This is a particularly good application, because a lined, earthen raceway (Fig. 25.4) is less expensive than the common concrete raceway. Liners also are used increasingly in broodstock, nursery, and fingerling ponds at hatcheries as a biosecurity measure. Despite bottom dry out and lime or chlorine application, disease organisms may survive between crops in earthen-lined, hatchery ponds. Lined ponds can be completely dried between culture cycles, and if necessary, chlorine or other disinfectant used to sterilize the dry liners before refilling.

**Fig. 25.4.** A lined, earthen raceway.

Partial lining of ponds with geotextile—mainly on erosion-prone areas of embankments—is often less expensive than installation of stone (rip-rap). Thus, in ponds where grass cover is difficult or impossible to establish, such as in ponds filled with brackishwater or seawater, partial lining with geotextile is an excellent alternative to traditional stone lining. The use of a non-porous liner over the inside slopes of embankments does not lead to greater phosphorus accumulation in pond water.

## Permeable Liners

Erosion is a particularly troublesome problem in small ponds such as those used on research stations or for the production of ornamental fish. A study was recently conducted at Auburn University to determine if relatively inexpensive, permeable geotextile could be used to stabilize pond earthwork. Two types of geotextile were studied, but the main difference between the two materials was the type of fabric—both had similar porosities. Although nitrogen and phosphorus concentrations did not differ greatly among control ponds and limed ponds, the lined ponds tended to have greater concentrations of chlorophyll *a* than the unlined, control ponds (Table 25.2). This suggests that more nutrients were available in the lined ponds than in the unlined ones. Fish production was quite similar in control and lined ponds (Table 25.2).

The liners were used for 2 years, and they were effective in controlling erosion. Unfortunately, after the production study was completed, the liners were removed, because the station superintendent did not like their appearance. Thus, the service life of the geotextile liners could not be evaluated.

The liners selected for the study were negatively buoyant and had very small openings. Both characteristics probably favored floating. As a result, the liners pulled their metal fasteners from over about 30 to 40% of the bottoms of several ponds and floated into the water column. A test of several geotextiles with a coarser weave revealed that they allow faster phosphorus uptake by soil than did one of the fine weave materials (Liner 2) used in the pond study (Table 25.3). The coarser weave materials should be tested, because they may interfere less with exchange of substances between bottom soil and water and be less likely to detach from pond bottoms and float up into the water column.

**Table 25.2.** Average concentrations of selected water quality variables and fish production in unlined earthen ponds and in ponds lined with two types of permeable geofabric.

| Variable | Unlined | Liner 1 | Liner 2 |
|---|---|---|---|
| Soluble reactive phosphorus (mg/L) | 0.025 | 0.040 | 0.040 |
| Total phosphorus (mg/L) | 0.15 | 0.11 | 0.13 |
| Total nitrogen (mg/L) | 0.44 | 0.58 | 0.73 |
| Total ammonia nitrogen (mg/L) | 0.12 | 0.14 | 0.14 |
| Chlorophyll $a$ (µg/L) | 225 | 386 | 510 |
| Turbidity (NTU) | 26 | 20 | 42 |
| Fish production (kg/ha) | 6,128 | 6,475 | 6,650 |

**Table 25.3.** Phosphorus concentrations remaining after 15 days in laboratory systems containing no soil, soil without liner, and soil with five, different, permeable geofabric liners. Initial phosphorus concentration in all systems was 1.0 mg/L.

| Description | Soluble reactive phosphorus (mg/L) |
|---|---|
| Control – no soil | 0.80 |
| Control – soil, no liner | 0.09 |
| Liner 2 (described in text) | 0.52 |
| Four liners of coarser weave than Liner 2 | 0.25-0.32 |

# References

1. Boyd, C. E. 1995. *Bottom Soils, Sediment, and Pond Aquaculture.* Chapman and Hall, New York, NY.
2. Boyd, C. E. 2009. Assessing, reducing pond seepage. Global Aquaculture Advocate 12(2):62-63.
3. Leonard, S. E. 1995. Water quality factors influencing striped bass (*Morone saxatilis*) production in lined ponds. Ph.D. Dissertation, Auburn University, AL.
4. McIntosh, R. P. 1999. Changing paradigms in shrimp farming: 1. General description. Global Aquaculture Advocate 2(4/5):42-47.
5. Browdy, C. L., J. A. Venero, A. D. Stokes, and J. Leffler. 2009. Superintensive bio-floc production technologies for marine shrimp *Litopenaeus vannamei*: technical challenges and opportunities, pages 1,010-1,028. In: G. Burnell and G. Allan (editors), *New Technologies in Aquaculture.* CRC Press, Boca Raton, FL.
6. Avnimelech, Y. 2010. Intensive production of shrimp, pages 233-246. In: V. Alday-Sanz (editor), *The Shrimp Book.* Nottingham University Press, Nottingham, UK.

# Chapter 26

# Flow-Through Systems

## Introduction

Flow-through aquaculture systems consist of tanks, troughs, raceways, or small ponds with water passing once through the culture unit.[1,2] Water entering the culture unit provides dissolved oxygen and water leaving the tank carries away waste products. Water may be reconditioned and reused as it passes through a series of culture units, but unlike recirculating aquaculture systems (Chapter 28), water is not reconditioned and passed through the same unit more than once. For this reason, flow-through systems are sometimes called *single-pass* systems.

If water temperature is in the proper range for the species being cultured, potential production is initially determined by water flow and dissolved oxygen concentration in the incoming water. Production can be increased by adding dissolved oxygen to water in the culture unit or to water flowing from one unit to another. In systems with oxygen supplementation, accumulation of ammonia, carbon dioxide or fine solids will eventually limit production. No natural foods are produced in flow-through systems and nutritionally complete diets are essential.

## Water Sources

Flow-through aquaculture requires large water volumes that must be the proper temperature for culture, because heating or cooling is impractical except in very small facilities. Water for flow-through facilities is usually diverted from streams, springs, artesian wells, or from intake structures in dams of large reservoirs (Fig. 26.1). Water then flows through the facility by gravity. Pumping water from wells or surface waters is too expensive for commercial use, although pumped water is sometimes used for seasonal hatcheries or research laboratories. Flow-through systems are most commonly used to grow coldwater fish, such as trout and the freshwater stages of salmon because sources of consistently cold water are easier to find than sources of consistently warm water, although locally important exceptions exist.[3] Other than research facilities, flow-through systems are not used to grow brackish or saltwater species.

Ground waters are good sources for flow-through aquaculture because they are usually free of suspended matter and fish pathogens, and are less likely to be polluted than surface waters. Groundwater temperatures and composition are relatively constant over time but vary with location and aquifer depth. Surface waters are common sources for flow-through facilities, but are less desirable than underground supplies. Surface water quality varies with time and some sources are susceptible to contamination with fish pathogens, water-borne predators, or pollution. Water quality depends on upstream geology and land-use practices, and sources from protected or undeveloped watersheds are preferred. Regardless of the source, water supplies of adequate volume and good quality (especially water temperature) are not common, which limits expansion of flow-through aquaculture.

Flow-through systems use more water for fish production than any other type of aquaculture. For example, average water use for trout culture in flow-through raceways is approximately 60 to 120 $m^3$/kg of fish produced, depending on how many times water is reused in serial raceways. This is 10-fold greater than channel catfish aquaculture in earthen ponds and more than 100-fold greater than fish culture in water-recirculating systems.[4] However, unlike ponds where large volumes of water may be lost to evaporation or seepage, flow-through facilities use water non-consumptively, meaning that essentially no water is lost as it is used to grow fish. Although quality may be altered as it passes through the system, effluent volume is essentially the same as inflow volume.[5]

**Fig. 26.1.** Iron Gate Hatchery on the Klamath River in northern California. The adult salmon and steelhead (anadromous rainbow trout) holding facility is in the center of the photograph at the base of Iron Gate Dam, with the dam's spillway on the left and a hydroelectric generating facility and associated penstock on the right. The dam blocks upstream migration of salmon and steelhead, which swim into the collection facility using the fish ladder to the left of the facility. Adult fish are held in round concrete flow-through tanks until manually spawned. Fertilized eggs are then transported to a hatchery about 500 m downstream (out of the picture) where fry and fingerlings are grown in flow-through raceways. Water for the collection facility and fingerling raceways is drawn from Iron Gate Reservoir at a depth of 30 m. (Photo credit: Thomas Dunklin)

# Culture Units

Culture units used in flow-through aquaculture can be functionally described based on water flow characteristics as either rotating or plug flow. Most round tanks have rotating water flow, with water entering tangentially near the tank perimeter and exiting in a center drain. Rotating flow—aided by the swimming activities of fish—produces a secondary radial flow that moves solids toward the center where they are removed in water leaving the tank through a center drain. The self-cleaning nature of round tanks is an advantage over units with plug flow. Also, because water in circular tanks is well mixed, environmental conditions (such as dissolved oxygen concentrations) are uniform throughout the culture unit, which is not the case in units with plug flow.

Rectangular culture units include tanks, troughs, and raceways. All are generally long, narrow, shallow containers in which water enters at one end and exits at the other. Water flow through raceways and other rectangular units is an approximation of plug flow. In ideal plug flow, water velocity is equal across any tank cross section down the length of the tank. In practice, friction losses at the air-water boundary and along the tank walls and bottom cause reduced water velocities at the surface, along the walls, and especially along the bottom. The flow of water along the long axis of the raceway causes a marked water-quality gradient from one end of the unit to the other. Best environmental conditions (highest dissolved oxygen concentration and lowest carbon dioxide, ammonia, and solids concentrations) are near the inflow and fish metabolism causes quality to deteriorate as water moves through the unit.

Raceways may be constructed of earth (Fig. 26.2), wood, plastic, fiberglass, or concrete (Fig. 26.3). Concrete is commonly used for commercial facilities. Raceway dimensions vary greatly but a 30:3:1 ratio of length-to-width-to depth is common for salmonid culture. Actual dimensions are determined by available water flow and desired

**Fig. 26.2.** Earthen raceways used to grow rainbow trout in the southern Appalachian Mountains of the United States. Photo credit: Jeffrey Hinshaw.

water velocity. A significant design consideration is the need to maintain adequate water velocity through the unit to sweep solid wastes down the raceway so that they do not accumulate in the culture unit.[6] A velocity of about 3 cm/second is a good compromise between conservative water use and adequate velocity for 'self-cleaning.' Water velocity is equal to flow divided by cross sectional area, so velocity can be manipulated by changing raceway width or depth.

Culture units can be configured in parallel, series, or both. In parallel arrangements, multiple culture units receive water from a common source, which is split so that water makes one pass through the each unit. Discharge from multiple units is then recombined into a common effluent. Advantages to parallel culture units include reduced opportunity for disease transmission among culture units and identical influent water quality in all units. The major disadvantage is low production efficiency because water is used only once before discharge. Parallel culture units are common in research facilities where biosecurity and uniform culture conditions are more important than production economics.

When culture units are arranged in a series, water flows by gravity from one unit into the next unit downstream. The drop from one unit to the next is used to aerate the water (Fig. 26.3). The number of serial reuses depends on the initial dissolved oxygen concentration, the effectiveness of aeration between serial reuses, fish biomass, and initial water chemistry. In practice, most commercial flow-through use multiple raceways arranged in parallel with serial reuse (Fig. 26.4).

**Fig. 26.3.** A group of two parallel sets of concrete raceways, each set with 14 raceways in a series, used to grow rainbow trout in the Appalachian Mountains of North Carolina. Water is diverted from a small permanent stream hidden in the trees on the left and is aerated as it falls over weirs between each raceway in the series. Photo credit: Jeffrey Hinshaw.

**Fig. 26.4.** A large, flow-through raceway facility producing rainbow trout in the Hagerman Valley, along the Snake River in Idaho. Six groups of raceways can be seen. The largest group has 30 parallel sets of raceways, each set with two raceways in a series. The facility is supplied by artesian springs emerging from the canyon walls. At least seven springs can be seen in this photograph. Photo credit: University of Idaho.

## Facility Design

*Carrying capacity* is the maximum biomass of fish that can be held in a culture unit without metabolic activities degrading water quality to the point where growth and health are adversely affected. At a given water temperature, carrying capacity is a function of flow rate because water flow determines the amount of dissolved oxygen available to meet fish metabolic demands and the rate at which wastes are diluted. Ultimately, facility productivity is determined by water temperature, carrying capacity, and stock manipulation.

Carrying capacity, water flow, and facility design (raceway size and number) are interdependent variables. For trout and salmon production—the most common type of flow-through aquaculture—relationships among these variables are refined to the point where rational design and production decisions are easily made. For example, flow rate for salmonid production facilities is based on proposed carrying capacity and production. Water flow should be adequate to provide at least four water exchanges per hour in each culture unit while maintaining a water velocity of 3 cm/second for solids management. If water flow, exchange rate, and water velocity are known, raceway dimensions can be calculated directly.[1,6]

## Carrying Capacity in Systems without Supplemental Oxygen

Carrying capacity in a single flow-through culture unit without supplemental aeration is easy to estimate because dissolved oxygen is almost always the first limiting factor and the dissolved oxygen budget is very simple: the only oxygen source is water inflow and the only significant loss is fish respiration. Carrying capacity is, therefore, a function of water flow rate because the amount of dissolved oxygen available to meet fish respiratory needs is the product of flow volume and influent dissolved oxygen concentration.

Fish carrying capacity can be estimated in four ways: 1) using established relationships between water flow and carrying capacity (this relationship is called the *flow index*); 2) using mass balance equations between dissolved oxygen supply and oxygen demand in fish respiration; 3) using relationships between fish respiration and amount of feed consumed; 4) through trial and error.

### Flow index

Flow index (F) describes the relationship among water flow (Q), maximum permissible total fish biomass (M) and average fish length (L):

$$F = \frac{M}{(Q)(L)}. \tag{26.1}$$

The factor, L, accounting for fish length is needed because small fish have a higher metabolic rate than bigger fish for the same total weight.

Flow indexes are empirical. One method of determining flow index for a single culture unit is to add increments of size-graded fish to a culture unit with constant inflow of water saturated with dissolved oxygen until the dissolved oxygen concentration in the effluent is reduced to a level deemed minimally acceptable. The final weight defines the carrying capacity and can be used with information on flow rate and average fish length to determine F using Equation 26.1.

Flow indexes in Table 26.1 were derived for salmonid culture in water initially oxygen-saturated and a minimum acceptable dissolved oxygen concentration of 5 mg/L. If the inflow is not saturated or another minimum dissolved oxygen criterion is used, the flow index must be corrected to account for changes in dissolved oxygen availability.[1,7] Indexes in Table 26.1 vary with water temperature and facility elevation because those

**Table 26.1.** Selected flow indexes for salmonid aquaculture in flow-through raceways as a function of water temperature and facility elevation. These indexes assume that the water inflow is 100% saturated with dissolved oxygen and the minimum acceptable dissolved oxygen concentration is 5 mg/L.

| Water temperature | | Facility elevation above sea level | | | | | |
|---|---|---|---|---|---|---|---|
| (°C) | (°F) | 0 m (0 ft) | | 610 m (2,000 ft) | | 1,830 m (6,000 ft) | |
| 5 | 41 | 0.12 | 2.6 | 0.11 | 2.4 | 0.10 | 2.1 |
| 10 | 50 | 0.09 | 1.8 | 0.08 | 1.7 | 0.07 | 1.4 |
| 15 | 59 | 0.06 | 1.3 | 0.06 | 1.2 | 0.05 | 1.1 |

factors affect dissolved oxygen solubility. Flow indexes in Table 26.1 are given for metric units (M in kg, Q in L/minute, and L in cm) in the left column under each altitude and for English units (M in pounds, Q in gallons per minute, and L in inches) in the right column.

The usefulness of the flow index is apparent when Equation 26.1 is rearranged so that fish biomass is a fish length-dependent function of water inflow:

$$M = (F)(Q)(L). \tag{26.2}$$

Equation 26.2 allows carrying capacity to be estimated from the flow index, water flow rate, and average fish length (Example 26.1). Rearranging Equation 26.1 also provides a method of estimating required water flow if a certain carrying capacity is desired:

$$Q = \frac{M}{(F)(L)}. \tag{26.3}$$

---

### Example 26.1
### Estimation of Carrying Capacity of Raceway based on the Flow Index

What is the carrying capacity (kg) for 10-cm trout held in a raceway at sea level with an inflow of 600 L/min of 10°C water? The flow index for that elevation and water temperature is 0.09 (Table 26.1). From Equation 26.2, for 10-cm trout:

$$M = (F)(Q)(L)$$

$$M = (0.09)(10)(600)$$

$$M = 540 \text{ kg.}$$

---

*Oxygen mass balance*

Flow indexes in Table 26.1 were developed at state and federal salmonid hatcheries in the United States and may not reflect desired tank carrying capacity for commercial facilities and for non-salmonid species. Another approach to estimating carrying capacity uses published estimates of fish respiratory rates (Example 26.2), which are available for many species.[8]

Note the similarity of carrying capacity estimates for trout of the same size using flow index in Example 26.1 and oxygen mass balance in Example 26.2. If initial assumptions are the same, as they are in these two examples, the two approaches should yield similar answers because both methods are based on matching oxygen use by fish to oxygen available in the incoming water. When using flow index to calculate carrying capacity, water flow is simply a surrogate for dissolved oxygen availability.

**347**

**Example 26.2**
**Estimation of Carrying Capacity of Raceway based on Fish Respiration Rate**

Assume a raceway at sea level is supplied with water at 10° C and a flow rate of 600 L/min. What weight of 10-cm (~11 g) trout can be held in the raceway while maintaining a minimum dissolved oxygen level of 5 mg/L? At 10°C, oxygen-saturated water contains about 11 mg/L dissolved oxygen at sea level and 11-g trout have a respiration rate of approximately 390 mg $O_2$/kg of fish per hr.[9]

First, calculate the mass of available oxygen in water flowing into the culture unit in 1 hr by subtracting the amount leaving the raceway from the amount entering, multiplying that number by the flow rate, and convert units to kg $O_2$/hr:

(11 mg $O_2$/L − 5 mg $O_2$/L)(600 L/min)(60 min/hr) = 216,000 mg $O_2$/hr.

Next, divide available oxygen per hour by the fish oxygen consumption rate per hour:

$$\frac{216,000 \text{ mg } O_2/\text{hr}}{390 \text{ mg } O_2/\text{kg fish per hour}} = 554 \text{ kg of fish.}$$

*Oxygen:feed ratio*

Oxygen use by fish is proportional to amount of feed consumed.[6,10] This provides another method for estimating carrying capacity if the following mass balance is established:

$$(M)(OFR)(FR) = [(DO_{in} - DO_{crit})(Q)(1440 \text{ min/day})(0.001 \text{ g/mg})] \qquad (26.4)$$

where M = fish carrying capacity (kg); OFR = oxygen:feed ratio (mg $O_2$/kg feed consumed); FR = daily feeding rate (kg feed/kg of fish per day); Q = water flow rate (L/min); $DO_{in}$ = influent dissolved oxygen concentration (mg/L); $DO_{crit}$ = critical minimum dissolved oxygen concentration (mg/L).

The left-hand side of Equation 26.4 is daily oxygen consumption by fish based on experimentally determined relationships between oxygen use and amount of feed consumed. The right-hand side of the equation is influent available dissolved oxygen.

Equation 26.4 can be rearranged to provide an estimate of carrying capacity:

$$M = \frac{(DO_{in} - DO_{crit})(Q)(1,440 \text{ min/day})(0.001 \text{ g/mg})}{(OFR)(FR)} \qquad (26.5)$$

Salmonid OFR values under typical culture conditions range from 200 to 300 g $O_2$/kg of feed consumed and are largely independent of fish size and temperature.[6] Values for other species, particularly warmwater species, are poorly documented but likely higher than those for salmonid culture. Daily feeding rate ranges from less than 0.01 to 0.05 kg feed/kg fish per day depending on fish weight (small fish eat more), water temperature (fish eat most in a narrow range of optimum water temperatures), and other factors.[6]

Carrying capacity estimated in Example 26.3 is greater than estimated in Examples 26.1 and 26.2 for the same conditions. However, available dissolved oxygen (the numerator in Equation 26.5) was calculated as the mean for a 24-hour day, whereas oxygen use by fish is greatest while feeding and shortly after fish are fed. Also, fish in many facilities are fed over an operational day of 12 to 18 hours rather than evenly throughout the day. Carrying capacity estimates based on feeding must therefore be adjusted by applying a *peaking factor* to reduce carrying capacity to levels that are safe during periods of highest oxygen use. Suggested peaking factors range from about 1.2 to 1.4.[6,10,11] Dividing the estimated carrying capacity in Example 26.3 (823 kg) by a peaking factor of 1.4 provides an estimate of 590 kg—an amount more in line with the estimates in Examples 26.1 and 26.2.

*Empirical carrying capacity estimates*

Carrying capacity calculations should be used as guidelines for planning. Actual carrying capacities and production potential are best determined empirically for specific facilities because they are influenced by site-specific factors such as seasonal variations in water temperature and source water quality. In fact, the flow indices explained above were developed in just that manner—by experimentation.

**Example 26.3**
**Estimation of Carrying Capacity of Raceway based on Available Dissolved Oxygen Inflow**

Assume a raceway at sea level is supplied with water at 10°C and a flow rate of 600 L/min. What weight of 10-cm trout can be held in the raceway while maintaining a minimum dissolved oxygen level of 5 mg/L? At 10°C, oxygen-saturated water contains about 11 mg/L dissolved oxygen at sea level. Assume an OFR of 300 g $O_2$/kg of feed consumed and a feeding rate of 0.021 kg feed/kg fish per day for trout of that size in 10°C water. Insert appropriate values into Equation 26.5:

$$W = \frac{(11 \text{ mg/L} - 5 \text{ mg/L})(600 \text{ L/min})(1{,}440 \text{ min/day})(0.001 \text{ g/mg})}{(300 \text{ g } O_2/\text{kg feed})(0.021 \text{ kg feed/kg fish per day})}$$

W = 823 kg of fish.

*Carrying capacity limitations other than dissolved oxygen*

Carrying capacity estimates described above assume that incoming water is the only source of dissolved oxygen. Under that condition, the assumption that carrying capacity is limited by dissolved oxygen availability is true for nearly all waters, except waters with exceptionally low or exceptionally high total alkalinity. If the source water has a very low total alkalinity (<5 mg/L), dissolved carbon dioxide produced in fish respiration will cause the water's pH to drop to a dangerous level before respiration causes dissolved oxygen to fall below critical concentrations. On the other hand, if the source water has a very high total alkalinity (>200 mg/L) that poises the initial pH above 8.8, un-ionized ammonia (the more toxic form of ammonia; see Chapter 16) will accumulate to undesirable levels before dissolved oxygen concentration falls below the minimum criterion.[10]

## *Carrying Capacity in Systems with Supplemental Dissolved Oxygen*

Carrying capacity can be increased by providing supplemental oxygen, either by aeration (exposing water to air) or oxygenation (exposing water to pure oxygen). Oxygen can be supplied directly to the culture unit or to water flowing between culture units when units are arranged in a series. Single culture units may be aerated by surface spray-type aerators or by diffusers introducing either air or pure oxygen. Aeration in serial raceways is usually accomplished by gravity fall over weirs between individual raceways (Fig. 26.5). The amount of oxygen added in weir aeration depends on fall height, water flow, weir geometry, and raceway depth.[12,13] Gravity aeration between culture units in serial-reuse systems replaces 50 to 70% of the oxygen lost in the previous unit. Available dissolved oxygen and carrying capacity therefore decreases with each serial reuse.

**Fig. 26.5.** Gravity aeration of water flowing over weirs between raceways in a series.

Dissolved oxygen concentrations can be restored to saturation (or higher) between culture units using pure-oxygen systems, such as low-head oxygenators (described in Chapter 28). Pure-oxygen systems can restore all oxygen consumed in previous culture units, which significantly increases carrying capacity and production in serial-reuse systems. Oxygenation is expensive, however, and is often not justifiable on commercial facilities.

Carrying capacity cannot be increased infinitely by providing supplemental oxygen because fish behavior and health may be affected at high densities even when water quality is excellent.[6,10] Also, at some point water quality variables other than dissolved oxygen concentration become limiting.

Depending on initial water quality and the type of aeration, carrying capacity in systems with oxygen supplementation will be limited by accumulation of dissolved carbon dioxide or ammonia produced during fish metabolism. In poorly buffered waters (low total alkalinity), dissolved carbon dioxide accumulation can cause pH to decrease to a dangerous level even though dissolved carbon dioxide itself is not of concern. The effect of carbon dioxide, ammonia and pH on carrying capacity is difficult to calculate because the variables interact with each other in complex ways (for example, dissolved carbon dioxide affects pH which in turn affects ammonia toxicity) and they interact with other water quality variables (for example, the affect of dissolved carbon dioxide on pH depends total alkalinity).

A further complication arises because dissolved carbon dioxide accumulation—a key variable having direct and indirect effects on carrying capacity—depends on the oxygen supplementation method (see Chapter 7). Some aerators remove considerable excess carbon dioxide in the process called degassing or stripping. On the other hand, pure-oxygen systems must be operated with as little exposure to air as possible to avoid losing expensive oxygen gas to the atmosphere. As a consequence, little excess dissolved carbon dioxide is stripped from water during oxygenation.

*Systems with aeration*

Dissolved oxygen availability does not limit carrying capacity in single culture tanks with vigorous aeration or in serial-reuse raceways with effective gravity aeration between culture units. As well as adding dissolved oxygen, aeration removes some dissolved carbon dioxide but ammonia is unaffected. The degree to which carbon dioxide accumulates (and, therefore, its affect on pH and carrying capacity) depends on the type and effectiveness of aeration. In systems with vigorous aeration provided by devices with a high gas-liquid ratio (see Chapter 7), most excess dissolved carbon dioxide can be stripped from the water and carrying capacity will be limited by ammonia accumulation, regardless of total alkalinity. If aerators are not effective at stripping dissolved carbon dioxide, carrying capacity is eventually limited by low pH or accumulation of dissolved carbon dioxide in low-alkalinity waters and by ammonia in high-alkalinity waters.[10]

*Systems with pure oxygen addition*

Dissolved oxygen availability never limits carrying capacity in properly operated systems with pure oxygen addition. But pure-oxygen systems are poor at removing dissolved carbon dioxide from water and, for most water sources, carrying capacity in flow-through facilities with pure oxygen addition is eventually limited by dissolved carbon accumulation. If the source water has low total alkalinity (<10 mg/L), dissolved carbon dioxide can quickly reduce pH to levels that limit carrying capacity; if the source water has high total alkalinity (>100 mg/L) and an initial pH above about 8.5, ammonia accumulation limits carrying capacity because a large proportion of ammonia exists in the more toxic un-ionized form.[10]

*Modeling water quality interactions*

A model has been developed describing relationships among dissolved oxygen, dissolved carbon dioxide, pH, and ammonia in serial-reuse raceways.[11] Model output can, in theory, be combined with water quality criteria to estimate the effects of water quality management practices on carrying capacity and productivity. The model's practical use is limited by lack of information on certain processes (such as carbon dioxide degassing rates for weirs and aerators) and by poor understanding of the sublethal affects dissolved carbon dioxide, ammonia, and pH.

*Practical examples*

The Hagerman Valley of the Snake River in Idaho is the major United States trout-producing area. Facilities are supplied by springs that provide a continuous supply of 15°C water with total alkalinities above 100 mg/L as $CaCO_3$. Water is gravity-aerated between uses in serial raceways (Fig. 26.4). Dissolved oxygen, dissolved carbon dioxide, and low pH do not limit production because weir aeration adds dissolved oxygen, removes some dissolved carbon dioxide, and the water's high total alkalinity prevents significant changes in pH caused by respired carbon dioxide. However, the water's high total alkalinity poises initial pH above 8.6 and ammonia accumulation eventually limits production. A typical facility can reuse water four to six times before ammonia accumulates to limiting levels, and maximum annual production is about 10 kg of trout per L/minute of flow.

Another major trout-producing area is the southern Appalachian Mountains. Most facilities are supplied with water diverted from permanent streams and water temperatures vary seasonally from 3°C to nearly 20°C. Most waters have very low total alkalinities (<10 mg/L as $CaCO_3$). The low total alkalinity poises initial pH at <7 and addition of respiratory carbon dioxide causes pH to drop significantly during use because the water lacks substantial buffering capacity. Under those conditions, ammonia is not limiting because low pH prevents accumulation of toxic, un-ionized ammonia. Although some dissolved carbon dioxide is removed by weir aeration, concentrations increase with serial reuse and eventually limit production. Despite variation in water temperature associated with these surface water sources, maximum annual production of about 17 kg of trout per L/minute of flow is greater than that of spring-fed facilities in Idaho because water can be serially reused 10 or more times before carbon dioxide becomes limiting.[2]

## Waste Management

Fish culture activities change the quality of water passing through a flow-through fish culture facility. Dissolved oxygen is consumed and wastes are produced. Wastes include solids (uneaten feed and fish fecal matter) and dissolved substances (ammonia, urea, phosphate, carbon dioxide, and others) excreted by the gills and kidneys. The goal of flow-through system management is to maintain a good environment for fish growth, which is accomplished by diluting the wastes with high water flows. Effluent water quality—as measured by waste concentrations—is typically very good. However, when concentrations are multiplied by the high water discharge volume from flow-through facilities, the result can be high waste mass loadings that may degrade receiving waters.

Flow-through systems do not retain water long enough for microbiological processes to remove solids and nutrients. Also, high water flow results in low dissolved nutrient concentrations, which makes removal difficult and expensive. Technologies have been developed for solids removal from flow-through systems but for economic and technical reasons, sedimentation (settling) is the most cost-effective waste-treatment process for commercial facilities.[5]

Solids management in flow-through aquaculture has two components. First, wastes must be removed rapidly from the fish culture unit before they decompose. Solids decomposition inside the culture unit consumes oxygen, degrades the environment, and impacts animal health. Decomposition also solubilizes nutrients and organic matter, making them much more difficult to remove before discharge. The second aspect of solids management is removal before water is discharged to the outside environment.

Solids removal is accomplished by making units self-cleaning. Circular tanks can be designed so that solids are rapidly concentrated in the bottom center of the tank and removed in a relatively small water volume.[14] Rectangular tank or raceway design should be based on water flow and dimensions necessary to achieve a water velocity of about 3 cm/second. This is a good compromise between low velocities that allow solids to settle and high velocities necessary to sweep settled solids out of the culture unit.[6]

Final solids removal takes place in either *full-flow* or *off-line settling basins* (Fig. 26.6). Settling basins provide an area with reduced water velocity where solids can settle for eventual collection and disposal. Basin size is determined mathematically from flow rate, solids settling characteristics, and desired solids removal percentage (Chapter 15).[5] Required basin size increases for higher flow rates (so that water velocity is reduced to the point where most solids can settle), for waters with slow-settling particles (to allow adequate retention time for settling), and when it is necessary (often by regulation) to remove a high percentages of total solids. Facilities usually have at least two settling basins so that one basin can be dewatered for solids removal while the other basin remains in use.

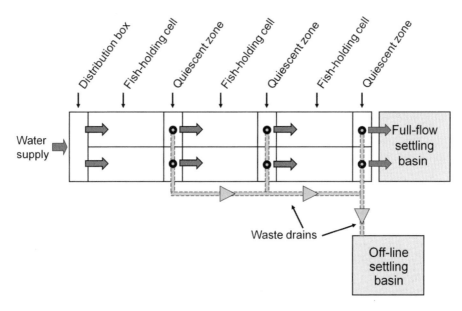

**Fig. 26.6.** Water and waste flow in two parallel sets of raceways, each set having three raceways in series. Solids produced during culture are settled and collected in quiescent zones at the end of each raceway coupled with either off-line or full-flow settling basins, or by full-flow settling basins without quiescent zones.

Full-flow settling basins remove solids from the entire facility water flow. They are most common on small facilities with low flow volumes (typically less than 300 L/second) because settling basin size becomes impractical for larger flow volumes. Off-line settling basins receive concentrated wastes from the culture unit. For example, off-line basins may receive concentrated waste streams discharged from the center drains of multiple, parallel round tanks or from quiescent zones of many raceways. Average flow to off-line settling basins is usually less than 1% of total facility flow over a 24-hour period.

Quiescent zones are areas at the downstream end of raceways or tanks that are separated from the rearing area with barriers to exclude fish and allow solids to settle undisturbed (Fig. 26.7). Quiescent zones are usually installed in every rearing unit but, at a minimum, a quiescent zone should be installed in the last rearing unit in a series to allow solids removal before final discharge. A combination of quiescent zones and off-line settling basins is the most common system of solids capture and removal on commercial flow-through facilities.

Solids capture can remove a large portion of the wastes generated in flow-through aquaculture. Additional measures can further reduce waste discharge. These measures include using high-quality feeds to optimize nutrient retention, careful feeding to avoid wasted feed, and managing fish populations within the system carrying capacity.[5]

**Fig. 26.7.** The quiescent zone is in the foreground, separated from the fish-holding area by a barred screen. Photo credit: Gary Fornshell.

# References

1. Soderberg, R. W. 1995. Flowing Water Fish Culture. Lewis Publishers, Boca Raton, FL.
2. Fornshell, G. J. Hinshaw, and J. H. Tidwell. 2012. Flow-through raceways, page 173-190. In J.H. Tidwell (editor), *Aquaculture Production Systems*. Wiley Blackwell, Ames, IA.
3. Ray, L. 1981. Channel catfish production in geothermal water, pages 192-195. In L .J. Allen and E. C. Kinney (editors), *Bio-Engineering Symposium for Fish Culture* (FCS Publ. 1). American Fisheries Society, Bethesda, MD.
4. Hargreaves, J. A., C. E. Boyd, and C. S. Tucker. 2002. Water budgets for aquaculture production, pages 9-33. In J. R. Tomasso (editor), *Aquaculture and the Environment in the United States*. United States Aquaculture Society, Baton Rouge, LA.
5. Fornshell, G. A. and J. M. Hinshaw. 2008. Better management practices for flow-through aquaculture systems, pages 331-388. In C. S. Tucker and J. A. Hargreaves (editors), *Environmental Best Management Practices for Aquaculture*. Wiley Blackwell, Ames, IA.
6. Westers, H. 2001. Production, pages 31-90. In G. A. Wedemeyer (editor), *Fish Hatchery Management, 2nd edition*. American Fisheries Society, Bethesda, MD.
7. Piper, R. G., I. B. McElwain, L. E. Orme, J. P. McCraren, L. G. Fowler, and J. R. Leonard. 1982. *Fish Hatchery Management*. United States Fish and Wildlife Service, Washington, D.C.
8. FishBase. Undated. Oxygen Consumption Studies. Available at http://www.fishbase.org/Topic/List.php?group=29. Accessed April 2013.
9. Liao, P. B. 1971. Water requirements of salmonids. Progressive Fish Culturist 33:210-215.
10. Colt, J. and K. Orwicz. 1991. Modeling production capacity of aquatic culture systems under freshwater conditions. Aquacultural Engineering 10:1-29.

11. Colt, J., B. Watten, and M. Rust. 2009. Modeling carbon dioxide, pH, and un-ionized ammonia relationships in serial reuse systems. Aquacultural Engineering 40:28-44.
12. Soderberg, R. W. 1982. Aeration of water supplies for fish culture in flowing water. Progressive Fish-Culturist 44:89-93.
13. Baylar, A. And T. Bagatur. 2000. Aerator performance of weirs. Water SA 26:521-526
14. Timmons, M. B., S. T. Summerfelt, and B. J. Vinci. 1998. Review of circular tank technology and management. Aquacultural Engineering 18:51-69.

# Chapter 27

# Cage Culture

## Introduction

Enclosures installed in natural water bodies have for many centuries been a traditional system for culturing fish. Net pens, the most basic form of enclosure, typically are made by attaching netting around poles driven into the bottom to form a pen into which fish are stocked. The simplest way of producing a net pen is to extend netting across a small embayment. Water exchange occurs between the large body of water and the embayment through the netting, and fish have access to the bottom of the water body within the enclosed area. Fish usually are stocked at low density and depend upon natural food, but in some cases, feed is applied.

Cages represent a more modern and intensive application of enclosure technology.[1] Cages usually are made of netting attached to a floating or submerged frame, and fish are suspended in the water column without access to the bottom. Fish are provided manufactured feed at regular intervals, and water quality is maintained in cages by natural water exchange.

Traditionally, cages were 25 to 100 m$^3$ in volume, and maximum fish densities were 2 to 30 kg/m$^3$. Modern cages used in freshwater bodies tend to be smaller (1 to 4 m$^3$) and fish densities are much greater (150 to 250 kg/m$^3$). However, large cages are still used, especially in the sea and in large lakes, but these cages also tend to be stocked at high densities.

Cage culture can be used in a variety of water bodies to culture most common species. For example, it has been used in freshwater lakes for tilapia culture throughout the tropics. Until recently in Vietnam, the pangasid catfishes, swai and basa, were cultured almost exclusively in cages installed in the Mekong River. Carp are cultured in cages in lakes and streams of several Asian countries. Most of the world's salmon production is performed in sea cages. In Scotland, trout are cultured in cages placed in lakes. There are other advantages of cage culture: the technology is simple, the infrastructure is relatively inexpensive, land is not necessary other than as a staging area, water consumption is limited to the water contained in fish biomass, and management logistics are facilitated by high fish density.

There are undesirable aspects of cage culture to include conflicts with other water users, loss of fish when cages are damaged by storms or predators, high susceptibility of fish in cages to water pollution, ease of disease spread within and between cages, and high degree of pollution potential by cage culture.[2] Nevertheless, these problems usually can be minimized through assessment and mitigation of possible negative impacts through good siting, design, and management. Cage culture is expected to increase in importance as a production method—especially for marine fish.

## Site Selection

Cages usually are installed in streams, lakes, reservoirs, or estuaries. These large systems have multiple uses and the aquaculturist has no control over water quality. Data should be collected for a year or more to ascertain if water quality is suitable for cage culture before a site is chosen. Important variables are water temperature, salinity, pH, total alkalinity, dissolved oxygen, carbon dioxide, total ammonia, nitrite, and types and abundance of phytoplankton.

Attention should be given to the pattern of thermal stratification and the volume of oxygen-depleted water in the hypolimnion. The typical stratification pattern in a lake or reservoir is discussed in Chapter 12 and illustrated in Fig. 27.1. In the temperate zone, lakes typically stratify in late spring or early summer and destratify in fall. In the tropics, lakes seldom stratify permanently. Sudden destratification and resulting dissolved oxygen depletion is a major risk to fish in cages in freshwater lakes and reservoirs (Fig. 27.2).

Cages are positioned at specific locations in water bodies, and these sites should be carefully selected. Cages should be installed in areas with good water circulation where they will be rapidly flushed and suspended and dissolved solids will be quickly diluted and transported away from the cages.[3]

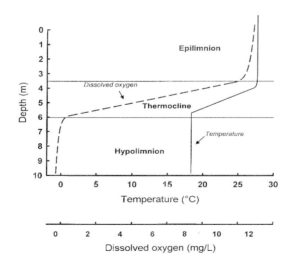

**Fig. 27.1.** Depth profiles for water temperature and dissolved oxygen concentration in a thermally-stratified water body.

Fig. 27.2. Massive fish mortality in cages caused by dissolved oxygen depletion following thermal destratification of a reservoir in Indonesia.

Sources of potentially toxic agricultural and industrial chemicals should be identified, for sites for cages ideally should be free of pollution. They should have relatively low primary productivity; that is, they should have clear or slightly turbid water with Secchi disk transparency greater than 100 cm. Lakes and reservoirs with moderate to dense plankton blooms and shallow, thermal stratification are particularly hazardous, and lakes with 50% or more of their volume devoid of dissolved oxygen during periods of thermal stratification should be avoided. Large changes in water level can jeopardize culture operations. Historical records of water levels in reservoirs and many natural lakes are available, as illustrated in Fig. 27.3 for Lake Yoja, Honduras.

## Cage Design

There are several types of cages.[1] The simplest are wooden boxes with openings between slats. Wire, plastic, or nylon netting provides more open space for water exchange than can be achieved with wooden slats. Cages can be made from stiff wire mesh or plastic-coated wire mesh (Fig. 27.4), but most cages are made from nylon or plastic mesh netting. Cages vary in size from 1 or 2 $m^3$ (Fig. 27.4) to 1,500 $m^3$ or more (Fig. 27.5). Cages commonly are moored to the bottom by ropes and anchors and float on the surface. Recent development of submersible cage technology allows cages to be suspended a sufficient depth to minimize effects of heavy seas.

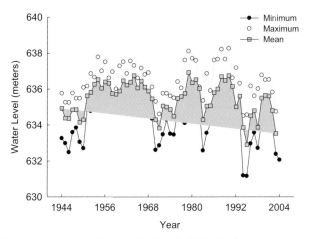

**Fig. 27.3.** Water level changes over a 60-year period in Lake Yoja, Honduras.

**Fig. 27.4.** Small, wire mesh cages.

**Fig. 27.5.** Large, circular cages in a lake.

Fish are crowded in cages, and water exchange for flushing out waste and renewing dissolved oxygen should be facilitated by cage design. Design features favoring water exchange are a high lateral surface area (LSA):volume (V) ratio (Fig. 27.6), and a large percentage open area in the netting. A high LSA:V ratio facilitates flushing as illustrated in Table 27.1. The highest LSA:V ratio is for a 1-m × 1-m × 1-m square cage or a 1-m diameter by 1-m deep circular cage. Square cages tend to be flushed better than circular cages of the same LSA:V ratio, because water tends to flow around circular cages (Fig. 27.7). Potential water exchange efficiency is less for rectangular cages than for square or circular ones. The potential efficiency of water exchange also decreases rapidly with increasing cage size for all shapes of cages. For example, a 16-m diameter by 3-m deep circular cage would be only 6.25% as efficient as a 1-m diameter by 1-m deep circular cage—assuming both cages have the same percentage open area in the netting.

**Table 27.1.** Lateral surface area (LSA):volume (V) ratios for cages of different shapes and sizes.

| Shape | Dimensions (m) | LSA ($m^2$) | V ($m^2$) | LSA:V | Potential water exchange efficiency (%) |
|-------|----------------|-------------|-----------|-------|------------------------------------------|
| Square | 1 × 1 × 1 | 4 | 1 | 4 | 100 |
| | 2 × 2 × 2 | 16 | 8 | 2 | 50 |
| | 4 × 4 × 4 | 64 | 64 | 1 | 25 |
| Rectangle | 2 × 1 × 1 | 6 | 2 | 3 | 75 |
| | 4 × 2 × 2 | 24 | 16 | 1.5 | 37.5 |
| | 8 × 4 × 4 | 96 | 96 | 1 | 25 |
| Circle | 1 × 1 | 3.1416 | 0.785 | 4 | 100 |
| | 2 × 2 | 12.57 | 6.28 | 2 | 50 |
| | 4 × 4 | 50.3 | 50.3 | 1 | 25 |
| | 16 × 3 | 150.8 | 603.2 | 0.25 | 6.25 |

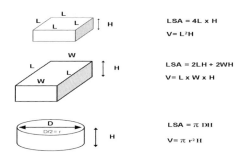

**Fig. 27.6.** Shapes of cages.[1]

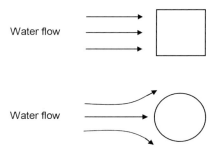

**Fig. 27.7.** Flow comparison for square and circular cages.[1]

The openings in nets should be as large as possible without risking escapes of fish. Large openings allow uneaten feed and feces to fall from cages and also favor efficient water exchange. The greatest percentage of open area usually is found in nylon netting. The great strength of this material allows small strands to be used to form the mesh (Fig. 27.8).

## Cage Position

Water exchange can be enhanced by positioning cages with regards to prevailing current and with respect to other cages.[1] Cages should be placed in areas where there is expected to be a continuous current, and the side of the cage with the maximum surface area should be parallel to the current. Some possible cage orientations are shown in Fig. 27.9. There is only one possible orientation of a circular cage (A) in the current. A square cage could be positioned with one side perpendicular to the current (B), but even more surface area can be exposed to the current if the cage diagonal is perpendicular to the current (C).

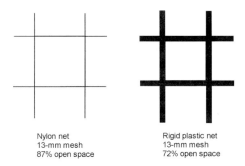

**Fig. 27.8.** Depiction of effect of size of stands in mesh netting on area of open space.[1]

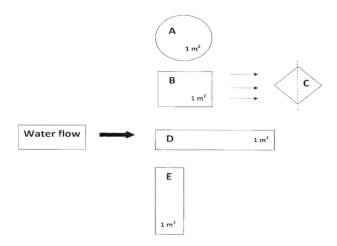

**Fig. 27.9.** Positioning of cages to maximize surface area facing current.[1]

The possible advantages of orientation C over orientation B may be negated if currents tend to deflect around the cage. The broad side of rectangular cages should be perpendicular to the current (compare D and E).

Stocking, feeding, and other management operations are easier when cages are grouped in a cluster (Fig. 27.10). The disadvantage of clusters is that water must flow through several cages, and dissolved oxygen concentration will decline and concentrations of metabolites will increase as water passes from one cage to the next in the cluster. Cages on the up-current side of a cluster usually have better water quality than other cages. The most efficient way of facilitating water flow through cages is to install cages in lines (Fig. 27.10), and if multiple lines are installed, a distance of 100 to 200 m should be allowed between adjacent lines.[1]

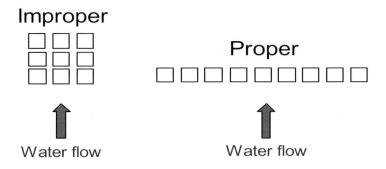

Fig. 27.10. Positioning of cages to maximize benefits of flushing on water quality.[1]

Wind patterns, storm frequencies, wave amplitudes and surges, and water currents should be understood. Cages should be installed in a manner to take advantage of water currents and wind action to flush cages and dilute wastes. Areas with restricted circulation (such as small embayments) usually should be avoided. Dense infestations of submersed aquatic plants also greatly restrict water movement. However, sites highly exposed to wind and wave action may also be unsuitable because of the high probability of cage damage.

Cages usually are placed in water bodies with multiple water uses, and conflicts may result. Cages should not interfere with navigation, fishing, recreation, tourism, or other traditional water uses. Cages also should be placed in areas where fish in them can be protected from predation by animals and poaching by humans.

## Water Quality in Cages

The discussion of site selection, cage design, and cage positioning has focused on locating sites with good water quality, achieving a high flushing rate to remove waste and replenish dissolved oxygen concentration in cages, and to dilute and transport wastes away from cages.[3] Nevertheless, dissolved oxygen concentration should be routinely monitored at minimum in the early morning and mid-afternoon at locations up current from the cages and within the cages. Dissolved oxygen concentration usually will be higher up current from cages than within cages because of fish respiration. Low dissolved oxygen concentration upstream of cages would indicate some problem with dissolved oxygen dynamics in the containing water body, such as low morning dissolved oxygen concentration in response to a dense phytoplankton bloom or extended period of cloudy weather, thermal destratification, or sudden phytoplankton die-off. Adequate dissolved oxygen concentration upstream of cages but low dissolved oxygen concentration in cages would indicate inadequate flushing for the density of fish in cages. Assuming that cages are designed and positioned properly, the obvious solution would be to lessen stock density.

Aeration is not a common practice in cage culture. Cages are open, water flushes through them rapidly, and dissolved oxygen added by aerators tends to be flushed out. Aeration has been used to avoid fish mortality in cages following dissolved oxygen depletion associated with thermal destratification. Plastic curtains can be installed, and during aeration, dropped along the outsides of cages to reduce water flow through them. A floating mechanical aerator is then operated in the cage (Fig. 27.11).

## Water and Sediment Quality in the Water Body

Nutrients in feeds that are applied to cages and not contained in fish at harvest enter the water body. Feed pellets not eaten by fish and feces quickly pass out of cages, and particles too large to remain suspended in the water settle to the bottom beneath or near cages. Fish excrete carbon dioxide, ammonia, and other metabolites that are soluble and pass into the surrounding water body.

The nutrient load imposed by cage culture is the amount of nutrients applied in feed minus the quantity harvested in fish over a specific time period. The *feed oxygen demand* of cage culture is calculated as shown on pages 142-144 in Chapter 11. Calculation of the pollution load from a cage culture operation is illustrated (Example 27.1).

There is no standard procedure for determining an acceptable, maximum daily feed input for a particular water body or site within that water body. There have been estimates that 2 to 5 kg feed applied daily to each hectare of water surface might not cause eutrophication in a lake or reservoir. However, lakes and reservoirs vary greatly in hydraulic retention time, depth, and ability to assimilate wastes. Natural and anthropogenic inputs of nutrients and organic matter also vary greatly among water bodies. Thus, assuming an average, acceptable daily feeding rate would be a risky way of establishing limits for cage culture.

**Fig. 27.11.** Floating, electric paddlewheel aerators in cages.

**Example 27.1**
**Calculation of the Pollution Load from a Cage Culture Operation**

A cage culture operation consists of several cages from which an annual production of 750,000 kg of fish is achieved at a feed conversion ratio of 1.80. The feed contains 45.0% C, 5.12% N, and 1.00% P, while the live fish contain 11.7% C, 2.25% N, and 0.80% P. The waste load is:

$Waste_{C,N,P} = Feed_{C,N,P} - Fish_{C,N,P}$

Feed C = 750,000 kg fish × 1.8 kg feed/kg fish × 0.45 kg N/kg feed = 607,500 kg
Fish C = 750,000 kg fish × 0.117 kg C/kg fish = 87,750 kg
Waste C = (607,500 – 87,750) kg = 519,750 kg C

Repeating the above for N and P gives:

Waste N = 52,245 kg
Waste P = 7,500 kg

The feed biochemical oxygen demand (BOD) is:

Feed BOD = (C waste × 2.67) + (N waste × 4.57)
Feed BOD = (519,750 kg C × 2.67 kg $O_2$/kg C) + (52,245 kg N × 4.57 kg $O_2$/kg N)
Feed BOD = 1,387,732.5 + 238,759.6 = 1,626,492.1 kg $O_2$.

Environmental monitoring provides a means for assessing changes in water quality over time to ascertain if eutrophication is progressing rapidly. The most important variables to monitor are patterns of thermal stratification, dissolved oxygen concentration at dawn in surface water, nitrogen and phosphorus concentrations, chlorophyll *a* concentration, and Secchi disk visibility. A decrease in the depth of the epilimnion, low morning dissolved oxygen concentrations, declining Secchi disk visibility, and increasing concentrations of nutrients and chlorophyll *a* suggest eutrophication (chlorophyll *a* concentration is an easily measured indicator of phytoplankton abundance). The relationship among concentrations of water quality variables and the trophic status of lakes is provided (Table 27.2). Ideal sites for cage culture would be oligotrophic or slightly mesotrophic water bodies. Eutrophic water bodies are not well suited for cage culture. However, cage culture in eutrophic and mesotrophic lakes and reservoirs usually is vigorously opposed by environmentalists on grounds that eutrophication will result.

When monitoring suggests that lakes are becoming more eutrophic, and effort should be made to lessen the input of nutrients. If cage culture is the main source of nutrients, fish producers should work together to reduce feed input. Ideally, a plan should be made to determine the acceptable amount of cage culture and allocate the amount among the different producers. Unfortunately, there are few good examples of how such a plan could work, and cage culture in many water bodies is largely uncontrolled.

Benthic impacts of cages can be minimized by fallowing for a few weeks to one year between crops to allow benthic communities to recover. Alternatively, cages may be moved to another site to allow benthic communities to recover. Methods for assessing benthic conditions include measurement of redox potential, organic carbon, abundance and composition of the benthos, and pictures or videos taken with an underwater camera to assess bottom condition.

**Table 27.2.** Trophic classification of lakes and reservoirs in relation to annual means of several variables.[4]

| Variable | Oligotrophic | Mesotrophic | Eutrophic |
|---|---|---|---|
| Total phosphorus (µg/L) | | | |
| Annual mean | 8.0 | 26.7 | 84.4 |
| Range | 3.0-17.7 | 10.9-95.6 | 16-386 |
| Total nitrogen (µg/L) | | | |
| Annual mean | 661 | 753 | 1,875 |
| Range | 307-1,630 | 361-1,387 | 393-6,100 |
| Chlorophyll $a$ (µg/L) | | | |
| Annual mean | 1.7 | 4.7 | 14.3 |
| Range | 0.3-4.5 | 3-11 | 3-78 |
| Secchi transparency depth (m) | | | |
| Annual mean | 9.9 | 4.2 | 2.45 |
| Range | 5.4-28.3 | 1.5-8.1 | 0.8-7.0 |
| Net primary production (mg C/m$^2$/day) | | | |
| Range | <300 | 300-1,000 | >1,000 |

# References

1. Schmittou, H. R. 1992. High density fish culture in low volume cages. American Soybean Association, St. Louis, MO.
2. Beveridge, M. C. M. 1984. Cage and pen fish farming. FAO Fisheries Technical Paper 255, Food and Agriculture Organization of the United Nations, FAO, Rome.
3. Boyd, C. E. 2010. Lake, reservoir characteristics affect cage culture potential. Global Aquaculture Advocate 13(5): 46-47.
4. Wetzel, R. W. 2001. *Limnology, 3rd Edition*. Academic Press, New York, NY.

# Chapter 28

# Recirculating Aquaculture Systems

## Introduction

Recirculating aquaculture systems confine aquatic animals in tanks at very high densities. Oxygenated water flows into the tank and water containing fish wastes flows out. A large portion of the water flowing from the culture tank is recycled back to the tank after dissolved oxygen is added and waste products are removed.[1]

Relative to other aquaculture systems, recirculating systems use little water from outside sources and wastes are concentrated into a small volume, allowing facilities to be located where water is scarce or where strict effluent regulations would preclude use of other culture systems. Predators and poachers can be excluded because the facility can be securely enclosed—usually indoors. Biosecurity measures to eliminate microbial pathogens are easy to implement because little water is exchanged with outside sources and overall system water volume is low. Recirculating systems offer flexibility in facility siting, allowing production near markets that may provide a better price for locally produced fresh products.

Despite numerous advantages, aquaculture production from recirculating systems is small relative to that from other culture systems, especially ponds. The expense of building and operating recirculating systems increases the cost of production to the point where many products cannot compete in the same markets as those grown in other systems. Carp, catfish, tilapia, trout, and salmon—which together comprise more than 90% of world finfish aquaculture production by weight—are usually grown at lower cost in other systems. Recirculating systems are currently used to produce specialty, high-value products (such as salmon smolts and ornamental fish) and fish for stock enhancement or restoration of threatened and endangered species. Recirculating systems also have been commercially successful where there is a dependable market for locally produced fresh fish that cannot be grown year-round in outdoor systems. For example, recirculating systems can be used to grow tilapia in regions with cold winters, trout in areas with warm summers, and marine species in inland areas.

## Water Quality in Recirculating Systems

Animals must be confined in recirculating systems at high densities and grown as rapidly as possible to offset relatively high costs of production. Rapid growth is obtained by providing high-quality feeds and maintaining, as nearly as possible, optimum environmental conditions for growth and health. Most important in this regard, water temperatures are controlled throughout the year. Past that, dissolved oxygen supply is the first water quality variable limiting production as culture intensity increases. After dissolved oxygen supply is increased, further increases in production are limited by accumulation of waste products, such as ammonia and carbon dioxide.

Rates of oxygen use and waste production can be estimated with good accuracy (Fig. 28.1), allowing precise design of engineering processes to recondition the water. Particulate solids are removed by clarifiers or filters, potentially toxic dissolved nitrogen compounds are transformed to nitrate by nitrification in biological filters, carbon dioxide is removed by gas strippers, and oxygen is added by aerators or oxygenators (Fig. 28.2).

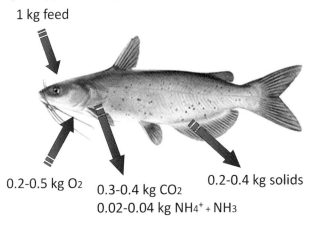

1 kg feed

0.2-0.5 kg O2    0.3-0.4 kg CO2    0.2-0.4 kg solids
0.02-0.04 kg NH4+ + NH3

**Fig. 28.1.** Ranges of oxygen use and waste production by fish as a ratio of amount of feed consumed.

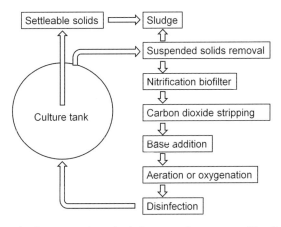

**Fig. 28.2.** Water flow and unit processes in recirculating aquaculture systems. Not all processes shown will be present in some systems and additional processes (nitrate reduction, for example) may be used in high-intensity systems.

Processes to control pH and alkalinity, remove nitrate and dissolved organic matter, and disinfect the water may also be required depending on system design, production goals, and the species cultured. In most facilities, monitoring and control devices oversee important processes so that environmental conditions never deviate from acceptable ranges.

There are great differences in engineering approaches to each process and in overall system design. There are, for example, many types of aerators, oxygenators, solids-removal filters, and biological filters (Table 28.1). The science of raising fish in recirculating systems is perhaps the best-developed aspect of aquaculture and excellent overviews of recirculating system theory and design are available.[1,2,3,4]

**Table 28.1.** Processes and examples of equipment used to control water quality in recirculating aquaculture systems.

| Process | Purpose | Equipment examples |
|---|---|---|
| Culture unit | Contain fish and collect settleable solids | Circular or octagonal dual-drain tanks<br>Linear flow raceways |
| Solids removal | Remove solids produced during grow-out | Low-flow center drains in culture tanks<br>Settling basins<br>Tube or plate settlers<br>Swirl separators<br>Microscreen filters<br>Floating bead filters<br>Foam fractionation |
| Biofiltration | Transform ammonia to nitrate | Rotating biological contactor<br>Trickling filters<br>Floating bead filters<br>Downflow bead filters<br>Fluidized sand filters<br>Moving bed filters |
| Aeration | Remove dissolved carbon dioxide and add dissolved oxygen by air contact | Mechanical surface agitators<br>Diffusers/bubblers<br>Packed columns |
| Oxygenation | Supersaturate water with dissolved oxygen by contacting water with pure oxygen | Diffusers/bubblers<br>U-tubes<br>Packed columns<br>Pressurized packed column<br>Oxygenation cones<br>Low-head oxygenators |

## Temperature

The ability to control water temperature at modest cost is a significant feature of recirculating aquaculture systems. Consistent water temperatures near the species' optimum allow rapid growth throughout the year. Temperatures can also be manipulated to control the reproductive cycle of broodstock. Temperature control is possible because low water volumes are exchanged with the outside environment and systems can be housed in well-insulated buildings. Depending on local climate and building design, waste heat produced by pumps in the system may be adequate to maintain temperatures for year-around production of warmwater fish in temperate climates. Boilers, heaters, heat pumps, and heat exchangers can be used to heat water if required.

Maintaining low water temperatures for culture of char, trout, or salmon in warm weather can be more challenging than raising warmwater fish in cold regions because waste heat generated by pumps may cause excessive water temperature increases in systems with low water exchange rates. Recirculating systems used to grow coldwater fish often use relatively high water exchange rates to dissipate waste heat.

## Solids

Waste solids include uneaten feed, fecal matter, and detritus derived from biofilm sloughed off the biological filter and other component surfaces. Solids production (dry weight) ranges from 20 to 40% of feed weight depending on species, animal size, feed formulation, and feeding practices. Oxygen is consumed and ammonia and carbon dioxide are produced as organic solids decompose. Rapid and effective solids removal is extremely important for efficient system operation, animal health, and reducing environmental impacts.[1,3,5]

For treatment purposes, solids are conveniently categorized as settleable solids, suspended solids, and dissolved solids. Settleable solids generally settle out of the water within 1 hour under non-turbulent conditions. Settleable solids should be quickly removed as they accumulate on the culture tank bottom. Using circular culture tanks with proper placement of double drains greatly enhances solids removal. Circular tanks have rotating flow that concentrates settled solids in the bottom center of the tank where they can be removed in a relatively low volume of water though a bottom-drawing center drain. Most of the tank overflow (containing suspended solids) leaves in a separate drain that may be located in the tank's center or along the tank sidewall. When properly designed, circular tanks with dual drains function effectively as swirl separators and are largely self-cleaning.[1,3,6]

Rapidly removing settleable solids from raceways or rectangular tanks is much more difficult than from circular tanks. Some of the solids moved along the raceway bottom can be collected and removed from quiescent zones at the end of raceway, but water velocities are too low to sweep all solids out of the raceway. Alternatively, solids can be kept in suspension by water currents or vigorous aeration and removed in a separate process external to the culture tank.

Settleable solids removed in the center, bottom-drawing drains of circular tanks or from quiescent zones of raceways can be further concentrated using settling basins or swirl separators. *Swirl separators*, or hydrocyclones, are sedimentation devices that inject water at the outside of the conical tank, establishing a spinning flow. Heavier solids move towards the walls and settle to the bottom where they are continuously removed. Swirl settlers work best to remove relatively heavy solids; the light solids generated in recirculating systems are less easily removed. The clarified water is then combined with the main flow stream leaving the tank.

After most of the settleable solids have been removed from flow exiting the culture tank, the remaining particulates—called suspended solids because they are not easily removed by settling—are removed by mechanical filtration. The most common filters used to remove suspended solids are microscreen filters and granular media filters (sand or pelleted media).

*Microscreen filters*, as the name implies, consist of a fine screen fabric that retains particles larger than the mesh openings. The most common variation is the microscreen drum filter (Fig. 28.3) where the screen forms the outside of a drum mounted in a tank. Recycled water flows by gravity into the inside of the drum and passes through the screen which removes particulate matter. Screens typically have openings of 60 to 100 μm. Clarified water is captured in the tank and leaves the unit by gravity flow. The drum rotates slowly or intermittently, and spray nozzles on the outside of the drum wash solids off the screen and into an internal collection trough leading to a waste drain. Drum filters rapidly remove solids from the recycled water, which reduces opportunities for decomposition or leaching. They are expensive but are the preferred solids-capture technology for large, commercial facilities because they have economies of scale and can be built to handle very high flows.

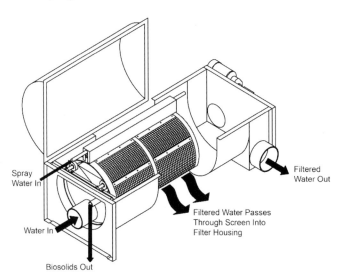

**Fig. 28.3.** Microscreen drum filter. Courtesy of PR Aqua, Nanaimo, British Columbia, Canada.

*Granular media filters* remove solids by passing water through a bed of plastic beads, sand, or diatomaceous earth. The solids are captured within pore spaces or adhere to the media. Filters eventually become clogged and require backwashing to expand the bed and release the solids. Sand and diatomaceous earth filters are seldom used in recirculating systems because they rapidly clog or foul with biological growth, requiring frequent backwashing and cleaning which wastes water. Floating bead filters, described below as a type of nitrification biofilter, are sometimes used in recirculating systems as a solids filter for relatively small flows.

## Dissolved Oxygen

For best growth, dissolved oxygen concentrations should be maintained above 4-5 mg/L for warmwater fish and above 6-7 mg/L for coldwater fish. Effective dissolved oxygen management in recirculating systems is critical because oxygen is consumed rapidly in the culture tank and even small reductions in oxygenated water inflow can cause rapid dissolved oxygen depletion and animal death. Recirculating systems have an additional dissolved oxygen criterion because nitrifying bacteria in the biological filter are aerobic and dissolved oxygen concentration in the filter must be maintained above 2.0 mg/L for efficient oxidation of ammonia to nitrate.

Oxygen consumption in recirculating systems is the sum of fish respiration, oxygen consumed by heterotrophic bacteria as they decompose wastes, and oxygen consumed by autotrophic nitrifying bacteria in the biological filter. Fish respiration ranges from 0.2 to 0.5 kg $O_2$/ kg of feed fed. In systems with poor solids removal, heterotrophic bacteria can remove an additional 0.5 kg $O_2$/kg of feed; in well-managed systems, it can be less than 0.1 kg $O_2$/kg of feed. Oxygen consumption by nitrifying bacteria varies with filter design, but a value of 0.2 kg $O_2$/kg of feed is representative. Overall oxygen consumption rates therefore vary from about 0.5 kg $O_2$/kg of feed in systems with efficient solids removal to more than 1.0 kg $O_2$/kg of feed when solids management is not good.

Oxygen can be supplied to culture tanks using aeration with atmospheric oxygen or oxygenation using a source of pure oxygen. Aerators increase oxygen concentrations only to near air-saturation levels (6 to 14 mg/L, depending on water temperature and salinity) and oxygen transfer efficiency decreases dramatically as dissolved oxygen concentration approaches saturation (see Chapter 13). To aerate water to levels near saturation therefore requires high energy input and, if the total oxygen demand of the system is high, large flows of water are needed to supply adequate oxygen. Increasing water flow requires larger pipes and pumps, and it also is costly. As such, aeration is practical only for systems with low to moderate fish biomass loading.

At high fish biomass loadings (generally above about 30 to 40 kg of fish/m$^3$), pure oxygen transfer technologies become more cost-effective than aeration. Well-designed oxygenators operated at atmospheric pressures can increase dissolved oxygen concentrations to levels nearly fivefold higher than aerators (air is about one-fifth oxygen). For example, at 20°C in freshwater, aeration can increase oxygen concentrations to about 9 mg/L, whereas oxygenation can increase concentrations to nearly 43 mg/L. In other words, the same mass of oxygen can theoretically be supplied in about one-fifth the water volume when pure oxygen technology is used rather than aeration. Dissolved oxygen concentrations can be increased even further when oxygenation equipment is operated at pressures greater than one atmosphere.

Air-stones and other diffusers are seldom used to deliver pure oxygen in culture tanks, except as emergency backups. Because of the short contact time for bubbles rising through shallow water in culture tanks, diffusers have relatively poor oxygen absorption efficiencies (oxygen absorption efficiency is the ratio of oxygen absorbed by water to amount of oxygen applied). Pure oxygen is expensive to purchase or generate, and for routine use it is imperative to attain high oxygen absorption efficiencies to reduce costs. Efficient oxygenation systems optimize the oxygen/water contact area and contact time. Modern oxygenation units designed specifically for aquaculture have excellent (75-90%) oxygen absorption efficiencies. The most common oxygenators used in recirculating aquaculture systems are packed columns, U-tubes, oxygenation cones, and multistage low-head oxygenators.[1,3] These devices are described in Chapter 13.

Oxygenation units are typically located just upstream of the culture tank so that other processes do not remove oxygen before it enters the tank. Oxygen-supersaturated water produced in the oxygenation process must be introduced into culture units at a controlled rate so that water with high total gas pressures in the flow is rapidly diluted throughout the culture tank to avoid gas bubble disease and loss of oxygen to degassing.

Although oxygenation is the most common technique used to provide oxygen in modern recirculating systems, aerators (such as packed columns; Fig. 26.4) are often used for the dual purposes of removing dissolved carbon dioxide and providing additional oxygen. Removing dissolved carbon dioxide may be necessary because pure-oxygen systems are ineffective at removing the gas, which may accumulate to high levels in intensive systems.

## *Ammonia, Nitrite, and Nitrate*

Ammonia is excreted from fish gills and produced when bacteria decompose organic matter within the system. Ammonia is toxic to most aquatic animals and toxicity increases at higher pH values because the un-ionized fraction is more toxic than the ammonium ion. Based on ammonia criteria for long-term exposures described in Chapter 16, total ammonia-nitrogen values should be maintained in the range of 1 to 2 mg N/L for pH values between 7 and 8, which is the range of pH values normally encountered in recirculating systems. Ebeling and Timmons[1] suggest that total ammonia-nitrogen should be maintained below 1 mg N/L for coolwater fish and below 2 to 3 mg N/L for warmwater fish. Lower total ammonia-nitrogen criteria will be needed if pH is consistently above 8. To maintain safe concentrations, ammonia must be removed from the culture tank at a rate equal to the rate of production within the system. Fish produce about 0.02 to 0.04 kg of total ammonia-nitrogen per kilogram of feed consumed, so the key is to define a production goal and then design an ammonia-removal process capable of removing all the ammonia that is produced during the period of highest feeding rates.

Bacterial nitrification is the most common method of removing ammonia from recirculating systems. This process—described in Chapter 16—consists of the sequential oxidation of ammonia to nitrite to nitrate by two groups of chemo-autotrophic bacteria. Nitrification is an acid-producing process, which has important implications for recirculating system management.

Nitrification occurs in biofilters, which are vessels filled with packing or media with a large surface area for nitrifying bacteria to attach and grow. All other conditions being equal, nitrification rate depends on the surface area available for attached growth. Accordingly, the medium should a high *specific surface area* (area per unit volume) to minimize biofilter size. However, water must pass through the filter easily and the filter must resist clogging, so the media must also have a high *void ratio* (the amount of space available for water flow through the media). The best medium must balance these two characteristics, as well as being inert, noncompressible, and non-biodegradable. Typical media include sand or plastic materials formed into beads, pellets, rings, plates or complex open shapes. Filters using fine media with high specific areas may be 'fluidized' by upwelling water or air bubbles to maintain adequate void space for good hydraulic performance. Six common biofilters are described below.[1,2,3,4]

*Rotating biological contactors* consist of a series of closely spaced, parallel discs mounted on a rotating shaft. The discs—usually corrugated to increase surface area—provide surfaces for attached growth and are partially submerged in a tank containing the recycled water. The discs rotate through the water and air. Exposure to air assures adequate oxygen for nitrification and rotation aerates water in the unit. Rotating biological contactors are simple and inexpensive to operate, but are costly to build. Over time, the biological film growing on the discs can become very heavy and may cause mechanical failure in poorly designed units.

*Trickling filters* consist of a column or tower filled with course plastic media. Recycled water sprayed over the top trickles through the media, which has a large void ratio. Air ventilated through the media provides oxygen for nitrification and also provides some aeration and carbon dioxide removal. Trickling filters are simple and have moderate capital and operating costs. However, they are relatively large, prone to clogging, and water flow through the filter can become channeled causing uneven water distribution and reduced nitrification efficiency.

*Floating bead filters* consist of a pressurized container filled with slightly buoyant plastic beads. Recycled water travels upward through the beads, which provide surface area for nitrifying bacteria and act as a mechanical filter for solids. The beads are periodically agitated by bubbles or propellers and then backwashed to remove trapped solids. Floating bead filters are compact, simple, relatively economical to operate, and provide the dual services of nitrification and solids removal. Combining nitrification and solids removal into one system component can also be a disadvantage because solids retained in the filter use oxygen as they decompose. If the system is operated improperly, nitrifying communities in the filter can become oxygen-limited and nitrification rates will be reduced.

*Downflow microbead filters* contain a bed of small (1- to 2-mm) polystyrene beads that float inside an unpressurized vessel. Recycled water is distributed over the top and trickles down through the bed. Downflow microbead filters are, in essence, a type of trickling filter, except the beads have a much higher specific surface area than traditional trickling filter media, which allows the filter to be smaller than comparable trickling filters. Downflow microbead filters are simple, energy efficient, and have low capital costs. They can be designed with a ventilated gas space above the microbead bed to provide aeration and carbon dioxide stripping.

*Fluidized sand filters* use finely graded sand as the medium for bacteria growth. Water is pumped upwards through the sand bed at a rate sufficient to lift and expand (fluidize) the bed. Turbulence within the bed abrades bacterial films on sand grains, making the filter self-cleaning. The fine sands used in fluidized beds have a high specific surface area, giving fluidized beds a high nitrification capacity in a compact unit. Filter sand also is also inexpensive. Disadvantages include the costs of pumping water to maintain adequate pressure to fluidize the bed and the lack of aeration within the unit.

*Moving bed bioreactors* are a hybrid between floating bead and fluidized sand filters. The beads are neutrally buoyant or slightly heavier than water, and are kept in suspension as water flows through the filter. The filter is aerated, which provides additional turbulence as well as some aeration and gas-stripping capability. The plastic media are larger than sand, so filters must be larger than fluidized sand units.

The ideal biofilter does not exist. All designs have advantages and disadvantages, and all the biofilters described above—and many others—have been used in recirculating aquaculture systems. Commercial recirculating systems must be operated at high biomass loadings to offset high capital and operating costs, and require compact, reliable, high-efficiency biofilters for cost-effective ammonia removal. Rotating biological contactors once were commonly used in recirculating aquaculture systems, but are not used in modern facilities because of size and high capital costs. Trickling filters and moving bed bioreactors provide nitrification and some aeration in one unit, but tend to be large and costly because the media used in those systems has a relatively low specific surface area. Current trends are to use bead or fluidized sand filters in large, commercial recirculating systems because they are compact and have high nitrification rates.

If the rate of the first nitrification step exceeds the rate of the second step, the intermediate product—nitrite—will accumulate. Nitrite is toxic to many fish species because blood-borne nitrite oxidizes hemoglobin to methemoglobin, which cannot transport oxygen. Nitrite toxicity, conditions that may cause nitrite accumulation, and methods of counteracting nitrite toxicity are discussed in Chapter 16.

Nitrate is the end production of nitrification and may accumulate within recirculating systems depending on the rate of dilution with makeup water. In systems with high rates of water reuse, nitrate concentration may reach 100 to 200 mg/L. Even higher nitrate concentrations occur if systems are operated with very low rates of water exchange to conserve water, heat, or salinity. Nitrate has low toxicity to most freshwater fish but some marine fish are much less tolerant. Further, effluent regulations may limit the amount of nitrogen discharged from facilities, and most of the nitrogen in recirculating systems will be in the form of nitrate. Although not widely practiced at this time, nitrate removal using denitrifying biological reactors may become more common as production intensifies and water-reuse rates increase.

Denitrification is the process where bacteria use nitrate as the terminal electron acceptor in respiration when oxygen is not available. The end product is nitrogen gas. Denitrification consumes acid and can offset some of the acid produced in nitrification (Chapter 16). Denitrification reactors consist of a container filled with a medium for bacterial growth. The reactors are operated in a flooded mode and anaerobic conditions are induced by flushing the reactor with nitrogen gas to displace oxygen or by operating the reactor with a long residence time so that bacteria consume all the oxygen in the feed water. Denitrification is a heterotrophic process and dissolved organic carbon availability limits denitrification rates in recirculating aquaculture. As such, an external carbon source (sugars or simple alcohols) is added to obtain adequate rates of nitrate reduction.[7]

## *Dissolved Carbon Dioxide*

Substantial respiration in indoor, water-recirculating aquaculture systems leads to high rates carbon dioxide production during fish respiration and decomposition of organic matter. Careful feeding and efficient solids removal can reduce the amount of carbon dioxide produced during organic matter decomposition.

Water exchange and vigorous aeration with air-contact aerators usually prevents dissolved carbon dioxide from accumulating to unsafe levels in systems with moderate fish loading densities. As system carrying capacity is increased by using pure-oxygen systems to overcome oxygen limitations, dissolved carbon dioxide problems may be because of the combination of high fish biomass, high levels of water reuse, and poor removal of carbon dioxide by oxygen-injection systems.

Carbon dioxide is difficult to strip from water because the gas is very soluble in water and its partial pressure in the normal atmosphere is low. In intensive aquaculture systems, dissolved carbon dioxide concentrations may be 25 to 100 times the concentration of dissolved carbon dioxide in water at equilibrium with the normal atmosphere (see Chapter 7), so large amounts of the gas can be lost from water during aeration. When carbon dioxide-supersaturated water droplets pass through air or when bubbles pass through water, gas lost from the water accumulates in the gas phase and carbon dioxide partial pressures can quickly rise far above that in normal air, especially if the volume of the gas phase is low compared to the volume of the liquid phase. When this happens, the carbon dioxide partial pressure gradient between water and air disappears and no more gas can be stripped from the water. Pure-oxygen injection systems work best as oxygenators when the ratio of the gas to liquid volumes is low; unfortunately, that also makes them inefficient at stripping carbon dioxide from water.

Carbon dioxide can be controlled in intensive culture systems using aeration devices that contact large air volumes with small water volumes (that is, the *gas-liquid ratio* is high).[8,9] In recirculating aquaculture systems, cascade-type packed-column aerators (see Chapter 7; Fig. 7.3) with large void volumes are often used to remove carbon dioxide. Columns are placed downstream of biofilters (where dissolved carbon dioxide concentrations are highest) and upstream of oxygenation devices (so that oxygen will not be removed in the degassing process). Columns work best with forced, counter-current air ventilation to maintain low carbon dioxide partial pressures in the gas phase by quickly removing the carbon dioxide-enriched off-gas. Off-gas from the column should be vented to the outside to prevent carbon dioxide from accumulating inside the building.

Carbon dioxide can also be removed from recirculation systems by adding sodium hydroxide (caustic soda), sodium carbonate (soda ash), or calcium hydroxide (hydrated lime).[8,10] Reactions of dissolved carbon dioxide with these chemicals are described in Chapters 7 and 21.

## pH and Alkalinity

The initial pH and alkalinity of a recirculating system depend on the quality of the water source and any amendments made to improve initial water quality. After fish culture begins, pH and alkalinity change in response to biological processes within the system. Dissolved carbon dioxide produced by respiring fish and microorganism causes pH to decrease, and the extent of pH reduction depends on the amount of carbon dioxide produced and the water's alkalinity (see Chapters 7 and 8). Dissolved carbon dioxide additions can depress pH to dangerous levels ($<$ pH 6) in waters of low alkalinity (see Example 7.1 on page 87), but this can be avoided by using aeration to strip carbon dioxide from recycled water and maintaining adequate alkalinity levels in the system.

Significant amounts of acid are produced in nitrification (see Chapters 8 and 16). Left unchecked, acid produced in nitrification will slowly destroy alkalinity and reduce pH. When nearly all of the alkalinity is destroyed, pH will then quickly fall to levels that can kill fish. Adequate bicarbonate alkalinity and pH levels above 7 must also be maintained for proper function of nitrification biofilters.

Total alkalinity should be maintained in the range of 50 to 100 mg/L as $CaCO_3$. Because alkalinity is constantly destroyed by acid produced in nitrification, it must be supplemented from outside sources—by addition of hydrated lime, quick lime, or sodium bicarbonate. Sodium bicarbonate (baking soda) is the safest and most convenient base, and simple methods are available to calculate dosages.[10,11] Rarely does makeup water contain enough base to satisfy the alkalinity requirement.

## Disinfection

Recirculating aquaculture facilities can be designed and managed to reduce the risk of introducing disease organisms from outside sources. However, if a disease outbreak occurs, it can spread rapidly throughout the facility because fish densities are high and culture tanks may share certain water treatment processes. Some chemicals used to treat fish diseases in other aquaculture systems are toxic to nitrifying bacteria within the biofilter and cannot be used in recirculating systems unless special precautions are taken to re-route water flows around the biofilter. Most commercial recirculating systems include continuous disinfection of the recycled water using ozone and ultraviolet irradiation.[3, 6]

Ozone is mentioned below as a treatment to remove dissolved organic matter. Ozone also has other positive effects on water quality, including oxidation of nitrite to nitrate. Although ozone is most often used to improve water quality—thereby providing indirect effects on fish health—ozone can also be used to disinfect water. Unfortunately, dissolved organic matter in recycled water expresses an 'ozone demand' and reduces the effectiveness of ozone as a disinfectant unless high levels are used. Several commercial ozone generators are available for recirculating aquaculture systems. Ozone is added in a contact chamber with adequate retention time to kill microorganisms. Residual ozone must then be destroyed or removed before water re-enters the culture tank because it is toxic to fish and crustaceans. Ozone is unstable and can be removed by allowing enough time for ozone destruction; ozone can be immediately destroyed by exposing water to intense ultraviolet radiation.

Ultraviolet (UV) irradiation kills microorganisms by denaturing DNA. Effectiveness depends on light intensity and exposure time. Light intensity decreases rapidly as it passes through water, particularly is the water contains dissolved or suspended organic matter. Ultraviolet disinfection units for recirculating systems have submerged, elongated UV lamps inside watertight quartz sleeves that are held within a small-diameter pipe so that water passes closely by the lamps. The quartz sleeve must be kept scrupulously clean to maintain high levels of disinfection.

### *Fine Solids and Dissolved Organic Matter*

Fine suspended solids (<50 μm) and dissolved organic matter are not removed by mechanical filtration and may contribute much of the total organic matter in the system, especially if the system is operated with high water reuse rates and solids are not efficiently and rapidly removed. These compounds cause the characteristic tea color of water in many recirculating systems. They express an oxygen demand, and certain dissolved organic materials may be harmful to fish at high concentrations.[12] Fine solids and some dissolved organic compounds can be removed by *foam fractionation* (also called protein skimming). In foam fractionation, air bubbles adsorb the materials and form a dirty foam at the water's surface. The foam and adsorbed material are then removed to a waste collection tank. Ozone can also be used to control these materials by oxidizing dissolved organic matter and flocculating fine solids, making them easier to remove by filtration.[3]

## System Design

The underlying principle for recirculating system design is that the effects of fish on water quality can be accurately quantified and a process can be designed to mitigate that effect. For example, dissolved oxygen consumption in the system can be estimated from the combined respiratory rate of fish and bacteria. Respiratory rate is based on known, empirical relationships with feeding rate because both fish and bacteria use oxygen to oxidize organic matter originating in feed—the only significant source of organic matter added to the system. If feeding rate is known, oxygen consumption rate can be estimated. An oxygenation system can then be designed to provide oxygen to match the consumption rate (in practice, designs have a safety factor and do more than merely offset calculated losses). The process of quantifying the amount of substance consumed and then matching that with an amount of substances added is called 'mass balance.' In the example above, oxygen is consumed in respiration and added in oxygenation. For wastes products, the equation is reversed: for example, ammonia is added by fish excretion and bacterial decomposition and it is consumed in the biofilter.

System design starts with identifying a production goal. For example, one may wish to produce 5 million kg of tilapia per year. Maximum daily feeding rate can then be calculated based on the production goal, production strategy (sequential single crops in one tank or staggered crops in multiple tanks), estimates of fish growth rate, and feed conversion efficiency. Maximum daily feeding rate is used to estimate maximum daily rates of oxygen use and production of ammonia, carbon dioxide and solids. These values are, in turn, used in mass balance equations to estimate process rates required to maintain oxygen, ammonia and carbon dioxide within predetermined limits[13] and to remove solid wastes. Ammonia removal rate in the biofilter determines the rate at which acid is produced in nitrification, which establishes the rate at which bases (such as sodium bicarbonate) must be added to stabilize alkalinity and pH. Fish growth rate and expected sizes at harvest can then be used to determine tank size, based on desired (or allowable) biomass densities. Biological activity is extremely high in recirculating systems and failure of filters, pumps, or other components can cause rapid water quality deterioration and crop loss. Ebeling and Timmons[1] present an excellent summary of the fundamental calculations needed to initiate the design process.

Selection of system components and integrating those components into an efficient, reliable system is challenging. Multiple solutions exist for each process (Table 28.1) and several combinations of components have been used successfully. Choice of components is based on species cultured, production goals, practical constraints, economics, and personal preference. Detailed information is available on system design[4] and only general guidelines for integrating components into an overall system are offered here:

- Dual-drain, circular culture tanks are highly preferred because a high percentage of total settleable solids can be quickly concentrated, collected, and removed before entering the rest of the system.

- Suspended solids should be removed from the recycled flow immediately after leaving the culture tank.

- Air-stripping to remove dissolved carbon dioxide should occur at the point where concentration is highest, which is immediately after the nitrification biofilter. Air-stripping should occur before oxygenation so that dissolved oxygen concentrations are brought to near saturation by aeration and expensive pure oxygen is used only to supersaturate the flow. Placing the aerator upstream of the oxygenator also prevents degassing of oxygen-supersaturated water, which would occur if the aerator was downstream of the oxygenator. Accordingly, air-stripping units are placed between the biofilter and oxygenation unit.

- Sodium bicarbonate or other bases added for pH and alkalinity control are best added immediately after dissolved carbon dioxide removal.

- Oxygenation should occur immediately before the recycled flow returns to the culture tank.

- Pumping should occur only once in each pass of recycled water through the system and pumps must be placed after the solids-removal process to avoid shearing solids into small particles that are difficult to remove by filtration. Flow between all other components should be by gravity to reduce costs and improve reliability.

- A system for continuous monitoring and control of critical processes should be part of all but the smallest recirculating systems. Facilities should also be equipped with a backup power supply, an emergency aeration system, and replacement parts for key components.

# References

1. Ebeling, J. M. and M. B. Timmons. 2012. Recirculating aquaculture systems, pages 245-277. In J.H. Tidwell (editor), *Aquaculture Production Systems*. Wiley-Blackwell, Ames, IA.
2. Summerfelt, S. T. 1996. Engineering design of a water reuse system, page 277-309. In R. C. Summerfelt (editor), *Walleye Culture Manual*. NCRAC Culture Series 101. North Central Regional Aquaculture Center, Iowa State University, Ames, IA.
3. Summerfelt, S. T., J. Bebak-Williams, and S. Tsukuda. 2001. Controlled systems: water reuse and recirculation, pages 286-395. In G. A. Wedemeyer (editor), *Fish Hatchery Management, 2nd edition*. American Fisheries Society, Bethesda, MD.
4. Timmons M. B. and J. M. Ebeling. 2010. *Recirculating Aquaculture, 2nd edition*. Cayuga Aqua Ventures LLC, Ithaca, NY.
5. Summerfelt, S. T. and B. T. Vinci. 2008. Better management practices for recirculating aquaculture systems, pages 389-426. In C. S. Tucker and J. A. Hargreaves (editors), Environmental Best Management Practices for Aquaculture. Wiley-Blackwell, Ames, IA
6. Losordo, T. M., M. M. Masser, and J. Rakocy. 1999. Recirculating aquaculture tank production systems: A review of component options. SRAC Publication No. 453, Southern Regional Aquaculture Center, Stoneville, MS.
7. van Rijn, J., Y. Tal, and H. J. Schreier. 2005. Denitrification in recirculating systems: Theory and applications. Aquacultural Engineering 34:364-376.
8. Grace, G. R. and R. H. Piedrahita. 1994. Carbon dioxide control, pages 209-234. In: M. B. Timmons and T. M. Losordo (editors), *Aquaculture Water Reuse Systems: Engineering Design and Management*. Elsevier, Amsterdam.
9. Summerfelt, S. T., B. J. Vinci, and R. H. Piedrahita. 2000. Oxygenation and carbon dioxide removal in water reuse systems. Aquacultural Engineering 22:87-108.
10. Bisogni, J. J., Timmons, M. B., 1994. Control of pH in closed cycle aquaculture systems, pages 235-246. In: M.B. Timmons and T.M. Losordo (editors), *Aquaculture Water Reuse Systems: Engineering Design and Management*. Elsevier, Amsterdam.
11. Loyless, J. C. and R. F. Malone. 1997. A sodium bicarbonate dosing methodology for pH management in freshwater recirculating systems. Progressive Fish-Culturist 59:198-205.
12. Colt, J. 2006. Water quality requirements for reuse systems. Aquacultural Engineering 34:143-156.

# Chapter 29

# Effluents

## Introduction

The world's population has been growing at a rapid rate for the last 100 years and there has been a corresponding increase in the demand imposed upon nature to supply resources and treat wastes. The World Wildlife Fund recently reported that it would take 1.3 earths to sustain the present global population at its current level of resource use. Unfortunately, at the present rate of human resource use and waste generation, the demand on the earth's resources will increase by 30% in the next four decades. Thus, environmental advocacy groups have initiated many programs to improve environmental awareness within private and public sectors. These efforts are probably a major reason for the willingness of many governments to focus more attention on environmental regulations and resource conservation.

Aquaculture has not avoided the scrutiny of environmentalists. The major concerns are wetland destruction, conversion of agricultural land to ponds, water pollution, loss of biodiversity, and excessive use of fish meal in feeds. Resources of the 'commons' are used by aquaculture and this has led to much discussion about possible negative socioeconomic impacts of aquaculture on rural communities in developing countries. Use of antibiotics and other potentially bioaccumulative chemicals in the culture of some species results in food safety concerns.

The list of resource-use, environmental, social, and food-safety issues is quite long. However, this book is about water quality in production systems and we will limit our discussion of environmental issues mainly to water pollution. This chapter will focus on aquaculture effluents and methods and approaches for minimizing waste discharge from aquaculture facilities into public waters.

## Culture Systems and Waste Discharge

As discussed in Chapters 3 and 4, organic fertilizers (manures and agricultural by-products), inorganic fertilizers, or nutrient-dense feeds are used to promote growth of fish, crustaceans, and other species. Only a portion of those inputs is recovered in the crop and—depending on the type of culture system—all or part of the remainder will be discharged to the outside environment. The pollution potential of feed-based aquaculture usually is much greater than that of fertilized ponds.[1,2]

The amount of waste produced by aquatic animals fed manufactured feed is approximately the same regardless of the type of culture system the animal is grown in. However, the amount of waste discharged from the facility into receiving water bodies varies greatly from one culture system to another. Cages and flow-through culture systems have very short hydraulic residence times and culture units have direct hydrological connections to effluent-receiving water bodies. As such, the potential for pollution is greater from these systems than for recirculating aquaculture systems and most ponds.

Effluent treatment is almost impossible in cage culture, and waste reduction relies on developing improved feeds and feeding practices. Nutrients and organic matter from feed that are not converted into fish biomass pass directly from cages into surrounding waters. Cage culture therefore has the greatest potential for causing pollution, although good site selection, periodic fallowing of cage sites, and good feed management practices can significantly reduce impacts (Chapter 27).[3]

In simple flow-through systems, water passes quickly through the culture unit and, as with cage culture, waste nutrients and organic matter are discharged directly into a receiving water body. However, flow-through systems offer greater opportunities for waste management than cages. In addition to reducing waste generation by using improved feeds and more efficient feeding practices, efficient (and relatively inexpensive) solids-removal technologies can be used to reduce waste discharge (Chapter 26).[4]

Most ponds have long hydraulic retention times and natural physical, chemical and biological processes assimilate wastes and lessen the proportion of feed wastes discharged into natural waters.[1] Suspended solids tend to settle to the pond bottom. Phytoplankton remove nutrients from the water, and bacteria decompose organic matter. Ammonia from animal excretions and bacteria degradation is lost from ponds by diffusion, converted to organic nitrogen in microbial biomass, and transformed to nitrate by nitrifying bacteria. Nitrate is converted to nitrogen gas through denitrification and lost to the air. Phosphorus is removed from water by microorganisms. It also is sequestered in sediment as relatively insoluble iron, aluminum, or calcium phosphates and as a component of dead organic matter. Practices that can reduce the pollution potential of pond effluents are discussed later in this chapter.

Recirculating aquaculture systems are similar to ponds in that most wastes produced during culture are treated within the facility rather than discharged directly to other water bodies. Whereas waste removal in pond systems relies on natural processes inherent in the pond ecosystem, wastes are removed from water-reuse systems by mechanical treatment or by chemical and biological processes that operate within discrete waste treatment units. Recirculating systems generate small volumes of concentrated waste that reduce the size and cost of wastewater treatment processes. In fact, it often is possible to discharge wastes directly to publicly owned treatment works. The high waste-capture efficiency of recirculating systems can be optimized by using high-quality feeds, efficient feeding practices, and good waste biosolids management (Chapter 28).[5]

# Waste Loads

The most common variables considered in discussions of aquaculture effluent quality are pH, dissolved oxygen, temperature, nitrogen, phosphorus, total suspended solids, 5-day biochemical oxygen demand (BOD$_5$), and salinity. Other variables may be used in place of salinity, such as total dissolved solids, specific conductance, or chloride. Most authorities recommend that the pH of effluents should not be below 6 or above 8.5, and effluents should not differ in temperature by more than 3 to 5°C from the receiving water, dissolved oxygen concentration should not be less than 5 mg/L, and brackishwater should not be discharged into freshwater. Common limits for other potential pollutants typically are 2 to 5 mg/L total nitrogen, 0.2 to 0.3 mg/L total phosphorus, and 20 to 30 mg/L total suspended solids and 5-day biochemical oxygen demand.[6]

Most of the effluent limitations are established in concentration units. This makes rule development and regulatory compliance monitoring easy but, from the standpoint of environmental protection, there is a serious disadvantage to using concentration-based limits for aquaculture effluents. The effect of effluents on receiving water bodies usually is related to the mass of pollutants added over time and not to the concentration of the pollutants. Also, compliance with concentration-based water quality criteria can be achieved by increasing inflow and flushing rate of culture units to reduce concentrations of potential pollutants by simple dilution, which does not reduce mass discharge.

Limits on daily loads of variables in an effluent sometimes are required in discharge permits. Load is calculated as follows:

$$\text{Load}_{Xe} \text{ (kg/day)} = (Q_e)(C_{Xe})(10^{-3} \text{ kg/g}) \tag{29.1}$$

where Load$_{Xe}$ = kg of pollutant X discharged per day; $Q_e$ = effluent discharge (m$^3$/day); $C_{Xe}$ = concentration of pollutant X in the effluent (g/m$^3$).

Waste loads vary greatly among aquaculture systems and calculating daily loads requires frequent monitoring of effluent volume and quality. An easier and more meaningful way of evaluating waste load from aquaculture is to estimate waste loads per metric ton (tonne) of production. With this information, it is possible to estimate waste loads that would be imposed upon receiving water bodies without resorting to effluent monitoring.[2] The procedure for estimating waste load indices depends on culture system type:

Watershed ponds and water reuse systems:

$$\text{Load}_{Xe} \text{ (kg/tonne)} = \frac{[(Q_e)(C_{Xe})(10^{-3})\text{kg/g}]}{P} \tag{29.2}$$

where Load$_{Xe}$ = kg of pollutant X discharged per tonne annual aquaculture production; $Q_e$ = effluent discharge (m$^3$/day); $C_{Xe}$ = concentration of pollutant X in the effluent (g/m$^3$); P = annual aquaculture production (tonne).

Raceways, embankment ponds, and ponds with water exchange:

$$\text{Load}_{Xe}\text{ (kg/tonne)} = \frac{\{[(Q_e)(C_{Xe})(10^{-3}\text{ kg/g})] - [(Q_1)(C_{Xi})(10^{-3}\text{ kg/g})]\}}{P} \qquad (29.3)$$

where $\text{Load}_X$ = kg of pollutant X discharged per tonne annual aquaculture production; $Q_e$ = effluent discharge (m$^3$/day); $C_{Xe}$ = concentration of pollutant X in the effluent (g/m$^3$); $Q_i$ = influent volume (m$^3$/day); $C_{Xi}$ = concentration of pollutant X in the influent (g/m$^3$); P = annual aquaculture production (tonne).

Cages and net pens:

$$\text{Load}_X\text{ (kg/tonne)} = \frac{\{[(F)(C_{Xf})] - [(B)(C_{Xb})]\}}{P} \qquad (29.4)$$

where $\text{Load}_X$ = kg of pollutant X discharged per tonne annual aquaculture production; F = feed used (kg); $C_{Xf}$ = concentration nutrient X in feed (decimal fraction), B = final animal biomass (tonne); $C_{Xb}$ = concentration of nutrient X in animal biomass (decimal fraction); P = annual aquaculture production (tonne).

Potential pollutant loads are provided for several species and culture systems in Table 29.1. Annually drained channel catfish ponds have much greater loads of total suspended solids, BOD$_5$, nitrogen, and phosphorus than ponds drained less frequently for harvest. When watershed ponds for channel catfish production are drained for harvest, the final 20 to 25% of discharge usually contains 75 to 80% of the loads of potential pollutants because harvest activities disturb pond bottom muds that contain large amounts of nitrogen, phosphorus and organic matter.[7] This pattern is not as pronounced during draining of embankment ponds, but there is a modest increase in the proportion of pollutants discharged during the final stage of draining.[8]

Waste loads for intensive shrimp ponds vary widely, with higher values for farms with high water-exchange rates (Table 29.1). Semi-intensive shrimp farms had greater BOD$_5$ loads than intensive farms—probably because the BOD$_5$ of pond water results mainly from phytoplankton. Semi-intensive ponds often have phytoplankton blooms nearly as dense as those in intensive ponds, but much lower shrimp production per unit of water volume—so production-based loads are higher. There were not great differences in nitrogen and phosphorus loads between intensive and semi-intensive ponds.

# Impacts of Waste Discharge

Water released from aquaculture facilities usually has relatively low concentrations of pollutants as compared to municipal sewage or industrial effluents. For example, pond effluents usually contain less than 20 mg/L BOD$_5$, while raw human sewage typically has a BOD$_5$ of 250 to 500 mg/L, and effluents from food processing operations have BOD$_5$ of 1,000 to 2,000 mg/L. In spite of low pollutant concentrations, aquaculture facilities often have large volumes of effluents that can lead to significant pollution loads.

**Table 29.1.** Approximate loads (kg/tonne) of annual production of potential pollutants from different aquaculture species and production systems. TSS = total suspended solids, $BOD_5$ = 5-day biochemical oxygen demand, TN = total nitrogen, TP = total phosphorus.

| Species and system | TSS | $BOD_5$ | TN | TP |
|---|---|---|---|---|
| Channel catfish | | | | |
|   Watershed pond | | | | |
|     Drained annually[7] | 2,300 | 40 | 20 | 0.8 |
|     Drained 6-8 years[6] | 190 | 13 | 7 | 0.7 |
|   Embankment pond | | | | |
|     Drained 6-8 years[6] | 70 | 6 | 5 | 0.2 |
| Shrimp ponds | | | | |
|   Intensive[9] | --- | --- | 25-120 | 15-40 |
|   Intensive[10] | 1,500 | 100 | 40 | 3 |
|   Semi-intensive[11] | --- | --- | --- | 8 |
|   Semi-intensive[12] | --- | 400 | 40 | --- |
| Rainbow trout | | | | |
|   Raceway[13] | 150-200 | --- | 40 | 7 |
|   Raceway[14] | 300-800 | --- | 50-100 | 5-20 |
| Salmon | | | | |
|   Cage[15,16] | --- | --- | 20-30 | 7 |
|   Cage[17] | --- | --- | 30 | 3 |
| Tilapia | | | | |
|   Cage[12] | --- | --- | 65 | 9 |

Impacts of waste discharge from aquaculture facilities vary from no impact to severe degradation of one or more aspects of water quality depending on production intensity, facility density, the hydraulic retention time and trophic state of receiving waters, and dilution rate. Effects often are difficult to discern because pollution loads tend to increase gradually, and negative effects are not observed until loads finally exceed the assimilative capacity of the receiving water, causing water quality to deteriorate. Potential adverse environmental effects include increases in phytoplankton abundance in response to elevated nutrient concentrations, increased variation in dissolved oxygen concentrations in response to increased phytoplankton abundance, increased frequency of dissolved oxygen depletion, reduced dissolved oxygen concentrations caused by the discharge of effluent with high biochemical oxygen demand, and changes to benthic communities caused by localized sedimentation of waste solids.

In many coastal areas, discharge from aquaculture production facilities represent one of many nutrient sources contributing to eutrophication and the relative contribution must be evaluated in terms of all sources and considered in the context of a watershed or whole-basin approach. In certain locations, particularly closed basins, aquaculture operations can be the primary contributor to localized eutrophication. The effects of effluent discharge tend to be localized near the discharge point. The susceptibility of receiving waters to eutrophication depends on trophic status prior to enrichment. For a given level of nutrient loading, oligotrophic waters are more susceptible to trophic state changes than mesotrophic waters. In general, nutrient enrichment is perceived to have negative consequences, although in some environments, eutrophication may be beneficial and perceived as desirable. The acceptability of changes in trophic state is a matter of perception, societal values, and policy.

Most discussions of waste loading from aquaculture consider the components of the waste stream (nutrients, organic matter, and so forth) but do not consider how the environment responds to waste loading. Aquatic environments have an inherent capacity to assimilate nutrients and other materials through well-known biological, physical, and chemical processes. In many areas, waste loading from aquaculture is low compared to the assimilative capacity of the effluent-receiving water body and no impact will be discernable. In some instances, aquaculture development may be so concentrated that much, or all, of the inherent assimilative capacity of receiving waters is used to remove wastes discharged by aquaculture facilities. Using public waters as a 'waste-treatment service' for aquaculture has been criticized on the basis that the cost of waste treatment is externalized by private operations and borne by society. The costs to society may include lower assimilative capacity for other potential pollutants (such as those from domestic or industrial wastewater), a degraded environment if the aquaculture waste discharge exceeds the assimilative capacity of the water body, and limits on options for other uses of the water (such as impacts on fisheries or recreational uses of the water). Fortunately, the negative environmental impacts of aquaculture can be avoided or lessened through selection of good sites, limits on production, and use of good management practices.[18,19]

# Managing Pond Effluents

Properly operated ponds have a high capacity for removing wastes produced during animal culture. Nevertheless, there may be ethical, marketing, or regulatory incentives for improving environmental performance of pond aquaculture by reducing waste discharge to an even greater extent. Four general approaches can be used to reduce quantities of substances discharged from ponds: 1) decrease waste production within the pond, 2) increase rate of waste treatment in the pond, 3) treat effluents after discharge to remove potential pollutants, or 4) reduce discharge volume. These options are described below.

It is important to recognize that ponds have two kinds of effluents and that treatment options depend on the type of effluent. One type occurs when water overflows from ponds when rainfall exceeds pond storage capacity or when water is pumped into the pond for intentional water exchange ('flushing'). The other type occurs when water is discharged intentionally when ponds are drained.

When rainfall exceeds pond storage capacity and causes ponds to overflow, the rate of water exchange during the event is usually low because the volume of most ponds is large relative to the volume of water added (except, however, for small ponds or prolonged, heavy rains). Therefore, the quality of most overflow effluents is similar to, or dilute, compared with water in the pond before the event causing overflow. Solids in overflow effluent are principally living and dead phytoplankton, suspended organic detritus, and finely divided clay derived from pond bank and watershed erosion. Because ponds act as their own settling basins and solids that settle rapidly are constantly removed from pond water, the solids that remain in overflow effluent have poor settling characteristics and are difficult to remove in post-discharge treatment. Reducing the volume of discharge is best accomplished by reducing effluent volume, reducing erosion, and using efficient feeding practices to reduce internal waste loading.

Quality, volume, and frequency of water discharged when ponds are drained are different from that discharged as overflow. Overflow effluents are unpredictable and discharge volume and frequency often are seasonal. Pond draining, on the other hand, is predictable and usually varies with the culture cycle. When ponds are drained, there are periods (often quite brief) when large amounts of solids from the pond bottom are discharged along with pond water. High-solids discharge may occur at the beginning of the draining process (when accumulated solids around the drain device inside the pond are dislodged) or at the end of the draining event (when harvest activities stir up pond bottom muds), or both. Water discharged during pond draining usually has much higher concentrations of solids, nutrients, and organic matter than overflow effluents.[7,8,20]

Frequency of pond draining depends primarily on the species or phase of culture. For some species, such as ornamentals and baitfish, crops are completely harvested annually (or more frequently) and ponds are drained to facilitate harvest and prepare the pond for the next crop. Ponds used to grow crayfish and juvenile phases of channel catfish and hybrid striped bass also are drained annually. In contrast, ponds used to grow food-sized channel catfish may be operated without draining for many years.

## Reduce Waste Production within Ponds

Despite the use of high quality manufactured feeds, relatively little of the nutrient content of the feed is ultimately converted to fish flesh and removed from the pond at harvest. Under commercial conditions, only about 10-15% of the carbon and 20-40% of the nitrogen and phosphorus in the feed is removed in animals at harvest (see Chapter 11). The remainder is the nutrient load to the ponds. Reducing the waste load in ponds can be accomplished by decreasing the amount of feed added to the pond or by increasing feed utilization efficiency.

### Feeding rates

Feed input is strongly correlated with deterioration of water quality in ponds. This relationship is thoroughly discussed in Chapter 11. In general, ponds with feeding rates less than approximately 30-40 kg/ha per day usually have few episodes of low dissolved oxygen concentrations. As feed inputs increase, phytoplankton abundance increases because feed wastes contain nutrients that stimulate plant growth and the need for mechanical aeration to offset dissolved oxygen deficits increases. When daily feeding rates exceed about 90 to 120 kg/ha, the capacity of the pond ecosystem to assimilate wastes is exceeded and metabolic byproducts such as ammonia and carbon dioxide may accumulate.[1] Poor water quality associated with excessively high feeding rates therefore affects animal health as well as increasing the pollutional strength of effluents.

*Feeds and feeding*

Considerable research has been conducted on methods of improving nutrient utilization in fish feeds with the goal of reducing waste production per unit of feed consumed. Most of the effort has concentrated on improving phosphorus utilization. There are obvious benefits of reduced waste phosphorus generation from fish cultured in facilities, such as raceways or cages, that discharge directly to the environment. However, the benefits of improved phosphorus utilization in static-water ponds with high fish densities are less clear. It appears that the reduction in phosphorus loading to the water possible by diet modification is overwhelmed by the complex fates of phosphorus within the pond ecosystem. As such, modest improvements in feed phosphorus utilization have not resulted in improved quality of potential pond effluents.[20] On the other hand, reducing waste nitrogen loading by increasing protein utilization efficiency or decreasing feed protein levels usually lessens the amount of total nitrogen (organic plus dissolved inorganic forms of nitrogen) in pond waters.[20]

The efficiency of feed utilization can be increased by using careful feeding practices. For example, improving the feed conversion ratio in channel catfish farming from 2.2 to 1.8 results in almost 25% less waste nitrogen added to ponds. Reductions in waste loading of this magnitude are possible by using improved culture practices, but are difficult to achieve simply by improving current feed formulations. Feeding fish more than they can consume in a relatively short period is wasteful and results in poor feed conversion. Because feed typically represents about 50% of production costs, inefficient feeding practices can have a profound effect on profitability. In addition, decomposition of uneaten feed exerts an oxygen demand and releases nutrients that contribute to the development of high phytoplankton abundance in the pond.

## Enhance Within-Pond Removal of Nutrients and Organic Matter

Natural biological and physicochemical processes within ponds act to reduce nutrient and organic matter levels in potential effluents far below the levels expected from the calculated mass balance of inputs and outputs. In effect, ponds act as their own water treatment system. Effluent quality could therefore be further improved if rates of these natural processes could be enhanced. Some approaches that have been examined include aeration to increase dissolved oxygen supply, precipitation of inorganic phosphorus from water using soluble calcium or aluminum salts; and use of bacterial or enzyme amendments (bioaugmentation).

*Aeration*

Mechanical aeration is usually the most important procedure for improving water quality in ponds. The primary goal of aeration is to prevent dissolved oxygen concentrations from falling to levels that negatively affect aquatic animal health, growth and survival. Aeration also reduces the pollutional strength of pond waters by increasing rates of organic matter decomposition in aerobic processes, increasing nitrification rate of ammonia to nitrate (which can then be lost from the pond through denitrification), and increasing the rate of phosphorus loss from pond water by maintaining a thin layer of oxidized surface sediment that prevents the release of orthophosphate from deeper, anaerobic layers of mud into the overlying water. The relationship between aeration and water quality is described in more detail in Chapter 13.

Despite the clear benefits of aeration, application of excessive aeration and circulation can have deleterious effects. Erosion of pond bottoms and levees by strong water currents produced by certain types of aerators can suspend large amounts of particles and potentially increase the suspended solid concentration in pond effluents.

*Phosphorus removal using chemical precipitation*

Alum (aluminum sulfate) is used in aquaculture to reduce clay turbidity (Chapter 15) and lower pond water pH (Chapter 8). Treatment of water with alum also quickly reduces the amount of phosphorus. Alum treatment increases the $Al^{3+}$ concentration in water, and $Al^{3+}$ quickly hydrolyzes to form flocculent aluminum hydroxide complexes of low solubility. Flocs of aluminum hydroxide adsorb phosphate ions and co-flocculate phosphorus-containing organic and inorganic particles. Phosphate is also removed by direct precipitation as low-solubility aluminum phosphate compounds.

In one study, treating channel catfish ponds with 20 mg/L alum (about 1.8 mg Al/L) reduced soluble reactive phosphorus concentrations by about 50% and total phosphorus concentrations by about 80%.[21] Despite the effectiveness in removing phosphorus, alum treatment has no residual activity and phosphorus concentrations quickly increase in aquaculture ponds in response to continuing inputs in feed. Frequent treatment would be needed for long-term control of phosphorus levels.

In naturally soft-water ponds, phosphate can be removed by increasing the concentrations of calcium, which forms poorly soluble calcium phosphates at pH values above neutrality. Gypsum is a relatively inexpensive and highly soluble source of calcium that has an advantage over alum because calcium is slowly lost from pond waters. As such, treatment of pond waters with gypsum should influence phosphorus levels for a longer period of time than alum treatment.[22] Note, however, that most of the phosphorus in aquaculture pond waters is present in the particulate organic fraction, principally inside living phytoplankton cells. Increasing the water hardness using gypsum will have little effect on phytoplankton abundance (and, by extension, total phosphorus concentrations) as evidenced by the fact that phytoplankton are abundant in nutrient-enriched waters with extremely high calcium concentrations.

*Bioaugmentation*

Static pond aquaculture is possible because the natural pond microbial community performs many of the functions required to maintain adequate environmental conditions for fish growth. These functions include the decomposition of organic wastes and the transformation and eventual loss of waste nitrogen from the pond. The central role of the microbiological community in pond ecology has led to the belief that water quality can be improved by augmenting the native microbial community with microorganisms produced in culture. As explained in Chapter 21, this approach to ecosystem manipulation—called *bioaugmentation*—usually fails to improve water quality in aquaculture ponds.

## *Treat Effluents to Remove Pollutants*

Many schemes for treating pond effluents or using the water discharged from ponds for a beneficial purpose have been proposed, including nutrient and organic matter removal by traditional wastewater treatment processes, use of water in hydroponics or to grow another crop of aquatic animal, use of water for irrigation of row crops or rice, treatment by wetlands and settling basins, and water reuse. It is important to emphasize that the intermittent nature of pond discharge and seasonal variation in discharge volume strongly impacts the cost and potential effectiveness of nearly all treatment options

Wastewater treatment procedures such as mechanical or biological filtration and activated-sludge processes are not economically feasible because the nutrient and organic matter concentrations in pond effluents are too dilute to make these treatment procedures effective. Another complicating factor is that average annual hydraulic loading to a treatment system will be low, but when discharge occurs, the volume may be large for a brief period. This is a difficult engineering problem because the treatment system must be designed to rapidly treat a large volume of dilute wastewater. The intermittent nature of pond discharges will also affect the economic performance of the treatment system because the system will be idle for many more days than it is used. In short, conventional wastewater treatment technologies are inefficient or too expensive to use with pond effluents.

Nutrients in fish pond effluents are not concentrated enough for use in hydroponics unless they are supplemented with additional nutrients, which defeats the purpose of using this procedure to treat effluents. Also, it is difficult to visualize hydroponics being developed to the scale where any significant proportion of the discharge from a large aquaculture facility can be treated in that manner. Filter-feeding fish and mollusks and certain plants have been successfully cultured in effluents, but this practice has seldom been economical (in part because of limited markets for the second crop), and it does not greatly improve effluent quality. Again, a significant limitation is the intermittent and seasonal nature of discharge.

The three procedures that have been considered for the treatment of pond effluents are wetlands, settling basins, and crop irrigation. Each of these three procedures has practical limitations.

### *Wetlands*

Using constructed wetlands to treat wastewaters is based on removal of nutrients and solids as the water is slowly passed through a shallow, vegetated impoundment. Nutrients are assimilated by wetland plants, removed by physicochemical processes (such as precipitation and adsorption reactions in the soil), and transformed and removed by biological reactions associated with the vast surface area provided by plant roots and above-ground plant biomass. Solids are removed by filtration and settling as water slowly passes through the system (Fig. 29.1).

Discharging pond effluents through wetland systems can significantly improve effluent quality, particularly when operated with long hydraulic retention times (2-4 days). Wetlands are relatively efficient in improving water quality even in winter when vegetation is dormant.[23] The disadvantage of constructed wetlands for treating aquaculture wastes is the large area necessary to provide adequate hydraulic retention time when the process is used on large farms. Economic studies show that constructed wetlands are one of the most costly treatment options for pond effluents, and they are not a feasible option for treating all of the discharge from fish farms.[24]

An alternative to using wetlands designed to treat all effluents from a farm would be to construct a small wetland to treat only the most concentrated effluents released when ponds are drained in the drier seasons—the time of greatest potential environmental impact because of low rates of dilution in effluent-receiving streams. In other words, effluents released during peak discharge periods would not be treated because of the large wetland area needed to provide an effective hydraulic retention time and the great dilution provided by high receiving stream flows. Using small wetlands to treat only the most concentrated effluents would minimize the land needed for constructed wetlands and significantly improve effluent quality during dry periods. However, the overall reduction in mass discharge of nutrients and organic matter, and the costs associated with this scaled-down approach are unknown.

**Fig. 29.1.** A constructed wetland used to treat effluents from a fish pond. The photograph was taken from the pond's dam. Water enters the center wetland cell near the bottom of the photograph, flow through the vegetation, and is discharged into the receiving stream hidden in the distant forest.

*Settling basins*

Settling basins are easier to construct and operate than wetlands because they do not have to be seeded with plants. More important, settling basins may be nearly as effective as constructed wetlands at removing potential pollutants from effluents discharged during pond draining, which often contain high concentrations of solids dislodged from the pond bottom by draining and harvest activities. Unfortunately, sedimentation may not be effective at removing potential pollutants from pond overflow because most of the solids, nutrients, and oxygen demand in those effluents is associated with phytoplankton that does not settle readily.

The feasibility of using settling ponds to treat effluents from pond draining alone or effluent from pond draining and storm overflow was studied for climate and soil conditions in Alabama.[25] Calculations were based on a settling pond with mean depth of 1.1-m and an 8-hr hydraulic retention time. Average settling basin areas to treat effluents from pond draining alone are 0.25 ha per ha of embankment pond and 0.28 ha per ha of watershed pond. Watershed ponds tend to be slightly deeper than levee ponds, which accounts for the need for a larger settling pond on a per-ha of production pond basis. Because of the effect of watershed area on runoff volume, settling pond areas required to retain and treat overflow from storms are much greater for watershed ponds than for levee ponds. For levee ponds, settling pond areas (per ha of production pond area) are 0.07 ha for rainfall from a 25-year storm, 0.08 ha for a 50-year storm, and 0.09 ha for a 100-year storm. Settling pond areas (per ha of production pond area) for watershed ponds are 0.43 ha for rainfall from a 25-year storm, 0.50 ha for a 50-year storm, and 0.57 ha for a 100-year storm.

Estimates of settling pond size were then used to calculate settling pond areas needed to treat draining effluent or draining effluent plus storm overflow for catfish farms of various sizes.[16] Percentages of the farm area devoted to settling ponds for draining effluent from levee ponds ranged from 0.7% for a 200-ha farm to 14% for a 10-ha farm. The corresponding range for watershed ponds is 0.8% to 15%. To treat overflow from a 25-year storm on farms greater than 25-ha, settling ponds would constitute 7% of the farm area for levee ponds and 43% of the farm area for watershed ponds.

Most catfish farms in Alabama extend downslope on watersheds to streams or property lines, which precludes installation of settling ponds unless existing ponds are taken out of production and reconfigured as settling ponds. Even where space is available, land and construction costs for settling ponds large enough to treat draining and overflow effluents usually are prohibitive for nearly all practical applications and that requiring their use would impose a disproportionate burden on small farms.[25,26]

For watershed ponds that must be partially drained to facilitate fish harvest, another possible approach—and one that does not require additional investment—is simply using the production pond as its own settling basin. When ponds are drained during fish harvest, most of the solids, organic matter, and nutrients are released in the last 20% of water discharged from ponds. So, when ponds are drained, the final volume of water may be held in the pond for 2 to 3 days to allow solids to settle before draining completely. Holding this last portion of water without discharge is even more desirable and can further minimize the potential environmental impacts of fish pond effluents.

Alternatively, the last 20% of water discharged from ponds can be held in farm drainage ditches for settling prior to final discharge.

*Crop irrigation*

Most pond aquaculture is practiced in areas already used for crop agriculture. As such, it appears logical that pond effluents could be used to irrigate terrestrial crops. The primary goal of integrating aquaculture and terrestrial agriculture would be to make productive use of pond effluents by supplementing the water supply for irrigation. Nutrients in the pond effluent might also be beneficial to the crop.

Using aquaculture pond water for irrigation is often not practical because peak water demand for irrigation (during droughts, for example) occurs at the time when there is little or no overflow from most fish ponds. Also, in some types of irrigation (such as flooding of rice fields), water is needed quickly, in relatively large volumes, and at a specific time—which may or may not correspond to the availability of water from fish ponds. Rapid delivery of large water volumes would require installation of large pumps and water distribution systems to convey water where it is to be applied in the required amounts. Nevertheless, when irrigation demand matches water availability from aquaculture ponds, irrigation can be an excellent use of water that might otherwise be a pollution problem.

## Reduce Effluent Volume

Effluent regulations often place limits on concentrations of potential pollutants that can be discharged. As explained above, a serious problem with concentration-based rules is that highly concentrated pollutants may be harmless if the volume of effluent is small, whereas dilute pollutants might be harmful if large volumes are discharged. In that respect, mass discharge—the product of concentration and volume discharged over time—is usually more important than concentration alone in determining the impact of an effluent on the environment.

From the discussion above, it should be obvious that reducing pollutant concentrations in pond effluents is difficult or expensive. Production of waste nutrients and organic matter is the inevitable consequence of using manufactured feeds to promote aquaculture production and short of drastic reductions in feeding rate—with concomitant reductions in animal production—little can be done to reduce internal nutrient loading. Further, the nature of pond effluents (dilute and intermittent) presents serious engineering challenges for post-discharge treatment. Overall, it is usually easier to reduce mass discharge by lessening discharge volume than it is to lessen waste concentrations.[19,27]

As mentioned above, total effluent volume consists of water discharged during intentional water exchange, water that overflows unintentionally during periods of excess rainfall, and water discharged when ponds are drained. All three sources of effluent can be controlled to some extent.

*Reducing overflow during water exchange*

Water exchange is a common practice in many aquaculture ponds and water lost during 'flushing' can constitute a substantial percentage of overall effluent volume. Displaced pond water represents a pollution load to receiving waters and consumptive use of a valuable resource. Furthermore, pumping requires energy and adds to the cost of growing the aquaculture crop. Accordingly, high rates of water exchange should not be used unless absolutely necessary. If water exchange is practiced as a dissolved oxygen management tool, pond aeration or mixing should be considered as a preferable option. Where technically feasible, discharged water should be circulated between a treatment or reservoir pond and production ponds.[18,19]

*Reducing overflow caused by excessive rainfall*

Although rainfall cannot be influenced by fish farmers, a degree of control can be exerted on the volume of overflow released from ponds as a result of rainfall. Overflow volume can be dramatically reduced simply by not refilling ponds completely when water is added to replace evaporation and seepage losses. This leaves some storage capacity in the pond so that rainfall is captured rather than allowed to overflow.[28] Maintaining storage capacity in ponds not only conserves water by capturing rainfall, but also reduces effluent volume and waste discharge. In one study, maintaining 7.5-cm of storage capacity in channel catfish embankment ponds in Mississippi reduced annual discharge of total nitrogen, total phosphorus, and organic matter by 70% compared with ponds not managed for rainfall storage.[27]

*Reducing water discharged during pond draining*

It is impossible to conduct pond aquaculture without occasionally draining the pond. Most commonly, ponds are drained to facilitate complete harvest of the aquaculture crop. Production schemes have, however, been developed for some species that allow multiple crops to be grown without draining the pond.[19,27] Using such systems dramatically reduces effluent volume and when natural microbial and physicochemical processes act over the long hydraulic retention time, a large proportion of the total waste loading to the pond is removed before water is discharged.

When it is necessary to completely drain ponds, it is may be possible to pump or drain water into adjacent ponds and store it. The water could then be drained or pumped back into an empty pond for reuse. On large farms, it may be possible to transfer water to a storage reservoir. Water quality would improve over time in the storage reservoir through natural water purification processes, and the water could then be reused.[18,19]

# Management Practices to Reduce Environmental Impacts

The unique nature of pond aquaculture poses challenges for effluent management. Reduction of discharge volume should be an important part of any set of best management practices for pond aquaculture because it is technologically difficult to achieve significant reductions in the concentrations of potential pollutants prior to discharge and most post-discharge treatment options are economically impractical. Aside from the obvious benefit of decreasing overall mass discharge, reducing discharge volume also conserves water and increases hydraulic retention time. Given a longer retention time, natural biological, chemical, and physical processes are provided a greater period of time in which to remove nutrients and organic matter from water before it is discharged. As such, a smaller percentage of the waste loading to ponds enters is actually discharged.

Below is a list of recommended management practices that will make farm operations more efficient and provide environmental protection.[1,18,19,29] A variety of culture techniques and culture facilities are used in pond aquaculture, so some practices may not be practical or economically justified in all situations.

## *Pond Operation and Management*

- Operate food-fish production ponds for several years without draining.

- Capture rainfall to reduce effluent volume.

- Eliminate or reduce water exchange.

- Use high-quality feeds and efficient feeding practices.

- Manage within the pond assimilative capacity.

- Provide adequate aeration and circulation of pond water.

- Position mechanical aerators to minimize erosion.

## *Harvest and Draining Practices*

- Allow solids to settle before discharging water.

- Reuse water that is drained from ponds.

- Treat pond effluents in constructed wetlands or settling basins prior to discharge.

- Use effluents to irrigate terrestrial crops.

## *Pond Construction and Renovation Practices*

- Optimize the ratio of watershed to pond area.

- Divert excess runoff from large watersheds away from ponds.

- Construct ditches to minimize erosion and establish plant cover on banks.

- Protect embankments in drainage ditches from erosion.

- Maintain plant cover on pond watersheds.

- Avoid leaving ponds drained in winter, and close valves once ponds are drained.

- Close drain valves when renovating ponds.

- Use sediment from within the pond to repair levees rather than disposing it outside of ponds.

- During pond renovation, excavate to increase operational depth, permitting increased water storage and greater fluctuation in water level.

# Effluent Regulations and Environment Stewardship Programs

## *Governmental Regulations*

Most governments have an agency responsible for water pollution abatement. Procedures used to establish and enforce regulations differ from country to country, but most countries focus more attention on municipal and industrial effluents than on agricultural and aquacultural effluents. In fact, effluent regulations are only beginning to be imposed on aquaculture in most countries. The United States is a good example; the United States Environmental Protection Agency (USEPA) only recently published a national aquaculture effluent rule.[30] The USEPA aquaculture effluent rule exempts operations not classified as concentrated aquatic animal production facilities (CAAPF). The definition of a CAAPF differs between coldwater and warmwater aquaculture, but it is based primarily on annual amount of production and frequency of discharge (Table 29.2). The discharge frequency provision of the definition is unclear, because USEPA failed to define excess runoff.

An aquaculture operation qualifying as a CAAPF must obtain a National Pollutant Discharge Elimination System (NPDES) permit. The USEPA makes effluent rules on an industry-by-industry basis, and for most industries, the rule will specify effluent limitation guidelines or limits on concentrations or loads of specific water quality variables allowed in effluents. For example, the rule for a particular industry might specify: pH 6-8.5; dissolved oxygen, >5 mg/L, 5-day biological oxygen demand, <30 mg/L; total dissolved solids <30 mg/L.

The USEPA aquaculture effluent rule did not specify effluent limitation guidelines. The reason for this approach seemed to be that there was no strong evidence that aquaculture effluents were contributing significantly to pollution to waters of the United States and that treatment of aquaculture effluents by standard wastewater treatment methodology would not be cost effective. The USEPA recommended the use of best management practices (BMPs) to reduce the volume and improve the quality of aquaculture effluents.[1]

Most states are NPDES-delegated meaning that federal effluent rules are enforced by the individual states. Although the USEPA aquaculture rule must be enforced by states, if individual states desire, they can impose stricter requirements than necessary for compliance with the federal rule. For example, individual states could require effluent limitations in permits for ponds classified as CAAPFs despite there being no effluent limitation guidelines for ponds in the USEPA rule.

There has been relatively little enforcement of the USEPA aquaculture effluent rule in most states. However, even before the USEPA finalized the aquaculture effluent rule, some states such as California, Idaho, and Texas already required aquaculture facilities to obtain effluent discharge permits.

The Food and Agriculture Organization (FAO) of the United Nations website describes environmental regulations for aquaculture for 47 countries—most major aquaculture countries are included. These country-level programs almost all include effluent standards, but it is not known how vigorously they are enforced, especially in developing countries.[31]

Environmental non-governmental organizations (NGOs) do not trust governments to adequately regulate potential pollution, including that from aquaculture effluents. They apparently feel that in developed countries, the aquaculture industry is able to influence rule making and enforcement policy. Moreover, they seem to think that governments of developing countries will not seriously enforce aquaculture regulations because of fear that export income would decline as a result.

**Table 29.2.** United States Environmental Protection Agency definitions of warmwater and coldwater concentrated aquatic animal production (CAAP) facilities.

| Warmwater CAAP Facilities |
|---|
| Includes ponds, raceways, or other similar structures which discharge at least 30 days per year but does not include: |
| • Closed ponds which discharge only during periods of excess runoff |
| • Facilities which produce less than 45,454 harvest weight kilograms per year |
| Coldwater CAAP Facilities |
| Includes ponds, raceways, or other similar structures which discharge at least 30 days per year but does not include: |
| • Facilities which produce less than 9,090 harvest weight kilograms per year |
| • Facilities which feed less than 2,272 kg during month of maximum feeding |

## Voluntary BMPs

In response to pressure from environmental NGOs, the aquaculture industry has taken actions that go beyond governmental requirement as a proactive measure to protect their image with consumers. Aquaculture associations, governmental agencies that support aquaculture, and international development organizations have worked with aquaculture producers to improve environmental stewardship. The main approach has been to promote aquaculture BMPs for voluntary adoption by producers. Education of producers on the need for better practices and gradual but widespread adoption of better practices by the industry is likely the most effective way of improving the environmental performance of aquaculture.[32] Of course, environmentalists do not approve of voluntary adoption programs because it is difficult to evaluate the degree of adoption of such programs or to determine their effectiveness.

## Buyer Specifications

Some large seafood buyers such as supermarket and restaurant chains have developed specifications for purchasing aquaculture products. These companies develop production standards that require aquaculture species to be reared by techniques that are environmentally acceptable to companies' customer bases. Aquaculture producers are found who are willing to comply with buyer standards, and agree to periodic inspections of facilities to verify compliance. These buyer programs contain specifications related to effluents—either BMPs or effluent quality standards.

## Eco-Label Certification

Several organizations have developed eco-label certification standards for aquaculture products.[33] These programs are designed to cover the entire range of environmental, resource use, social, and food safety issues discussed in the introduction, and they all have standards for effluents. In some programs, compliance with the effluent standards may be implementation of specific best management practices, but other eco-label programs may contain effluent limitation guidelines.

The Global Aquaculture Alliance's *Best Aquaculture Practices* (BAP) program and the Global GAP program have probably developed eco-label standards for more species and certified more production facilities than other eco-label certification programs. The BAP standards include effluent standards with water quality concentration limits (Table 29.3). Water samples must be collected and analyzed according to specific instructions (http://gaalliance.org/bap/standards.php) at 3-month intervals in order to demonstrate compliance with the limits and maintain good standing in the program. The guidelines for the BAP program include suggestions for changes in production practices and farm management that will assist producers in complying with the effluent standards. The Global GAP program relies mostly on record-keeping and does not have particularly strong water quality standards.

Environmental NGOs do not trust the GAA and other private organizations that are working on eco-label certification. They do not believe that the methods used for developing standards involve all stakeholders, and they do not believe that certifiers will be objective. Nevertheless, the World Wildlife Fund, a well-known NGO with a long history of involvement in international food production, through its Aquaculture Dialogues developed aquaculture eco-label certification standards—including effluent standards—for several internationally-traded species. These standards are used by an aquaculture eco-label certification program called the Aquaculture Stewardship Council. The program is growing and will no doubt compete with the GAA program of BAP certification and Global GAP certification.

**Table 29.3.** Effluent limitation guidelines of the Global Aquaculture Alliance shrimp certification standards.[4]

| Variable (units) | Initial standard | Target standard | Measurement frequency |
|---|---|---|---|
| pH (standard units) | 6.0-9.5 | 6.0-9.0 | Monthly |
| Total suspended solids (mg/L) | 100 or less | 50 or less | Quarterly |
| Soluble phosphorus (mg/L) | 0.5 or less | 0.3 or less | Monthly |
| Total ammonia nitrogen (mg/L) | 5 or less | 3 or less | Quarterly |
| 5-day biochemical oxygen demand (mg/L) | 50 or less | 30 or less | Quarterly |
| Dissolved oxygen (mg/L) | 4 or more | 5 or more | Monthly |
| Salinity (ppt) | No discharge of water above 1.5 ppt salinity into freshwater[a] | No discharge of water above 1.5 ppt salinity into freshwater[a] | Monthly |

[a]Freshwater is defined as water less than 1 ppt salinity or specific conductance less than 1,500 μmhos/cm.

# References

1. Boyd, C. E. and C. S. Tucker. 1998. *Pond Aquaculture Water Quality Management*. Kluwer Academic Publishers, Boston, MA.
2. Boyd, C. E., C. Tucker, A. McNevin, K. Bostick, and J. Clay. 2007. Indicators of resource use efficiency and environmental performance in aquaculture. Reviews in Fisheries Science 15:327-360.
3. Belle, S. M. And C. E. Nash. 2008. Better management practices for net-pen aquaculture, pages 261-330. In: C. S. Tucker and J. A. Hargreaves (editors), *Environmental Best Management Practices for Aquaculture*. Wiley Blackwell, Ames, IA.
4. Fornshell, G. And J. M. Hinshaw. 2008. Better management practices for flow-through aquaculture systems, pages 331-388. In: C. S. Tucker and J. A. Hargreaves (editors), *Environmental Best Management Practices for Aquaculture*. Wiley Blackwell, Ames, IA.
5. Summerfelt, S. T. And B. J. Vinci. 2008. Better management practices for recirculating aquaculture systems, pages 389-426. In: C. S. Tucker and J. A. Hargreaves (editors), *Environmental Best Management Practices for Aquaculture*. Wiley Blackwell, Ames, IA.
6. Boyd, C.E. 2000. *Water Quality, An Introduction*. Kluwer Academic Publishers, Boston, MA.
7. Schwartz, M. F. and C. E. Boyd. 1994. Effluent quality during harvest of channel catfish from watershed ponds. Progressive Fish-Culturist 56:25-32.

8. Hargreaves, J. A., C. S. Tucker, and S. K. Kingsbury. 2005. Pattern of discharge and mass loading during drainage of excavated ponds used for foodfish production of channel catfish. North American Journal of Aquaculture 67:79-85.

9. Lin, C. K., P. Ruamthaveesub, and P.Wanuchsoontorn. 1993. Integrated culture of the green mussel (*Perna viridis*) in wastewater from an intensive shrimp pond: Concept and practice. World Aquaculture 24(2):68-72.

10. Dierberg, F. E. and W. Kiattisimkul. 1996. Issues, impacts, and implications of shrimp aquaculture in Thailand. Environmental Management 20:649-666.

11. Boyd, C. E., K. Corpron, E. Bernard, and P. Pensang. 2006. Estimates of bottom soil and effluent load of phosphorus at a semi-intensive marine shrimp farm. Journal of the World Aquaculture Society 37:41-47.

12. Boyd, C.E. Unpublished data.

13. Bergheim, A., and A. Brinker. 2004. Effluent treatment for flow-through systems and European environmental regulations. Aquacultural Engineering 27:61-77.

14. Axler, R. P., C. Tikkanen, J. Henneck, J. Schuldt, and M. E. McDonald. 1997. Characteristics of effluent and sludge from two commercial rainbow trout farms in Minnesota. Progressive Fish-Culturist 59:161-172

15. Johnsen, F. and A.Wandsvik. 1991. The impact of high energy diets on pollution control in the fish farming industry, pages 51-62. In: C. B. Cowey and C. Y. Cho (editors), *Nutritional Strategies and Aquaculture Waste, Proceedings of the First International Symposium on Nutritional Strategies in Management of Aquaculture Waste*. University of Guelph, Ontario, Canada.

16. Johnsen, R. I., O. Grahl-Nelson, and B. T. Lunestad. 1993. Environmental distribution of organic waste from a marine fish farm. Aquaculture 118:229-244.

17. Hardy, R. W. 2001. Urban legend: are we one? Aquaculture Magazine 27(7):52-56.

18. Boyd, C. E. 2008. Better management practices for marine shrimp aquaculture, pages 227-260. In: C. S. Tucker and J. A. Hargreaves (editors), *Environmental Best Management Practices for Aquaculture*. Wiley Blackwell, Ames, IA.

19. Tucker, C.S., J.A. Hargreaves, and C.E. Boyd. 2008. Better management practices for freshwater pond aquaculture, pages 151-226. In: C. S. Tucker and J. A. Hargreaves (editors), *Environmental Best Management Practices for Aquaculture*. Wiley Blackwell, Ames, IA.

20. Tucker, C. S., C. E. Boyd, and J. A. Hargreaves. 2002. Characterization and management of effluents from warmwater aquaculture ponds, pages 35-76. In: J. R. Tomasso (editor), *Aquaculture and the Environment in the United States*. World Aquaculture Society, Baton Rouge, LA.

21. Masuda, K. and C. E. Boyd. 1994. Effects of aeration, alum treatment, liming, and organic matter applications on phosphorus exchange between pond soil and water in aquaculture ponds. Journal of the World Aquaculture Society 25:405-416.

22. Wu, R. and C. E. Boyd. 1990. Evaluation of calcium sulfate for use in aquaculture ponds. Progressive Fish Culturist 52:26-31.

23. Schwartz, M. F. and C. E. Boyd. 1995. Constructed wetlands for treatment of channel catfish pond effluents. Progressive Fish-Culturist 57:255-266.

24. Kouka, P.-J. and C. R. Engle. 1996. Economic implications of treating effluents from catfish production. Aquacultural Engineering 15:273-290.

25. Boyd, C. E. and J. F. Queiroz. 2001. Feasibility of retention structures, settling basins, and best management practices for Alabama channel catfish farming. Reviews in Fisheries Science 9(2):43-67.

26. Engle, C. R. and D. Valdarrama. 2003. Farm-level costs of settling basins for treatment of effluents from levee-style catfish ponds. Aquacultural Engineering 28:171-199.

27. Tucker, C. S., S. K. Kingsbury, J. W. Pote, and C. L. Wax. 1996. Effects of water management practices on discharge of nutrients and organic matter from channel catfish (*Ictalurus punctatus*) ponds. Aquaculture 147:57-69.

28. Pote, J. W., C. L. Wax, and C. S. Tucker. 1988. Water in catfish production: sources, uses, conservation. Special Bulletin 88-3, Mississippi Agricultural and Forestry Experiment Station, Mississippi State University, MS.

29. Tucker, C. S. and J. A. Hargreaves. 2003. Management of effluents from channel catfish (*Ictalurus punctatus*) embankment ponds in the southeastern United States. Aquaculture 266:5-21.

30. Federal Register. 2004. *Effluent Limitation Guidelines and New Source Performance Standards for the Concentrated Aquatic Animal Production Point Source Category: Final Rule.* Federal Register:August 23, 2004, Vol. 69, Number 162, pages 51,892-51,930. Office of the Federal Register, National Archives and Records Administration, Washington, DC.

31. Boyd, C. E. and A. McNevin. 2011. An early assessment of the effectiveness of aquaculture certification and standards. Report to RESOLVE, Washington, DC.

32. Clay, J. 2008. The role of better management practices in environmental management, pages 55-72. In: C. S. Tucker and J. A. Hargreaves (editors), *Environmental Best Management Practices for Aquaculture.* Wiley Blackwell, Ames, IA.

33. Boyd, C. E. 2008. Better management practices in international aquaculture, pages 73-90. In: C. S. Tucker and J. A. Hargreaves (editors), *Environmental Best Management Practices for Aquaculture.* Wiley Blackwell, Ames, IA.

# Chapter 30

# Volume Measurements and Calculations

## Introduction

Evaluations of source water requirements and calculations of water exchange rates, doses of pond amendments, volumes of effluents, and other water quantity-related variables often are made in aquaculture. Measurements of some water quantity variables were discussed in previous chapters—especially Chapter 2. The purpose of this chapter is to provide additional details on measurements and calculations used in aquaculture water quality management.

## Water Volume

### Small Vessels

The volume of water in tanks and other small vessels can be estimated from their dimensions:

Square vessel, $V = L^2h$                                                     (30.1)

Rectangular vessel, $V = LWh$                                      (30.2)

Circular vessel, $V = \pi r^2h$                                          (30.3)

where $V$ = volume; $L$ = length; $W$ = width; $h$ = height; $r$ = radius or half the diameter; $\pi$ = 3.1416; units must be the same for each variable but can be either metric or English.

### Ponds

The surface area of aquaculture ponds is usually known from design and construction data. However, even if area and average depth were known for a newly-constructed pond, the estimate is not usually reliable in older ponds because area may increase slightly due to bank erosion and sedimentation reduces average depth. Standard surveying techniques usually are not practical for estimating water volume for routine management purposes. A simple way to obtain average depth is to make many soundings (50-100) along a grid-shaped pattern over the pond surface and average them. Alternatively, fewer soundings (15-25) may be made at intervals along an S-shaped pattern and averaged. The volume of a pond is estimated as area multiplied by average depth.

It is relatively easy to gauge volumes of embankment ponds if the inflow rate can be estimated with weirs, water meters, or pumping data (pump discharge × hours of pump operation). A staff gauge can be installed in the pond near the discharge gate and the volume of water necessary to fill the pond to different depths can be recorded (Example 30.1). Provided pond depth does not change as a result of sedimentation, volume can be estimated in the future from staff gauge readings.

# Water Inflow

## Pumps

Discharge of pumps can be obtained from manufacturer's pump curves and pumping head. It also is possible to determine pump discharge from the time to fill a container (even a pond) of known volume.

---

### Example 30.1
### Depth-Volume Rating of Embankment Pond

A small, empty embankment pond is 1.4 m deep at the top of the overflow gate that consists of a concrete structure with dam boards. One side of the concrete structure is marked at 1.4 m and at 0.2 m intervals to the floor. The dam boards are installed and water is introduced with a pump delivery of 7,500 L/min (7.5 m$^3$/min). The pumping time required to incrementally fill the pond and the resulting volumes of water are presented below:

| Depth increment (m) | Pumping time (min) | Volume (m$^3$) | Accumulative volume to top of increment (m$^3$) |
|---|---|---|---|
| 0-0.2 | 20 | 150 | 150 |
| 0.2-0.4 | 45 | 338 | 485 |
| 0.400.6 | 49 | 368 | 856 |
| 0.6-0.8 | 60 | 450 | 1,306 |
| 0.8-1.0 | 62 | 465 | 1,771 |
| 1.0-1.2 | 64 | 480 | 2,251 |
| 1.2-1.4 | 66 | 495 | 2,746 |

---

## *Pipes*

Pipe discharge also may be measured by time to fill a container of known volume. Water flow meters, pilot tubes, or orifices can be attached to the ends of pipes to measure discharge.[1] However, fairly reliable estimates of flow rate can be determined from the shape of the discharge stream from vertical or horizontal pipes under free flow conditions. The procedures are called coordinate or trajectory methods and consist of measuring the horizontal and vertical coordinates of a point in the jet (stream) issuing from the end of a pipe and using these coordinates to estimate discharge for the particular pipe diameter from a nomograph.[1] The instructions for use of the coordinate method can be found on-line. One excellent resource is from the USBR Water Measurement Manual: (http://www.usbr.gov/pmts/hydraulics_lab/pubs/wmm/chap14_13.html).

## *Open Channels*

Water may be delivered to aquaculture facilities through open channels. There are several ways of measuring flow in open channels, and most are based on application of the fact that discharge is the product of cross-sectional area and velocity of flow:

$$Q = Av \tag{30.4}$$

where Q = discharge ($m^3$/sec or $ft^3$/sec); A = cross-sectional area ($m^2$ or $ft^2$); v = velocity (m/sec or ft/sec). In a channel with a cross-sectional area of 10 $m^2$ and velocity of 0.1 m/sec, discharge is 1 $m^3$/sec.

The discharge equation also can be applied in measuring stream discharge. In a straight section of a stream or channel, each depth (stage height) corresponds to a unique, cross-sectional area and velocity. By measuring cross-sectional area and velocity of flow at a number of stage heights, a stream-specific graph relating stage height to flow rate can be prepared (Fig. 30.1). The graph in Fig. 30.1 is called a rating curve; it can be used to estimate stream discharge from measurements of stage height.

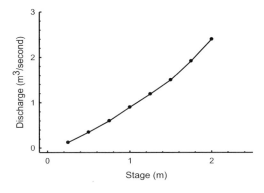

**Fig. 30.1.** A rating curve can determine channel or stream flows.

The float method may be applied in small streams and channels where it is not necessary to obtain frequent measurements of discharge.[2] A straight stretch of channel is selected, the width is measured, and the average depth is obtained from five to ten soundings made across the stream. The time required for a float (an orange or grapefruit is an excellent float) to travel a measured distance in the stream is determined and the surface velocity calculated. The surface stream velocity must be adjusted for depth by using the appropriate coefficient from Table 30.1. The following expression (Equation 30.5) can be used to estimate stream discharge:

$$Q = (W)(H)(\frac{d}{t})(C) \tag{30.5}$$

where Q = discharge (m³/sec or ft³/sec); W = stream width (m or ft); H = average depth (m or ft); d = distance flow travels (m or ft); t = time for float to travel distance d (sec); C = coefficient from Table 30.1. An exemplary calculation is made in Example 30.2.

**Table 30.1.** Velocity coefficients for the float method of determining channel velocity.

| Average flow depth (m) | Coefficient |
|---|---|
| 0.25 | 0.64 |
| 0.50 | 0.67 |
| 0.75 | 0.70 |
| 1.00 | 0.71 |
| 1.50 | 0.74 |
| 2.00 | 0.76 |
| 3.00 | 0.77 |
| 4.00 | 0.78 |
| 5.00 | 0.79 |

**Example 30.2**
**Illustration of Float Method Calculation of Stream Flow**

A channel of 8 m in width has an average depth of 1.5 m. A float travels 10 m in the channel in 85 sec. Stream discharge estimated with Equation 30.5 is:

$$Q = (8 \text{ m})(1.5 \text{ m}) \left( \frac{10 \text{ m}}{85 \text{ sec}} \right) (0.74)$$

$$Q = 1.04 \text{ m}^3/\text{sec}.$$

Weirs may be installed in streams or channels to measure discharge. A weir is a barrier plate that constricts flow in an open channel through a fixed-sized opening.[2] Common shapes of weirs are rectangular, trapezoidal, and triangular (Fig. 30.2). The bottom edge of the opening through which the water flows is the weir crest (L). The depth of water above the elevation of the bottom of the crest is the head (H). The stream of water passing through the weir opening is the *nappe*. The nappe must maintain free discharge if an accurate measurement is to be obtained. This means that the water level must be lower downstream of the weir plate than upstream of it so that there is air flow under the nappe.

There are two types of rectangular weirs (Fig. 30.2). The weir crest is exactly the same width as the channel for a non-contracted, rectangular weir. In a contracted, rectangular weir, the weir crest is not as wide as the channel, and the entering flow is constricted by the end contractions. The V-notch weir (Fig. 30.2) does not have a crest for the water flows through a V-notch. A V-notch weir is especially applicable for small flows because a greater head is achieved at low flow.

| Weir type | Views | | Formula |
|---|---|---|---|
| Rectangular (without contraction) | 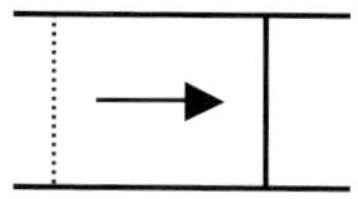 <br>Top view | | Metric<br>$Q = 0.0184\ LH^{1.5}$<br><br>English<br>$Q = 3.33\ LH^{1.5}$ |
| Rectangular (with contraction) | 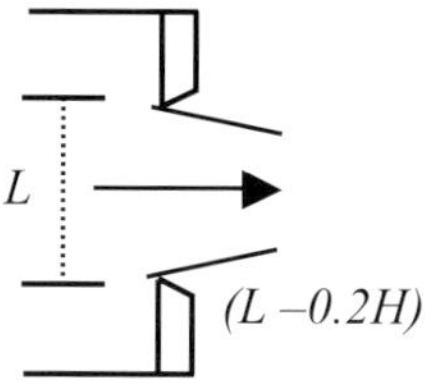 <br>Top view | 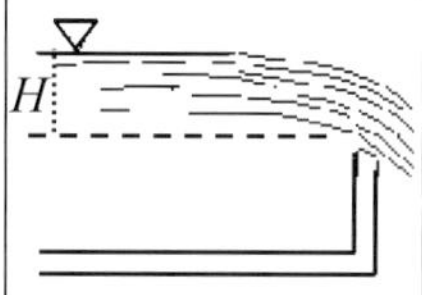 <br>Side view | Metric<br>$Q = 0.0184(L{-}0.2H)H^{1.5}$<br><br>English<br>$Q = 3.33(L - 0.2H)H^{1.5}$ |
| Trapezoidal | 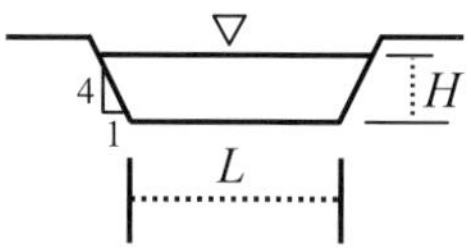 <br>End view | | Metric<br>$Q = 0.0184\ LH^{1.5}$<br><br>English<br>$Q = 3.37LH^{1.5}$ |
| 90°Triangular | 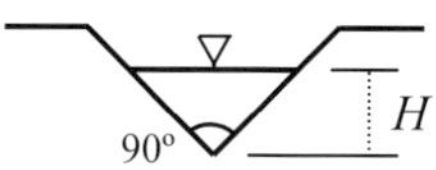 <br>End view | 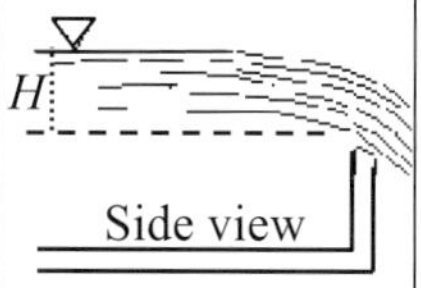 <br>Side view | Metric<br>$Q = 0.0138H^{2.5}$<br><br>English<br>$Q = 2.48H^{2.5}$ |

**Fig. 30.2.** Weir types, designs, and equations.

The discharge from weirs is estimated with equations (Fig. 30.2), and weir plates must be constructed precisely to the specified geometric shape and installed with the weir crest level. The head must be measured at a point at least four times the head upstream from the crest, because the water surface slopes downward as it approaches and flows over the crest. For example, if the head is 25 cm, the head measurement must be made at least 100 cm upstream of the crest. The channel depth between the weir plate and point for head measurement must be at least twice the maximum expected head (Fig. 30.2).

Ponds often have rectangular water inlet gates that are used as weirs even though they frequently do not exactly meet the assumptions for the rectangular weir equation. The accuracy of inflow estimates made with weir equations can be evaluated by comparison of direct estimates of inflow to the pond made from the time required to increase water level in the pond by a specified amount (Example 30.1). Example 30.3 illustrates how the accuracy of a weir could be checked. Of course, the accuracy of the weir ideally should be checked for four or five different values of H over the range in head.

## Rainfall

Measurement of rainfall is discussed in Chapter 2, but it is worth repeating that depth of rainfall is converted to volume by multiplying rainfall depth over the hydrologic unit of interest by the surface area of that unit. The depth of a single rainfall event seldom exceeds 10 cm, but expanded over a large area, the volume is large, e.g., 2-cm of rainfall over an aquaculture farm with a water surface of 100 ha represents $20,000$ $m^3$ of water.

---

**Example 30.3**
**Evaluation of Accuracy of an Inlet Gate Weir**

A 1-ha pond has an inlet gate with a 2-m wide crest and the gate functions as a contracted, rectangular weir. For a head of 10 cm, the inflow is estimated as follows:

$$Q = 0.0184 (L - 0.2H)H^{1.5}$$

$$Q = 0.0184[200 \text{ cm} - 0.2(10)]10^{1.5}$$

$$Q = 0.0184(198)31.62 = 115.2 \text{ L/sec } (6.91 \text{ m}^3/\text{min})$$

Inflow can be measured directly by lowering the pond water level a few centimeters and estimating the time required to replace the water with an inflow head of 10 cm. Suppose that the water level is drawn down 15 cm. This is a volume of 1,500 $m^3$ (1 ha × 10,000 $m^2$/ha × 0.15 m). If the weir discharges in accordance with the weir equation, it should take 217 min (1,500 $m^3$ ÷ 6.91 $m^3$/min) to replace the water.

Suppose the time to replace 10 cm of water in the pond requires 250 min. The factor 217 min/250 min can be used to adjust the weir equation to fit the actual weir conditions.

---

## Runoff

Runoff measurement is difficult and seldom necessary except for hydrologic studies of watershed ponds. It can be estimated from stream flow and catchment area, by subtracting annual evapotranspiration from annual precipitation, by the curve number method, or by the soil moisture accounting technique[1]; however, these methods are too complex to explain here and too complicated for most aquaculture purposes.

The only simple method for runoff that could be applied to aquaculture ponds is the water increase after a storm less the amount of rain falling directly into the pond during a period when there is no overflow or the overflow rate is unknown. This procedure is illustrated in Example 30.4.

# Water Losses

## Evaporation

Evaporation usually is measured using an evaporation pan (see Chapter 2). Like rainfall, it is measured in depth, and daily evaporation rates are small. Evaporation from a pond would seldom exceed 0.75 cm/day (75 $m^3$/ha/day), but average evaporation of 0.3 cm/day during a summer month would be equivalent to 900 $m^3$ of water. Evaporation is a major water loss from ponds.

---

**Example 30.4**
**Estimation of Runoff into a Watershed Pond**

A watershed pond has an area of 1 ha with a 15-ha watershed. A staff gauge in the pond registers 1.60 m before and 1.95 m after a 10-cm rainfall event that did not cause overflow.

The water level increased by 0.35 m, but 0.10 m was from direct rainfall into the pond – runoff amounted to 0.25 m (0.35 m – 0.10 m). Runoff was equal to a volume of 2,500 $m^3$ (0.25 m × 1 ha × 10,000 $m^2$/ha).

Runoff can be expressed in terms of depth over the watershed by dividing volume of runoff by area of catchment:

$$\frac{2,500 \ m^3}{15 \ ha \times 10,000 \ m^2/ha} = 0.0167 \ m = 1.67 \ cm$$

Runoff equaled 16.7% of precipitation falling on the pond's watershed.

---

## *Seepage*

Seepage usually results in a net loss of water, and sometimes the loss may be excessive. Ponds constructed in sandy areas or other sites with permeable soils are most likely to have high seepage rates. However, ponds built in almost any kind of soil may seep too much if they were constructed improperly. Water also can seep into ponds where bottoms are excavated below the water table, when ponds constructed at higher elevations seep into ponds constructed below them, or where a pond within a complex of ponds is drained but adjacent ponds are full of water.

Compaction applied during construction is important for reducing seepage. Soils of pond embankments and bottoms should be compacted at about 95% of their optimum moisture content as determined in a standard proctor test (see Chapter 23). Soils that are too moist should not be compacted until they are dry enough, and water should be applied to excessively dry soil before compaction.

A seepage cut-off core made of soil of high clay content can be installed in a trench and extended upward into dams or embankments to lessen seepage between the former land surface and the earthwork. Where pond bottoms are expected to seep excessively, soil of adequate clay content can be brought in and a soil blanket 20- to 30-cm thick installed over the bottom and compacted.

Drain pipes placed through embankments or dams should have anti-seepage collars to avoid seepage along the pipe and through the embankment. Water also may seep along the junction between earthwork and rock, so large stones should be removed from dams and embankments. Trees should not be allowed to grow in dams or embankments because water can seep along roots or channels resulting from dead, decomposing roots. Nevertheless, in spite of attention to construction details and maintenance, ponds still seep and some may seep excessively.

Seepage data were reviewed for 39 ponds in Honduras, Panama, and several regions of the United States.[3] Watershed ponds and embankment ponds used for sportfishing, livestock watering, aquacultural research, and commercial aquaculture were included in the data. Soils at pond sites varied in texture from clayey to sandy. Seepage rates differed greatly with a range of 1.5 to 176.5 cm/month (Fig. 25.1). The data were skewed to the left towards lower seepage rate. The highest seepage rates were for ponds on sandy soil at a fisheries research station in Panama. The lowest seepage rates were for watershed ponds constructed in the Blackland Prairie region of Alabama on soils with a high concentration of expandable, smectite clay. The average seepage rate calculated from the entire data set was 23.1 cm/month with a standard deviation of 33.7 cm/month. Seepage rate categories were proposed (Table 30.2); normal seepage was considered to be less than 20 cm/month.

Pond managers who feel that one or more of their ponds seeps too much should measure seepage rate and compare the results with pond seepage categories (Table 30.2.). An estimate of seepage loss can be made fairly easily. A staff gauge or a ruler can be mounted vertically in a pond so that the decline in water depth can be measured over several days when there is no rainfall or other water additions and no overflow or intentional discharge. Usually 3 to 7 days will be required for the water level to decline

**Table 30.2.** Pond seepage rate categories.

| Seepage rate (cm/month) | Category |
|---|---|
| < 8 | Low |
| 8-20 | Moderate |
| 20-40 | High |
| > 40 | Extreme |

enough for an accurate reading. The water level decline will represent both seepage and evaporation. Class A pan evaporation multiplied by 0.8 is a good approximation of pond evaporation. It will rarely be possible to obtain data on Class A pan evaporation at a locality. An alternative is to install a small, floating, plastic pan of water in the pond and measure the depth of water lost from the pan with a ruler. It is important for no more than 2 or 3 cm of the sides of the pan extend above the water surface to minimize the effect of the sides of the pan on air movement that greatly affects evaporation rate. Water loss through evaporation varies greatly, but when water temperatures are between 25°C and 35°C, typical rates for ponds are 0.6 to 0.7 cm/day. Seepage per month can be estimated as follows:

$$S_{out} = (WL - E) \times \frac{D}{d} \tag{30.6}$$

where $S_{out}$ = seepage out (cm or in); WL = water level (cm or in); E = pond evaporation (cm or in); D = days in month; d = days in period of measurement.

Seepage rates tend to decline as ponds age and organic matter accumulates in their bottoms to seal off pore space in the soil.

### *Discharge through Water Control Structure*

Water may overflow from ponds after heavy rainfall, and it may be intentionally discharged for water exchange or in preparation for harvest. Weir equations also can be used to estimate discharge through outlet gates with configurations compatible with weir equations. A standing drain pipe can function as an uncontracted rectangular weir if the pipe is not filled with overflow. The circumference of the pipe is L for the weir equation and H is the distance of the water surface above the top of the pipe.

## Water Balance

Water balance in ponds or other aquaculture units may be assessed from data on inflows: precipitation, runoff, and intentional additions; outflows: precipitation, evaporation, seepage out, and intentional withdrawal or discharge; change in storage volume over the period of measurement. The general hydrologic equation which states that inflows equal outflows plus or minus the change in storage volume; it is used in its expended form to estimate any single term that cannot be measured:

$$P + RO + S_i + A = E + S_o + OF + W + \Delta V \qquad (30.7)$$

where P = precipitation; RO = runoff including stream inflow; $S_i$ = seepage in; A = intentional additions from stream, well, or other external source; E = evaporation from pond surface; $S_o$ = seepage out; OF = overflow; W = intentional withdrawal or discharge; $\Delta V$ = stage in storage volume over period of measurement.

A single pond or other aquaculture system will seldom have all inflows and outflows included in Equation 30.7. The terms in the equation may be omitted as dictated by a particular situation, but the values that are substituted for the remaining terms must all have the same dimensions—usually either centimeters or inches of depth or cubic meters or cubic feet of volume. Examples 30.4, 30.5, 30.6, and 30.7 illustrate use of Equation 30.7 in estimating water supply requirements for aquaculture.

---

**Example 30.5**
**Calculation of Minimum Watershed Area for a Watershed Pond**

Minimum watershed size will be estimated for a 1-ha pond of 2-m average depth (V = 20,000 $m^3$) in a region where rainfall is 1,200 mm/yr, evapotranspiration is 900 mm/yr, and class A pan evaporation is 1,200 mm/yr. The pond is expected to have a seepage loss of 10 cm/month (120 cm/yr) or less.

Water expected from rainfall on pond area:
Input – Output = Storage
P – (E + S) = Storage
1,200 mm – [(1,200 × 0.8) + 120 mm] = 120 mm.

Water needed from watershed to fill pond:
20,000 $m^3$ – (10,000 $m^2$ × 0.12 m) = 18,800 $m^3$.

Runoff from watershed:
RO = P – ET = (1,200 – 900) mm/yr = 300 mm/yr
V = (0.3 m/yr)(10,000 $m^2$/ha) = 3,000 $m^3$/ha/yr.

Area of watershed:

$$A = \frac{V \text{ required}}{V/ha} = \frac{18,800 \text{ m}^3}{3,000 \text{ m}^3/ha} = 6.27 \text{ ha.}$$

## Example 30.6
## Estimation of Maximum Pond Area for Available Water Supply

A well that can yield 5 m³/min (7,200 m³/day) will supply a pond aquaculture facility. In this area, rainfall is 800 mm/yr, while pond evaporation plus seepage is expected to be 1,200 mm/yr (100 mm/month). Ponds will be drained annually, and it is desired to be able to refill them in 30 days. The maximum surface area of ponds (1 m deep) is estimated.

Water availability = 7,200 m³ × 30 days = 216,000 m³

Equivalent pond surface area (assuming no rainfall during filling period of 30 days) =

$$\frac{216,000 \text{ m}^3}{1 \text{ m}} - \left[0.1 \text{ m/month} \times \frac{216,000 \text{ m}^3}{1 \text{ m}}\right] = 194,400 \text{ m}^2 \text{ (19.4 ha)}.$$

## Example 30.7
## Water Supply Requirement for Water Exchange

Water exchange of 5% will be used at a shrimp farm with 200 ha (2,000,000 m²) of pond water surface area. Evaporation and seepage is 0.6 cm/day on average. The water supply requirement for water exchange (assuming no rainfall) will be:

Inputs = outputs + storage change

Pumped water = water exchange + seepage and evaporation + 0.0
= (0.05 m/day × 2,000,000 m²) + (0.006 m /day)(2,000,000 m²)
= 112,000 m³/day.

# Pond Effluents

Pond effluents result mainly from three events: overflow after heavy rains, water exchange, and draining for harvest. Unless outflow structures can be rated as weir, it is difficult to measure overflow following rainfall events, but the annual overflow from ponds can be estimated using Equation 30.7 (Example 30.8). Water exchange effluent can be estimated by adjusting inflow for seepage, evaporation and rainfall, but for practical purposes, it usually can be assumed that inflow equals outflow when daily water exchange is used. Thus, the pumping volume can be used as the effluent volume (Example 30.9).

**Example 30.8**
**Calculation of Overflow from Watershed Pond**

An 8,000-m$^2$ pond of 1.4 m average depth has a 12-ha watershed. Rainfall in the region is 1,100 mm/yr and evapotranspriation is 850 mm/yr. Average seepage plus evaporation for the pond was determined as 900 mm/yr. The pond is full on 1 January and 31 December.

Runoff:
RO = P − ET = (1,100 − 850) mm/yr = 250 mm/yr
RO = 0.25 m/yr × 120,000 m$^2$ = 30,000 m$^3$

Pond water budget:
P + RO = (S + E) + OF + ΔS

(1.1 m × 8,000 m$^2$) + 30,000 m$^3$ = (0.9 m × 8,000 m$^2$) + OF + ΔS
38,800 = 7,200 m$^3$ + OF + 0.0
OF = 31,600 m$^3$.

**Example 30.9**
**Calculation of Water Exchange Rate**

A shrimp farm has a combined pond water surface of 500 ha and ponds average 1.3 m deep. The farm practices daily water exchange and has a pumping capacity of 400,000 m$^3$/day. The approximate, maximum, attainable, daily, water exchange for the farm would be:

$$\text{Exchange rate} = \frac{\text{Pumping capacity}}{\text{Pond volume}} \times 100$$

$$\text{Exchange rate} = \frac{400{,}000 \text{ m}^3/\text{day}}{500 \text{ ha} \times 10{,}000 \text{ m}^2/\text{ha} \times 1.3 \text{ m}} \times 100 = 6.15\%.$$

# Chemical Treatments

Managers may treat aquaculture ponds with fertilizers, liming materials, osmoregulatory enhancers, coagulants, oxidants, or algicides.[4] Dosages of these materials should be calculated accurately to avoid waste, assure efficacy, and prevent possible damage to the culture species or the environment. Various chemical treatments also may be applied to other types of holding and grow-out units. Fertilizers and liming materials usually are applied on a weight to pond area basis, but other treatments usually are made on a concentration basis. Some products used for pond treatments are solid, particulate materials such as agricultural limestone, lime, traditional fertilizers, copper sulfate, and potassium permanganate. Others are liquids, some examples of which are fluid fertilizers, chelated copper solutions, formalin, calcium hypochlorite solutions, and molasses.

Pond treatment products seldom contain 100% of the active ingredient. Liming materials are applied on the basis of their neutralizing value or percentage calcium carbonate equivalence—the neutralizing value of different liming products can range from less than 75% to more than 150%. The active ingredients of fertilizers are their nutrients, especially nitrogen and phosphorus.

Although many farmers still apply fertilizers on a quantity-per-hectare basis, the growing tendency is to apply a specific quantity of nutrients per hectare or dose of fertilizer calculated to increase the concentration of nutrients in the pond water by a specific amount. Copper sulfate may be applied to provide a certain concentration of copper; copper sulfate contains only 25% of the active ingredient copper. Crusher rock salt (sodium chloride) is applied to ponds to raise the chloride concentration to a specific level to combat nitrite toxicity. This product is seldom less than 97% pure, and pure sodium chloride is nearly 61% chloride. The active ingredient content of the salt applied to ponds is about 58-59%.

The specific gravity of liquid products used in aquaculture often differs from that of water (1 g/m$^3$). Fluid fertilizers have specific gravities around 1.4—they are 1.4 times denser than water. A product with a specific gravity of 1.0 and 50% active ingredient (AI) would contain 0.5 kg AI/L, but a product with specific gravity of 1.4 with the same percentage of the active ingredient would contain 0.7 kg AI/L. Thus, adjustments must be made for percentages of active ingredients in solid products, and for both active ingredient contents and specific gravities of liquid products. A typical calculation is illustrated in Example 30.10, and equations are given for estimating pond treatment rates (Table 30.3).

Liming materials can be applied to bottoms of empty ponds or to the surfaces of full ponds. In either case, liming material should be spread uniformly over the entire pond area. Fertilizers and most other granular materials will settle to the pond bottom before completely dissolving if broadcast over pond surfaces. Solubility in pond water will be improved if these products are pre-dissolved by mixing with water (1 part product:10 parts water) and spreading the mixture uniformly over pond surfaces. Liquids that are denser than water settle to the bottom without completely dissolving in the water column if splashed directly over the pond surface. Thus, liquid fertilizers and other fluid products also should be pre-mixed with water and spread over pond surfaces. The mixture can be splashed over the surface, released into the turbulence caused by the propeller of an outboard motor while the boat is driven in a zigzag pattern over the pond surface, or sprayed over the pond surface. In small ponds, mixtures also can be sprayed or splashed over pond surfaces from the edges, but a boat should be used to make applications in a large pond. The operation of mechanical aerators in ponds following application of pond treatments encourages mixing of the product throughout the water volume.

Equations are provided in Table 30.4 for the calculation of the amounts of substances necessary for treating small ponds or other fish production units.

---

**Example 30.10**
**Calculation of Treatment Dose of a Liquid Product**

A copper algicide with a specific gravity of 1.1 and 15% copper content is to be applied to 2,500 m² pond of 1.5 m average depth. The volume of algicide needed to provide 0.1 mg/L of copper will be calculated:

Pond volume = 2,500 m² × 1.5 m = 3,750 m³

Copper dose = 3,750 m³ × 0.1 g/m³ = 375 g Cu

Copper concentration in algicide = 1.1 g/cm³ × 0.15 g Cu/g = 0.165 g Cu/cm³

Algicide dose = 375 g Cu ÷ 0.165 g Cu/cm³ = 2,273 cm³.

---

Table 30.3. Equations for calculating chemical treatment amounts for large ponds.

| State of chemical | Type of treatment | Units for amount | Equation for calculating amount Metric[a] | English[b] |
|---|---|---|---|---|
| 1. Solid | Weight/area | kg or lb | $\frac{(A)(R)}{\% AI/100}$ | Same |
| 2. Solid | Weight/volume | kg or lb | $\frac{(A)(D)(C)(10)}{\% AI/100}$ | $\frac{(A)(D)(C)(2.71)}{\% AI/100}$ |
| 3. Liquid | Volume/volume | L or gal | $\frac{(A)(D)(C)(10)}{(\% AI/100)(SG)}$ | $\frac{(A)(D)(C)(2.71)}{(\% AI/100)(SG)}$ |

[a]A = area (ha); D = average depth (m); R = treatment rate for active ingredient (kg/ha); C = treatment concentration of active ingredient (g/m³, which is equivalent to mg/L); % AI = percentage active ingredient; SG = specific gravity (relative to water with a density of 1 kg/L); 10 = factor for converting g/m³ to kg/ha-m).

[b]A = area (acres); D = average depth (ft); R = treatment rate for active ingredient (lb/acre); C = treatment concentration of active ingredient (ppm, which is equivalent to g/m3); % AI = percentage active ingredient; SG = specific gravity (relative to water with a density of 8.34 lb/gal); 2.71 = factor for converting ppm to lb/acre-ft.

**Table 30.4.** Equations for calculating chemical treatment amounts for small holding or culture units.[4]

| State of chemical | Type of treatment | Units for amount | Equation for calculating amount | |
|---|---|---|---|---|
| | | | Metric[a] | English[b] |
| 1. Solid | Weight/area | g or oz | $\dfrac{(A)(R)}{\% \text{AI}/100}$ | Same |
| 2. Solid | Weight/volume | g or oz | $\dfrac{(V)(C)}{\% \text{AI}/100}$ | $\dfrac{(V)(C)(0.001)}{\% \text{AI}/100}$ |
| 3. Liquid | Volume/volume | mL or fluid oz | $\dfrac{(V)(C)}{(\% \text{AI}/100)(\text{SG})}$ | $\dfrac{(V)(C)(0.001)}{(\% \text{AI}/100)(\text{SG})}$ |

[a]A = area ($m^2$); R = treatment rate for active ingredient ($g/m^2$); C = treatment concentration for active ingredient ($g/m^3$, which is equivalent to mg/L); % AI = percentage active ingredient; SG = specific gravity (relative to water with a density of 1 g/mL).

[b]A = area ($ft^2$); R = treatment rate for active ingredient ($lb/ft^2$); C = treatment concentration of active ingredient (ppm, which is equivalent to $g/m^3$); % AI = percentage active ingredient; SG = specific gravity (relative to water with a density of $1.^{042}$ oz/fluid oz); 0.001 = factor for converting ppm to $oz/ft^3$.

# References

1. Yoo, K. H. and C. E. Boyd. 1994. *Hydrology and Water Supply for Aquaculture.* Chapman and Hall, New York, NY.
2. Boyd, C. E. 2005. Measuring water flow. Global Aquaculture Advocate 8(5):76-77.
3. Boyd, C. E. 2009. Assessing, reducing pond seepage. Global Aquaculture Advocate 12(2):62-62.
4. Boyd, C. E. 2009. Calculating chemical treatments for aquaculture production. Global Aquaculture Advocate 12(3):52-54.

# Chapter 31

# Conversion Factors

## Introduction

Aquaculturists in the United States typically make measurements in English units. In other countries, aquaculturists normally use the metric system of measurement, although there is increasing use of the metric system in the United States, this chapter contains factors for converting measurements made in the English system to metric equivalents and vice versa. Information also is provided on relationships among different length, weight, and volume measurements in both measurement systems.

Accuracy and precision of measurements do not depend upon the system of measurement, but rather upon accuracy and precision of instruments used for making measurements. For example, a balance that records the weight of 1 L of water as 900 g is not very accurate because the true weight is 1,000 g. But, suppose the balance is used to make three successive measurements of 1 L of water and the values are 900 g, 900.5 g and 899.59 g. The balance would be fairly precise even thought it has poor accuracy. A device for measuring water volume that is calibrated in gallons can have less, equal, or greater accuracy and precision than a device calibrated in liters and vice versa. The advantage of the metric system over the English system results from metric units being related to each other by powers of 10; for example, $1 \text{ m}^3 = 1,000 \text{ L} = 1,000,000 \text{ mL}$. This is much simpler than in the English system in which there is no consistency in relationships among units. For example, $1 \text{ yd}^3 = 27 \text{ ft}^3 = 202 \text{ gal} = 6,464$ fluid oz.

## Relationships among Metric Units

### Volume

$$1 \text{ cm}^3 = 1 \text{ mL}$$

$$1 \text{ mL} = 1,000 \text{ μL}$$

$$1 \text{ L} = 1,000 \text{ mL}$$

$$1 \text{m}^3 = 1,000 \text{ L}$$

$$1 \text{ ha·m} = 10,000 \text{ m}^3$$

Note:   A 1-ha pond with an average depth of 1 m has a volume of 1 ha-m.

## *Weight*

$$1 \text{ mg} = 1,000 \text{ μg}$$
$$1 \text{ g} = 1,000 \text{ mg}$$
$$1 \text{ kg} = 1,000 \text{ g}$$
$$1 \text{ tonne} = 1,000 \text{ kg}$$

Note: Tonne refers to a metric ton that sometimes is sometimes called a long ton in the United States.

## *Length*

$$1 \text{ mm} = 1,000 \text{ μm (microns)}$$
$$1 \text{ cm} = 10 \text{ mm}$$
$$1 \text{ m} = 100 \text{ cm}$$
$$1 \text{ km} = 1,000 \text{ m}$$

## *Area*

$$1 \text{cm}^2 = 100 \text{ mm}^2$$
$$1 \text{ m}^2 = 10,000 \text{ cm}^2$$
$$1 \text{ are} = 100 \text{ m}^2$$
$$1 \text{ ha} = 100 \text{ are} = 10,000 \text{ m}^2$$
$$1 \text{ km}^2 = 100 \text{ ha}$$

Note: 1 ha is equal to a square with 100 m sides.

## *Volume of Weight Conversions for Water*

$$1 \text{ mL} = 1 \text{ g at } 4°\text{C}$$
$$1 \text{ L} = 1 \text{ kg at } 4°\text{C}$$
$$1 \text{ m}^3 = 1 \text{ tonne } 4°\text{C}$$

Note: The density of water decreases above and below 4°C (see Table 2.2 on page 8). For aquaculture applications, the change in density with temperature is insignificant in most calculations.

# Relationships among English Units

## *Volume*

$$1 \text{ fluid ounce (oz)} = 1.804 \text{ in}^3$$

$$1 \text{ fluid ounce} = 6.035 \text{ teaspoons}$$

$$1 \text{ tablespoon} = 3 \text{ teaspoons}$$

$$1 \text{ cup} = 14.43 \text{ in}^3 = 8 \text{ fluid oz}$$

$$1 \text{ pint} = 2 \text{ cups}$$

$$1 \text{ quart (qt)} = 2 \text{ pints}$$

$$1 \text{ gal} = 4 \text{ qt} = 231 \text{ in}^3$$

$$1 \text{ ft}^3 = 7.481 \text{ gal}$$

$$1 \text{ cubic yard (yd}^3) = 27 \text{ ft}^3$$

$$1 \text{ acre·ft} = 43{,}560 \text{ ft}^3 = 325{,}872.4 \text{ gal}$$

Note: The volume of water present in a 1-acre pond with an average depth of 1 ft is 1 acre-ft.

## *Weight*

$$1 \text{ dram} = 27.3 \text{ grains}$$

$$1 \text{ oz} = 16 \text{ drams} = 436.8 \text{ grains}$$

$$1 \text{ lb} = 16 \text{ oz}$$

$$100 \text{ lb} = 1 \text{ hundredth-weight}$$

$$1 \text{ ton} = 2{,}000 \text{ lb}$$

Note: Ton is an English ton that is sometimes called a short ton in the United States.

## *Length*

$$1 \text{ mil} = 0.001 \text{ in}$$

$$1 \text{ ft} = 12 \text{ in}$$

$$1 \text{ yd} = 3 \text{ ft}$$

$$1 \text{ rod} = 16.5 \text{ ft} = 5.5 \text{ yd}$$

$$1 \text{ mile (mi)} = 5{,}280 \text{ ft}$$

$$1 \text{ nautical mile} = 6076.12 \text{ ft}$$

Note: 1 statute mile = 1 mi (5,280 ft).

*Area*

$$1 \text{ ft}^2 = 144 \text{ in}^2$$
$$1 \text{ yd}^2 = 9 \text{ ft}^2$$
$$1 \text{ acre} = 43{,}560 \text{ ft}^2 = 4{,}840 \text{ yd}^2$$
$$1 \text{ mile}^2 = 640 \text{ acres} = 1 \text{ section}$$
$$36 \text{ sections} = 1 \text{ township}$$

Note: 1 acre is equal to a square with 208.71 ft sides.

*Volume to Weight Conversions for Water*

$$1 \text{ gal} = 8.344 \text{ lb at } 4^\circ\text{C } (39.2^\circ\text{F})$$
$$1 \text{ gal} = 8.319 \text{ lb at } 25^\circ\text{C } (77^\circ\text{F})$$
$$1 \text{ ft}^3 = 62.414 \text{ lb at } 4^\circ\text{C}$$
$$1 \text{ ft}^3 = 62.234 \text{ lb at } 25^\circ\text{C}$$
$$1 \text{ acre·ft} = 2{,}719{,}000 \text{ lb at } 4^\circ\text{C}$$
$$1 \text{ acre·ft} = 2{,}711{,}000 \text{ lb at } 25^\circ\text{C}$$
$$1 \text{ ton water at } 25^\circ\text{C} = 32.14 \text{ ft}^3 = 240.42 \text{ gal}$$

# Relationships among Metric and English Units

Basic relationships between English and metric units are given below. Conversion factors presented in Table 31.1 may be used to quickly convert between English and metric units.

*Volume*

$$1 \text{ qt} = 0.9464 \text{ L}$$
$$1 \text{ gal} = 3.785 \text{ L}$$
$$1 \text{ ft}^3 = 28.317 \text{ L} = 0.02932 \text{ m}^3$$
$$1 \text{ acre·ft} = 1{,}233.6 \text{ m}^3$$

*Weight*

$$1 \text{ lb} = 453.6 \text{ g} = 0.4536 \text{ kg}$$
$$1 \text{ kg} = 2.20462 \text{ lb}$$
$$1 \text{ tonne} = 2{,}204.6 \text{ lb}$$

## Length

$$1 \text{ in} = 2.54 \text{ cm}$$

$$1 \text{ ft} = 30.48 \text{ cm} = 0.3048 \text{ m}$$

$$1 \text{ yd} = 0.9144 \text{ m}$$

$$1 \text{ mile} = 1,609.34 \text{ m}$$

## Area

$$1 \text{ ft}^2 = 0.0929 \text{ m}^2$$

$$1 \text{m}^2 = 10.76 \text{ ft}^2$$

$$1 \text{ acre} = 4,047 \text{ m}^2 = 0.4047 \text{ ha}$$

$$1 \text{ ha} = 2.471 \text{ acre}$$

## Flow Rates

1 gal/min = 0.00223 ft$^3$/sec = 0.00442 acre·ft/day = 0.0631 L/sec = 5.42 m$^3$/day

1 ft$^3$/sec = 449 gal/min = 1.98 acre·ft/day = 28.3 L/sec = 0.0283 m$^3$/sec = 2,450 m$^3$/day

1 acre·ft/day = 226 gal/min = 0.505 ft$^3$/sec = 14.2 L/sec = 1,230 m$^3$/day

1 L/sec = 15.9 gal/min = 0.0353 ft$^3$/sec = 0.0703 acre·ft/day = 86.4 m$^3$/day

1m$^3$/sec = 15,800 gal/min = 35.3 ft$^3$/sec = 70.0 acre·ft/day = 86,400 m$^3$/day

## Pressure

Standard conditions for a gas refer to 1 atmosphere (atm) of pressure at 0°C. The average atmospheric pressure at mean sea level and 0°C is 1 atm. Pressure may be expressed in several ways as follows:

1 atm = 1,013.2 millibars (mb)

1 atm = 760 mm Hg = 33.898 ft of water = 14.7 pound per square inch (psi)

1 atm = 1,033.2 g/cm$^2$ = 14.696 lb/in$^2$

1 lb/in$^2$ = 70.307 g/cm$^2$ = 0.06804 atm

## *Power*

$$1 kW = 1.34 hp$$

$$1 hp = 0.746 kW$$

**Table 31.1.** Conversion factors for English and metric units.

| To convert column 1 to column 2, multiply by | Column 1 | Column 2 | To convert column 2 to column 1, multiply by |
|---|---|---|---|
| | | Length | |
| 2.540 | Inches | Centimeters | 0.3937 |
| 0.3048 | Feet | Meters | 3.281 |
| 1.609 | Miles (statute) | Kilometers | 0.6214 |
| 30.48 | Feet | Centimeters | 0.0328 |
| 0.9144 | Yards | Meters | 1.094 |
| | | Area | |
| 0.4047 | Acres | Hectares | 2.471 |
| 6.452 | Square inches | Square centimeters | 0.1550 |
| | | Volume | |
| 0.9463 | Quart, liquid, U.S. (32 ounce) | Liters | 1.057 |
| 1.136 | Quart, imperial (40 ounce) | Liters | 0.8799 |
| 3.785 | Gallon, U.S. (4 quarts) | Liters | 0.2642 |
| 4.546 | Gallon, imperial | Liters | 0.2200 |
| 29.57 | Ounce (U.S. fluid) | Milliliters | 0.0338 |
| | | Weight | |
| 28.35 | Ounces (avoirdupois) | Grams | 0.0353 |
| 0.4536 | Pounds (avoirdupois) | Kilograms | 2.205 |
| 1.016 | Tons (gross or long) | Metric ton | 0.9842 |
| 0.9072 | Tons (short or net) | Metric ton | 1.102 |
| | | Pressure | |
| 70.31 | Pounds per square inch | Grams per square centimeter | 0.0142 |
| 0.0703 | Pounds per square inch | Kilograms per square centimeter | 14.22 |
| | | Other conversions | |
| 1.12 | Pounds per acre | Kilograms per hectare | 0.892 |
| 10.76 | Foot candles | Lux | 0.0929 |
| | | Power | |
| 0.746 | Horsepower | Kilowatt | 1.34 |

## Temperature

The freezing and boiling points of water on the Centigrade and Fahrenheit scales are 0°C and 32°F and 100°C and 212°F, respectively. The difference between the boiling and freezing points is 100 Centigrade degrees, but 180 Fahrenheit degrees. A Fahrenheit degree is 5/9 of a Centigrade degree, so

$$°C = 5/9 \ (°F - 32) \tag{31.1}$$

$$°F = 9/5°C + 32. \tag{31.2}$$

Table 31.2 may be used to convert °F to °C, while Table 31.3 may be used to convert °C to °F for the temperature range normally encountered in pond waters.

**Table 31.2.** Conversions of degrees Fahrenheit (°F) to degrees Centigrade (°C).

| °F | °C | °F | °C | °F | °C | °F | °C |
|----|----|----|----|----|----|----|----|
| 32 | 0.0 | 52 | 11.1 | 72 | 22.2 | 92 | 33.3 |
| 33 | 0.6 | 53 | 11.7 | 73 | 22.8 | 93 | 33.9 |
| 34 | 1.1 | 54 | 12.2 | 74 | 23.3 | 94 | 34.4 |
| 35 | 1.7 | 55 | 12.8 | 75 | 23.9 | 95 | 35.0 |
| 36 | 2.2 | 56 | 13.3 | 76 | 24.4 | 96 | 35.6 |
| 37 | 2.8 | 57 | 13.9 | 77 | 25.0 | 97 | 36.1 |
| 38 | 3.3 | 58 | 14.4 | 78 | 25.6 | 98 | 36.7 |
| 39 | 3.9 | 59 | 15.0 | 79 | 26.1 | 99 | 37.2 |
| 40 | 4.4 | 60 | 15.6 | 80 | 26.7 | 100 | 37.8 |
| 41 | 5.0 | 61 | 16.1 | 81 | 27.2 | 101 | 38.3 |
| 42 | 5.6 | 62 | 16.7 | 82 | 27.8 | 102 | 38.9 |
| 43 | 6.1 | 63 | 17.2 | 83 | 28.3 | 103 | 39.4 |
| 44 | 6.7 | 64 | 17.8 | 84 | 28.9 | 104 | 40.0 |
| 45 | 7.2 | 65 | 18.3 | 85 | 29.4 | 105 | 40.6 |
| 46 | 7.8 | 66 | 18.9 | 86 | 30.0 | 106 | 41.1 |
| 47 | 8.3 | 67 | 19.4 | 87 | 30.6 | 107 | 41.7 |
| 48 | 8.9 | 68 | 20.0 | 88 | 31.1 | 108 | 42.2 |
| 49 | 9.4 | 69 | 20.6 | 89 | 31.7 | 109 | 42.8 |
| 50 | 10.0 | 70 | 21.1 | 90 | 32.2 | 110 | 43.3 |
| 51 | 10.6 | 71 | 21.7 | 91 | 32.8 | | |

**Table 31.3.** Conversions of degrees Centigrade (°C) to degrees Fahrenheit (°F).

| °C | °F | °C | °F | °C | °F | °C | °F |
|----|----|----|----|----|----|----|----|
| -20 | -4.0 | 0 | 32.0 | 20 | 68.0 | 40 | 104.0 |
| -19 | -2.2 | 1 | 33.8 | 21 | 69.8 | 41 | 105.8 |
| -18 | -0.4 | 2 | 35.6 | 22 | 71.6 | 42 | 107.6 |
| -17 | 1.4 | 3 | 37.4 | 23 | 73.4 | 43 | 109.4 |
| -16 | 3.2 | 4 | 39.2 | 24 | 75.2 | 44 | 111.2 |
| -15 | 5.0 | 5 | 41.0 | 25 | 77.0 | 45 | 113.0 |
| -14 | 6.8 | 6 | 42.8 | 26 | 78.8 | 46 | 114.8 |
| -13 | 8.6 | 7 | 44.6 | 27 | 80.6 | 47 | 116.6 |
| -12 | 10.4 | 8 | 46.4 | 28 | 82.4 | 48 | 118.4 |
| -11 | 12.2 | 9 | 48.2 | 29 | 84.2 | 49 | 120.2 |
| -10 | 14.0 | 10 | 50.0 | 30 | 86.0 | 50 | 122.0 |
| -9 | 15.8 | 11 | 51.8 | 31 | 87.8 | 51 | 123.8 |
| -8 | 17.6 | 12 | 53.6 | 32 | 89.6 | 52 | 125.6 |
| -7 | 19.4 | 13 | 55.4 | 33 | 91.4 | 53 | 127.4 |
| -6 | 21.2 | 14 | 57.2 | 34 | 93.2 | 54 | 129.2 |
| -5 | 23.0 | 15 | 59.0 | 35 | 95.0 | 55 | 131.0 |
| -4 | 24.8 | 16 | 60.8 | 36 | 96.8 | 56 | 132.8 |
| -3 | 26.6 | 17 | 62.6 | 37 | 98.6 | 57 | 134.6 |
| -2 | 28.4 | 18 | 64.4 | 38 | 100.4 | 58 | 136.4 |
| -1 | 30.2 | 19 | 66.2 | 39 | 102.2 | 59 | 138.2 |

# Atomic Weights

Atomic weights of selected elements are presented in Table 31.4.

**Table 31.4.** Selected atomic weights.

| Element | Symbol | Atomic weight | Element | Symbol | Atomic weight |
|---|---|---|---|---|---|
| Aluminum | Al | 26.9815 | Manganese | Mn | 54.9380 |
| Arsenic | As | 74.9216 | Mercury | Hg | 200.59 |
| Barium | Ba | 137.34 | Molybdenum | Mo | 95.94 |
| Boron | B | 10.811 | Nickel | Ni | 58.71 |
| Bromine | Br | 79.904 | Nitrogen | N | 14.0067 |
| Cadmium | Cd | 112.40 | Oxygen | O | 15.9994 |
| Calcium | Ca | 40.08 | Phosphorus | P | 30.9738 |
| Carbon | C | 12.01115 | Platinum | Pt | 195.09 |
| Chlorine | Cl | 35.453 | Potassium | K | 39.102 |
| Chromium | Cr | 51.996 | Selenium | Se | 78.96 |
| Cobalt | Co | 58.9332 | Silicon | Si | 28.086 |
| Copper | Cu | 63.546 | Silver | Ag | 107.868 |
| Fluorine | F | 18.9984 | Sodium | Na | 22.9898 |
| Gold | Au | 196.967 | Strontium | Sr | 87.62 |
| Helium | He | 4.0026 | Sulfur | S | 32.064 |
| Hydrogen | H | 1.00797 | Thallium | Tl | 204.37 |
| Iodine | I | 126.9044 | Tin | Sn | 118.69 |
| Iron | Fe | 55.847 | Tungsten | W | 183.85 |
| Lead | Pb | 207.19 | Uranium | U | 238.03 |
| Lithium | Li | 6.939 | Vanadium | V | 50.942 |
| Magnesium | Mg | 24.312 | Zinc | Zn | 65.37 |

# Index